We need a new generation of business leaders willing to take responsibility for solving the problems of climate change and poverty. And we need bold new programmes and partnerships in business management education to support these leaders. A sustainable company can be more successful than one that pursues profits alone. *Sustainable Business: A One Planet Approach* makes a valuable contribution to redefining what it means to be a successful company, and the kind of curricula we need to shape it.

Paul Polman
CEO, Unilever

The beauty of the book is that it is a collaborative work by multiple thought leaders who bring phenomenal insights in a comprehensive way. The well-researched and connected topics show how to build institutions for the 21st century rather than just business-as-usual.

Arun Jain
Executive Chairman, Intellect Design

Sustainability has gone from a nice-to-do to a must do. Tomorrow's business leaders need to transform their business models in to ones that create value for their customers and society within the limits of the planet. In a world challenged by climate change, scarce resources and inequality there is no room for half measures. A One Planet Approach will help MBA students develop the background and the thinking to help lead this transformation.

Steve Howard
Chief Sustainability Officer, IKEA

Businesses with a higher purpose are discovering that there are better, and often unexpected ways, of doing business that can alleviate poverty, address environmental challenges, and still be profitable. *Sustainable Business: A One Planet Approach* argues for new business models that will help regenerate our economy in ways that are pro-poor, pro-planet and pro-prosperity.

Miriam Turner
AVP Co-Innovation, Interface

9 billion people living well on a healthy planet can only be achieved by the greatest wave of entrepreneurial innovation ever seen. One Planet thinking does something unique – it acknowledges physical limits but uses them to inspire global action. This book rightly encourages business to be at the forefront of this change.

Oliver Greenfield
Convenor, Green Economy Coalition

In 3M we have proved that reducing waste can save companies billions of dollars over the years. But we also know that sustainability can be a driver of good leadership, innovation and success over the longer term – beyond eco-efficiency arguments. We need a new generation of business leaders who know how to integrate sustainability issues into their business DNA in smart and strategic ways. This new textbook helps point the way.

Pip Frankish
Corporate Communications Manager, 3M Europe

Business in the 21st Century is vastly different from that of even the late 20th Century. This book is for managers who want to lead organizations and transform how business is conducted in this networking, information age, with its different dynamics, challenges and rapid changes. These challenges are why we at Texas A&M Univ. – Central Texas are making innovative changes to incorporate the concepts of sustainability and socially responsible management deep into our curriculum to bring about these much needed innovations in business education - this book provides many of the core concepts and techniques we need.

Larry Garner, Ph.D.
Dean, College of Business Administration, Texas A&M Univ.
Central Texas, USA

Sustainability is no longer simply about complying with environmental regulations or CSR, it is becoming central to way business is done. It is shaping strategy, innovation, operations, finance and accounting. The One Planet MBA, co-founded with WWF, offers global perspectives on the sustainability challenges facing us all, and the business opportunities that are generated by embracing change for good.

Fuji Kimura
Global Insights Manager at Google, and One Planet MBA alumna

This important new textbook highlights the urgent need to develop new economic and business models that will contribute to achieving the UN Sustainable Development Goals. These address the 3 major challenges facing humanity - eradicating poverty, sharing prosperity, and safeguarding the environment. Business has a crucial role to play in delivering these goals, and as this book reveals, progressive businesses are already leading way.

Sheng Fulai
Head, Economic Research Unit, United Nations Environment Programme (UNEP)

Business people need to think about a more sustainable society from a new and different point of view, namely a One Planet Approach. This book shows what this means for each of the main functions of a business - a most valuable guide.

Kentaro Iijima
Senior Advisor, former Corporate Senior Vice President, Fujitsu Marketing

Sustainable Business: A One Planet Approach is a holistic approach to life and leadership, which invites us to lead internally and externally, to realize that we live in a deeply interconnected world, and above all, to make a meaningful difference to self, the community and the planet. A must read for all.

V. R. Ferose
Senior Vice President, SAP SE and Co-author of 'Gifted'

This is a new generation business textbook, that makes the case for a transition to radically different economic and business models - ones that address social inequality and environmental degradation, and promotes new understandings of prosperity. Business leaders and students need access to new ideas and fresh perspectives if business is to become a force for public good, rather than private gain.

Mark Goldring
Chief Executive, Oxfam GB

You just have to do it! How often have we heard it said, and how often have we said it ourselves: that doing business in more human, more environmentally sustainable ways is the great adventure of our times. Here is a textbook that assumes a new normal. Start with the assumption that we have just one beautiful planet, and business suddenly becomes sane again. I recommend this book to all who want to do proper, value-adding business

Jan van Betten
Founder, Nudge.nl

When leading minds get together to challenge established ways of thinking about the purpose of business in today's world, it is a sign that existing systems boundaries are being pushed and redrawn. This urgently needed book brings to the surface comprehensive and game-changing approaches that will enable business leaders to steer their organizations with care, responsibility, value and success through rapidly changing societal and environmental complexities. Most importantly though, the authors courageously address the most difficult barrier we face in creating change for a sustainable future – the role that our own mindsets, values and behaviours play. This is the textbook for business and management educators who want to be on the right side of history.

Isabel Sebastian
Senior Research Consultant, Institute of Sustainable Futures
University of Technology Sydney, Australia

SUSTAINABLE BUSINESS
A One Planet Approach

EDITED BY

Sally Jeanrenaud

Jean-Paul Jeanrenaud

Jonathan Gosling

In association with

WILEY

To the Goodness, Truth and Beauty of People and Planet,
and for the wisdom to co-create for the benefit of all.

CONTENTS

Foreword   xiii
Preface   xv
About the Authors   xxiii

1   Challenging   **1**
Sally Jeanrenaud & Jean-Paul Jeanrenaud

1.0 Stories about the Future   2
2.0 Planet   7
3.0 People   18
4.0 Profit   28
5.0 Power   35
6.0 Conclusion: The Case for Change   42
References   46

2   Changing   **53**
Sally Jeanrenaud & Jean-Paul Jeanrenaud

2.0 Changing from the Outside-In and the Inside-Out   53
2.1 Business   54
2.2 Economy   56
2.3 Self   57
2.4 Transformations   59
2.5 Conclusion: Metamorphosis   81
References   83

3   Leading   **87**
Jonathan Gosling & Prasad Kaipa

Introduction   87
3.0 Sustainability and Leadership   89
3.1 What is Leadership?   90
3.2 Some Nagging Questions about Leadership   100
3.3 Bringing it All Home: How to Conduct Yourself in Leadership 111
Summary   115
References   116

4 **Valuing**   119
   Catherine Cameron

   Introduction   120
   4.0 The Limits to GDP and GNP as Measures of Value   122
   4.1 The Range of Alternative Measures and Current Practice   130
   4.2 Rethinking Growth   143
   Summary   146
   References   147

5 **Collaborating**   149
   Ward Crawford

   Introduction   150
   5.0 Images of Working Together   150
   5.1 Choosing Collaboration   157
   5.2 The Theory and Practice of Collaboration   162
   5.3 Managing Collaborative (Dis)Agreement   169
   Summary   174
   References   175

6 **Strategizing**   177
   Nadya Zhexembayeva & Judith Jordan

   Introduction   177
   6.0 Oil, Water, and a Touch of Hurricane Katrina: The New
        Business Reality   178
   6.1 Searching for a Disappeared Resource? Check your landfill   181
   6.2 The Strategic Challenge of Sustainability: Stakeholders are calling   182
   6.3 Strategic Responses: What Strategies Have Businesses Adopted?
        What More Can They Do?   190
   Summary   201
   References   201

7 **Organizing**   205
   Morgen Witzel

   Introduction   205
   7.0 Organizations and Sustainability   206
   7.1 Motivating People   208
   7.2 Organizational Culture   215
   7.3 Requisite Knowledge   218
   7.4 The Employer Brand   220
   Summary   221
   References   223

8 Investing   **225**
Rory Sullivan

Introduction   225
8.0   Mechanics of Influence: How do Investors Influence Companies?   227
8.1   What is Responsible Investment?   228
8.2   So What Can Responsible Investment Deliver?   235
8.3   Conclusion   240
Summary   240
References   241

9 Innovating   **243**
John Bessant & Palie Smart

Introduction   243
9.0   Innovation Strategy   245
9.1   How Can We Innovate? Innovation as a Management Process   255
Summary   261
References   262

10 Operating   **265**
Mickey Howard, Fu Jia & Zhaohui Wu

Introduction   265
10.0   Transition to the Triple Bottom Line   266
10.1   Industrial Ecology and Closing the Loop   268
10.2   Sustainability Standards, Certification and Measures   271
10.3   Stakeholder Management   278
Summary   291
References   292

11 Marketing   **293**
Ken Peattie and Frank-Martin Belz

Introduction   294
From 20th to 21st Century Marketing   295
11.0   Sustainability and Marketing: An Evolving Relationship   296
11.1   Sustainability Marketing: Marketing for the 21st Century   298
11.2   From Products to Customer Solutions   305
11.3   From Price to Consumer Cost   307
11.4   From Place to Convenience   309
11.5   From Promotion to Communication   311
11.6   Sustainability Marketing as a Transformational Force   314
11.7   Conclusion   315
Summary   317
References   318

12 Accounting   **319**
Stephen Jollands

Introduction   319
12.0 Accounting and Sustainability   320
12.1 Financial Accounting   326
12.2 Management Accounting   335
12.3 Conclusion: Addressing the meta- and sub-questions   341
Summary   343
References   344

13 Entrepreneurship   **347**
Tony Cooke

Introduction   347
13.0 The 'Cult' of Entrepreneurship?   348
13.1 A Brief History of Entrepreneurship Theory   350
13.2 Towards One Planet Entrepreneurship   357
Summary   377
References   378

14 Transitioning   **381**
Thomas Dyllick & Katrin Muff

Introduction   381
14.0 Sustainable Business and Sustainable Development:
     The Big Disconnect   382
14.1 Understanding Our Global Sustainability Challenges   385
14.2 Different Approaches to Framing Business Sustainability   387
14.3 Introducing a Typology for Business Sustainability   391
14.4 Managing Business Sustainability: Organizational Characteristics   400
14.5 Conclusion   401
Summary   404
References   405

15 Conclusion   **409**
Sally Jeanrenaud, Jean-Paul Jeanrenaud & Jonathan Gosling

15.0 The Challenges: The One Planet Predicament   409
15.1 Sustainable Business: A One Planet Approach   411
15.2 Change for Good   414
15.3 Transforming Business Management Education   416
References   419

Index   421

FOREWORD

Global wildlife populations have declined by more than half in the last 40 years, climate change and extreme weather events threaten the long-term stability of the planet and society. We should be in no doubt as to the scale of the challenges we are facing.

The crisis is global and the impacts of our unsustainable lifestyles are being felt everywhere in resource scarcity, poverty, civil unrest and war. These pose major risks to business and society but also provide opportunities for innovation, and new kinds of growth and prosperity. The solution is inspiring and exciting - learning how to live sustainably on our One Planet.

If we are to ensure that the Earth, our only home, continues to provide us with all we need to survive and prosper, then we will need to create a new, just, and equitable economic system that will be sustainable in perpetuity.

This timely book makes a powerful argument for a radical shift in the focus of Management Education away from a narrow emphasis on financial growth, to one that puts equity, and prosperity for all at centre-stage. Although corporations have a key role to play in shaping a sustainable future for people and planet, it is not always easy to strike the right balance between our ideals and values, and running a successful business. All too often the quest for profits can obscure wider social benefits. However, I am convinced that the private sector can, and must, be a principle driver of change for good. I believe we are already witnessing the first signs of this paradigm shift spearheaded by pioneering NGOs, governments and businesses. More and more people understand that working in ways that protect the environment is good for business, good for society, and good in itself.

We are witnessing a growing movement to disinvest from our dependency on fossil fuels to a world based on renewable energy. WWF's Seize Your Power campaign has played a part, helping to spur divestment from dirty fossil fuels and investment into clean, abundant renewable energy. This is not just about protecting the environment it also makes sound economic sense, especially when oil and gas reserves are increasingly likely to become stranded assets.

To stop the degradation of the planet's natural environment and to build a future in which people live in harmony with nature: that is WWF's mission. And it is one that touches all areas of our lives. For the natural environment is ultimately the basis of our economic prosperity, our social progress and our personal well-being.

We are not alone in our mission, nor in our message. It is increasingly echoed by a wide range of voices, in many spheres and many sectors. By civil society organizations, scientists, communities and millions of concerned global citizens; by village councils and UN bodies; by businesses, banks and economists. We are all potential allies as we grapple with the big planetary challenges – climate and energy issues, protecting species and ecosystems, curbing unsustainable resource use and securing water supplies for all. We cannot achieve the change we need alone, but when we come together with others, anything is possible.

Yolanda Kakabadse

President of WWF

PREFACE

Introduction

There are at least five major strands of thought that shape the content and style of this book.

1. Business Serving Society

The overall goal of *Sustainable Business: The One Planet Approach* is to help train MBA students to manage and lead companies and organizations that serve wider society and work towards the common good, in ways that increase human well-being, reduce poverty, inequality and ecological degradation, and are nonetheless profitable. Corporate scandals, growing inequalities between the rich and the poor, mounting environmental risks and ecological scarcities, and the risk of financial recession, underpin the arguments that 'the corporation' has become dysfunctional, de-linked from its social purpose, focused on financial gain at the expense of ethical practice and environmental health, and is in danger of losing its status as a trusted social institution.

There is a growing consensus that, while firms need to remain profitable to stay in business, their owners and managers need to take responsibility for their social and environmental impacts, and define a higher purpose that expresses the inherent aspiration for the good. Others claim that capitalism itself is at a crossroads, and that we are in a profound transition from an old to a new economy, in how we create and measure value, and define success, which will have profound implications for business, society and self.

This book, then, aims to promote and support an understanding of a transition to a more sustainable economy, and to position itself in the wider debate about the changing role of business in society. Its goal is not to prepare students to work in companies that operate within the same cost-externalizing, profit-maximizing business logic of the last 50 years, nor to adopt the same ethically myopic practices of the past. Nor does it aim to mainstream sustainability considerations into business practice simply to enhance competitive advantage, nor to prepare students to become better corporate social responsibility (CSR) managers (although it may include this). Rather, it recognizes that business management education needs to radically evolve and transform to reflect new aspirations, knowledge and practices. The leitmotif of the book may be considered change or transition from business as usual to business models that will have a net positive impact. It promotes pro-business, pro-people and pro-planet approaches.

2. Integrating Planetary Boundaries and Social Foundations

Sustainable Business is rooted in an understanding of the concept of planetary boundaries. Scientists have identified nine boundaries of the planet's biophysical subsystems or processes that define a stable environment conducive to life and a 'safe operating space' for humanity. This approach recognizes that 'nature has its own budget', and that current patterns of production and consumption are pushing us across certain biophysical thresholds, such as safe thresholds of CO_2 in the atmosphere, with unknown but potentially disastrous consequences for humanity.

The concept of 'planetary boundaries' is often combined with a parallel notion of 'social foundations', which identifies 11 social priorities for human development, below which lies unacceptable human deprivation, such as hunger, ill-health and income poverty. The concept of a 'safe and just space for humanity' within which our institutions have to work is sometimes referred to as the 'Oxfam doughnut model'. The concepts of planetary boundaries and social foundations are introduced in more detail in *Chapter 1*. Our efforts in this book thus take into account these factors for corporate sustainability.

Basically, business has tended to operate on the assumption that natural resources are infinite, but that enterprise(s) are bounded. Actually the opposite is the case: the planet is bounded (notwithstanding the practically endless energy from the sun), while human imagination and enterprise are free. Some scholars propose how metrics for organizational performance could be applied to strategic and operational decisions, in the preferred metaphor of some authors providing a 'dashboard' on how each company's operations take us towards or back from these nine crucial boundaries. Why is this important? Because it begins to show how businesses might evaluate their contributions to global wealth, more broadly defined.

Of course all these boundaries and foundations are socially constructed in the normal context of the political economy; and how business and regulations work in relation to them is not straightforward. Many will choose not to be mindful of such criteria, so one important aspect of 'one planet business' must be a willingness to contest the status quo. But the point we want to make is that our book should speak to those who want to work differently; who choose to take a critical stance in relation to promises of 'responsible capitalism', 'sustainable business', and 'escape through technical innovation'. We should help these people to articulate their aspirations, and to figure out how to work in what might be radically different ways.

3. Supporting the Transformation of Business and Management Education

The book aims to make a contribution to the transformation of business and management education. We recognize that business and management education have been blamed for various dysfunctions of the modern corporation, and that there is a need to challenge and transform the way business and management are taught. It is currently in a state of transition worldwide. Business schools have been responsible for failing to foster ethically-informed leadership, sustainability, and accountable business practices. They have even been blamed for creating financial crises and recessions. Managers and recruiters are increasingly questioning conventional business education. Various student-led initiatives, such as the MBA Oath, are seeking to restore ethics and higher purpose in the field of management education. With the exception of the emerging economies, applications to MBA programmes have declined as economic uncertainty is leaving students wary of investing in business programmes.

Several organizations are taking a lead in articulating the rationale for transforming business school education. For example, the goal of the United Nations PRME initiative (Principles for Responsible Management Education) is to inspire and champion responsible management education, research and thought leadership globally. It claims that corporate responsibility and sustainability have entered but not yet become embedded in the mainstream of business-related education, and calls on business schools to address new business challenges and opportunities. It has developed six new principles of responsible business education (related to purpose, values, method, research, partnership, dialogue) with over 650 participating institutions.

The 50+20 Group's manifesto *Management Education for the World*, prepared for Rio+20, describes a vision for the transformation of management education in which the common tenet of being best *in* the world is revised in favour of creating businesses which are designed to achieve the best *for* the world. It lays out three new roles of management education: the education of globally responsible leaders; the transformation of research into an applied field to serve the common good; and, the role of management educators in transforming business and the economy through open space action learning and research.

Business schools worldwide are revamping their curricula in attempts to rebuild reputation and trust. New modules on ethics, CSR and sustainability are being developed, and many are rethinking and extending MBA curricula beyond a bolt-on sustainable development module. However, beyond these preliminary efforts, there are deeper transformations of economy and society underway. These changes will affect how every business discipline is taught. This book aims to contribute to this transformation of business management education, and to produce a useful resource to help, support and guide students who want to adopt a 'one planet' approach.

4. Mainstreaming Sustainability within the MBA Curricula

This text is based on the belief that sustainability is emerging as a concern in every discipline, and needs to be embedded within all modules, rather than considered as an add-on module to an existing MBA programme. We understood that the relationship between society, economy and ecology is framed in various ways in the diverse literatures, but that the interconnections between human and natural systems are increasingly recognized in every field. Thus, we are dependent on nature's life support systems for our own survival (the air we breathe, the water we drink, the soil in which we grow our crops) and ecosystems provide us numerous goods and services critical to the economy, but are often taken for granted and are economically invisible (e.g. pollination, production of oxygen, sequestration of carbon dioxide). Sustainability cannot be considered as something nice to have, or as extra to life. It is more than a set of resources; it is the basis of life. Learning how to be sustainable is more a rite of passage that every species has to go through if it wants to remain on the planet over the long haul, and needs to be considered by and within every discipline.

We aim to capture some of the results of this thinking within the business education world, and in particular the implications for teaching leadership, economics, strategy, collaboration, innovation, operations, organization, marketing, finance, entrepreneurship and accounting, amongst others. However, *Sustainable Business* does not aspire to put forward a complete reworking of the MBA curriculum. The collection of chapters should be considered as a modest contribution to a learning journey. It recognizes that the economy and business practices are in a state of transition, and that the book's efforts to capture some of these changes across a range of MBA modules should be seen as a work in progress.

This work also supports the development of new and diverse pedagogies, which will encourage students to be more politically, culturally and ecologically aware, to challenge old assumptions, values, and ways of working, and to adopt new perspectives and tools in order to realign company interests with wider social goals.

5. Respecting Diversity of Voices

We sought to work with a wide group of authors and practitioners who are pioneering sustainable business in their research, teaching, and work. The text is international in scope, and draws on the work of academics and practitioners from across the globe. We also wished to acknowledge and respect distinctive intellectual perspectives, and practical approaches to sustainability and business transformation. We welcomed a diversity of views and voices in this emerging field, understanding that the contributing authors rationalized or communicated sustainability, or business transformation, in different ways. Each contributing author has been free to develop and articulate their preferred perspectives and material in their own style.

Structure of the Book

Each of the chapters broadly covers a traditional MBA curriculum. But instead of naming each in terms of an academic discipline (e.g. economics, finance, accounting, etc.) they are titled according to the problems they are trying to solve. In each chapter we have addressed the problems as they are conceived in our contemporary world, with an emphasis on new framings and emerging solutions. The first chapter outlines the main sustainability challenges and the case for change, while the second chapter outlines some of the principles and examples of new economic and business approaches. Some readers may prefer to begin with the *Chapter 2*.

In **Challenging**, *Chapter 1*, Sally and Jean-Paul Jeanrenaud outline a big picture overview of our 'one planet predicament'. They introduce the interconnected impacts of business as usual on planet, people, profit and power, which have been described as unsustainable, unfair, unstable and undemocratic, and which pose risks to business and society. They challenge the ideas that we can grow now and clean up later; that wealth trickles down, that rising GDP increases well-being; that growth creates jobs; and that competitive capitalism is a vehicle of democracy. Such challenges help create the case for change to new economic and business models, or what might be called a 'one planet approach'.

In **Changing**, *Chapter 2*, Sally and Jean-Paul Jeanrenaud outline three interlinked domains of change: business, economy, and the self, and highlight the importance of changing from the 'inside-out' as well as the 'outside-in'. They illustrate 10 ways in which thinking and practice is shifting in business, relating to mindsets; purpose; governance; capitals; nature; labour, production, consumption; energy and technologies. These represent a fresh integration of inner and outer realms, which is helping us reconnect to ourselves, each other, and to nature.

In **Leading**, *Chapter 3*, Jonathan Gosling and Prasad Kaipa show how the art of influencing people towards shared goals is rooted in culturally and historically specific settings. A development towards eco-leadership is charted and described. Because leadership involves relationships imbued with feelings about power, dependency and trust, people are usually and rightly ambivalent about their leaders. Often there is a mismatch of expectations throughout a hierarchy, and differences between unitary, plural and radical conceptions of organizations. The argument that leadership should adapt to the situation is criticized on the grounds that defining the situation – as wicked, tame or critical – is a leadership function with important political outcomes. While new leadership thinking hails a shift from hero to host, from conqueror to carer, the abiding responsibility is to face uncertainty with wisdom. The chapter concludes with an explanation of why mindfulness is important in developing responsible and wise leadership towards more integral purposes.

In *Chapter 4* on **Valuing**, Catherine Cameron explores the concept of economic growth, and new ways of measuring what matters, arguing why reframing growth is essential in the 21st century, and the implications for business and management students. She discusses the limits to GDP as a measure of value; broader approaches to value, including new ways of valuing the contribution of nature and ecosystem services to business; and examples of companies and alliances of companies at the forefront of the practical work of revaluing, and measuring what matters.

In **Collaborating**, *Chapter 5*, Ward Crawford explores how social interactions can be transformed into collaborations between people, organizations and stakeholders, and how these can contribute towards addressing sustainability challenges. He explores the theory and practice of collaboration, including how to manage collaborative disagreements. The development of relationships built on respect, inclusivity, equity and trust, encourage the integration of interests and a commitment to a shared goal; while the recognition of different dimensions of value can underpin the co-creation of new value for individuals as well as a wider group.

Nadya Zhexembayeva and Judith Jordan, in **Strategizing**, *Chapter 6*, highlight the risks of doing business in a resource-constrained world with more stakeholder demands, and what this means for business strategy today. They explore different strategic responses of companies, such as trade-offs, bolt-on sustainability, embedding sustainability, and what they call the Overfished Ocean Strategy, which transforms challenges into opportunities, and gives rise to a new economy, transforming the collapsing linear throwaway economy into a more lasting, more abundant, more sustainable one.

Morgen Witzel, in **Organizing**, *Chapter 7*, defines organizations as dynamic socio-technical systems comprised of people with their own individual needs and wants. He argues that there is no one 'right' form of organizing for sustainability. Once an organization has set its strategy, it then adapts itself to best meet that strategy. This involves understanding and managing the roles of personal motivations, culture, knowledge and communication, as well as the concept of employee brand in helping drive organizations towards their goals.

In **Investing**, *Chapter 8*, Rory Sullivan explores different responsible investment strategies, and their relationship to mainstream investment practice, and discusses the potential contribution that responsible investment might make to the goals of a more sustainable economy. He argues that the growth in the number of investors that have made commitments to responsible investment is yielding good results. However, many challenges remain such as the pressures on investors to deliver short-term financial returns, the focus on risk and opportunity at the portfolio level, and the weaknesses in wider policy frameworks for sustainable development.

In **Innovating**, *Chapter 9*, John Bessant and Palie Smart examine the key concepts and theory relating to sustainability orientated innovation, and how sustainability is helping generate new forms of value in organizations and systems. They explore the innovation imperative, innovation strategy, and innovation as a management process, and challenge. And they outline a range of contexts in which sustainability-orientated innovation takes place, from operational optimization, organizational transformation, and systems building for societal change, and include examples of innovations inspired by nature.

Mickey Howard, Fu Jia and Zhaohui Wu, in **Operating**, *Chapter 10*, explore the transition to the triple bottom line and what this means for the sustainable supply chain. New operational approaches are evolving built on reducing energy and waste, developing sustainable supply systems, and fostering a transition to a circular economy. In particular they outline the principles of industrial ecology and closing the loop, sustainability standards, certification and measures, and stakeholder management in the context of supply chain management.

In **Marketing**, *Chapter 11*, Ken Peattie and Frank-Martin Belz outline the relationship between marketing and sustainability, and argue that the concept of sustainability marketing requires different approaches to traditional marketing ideas and concepts, creating a number of political challenges. They explore how sustainable companies are creating innovative approaches to marketing that can transform markets and consumer behaviour, and generate greater competitive advantage.

In **Accounting**, *Chapter 12*, Stephen Jollands argues that accounting means much more than preparing a narrowly-focused financial account. He critically explores new accounts, tools and techniques that are being developed in the name of sustainability and highlights a range of issues associated with them. Accounts give visibility to certain elements, while making others invisible. He argues that actions resulting from accounts are more important than accounts themselves, and that organizations need visibility over different sustainability dimensions.

Tony Cooke, on **Entrepreneurship**, *Chapter 13*, explores the concept of the entrepreneur and the wide variety of organizational and social contexts where entrepreneurship has an impact, where it is widely perceived as a positive force for change. He develops the concept of a One Planet Entrepreneur, as an innovator pursuing opportunities to create positive social, environmental and economic value, and he encourages readers to consider their own entrepreneurial attributes and intentions.

In **Transitioning**, *Chapter 14*, Thomas Dyllick and Katrin Muff point out that despite the fact that more companies are integrating sustainability into their management, the state of the planet is not improving. This 'big disconnect' is related to the way business sustainability has been framed and developed in theory and in practice. They propose a new typology for business sustainability, ranging from Business-as-Usual to Business Sustainability 1.0 (Refined Shareholder Value Management);

Business Sustainability 2.0 (Managing for the Triple Bottom Line); and Business Sustainability 3.0 (Truly Sustainable Business). A truly sustainable business shifts from seeking to minimize its negative impacts to creating a positive impact on people and planet.

In summary, *Sustainable Business: The One Planet Approach* promotes the development of businesses with higher purpose that serve the common good, that operate within planetary boundaries, recognize social foundations, that internalize the negative externalities of business, and which contribute to building human, social, natural, manufactured and financial capital. This book aims to promote one planet business approaches that are pro-people, pro-planet and pro-prosperity, and which help achieve the United Nations Sustainable Development Goals (SDGs).

S. Jeanrenaud, J. Gosling, J-P. Jeanrenaud
January 2017

ABOUT THE AUTHORS

Frank-Martin Belz holds the Chair of Corporate Sustainability at the Technische Universität München (TUM School of Management), Germany. He focuses his research and teaching on sustainable entrepreneurship, innovation and marketing. Together with Ken Beattie (Cardiff Business School, UK) he published the award-winning text book *Sustainability Marketing: A Global Perspective*.

John Bessant, originally a chemical engineer, currently holds the Chair in Innovation and Entrepreneurship at the University of Exeter. He's been researching, teaching and consulting about innovation management for over 35 years and is the author of 30 books and many articles, including the standard text *Managing Innovation*, published by John Wiley and now in its 5th edition.

Catherine Cameron is a practitioner and advocate for a climate resilient, sustainable future. She leads the Living the Dream programme, building aspirational, positive narratives of sustainable living. She works across the public, private, academic and third sectors as a connector and enabler. She advises, teaches, writes, convenes, innovates and changes as Adviser, Chair, Director, Fellow or Professor in 45 countries.

Tony Cooke is the founding CEO of the One Planet Education Network ('OPEN') for Business which aims to make responsible business practice the norm. He has a background as a strategy consultant and social entrepreneur having worked internationally across the private, public and not-for-profit sectors. He holds a One Planet MBA from the University of Exeter Business School.

Ward Crawford has taught on the One Planet MBA at University of Exeter since its inception, leading two modules in Collaboration, Partnering & Negotiation, and Marketing & Customer Engagement. Prior to this he held senior executive strategic and commercial roles in the UK, Japan, and Malaysia, in the FMCG and Consumer Durable sectors.

Thomas Dyllick is Professor of Sustainability Management at University of St. Gallen, Switzerland. He is a Managing Director of the Institute for Economy and the Environment, and University Delegate for Responsibility and Sustainability. He was Dean of the Management Department and Vice President of the University. He codirected the 50+20 Initiative, a vision of management education for the world.

Jonathan Gosling is Emeritus Professor of Leadership and co-founder of the One Planet MBA at University of Exeter, UK. He has been involved in leadership education for over 25 years, consultant to many international companies and NGOs, and was founding secretary of the European Conference on Peacemaking and Conflict Resolution. He currently works on the delivery of public health in crisis zones.

Mickey Howard is Professor of Supply Management at the University of Exeter Business School, UK. His research interests include the circular economy and sustainable supply chain management. He is co-founder of the Circular Economy Business Forum, and co-author of several books: *'Purchasing & Supply Chain Management: A Sustainability Perspective'* (2014) Routledge UK, and *'Procuring Complex Performance'* (2011) Routledge NY.

Jean-Paul Jeanrenaud has worked for WWF for over 25 years as Director of Corporate Relations and education projects. He has lived and worked in Asia, Africa and Europe. He co-founded the Forest Stewardship Council (FSC); One Planet Leaders; the award winning One Planet MBA; and OPEN for Business (One Planet Education Network). He is also a qualified Mindfulness teacher.

Sally Jeanrenaud is Senior Research Fellow in Sustainability, Business School, University of Exeter, UK. She has worked in Nepal, Rwanda, Cameroon and Europe, in field-based and international positions. She helped establish Exeter's One Planet MBA, and co-founded the Green Economy Coalition, and OPEN for Business. She researches sustainability-orientated innovation processes, including the psychological dimensions of social change.

Fu Jia is a Senior Lecturer in Supply Network Management, Business School, University of Exeter, UK. He co-founded the Business, Nature and Value Research Centre, which focuses on relationships between business, nature and value creation. He researches sustainable supply chain management, relationships and innovation in agricultural and industrial contexts. He is Associate Editor of Journal of Purchasing and Supply Management.

Stephen Jollands joined the University of Exeter, UK as a Lecturer in 2011 after completing his PhD at The University of Auckland. Stephen has a variety of practical experience including two years working for Ernst and Young. His research and professional interests primarily rest in issues related to accounting for sustainable development and accounting for social and ecological sustainability.

Judith Jordan is a Senior Teaching Fellow at the University of Bristol, specializing in Strategy, and has a wealth of experience in developing and delivering executive strategy programmes. She is the co-author of a popular strategy textbook *Foundations of Strategy* (Wiley), and has a keen interest in strategy and innovation and case study approaches in research.

Prasad Kaipa is an advisor to CEOs in the area of leadership, innovation and transformation and has taught executive programmes in Indian School of Business, USC, INSEAD, Tuck and LBS. Prasad co-wrote an international best-seller *"From Smart to Wise"* (Wiley 2013) and *"You Can"* (Bloomsbury 2016). He integrates brain research, management principles and spiritual perspectives in his writings.

Katrin Muff is Dean of Business School Lausanne, Switzerland, implementing a values-based approach to sustainability, responsibility and entrepreneurship. Her business experience includes M&A and international General Manager positions with Alcoa, Iams Pet Food, and a start-up incubator. She codirected the global 50+20 Initiative (www.50plus20.org). Her research focuses on the convergence of responsibility and sustainability and transformational learning environments.

Ken Peattie is Professor of Marketing and Strategy at Cardiff Business School and Co-Director of Cardiff University Sustainable Places Research Institute, UK. His research focuses on sustainability and marketing; social marketing for sustainable lifestyles; social enterprise and corporate social responsibility. Through books, book chapters, journal articles, teaching and presentations he has tried to promote business sustainability for over 25 years.

Palie Smart is Reader and Director of PhD Programme at Cranfield School of Management. She is the Principal Investigator for an EPSRC project exploring sustainability-led innovation. She has published in journals such as *Research Policy, British Journal of Management, International Journal of Operations and Production Management, R&D Management, International Journal of Production Economics, and International Journal of Management Reviews.*

Rory Sullivan is an internationally recognized expert on responsible investment, and climate change. Dr Sullivan is the author/editor of seven books and many papers and reports on responsible investment, climate change and related issues, including *Valuing Corporate Responsibility: How Do Investors Really Use Corporate Responsibility Information?* (Greenleaf Publishing, 2011), and *Corporate Responses to Climate Change* (editor, Greenleaf Publishing, 2008).

Morgen Witzel is a Fellow of the Centre for Leadership Studies at the University of Exeter Business School, and a lecturer on the One Planet MBA programme. He is the author of more than 20 books on management and leadership.

Zhaohui Wu is Professor of Supply Chain & Operations Management at Oregon State University, USA. He has considerable experience of conducting research in supply networks, environmental management strategy in operations, alternative/sustainable food systems and agricultural cooperatives. He is currently the Associate Editor for the *Journal of Supply Chain Management* (2015-) and *Journal of Operations Management* (2007-).

Nadya Zhexembayeva is a business owner, educator, speaker and author, specializing in reinvention. She was Coca-Cola Chaired Professor of Sustainable Development at IEDC, Slovenia, and teaches in CEDEP (France) and IPADE Business School (Mexico). She helps companies reinvent products, processes, and leadership practices. She has been called 'The Reinvention Guru' (*Ventures* magazine) and 'The Queen of Reinvention' (TEDx Navasink).

1 Challenging: An Overview of Our One Planet Predicament

Sally Jeanrenaud and Jean-Paul Jeanrenaud

'Enough of the imbalance that is destroying our democracies, our planet and ourselves.'

Henry Mintzberg, 2015

LEARNING OUTCOMES

This chapter provides a big picture, multidisciplinary overview of our one planet predicament and its implications for business and society, and makes the case for new economic and business approaches. By the end of the chapter you will be familiar with:

1. Stories about the future: scenarios and perspectives on the role of business in social change; and the contested concept of sustainable development.

2. Planet: the environmental challenges facing business and society; concepts such as planetary boundaries, ecological footprint, and systemic risk. Case Study: Lafarge.

3. People: the social challenges facing business and society; concepts such as poverty, social inequality, consumerism and the happiness paradox. Case Study: Interface.

4. Profit: the economic challenges facing business and society from a sustainability perspective; and concepts such as natural capital, negative externalities, and short-termism.

5. Power: the challenges relating to the power of multinational corporations from a sustainability perspective; and concepts such as corporate lobbying, the revolving door, and the democracy deficit. Case Study: SumOfUs and Avaaz.

You can use the chapter in various ways. First, each section can be used to provide a daily focus for a five-day module. Second, a number of issues can be selected from the sections to address a particular question from a multidisciplinary perspective (e.g. the concept of economic growth). The issues presented here are quite succinct – more could be said about each one – and many are dealt with in greater depth in the following chapters. All the ideas in this chapter are open to interpretation, and readers are encouraged to reflect critically upon them all. If you are familiar with the interlinked problems facing business and society, then you can skip *Chapter 1*, and go directly to *Chapter 2*, which introduces new business and economic approaches.

1.0 Stories about the Future

We tell ourselves many different stories about the future. Leading organizations and companies – such as the World Business Council for Sustainable Development, United Nations Environment Programme, and Shell – develop scenarios to help guide their strategic planning. These draw on a knowledge of trends in demography, economics, social and culture issues, technology, environment and governance, and develop alternative, plausible narratives about possible outcomes. Such scenarios can be helpful to business in directing decision-making towards desirable outcomes.

According to the Tellus Institute (2015) there are three broad classes of scenarios: Conventional Worlds, Barbarization, and Great Transitions. They each have a different view on the role of business in society.

Conventional World Scenarios: these envisage that the dominant values and relationships of the global industrial and economic system will continue to evolve in the 21st century through incremental market and policy adaptations. Fundamental or radical transformations are not foreseen. Volans (2013) describes these as 'Change-as-Usual' stories, and argues that they frequently fail to identify the systemic nature of challenges to society, or risks to business. These conventional world scenarios imply business-as-usual approaches, in which business responds to sustainability challenges as a result of changes in legislation, policies and markets, and via piecemeal, incremental innovation.

Barbarization Scenarios: these envisage the deterioration of ethical, socio-economic, environmental and governance systems, and crises that overwhelm the coping capacity of the market or the state. This can lead to social unrest and collapse, and/or to a 'fortress world', as analysed by Jared Diamond (2011) in his book *Collapse*. Volans (2013) describes this as 'Breakdown', and claims that such collapse is increasingly apparent and that there are links between these challenges (e.g. slow recovery from recession, financial turmoil, youth unemployment, social conflict, spread of chronic disease, climate change, declining resources). The barbarization scenarios help explain the rise of so-called 'doom capitalism', in which some businesses develop a financial interest in exploiting and sometimes even exacerbating crises in order to generate value (Klein, 2007).

Great Transition Scenarios: these imagine visionary solutions to sustainability challenges, including a transformation of values; increased levels of welfare and more equitable distribution; eco-friendly production and consumption systems; the conservation and restoration of natural systems; new governance systems; enabling policies; fiscal regimes, incentives and metrics. Such scenarios include variants such as face-to-face democracy, appropriate scale technology and economic independence, relocalization of the global economy, and the new sustainability paradigm, which involves the transformation of markets and policies to serve sustainable development.

1.1 Perspectives on the Role of Business

As major actors in the political economy, companies play a key role in shaping and adapting to the world around them, and this role is framed in diverse ways in stories about the future.

Business Must Adapt. A mainstream perspective is that companies need a rigorous understanding of global megatrends and disrupters in order to manage complexity, navigate risks and grow their businesses in fragile and challenging environments (PwC, 2015). According to the futurist Bob Johansen, business is now operating in a VUCA world, an environment of Volatility, Uncertainty, Complexity and Ambiguity. The acronym VUCA, borrowed from the military, describes the chaotic, turbulent, and rapidly changing business environment which some argue has become the 'new normal'. There are many interconnected factors shaping a VUCA world, which have the potential to profoundly disrupt or destroy business (see Definition box). Of the Fortune 500 companies listed in 1955, only 12.2% (61 companies) were still on the list in 2014 (Perry, 2014). It is predicted that 50% of today's top Fortune 500 businesses will have disappeared by 2030 (Frey, 2013). In such a VUCA world, businesses need to prepare *for* change, adapt or die.

A VUCA WORLD

- Climate disruption, decline in biodiversity, water and energy insecurities, resource scarcities, natural disasters and epidemics.
- Demographic changes, rapid urbanization, shifting consumer values, the rise of the fast-growing BRICS economies (Brazil, Russia, India, China, South Africa) and a shift in economic power from West to East; unstable political regimes.
- Volatile prices and financial markets, increasing risk and complexity in supply chains, rapid technological changes, risks of 'boom and bust' cycles and global economic recession.

Business is the Problem. An alternative perspective is that business is actually to blame for major social and planetary disruptions, and that business urgently needs reforming. In his provocative book and film *The Corporation: The Pathological Pursuit of Profit and Power,* Joel Bakan (2004) argues that if the corporation were a person it would be a psychopath, causing harm to society because of the way it has been created and protected under the law. Its unethical behaviour includes low wages in developing countries, environmental damage, subversion of the democratic process through donations and lobbying, insidious marketing, and wielding power over society. He argues for restoring the balance of power from corporations back to the people, and proposes a number of reforms. As Paul Hawken (1993) puts it: '*There is no polite way to say that business is destroying the world.*' However, he also argues that while business is the principle instrument of global destruction, it is also the only institution large enough, wealthy enough, and pervasive and powerful enough to lead humankind out of the mess we are making (cited in Anderson & White 2009, p.14).

Business is the Solution. Others promote a normative view of business in shaping the world. Two major international business platforms, the World Business Council for Sustainable Development (WBCSD) and the United Nations Global Compact (2015) both believe that corporations have a responsibility to make a contribution to sustainable development. In its Vision 2050 document, the WBCSD foresees that by 2050 '*some 9 billion people live well and within the limits of the planet*', and that business will make a major contribution to achieving this goal (WBCSD, 2010). Similarly, the aim of the UN Global Compact, which has over 8,000 members, is to work with business '*to transform the world, and to create a sustainable and inclusive global economy that delivers lasting benefits to people, communities and markets*'. Both organizations are helping companies define their role in delivering a new set of 17 global sustainable development goals agreed in 2015. As Peter Bakker, CEO of WBCSD put it in 2012: '*The future of the planet rests on business*' and '*business offers the best opportunity to save the world*' (cited in Confino, 2012). These views are controversial, since what is good for big business is not necessarily good for society as a whole. From this perspective, business has a key role to play but needs to prepare *to* change.

Whether you believe that the economy is now 'better than ever', that 'things are getting worse' or that we are 'in a transition to a more sustainable world', that business is 'part of the problem' or 'part of the solution', the assumptions and theories that supported the development of business and markets over the past 50 years are being challenged and reshaped in response to new forces. Radically new economies and new business mindsets and models are emerging which are recasting the purpose of business, the ways of producing, consuming, leading, relating, valuing and measuring, many of which seem to promise 'change for good', *and these are addressed in later chapters.*

1.2 Sustaining Development?

QUESTIONS FOR CLASS DISCUSSION

1. How would you define 'sustainable development'?
2. What is the 'development' that we want to sustain?

GROUP EXERCISE

RICH PICTURES: DRAWING SUSTAINABLE DEVELOPMENT AND SUSTAINABLE BUSINESS

See Exercise 1.2 at the end of the chapter.

Normative views about 'the world we want' are often framed as 'sustainable development'. This concept has become a major topic of international debate since the 1980s, and a key influence on governments, businesses, NGOs, and citizens worldwide. However, historical research, as well as an understanding of indigenous peoples' wisdom, suggests that ideas about how to live well on the planet have been considered since the dawn of civilization.

The term 'sustainable development' was popularised in 1987 by the book *Our Common Future* by the World Commission on Environment and Development (WCED), also known as *The Brundtland Report*, named after the Chair of the Commission and former Prime Minister of Norway, Gro Harlem Brundtland. It famously defined sustainable development as '*development that meets the needs of the present, without compromising the ability of future generations to meet their own needs*' (WCED, 1987, p. 43).

The Brundtland Report drew attention to a number of key issues. Significantly, it highlighted the interdependence of development and environment – the idea that economic progress cannot be considered in isolation from environmental

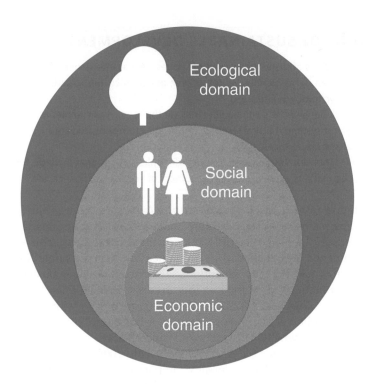

FIGURE 1.1 Strong Model of Sustainability.

degradation. It stressed the needs of the poorest nations and promoted the idea of global equity. And it famously emphasized the concept of intergenerational justice, or the idea that in the process of meeting the needs of the current generation, we should not undermine the ability of future generations to meet their own.

There are many definitions of sustainable development. Another simple definition provided by Hopkins (2010) is: '*Enough, For All, For Ever.*' 'Enough' implies an economic sufficiency (though not wasteful excess); 'For All' evokes both social equity and consideration for the non-human inhabitants of shared ecosystems; 'Forever' signals respect for natural resource limitations as well as the pursuit of 'intergenerational justice'.

Models of sustainable development typically include three dimensions of sustainability: the social, environmental, and economic sectors (see Definition box). These were first conceptualized by Edward Barbier in 1987 in the famous diagram of 'three inter-locking circles', but they are also portrayed as 'three pillars', as a 'three-legged stool', and more recently as a series of 'nested circles', reflecting different ways of thinking about these relationships.

This book widely employs the nested model of sustainable development, illustrated as a series of concentric circles, with the economy nested in society, which in turn is embedded in nature. This is sometimes referred to as the 'strong' model of sustainability (see Figure 1.1), and is one that recognizes that society and the economy are physically dependent on nature for life support systems: the air we breathe, water we drink, the soil we need in which to grow crops. If these services fail we would not be alive or have an economy at all; whereas the natural world would survive without us.

DIMENSIONS OF SUSTAINABLE DEVELOPMENT

- The social dimensions of sustainability include issues such as intergenerational justice, equity, basic needs, human rights, gender, values, power, governance, participation, and are studied by sociology, psychology, politics, etc.
- The ecological dimensions of sustainability include topics such as climate, water, biodiversity, waste, life support systems, natural resources, ecological footprint, and are studied through by the ecological and life sciences.
- The economic dimensions of sustainability include topics such as growth, trade, finance, profit, prosperity, jobs, markets, power, and are the subject of economics, finance, etc.

John Elkington (1997), in his book *Cannibals with Forks*, was one of the first thinkers to bring mainstream sustainability concepts into business management, by defining the significance of 'the triple bottom line' to business. This emphasizes social, environmental and economic performance instead of a single financial bottom line, and this has become an influential concept in new business metrics. These are also sometimes described as the three Ps: People, Planet and Profit; or the 3 Es: Equity, Ecology and Economy. Not everyone agrees with the significance of the triple bottom line concept. For example, it has been critiqued for providing a smokescreen behind which firms can avoid truly effective social and environmental reporting and performance (Norman & MacDonald 2003). We maintain, however, that change for good must have a positive impact on people and planet, as well profit, or put another way – prosperity – which includes wellbeing as well as wealth.

While the concept of sustainable development provides a normative view of change for business and society, it is important to be aware of its limitations. Narratives tend to get coopted and shaped by powerful institutions for their own ends, and it is important to uncover ideological assumptions and positions. There are political questions related to how 'needs' are defined, who defines them, and how they are met. Some fail to distinguish between growth (getting bigger) and development (getting better). The concept is seen as an 'oxymoron', as well as a 'wicked problem', one which is complex, changing, contradictory and subject to different stakeholder perspectives. There is also confusion between becoming a 'sustainable business', and the 'contribution business makes to sustainable development', which shape different corporate aims and outcomes.

Sustainable development is also considered boring to those who are more interested in fecundity and celebrating nature's abundance and designs that enrich life, rather than 'maintenance' or 'living within our means'. The concept and language can be off putting in corporate settings; practitioners have discovered it can be more effective to use a 'silent S' approach and promote 'smart' or 'future proofed' rather than 'sustainable' business practices. And in the context of climate change it may be more appropriate to support humanity's need to adapt, and to foster resilience in the face of growing inequalities, climate disruption, biodiversity loss, and increasing water, energy and resource scarcity.

Given that the concept was originally conceived and shaped as a counterpoint to the logic and values of a neo-liberal economic and global development agenda in the 1980s, it is questionable whether it is still as relevant today. This agenda has arguably lost much of its moral if not economic power, and has already undermined the ability of future generations to meet their own needs. There are many alternative economies emerging at regional and local levels, with culturally rich versions of prosperity and well-being, which challenge the need for global definitions and agendas. Some claim that the concept of sustainable development is dead, while other thinkers and practitioners have made efforts to define a new development paradigm (NDP, 2013).

We contend, however, that the basic principles and values of sustainable development, such as social justice, caring for nature, and prosperity are sound, and argue that if the term is dropped, just as more businesses are beginning to understand it, there is a risk of losing important ground and hard won awareness. The concept certainly needs to evolve and be enriched by alternative framings of development, so our approach is: keep it, but fix it!

But let's look at the case for change in more detail. The following sections present evidence for the need for transition, through understanding the challenges to Planet, People, Profit and Power. These introduce key environmental, social, economic and political concepts and issues from a sustainability perspective, and help illustrate the interlinked nature of our one planet predicament.

2.0 Planet

'There is no business to be done on a dead planet.'

David Brower, the late leading
American environmentalist

'We're running Genesis *backward, decreating.'*

Bill McKibben, American environmentalist
and founder of 350.org

QUESTIONS FOR CLASS DISCUSSION

1. What are the major global ecological challenges facing society today?
2. What are the implications of ecological risks for business?
3. Is it okay to grow now and clean up later?

2.1 Environmental Dimension

Scientific research indicates that the planet has undergone many eras of significant environmental change in its 4.6 billion years of history. But for the last 10,000 years there has been a period of relative stability in which the planet's systems regulated temperatures, fresh water, and chemical flows within a relatively narrow range. This period, known as the Holocene, created conditions that allowed human civilization to evolve and flourish (Rockström *et al.*, 2009).

However, since the Industrial Revolution, and the burning of fossil fuels, coupled with the 'Great Acceleration' in industrialization and energy use that followed WWII, human activities have become a major cause of environmental

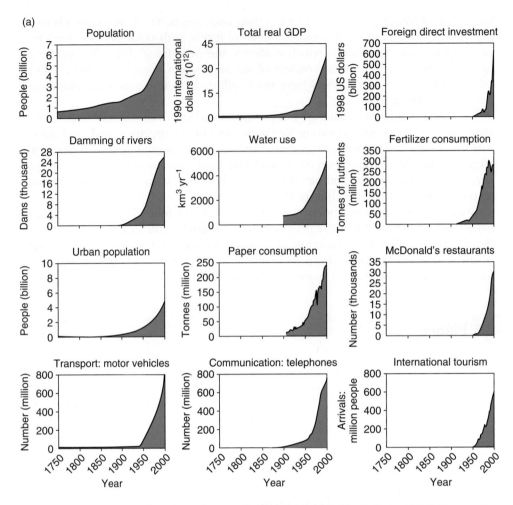

FIGURE 1.2 Economic Acceleration. *Source:* Steffen *et al.* (2011). Philosophical Transactions of the Royal Society, 369, 842–867.

change (see Figure 1.2(a) and (b)). These changes are affecting the regulatory systems that kept the earth in a stable state. Scientists have called this new era the 'anthropocene', a term proposed to cover an era in which human activities are the main drivers of change shaping the planet's geological and biophysical systems with potentially catastrophic consequences for all life on earth (Steffen *et al.*, 2007).

Human economic activities are affecting our global climate, biodiversity, the availability of key resources (such as water), and our waste systems. See Table 1.1, which presents consensus around key data. Out of all the changes shaping the planet, climate change is widely considered by the United Nations to be the 'defining challenge of our time'. Some scientists consider the climate change data presented below to be conservative. The current environmental challenges present huge and potentially catastrophic risks to business and society. *See Table 1.1 for major environmental trends.*

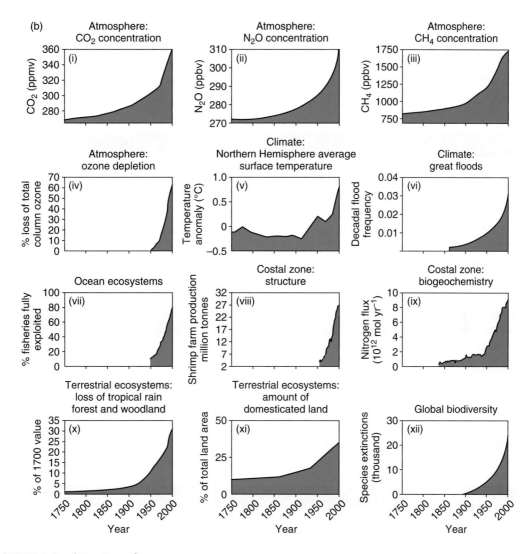

FIGURE 1.2 (*Continued*)

TABLE 1.1   Key Environmental Challenges

Climate
2.5–7.8 °C: how much average surface temperatures are expected to increase by the end of the century, based on a range of scenarios (IPCC, 2014).
2 °C: the increase in global temperature above pre-industrial levels that we need to keep below, to avoid catastrophic climate change (UNFCCC, 2010).
50%: the percentage increase in carbon emissions between 1990 and 2012 (United Nations, 2015).
400 parts per million: the current concentration of carbon dioxide (CO_2) by volume in the atmosphere, the highest it has been for about 650,000 years (NOAA, 2015).

(*Continued*)

TABLE 1.1 *(Continued)*

1 metre: an estimated sea level rise by 2100, resulting from climate change threatening islands, coastal cities and economies (IPCC, 2014).

80%: the amount of current coal reserves that should remain unused from 2010 to 2050 in order to meet the 2 °C target (McGlade & Ekins, 2015).

Water

40%: the amount by which global freshwater demand is projected to exceed current supply by 2030 (WRG, 2012).

2 billion: the number of people at risk from water stress, as a result of climate change, by the beginning of the 2030s (WWAP, 2015).

70%: the percentage of industrial wastes that are dumped into waters in developing countries, where they pollute the usable water supply (IFAD, 2015).

13,000–15,000: the number of litres of water it takes to produce one kilo of grain-fed beef, in contrast to the 1,000 to 3,000 litres to produce one kilo of rice (IFAD, 2015).

Biodiversity

1,000–10,000 times higher: the estimated rate of species extinction above the natural extinction rate levels (IUCN, 2007).

52%: the drop in wildlife populations of mammals, birds, reptiles, amphibians, and fish around the globe between 1970 and 2010 (WWF, 2014).

60%: the percentage of global ecosystem services (such as pollination) that are being degraded or used unsustainably (Millennium Ecosystem Assessment (MA), 2005).

13 million hectares: annual deforestation rate between 2000 and 2010. We have lost or severely degraded more than half the planet's original, post-ice age forest cover (FAO, 2010). This is equivalent to losing 36 football fields per minute (WWF, 2008).

Resource depletion

'Peak Oil': the prediction by Shell geologist M. King Hubbert that US oil production would peak in the 1970s and then decline. This has been offset by tar sands extraction and fracking, both of which have major negative environmental and social impacts.

'Peak Everything': a phrase coined by Heinberg (2007) to highlight the global decline in many key resources for the global economy – oil, natural gas, coal; metals and minerals, such as uranium, phosphorous, rare earths; food and water.

90%: the amount of fish stocks that are overfished or fully exploited, leaving about 10% underexploited (FAO, 2014). The global fish catch has increased from 19 million tonnes in 1950 to 90 million tonnes in 2012 (Roney, 2012).

Waste

20–50 million: the tonnes of E-waste generated per annum. It is the fastest growing waste stream in the world (Greenpeace, 2015).

1.3 billion: the tonnes of food wasted per year, with an annual cost of $750 billion* to food producers (FAO, 2013).

1 billion: the tonnes of plastic that have been discarded since the 1950s. Plastic is a material that can persist in the biosphere for thousands of years (Weisman, 2007).

248,000: the quantity of chemical products that are commercially available, but for which there is a lack of data on the effects of exposure on health and ecosystems (UNEP, 2013).

*Note that $ refers to US$ throughout the book.

2.2 Key Planet Concepts and Issues

2.2.1 Ecosystem Services   Humans obtain multiple benefits from the biosphere known as ecosystem services, which deliver huge (although largely invisible) economic benefits, such as *provisioning services*, including the production of food, water and raw materials; *regulating services*, such as the control of climate and disease; *supporting services*, such as crop pollination and nutrient recycling; and *cultural services*, such as spiritual and recreational benefits. Some 15 of the planet's 24 ecosystem services are being used unsustainably and are in decline (MA, 2005). It is, however, important to consider 'nature' as more than a set of *resources* for business and industry – it is the *source* of our life support systems, which we depend on and participate in. We have a relationship with and a responsibility towards what WWF calls a 'living planet' (WWF, 2014).

2.2.2 Take-Make-Waste Economy   One of the major physical problems of the current economic system is our creation of, and dependence on, a fossil-fuel based, linear, take-make-waste or 'cradle to grave' production process, in which raw materials are extracted or cut down, manufactured into products and packaging, and eventually disposed of in landfills or incinerators. This linear process is leading to resource scarcity and toxic pollution, and squanders enormous quantities of embodied energy. This economy has long relied upon cheap inputs and readily available resources to create conditions for growth. But as Meadows *et al.* (1972) have long pointed out, this model is unsustainable over the long term and leads to 'limits to growth'. Businesses are increasingly affected by growing commodity prices, which will make the take-make-waste economic model less tenable in the future. *For illustrations see YouTube videos:* Annie Leonard on *The Story of Stuff,* or Steve Cutts' *Man.*

2.2.3 Ecological Footprint   The ecological footprint is a measure of humanity's demand on the planet – indicating how much we consume versus how much we have (see Figure 1.3). It compares the earth's biocapacity to supply renewable goods and services – including the capacity to absorb waste – against humanity's demand on those goods and services (Global Footprint Network, 2015). Since the 1970s, our demand on the natural world has exceeded what the earth can renew in a year,

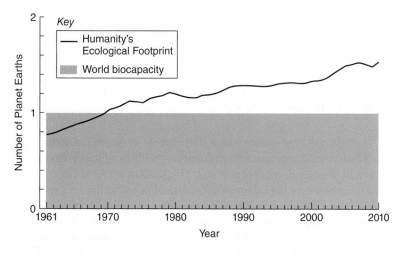

FIGURE 1.3   Humanity's Ecological Footprint. *Source:* Global Footprint Network, 2014.

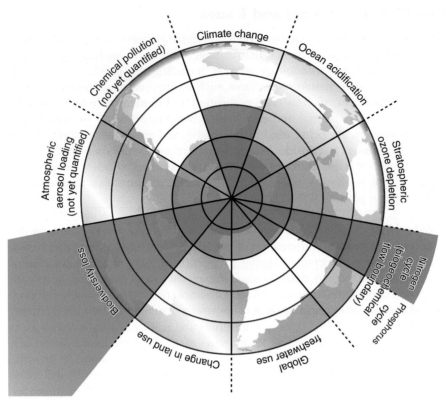

The inner shaded circle represents the proposed safe operating space for nine planetary systems. The darker wedges represent an estimate of where planetary boundaries have already been exceeded.

FIGURE 1.4   Planetary Boundaries. *Source:* Rockstrom et al., 2009.

resulting in what is called 'ecological overshoot'. Globally, we are currently using the productive capacity of more than 1.5 planets to satisfy our current levels of consumption. It now takes the earth one year and six months to regenerate what we use in a year (WWF, 2014). In other words, the economic system is using more resources than the earth can replenish, and putting more waste into the system than can be absorbed by natural processes. To use economic metaphors, we are exceeding 'nature's budget'; or drawing down the capital of a savings account, rather than just taking off the interest, which is clearly unsustainable in the long term. Or to put it another way, the invisible hand of the market is resulting in a very visible ecological footprint (Sukhdev, 2012). *See Table* 1.1 for details of some of the major impacts on climate, water, biodiversity, resources and waste.

2.2.4 Planetary Boundaries   Scientists claim that current economic activities are pushing us outside a 'safe operating space for humanity', with potentially disastrous consequences for human development and survival. The Stockholm Resilience Centre has identified nine boundaries of the planet's biophysical subsystems or processes which define a stable environment conducive to life (see Figure 1.4). Many of the earth's subsystems are particularly sensitive around threshold levels of key variables. Once these thresholds are breached, earth systems may react in abrupt and irreversible ways, and cause the system to collapse or change into a distinctly different system. These are sometimes known as 'tipping points'. Our economy is putting pressure on the resilience of these earth subsystems, and four of the nine interlinked planetary boundaries have already been breached: climate change, biodiversity loss, the nitrogen and phosphorous cycles, and land-use change (Steffen *et al.*, 2015). In other words, economic activities are destabilizing our planet's life support systems.

2.2.5 Systemic Risk   Systemic risk is where the negative impacts of change add up to create 'breakdowns in an entire system, as opposed to breakdowns in individual parts and components' (Kaufman & Scott, 2003, p. 371). Scientists warn that we cannot consider individual earth subsystems in isolation – the boundaries of the systems are tightly coupled. Environmental problems are exacerbated as a result of complex inter-actions and feedback loops between conditions. For instance, significant land-use changes in the Amazon could influence water resources as far away as Tibet (Rockstrom *et al.*, 2009). A water-food-energy-climate nexus suggests that increasing demand from a growing population will increase pressure on a range of resources including, land, water, and energy. Climate change is already adversely affecting these resources; and increased warming will put extra pressure on them through negative feedback loops. Climate change will have serious impacts on hydrological cycles which, together with increasing demand, will result in shrinking supplies of freshwater (WEF, 2011).

2.2.6 Disproportionate Impact   The risks of climate change and the degrada-tion of natural systems are unevenly distributed and tend to have a disproportionate impact on disadvantaged and poorer communities in low-income countries who cannot 'buy their way out of trouble'. Ecological overshoot and the breaching of planetary boundaries have adversely affected the availability of resources, sparking conflicts, provoking the spread of disease and epidemics, famines and, increasingly, driving population migrations. The rapid pace of change makes it difficult for people and nature to adapt to new conditions. These biophysical changes are undermining life support systems and clearly have profound implications for all life on earth, as well as for the future of business.

2.2.7 Grow Now, Clean Up Later?   The global interconnectedness and the scale of environmental problems challenge widely held views that we can 'grow now, and clean up later'; or that countries are 'too poor to be green', or that 'environmental con-cerns are mainly for the rich'. Earlier thinking, influenced by the so-called Environmental Kuznets' Curve, proposed that while early stages of development use large quantities of natural resources and produce large amounts of waste, these decline as people get richer and demand better environmental quality, as technologies improve, and as insti-tutions are formed to manage environmental problems. Subsequent research has shown that while the relationship may hold true for some local pollutants, the theory cannot be generalized across all resources and wastes. There is no evidence that eco-logical footprint is falling with rising income, and pollutants such as greenhouse gas emissions (GHGs), affect the whole planet irrespective of borders.

2.3 Environmental Risks to Business

According to Willard (2012) there are four major categories of risk that need to be assessed in risk management: Strategic, Operational, Compliance, and Financial.

1   **Strategic** risks are those that relate to a company's business plans and strategies, including reputational risks associated with its markets and demand for its products and services, competitive threats, technological and product innovations.

2   **Operational** risks are those that relate to external events that could affect a company and its bottom line, including threats from the supply chain, or other factors that threaten the staff, systems and processes.

3   **Compliance** risks are those that relate to stricter government regulations on waste, carbon emissions, use of chemicals, impact on biodiversity, and working conditions, which potentially force the company to change its behaviour to become compliant.

4   **Financial** risks are those that relate to a company's ability to meet its financial obligations, and mitigate its credit risk, liquidity risk and exposure to financial market risks.

UNEP (2013) provides a useful overview of major environmental trends and key implications for business related to supply chains, logistics, operations, reputation, and regulatory pressures, all of which affect a company's finances and social license to operate. These are analyzed across different corporate sectors including building and construction; chemicals; power; extractives; finance; food and beverages; healthcare; information and communication technologies; tourism; and transportation. UNEP argues that without unexpected shifts in the drivers of environmental trends, the environmental pressures will increase in the foreseeable future. *Some illustrations are given below.*

Supply Chains: will be disrupted as warming temperatures affect yields of major crops such as coffee, cotton, maize, wheat and soybean and other commodities; as water becomes scarcer; and as ecosystem services are lost as a result of declining biodiversity. This will generate higher and fluctuating commodity prices and stricter regulatory controls. Starbucks, for example, has reported that climate change threatens future coffee supply as temperatures increase, rainfall patterns change and insects become more resistant (Goldenberg, 2011). Walmart's UK supermarket chain Asda has reported that 95% of its global fresh produce is at risk from global warming (Confino, 2014). Coca Cola has developed a Water Stewardship Strategy, and aims to become water neutral by 2020. It is now a requirement that each of Coca Cola's 859 bottling plants around the world conducts a water Source Vulnerability Assessment (SVA) and begins implementing a Source Water Protection Plan (SWPP). The global clothing company Gap reports that drought in China leads to lower cotton yields and higher cotton prices, which has an impact on their unit costs and gross margins. While companies use various hedging strategies and pricing arrangements to help stabilize commodity prices, risks are passed through the supply chain and ultimately passed onto the consumers (CDP, 2014a).

Logistics and Operations: will be disrupted as extreme weather events, such as flooding, storm surges and rising sea levels, cause damage to public and private infrastructure, increasing the cost of transportation, operations, and reinsurance. For example, Hurricanes Katrina and Rita, which hit the US Gulf Coast in 2005, caused a local utility, Entergy, to incur some $1.5 billion in restoration costs, and forced it to repair more than 120,000 kilometres of transmission lines and distribution circuits, and relocate its headquarters from New Orleans (UNEP, 2013). Floods in Thailand in 2011 led to estimated losses of $15–20 billion for badly damaged global parts suppliers, which hit the bottom lines of Ford, Toyota, Dell and Honda (Coffee, 2014).

Reputation: will be at risk as environmental trends generate more stakeholder conflicts. NGOs and consumers are likely to increase pressure to reduce carbon emissions, manage waste, protect critical natural habitats and resources, manage conflicts with local stakeholders, and demand greater transparency. For example, in 2010 Greenpeace, the environmental campaigning organization, produced a YouTube video targeting Nestlé's Kit Kat brand, which satirized the 'Have a break – have a Kit Kat' slogan, to highlight the impact on wildlife resulting from forest clearance to produce palm oil. Messages were also posted on Twitter and Facebook. Nestlé was sourcing palm oil from Sinar Mas, an Indonesian supplier that was acting unsustainably. In the video, an office worker bites into a finger of Kit Kat that turns out to be the bloody finger of an orang-utan, a species threatened by deforestation. Nestlé initially forced the video to be withdrawn from YouTube, which led to an outbreak of criticism. Greenpeace then posted the video on Vimeo, which had 78,500 views within hours. Greenpeace's campaign pushed Nestlé into suspending sourcing from Sinar Mas; to hold meetings with Greenpeace to disclose details of its palm oil supply chains; and to join the Roundtable for Sustainable Palm Oil. It now has a goal of using only palm oil certified as sustainable (Ionescu-Somers & Enders, 2012).

Compliance: regulatory pressure will increase as governments seek to influence product efficiency, resource and water use, control of waste, and health impacts. For example, in response to concerns about the impact of toxic chemicals on health, water, the atmosphere and wildlife, the EU is establishing regulations that restrict the use of some chemical products. The Registration, Evaluation, Authorization and Restrictions of Chemical substances (REACH), which came into force in 2007, is phasing out those chemicals considered to pose serious dangers to human health and the environment. Companies will be obliged to give new data on 30,000 chemicals, and will have to prove adequate control of many toxic substances. The new regulations will be phased in over 11 years, and the full legal package will be in place by 2022.

Financial: Ecological threats, such as climate change or the declining availability of resources, affect the bottom line through impact on the price and price volatility of foods and other commodities, operational costs, loss of productivity, reduced demand for goods and services, and costs of insurance. A CDP (2014a) study into climate change disclosures from public companies, on behalf of investors, revealed that of 767 institutional investors with $92 trillion in assets in S&P 500 companies, the physical risks from climate change are increasing in urgency, and that the impacts are already hitting the bottom line (the S&P 500, or the Standard & Poor's 500, is an American stock market index). There is also increased pressure on lenders and investors to take into account and disclose a client's company's impact on the environment and communities.

2.4 Planet-changing Economy

How are companies responding to environmental challenges and risks? Governments and international agencies have established hundreds of environmental laws and regulations to control pollution (international and domestic) such as the Kyoto Protocol, an international treaty which commits state parties to reduce greenhouse gas emissions. Environmental management standards have been formulated, such as the ISO 14000 series, which provides practical tools for companies and organizations looking to manage their environmental responsibilities. New markets have been established, such as the European Union Emissions Trading Scheme (EU ETS), which trades greenhouse gas emission allowances. There are proposals to create a carbon tax. NGOs have launched campaigns to persuade people to change environmental behaviours, such as divesting from fossil fuel companies, and 350's campaign to 'keep fossil fuels in the ground'. A Science Based Targets initiative has been established to help companies to set greenhouse gas (GHG) emissions targets in line with the level of decarbonization required to limit global warming to less than 2 °C compared to pre-industrial levels.

Many businesses are working to reduce their environmental footprint through voluntary corporate social responsibility (CSR) programmes, often with NGO support (see Case Study 1.1 on Lafarge). Product certification schemes, such as the Forest Stewardship Council (FSC) and Marine Stewardship Council (MSC) have been developed, and supply chain initiatives such as the Palm Oil initiatives have been established to foster more sustainable practices. More companies are beginning to measure and disclose their emissions and use of resources, by reporting to organizations such as the CDP (2014b). New markets for efficient and eco-friendly products and services have evolved; and more companies are reporting their achievements through new metrics such as those developed by the Global Reporting Initiative (GRI). However, despite decades of sustainable business efforts, the scale of global environmental challenges are getting worse, not better. After a slight decline in 2009, as a result of the global economic recession, carbon emissions soared by 5.9% in 2010, the largest increase since the industrial revolution (Klein, 2014).

However, beyond the incremental innovations to the old linear, take-make-waste economy, radically different production and consumption approaches are emerging, such as the **Circular Economy** (Ellen MacArthur Foundation, 2012; Webster, 2015). This is a regenerative economy model, which recovers, recycles and refurbishes products; designs out of waste; and increases resource productivity. This has the potential to transform economic and business models, and generate new markets and values. *It is discussed in more detail in Chapter 2, and elsewhere in the book.*

CASE STUDY 1.1
Lafarge: Addressing Carbon and Climate

In 2015 the two biggest global manufacturers of building materials Lafarge and Holcim merged to form LafargeHolcim, now the largest producer of cement, aggregates and concrete in the world. LafargeHolcim is headquartered in Switzerland, operates in 90 countries, has over 100,000 employees, and had sales of CHF 29.5 billion in 2015. This case study describes the years before the merger, when Lafarge partnered with WWF International, the global conservation NGO, to reduce its greenhouse gas emissions and address the issue of climate change.

In 1999 Lafarge was the world's biggest cement producer and had a CO_2 footprint that contributed 2% of global emissions, roughly twice those of Switzerland.

In late 1999 Lafarge approached WWF International asking for their collaboration on a project 'to plant a tree for every employee' to mark the new millennium. In 2000 WWF agreed to enter a five-year partnership with Lafarge to help restore forests worldwide through their *Forests Reborn* initiative. Later that year, following inputs from other WWF experts, the agreement was extended to include two new work-streams on Persistent Pollutants and Climate Change.

After several months of negotiations, two CO_2 reduction targets were agreed by the partners:

1   To reduce CO_2 from cement production in OECD countries by 10% (double that called for under the Kyoto Protocol) below 1990 levels by 2010 and;

2   To reduce emissions globally by 20% net per tonne of cement produced, using the same benchmark and timeline.

This was the first time that a large multinational company in a heavy industrial sector had set such ambitious targets, and some senior managers at Lafarge doubted whether the targets could be achieved within the timeline.

However, Lafarge's leadership was influential. Following the press conference announcing the targets, other companies, such as their major competitor Holcim, quickly followed suit. In 2002, Lafarge's CEO was also asked to co-chair WBCSD's newly-founded Cement Sustainability Initiative (CSI).

Having set the targets, the next step was to find ways of reducing emissions across their operations. Several strategies were adopted, including: improvements in kiln energy efficiency; the use of biomass and waste as fuels (14% of fuel mix in 2012); product development and innovation to bring lower carbon cement solutions to market (clinker factor reduced by 12% below 1990 levels in 2012); and the introduction of new products such as Aether, which performs like Ordinary Portland Cement while achieving up to 30% reduction in CO_2 emissions.

Progress towards the targets was independently monitored and verified by Ecofys (a leading consultancy in energy and climate policy, recommended by WWF) on an annual basis. The results were then audited and assured by Ernst and Young and the figures published in the company's sustainability report.

By 2009, Lafarge had exceeded both targets a year ahead of time, achieving reductions of 12% (developed economies) and 21.7% per tonne of cement produced globally.

In June 2011 Lafarge announced two new targets:

◆   A 33% reduction per tonne of cement by end-2020 below 1990 levels;

◆   The development of sustainable construction solutions by 2015, consisting of ten new ranges of innovative products and solutions; and involvement in the design and delivery of 500 energy-efficient construction projects around the world.

In 2012 Lafarge made a commitment to becoming a restorative or 'net positive' company, which gives back more to society and the environment than it takes. This is visionary, but it remains to be seen how this will be achieved. Lafarge is working with Accenture and WWF to develop the goals, milestones and metrics that will help determine the outcome.

Lessons learned

Partnerships with NGOs often catalyse the development of a shared sustainability agenda that delivers triple bottom line benefits. ('Triple bottom line' is defined as an accounting framework that incorporates three dimensions of performance: social, environmental and financial.) The NGO can act as a 'critical friend', challenging the company to go further than it would otherwise.

◆   It is crucial that the CEO and senior managers initiate and lead the change process.

◆   The company can gain a first-mover advantage, with potential access to new markets, by setting the benchmark that others in the sector must follow.

◆   Stretch targets may appear unattainable at the outset but stimulate employees to focus, resulting in much higher achievements than if more 'realistic' targets are set.

◆   Employees' performance appraisals and bonuses must reflect the priority given to implementing sustainability measures.

◆   Operational optimization is important for reducing ecological footprint but insufficient to effect the broader and urgent systemic change required for a sustainable economy.

3.0 People

'The World Economic Forum identifies severe income disparity and high structural unemployment as two of the top five greatest global risks.'

WEF, 2014

'The world has enough for everyone's need, but not enough for everyone's greed.'

Mahatma Gandhi

QUESTIONS FOR CLASS DISCUSSION

1   What are the major global social challenges facing society today?

2   What are the positive and negative impacts of business on people?

3   Does wealth trickle down?

3.1 Social Dimensions

Since WWII it is claimed that we have seen an era of unprecedented social progress with improved standards of living, better education opportunities, health care, communications and transport. According to the United Nations (2015) more than a billion people have been lifted out of extreme poverty since 1990, and the proportion of undernourished people in the developing regions has fallen by almost half since 1990. The primary school enrolment rate has reached over 90%, up from 83% in 2000. Maternal mortality rates, and under-five mortality rates, have fallen. Some 2.6 billion people have gained access to improved drinking water. Many mainstream economists credit free market economies and trade liberalization for lifting people out of poverty because they enable private businesses and economies to grow, and this growth supposedly eases destitution. However, some of the assumptions of mainstream economics such as 'wealth trickles down', and that 'rising GDP increases human welfare' are increasingly contested. These, and other major social challenges (see Table 1.2) facing business and society, are introduced below.

TABLE 1.2   Key Social Challenges

Population dynamics
7+ billion: the number of people currently living on the planet. Population is expected to reach 9.5 billion in 2050 (UNDESA, 2015).
3 billion: the anticipated growth of middle class consumers in emerging markets by 2020 (Pezzini, 2012).
54%: the percentage of people across the globe living in urban areas in 2014. The number of people living in cities will almost double to some 6.4 billion by 2050 (IOM, 2015).
25%: the percentage decline in global linguistic diversity since the 1970s. The world is undergoing a massive extinction of human languages and cultures, with a corresponding erosion of traditional sustainability knowledge (Amano *et al.*, 2014).
200 million: the estimated number of climate change refugees by 2050 (Christian Aid, 2007).

Poverty and inequality

1 billion: about 1 billion people live in extreme poverty, on less than $1.25 a day. More than 2 billion people live on less than $2 per day (World Bank, 2015).

1%: the percentage of the world's population that owns almost half the world's wealth (Hardoon, 2015).

7%: the percentage of richest people who account for about half the world's carbon emissions. The poorest 3 billion account for 7% of carbon emissions (Pearce, 2009).

81 years: the number of years to achieve gender parity in economic participation. Progress on gender equality has been unacceptably slow in the past 20 years, with areas of stagnation and regression. It will take some 50 years to reach parity in parliamentary representation (UN Women, 2015).

300:1: the ratio of top CEOs' earnings to that of the typical worker in the USA in 2015. The ratio is up from 20:1 in 1965 (Mishel & Davis, 2015).

Exploitation

21 million: the number of victims of forced labour worldwide resulting from human trafficking, slavery, bonded labour and prostitution. They generate $150 billion in illegal profits (ILO, 2014).

11%: the percentage of UK firms who believe slavery in the supply chain is likely (Noble, 2014).

215 million: the number of child labourers under 18 who work full time. Nearly 1 in 4 children between 5 and 14 are engaged in labour that is considered detrimental to their health and development in Sub-Saharan Africa (UNICEF, 2014).

1,134: the number of textile factory workers who were killed in the Rana Plaza building collapse, Dhaka, Bangladesh in April 2013 (Hoskins, 2015).

Well-being

60%–90%: the percentage of doctor visits related to stress (Perkins, 1994).

350 million: the number of people affected by depression in the world (WHO, 2014).

1 million: the number of people worldwide who die by suicide each year. It is the leading cause of death, especially among young people (WHO, 2014).

96%: the percentage of senior leaders who felt 'burned-out', with one third of those describing their burn out as extreme (Kwoh, 2013).

10%: the percentage of American adults who use antidepressants. In China, the antidepressant market has grown by about 20% for each of the past three years, albeit from a lower base (Boseley *et al.*, 2013).

$300 billion: the amount the US economy loses per annum in lost work hours due to stress (Mattenson & Ivancevich, 1987).

3.2 Key Social Concepts and Issues

3.2.1 Demographic Dynamics Current world population is 7.4 billion, and is expected to grow to about 10 billion by the middle of the century. Population is growing rapidly in some areas, such as Africa, China and India, but is aging and declining in others (e.g. Japan), creating different sets of social problems (and business opportunities). There is a predominant school of thought that blames world population growth for causing poverty and environmental degradation. But this causal link is too simplistic, and it is important to consider the institutional factors that drive high fertility rates, and encourage unsustainable activities. Higher birth rates are known to be a function of poverty, since poor people depend on children for income and security in old age; a lack of education for girls; and a lack of access to reproductive health care. The demographic transition, which results in a decline in the population growth rate, is closely related to the education and transformation of the role of women in society, changes in social norms, and effective social nets, such as the provision of health insurance and pensions.

3.2.2 Growing Consumption The debate about population growth must also be considered in the context of consumption habits. People in richer countries consume far more per capita than people in developing countries, and they have a far higher ecological footprint. The Global Footprint Network calculates that if everyone on the earth lived the lifestyle of the average American citizen, we would need about four planets to sustain us; while if we consumed like an average person in countries such as India or Uganda, even with high population growth rates, we would not even use one planet's worth of resources (GFN, 2015).

Indeed, it is argued that it is overconsumption, not overpopulation, that is the real threat to the environment; and that we have an economic system that creates and depends on unsustainable consumption (*Simms et al.*, 2009) *(see section 3.2.7 on Consumerism)*. The geography of consumption is expected to shift over the coming decades, as the number of consumers in fast growing economies is expected to rise. The growth of the global middle class in emerging markets is expected to grow 3 billion by 2003, with the bulk of this growth taking place in Asia (Pezzini, 2012), and this is expected to contribute to a shift in economic power from West to East over the coming decades, driving both risks and opportunities for business.

3.2.3 Poverty Poverty is a multidimensional concept, which includes social, economic and political elements, and is characterized by far more than just a lack of money'. Extreme poverty refers to the deprivation of basic human needs, such as food, water, sanitation, clothing, shelter, health care. Poverty is also experienced as insecurity, marginalization and oppression, lack of voice in political processes, lack of opportunities to better one's life, as well as susceptibility to violence. The World Bank controversially defined an absolute international poverty line (IPL) as $1.25 per day, although it is argued that this is not adequate to survive on, and the amount of wealth required for survival is not the same in all places and time periods. Poverty is also a relative concept, which depends on social context, and is closely associated with income inequalities in any given county, which are measured by indicators such as the Gini coefficient (a measurement of the income distribution of a country's residents, which helps to define the gap between rich and poor).

Critics claim that the UN narratives about cutting poverty are misleading. While millions have stepped out of absolute poverty, some 71% of the world's population lives on $10 or less per day, suggesting that the global middle class is more of a promise than a reality (Kochhar, 2015). Some claim that poverty 'goalposts' have been moved from absolute numbers to proportions of populations in developing countries, definitions have evolved, and statistics have been 'massaged', and in ways that help reinforce the present economic order and development policies (Hickel, 2014). Others demonstrate that eradicating poverty, even under the most optimistic and favourable growth and policy assumptions, will take at least 100 years at $1.25-a-day, and 200 years at $5-a-day, but even this progress is likely to be offset by the adverse effects of climate change and the costs of adaptation (Woodward, 2015). Tackling poverty in an increasingly carbon and resource constrained world will require cultivating fundamentally new development agendas, and economic and business approaches.

3.2.4 Exploitation Exploitation means taking unfair advantage of someone. The globalization of the economy, and business models designed to keep labour costs down and margins high, have enabled companies to profit unfairly from goods that workers produce, and are responsible for a number of exploitative practices and human rights abuses. The so-called 'sweatshops', characterized by long hours, dangerous work, the use of child labour, and very low wages are familiar forms of labour exploitation. But there are other more insidious forms such as gender discrepancies in pay, failing to pay the minimum wage, zero hour contracts, the unfair use of interns and poor working conditions, which violate international labour standards and labour rights, such as the right to form unions to improve work conditions. Freedom of Association is enshrined in the Universal Declaration of Human Rights, and is at the core of ILO values, although many are denied these rights.

In the worst cases, business supply chains also involve human trafficking, bonded labour and slavery, such as the Asian slave labour syndicates which are known to be involved in producing seafood for supermarkets worldwide *(see section 3.3 on reputational risks to business)*. Corporations are also associated with violations of indigenous peoples' rights, land grabs that deprive local and indigenous people of their homes and livelihoods, habitat destruction, pollution, and other exploitative practices including cartels, price-fixing, and support for despotic regimes. Exploitative practices expose business to many risks and ethical dilemmas, and human rights abuses can seriously damage a company's reputation and brand, and undermine its social licence to operate. Companies such as Glencore, Walmart, Suncor, Nestlé, Barclays Bank, AbitibiBowater, Domtar, Nike, Apple & Foxconn, APRIL and Shell have all been the subject of activist campaigns and consumer boycotts.

3.2.5 Rapid Urbanization Another major social challenge facing society is the rate of urbanization. For the first time in history more people live in urban areas than rural areas, a threshold that was crossed in 2007. In the 1800s just 2% of the world's population lived in cities. In 2014 it was 54%, while in 2050 it is expected to be 66%. More than 1 million people migrate to cities every week, in search of employment and better opportunities. In China alone, more than 250 million rural people will migrate to urban areas in the next 15 years. Rapid urbanization is leading to problems of poverty, congestion and pollution, with profound implications for social well-being.

While cities cover 0.5% of the world's surface they consume 75% of the world's resources, with implications for urban and rural environmental sustainability. Rapid urbanization puts huge pressures on urban food, water, sanitation, energy, and transport systems, and smart city planning is vital to improve the livability and resilience of cities, and to reduce ecological footprint. Companies have opportunities to refocus their business offerings towards the distinct needs and habits of urban dwellers, and to collaborate with urban communities to co-create solutions to water, food, energy and transport issues (PwC, 2015).

3.2.6 Growing Inequality

3.2.6 Growing Inequality Inequality relates to disparities in wealth between countries, within countries, and between people across the world. Recent research indicates that social inequalities have increased since WWI; that there is an accumulation of wealth in the hands of fewer and fewer people, and a growing global divide between the rich and the poor. For example, Piketty (2014), who has studied wealth concentration and distribution over the past 250 years, demonstrates that the rate of capital return in developed countries is greater than the rate of economic growth, and that this causes inequalities to increase over time. An ever-increasing concentration of wealth is not self-correcting, and inequalities can threaten economic growth and democratic order.

Oxfam reports that 1% of the world's population now owns almost half the world's wealth (Hardoon, 2015). In the US, the wealthiest 1% has captured 95% of post-financial crisis growth since 2009, while the bottom 90% has become poorer. The slogan 'We are the 99%' became a rallying call for the Occupy movement in 2011 (Stiglitz, 2011, 2013, 2015). Hunger and poverty are also affecting an increasing number of unemployed and low paid workers in the UK. The Trussell Trust, which provides emergency food and support for people in crisis, reports that over 1 million people received three days' food from a network of over 400 food banks in the UK in 2014–2015, and that the use of food banks has increased by 19% year-on-year, despite signs of economic recovery (Trussell Trust, 2015).

In their book *The Spirit Level*, epidemiologists Wilkinson and Pickett (2009) argue that inequality has pernicious effects on societies, such as eroding trust, increasing anxiety and illness, and encouraging excessive consumption. They argue that the cost of health and social problems, across several important domains such as mental health and drug use, physical health and life expectancy, obesity, educational performance, teenage births, violence, imprisonment and punishment, social mobility, and community life, are significantly higher in more unequal rich countries. Indeed, income inequality is getting so bad that the G20 have recently highlighted it as a growing concern, and the World Economic Forum describe it as '2015's most worrying trend', because it is considered to lead to dangerous economic and political instability in the long run.

The dynamics of growing inequality in the 21st century challenge a common assumption of neo-liberal economic theory that 'wealth trickles down' and that the current economic system improves the lives of everyone. Piketty's (2014) work, for example, challenges Kuznet's inequality hypothesis of the 1950s that claimed that as economies grow, market forces first increase and then decrease inequalities. Since the increasing concentration of wealth is not self-correcting, Piketty proposes government intervention and redistribution through a progressive tax on wealth.

3.2.7 Consumerism

3.2.7 Consumerism By consumerism we mean the belief that consuming more makes you happy. A 'culture' of consumerism is often blamed for driving unsustainable production and resource degradation, and there are calls to change behaviour and to live more simply (Worldwatch Institute, 2010). However, there are complex relationships between business models, advertising, and consumer behaviour, which foster a 'hedonic treadmill' and make the problem of consumerism more than just a cultural issue. Current growth strategy is based on selling fast-moving consumer goods and products that often have built-in obsolescence, and business models that are based on continuous innovation to serve short-term needs. Smith (2014) argues that '*it's not the culture that drives the economy so much as the economy that drives the culture*', and '*most things are not designed for the needs of people, but the needs of manufacturers to sell to people.*'

Global marketing and advertising use sophisticated sales strategies to create and shape demand, 'turning wants into needs', and are responsible for driving a culture of materialism which feeds economic growth. According to Dawson (2004), American big business spends a trillion dollars a year on marketing, which has come to dominate personal lives. Others claim that while markets provide us with well-being, they also hurt us. Markets are manipulated and full of deception, and take advantage of consumers' weaknesses and vulnerabilities (Akerlof & Shiller, 2015). Consumerism creates problems of 'affluenza' (the diseases of affluence), and is unfulfilling for those who do not buy into the culture. As Dave Ramsey skeptically points out: 'We buy things we don't need, with money we don't have, to impress people we don't like.' There are calls to develop more responsible and accountable advertising, which focuses on marketing goods and services that have a positive impact on society and the environment, and discloses full product information to consumers (Sukhdev, 2012).

3.2.8 Happiness Paradox   Decades of research into happiness and well-being reveal the anomaly that once a certain wealth threshold has been achieved, as societies become richer they do not necessarily become happier. Over the last 50 years, despite an increase in GDP, there has not been a corresponding increase in life satisfaction, and many countries have seen stagnation in individual happiness even as average incomes have more than doubled (Easterlin, 1974, 1995, 2003; Layard, 2006). This suggests that the factors that contribute to well-being have a relatively low correlation with material wealth once a certain level of development has been achieved (Diener & Seligman, 2004). Maslow's famous Hierarchy of Needs theory also supports the idea that humans are motivated by many needs beyond the material: physiological, safety, love and belonging, esteem, self-actualization, and self-transcendence, and that life satisfaction depends on more than rising income and consumption. The concept of well-being has become an important area of research, and the goal of well-being has also been incorporated into post-2015 United Nation's Sustainable Development Goals (SDGs), as well as some new business metrics.

3.2.9 Work-related Stress   Rather than a growth in well-being, research indicates that there has been an increase in anxiety, stress and depression in the last few decades. Stress has become a number one health concern in the western world, and is also rising in fast-growing economies, such as China and India. The main causes of work-related stress are too much work, long hours, job security (such as terms of employment), and work relationships. Work-related stress affects performance and productivity, accidents at work, aggression, and job turnover. It is also expensive, leading to absenteeism, and loss of work hours. If prolonged it may also result in serious health problems such as cardiovascular or musculoskeletal diseases. Business cultures which focus on the bottom line and high performance, at the expense of other values, have been blamed for glorifying an approach to measuring success, that leads to stress, depression, and 'burnout', a condition described as persistent fatigue, detachment or resentment triggered by excessive work and stress (Kwoh, 2013; Huffington, 2014). The use of antidepressants has surged across the rich world over the past decade, increasing by 25% in the last three years (OECD, 2013).

The arguments that decouple GDP growth and growth in happiness and well-being provide yet a further critique of the prevailing economic orthodoxy, and have significant implications for public policy and business approaches. It is suggested that once human needs have been met, governments should focus on increasing life satisfaction; and that business needs to develop new non-consumptive business models (Sebastian, 2015).

3.2.10 A Safe and Just Space for Humanity In 2012 Raworth produced a framework for environmental sustainability and social justice known as the 'Oxfam Doughnut' (see Figure 1.5), which brings together the planetary boundaries concept

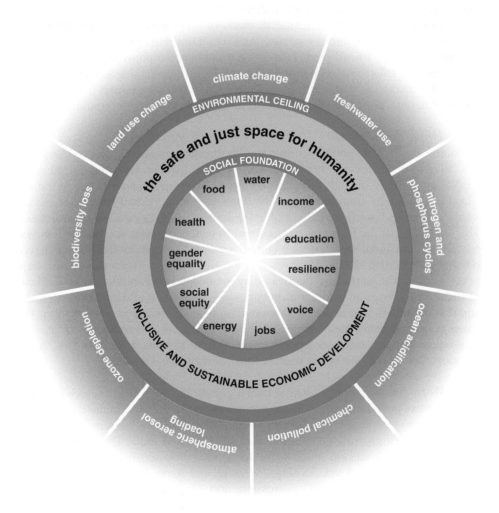

FIGURE 1.5 The Safe and Just Space for Humanity Concept: the Oxfam Doughnut Model. *Source:* Raworth, 2012.

with the idea that there is a social foundation (of 11 social priorities) for human development, below which lies unacceptable human deprivation, such as hunger, ill-health and income poverty. The concept of a safe and just space for humanity is significant in that it combines issues of social justice and environmental sustainability in one model. The model also highlights the need for an economy which achieves certain standards of health, wealth, power and participation for all its citizens, rather than pursuing economic growth without regard for its quality or distribution.

3.3 Reputational Risks to Big Business

Exploiting Labour: Apple is under constant pressure to improve the working conditions of employees in Foxconn factories in China, which assemble iPhones and iPads, as well as manufacturing parts for other brands such as Dell and Sony. Poor working conditions at Foxconn came to light in 2010 after a series of suicides at Foxconn factories, and the erection of so-called 'suicide nets' around its buildings to stop workers committing suicide on company premises. Various audits of Foxconn factories, as well as undercover reporting for the BBC, revealed illegal working conditions, including excessive work hours (sometimes 70 hours per week); working for up to 18 days without a rest; unpaid overtime; health and safety failings; plus low wages and harsh management. Apple has stated that it is committed to improving its supply chain (Arthur, 2012; Apple, 2014).

Financing Conflict: So-called conflict minerals, such as gold, tantalum, tungsten and tin, used in electronic equipment such as mobile phones and laptops, are mined in conflict areas, such as the Democratic Republic of Congo (DRC), Colombia, and Zimbabwe. Minerals are extracted from hundreds of small-scale mines, many of which are managed legally, but others are held by armed groups, which use enforced labour, including child labour, under appalling work conditions that fuel human rights abuses. Conflict minerals from DRC are smuggled out through Uganda and Rwanda and sold on to the suppliers of big companies from the United Arab Emirates. It is often difficult to distinguish between conflict and conflict-free minerals. Proceeds from sales of conflict-minerals are used to finance rebel activities in DRC. Although the USA has legislation in place that requires listed companies to check that sources of minerals are not from conflict areas, the EU rules relating to the sourcing of minerals are only voluntary. A new certification framework, developed by a group of African nations, promises to make it easier for companies to eliminate conflict minerals from their supply chain (Moodie, 2015).

Supply Chain Slaves: Thailand is one of the world's largest exporters of seafood, with annual sales of about $7.3 billion. The Thai fishing industry, which extends into international waters around Indonesia, employs more than 650,000 people, most of whom are migrants. Prawns (known as shrimp in the USA) are sold to many supermarkets around the world, including the top four global retailers: Wal-Mart, Carrefour, Costco and Tesco. Thailand exports about 500,000 tonnes of prawns every year. The world's largest prawn farmer is Thai-based Charoen Pokphand (CP) Food, which raises its own prawns fed with fishmeal. It is responsible for nearly 10% of the prawn exports, and supplies international supermarkets with frozen or cooked prawns and ready-made meals, such as prawn stir-fry. It has an annual turnover of $33 billion.

Although slavery is illegal in Thailand, investigations have revealed that CP Food, amongst others, buys its fishmeal from suppliers of cheap fish that own, or operate, illegal fishing vessels manned by slaves in the international waters off Thailand. Migrants from countries such as Myanmar and Cambodia come to Thailand looking for work, and are vulnerable to being deceived by brokers involved in human trafficking syndicates, often implicating Thai officials. Brokers sell migrants to ships' captains for a few hundred dollars. Captains keep workers on the ships against their will, without pay, and under horrific conditions, including being deprived of adequate food and shelter, being chained, 20-plus hour shifts, beatings, torture, and execution of those who attempt to escape. Some workers are kept at sea for years. As fish stocks decline, the boats are also turning to the more lucrative trade in human trafficking at sea. International campaigns continue to challenge the Thai government, retailers and consumers to address the situation. Costco was sued in 2015 for retailing shrimp which had involved slave labour in the supply chain (Hodal *et al.*, 2014; Cotchettpitre & McCarthy LLP, 2015).

3.4 People-changing Economy

How are companies responding to social challenges and risks? Research shows that the vast majority of people, in fact well over 80% of consumers from Shanghai to London, New Delhi to New York, feel strongly that companies and brands must actively lead social change (Pigott, 2014). Companies are participating in Fair Trade initiatives, such as The Rainforest Alliance, and Max Havelaar, the world's first fairtrade mark, which aims to improve the living and working conditions of small farmers and agricultural workers in disadvantaged regions. Corporations are leveraging synergies between business and social development, and concepts such as a 'social business' (Yunus, 2009), business at the 'base of the pyramid' (London & Hart, 2010), and 'creating shared value' (Porter & Kramer, 2011) have evolved to address social and environmental problems as well as make a profit. Some of these are explored in *Chapter 2*.

Conflicts over scarce resources, such as water, are encouraging companies, such as Coca Cola, to enter into shared governance or stewardship arrangements. There is a shift away from merely serving shareholders to considering a greater number of stakeholders; for example, through the rise of the Benefit Corporation (B Corp), which aims to be the best *for* the world, rather than *in* the world *(see Chapter 2)*. There has been a rise in the number of values-led businesses and social enterprises that serve both people and profit. Happiness is also becoming a measure of success in some companies, where it is found that happy employees are more engaged, creative, collaborative and productive. New workplace cultures are arising which encourage a better work-life balance, and provide time and space for creativity, mindfulness and reflection, such as Google's 'Search Inside' programme. See Case Study 1.2 on Interface, Inc. for an example of a company proactively seeking to do good for people as well as the planet.

But beyond incremental changes in business practices, radically new economies and cultures are emerging. For example, new models of collaborative consumption are emerging through what is called the **Sharing Economy** (Botsman & Rogers, 2010), which gives a greater number of people access to the economy, and involves innovative ways of sharing human and physical assets. This is bypassing established companies and disrupting 'business as usual'. Similarly the **Caring Economy** (Eisler, 2008) is reframing economics around values and true-wealth partnerships of care. *The Sharing Economy is explored in more detail in Chapter 2.*

CASE STUDY 1.2
Interface: 'Getting the Social into the Product'

Interface, Inc. is the world's largest manufacturer of commercial and residential carpet tiles. It was founded in the US in 1973; has an annual turnover of $1billion; and is represented in 130 countries around the globe. Interface's founder and former CEO Ray Anderson famously committed the company to its bold sustainability 'Mission Zero' goals in 1994, which promised to eliminate any negative impact of the company on the environment by 2020. Since then, the company has radically improved energy efficiency, reduced greenhouse gas emissions, eliminated waste, improved water efficiency, as well as cultivating a passionate culture of sustainability amongst its employees, which has saved the company millions of dollars – making it an outstanding example of a company committed to sustainability (Anderson & White, 2009).

More recently Interface has been pioneering a 'restorative economy' approach, intended to help make the world better while growing business, and which engages more deeply with recycling and local communities. The Net-Works initiative in the Philippines works with poor coastal fishing communities to recycle discarded fishing nets into new yarn for its commercial carpet tiles. This helps clean up the environment and generates income opportunities for the poor in commercially viable ways. Interface is undertaking this restorative economy initiative in collaboration with the Zoological Society of London (ZSL), Project Seahorse Foundation for Marine Conservation, and the yarn manufacturer Aquafil.

Net-Works is located near the Danajon Bank, a double barrier reef, once rich in biodiversity but now one of the world's most degraded coral reefs due to unsustainable fishing practices and the dumping of old nylon fishing nets. According to Davis (2013) there are enough old nets to circle the entire earth 1.5 times when laid out end to end. When nets are discarded into the ocean they continue to trap fish and other marine life, a phenomenon known as 'ghost fishing', which damages marine ecosystems and fisheries and thus undermines the economy.

The local communities have limited access to productive assets, finance or markets, little social security, and few opportunities to break out of cycles of poverty. They were once dependent on the marine environment for their livelihoods, but the decline of their fisheries in the last few years has made them very vulnerable. Family incomes in the area are typically less than $157 a month (Conlin & Chandra, 2013). The Net-Works project started in 2012, and has helped organize the communities into groups to collect, clean, bale and transport old nylon fishing nets in return for individual payments or deposits into a community bank, that is used to help fund livelihood development schemes and education. Since its inception the initiative has engaged with hundreds of poor households, and helped establish community banking centres in 26 poor fishing villages in the region (Davis, 2013).

The collected fishing nets become part of the supply chain for Aquafil's innovative Econyl Regeneration system, which uses non-virgin nylon-6 resources, such as carpet waste, fishing nets and industrial scrap. These are recycled into new carpet fibre, with the durability required for commercial carpet, thus reducing the environmental footprint associated with making the yarn from virgin oil. Life Cycle Analysis (LCA) reveals that nylon from the Philippines has 56% less climate change impact than virgin nylon, even taking into account the transportation footprint (Davis, 2013). And, as Miriam Turner, Assistant Vice President Co-Innovation at Interface (2012) puts it, referring to the social dimensions of sustainability, using the fishing nets and improving the livelihoods of the poor 'helps get the social into the product'.

(Continued)

Videos

Net-Works: A Community-Based Supply Chain for Discarded Fishing Nets

   https://www.youtube.com/watch?v=zFQdcDqv5jg

(2 minutes).

Net-Works: Turning Waste Nets into Carpets

   https://www.youtube.com/watch?v=DX6Uidpg3VM

(4 minutes).

4.0 Profit

'Socialism collapsed because it did not allow prices to tell the economic truth. Capitalism may collapse because it does not allow prices to tell the ecological truth.'

   Oystein Dahle, former Exxon Vice President for Norway and the North Sea

'The brands that will thrive in the coming years are the ones that have a purpose beyond profit.'

   Richard Branson

QUESTIONS FOR CLASS DISCUSSION

1 What are the major economic challenges facing society today, from a sustainability perspective?

2 Can the economy keep on growing?

3 Are companies truly 'profitable'? What are the costs to society?

4.1 Economic Dimensions

Over the last 25 years the global economy has quadrupled, and in the last ten years alone global GDP has almost doubled from $43 trillion in 2004 to $77.6 trillion in 2014 (Statistics Portal, 2015). Emerging markets have accounted for over half this growth. The IMF (2015a) predicts that global growth will be about 3.5% over the next year, but will be uneven across many countries and regions of the world. The decline in oil prices is expected to boost economic activity, while geopolitical tensions, shifts in commodity prices, weaker investments, and an ageing population are seen to depress growth.

    The pursuit of economic growth is seen as a good and necessary public policy goal, and promoted by politicians and mainstream economists. It is seen as key to generating wealth, meeting peoples' aspirations, creating jobs, improving living standards, and alleviating poverty. But, *as discussed in section 2.0, 'Planet'*, there are long standing critiques of growth models that are destroying the world. As some economists put it: 'One can't have infinite growth on a finite planet.' Similarly, *as discussed in section 3.0, 'People'*, growth models are critiqued for exploiting people, benefiting the few, and not necessarily making us any happier. In addition, there is growing disillusionment with economic theory that treats nature as a free good, and externalizes its costs. Some of the economic challenges facing society today, from a sustainability perspective (see Table 1.3), *are introduced below, and addressed in more detail in Chapter 4 on Valuing.*

TABLE 1.3   Key Economic Challenges

Natural capital

$72 trillion: the estimated worth of free goods and services from nature per annum, unaccounted for in business and government decisions (Corporate EcoForum & TNC, 2012).

$190 billion: the estimated value of pollination by insects of agricultural crops per annum, which is economically invisible (TEEB, 2010).

25%–50%: the percentage of the value of $640 billion pharmaceutical market derived from components sourced directly from plants and animals (TEEB, 2009).

Negative externalities

$6.6 trillion: the cost of negative externalities (e.g. environmental pollution) resulting from economic activities, equivalent to 11% of global GDP in 2008 (UNEP, 2011a).

$2.15 trillion: the global environmental costs of 3,000 large public companies in 2008, which equates to nearly 7% of their combined revenues (UNEP, 2011b).

$34–$670 billion: the estimated loss of ecosystem services in the Mississippi River Delta, resulting from the BP Oil Spill in the Gulf of Mexico in 2010, including damage to commercial fisheries, tourism, and ecological services (Costanza *et al.*, 2010).

Phantom wealth

$1.5 quadrillion: the total value of global foreign exchange transactions in 2010, generating 'phantom wealth', and driving boom and bust cycles (Korten, 2010).

Perverse subsidies

$550 billion: the amount spent on subsidizing fossil fuels per annum (IEA, 2014).

$1 trillion: the amount of government money spent on fossil fuel, agricultural and fisheries subsidies per annum (Sukhdev, 2012).

$5.3 trillion: the amount countries spent on subsidizing oil, gas and coal in 2015. This cost takes into account the 'true cost' of consumption including the costs of treating people suffering from pollution (IMF, 2015b).

Tax avoidance

9%: the percentage of all taxes paid by corporations in the US in 2010, down from 32% of all taxes paid by corporations in 1952 (Mintzberg, 2015).

$100–$160 billion: the estimated amount of annual corporate tax dodging (Christian Aid, 2014).

$18.5 trillion: the amount of money estimated to be hidden by wealthy individuals in tax havens worldwide, representing a loss of more than $156 billion in tax revenue that could be used to fight poverty (Rousell, 2013).

4.2 Key Economic Concepts and Issues

4.2.1 Natural Capital Natural capital is the value of the planet's ecosystem services and its capacity to process waste. One of the reasons we continue to degrade and lose our ecosystem goods and services is that their value is economically invisible. Nature provides many services such as plant and animal production, climate regulation, pollination, water purification, nutrient recycling, flood control, pest and disease control. These may be considered a kind of 'natural infrastructure', just as valuable as manufactured infrastructure. Nature's services are economically significant, producing an estimated $72 trillion worth of free goods and services essential to the well-being of the global economy (Corporate EcoForum & TNC, 2012). However, because these are predominantly public goods with no markets, they do not command a price and are left unaccounted for in the conventional market system. Natural capital is declining in 116 out of 140 countries (UNU-IHDP/UNEP, 2014). Understanding the size of nature's economic contributions has led to claims that nature, rather than the financial sector, is 'too big to fail', and we need to redirect financial flows away from assets that deplete natural capital, and towards those that grow it (UNEP, 2015). While some critics argue strongly against the idea of giving nature's goods and services a monetary value, others claim that we need improvements in such valuations to ensure that markets incorporate the full value of environmental services (Schröter *et al.*, 2014).

4.2.2 Externalities – Is Business Really 'Profitable'? Business activities impose costs on society known as negative externalities. A negative externality is a cost not transmitted through prices, incurred by a party who did not agree to the action causing the cost. In other words they are largely external to financial accounts. Corporations are chiefly responsible for two categories of negative externalities: (i) damage to the environment through greenhouse gas (GHGs) emissions, deforestation, water pollution, and waste, among others; (ii) damage to human health through toxic emissions and waste, and the manufacture and sale of products that are deleterious to human health and well-being (Sukhdev, 2012) *(see Table 1.3)*. Thus, in his review of the economics of climate change, Nicolas Stern famously argued that 'climate change is a result of the greatest market failure that the world has ever seen', because those who damage others by emitting greenhouse gases generally do not pay.

Tru Cost (2013) examined the profits earned by the biggest industries on the planet, and compared these with the costs to the environment, such as water use, GHG emissions, waste, land and water pollution. Huge profit margins are made by big businesses, but if they had to internalize these costs, and pay for the damage they were causing, none of the industries would be making a profit. For example, the profits from cattle ranching and farming (for meat) in South America are about $16 billion, while the natural capital costs are nearly $354 billion. The profits of coal power generation in Eastern Asia are estimated to be $443 billion, while the natural capital costs are estimated to be almost $453 billion. While profits go to the shareholders, society has to bear the costs. As Orr (2006) says, 'We are privatizing the gains, while socializing the costs.' Pioneering economists are calling for all externalities, positive and negative, to be measured, disclosed, and managed (Sukhdev, 2012; UNEP, 2011b).

4.2.3 Phantom Wealth   According to Korten (2010) we live in an era of 'phantom wealth', rather than real wealth, or one that has intrinsic value, such as fertile soils, pure water, clean air, caring relationships, quality education, affordable health care, fulfilling opportunities for creativity and service, most of which are beyond price. Phantom wealth, on the other hand, refers to financial assets that result from manipulating accounting entries; generating money through complex trading and lending schemes that overvalue assets as collateral for loans; inflating asset bubbles (such as housing or high-tech stock); and devices such as debt pyramids, to create money that is unrelated to anything of real value. Those engaged in phantom wealth creation receive high performance fees for their services and bear none of the costs when the bubble bursts and borrowers default on debts and are often bankrupted. Such speculative trading creates boom and bust cycles in the economy, and does not encourage investment in companies that produce real wealth based on goods and services that have intrinsic value.

4.2.4 Short-termism   Short-termism refers to an excessive focus on short-term results at the expense of long-term interests and value creation. Quarterly reporting by modern business is often blamed for short termism because decisions are made to hit quarterly earnings targets to meet shareholder demands. This pressure leads corporate leaders to make decisions that discount the future, and undermine longer-term value creation. Quarterly reporting was designed to increase transparency and accessibility of up-to-date financial information, and accurate information is thought to make markets more efficient. However, it encourages increased price volatility, higher compliance costs and administrative burdens, and does not reward businesses that want to adopt medium- to long-term sustainability strategies (Barton, 2011). Short termism affects investors too. Mark Carney, the Governor of the Bank of England, has warned: '*The central bank time horizon is relatively short – but the real challenges to prosperity and economic resilience from climate change will manifest well beyond this. We face a "tragedy of horizons".*' As UNEP (2015) put it, short-termism remains a significant driver of instability and a reason why longer-term sustainability risks are being sidelined in financial decision making (UNEP, 2015). The EU scrapped quarterly reporting for listed companies in 2013, but it is still mandatory in the US.

4.2.5 Enabling Conditions   A powerful economic barrier to making a transition to a sustainable economy is that those businesses wanting to do good for people and planet, face a multitude of policies that support business as usual. These include perverse subsidies, unsupportive fiscal regimes, and an inadequate financial system that misprices environmental risk. Government fiscal regimes are frequently aligned around taxing incomes and profits rather than taxing resource extraction and pollution, rewarding 'cutting, digging and burning' at the expense of 'conserving, recycling and innovating'. There is a need for tax reforms that support a shift away from taxing 'goods' to taxing 'bads' (Sukhdev, 2012). There is also a need for a sustainable financial system, one which moves away from mispricing environmental risk and short-termism, towards supporting sustainable development. Despite historically low interest rates and a growing surplus of capital seeking secure returns, our current financial system is not investing in the transition to an efficient, effective and resilient low carbon economy (UNEP, 2015).

4.2.6 Perverse Subsidies   A subsidy is a type of financial support given to a producer or consumer, with the aim of promoting economic and social policy. Subsidies can take various forms such as market price support, tax breaks, depreciation write-offs, etc. Perverse subsidies are those that have significantly adverse economic and environmental effects, and some of the most controversial are those supporting fossil fuel production and consumption. For example, the International Energy Agency (IEA, 2014) estimated that subsidies for fossil fuels amounted to $550 billion per annum in 2014, while subsidies for renewables amounted to $121 billion. Analysis shows that the rich benefit overwhelmingly from such subsidies, with only 8% reaching poor consumers.

More recent figures from the IMF (2015b) are substantially higher, with countries spending $5.3 trillion subsidizing oil, gas and coal in 2015, versus $2 trillion in 2011. These figures also take into account the 'true costs' of energy consumption, including the damage that energy consumption inflicts on people and the environment, such as the health effects of air pollution, and the effects on traffic congestion, traffic accidents, and road damage. Most of these externalities are borne by local populations. That is equivalent to 6.5% of global GDP, which is more than governments across the world spend on health care. The IMF estimates that if the subsidies were cut, global CO_2 emissions would fall by over 20% and government revenues would increase by $2.9 trillion, or 3.6% of GDP.

The figures spent on subsidizing fossil fuels are shocking, given the catastrophic risks of climate change, and the fact that they are holding back investments in renewables. The G20 agreed to phase out subsidies in 2009, and some countries are making progress in this area although it is a politically contentious process. As Sukhdev (2012) points out, the fossil fuel subsidies, as well as those for fisheries and agriculture, distort the playing field for companies wanting to promote renewable energy, and sustainable practices.

4.2.7 Jobless Growth   Unemployment is a significant global concern. According to the ILO (2015) the number of unemployed is predicted to increase to 212 million people by 2019. Young people are disproportionately affected by unemployment and underemployment across the world, and countries facing high youth unemployment are especially vulnerable to social unrest. Jobless growth refers to economies that experience growth without an expansion of job opportunities. This may occur as a result of cyclical recovery from a recession, or deeper structural changes in the economy. There are increasing concerns about the phenomenon of 'persistent jobless growth', in which economies emerging out of recession merely maintain or, in some cases decrease, their level of employment (Summers, 2015). The World Economic Forum (2014) has ranked structural employment as the third most concerning trend.

The arguments that economic growth creates wealth, generates jobs and lifts people out of poverty are pervasive, although orthodox views are increasingly challenged. Some analysts claim that growth does not create jobs, but may actually destroy them. The constant drive to increase productivity requires manufacturers to reduce input costs such as labour (Maxton, 2015). Even in areas of economic growth, unemployment rates have actually increased. For example, fast-growing China has seen manufacturing employment decline over the last 20 years, as a result of use of technology and automation. Disruptive technologies such as robotics and 3D printing could accelerate this trend still further in developed and developing economies. One

study of future employment predicts that almost half of all jobs are at risk of roboti-
zation in the next 20 years (Frey & Osborne, 2013).

4.2.8 Tax Avoidance   Tax avoidance is a way of using a tax regime, within the
confines of the law, to reduce the amount of tax paid. Current patterns of globalization have enabled multinational corporations (MNCs) to arrange their affairs across
the countries in which they operate, and allowed them to reduce their tax bills. For
example, American online retail giant Amazon channelled purchases through a subsidiary in Luxembourg where it had a low tax agreement; and while Google has its
headquarters in Ireland, it remits its non-US revenues through the Cayman Islands.
Google's CEO, Larry Page, has argued that its main responsibility is to maximize
returns to shareholders and to reduce its tax obligations.

Many critics argue that tax avoidance by big companies is unfair. It reduces the
money available for governments to tackle poverty, climate change and other issues of
public concern. And, as a result of public austerity measures, governments have cut
public spending and development aid, which hurts ordinary people, but have let rich
people and corporations off the hook. In 2015 US Senator Bernie Sanders released a
report revealing 18 big American companies that have avoided paying tax, outsourced
thousands of jobs to low wage countries, and yet received billions of dollars in Federal
Reserve bailouts, and tax refunds. These included Bank of America, Goldman Sachs, JP
Morgan Chase, General Electric, Boeing, and Microsoft, amongst others (Sanders, 2015).

According to Christian Aid (2014) developing countries lose an estimated $100 to
$160 billion annually to corporate tax avoidance, and this is entrenching poverty and
weakening developing country economies. There are calls for MNCs to be more
transparent in their tax planning; for governments to clamp down on tax evasion
and corruption that is draining poor country economies; and to give poor countries
a real voice in tax negotiations.

4.2.9 Metrics – Measuring what Matters   Gross Domestic Product (GDP) is a
measure of the market value of all officially recognized goods and services produced
within a country in a given period. The GDP measure was developed in the 1930s,
when recessionary times prioritized maximizing the productive capacity of the economy. It quickly became a standard, convenient and robust benchmark used by
policy-makers throughout the world to compare economies. However, GDP has also
come to be used as a proxy indicator for overall social development and progress –
the more it grows the better the country and its citizens are meant to be doing.

The metric is increasingly critiqued, however. It tends to prioritize things that are
easy to count (quantities rather than qualities) and the short term, and ignores many
significant social and environmental values. The critique of GDP as a limited and
misleading measure of prosperity is not new *(see YouTube video Robert Kennedy
Challenges GDP in 1968)*. Generating goods and services to deal with crime, health
problems, pollution, or dealing with the aftermath of wars and other man-made and
natural disasters, can show up as increasing GDP. It ignores negative effects on our
well-being such as longer working hours, rising levels of indebtedness, the breakdown
of families and communities; and it does not take into account environmental degradation and pollution. Gertner (2010) argues that it has skewed global political objectives toward the single-minded pursuit of economic growth and does not capture the
wellbeing of 21st century society. As Paul Hawken puts it: 'At present, we are stealing
the future, selling it in the present, and calling it GDP.' Several public policy initiatives

are exploring new metrics of progress beyond GDP at a global level, *and these are explored in more detail in Chapter 4.*

4.3 Economic Risks to Business

The challenges outlined above point to an economic disconnect between the dominant economic paradigm and nature. They can be seen as symptoms of an outmoded economic mindset that takes nature for granted, or treats it as a free good. The pursuit of growth, short-termism, the provision of perverse subsidies, the mispricing of environmental risk, fiscal regimes which tax 'goods' rather than 'bads', and flawed metrics of prosperity destroy sources of real wealth, and serve to undermine our life support systems. The 'playing field is tilted in favour of business as usual' (Sukhdev 2012), making it difficult for more sustainable business approaches and models to establish a secure foothold in the market. It also threatens the viability of business, and economic and financial stability over the long term. We need new economic theories and policies, and proactive governments to put in place enabling conditions to facilitate the transition. As Klein (2014) puts it: 'Our economic model is at war with life on Earth. We can't change the laws of nature, but we can change our broken economy.'

4.4 Profit-changing Economy

The dysfunctions of old economic theories are stimulating alternative economic theories, models, and business approaches, and driving new sustainable public policy initiatives. There is growing understanding of the value of natural and social capital; new markets in ecosystem services; and growing interest in new metrics beyond GDP. Some companies such as Unilever and Nestlé have made the decision to shift to longer reporting cycles, rejecting quarterly reporting and focusing on the longer term by issuing reports annually. Puma is adopting new metrics such as true cost accounting that take into account the costs of negative externalities. Patagonia, which is privately owned, has made the decision to limit growth, seeking quality of life and relationships above the maximization of profits and is content with being medium sized. New technologies are disrupting the business models of banks through peer-to-peer lending, and of insurance companies through the rise of 'big data' for pricing risk. Governments are exploring new metrics of success, such as Genuine Progress Indicators (GPIs); the OECD Better Life Initiative; and Bhutan's Gross National Happiness.

There is also growing global interest in what is known as the **Green Economy** (UNEP, 2011b), based on a new macroeconomics of nature, which helps reconnect the economy and the environment, and which challenges the myth that there is a trade-off between environmental sustainability and economic progress. A number of key public policy institutions such as UNEP (2011b), the OECD (2011), the World Bank (2012), and the Global Green Growth Institute (GGGI) are promoting green growth strategies which foster growth, income, employment, and well-being while reducing carbon emissions, inefficient use of resources, pollution, and the destruction of biodiversity. Such strategies aim to decouple growth from resource use ('doing more with less'), and to support renewable energies and smart grids, recycling and clean production, sustainable food, construction, and transport. The debate and dilemmas about 'growth' and 'green growth' are still contested by many environmental economists, *and this issue is discussed further in Chapter 4* in more detail.

5.0 Power

'We have the best Congress that money can buy.'

Will Rogers, 1924

'This fight . . . was never going to be settled on the grounds of justice or reason. We won the argument, but that didn't matter: like most fights it was, and is, about power.'

Bill McKibben

'When the power of love overcomes the love of power, the world will know peace.'

Jimi Hendrix

QUESTIONS FOR CLASS DISCUSSION

1 Do you think large MNCs have too much power?
2 Do you think MNCs are more likely to change as a result of voluntary initiatives, government regulations, or NGO/citizen/consumer pressure?

5.1 Power Dimensions

It has been claimed that economic and political freedoms are inextricably linked. Milton Friedman (2002), for example, influentially argued that competitive capitalism serves as both a device for achieving economic freedom, and a necessary condition for political freedom. Mandelbaum (2003) claims that the institutions, skills and values needed to operate a free market economy are those that constitute democracy. Coyne (2007) contends that free trade in goods and services is a means of exporting the foundations of liberal economic, political and social institutions. However, such views are highly controversial.

Others see a far more fragile relationship between capitalism and democracy, neoliberal economy theory and social well-being, and challenge the myth that the two are historically interdependent. Piketty (2014) demonstrates that capitalism's inherent dynamic propels powerful forces that actually threaten democratic societies. Klein (2007) argues that free market policies have not succeeded democratically, but have come to dominate the world through the exploitation of disaster-shocked people and countries, through what she calls the rise of 'disaster capitalism'. Korten (2001, 2010) argues that while democracy is usually seen as 'one person, one vote', the system in the US actually reflects 'one dollar, one vote', and that the growth and concentration of corporate wealth and power is fundamentally an anti-market and anti-democratic movement. He claims we are now living in a plutocracy, a system ruled and dominated by a small minority of the wealthiest citizens, and this is a real threat to democratic freedoms.

Much of today's debate relates to the rapid rise, influence and unaccountable political power of large corporations in the current political economy, raising significant concerns about a 'governance deficit' or 'corporate governance problem'. In making the case for a transition to a new economy, it is crucial to understand some of the issues relating to how big business exerts its power in the political arena, and the calls to control corporate power.

TABLE 1.4 The Challenges of Corporate Power

Number and size

75,000: the estimated number of MNCs operating worldwide in 2005. These have hundreds of subsidiaries and associates (UNCTAD, 2006).

$162 trillion: the combined value of assets of the top 200 companies in 2015. They had a combined revenue of $39 trillion, profits of $3 trillion, and a market value of $48 trillion (Forbes, 2015).

686%: the increase in the value of capital assets owned by the world's largest 50 companies between 1983 and 2001 (Roach, 2007).

Concentration

1000: the number of MNCs that controlled half the market value of some 60,000 publicly traded companies, representing $32 trillion in revenues in 2012 (Eccles & Serafeim, 2013).

147: the number of a 'super-entity' of tightly-knit companies that control 40% of the total wealth of a global network of 43,000 MNCs (Vitali *et al.*, 2011).

300–500: the number of companies that control 70% of global trade in 15 key commodities such as palm oil, cotton, biofuels, sugar cane, pulp and paper, sawn wood, dairy, beef (Clay, 2015).

Corporate lobbying

$2.6 billion: the amount US corporations spend a year on lobbying government, more than the $2 billion budget which funds the House of Representatives and the Senate (Drutman, 2015).

$3 billion: the amount electric utilities as well as oil and gas companies spent on lobbying government between 1998 and 2001. This was four times as much as was spent on research and development (Sukhdev, 2012).

$39 million: the amount General Electric spent in lobbying expenses in 2010 in the US; ExxonMobil spent $29 million, and Monsanto spent nearly $9 million in lobbying expenses in 2008 (Center for Responsive Politics, 2015).

75%: of the declared lobby meetings between European Commission officials were with corporate lobbyists. This compares to 18% with NGOs, 4% with think-tanks and 2% with local authorities (Transparency International, 2015).

$900 million: the amount the Koch Brothers (and climate deniers) plan to spend on the 2016 US political campaign (Gold, 2015).

5.2 Key Power Concept and Issues

5.2.1 Bigger than Nations One study, which compared annual revenues of MNCs with the GDP of nations, claimed that of the largest 100 economies in the world, 51 were global corporations and 49 were nations, suggesting that large corporations now have the power of nations (Anderson and Cavanagh, 2000). Revenues and GDP data are not strictly comparable since GDP is measured in terms of value-added (revenues minus the cost of inputs). But when value-added was taken into account, 29 of the world's largest 100 economies are companies. In 2000 the world's largest MNC, ranked by value-added, was ExxonMobil, with an added value of $63 billion. This was larger than the GDP of countries such as Pakistan, New Zealand,

Hungary and Vietnam (Roach, 2007). The disturbing aspect of this situation is that these corporations are mostly unaccountable to either governments or civil society and serve private rather than public interests.

In 2015, *Forbes* reports that Chinese banks appear in the top positions for the first time, with the Industrial and Commercial Bank of China (ICBC) in the lead. Other top companies include the banking, oil and gas, conglomerates, automotive, and consumer electronics sectors. China's GDP has tripled since the turn of the century, and analysts claim that economic power is now shifting from West to East – for the first time since the industrial revolution. By 2030 the Asia Pacific region will have a larger middle class than Europe and North America combined, and is expected to dominate the global economy (PwC, 2015).

5.2.2 Concentration of Wealth   Economic globalization has led to a huge concentration of economic power, with just 1,000 businesses now responsible for half of the total market value of the world's some 60,000 publicly traded companies, representing $32 trillion in revenues, up from $2.64 trillion in 1980. Eccles and Serafeim (2013) claim that large corporations virtually control the global economy.

In their study, Vitali *et al.* (2011) have shown that out of some 43,000 MNCs, a core of 1,318 companies form the core of the global economy. Each of these had ties to two or more other companies and on average were connected to 20 through their shareholdings. This group appears to collectively own the majority of the world's large blue chip and manufacturing firms. Deeper analysis of ownership reveals a 'super-entity' of 147 even more tightly-knit companies. All of their ownership was held by other members of the super-entity that controlled 40% of the total wealth in the network. Most of the smaller group were financial institutions, such as Barclays Bank, JPMorgan Chase & Co, and the Goldman Sachs Group.

While wealth and ownership does not necessarily equate with power or control of the economy, it does reveal a level of tight interconnections between companies, and the potential instability of the system, suggesting that if one company suffers, it will affect the system as whole. It also gives an idea of the scale and influence of MNCs on the world stage.

5.2.3 Corporate Empowerment   Global corporations have not always been so rich and powerful. In the 1800s in the US corporations were originally charted as public rather than private entities, which ensured that they served wider interests. The power of corporations started growing after the late 19th century, when businesses were granted legal rights similar to individuals; and as the laws and restrictions governing the size of corporations were relaxed, allowing them to achieve far greater economies of scale and scope (Roach, 2007; Sukhev, 2012).

Over the years, corporations have benefited from reduced corporate tax rates, intracompany trade and price transferring (allowing companies to avoid market mechanisms), the declining power of labour unions, and removal of international trade barriers. These trends have been driven by powerful corporations, but also supported by conservative political regimes in the US and UK in the 1980s, which have promoted the privatization of public assets, and the deregulation of markets. The fall of the Soviet Union and other Eastern Bloc countries in the 1980s, and the so-called 'end of history' (Fukuyama, 1989), gave rise to a culture of 'market triumphalism' in the 1990s. A growing alignment of major economic institutions such as the World Bank and the World Trade Organization (WTO) emerged, known as the 'Washington consensus', which continues to drive free trade and privatization policies, and has served to bolster the profits, power and influence of large MNCs.

5.2.4 Economic Globalization Since WWII trade barriers between nations have gradually been removed through a series of international trade agreements, such as the General Agreement on Tariffs and Trade (GATT) and the North American Free Trade Agreement (NAFTA), precursors of the WTO. These have had worldwide reach and impact, and increased the value of world trade and GDP. The WTO, which was formed in 1995, deals with the trade rules between nations. Agreements are negotiated and signed by most of the world's trading nations and ratified in their parliaments. When trade rules are violated they are disputed and settled by the WTO panels, and can result in penalization by harsh trade sanctions.

The deregulation and dismantling of legal and administrative controls, as well as investment rules, has a number of advantages and disadvantages. It has allowed goods and services to be produced efficiently across a diverse range of countries, and it has provided consumers with a wider variety of competitively priced products. It has given companies the flexibility to shift to countries where input and production costs are low, and to find new markets for goods and services. However, it has also allowed MNCs to outsource jobs to countries where wages are low, resulting in large number of job losses in home countries. It has allowed them to take advantage of weak labour and environmental standards in host countries, and not to be held accountable for any abuses, and to avoid paying taxes. According to Khor and Khor (2001) the whole logic of the prevailing economic system has no connection to the real needs of people, and benefits western countries rather than developing countries, and has been at the expense of the poor and voiceless. Deregulation is accused of driving environmental destruction and increased inequality since the 1980s.

5.2.5 Corporate Lobbying Lobbying, the act of attempting to influence government decision-making, is done by a wide variety of interest groups, and is accepted as a legitimate, albeit controversial, part of democratic activities (Holman & Luneburg, 2012). However, over the last generation large finance, health, electronics and energy corporations have spent massive amounts of money on lobbying in the US, Europe, the UK and elsewhere, which has allowed them to develop unparalleled influence on public policy decision-making. Mintzberg (2015) argues that the visible claw of lobbying has replaced the invisible hand of competing.

Drutman (2015) reports that $2.6 billion is spent on lobbying each year in the US, and that the biggest companies have upwards of 100 lobbyists representing them, allowing them to be everywhere, all the time. Corporate lobbying budgets vastly exceed those of other interest groups. For every dollar spent on lobbying by labour unions and public-interest groups together, large corporations and their associations now spend $34. Of the 100 organizations that spend the most on lobbying, 95 consistently represent business (Drutman, 2015). This weakens the ability of other groups to have their voices heard through the democratic process.

Corporate lobbying takes place in other countries and regions too. Lobbying is a billion-euro industry in Brussels, where 75% of lobby meetings with policy-makers are with corporations (Transparency International, 2015). In India, the ties between politicians, bankers and businesspeople is an open secret. Ramanna and Muthuram (2013) document the controversy following the revelation by Wal-Mart that it had spent $28 million in lobbying to enhance market access for investment in India.

There are worries about the cozy links between Brazilian politics and business, in which the country's 'commercial and political elites are joined at the hip' (*Economist*, 2015). The WTO in Geneva also attracts large numbers of corporate lobbyists, and unlike government lobbyists in the US, they are not required to register. Many industry groups maintain lobbying offices in Geneva, and also travel to WTO meetings around the world (Sukhdev, 2012).

Corporate lobbying translates into policies, tax breaks, subsidies, legislation, deregulation, the commissioning of research to shape public opinion, influence on media and election campaigns, and hundreds of other benefits. It amounts to what some describe as 'corporations writing their own rules', the 'erosion of the independence of the civil service', threatening democracy, and opening the door to corruption, particularly when unregulated.

5.2.6 The Revolving Door   The 'revolving door' concept refers to the movement of employees between government and business, and between business and government, where civil servants join the private sector, and where businesspeople are loaned or 'seconded' to government departments. It gives those people opportunities to influence public policy decisions. Sukhdev (2012) describes how the interdependence between corporations and governments works. Today's corporate's mantra of 'more is better' needs and feeds the mantra of the economic model, 'GDP growth'. The private sector delivers nearly 60% of GDP worldwide and employs 70% of workers. Politicians' 'grades' on growth, employment, and budgets are largely written by corporations. The revolving door gives private sector employees access to documents, meetings behind closed doors, and to decision-making processes. While the majority of government officials are dedicated to public service, it can risk putting them in the pockets of wealthy corporations, promote private interests over public interests, and distort democratic principles and processes.

5.2.7 Democracy Deficit   By 'democracy deficit' we mean the lack of accountability and regulation of MNCs in the global political economy, and the threat to democratic principles and practices. Controversially, free trade agreements have allowed big corporations to override national sovereignty and domestic legislation, and sue governments before private arbitration panels composed of trade lawyers if governments change their policies which then affect corporate investment or intellectual property. For example, the Swedish energy company Vattenfall is suing the German government for €3.7 billion for its decision to phase out nuclear power. The US tobacco company Philip Morris is suing the Australian government for billions in damages over measures to reduce smoking.

The threat to democracy is at the heart of the hotly contested Transatlantic Trade and Investment Partnership (TTIP), a series of trade negotiations between the US and EU which aim to promote economic growth. Companies can use TTIP to bring an arbitration case against governments where there is a risk to their investments, and disputes are addressed through Investor State Dispute Settlements (ISDS). These involve a panel of trade lawyers, one of which is chosen by the company. The chair of the panel has authority to award unlimited compensation to companies, and there is no right of appeal. Critics claim that TTIP threatens existing environmental legislation based on precautionary approaches, banking regulations and the sovereign powers of individual nations. Trade disputes, which bypass domestic courts and override the will of parliaments, are considered a 'full frontal assault on democracy' (Monbiot, 2013).

5.2.8 Trade Trumps People and Planet   Klein (2014) argues that the three pillars of the neo-liberal economic agenda – the privatization of the public sphere, deregulation of the corporate sector, and lowering of corporate taxes – have formed an ideological wall that has blocked serious response to climate change or efforts to safeguard the environment. She documents how 'trade trumps climate', how trade deals (often negotiated with little public scrutiny) and decisions by organizations such as the WTO have far greater influence than other international agreements, such as those negotiated under the Intergovernmental Panel on Climate Change (IPCC), and how trade deals lock society into dozens of agreements that undermine our capacity to respond effectively to environmental crises, and local needs, and even make that response illegal. She claims that we have all been thinking about the climate crisis the wrong way around: it's actually about capitalism – not carbon. As Klein (2014: 18) puts it:

> *We have not done the things that are necessary to lower emissions because those things fundamentally conflict with deregulated capitalism, the reigning ideology of the whole period we have been struggling to find a way out of this crisis. We are stuck because the actions that would benefit the vast majority are extremely threatening to an elite minority that has a stranglehold over our economy, our political process, and most of our media outlets.*

In this chapter we have argued that the growing wealth and power of big corporations (see Box 1.1), coupled with an intimate relationship with government and public institutions, is preserving the *status quo* and 'business as usual', blocking a transition to a more sustainable economy, and threatening democracy. Such a transition requires not only the environmental, social and economic reforms suggested in

BOX 1.1
Characteristics of Corporation 1920

Pavan Sukhdev (2012) reveals how the model for today's corporation has evolved over the last two centuries. Some interdependent and mutually reinforcing characteristics of what he calls 'Corporation 1920' include:

Purpose: profit and self-interest have become established as the *raison d'être* of large corporations, which have freed companies from higher social purpose.

Governance: shareholders have achieved limitations on liability, and corporate 'personhood' has been established, freeing a company from wider accountability.

Products: constant technological innovation ensures a rapid supply of novel and changing products, often involving built-in obsolescence.

Demand: extensive advertising creates consumer demand by 'turning wants into needs', often unhindered by ethical considerations.

Profits: companies leverage profit in all aspects of operations: sourcing of raw materials, cheap labour, low-cost production, sale of branded goods, investments.

Power: companies use their power and funds to lobby aggressively for regulatory and competitive advantages.

Scale: successful corporations have multinational presence and pursue size and economies of scale and scope in order to achieve market dominance, outcompeting local businesses.

the sections Planet, People and Profit, but also a reform of governance between governments, business and civil society.

5.3 Power-changing Economy

In *Rebalancing Society*, Mintzberg (2015) claims that current political imbalances are destroying our democracies, our planet and ourselves. He argues for a radical renewal, through empowering the plural (social) sector to balance the power of the private and public sectors. To Mintzberg this means individuals acting together, engaging in social movements to replace destructive practices with constructive ones. As he puts it: 'We need to cease being human resources in the service of imbalance, and instead tap into our resourcefulness as human beings, in the service of our progeny and planet' (2015, p. xi).

Social media is enabling people to tackle the negative aspects of globalization and the worst abuses of corporate power. Business campaign platforms have unprecedented reach and help grow and support citizen movements, community action, and climate marches (see Case Study 1.3). Fast-growing social movements

---

CASE STUDY 1.3

Online Campaigns

A rapid rise in online campaigns over the last decade has helped challenge the worst abuses of power of the big MNCs. Global online campaigns, which operate with unprecedented scale and speed, can potentially destroy the reputation of high-profile companies almost overnight. They have the power to influence consumers, investment flows, and reverse company strategies, and push companies to be more environmentally and socially responsible. Dealing with such reputational risk is becoming a business imperative; and many companies discover that engaging with critics is more effective than trying to shut down discussion on social media.

For example, SumOfUs, founded in 2011, is a movement of consumers, workers and shareholders speaking with one voice to counterbalance the growing power of large corporations. It has about 10 million members worldwide, and has run campaigns on companies such as Apple, Google and Amazon, and the highly controversial trade deal known as the Trans-Pacific Partnership (TPP) which gives companies unprecedented power to decide laws, and open up local and national government to corporate lawsuits. SumOfUs has helped reverse company practices; for example, over 160,000 signatories urged Costco, Wal-Mart and Carrefour to stop selling shrimp whose production relies on slave labour in South-east Asia.

Avaaz, which means 'voice' in several languages, is a global web movement, which brings people-powered politics to political decision-making. It was founded in 2007 and now has over 43 million members in 194 countries. It has a democratic mission to organize citizens of all nations 'to close the gap between the world we have and the world most people everywhere want'. Its campaigns collect signatures and exert pressure through profiling stories in the media, organizing demonstrations, and political lobbying. Avaaz helped organize the biggest climate change march in 2014, and its Executive Director, Ricken Patel, delivered a 2 million-strong petition to UN Secretary General Ban Ki-moon, calling for 100% clean energy worldwide.

are also helping relocalize the economy and trade, which undercuts the power of large MNCs. For example, the rise of Local Living Economies, such as the North American Business Alliance for Local Living Economies (BALLE), founded in 2011 and consisting of about 20,000 members, aims to build a new economy from the bottom up, and is one of the fastest-growing movements in the US.

GROUP EXERCISE

What are the sustainability challenges and opportunities facing your company?
  See Exercise 1.3 at the end of the chapter.

6.0 Conclusion: The Case for Change

Science reveals that we are at a significant juncture in the history of the human species on the planet. Research from across every discipline is revealing how we are faced with a series of interlinked ecological, social, economic and political challenges: or a 'perfect storm' of crises which are disrupting economic and business models across the globe, and involve us all.

This chapter acknowledges that the free market and economic globalization have helped generate wealth, created jobs, and lifted millions of people out of poverty, and that business is a significant and powerful actor in the political economy, providing useful goods and services. However, current patterns of economic growth are generating huge negative ecological and social costs, which threaten to undermine prosperity over the longer term.

While business is an important and powerful actor in the political economy, providing numerous goods and services to society, many are based on business models that are unsustainable over the long term. The rise of large MNCs, and strong links between big business and governments, have created patterns of vested interests that make it hard to shift the balance of power required to make the transition to more sustainable economies.

The evidence provided in this chapter challenges several mainstream economic orthodoxies, such as:

- *Planet:* the scale of global ecological crises, which extend beyond borders, challenge the argument that we can 'grow now and clean up later'.
- *People:* social science research challenges the ideas that 'wealth trickles down', and 'that rising GDP increases well-being'.
- *Profit:* new economic theories challenge the ideas that 'business is truly profitable', 'the economy creates value over the long term' or that 'growth creates jobs'.
- *Power:* political dynamics challenge the idea that 'competitive capitalism is a vehicle of democracy'.

An increasing number of thinkers are pointing to a 'crisis of capitalism', and are arguing that the prevailing capitalist system needs a massive overhaul in order to deliver a sustainable future. As Townsend and Zarnett (2013) put it, we need to evolve from Capitalism 1.0 to 2.0 or, put in a better way, to make a transition to a sustainable economy.

And a growing number of business leaders recognize that a new social contract between business and society must be forged if we are to transcend the prevailing one planet crises. We need a new corporate DNA fit for the 21st century, or a shift from Corporation 1920 to 2020 as Sukhdev (2012) describes it.

Sustainability challenges present both risks and opportunities for business today. There is clear a business case for sustainability, as businesses seek to manage risks and as sustainability becomes a driver of innovation and value creation. But, beyond corporate social responsibility (CSR) programmes, incremental innovation, and the arguments that it 'pays to be green', current crises and new technologies are profoundly disrupting the dominant economic and development paradigm, and catalysing new ones.

There are many new articulations of what a new economy could look like, each with a different focus, but each addressing the environmental, social, economic and accountability failures of outdated and broken approaches. These include, amongst others, the Circular Economy, the Sharing Economy, and the Green Economy *(explored in more detail later)*.

In this chapter we conclude that our one planet predicament is essentially a symptom of 'disconnection'. Despite their supposed strengths, conventional economic and business approaches have (perhaps unwittingly) driven a profound divide between people and nature, self and others, money and real wealth, people and place, between self and authentic self.

But there is plenty of evidence that new pro-people, pro-planet, pro-prosperity approaches are emerging, and that these are driving a conscious 'reconnection' or 'restoration'. New mindsets and models are about reconnecting nature and people, others and self, real wealth and the economy, place and people, and between authentic self and self. Some of the principles of change for good, or one planet approaches, are explored in more detail throughout the rest of this book.

GROUP EXERCISE 1.1
Deep listening: a mindful practice with a partner

Do you think that the world is better now than it ever has been in the past?

Description

This is a short exercise, which practises deep listening skills, with a partner. Deep listening is non-judgemental listening to understand another, which tunes into the speaker's deeper thoughts and feelings, and attempts to let go of usual assumptions and desires to control the conversation. It is a practice of being fully present and giving quiet mindful attention to another.

Aim

◆ To develop the capacity for deep listening.

◆ To experience being attentively listened to, without any interruption.

◆ To foster *respect* for diverse views related to the question about the state of the world (i.e. the aim is not to create agreement).

(Continued)

Set up

◆ Invite people to sit next to a partner, preferably someone they do not know very well.

◆ Allow about 15–20 minutes for this exercise (depending on the size of the group).

Process

Invite individuals to quietly reflect on the question: Do you think that the world is better now than it ever has been in the past? The question could be enriched by adding, for example: 'What do you think is improving?' 'What do think is getting worse?' (Allow about 1–2 minutes to allow people to collect their thoughts.)

◆ Invite the first person to speak to their partner on their reflections, without interruption, for 3 minutes.

The listening partner should aim to be fully attentive but not comment or ask questions.

◆ The partners exchange roles after 3 minutes.

◆ In plenary session, invite feedback on the experiences of deep listening. For example: 'What does it feel like to be listened to for a full 3 minutes without interruption?' 'What does it feel like to listen without verbally engaging?' 'What happens when you are given permission to speak for a full 3 minutes without interruption?'

◆ Additionally, if required, the module leader can capture key perspectives related to the question on a board. The outcomes can be used as a transition to the discussion on Stories about the Future (see section 1.0).

GROUP EXERCISE 1.2

Rich pictures: drawing sustainable development and sustainable business

Description

This is a group exercise in which small teams of people draw pictures, sketches or diagrams of 'sustainable development' and 'sustainable business'. The technique encourages the creator(s) to think deeply about an issue and to record their understanding pictorially.

Aims

◆ To facilitate learning about complex multifaceted issues, that can be difficult to define verbally.

◆ To encourage groups to think deeply about an issue, and record learning pictorially.

◆ To critically reflect on any similarities and differences between representations of 'sustainable development' and 'sustainable business'.

Set up

◆ **Materials:** Flip chart paper, flip chart stands, white tack, coloured pens.

◆ **Groups:** Divide the class into an equal number of teams of about 3–4 people.

◆ **Time:** Allow about 45 minutes for the exercise, depending on the size of the group.

Process

◆ **Instruction:** Invite half of the teams to discuss and draw what 'sustainable development' looks like; and invite the rest of the teams to discuss and draw what 'sustainable business' looks like (i.e. in other words each team reflects and draws only one concept, not both). It is helpful to write

(Continued)

these two concepts on the flip chart sheets before they are handed out. Allow at least 20 minutes for the teams to discuss and draw their concept.

◆ **Feedback:** Invite participants to stick their sheets on the wall, and make a 'gallery tour' with the whole group. Invite a representative from each group to share main points from their pictures to help make collective knowledge visible. Encourage additional comments from that team.

◆ **Conclusion:** Invite further insights and reflections from the whole group on similarities and differences between the two sets of pictures, including any important missing points.

GROUP EXERCISE 1.3
What are the sustainability challenges and opportunities facing your company?

Description

This is a small group exercise involving collaboration in researching, designing and making a presentation (any media), with supporting written notes on the question 'What are the sustainability challenges and opportunities facing your company?' The exercise can take place over the course of the module.

Aims

◆ To encourage learning about key sustainability challenges and opportunities facing business, key stakeholder perspectives, and evolving business approaches.

◆ To foster group work in gender- and culturally-diverse teams.

◆ To practise creative and effective presentation skills.

Set Up

◆ **Create groups:** Module leader divides group into diverse teams of 4–5 people, ensuring gender- and cultural-diversity.

◆ **Assign companies:** Module leader assigns a company to each team, ensuring diversity of company sector, region, and governance (e.g. Huawei; TATA Motors; Shell; Lafarge/Holcim; SAB Miller; Unilever; HSBC; Syngenta; Thomson Reuters; H&M; IKEA; Novo Nordisk; McDonald's; Google; IBM, etc.).

◆ **Manage time:** Module leader allocates time during the programme for teams to research the company and prepare the presentation. Advise students that they may also want to meet outside the allocated times, for example, during lunch breaks or some evenings. Allocate at least 5 hours across the course of the module to work on the exercise.

Process

◆ **Team preparation:** Before teams start working together, encourage individuals to spend a few minutes reflecting individually on how they work best in a group situation, and then to share this with their team members. This is an opportunity to reflect on individual skills, to practise deep listening within a team, and to consider how to play to the strengths of the participants in the group.

◆ **Choice of media:** Encourage students to think creatively about the use of different formats and media to present their ideas. Encourage students to think about going beyond simply using PowerPoint Presentations (PPT), or how to use PPTs to *support* a presentation, rather than *drive* a presentation.

(Continued)

◆ **Stakeholders:** The objective of thinking about different company stakeholders is to build an appreciation of the diverse interests and the dynamics shaping sustainability challenges and opportunities. The groups might wish to represent some of the following: CEO/CFO/COO; Shareholder; Investor; NGO/Civil Society (social or environmental); Government (local or national); Employees/Union; Customers, etc.

◆ **Self-organize:** Teams self-organize to decide on a presentation format, and on how to divide the tasks between themselves.

◆ **Written notes:** Teams also prepare written notes, up to 1,000 words, which must be completed and submitted to the module leader before the start of the group presentations. Speaking notes are sometimes required by outside examiners.

◆ **Presentation:** Teams make a 15-minute presentation to the entire group at the end of the module, to be assessed by a panel of judges, including course tutors and invited participants, according to predefined marking criteria.

References

Akerlof, G., & Shiller, R. (2015). *Phishing for phools: Economics of manipulation and deception*. New Jersey: Princetown University Press.

Anderson, S., & Cavanagh, J. (2000). *top 200: the rise of global corporate power*. Global Policy Forum. Retrieved from https://www.globalpolicy.org/component/content/article/221/47211.html

Anderson, R., & White, R. (2009). *Confessions from a radical industrialist: Profits, people, purpose – doing business by respecting the earth*. New York: St. Martin's Press.

Amano, T., Sandel, B., Eager. H., Bulteau, E., Svenning, J-C., Dalsgaard, B., Rahbek, C., Davies, R., & Sutherland, W. (2014). Global distribution and drivers of language extinction risk. *Proceedings of the Royal Society*. B 281: 20141574. Retrieved from http://rspb .royalsocietypublishing.org/content/royprsb/281/1793/20141574.full.pdf (accessed 2015, October 17).

Apple. (2014). *Supplier responsibility 2014 progress report*. source

Arthur, C. (2012). Apple faces its Nike moment over working conditions in Chinese factories. *The Guardian* (2012, February 20). Retrieved from http://www.theguardian .com/technology/2012/feb/20/foxconn-raise-wages-apple-contractor (accessed 2015, October 27).

Bakan, J. (2004). *The corporation: The pathological pursuit of profit and power*. US: Simon and Schuster Inc.

BALLE (Business Alliance for Local Living Economies):. Retrieved from https://bealocalist.org/ (accessed 2015, October 29).

Barbier, E. (1987). The concept of sustainable economic development. *Environmental Conservation*, *14*(2), 101–110.

Barton, D. (2011, March). Capitalism for the long term. *Harvard Business Review*. . Retrieved from https://hbr .org/2011/03/capitalism-for-the-long-term

Boseley, S., Chalabi, M., & Rice-Oxley, M. (2013). Antidepressant use on the rise in rich countries, OECD finds. *The Guardian* (2013, November 20). Retrieved from http://www.theguardian.com/society/2013/nov/20/antidepressant-use-rise-world-oecd (accessed 2015, October 27).

Botsman, R., & Rogers, R. (2010). *What's mine is yours: The rise of collaborative consumption*. New York: Harper Collins.

CDP. (2014a). *Major public companies describe climate-related risks and costs: A review of findings from CDP 2011–2013 disclosures*. London, CDP.

CDP. (2014b). *Climate action and profitability. CDP S&P 500 Climate Change Report 2014*. London: CDP.

Center for Responsive Politics. (2015). Lobbying database. OpenSecrets.org. Retrieved from https://www .opensecrets.org/lobby/ (accessed 2015, October 8).

Christian Aid. (2007). *The real migration crisis*. London: Christian Aid.

Christian Aid. (2014). $160bn – the price of tax dodging in developing world. Retrieved from http://www .christianaid.org.uk/pressoffice/pressreleases/comment/the-price-of-tax-dodging-in-the-developing-world.aspx (accessed 2015, October 27).

Clay, J. (2015). Food for thought: Sustainability as a precompetitive issue. World Food Day (2015, October 16). Retrieved from http://www.worldfooddayusa.org/food_ for_thought_sustainability_as_a_precompetitive_issue (accessed 2015, October 18).

Coffee, J. (2014) Climate change a growing concern for companies expanding their footprint. *Guardian Sustainable Business* (2014, April 28). Retrieved from http://www.theguardian.com/sustainable-business/hubs-water-climate-change-siting-drought-flood-business (accessed 2015, September 30).

Confino, J. (2012) Rio+20: WBCSD president says the future of the planet rests on business. *Guardian Sustainable Business* (2012, June 22). Retrieved from http://www.theguardian.com/sustainable-business/rio-20-business-sustainable-development (accessed 2015, October 7).

Confino, J. (2014). More big companies say they're concerned about climate risks. *Guardian Sustainable Business* (2014, May 16). Retrieved from http://www.theguardian.com/sustainable-business/blog/climate-change-business-risks-costs-natural-disasters-cdp (accessed 2015, September 30).

Conlin, J., & Chandra, S. (2013). Interface, Inc. and the Zoological Society of London pilot in the Philippines hailed a success. Market Wired (2013, January 7). Retrieved from http://www.marketwired.com/press-release/interface-inc-zoological-society-london-pilot-philippines-hailed-success-nasdaq-ifsia-1742647.htm (accessed 2014, February 11).

Corporate EcoForum & The Nature Conservancy (TNC). (2012). *The new business imperative: Valuing natural capital.* E-book. Retrieved from http://www.corporateecoforum.com/valuingnaturalcapital/ (accessed 2014, October 27).

Costanza, R., Batker, J., Day, J., Feagin, R., Martinez, M.L., & Roman, J. (2010). The Perfect spill: Solutions for averting the next Deepwater Horizon. *Solutions,* 1(5), 17–20. Retrieved from http://www.thesolutionsjournal.com/node/629 (accessed 2015, October 17).

Cotchettpitre & McCarthy LLP. (2015). Costco taken to court for knowingly selling slave labor shrimp to unsuspecting Californians. News Centre (2015, August 19). Retrieved from http://www.cpmlegal.com/pp/news-452.pdf

Coyne, C. (2007). *After war: The political economy of exporting democracy.* Stanford, US: Stanford University Press.

Davis, M. (2013). How Net-Works fishes for a triple bottom line. Greenbiz.com (July 2013, July 19). Retrieved from http://www.greenbiz.com/blog/2013/07/19/how-net-works-fishes-triple-bottom-line (accessed 2014, February 11).

Dawson, M. (2004). *The consumer trap: Big business marketing in American life.* Urbana and Chicago: University of Illinois Press.

Diamond, J. (2011). *Collapse: How societies choose to fail or succeed.* London: Penguin.

Diener, E., & Seligman, M. (2004). Beyond money: Toward an economy of well-being. *Psychological Science in the Public Interest,* 5, 1–31.

Drutman, L. (2015). *The business of America is lobbying: How corporations became politicized and politics became more corporate.* New York: Oxford University Press.

Easterlin, R. (1974). Does economic growth improve the human lot? Some empirical evidence. University of Pennsylvania. Retrieved from http://huwdixon.org/teaching/cei/Easterlin1974.pdf

Easterlin, R. (1995). Will raising the incomes of all increase the happiness of all? *Journal of Economic Behavior and Organization,* 27, 35–57.

Easterlin, R. (2003). Explaining happiness. *Proceedings of the National Academy of Sciences of the United States of America (PNAS) (2003, September 16).* 100(19), 11176–11183.

Eccles, R., & Serafeim, G. (2013, May). The performance frontier: Innovating for sustainable strategy. *Harvard Business Review.* Retrieved from http://www.eticanews.it/wp-content/uploads/2013/07/Harward-Articolo.pdf

Economist. (2015). Business in Brazil, courting the state: The upside of professional lobbying. *The Economist* (2015, May 16).

Eisler, R. (2008). *The real wealth of nations: Creating a caring economics.* San Francisco: Berrett-Koehler Publishers.

Elkington, J. (1997). *Cannibals with forks: The triple bottom line of twenty-first century business.* Oxford: Capstone Publishing Ltd.

Ellen MacArthur Foundation. (2012): *Towards the Circular Economy Vol. 1: An economic and business rationale for an accelerated transition.* Isle of Wight, UK: Ellen MacArthur Foundation Publishing.

FAO. (2010). *Forestry paper 163. Global forest resources assessment 2010. Main report.* Rome: Food and Agriculture Organization of the United Nations.

FAO. (2013). *Food wastage footprint: Impact on natural resources. Summary report.* Rome: Food and Agriculture Organization of the United Nations.

FAO. (2014). *The state of world fisheries and aquaculture: Opportunities and challenges.* Rome: Food and Agriculture Organization of the United Nations.

Forbes. (2015). *Global 500.* Retrieved from http://fortune.com/fortune500/

Friedman, M. (2002). *Capitalism and freedom* (40th anniversary ed.). Chicago: University Of Chicago Press.

Frey, C., & Osborne, M. (2013) The future of employment. How susceptible are jobs to computerization? Oxford Martin School, Programme on the Impacts of Future Technology. University of Oxford. Retrieved from http://www.oxfordmartin.ox.ac.uk/downloads/academic/The_Future_of_Employment.pdf

Frey, T. (2013). 33 dramatic predictions for 2030. Futurist Speaker. Retrieved from http://www.futuristspeaker.com/2013/12/33-dramatic-predictions-for-2030/ (accessed 2015, September 30).

Fukuyama, F. (1989).The end of history? *The National Interest,* 16(1989, Summer), 3–18.

Gertner, J. (2010). The rise and fall of the GDP. *The New York Times* (2010, May 27). Retrieved from http://www.nytimes.com/2010/05/16/magazine/16GDP-t.html?_r=0

Greenpeace International. (2015). The e-waste problem. Retrieved from http://www.greenpeace.org/international/

en/campaigns/detox/electronics/the-e-waste-problem/ (accessed 2015, October 15).

Gold, M. (2015). Koch-backed network aims to spend nearly $1 billion in run-up to 2016. *Washington Post* (2015, January 26). Retrieved from http://www.washingtonpost.com/politics/koch-backed-network-aims-to-spend-nearly-1-billion-on-2016-elections/2015/01/26/77a44654-a513-11e4-a06b-9df2002b86a0_story.html (2015, October 8).

Global Footprint Network. (2015). Retrieved from http://www.footprintnetwork.org/en/index.php/GFN/

Goldenberg, S. (2011). Starbucks concerned world coffee supply is threatened by climate change. *Guardian Sustainable Business* (2011, October 13). Retrieved from http://www.theguardian.com/business/2011/oct/13/starbucks-coffee-climate-change-threat (accessed 2015, September 30).

Hardoon, D. (2015). *Wealth: Having it all and wanting more. Oxfam Briefing Issue*. Oxfam UK. Retrieved from https://www.oxfam.org/sites/www.oxfam.org/files/file_attachments/ib-wealth-having-all-wanting-more-190115-en.pdf

Hawken, P. (1993). *The ecology of commerce: A declaration of sustainability*. New York: HarperCollins.

Heinberg, R. (2007). *Peak everything: Waking up to the century of declines*. Canada: New Society Publishers.

Hickel, J. (2014). Exposing the great 'poverty reduction' lie. Aljazeera. Retrieved from http://www.aljazeera.com/indepth/opinion/2014/08/exposing-great-poverty-reductio-201481211590729809.html (accessed 2015, October 1).

Hodal, K., Kelly, C., & Lawrence, F. (2014). Revealed: Asian slave labour producing prawns for supermarkets in US, UK. *Guardian Sustainable Business*, (2014, June 10). Retrieved from http://www.theguardian.com/global-development/2014/jun/10/supermarket-prawns-thailand-produced-slave-labour

Holman, C., & Luneburg, W. (2012). Lobbying and transparency: A comparative analysis of regulatory reform. *Interest Groups & Advocacy*, *1*, 75–104.

Hopkins, C. (2010). Enough, for all, forever: The quest for a more sustainable future. *Education Canada*, *49*(4). Canadian Education Association. Retrieved from www.cea-ace.ca

Hoskins, T. (2015). Reliving the Rana Plaza factory collapse: A history of cities in 50 buildings, day 22. *Guardian Sustainable Business* (2015, April 23). Retrieved from http://www.theguardian.com/cities/2015/apr/23/rana-plaza-factory-collapse-history-cities-50-buildings (accessed 2015, October 7).

Huffington, A. (2014). *Thrive: The third metric to redefining success and creating a life of well-being, wisdom, and wonder*. US: Harmony.

IEA (International Energy Agency). (2014). World energy outlook: Energy subsidies. Retrieved from http://www.worldenergyoutlook.org/resources/energysubsidies/

IFAD (International Fund for Agricultural Development). (2015). *Water facts and figures*. Retrieved from http://www.ifad.org/english/water/key.htm

ILO (International Labour Organization). (2014). *Profits and poverty: The economics of forced labour*. Geneva: International Labour Office.

ILO (International Labour Organization). (2015). *World employment social outlook: The changing nature of jobs*. Retrieved from http://www.ilo.org/global/research/global-reports/weso/2015-changing-nature-of-jobs/WCMS_368626/lang--en/index.htm

IMF (International Monetary Fund). (2015a). *World economic outlook. Uneven growth: Short- and long-term factors*. Retrieved from http://www.imf.org/external/pubs/ft/weo/2015/01/

IMF (International Monetary Fund). (2015b). *Counting the cost of energy subsidies*. Retrieved from http://www.imf.org/external/pubs/ft/survey/so/2015/new070215a.htm

IOM (International Office for Migration). (2015). Migration and cities: New partnerships to manage mobility. World Migration Report 2015. Retrieved from https://www.iom.int/world-migration-report-2015

Ionescu-Somers, A., & Enders, A. (2012). How Nestlé dealt with a social media campaign against it. *Financial Times* (2012, December 12). Retrieved from http://www.ft.com/intl/cms/s/0/90dbff8a-3aea-11e2-b3f0-00144feabdc0.html#axzz3nCgM0br2 (accessed 2015, September 30).

IPCC (Intergovernmental Panel on Climate Change). (2014). Climate change 2014: Mitigation of climate change. *Contribution of Working Group III to the Fifth Assessment Report of the Intergovernmental Panel on Climate Change*. Cambridge, UK and New York, NY, US: Cambridge University Press.

IUCN. (2007). Species extinction – the facts. Retrieved from https://cmsdata.iucn.org/downloads/species_extinction_05_2007.pdf

Kaufman, G., & Scott, K. (2003). What is systemic risk, and do bank regulators retard or contribute to it? *Independent Review*, *7*(3), 371–391.

Khor, M., & Khor, K. (2001). *Rethinking globalization: Critical issues and policy choices*. New York: Zed Books.

Klein, N. (2007). *The shock doctrine: The rise of disaster capitalism*. London: Penguin Group.

Klein, N. (2014). *This changes everything: Capitalism vs the climate*. New York: Simon & Schuster.

Kochhar, R. (2015). Seven-in-ten people globally live on $10 or less per day. Pew Research (2015, September 23). Retrieved from http://www.pewresearch.org/fact-tank/2015/09/23/seven-in-ten-people-globally-live-on-10-or-less-per-day/ (accessed 2015, November 2).

Korten, D. (2001). *When corporations rule the world* (2nd ed.). San Francisco: Berrett-Koehler Publishers, Kumarian Press.

Korten, D. (2010). *Agenda for a new economy: From phantom wealth to real wealth*. San Francisco: Berrett-Koehler Publishers Inc.

Kwoh, L. (2013). When the CEO burns out. *The Wall Street Journal* (2013, May 7). Retrieved from http://www.wsj.com/articles/SB10001424127887323687604578469124008524696 (accessed 2015, October 7).

Layard, R. (2006). *Happiness: Lessons from a new science*. London: Penguin.

London, T., & Hart, S. (2010). *Next generation business strategies for the base of the pyramid: New approaches for building mutual value*. New Jersey: Pearson FT Press.

Mandelbaum, M. (2003). *The ideas that conquered the world: Peace, democracy, and free markets in the twenty-first century*. New York: Public Affairs.

Mattenson, M., & Ivancevich, J. (1987). *Controlling work place stress: Effective human resource and management strategy*. San Francisco: Jossey Bass Publications.

Maxton, G. (2015). Economic growth doesn't create jobs, it destroys them. *Guardian Sustainable Business* (2013, April 21). Retrieved from http://www.theguardian.com/sustainable-business/2015/apr/21/jobs-economic-growth-inequality-environment-club-of-rome

McGlade, C., & Ekins, P. (2015). The geographical distribution of fossil fuels unused when limiting global warming to 2 °C. *Nature, 517*, 187–190.

Meadows, D. H., Meadows, D. L., Randers, J., & Behrens III, W. (1972) *Limits to growth*. New York: New American Library.

Millennium Ecosystem Assessment (MA). (2005). *Ecosystems and human well-being: Synthesis*. Washington, DC: Island Press.

Mintzberg, H. (2015). *Rebalancing society: Radical renewal beyond left, right and centre*. Oakland: Berretr-Koehler Publishers, Inc.

Mishel, L., & Davis, A. (2015). Top CEOs make 300 times more than typical workers. Economic Policy Institute Report. *Wages Income and Growth* (2015, June 21). Retrieved from http://www.epi.org/publication/top-ceos-make-300-times-more-than-workers-pay-growth-surpasses-market-gains-and-the-rest-of-the-0-1-percent/ (accessed 2015, October 27).

Monbiot, G. (2013). This transatlantic trade deal is a full-frontal assault on democracy. *The Guardian* (2015, November 4). Retrieved from http://www.theguardian.com/commentisfree/2013/nov/04/us-trade-deal-full-frontal-assault-on-democracy (accessed 2015, October 27).

Moodie, A. (2015). African nations work together to rid supply chains of conflict materials. *Guardian Sustainable Business* (2015, September 14). Retrieved from http://www.theguardian.com/sustainable-business/2015/sep/14/conflict-minerals-africa-dodd-frank-apple-ford

New Development Paradigm (NDP) Steering Committee and Secretariat. (2013). *Happiness: Towards a new development paradigm*. Report of the Kingdom of Bhutan.

NOAA. (2015). Greenhouse gas benchmark reached. Retrieved from http://research.noaa.gov/News/NewsArchive/LatestNews/TabId/684/ArtMID/1768/ArticleID/11153/Greenhouse-gas-benchmark-reached-.aspx (accessed 2015, October 15).

Noble, D. (2014). 11% of UK businesses say slavery in their supply chains is likely. *Guardian Sustainable Business* (2014, August 18). Retrieved from http://www.theguardian.com/sustainable-business/2014/aug/18/11-of-uk-businesses-say-slavery-in-their-supply-chains-is-likely (accessed 2015, October 27).

Norman, W., & MacDonald, C. (2003). Getting to the bottom of the 'triple bottom line'. *Business Ethics Quarterly, 14*(2), 243–262.

OECD (Organization for Economic Co-operation and Development). (2011, May). *Towards green growth: A summary for policy makers*. Retrieved from http://www.oecd.org/greengrowth/48012345.pdf

OECD (Organization for Economic Co-operation and Development). (2013). *Health at a glance 2013, OECD indicators*. OECD Publishing. Retrieved from http://dx.doi.org/10.1787/health_glance-2013-en

Orr, D. (2006). *The design revolution: Notes for practitioners*. Washington: Island Press.

Pearce, F. (2009). Consumption dwarfs population as main environmental threat. Environment 360. Retrieved from http://e360.yale.edu/feature/consumption_dwarfs_population_as_main_environmental_threat/2140/ (accessed 2015, October 1).

Perkins, A. (1994). Savings money by reducing stress. *Harvard Business Review, 72*(6), 12.

Perry, M. (2014). Fortune 500 firms in 1955 vs.2014. American Enterprise Institute. Retrieved from http://www.aei.org/publication/fortune-500-firms-in-1955-vs-2014-89-are-gone-and-were-all-better-off-because-of-that-dynamic-creative-destruction/ (accessed 2015, September 29).

Pezzini, M. (2012). An emerging middle class. *OECD Year Book 2012*. Retrieved from http://www.oecdobserver.org/news/fullstory.php/aid/3681/An_emerging_middle_class.html

Pigott, T. (2014). Marketing is failing to address social change . . . why? *Guardian Sustainable Business* (February 2014, February 5). Retrieved from http://www.theguardian.com/sustainable-business/marketing-failing-to-address-social-change

Piketty, T. (2014). *Capital in the twenty first century*. Cambridge, Massachusetts: The Belknap Press of Harvard University Press.

Porter, M. E., & Kramer, M. R. (2011). Creating shared value. *Harvard Business Review*, January/February. Retrieved from http://www.waterhealth.com/sites/default/files/Harvard_Business_Review_Shared_Value.pdf

PwC. (2015). Five global megatrends. Retrieved from http://www.pwc.com/gx/en/issues/megatrends.html (accessed 2015, September 29).

Ramanna, K., & Muthuram, V. (2013, September). Wal-Mart lobbying in India. *Harvard Business School Case* 114–023.

Raworth, K. (2012, February). *A safe and just space for humanity*. Oxfam Discussion Paper. Retrieved from https://www.oxfam.org/sites/www.oxfam.org/files/dp-a-safe-and-just-space-for-humanity-130212-en.pdf

Roach, B. (2007). *Corporate power in a global economy*. Global Development and Environment Institute. MA, US: Tufts University.

Rockström, J., Steffen, W., Noone, K., Persson, Å., Chapin III, F. S., Lambin, E., Lenton, T. M., Scheffer, M., Folke, C., Schellnhuber, H., Nykvist, B., De Wit, C. A., Hughes, T., van der Leeuw, S., Rodhe, H., Sörlin, S., Snyder, P. K.,

Costanza, R., Svedin, U., Falkenmark, M., Karlberg, L., Corell, R. W., Fabry, V. J., Hansen, J., Walker, B., Liverman, D., Richardson, K., Crutzen, P., & Foley, J. (2009). Planetary boundaries: Exploring the safe operating space for humanity. *Ecology and Society, 14*(2), 32.

Roney, J. (2012). Taking stock: World fish catch falls to 90 million tons in 2012. Rutgers University: Earth Policy Institute.

Rousell, K. (2013). Tax on the 'private' billions now stashed away in havens enough to end extreme world poverty twice over. Oxfam International. Retrieved from https://www.oxfam.org/en/pressroom/pressreleases/2013-05-22/tax-private-billions-now-stashed-away-havens-enough-end-extreme (accessed 2015, October 7).

Sanders, B. (2015). Top corporate tax dodgers. United States Senate. Retrieved from http://www.sanders.senate.gov/imo/media/doc/102512%20-%20JobDestroyers3.pdf

Schröter, M., van der Zanden, E., van Oudenhoven, A., Remme, R., Serna-Chavez, H., de Groot, R., & Opdam, P. (2014). Ecosystem services as a contested concept: A synthesis of critique and counter-arguments. *Conservation Letters, 7*(6), 514–523.

Sebastian, I. (2015, April). Doing business in a wellbeing economy. In Reframing the Game: The Transition to a New Sustainable Economy. *A Special Issue of Building Sustainable Legacies, 5.*

Simms, A., Johnson, V., Smith, J., & Mitchell, S. (2009). *The consumption explosion.* The Third UK Interdependence Report. The New Economics Foundation. Retrieved from http://b.3cdn.net/nefoundation/41a473dfbe880a0742_ucm6i4n29.pdf

Smith, R. (2014). Green capitalism: The god that failed. Truthout. News Analysis (2014, January 9). Retrieved from http://www.truth-out.org/news/item/21060-green-capitalism-the-god-that-failed

Statistics Portal. (2015). Global Gross Domestic Product (GDP) from 2010 to 2020 (in billion U.S. dollars). Retrieved from http://www.statista.com/statistics/268750/global-gross-domestic-product-gdp/

Steffen, W., Crutzen, P., & McNeill, J. (2007). The anthropocene: Are humans now overwhelming the great forces of nature? *Ambio, 36*(8), 614–621.

Steffen, W., Richardson, K., Rockström, J., Cornell, S., Fetzer, I., Bennett, E., Biggs, R. , Carpenter, S., de Vries, W., de Wit, C., Folke, C., Gerten, D., Heinke, J., Mace, G., Persson. L., Ramanathan, V., Reyers, B., & Sörlin, S. (2015). Planetary boundaries: Guiding human development on a changing planet. *Science, 347*(6223).

Stiglitz, J. (2011). Of the 1%, by the 1%, for the 1%. *Vanity Fair.* Retrieved from http://www.vanityfair.com/news/2011/05/top-one-percent-201105

Stiglitz, J. (2013). *The price of inequality: How today's divided society endangers our future.* London: Penguin.

Stiglitz, J. (2015). *The great divide: Unequal societies and what we can do about them.* New York: W.W. Norton and Company.

Sukhdev, P. (2012). *Corporation 2020: Transforming business for tomorrow's world.* Washington: Island Press.

Summers, L. (2015). *Persistent jobless growth. Outlook on the global agenda 2015. Top 10 trends of 2015.* Geneva: World Economic Forum. Retrieved from http://reports.weforum.org/outlook-global-agenda-2015/top-10-trends-of-2015/2-persistent-jobless-growth/

Tellus Institute. (2015). Retrieved from http://www.tellus.org/ (accessed 2015, September 29).

The Economics of Ecosystems and Biodiversity (TEEB). (2009). *TEEB for Policy Makers – Summary: Responding to the Value of Nature.* Retrieved from http://www.teebweb.org/publication/teeb-for-policy-makers-summary-responding-to-the-value-of-nature/

The Economics of Ecosystems and Biodiversity (TEEB). (2010). *TEEB for Business. Executive Summary.* Retrieved from http://www.teebweb.org/publication/teeb-for-business-executive-summary/

Townsend, M., & Zarnett, B. (2013). *A journey in search of Capitalism* 2.0. Earthshine & Toronto Sustainability Speaker Series. Retrieved from http://www.earthshinesolutions.com/docs/A-Journey-in-Search-of-CAP2_Clean-Slate_Oct_2013.pdf (accessed 2015, January 16).

Transparency International. (2015). Lobby meetings with EU policy-makers dominated by corporate interests. Retrieved from http://www.transparency.org/news/pressrelease/lobby_meetings_with_eu_policy_makers_dominated_by_corporate_interests (accessed 2015, October 17).

Tru Cost. (2013). *Natural capital at risk: The top 100 externalities of business.* Retrieved from http://www.trucost.com/published-research/99/natural-capital-at-risk-the-top-100-externalities-of-business

Trussell Trust. (2015). Foodbank use tops one million for first time. Press release (2015, April 22). Retrieved from http://www.trusselltrust.org/resources/documents/Press/Trussell-Trust-foodbank-use-tops-one-million.pdf

Turner, M. (2012). Assistant Vice President Co-Innovation at Interface. *Personal communication.*

United Nations Global Compact. (2015). Retrieved from https://www.unglobalcompact.org/ (accessed 2015, October 27).

United Nations. (2015). *The millennium development goals report. Summary.* Retrieved from http://www.un.org/millenniumgoals/2015_MDG_Report/pdf/MDG%202015%20Summary%20web_english.pdf

UNCTAD (United Nations Conference on Trade and Development). (2006). *World investment report 2006. FDI from developing and transitional economies: Implications for development.* New York and Geneva: United Nations.

United Nations Department of Economic and Social Affairs (UNDESA). (2015). World population projected to reach 9.7 billion by 2050. Retrieved from https://www.un.org/development/desa/en/news/population/2015-report.html (accessed 2015, October 7).

UNEP (United Nations Environment Programme). (2011a). *Universal ownership: Why environmental externalities matter to institutional investors.* Retrieved from http://www.unepfi.org/fileadmin/documents/universal_ownership_full.pdf

UNEP (United Nations Environment Programme). (2011b). *Towards a green economy: Pathways to sustainable development and poverty eradication*. Retrieved from http://www.unep.org/greeneconomy/ GreenEconomyReport/tabid/29846/Default.aspx

UNEP (United Nations Environment Programme). (2013). *GEO-5 for business: Impacts of a changing environment on the corporate sector*. Nairobi, Kenya: United Nations Environment Programme. Retrieved from http://www .unep.org/geo/pdfs/geo5/geo5_for_business.pdf

UNEP (United Nations Environment Programme). (2015). *The financial system we need: Aligning the financial system with sustainable development*. Retrieved from http:// unepinquiry.org/publication/inquiry-global-report-the-financial-system-we-need/ (accessed 2015, October 27).

UNFCCC (United Nations Framework Convention on Climate Change (2010). *Draft Decision/CP. 15 Copenhagen Accord. December 2010. Source?*

UNICEF (United Nations Children's Fund). (2014). *Child labour and UNICEF in action: Children at the centre*. Retrieved from http://www.unicef.org/protection/files/ Child_Labour_and_UNICEF_in_Action.pdf

UNU-IHDP/UNEP. (2014). *The inclusive wealth report: Sustainable development policy and practice*. Cambridge: Cambridge University Press.

UN Women (United Nations Women). (2015). Collective failure of leadership on progress for women. UN Women press conference (2015, March 6). Retrieved from http:// www.unwomen.org/en/news/stories/2015/3/collective-failure-of-leadership-on-progress-for-women#sthash. hVC4RyrV.dpuf (accessed 2015, October 7).

Vitali, S., Glattfelder, J., & Battison, S. (2011). The network of global corporate control. *PLoS ONE, 6*(10), e25995. Retrieved from http://arxiv.org/pdf/1107.5728.pdf

Volans. (2013). *Breakthrough: Business leaders, market revolutions*. London:Volans.

WBCSD (World Business Council for Sustainable Development). (2010). *Vision 2050: The new agenda for business*. Geneva, Switzerland: WBCSD.

WCED (World Commission on Environment and Development). (1987). *Our common future*. Oxford: Oxford University Press.

Webster, K. (2015). *The Circular Economy: A wealth of flows*. Isle of Wight, UK: Ellen MacArthur Foundation Publishing.

Weisman, A. (2007). *The world without us*. New York: Thomas Dunne Books/St. Martin's Press.

WHO (World Health Organization). (2014). *Preventing suicide: A global imperative*. Geneva: World Health Organization.

Wilkinson, R., & Pickett, K. (2009). *The spirit level: Why equality is better for everyone*. London: Allen Lane/ Penguin.

Willard, B. (2012). *The new sustainability advantage: Seven business case benefits of a triple bottom line*. Gabriola Island, BC. Canada: New Society Publishers.

Woodward, D. (2015). *Incrementum ad absurdum*: Global growth, inequality and poverty eradication in a carbon-constrained world. *World Economic Review, 4* (2015, February 9). Retrieved from http://wer .worldeconomicsassociation.org/papers/incrementum-ad-absurdum-global-growth-inequality-and-poverty-eradication-in-a-carbon-constrained-world/

World Bank. (2012). *Inclusive green growth: The pathway to sustainable development*. Retrieved from http:// siteresourccs.worldbank.org/EXTSDNET/Resources/ Inclusive_Green_Growth_May_2012.pdf

World Bank. (2015). Poverty overview. Retrieved from http:// www.worldbank.org/en/topic/poverty/overview (accessed 2015, October 7).

World Economic Forum. (WEF). (2011). *Water security: The water-food-energy-climate nexus*. Geneva: World Economic Forum.

World Economic Forum (WEF). (2014). *Global risks 2014* (9th ed.). Retrieved from http://reports.weforum.org/ global-risks-2014/

Worldwatch Institute. (2010). *State of the world* 2010. *Transforming cultures: From consumerism to sustainability*. New Jersey: W. W. Norton & Company.

WRG (Water Resources Group). (2012). *Background, impact and the way forward*. Briefing report prepared for the World Economic Forum, Switzerland.

WWAP (United Nations World Water Assessment Programme). (2015). *The United Nations world water development report 2015: Water for a sustainable world*. Paris: UNESCO.

WWF. (2014). *Living planet report: Species and spaces, people and places*. Gland, Switzerland. Retrieved from http://wwf.panda.org/about_our_earth/all_publications/ living_planet_report/

WWF. (2008). Zero net deforestation by 2020: A WWF briefing paper. Retrieved from http://awsassets.panda.org/ downloads/wwf_2020_zero_net_deforest_brief.pdf (accessed 2015, October 27).

Yunus, M. (2009). *Creating a world without poverty: Social business and the future of capitalism*. New York: Public Affairs.

2 Changing: Towards a One Planet Approach

Sally Jeanrenaud and Jean-Paul Jeanrenaud

'Change or be changed. But make no mistake, this changes everything.'
Naomi Klein

'You never change things by fighting the existing reality. To change something, build a new model that makes the existing model obsolete.'
R. Buckminster Fuller, 20th century American inventor and visionary

LEARNING OUTCOMES

The aim of this chapter is to understand how new economic and business opportunities are emerging in response to the ecological, social and economic challenges *introduced in Chapter 1*, and how these involve different dimensions of change. It has three main objectives:

1. To frame three dimensions of change including business, economy, and self, to highlight transformation from the 'outside-in' and 'inside-out'.

2. To provide an overview of new business and economic approaches, and to illustrate how thinking and practice are shifting in relation to mindsets, purpose, governance, capital, ways of producing and consuming.

3. To encourage critical reflection on new opportunities of 'change for good'.

2.0 Changing from the Outside-In and the Inside-Out

Chapter 1 helped frame our one planet predicament, and explored the interlinked environmental, social, economic and political challenges facing business and society globally. Many see these sustainability challenges as catalysts of profound change, which are provoking a fundamental rethink of 'business', 'economy' and 'self'. As Klein (2014) says when commenting on climate change: 'Change or be changed. But make no mistake, this changes everything.' For an illustration see YouTube video

This Changes Everything: Capitalism vs the Climate, Naomi Klein (1 minute), https://www.youtube.com/watch?v=WPQI1Lui42c.

'Change' is a complex process. Transition scholars and practitioners recognize that transformational change occurs at many levels – personal, cultural, organizational, institutional, and systematic - and that there are complex interdependencies between them. O'Brien and Sygna (2013) outline three interacting spheres of transformation in dealing with sustainability challenges, relating to practical, political and personal spheres, suggesting a need for transformations from both the 'outside-in' and the 'inside-out'.

In transforming business, society and self, Scharmer and Kaufer (2013) outline a threefold transformation of the old paradigm – personal, relational and institutional. Pirson *et al.* (2014) outline three major levels involved in the transformation of capitalism: the systemic, institutional, and individual levels. We recognize that while the definitions of these domains are complex, and the boundaries between them are not always clear, it is helpful to bear in mind at least three major intersecting areas of change – business, economy and self. These are outlined in the following sections.

2.1 Business

GROUP EXERCISE

WHAT DOES A ONE PLANET BUSINESS LOOK LIKE?

See Exercise 2.1 at the end of the chapter.

A positive view of the current corporate model is that it creates useful goods and services for customers, wealth for shareholders, lowers the prices of goods, invests in research and development, helps solve problems, and contributes to the growth of the economy. A contrasting view of big business is that it exernalizes its costs, exploits workers, undermines cultural values and interferes with public policy processes. While sustainability challenges certainly present risks *to business*, many business approaches also present a growing risk *to people and planet*. As Sukhdev (2012) points out however, the model of today's corporation might be broken, but we are not stuck with it. Business needs a new DNA and is quite capable of transforming itself with the right enabling conditions.

There are so many innovative ideas, platforms and initiatives promoting new corporate models, and alternative ways of doing business (see Table 2.1). Here is a flavour of some new approaches. In *Corporation 2020*, Sukhdev (2012) explores how a new corporate model can be built that incorporates externalities, cares for all the capitals, undertakes responsible advertising, and limits financial leverage to help shape a more sustainable world. In their book *Firms of Endearment*, Sisodia *et al.* (2014) focus on transforming the way business is done, by generating new forms of value that matter (emotional, experiential, social, and financial) for all stakeholders. This involves conscious leadership, putting meaning into the workplace, new marketing paradigms, and stakeholder integration.

In *Breakthrough: Business Leaders, Market Revolutions*, Volans (2013) sets out a breakthrough manifesto for business, and explores what top businesses are doing, in the context of the transformation of capitalism. It outlines seven vectors of systems change where solutions are evolving, in the domains of science, activism, institutions, access, finance, economics and culture. *The B Team*, an initiative founded by Richard Branson and Jochen Zeitz in 2013, believes business can be a catalyst for change for good if it prioritizes people and planet alongside profit, and addresses key challenges such as transparency, collaboration, restoring nature, true accounting, building communities, redefining market incentives, reward systems, dignity and fairness, and leading for the long run. Some examples of new ways of doing business that are good for people, planet and prosperity are explored *in the following sections*.

TABLE 2.1   Differences between the Firm of the Past and the Firm of the Future

	Firm of the past	Firm of the future
Beneficiaries	Shareholders	Stakeholders
Bottom line	Single financial bottom line	Triple bottom line People, planet and prosperity
Boundaries	The firm	Value chain Product life cycles
Communities	Corporate social responsibility	Creating shared value Social enterprise Building community
Capitals	Financial Manufactured	5 capitals
Sources of capital	Stock market Financial institutions Absentee owners	Stock market Customers Crowd-sourcing
Negative externalities	Externalized	Internalized
Operations	Linear: take-make-waste	Circular: closed loop Servitization Production-on-demand
Market forces	Global	Global Local
Growth	Infinite	Green growth Limited growth Degrowth
Reporting	Short-term quarterly Financial	Longer term – annually Triple bottom line
Advertising	Turning wants into needs	Responsible advertising
Leadership	Heroic	Responsible leadership Servant leadership

2.2 Economy

The traditional view of the prevailing competitive, globalized, free market economy, based on private property, deregulated markets, and shareholder wealth, is that it is a superior means of organizing economic activities compared to centrally planned systems. The capitalist system is considered to allocate resources efficiently, match supply and demand, generate wealth, and reward hard work and innovation, and is seen by many to deliver well-being, and catalyse higher forms of civilization. However, it is increasingly argued that all is not well with the current system, that 'capitalism is in crisis', and is incapable of delivering a sustainable future (Korten, 2001; Porritt, 2005; Hart, 2005; Kotler, 2015).

There are many new articulations of how to transform capitalism, and develop new forms, sometimes called 'conscious capitalism'. Various reforms have been outlined to develop a future-proofed economy in which 9 billion people can live well within the limits of one planet. Most agree that we need to work with free market structures and free choice; while serving the needs of all stakeholders. There is a need to restructure markets, property and ownership models. Financial and investment systems, and incentive structures, need to encourage long-term behaviour. Metrics need to integrate environmental, social and governance dimensions, and we need production systems that work in sync with nature. There are also calls to relocalize the economy and to develop more life-centred, democratic, community-oriented enterprises (Porritt, 2005; Korten, 2010; Gore & Blood, 2012; Townsend & Zarnett, 2013; Scharmer & Kaufer, 2013; Pirson *et al.*, 2014; Kotler, 2015).

There are some compelling new narratives of what a new economy might look like. Each of these new economies has a different label and conceptual focus, but each addresses one or more of the ecological, social and economic flaws of the existing paradigm. Amongst others, these include:

- **The Circular Economy** (Ellen MacArthur Foundation, 2012): associated with Cradle-to-Cradle (C2C) manufacturing, focuses on material flows of two types – biological nutrients, designed to re-enter the biosphere safely, and technical nutrients, which are designed to circulate at high quality without entering the biosphere.

- **The Sharing Economy:** also called 'collaborative economy' (Botsman & Rogers, 2010), which focuses on creating value out of sharing human and physical assets, such as spare rooms, cars, equipment, clothes, and skills, with the potential to give more people access to the economy, and to reduce resource use.

- **The Green Economy** (UNEP, 2011): which focuses on a new macroeconomics of nature, to help reduce environmental risks and ecological scarcities, and to improve well-being and equity. It is a low carbon, resource efficient, socially inclusive economy, which values and invests in natural and social capital, for growth and jobs.

- **From Ego-System to Eco-System Economies** (Scharmer & Kaufer 2013): which addresses updating our economic logic, and moving from an obsolete 'ego-system' mindset, focused on personal interests, to an 'eco-system' awareness that emphasizes the well-being of the whole.

Based on the work of many pioneering leaders, Townsend and Zarnett (2013) have developed an initial synthesis of nine design principles underpinning a new sustainable economy:

1   Less growth, more well-being.
2   A broader view of what capital means.
3   Based on responsible enterprise, adding real value, where it is needed.
4   Holistic systems thinking, aligned with the circular economy.
5   Enabled by a well-functioning money system.
6   Away from speculative bubbles, towards creating longer-term real wealth.
7   Shared ownership and distribution of resources and wealth.
8   Based on collaboration and striving together.
9   Founded on new institutions and greater systemic resilience.

2.3 Self

The further sphere of transformation involves the personal, inner or micro dimensions of change. At an individual level, what kinds of mindsets and values do we need if we are going to transition into a sustainable future?

For many good reasons the received wisdom about solutions is that we need to transform 'external' conditions 'out there': the political, economic, social and technical systems, in order to '*breakthrough*' into a new sustainable economy (Volans, 2013). This approach often projects 'the blame' onto structures or other actors in the system, and undervalues the role that self-awareness, mindsets and values play in system transformation. Here we propose that we need to '*open up*' to the inner world of aspiration, attention and intention, and also work on the inner dimensions of social change, or 'change from the inside-out'.

Townsend (2013) points out, the further we advance on the sustainable business journey the more we meet deeper constraints, and challenges, in addition to the need for systems change. Eventually, we come to recognize the imperative for a fundamental change in human behaviour, and the ultimate barrier to change – ourselves – and hence, the consequent challenge of personal transformation. Could it be that we must first undergo individual transformation in order to unlock wider social change?

In his book *The Sustainable Self*, Murray (2011) emphasizes the key role of the personal dimensions of sustainability as well as the professional ones. He explores the relationship between personal core values and sustainability issues, and outlines how personal motivations, values, attitudes and beliefs influence our potential to drive change.

Transformation of the personal sphere is integral to Scharmer and Kaufer's (2013) work on new economies at MIT's Presencing Institute. In *Leading from the Emerging Future: From Ego-System to Eco-System Economies*, they emphasize 'attending to your attention' and 'shifting *the inner place* from which we operate'. Scharmer and Kaufer make the case that the evolution of our economy mirrors the evolution of human consciousness; and that in order to transform the current unsustainable, unjust and unstable economic model, we need to reclaim our attention and intention through mindful practices. Thus from an agency perspective, the evolution of the economy requires an 'inversion journey', which involves bending the beam of attention back onto ourselves and the sources of self. This social transformational journey (known as the U Process) emphasizes the importance of engaging with an open mind, heart, and will. The 'inversion journey', involving mindful practices, can help cultivate presence, awareness, and compassion, which underpin people- and planet-focused mindsets, values, and intentions.

Mind: by mind we mean the cognitive power that 'knows', 'understands' and 'sees' (although it is also recognized that the heart and body have their own ways of 'knowing'). The mind relates to states of consciousness, attention, curiosity, and awareness. Many of the challenges we now face result from a narrow adherence to the beliefs and assumptions of old theories, concepts, ideologies, and stories. While our education system is good at training specialists, which is useful when an expert is required for a particular job, it can tend towards reductionism. This can lead to 'silo thinking' which fails to perceive whole systems resulting in 'systems blind spots'. Individual transformation thus implies training the attention, transcending old concepts and cognitive boundaries, and opening the mind to alternative and holistic worldviews. An open mind reflects a shift from judgement to humility and curiosity. This will help facilitate a growth in consciousness from 'silos to systems', from 'parts to wholes', to more integrative perspectives – in other words, a One Planet Mindset.

Heart: by heart we mean an inner power that 'feels' and 'aspires'. It is a key faculty that relates to values, desires, affections and emotions (*e-movere:* to move out from your/a centre). When aspirations and values are narrow there is a tendency to focus on individual enjoyment, pleasure and satisfaction, which can result in a lack of respect and compassion for others. Old business and economic approaches have tended to prioritize extrinsic values, such achievement, wealth, and status, at the expense of intrinsic ones, such as relationships, responsibility and well-being. At the same time business environments have been dominated by top down, competitive and individualistic cultures, at the expense of ones that are more collaborative and community-minded. In the transition to a new economy, the personal transformation involves opening the heart, transcending relational boundaries, and cultivating more compassionate, caring, and collaborative relationships. An open heart reflects a shift from cynicism to compassion. As psychologist Dan Seigel (2014) explains it, while we need to nurture the differentiated aspects of our inner selves, we also need to shift to a more integrated and interpersonal sense of self, from 'me' to 'we' to 'MWe'.

Will: by will we mean the purposive and elective powers, which direct attention and action. It is the faculty that relates to motives, intentions, purpose and resolve, which in turn drives behaviour and directs action towards particular goals. Individuals and groups exert their will to seek 'the good' (however framed), and this can be narrowly or altruistically focused, including material and spiritual dimensions. Old economic and business models have focused on the private good, typically at the expense of the public good, and have sought profits over a higher social purpose. New business models, which harness markets to deliver prosperity for people and the planet, represent an evolution of purpose. In the transition to a new economy the personal element of transformation involves opening up the will, transcending the boundaries of the small will, to larger spheres of meaning. An open will reflects a shift from fear and craving, to courage and inner peace. It involves cultivating a higher sense of purpose, and serving community through more people- and planet-minded approaches.

The attention given to these inner faculties resonates with many of the world's wisdom traditions, which variously refer to three interior human faculties and their cultivation: the will, the mind, and the heart, which address themselves to the 'good', the 'true' and 'beautiful' respectively (Addey, 2005). These faculties give us the ability to engage with the ethical, intellectual and aesthetic dimensions of life. HH Pope Francis refers to them in the Encyclical Letter *Laudato Si'* (2015): 'No system can completely suppress our openness to what is good, true and beautiful . . . I appeal to everyone throughout the world not to forget this dignity which is ours. No one has the right to take it from us.'

Beyond the dogma of any one religion, neuroscientist Jean-Pierre Changeux, who writes on the connection between the mind and the brain, claims that while it will be a long time before we understand the nature of consciousness and how we perceive things, there is a reciprocity and causal relationship between ideas, neurons and the evolution of the brain. He places the good, the true and the beautiful within the characteristic features of the brain's neuronal organization, showing that humans strive for a life of 'goodness' through ethics; seek universal 'truth' through science; and seek interpersonal communication of 'beauty' through art (Changeux, 2012).

Thus we argue that transformation involves both change from the inside-out (self) as well as the outside-in (economy). The domains of business, economy and self are connected, and processes of change are reflexive and interdependent. Greater self-realization generates new mindsets and values, which inform new ways of producing and consuming, which in turn influence thoughts and aspirations. A transition to a sustainable economy calls for a deepening of the self, which requires interior as well as outer action. If we take up this challenge, the emergent paradigm promises to be an expression of a transformed way of being, based on compassion and understanding, and founded on mutual respect – respect for each other, for the earth, and for different ways of seeing and being.

2.4 Transformations

Einstein famously remarked that 'we cannot change our problems with the same thinking we used when we created them'. What is the new thinking we need to solve the problems we have created? The *following subsections* introduce ten examples of transformation, which emerge from significantly different mindsets and values, and represent a new integration of inner and outer realms *introduced in section 2.3*. They illustrate how some of the classic factors of production are being reframed. Each subsection introduces one or two seminal ideas from the literature, and includes some short case studies to illustrate the points.

2.4.1 Mindsets: Towards an Ecology of Mind

'A mind is like a parachute; it doesn't work unless it's open.'

Frank Zappa

What is a 'mindset'? And how are business mindsets shifting in response to the sustainability challenges *outlined in Chapter 1*? Mindsets are defined in various ways. For example, Meadows (1999) describes mindsets as the shared ideas in the mind of society; the deepest set of beliefs about how the world works, or shared social agreements about the nature of reality. Korten (2015) describes similar elements as 'stories' and argues that human beings live by shared cultural stories: 'They are the lens through which we view reality. They shape what we most value as a society and the institutions by which we structure power.' Scharmer and Kaufer (2013) make the case that the evolution of our economy mirrors the evolution of human consciousness, and that inner transformation is involved in the transition to a new economy.

Mindsets give rise to systems, which structure our businesses and economies. Ideas such as 'one can own land' or 'nature is a stock of resources to be converted to human purposes', or 'growth is good' may be taken for granted by some societies, but may completely dumbfound others (Meadows, ibid.). Changing mindsets is considered one of the most powerful ways of changing a system – more powerful than changing rules, incentives or infrastructures. And change agents who work at the level of transforming mindsets have the potential to transform entire systems, although society tends to resist challenges to its paradigms harder than it resists anything else. Changes in a single individual, however, can happen in a split second, involving: 'a falling of scales from the eyes, a new way of seeing' (Meadows, ibid., p. 18). Some business leaders such as Ray Anderson, former CEO of Interface, or Richard Branson of Virgin, talk of similar experiences; and such shifts in mindsets have gone on to inspire radically new sustainability approaches both within a company, such as Mission Zero in Interface, and international sustainability initiatives such as the *Carbon War Room* and the *B Team* founded by Branson.

We argue that a One Planet Mindset represents responsible, people-and-planet friendly approaches to business and economy. It values triple bottom line benefits to nature, society, and the economy (Jeanrenaud *et al.*, 2015). Such a mindset is expressed through various narratives, values and metaphors. For example, an old mindset might typically cast the environment as a threat, risk or cost to business, and people who are seen to care about nature are portrayed as anti-progress 'bunny lovers', 'tree huggers', or the 'hair shirt brigade', who seem to want society to go backwards and 'live in caves' again.

New business mindsets have a better understanding of the interdependence of environment and development. Sustainability challenges are being recast as 'business opportunities', as 'clouds with silver linings', the environment as an 'engine of growth', and sustainability as a 'driver of innovation and value creation'. New metaphors of nature as a 'living planet' or as a 'self-organizing, living system' rather than a set of resources are also emerging, as we shift from traditional silo thinking to systems thinking, or from understanding the individual parts of the problem to appreciating the whole.

Similarly, the language relating to people is shifting from the celebration of individualism and competition, to one that puts greater value on social relationships and on cross-sector collaboration and co-creation. It is a shift that recognizes that people are not islands unto themselves but are embedded in broader society, and thus have a responsibility to society as a whole. As Scharmer and Kaufer (2013) put it: we need an evolution from an outmoded 'ego-system', focused on the well-being of oneself, to an 'eco-system' awareness that emphasizes the well-being of the whole. New narratives, which recognize the interdependent relationships between all living things, reveal, perhaps, a gradual movement towards developing what Gregory Bateson

(1972) once described as 'an ecology of mind', which inspires a whole new way of understanding our place in nature, and the value of our social relationships.

However, it is also known that people and institutions can hide behind words, that narratives cannot be taken at face value, but can become co-opted, and used as even more insidious forms of control (Jeanrenaud, 2002). It is important to look critically beyond the words and metaphors to see how ideas and values are expressed in practice. A number of indicators of a transition to a One Planet Mindset within business can be identified. A first stage is expressed through 'do less harm', or 'doing more with less', which drives eco-efficiency initiatives and attempts to reduce corporate footprint. The second stage is expressed as 'do no harm', which drives the shift to zero footprint. A third stage can be expressed as 'do good' or a 'net positive approach' in which a company would give back more than it takes from society and the environment. A shift in mindsets will thus be embodied in all business practices, from defining corporate purpose and mission, through operations to metrics. *Some of these are discussed it the following sections.*

2.4.2 Purpose: Profit with a Purpose

What are companies for? How is the purpose of business evolving? It is still widely assumed that the 'business of business is business' or that the only social responsibility of business is to make a profit for its shareholders. As the influential economist Milton Friedman (1970) once argued: 'there is one and only one social responsibility of business – to use its resources and engage in activities designed to increase its profits so long as it stays within the rules of the game.' But this hasn't always been the case. The introduction of limited liability laws, the establishment of corporate personhood, the deregulation and innovation in trade and capital markets since the 1800s, freed corporations from wider accountability and social purpose and allowed them to become agents of free market capitalism. Growth, profit and self-interest have evolved to become the *raison d'être* of large corporations (Sukhdev, 2012).

However, many thinkers and business practitioners are reframing and reclaiming the core purpose of business. In their paper *Corporate Design: The Missing Business and Public Policy Issue of Our Time,* Kelly and White (2007) argue that corporate design starts with purpose, and that the corporate design challenge of the 21st century is to define a socially relevant purpose. They ask: 'How can corporations be designed so as to blend social, environmental, and financial mission at their very core?' They claim that a fundamental principle in redesigning the corporation of the future 'is to harness private interests to serve the public interest'.

The idea of a company having a social or higher purpose is not a new one. In the early years of industrialization the original aim of many corporations was to serve social goals, and this is still explicit in the mission and values of some long-standing corporations. Tata Group in India, founded in 1868, is particularly well known for its strong sense of values. As Jamsetji Nusserwanji, Tata Founder, said: 'In a free enterprise, the community is not just another stakeholder in business but is in fact the very purpose of its existence.' British retailer Marks and Spencer (M&S), founded in 1884, had strong values of fair trading, building good relationships with staff, suppliers and customers, and making generous contributions to charities and community causes. The father and two brothers who founded Philips in 1891 are known to have cared very much about the community in which they lived.

The idea of harnessing private interests to serve the public interest is a key principle in new versions of environmentally and socially sustainable business (e.g. Elkington, 2012; Volans 2013; Mackey & Sisodia 2014). Business leaders are recognizing that doing good and making money are not polar opposites. Purpose is recognized as a critical human need, a driver of innovation, and is inspiring a new generation of values-based businesses such as Seventh Generation, Toms, and Etsy. As Townsend (2012) put it: 'We will increasingly see businesses taking a values-based approach, putting money and business back in the service of people and planet, to support social and environmental balance, and generate real, living wealth – what might be called profit with a purpose.' And as Paul Polman, CEO of Unilever, points out, 'winning on its own is not enough, it's about winning with purpose' (Confino, 2011). See Case Study 2.1.

CASE STUDY 2.1
Ikea's Sustainability Strategy: People and Planet Positive

Ikea is the world's largest family-owned multinational furniture retail company, founded in Sweden in 1943, which had €30 billion in sales in 2014. In 2012 the Ikea Group launched an ambitious sustainability strategy, *People and Planet Positive*, which is designed to be an integral part of the Group's long-term growth direction, and builds on its long history of working with sustainability. This might be considered an example of a mission which links social purpose with profit. It has three main goals and areas of action up to 2020.

More Sustainable Life at Home: Ikea aims to inspire and enable millions of people to live a more sustainable life at home, by offering products and solutions that help customers to save money by using less energy and water and reducing waste. For example, it aims to only sell energy-efficient LED bulbs by 2016. These last for 20 years and use up to 85% less electricity than other bulbs. Ikea uses 1% of the world's commercially logged wood, and has made a commitment to become forest positive by 2020, by growing as many trees as it uses and increasing its use of certified wood products. It is also making progress on using cotton goods from sustainable sources, which increased from 34% in 2012 to 75% in 2014.

Energy and Resource Independent: Ikea aims to generate 70% of its energy from renewables by 2017, and 100% by 2020. It has invested €1.5 billion in renewable energy since 2009, and in 2015 it announced that it will invest a further €600 million on wind and solar power installations. It has already signed up to own and operate 314 wind turbines and has 700,000 solar panels on its roofs. The charitable arm of the group also plans to invest €400 million by 2020 to support families and communities in nations vulnerable to the impacts of climate change such as floods, droughts and desertification.

Better Life for People and Communities: Ikea aims to support the development of good places to work throughout the IKEA Group supply chain, and encourages suppliers to not only focus on compliance but also shared values. For example, Ikea actively works to prevent child labour in its supply chain. Since their IWAY Supplier Code of Conduct was introduced in 2000 there have been more than 165,000 audited improvements in environment and working conditions in supplier factories around the world. Ikea will also introduce the 'living wage' for all its UK staff from 2016.

Source: IKEA (2015).

2.4.3 Governance: From Shareholders to Stakeholders

Who are companies for? Can companies create value by serving stakeholders? Under shareholder capitalism the main objective of the corporation is to maximize shareholder wealth. The success of a company is measured by its share price, its dividends and overall profit. Milton Friedman once claimed that any activities not directly related to generating shareholder wealth are considered a waste of shareholders' money and, potentially, unethical because they amount to stealing from owners. He argued that solving social problems was the responsibility of other actors such as the state and non-government organizations. The predominance of the shareholder perspective has been enshrined in law and tested in US courts in the well-known legal case between Dodge and Ford in 1919, which helped establish the primacy of corporate self-interest over any form of social responsibility (see Definition box).

SHAREHOLDERS AND STAKE HOLDERS

Shareholders (or stockholders) are individuals or institutions that legally own a share of stock in a private or public corporation, and have the legal right to make decisions about a company. They frequently push to increase financial returns. Corporate stakeholders are groups, internal and external to the company, who can affect or be affected by the actions of a business as a whole, such as employees, customers, suppliers, investors, and the wider community.

The shareholder model of capitalism is widely blamed for many of the negative impacts of business on people and the environment. Decision-making processes are usually influenced by a small number of shareholders, and are dominated by short-term interests and quarterly reporting requirements. Although registered in a home state, the subsidiaries of MNCs are often outside the reach of national legal regulatory systems. Weak governance and civil society structures in many host countries make it difficult for people to hold companies accountable for social and environmental abuses, or the loss of livelihoods. It is seen as a model that externalizes its costs while privatizing its benefits, and constrains the movement towards being more sustainable.

Corporations wishing to shift towards more sustainable practices can face resistance from their shareholders. For example, in 2014 Apple CEO Tim Cook told the National Center for Public Policy Research (NCPPR), a campaign group against action to tackle climate change, that they should sell their stock if they did not support Apple's pledge to reduce greenhouse gas emissions: 'If you want me to do things only for ROI [return on investment] reasons, you should get out of this stock' (Shankleman, 2014). Progressive companies are beginning to be more selective about the kind of shareholders they want to attract as investors, in attempts to align their shareholders' values with company values.

According to Jay Cohen Gilbert, founder of the B Corporation (see Case Study 2.2), the zeitgeist of our era is the story about the evolution of capitalism. This involves a movement away from an outdated 20th century model of shareholder or stockholder capitalism, one which has dominated business practice over the last hundred years, to a new model of stakeholder capitalism which harnesses the power of business to generate wealth for people and the planet. Besides new governance features, the shift to stakeholder capitalism also presents a different model of how value is created and traded, and takes a larger view of the role and responsibilities of business in society (Freeman *et al.*, 2007).

CASE STUDY 2.2
The B Corps

The 'Benefit Corporation' or 'B Corp', which emerged in the US in 2010, has created a new legal form to allow it to go beyond benefiting shareholders to benefiting wider society and the environment. B Corps legislation 'helps return business to its proper role in society to create shared and durable prosperity' (B Corps, 2013). Certified B Corps are required to make decisions that have a positive material impact on society and the environment. The B Corps website (2013) claims:

Government and the nonprofit sector are necessary but insufficient to address society's greatest challenges. Business, the most powerful man-made force on the planet, must create value for society, not just shareholders. Systemic challenges require systemic solutions and the B Corp movement offers a concrete, market-based and scalable solution. It encourages companies to compete not just to be the best in the world, but to be **the best for the world**.

There are now over 1,000 Certified B Corps from over 30 countries and 60 industries working toward redefining success and corporate purpose (B Corps, 2015). B Corp companies include: ice cream producer Ben & Jerry's, e-commerce platform Etsy, Guayali Sustainable Rainforest Products, Sungevity, and DIRTT Environmental Solutions. B Corps was launched in Europe in 2015. B Corps companies have a statistically significant revenue growth rate that has outpaced the average revenue growth of the public companies of a similar class to B Corps.

Source: B Corps (2015); Chen and Kelly (2015).

Stakeholder models recognize the role of building good social relationships, with groups such as employees, customers, suppliers, investors, regulators, and local communities, in generating wealth, and in a company's social licence to operate. Stakeholder theories date from the late 1970s and early 1980s, when researchers began developing alternative theories of value that challenged the model that puts the maximization of shareholder value first. Freeman *et al.* (ibid.), for example, argue that by looking at all the factors responsible for business success, and taking the interests and welfare of all its stakeholders into account, the firm would do better than by simply focusing on shareholder interests. If a firm creates value for its stakeholders, it will create value for its shareholders too.

2.4.4 Capital: Growing All the Capitals Together

What is capital? How can our understanding of capital be broadened? Wealth is derived from the old English word *weal*, which means sound, healthy and prosperous. It is a multidimensional concept, usually measured through its 'stocks' or 'capital'. Over the past hundred years, the notion of wealth has become almost solely equated with the sum of the financial and manufactured capital privately held by companies. It has ignored other forms of capital as well as the value of public goods and services not priced by markets, such as ecosystem services.

In *Corporation 2020* Sukhdev (2012) argues that we need to expand the scope of what is considered capital; think beyond the traditional boundaries of what creates value, and think in terms of 'three-dimensional capitalism'. This recognizes that human, social and natural capital are just as able to produce value as financial capital. He argues that tomorrow's corporation needs to be a 'capital factory', not just a goods and services factory, but one that grows all its assets – financial, human, social and natural capital for its shareholders and its stakeholders.

Porritt (2005) outlines five types of capital from which we derive goods and services needed to improve our lives, which are all important to the success of companies. New economic thinking aims to maximize the value of each capital and to avoid making trade-offs between them, see Forum for the Future (2015). The five types of capital are:

1   **Financial Capital:** this is the value of currency owned and traded, shares, bonds, and banknotes, and is meant to reflect the productive power of other types of capital. It is the traditional measure of business performance (the original single 'bottom line') and is used in reporting to shareholders, investors, regulators, and government. Financial capital often reflects and depends on other types of intangible assets such as brand, as well as natural capital.

2   **Manufactured Capital:** this is the value of buildings, infrastructure, transport, communications, and technologies. It is highly valued as a key source of innovation, the capacity to quickly transport goods to market and reduce resource use. It can be enhanced through using natural resources efficiently; reducing carbon emissions; reducing waste; generating power from renewable energy; moving from selling products to services.

3   **Human Capital:** this refers to the value of knowledge, skills, creativity, motivation, and passion that is employed by corporations to create economic value. Good corporations value it for the health of its workforce; bad companies undermine it through the abuse of human and labour rights. Corporations can grow human capital by training their employees, enhancing their earning potential, respecting human rights, health and safety, and ensuring fair wages.

4   **Social Capital:** this is the value of human relationships, families, communities, schools, unions, networks and partnerships, that fosters a culture of shared values, and trust, needed for cohesive and effective work, as well as a company's social licence to operate. It can grow by encouraging new communities among staff, suppliers, customers and other stakeholders, and developing safe, family-friendly policies; good governance; and community services (see Case Study 2.3).

5   **Natural Capital:** this is the value of the planet's natural resources, ecosystem services, and its ability to process and assimilate wastes. Companies currently benefit from natural capital free of charge, externalize their costs, and privatize value at the expense of the commons. Companies can help protect and grow natural capital through reducing, recycling and reusing resources, by committing to the circular economy, and by restoring biodiversity.

The value of protecting and investing in natural capital is illustrated by the example of the Catskill watershed, a major source of New York City water. If engineers had to build a filtration plant required to clean the water, to replace the services of the natural watershed, it would cost about $6 billion, along with ongoing annual costs of operating such a plant. However, to restore the natural watershed would cost between $1 and $2 billion, which is considered a bargain compared to building an artificial filtration plant.

CASE STUDY 2.3
Natura, Brazil – Growing Social Capital

Natura is a large Brazilian cosmetics company that was founded in 1969 by Luiz Seabra (now a billionaire), with its headquarters in Cajamar, São Paulo, Brazil. In 2013 it had an annual revenue of about $3 billion, and net income of about $356 million. It has always been a community and eco-friendly company. It sources about 80% of its ingredients from rainforest flora, and partners with more than 5,000 suppliers, as well as with 32 supplier communities and over 3,000 families to access ingredients.

What also makes Natura so special is their direct sales model (similar to Avon), which uses mainly women to sell products to friends, relatives and neighbours. There are about 1 million saleswomen, who Natura call 'consultants', who work throughout Latin America. They earn some $900 million per year in commissions, which is about one third of Natura's turnover.

Natura's model has allowed women to participate in the labour market in a flexible manner, which is particularly helpful to those with children, and empowered them economically and socially. Giving women employment and income has had a profound effect on household welfare and local economies, which has a positive long-term impact on the health of Brazilian society and other Latin American countries.

Natura became the largest and first publicly-traded company to become a B Corps in 2014, further consolidating its sustainability brand. It is 'identified with the community of people who are committed to building a better world, based on better relationships with themselves, with other people, with the nature they are part of, and with the whole.'

Source: Natura (2014); Watson (2014).

Labelling humans, society and nature as types of 'capital' is contested by some. See Schröter *et al.* (2014) for a comprehensive discussion of the arguments relating to valuing nature and ecosystem services. While some economists argue that it makes nature's role and contributions visible and therefore valuable, others contend that it leads to the commodification of nature, and new forms of human-nature exploitation.

Porter and Kramer (2011) argue that many companies are trapped in an outdated approach to value creation. Such approaches continue to view value creation narrowly, optimizing financial performance in a bubble, and ignoring the wider context that determines their long-term success. By overlooking the needs of customers and depleting natural resources they are undermining the long-term success of their business. They argue that we need new ways of 'creating shared value' (CSV), which they define as: 'Policies and operating practices that enhance the competitiveness of a company while simultaneously advancing the economic and social conditions in the communities in which it operates.'

CSV has three dimensions:

1 *Reconceiving products and markets.* This entails meeting social needs while better serving existing markets and providing access to new markets. Costs are lowered through innovation.

2 *Redefining productivity in the value chain.* This involves improving quality, quantity, cost and reliability of inputs and distribution. Corporations may act

as stewards for essential natural resources and drive economic and social development.

3   *Enabling local cluster development.* This helps ensure reliable local supplies of materials and services; good infrastructure of roads and telecommunications; access to talent; and an effective and predictable legal system.

CSV is not without its critics. It is arguably a firm-centric approach to creating value, and others such as Crane *et al.* (2014) see it as unoriginal, ignoring the tensions between social and economic goals, naïve about the challenges of business compliance, and based on a shallow conception of the corporation's role in society.

2.4.5   Nature: Working with the Grain of Life

'Our planet is alive and the wondrous web of biodiversity provides us with all that we need: clean air, water, soil and energy, as well as food, medicine and resources . . . the way to genuine sustainability is by the study of nature and mimicking her ways.'
                              David Suzuki, Canadian academic and environmentalist

How can businesses learn from nature and work with the grain of life, rather than against it? It is widely argued that humans, particularly in western culture, have become divorced or disconnected from nature, through the effects of centuries of reductionist thinking, industrialization and mechanization. This disconnect has created what Louv (2005) calls a 'nature deficit disorder', which he argues undermines human health and well-being. One of greatest challenges today is to realize the illusion of this separation, and to develop a new consciousness through rediscovering and restoring our relationship with nature and the web of life (Louv, 2005; Charles HRH The Prince of Wales, 2010; Hutchins, 2014).

In their pioneering book *Natural Capitalism: Creating the Next Industrial Revolution*, Hawken, Lovins and Lovins (2000) outline four key ways in which business is developing new relationships with nature, which can contribute to solving many sustainability problems, and which can generate a business profit too. These include:

1   *Dramatically increasing the productivity of resource use.* Reducing the wasteful consumption of resources can stretch the use of energy, minerals, water and materials by 5, 10 or even 100 times, and yield higher profits.

2   *Shifting to biologically inspired models*, a movement known as biomimicry. In nature there is no such thing as waste; every output is returned harmlessly to the ecosystem as a nutrient. Business can learn from nature to improve and develop new products, processes and systems.

3   *Shifting to providing services rather than products.* Traditional business models rely on the sale of products; but value can also be generated through the flow of services which saves resources.

4   *Investing in natural capital.* Business needs to protect, manage and restore the planet's ecosystems which provide numerous provisioning, regulating, cultural and supporting goods and services (such as climate regulation, water purification, disease regulation, pollination, etc.).

Biomimicry and innovation inspired by nature has become a source of design inspiration for a whole new industrial paradigm that seeks to work with the laws of nature, rather than against them (Benyus, 1997). Biomimicry literally means 'to imitate life'. It recognizes that life has been on the planet for 3.8 billion years, that successful organisms have learned to adapt to the planet, and that a natural sustainable economy already exists. Biomimetic design thus encourages innovators to think outside the box and look at the ways nature solves problems and meets energy needs. It asks the question, 'How would nature do business?' There are countless examples of companies successfully applying biomimetic design techniques to solve resource, energy, and engineering problems, by mimicking natural forms, processes and systems. See Case Study 2.4, for one example.

Biomimicry is not 'new' discipline, in the sense that inventors have always looked at nature's patterns and processes to inspire new designs. For example, Leonardo de

CASE STUDY 2.4

The Japanese Shinkansen: Innovation Inspired by Nature

The Shinkansen is a network of high-speed railway lines in Japan, sometimes known as the 'bullet train' in English, which has speeds of up to 320 km/hr. The network links most of the major cities on the Islands of Honshu and Kyushu, transports millions of passengers a year, and has had a profound impact on the Japanese economy, society and the environment. The sound levels of earlier models of the train exceeded Japan's strict environmental standards. The largest source of noise came from the connection between the train and the overhead wires which provided electricity (the pantograph). Another source of noise came from the emergence of the train from tunnels. This was due to an atmospheric pressure wave forced in front of the train as it travelled through a narrow tunnel, creating a sonic boom at the exit, which could be heard by residents 400 metres away.

The engineer Eiji Nakatsu was a birdwatcher, and used his knowledge of owls and kingfishers to innovate structural adaptations to the train to minimize noise levels. For example, owls have noise-dampening feather parts (fimbriae) which are a comb-like array of serrations grown on the leading edge of the primary wing feathers. These serve to break down the air rushing over the wing into micro-turbulences, which muffles the sound that typically occurs in wings without this feature. His team tested prototype pantographs that mimicked these natural forms and, in 1994, a new 'wing-graph' replaced the traditional pantograph and was a great success. The train can now run at 320 km/hr and meet the stringent noise standard set by the government.

Similarly, Nakatsu recalled that the kingfisher could dive at high speed from one fluid (air) to another that is 800 times denser (water) with barely a splash. He deduced that the streamlined shape of its beak allowed the bird to dive cleanly into the water, since it allowed the water to flow past the beak rather than being pushed in front of it. Because the train faced the same challenge, moving from low-drag open air to high-drag air in the tunnel, Nakatsu successfully designed the front of the bullet train based on the kingfisher's beak in 1997. The more streamlined bullet train now travels more quietly and also 10% faster, and uses 15% less electricity than before.

Source: Mckeag (2012).

Vinci (1452–1519) was a keen observer of the anatomy and flight of birds, although he never managed to invent a 'flying machine'. The Wright Brothers, who finally did succeed in creating the first aeroplane in 1903, also took inspiration from observations of bird flight. However, one of the reasons biomimicry has become such a popular and compelling new narrative is because of its inherent promise that if we look to nature, we can potentially solve many of the sustainability problems that we are confronted with today.

Other ecological design frameworks have been also been developed to help business innovate according to nature's principles, such as The Natural Step, founded by Karl-Henrik Robért in Sweden; and Cradle-to-Cradle design, founded by Bill McDonough and Michael Braungart, and these have formed the basis of many lucrative business consultancies and innovations. The DaVinci 2.0, an index which monitors global activity in the bioinspiration field, shows an annual growth rate in this sector of 15.3% between 2000 and 2012. The top 100 biomimetic products netted $1.5 billion in profits between 2005 and 2008. By 2030 bioinspiration could account for $425 billion of US GDP, and globally it could generate $1.6 trillion of total GDP (DaVinci 2.0, 2014). Important questions remain, however, as to whether mimicking natural forms and processes can effectively restore our relationship with nature, and whether biomimicry can contribute to the triple bottom line benefits for people and planet, as well as profit.

2.4.6 Labour: Living Livelihoods

What are the new ways of thinking about work and jobs in a transition to a sustainable business? Labour is one of the key factors of production in neo-classical economics, which states that economic value creation is generated through applying work to nature. Economic growth is assumed to be good because it creates jobs, and work creates wealth. However, *as mentioned in Chapter 1*, research indicates that despite economic growth, unemployment rates are increasing globally.

In a transition to a green economy, Poschen (2015) argues that the twin challenges of generating decent work and achieving environmental sustainability are closely aligned, and require an integrated approach, involving the active contribution of workers. Green jobs can be a key economic driver, as the world makes a transition to building a sustainable and low-carbon global economy. IRENA (2015) report that clean energy jobs reached an estimated 7.7 million across the world in 2014 (excluding large hydropower), an increase in 18% from the year before. The solar PV sector accounted for 2.5 million jobs, of which two thirds were in China. Poschen (ibid.) claims that enterprises, workers and governments are key essential agents of change in the great transformation that is urgently needed in our economies. They can develop new ways of working in sustainable enterprises that safeguard the environment, create decent jobs and foster social inclusion (see Case Study 2.5).

The debate about work and jobs in the new economy, however, goes beyond the importance of generating 'green jobs' and ensuring 'living wages', important as these are, to rethinking the purpose of work in society. Our ideas about work have been profoundly shaped by the logic of the capitalist system, in which we participate in purely economic transactions where labour is exchanged for wages; promotion and bonuses are tied to economic targets; and which can end up creating a disconnect between what we do for a living and what we really care about.

CASE STUDY 2.5
Dharma Life, India

Dharma Life is a social enterprise, founded in 2009 by Gaurav Mehta, with it main office in New Delhi, India. Gaurav is an 'accidental entrepreneur' who originally worked in the finance sector but after a life-threatening illness decided he wanted to help create livelihoods that served a social goal. He and several MBA class-mates set up Dharma Life in India to foster sustainable livelihoods by creating social entrepreneurs who sell socially useful products and services to consumers at an affordable price. It seeks to:

1   Build a national network of rural entrepreneurs (Dharma Life Entrepreneurs) by providing business training, mentoring and support to people with high potential in rural villages.

2   Activate market demand by raising awareness of the economic and social value of these products to rural customers.

3   Create a sustainable value chain for 'social impact' products by working with manufacturers, distributors and local retailers.

It currently has a network of over 3,000 mainly female village entrepreneurs operating across six Indian states, who sell products such as:

◆   Clean lighting where there is no access to grid electricity;

◆   Improved cooking stoves which reduce smoke by 80% and improve indoor air quality;

◆   Health and hygiene products, such as iron-fortified drinks, and sanitary napkins;

◆   Water purifiers which provide clean, safe and cheap drinking water;

◆   Livelihood products such as sewing machines, mobile phones and bicycles.

Dharma Life recruits people with basic education, who are in need of money and who do not have a full-time job – typically subsistence farmers and women. The enterprise gives their recruits sales and educational training, and also actively seeks feedback from the entrepreneurs to improve the enterprise. Entrepreneurs earn a monthly income of between ₹2,000 and ₹8,000 depending on their sales. Dharma earns a margin from the sales.

The enterprise partners with corporates such as Singer, Hero and Bata to source their products. It then ships them to distribution points in a district where an enterprise leader (on the company's payroll) and local distributor ensure that the goods reach the local entrepreneurs. If a product fails to sell among villagers the entrepreneur returns the unsold items to Dharma, which bears the loss.

Dharma Life has already improved over 2 million livelihoods, and is helping drive sustainable economic growth in rural India. By 2020 it aims to create a network of 100,000 Dharma Life entrepreneurs of which 50% will be female; serve 50 million rural, low-income consumers; and expand its network across India and globally. In 2013 its income stood at about 3.1 Crore Indian ₹s (or roughly US$ 465,000).

Source: Dharma Life (2015); Hussain (2014).

The upsurge of interest in socially responsible enterprises, social entrepreneurship, and what some call 'right livelihoods' (the latter concept inspired by Buddhist ethics), reflects a strong drive to realign work with creative energy and purpose, to serve real community needs, and to 'do what you love, and love what you do', rather than simply 'working for money' (Scharmer & Kaufer 2013). A recent *Brookings*

Report showed that 64% of millennials (people born after the 1980s) would be prepared to take a pay cut to work in a job they value, and 63% want their employers to contribute to social and ethical causes (Winograd & Hais, 2014). Similarly, the *Deloitte Millennial Survey* (2015) indicates that 'a sense of purpose' is part of the reason millennials chose to work for their current employers. Business should focus on people and purpose, not just products and profits, in order to attract millennials in the 21st century. This is because there is an increasing aversion to 'leaving your values on the doorstep' when you go to work.

2.4.7 Production: Cycling the Future

What will production look like in the future? How can we design manufacturing systems that are good for people and the planet? *As we noted in Chapter 1*, current manufacturing processes are locked into a damaging, linear, take-make-waste approach, which is highly inefficient and wasteful of materials and energy. We need to rapidly shift to new production systems that are built on sustainable supplies of renewable and non-renewable resources, and which reduce the pollution associated with manufacturing.

In their inspiring and influential book *Cradle-to-Cradle: Rethinking the Way We Make Things*, McDonough and Braungart (2002) outline a design strategy for creating beneficial products and systems. The phrase 'cradle to cradle' (C2C) was actually coined by Swiss architect Walter R. Stahel in the 1970s. It draws its inspiration from biomimicry and the examination of nature's living systems where there is no such thing as waste, where everything is recycled, and production is powered by solar energy. This is in direct contrast to our current 'cradle to grave' manufacturing models.

McDonough and Braungart (ibid.) argue that toxic chemicals also need to be phased out of production, and that material inputs should be treated as either 'biological or technical nutrients' which are kept separate and cycled back into their respective metabolisms. C2C models aim to extend the service-life of goods through reusing, repairing, refurbishing, repurposing, remanufacturing. Their C2C design concept is founded upon three principles: (1) Waste = Food; (2) Use Current Solar Income; (3) Celebrate Diversity. They go beyond the older corporate concerns with 'eco-efficiency' (doing more with less) and elaborate a new concept of 'eco-effectiveness' which aims to create a beneficial human footprint. They have helped shift the conversation about business 'being less bad' towards 'doing good'. These and similar ideas have been integrated into the concept of a 'Circular Economy' (CE), a term coined by the Ellen MacArthur Foundation.

Progressive businesses are beginning to tap into the opportunities of closed loop systems, and many are beginning to work together in business ecosystems which build business through an exchange of 'nutrients' between businesses. But C2C systems are still new and have many challenges. The prevailing economic and social conditions favour linear throughput models; products are hard to recycle; reverse logistics are hard to operationalize; legislation is weak; knowledge and capacity are limited; and innovation is fragmented. However, the potential of the Circular Economy to eliminate waste, generate new local and regional jobs, and make huge savings is enormous (see Case Study 2.6). It is calculated that the Circular Economy could generate $1 trillion annually by 2025. It could generate $500 million in material cost savings, 100,000 new jobs and prevent 100 million tonnes of waste globally within five years, and increase European competiveness (WEF, 2014).

CASE STUDY 2.6
China and the Circular Economy

China's fast pace of industrialization in recent decades has resulted in serious environmental and resource problems. Air pollution in Beijing is many times higher than the safe levels recommended by the World Health Organization; one fifth of the country's rivers are toxic, while two fifths are classified as seriously polluted; and China's rapid growth is consuming 40% to 50% of the world's coal, copper, steel, nickel, aluminum and zinc (Collot d'Escury, 2014; Lin, 2014). However, such challenges are providing a fertile context for developing pioneering circular and green economy approaches.

The concept of the Circular Economy was first proposed in China in 1998, and was originally promoted by the State Environmental Protection Agency (SEPA) which launched a series of Eco Industrial Parks (EIPs) across the country, the first at Guigang Guanxi in the Zhuang Autonomous Region in 2000. The CE has subsequently become a major focus of government development policy as a means of helping China leapfrog to new sustainable models, and it has passed a number of laws and regulations to promote the concept, helping to develop new enterprises and jobs (Yuan *et al.*, 2006; Geng & Doberstein, 2008).

For example, the Ziya Circular Economy Industrial Park, which lies between Beijing and Tianjin, was established in 2001 and is helping create a new regenerative economy based on recycling electronic equipment, creating value for people and the planet. The town of Ziya used to suffer from heavy pollution from the local recycling industry, which depended on primitive recycling methods such as burning wire and appliances to reclaim the metals. The water and soil were contaminated, and the local population suffered from a high rate of lung cancer.

The new industrial park has a planned space of 135 square kilometres. The largest of its kind in northern China, it is based on renewable energy, zero emissions and non-polluting models. It has large areas set aside for manufacturing, forestry, scientific research and accommodation. Some 231 companies had moved into Ziya's Circular Economy Industrial Park by 2013. Clean, efficient technologies are used to recycle waste electrical items such as computers, refrigerators, televisions and cars, as well as plastics and rubber. Valuable components such as copper, aluminum, gold, silver and iron, and rubber materials are retrieved and reprocessed.

The company TCL-AOBO, for example, has an annual processing capacity of 2.4 million machines, disassembling, sorting, and treating products on 18 automated disassembling lines. These retrieve high volumes of recyclable materials out of electronic scraps, as well as clean up the waste produced in the process.

The park has the capacity to recycle about 1.5 million tonnes of waste per annum, and is currently providing the market with 457,000 tonnes of copper, 300,000 tons of iron, 300,000 tons of rubber and plastic, 250,000 tons of aluminum, and 200,000 tons of other materials. Its annual production of reclaimed copper equals the output of a large copper mine. Recycling waste saves 5.24 million tons of coal and 1.8 million tons of petroleum per year. The process also reduces emissions of CO_2 by 1.66 million tons and SO_2 (sulphur dioxide) by 100,000 tons.

Local forests have been preserved, and trees are planted throughout the industrial park. The initiative has also invested in a waste water treatment plant, which will be able to treat 81,000 tonnes of water daily, and a solid waste treatment centre which can dispose of 40,000 tons of waste annually. Geothermal pumps and solar heating systems have been installed in public facilities and private apartments. A green belt of 20 square kilometres separates the living area and the industrial zone to improve the neighborhood environment. The area is also building a new town to accommodate 16,000 people from the nine villages nearby. The EIP offers employment opportunities, schools, houses, insurance and pensions with long-term benefits (Xiaofei, 2014).

(Continued)

Peter Lacy, who leads Accenture's strategy and sustainability practice in the Asia Pacific region, says:

> With demand for resources in China growing more than twice as fast as the world average, we see disruptive innovation in circular approaches to production and consumption and the emergence of new business models. Our research shows that in the coming decade between 6 and 7 million jobs will be created in the circular economy in China alone. And we are only just beginning.

Cited in Collot d'Escury, 2014.

Developing circular economy systems takes time and there are still a number of institutional, technological and economic challenges to implementing the CE in China, but there are signs of rapid growth in the popularity of the concept, and indications that China could become a global leader in this area. The China Association of Circular Economy, consisting of a group of government, academic and business partners, established in 2013 to promote the CE, estimates that it grew by 15% annually between 2006 and 2010, and that projects will almost double from $164 billion in 2010 to $293 billion in 2015 (*Global Times*, 2013).

2.4.8 Consumption: Conscious Consumer

Can we find new ways of consuming which don't destroy the planet but which still deliver goods and services that people want in fair ways? *Chapter 1* argued that current economic and business models are fuelling a culture of consumerism. Our current consumption patterns are already unsustainable but set to increase, with the growth in the number of middle class consumers predicted to rise by 3 billion by 2025. Moreover, an increase in material consumption does not necessarily improve contentment, happiness and well-being. However, as UNEP (2015) points out, models of sustainable consumption do not necessarily mean consuming less, but consuming better.

Sebastian (2015) insightfully points out that current business models that trap people on a consumer treadmill and foster consumption-addiction cycles are ultimately unfulfilling from a human happiness and well-being perspective. Businesses aspiring to operate within a new economy need to let go of old paradigms and look for opportunities to shape prosperity and well-being, beyond fulfilling humanity's immediate material needs, in non-consumptive ways. For example, it is hopeful to see that the LOHAS (Lifestyles of Health and Sustainability) sector is growing rapidly. This area focuses on goods and services related to the environment, social justice, personal development, sustainable living. It is already worth $290 billion globally (LOHAS, 2015).

More recently, other disruptive markets and business models are transforming the way we think about consumption, and the role of consumers in the value chain. In their book *What's Mine is Yours: The Rise of Collaborative Consumption*, Botsman and Rogers (2010) explore the rise of new consumer behaviour based on sharing, swapping and renting personal assets, such as spare rooms, cars, equipment, clothes, and skills. The so-called Sharing Economy is based on the idea of 'access over ownership' and is defined as an economy that 'creates value out of shared and open resources in ways that balance personal self-interest with the good of the larger community'.

CASE STUDY 2.7
Patagonia

One of the most famous examples of the dilemmas facing a company trying to tackle unsustainable consumption and grow a business at the same time is Patagonia. This is a sustainable company which sells outdoor clothing and gear. Founder and owner Yvon Chouinard and Gallagher (2004) say: 'Our idea is to make the best product so you can consume less and consume better.' On Black Friday in 2011, the company controversially ran an advertisement in the *New York Times* featuring a Patagonia jacket under the headline, 'Don't buy this jacket'. The advert gave statistics on how much water was used and how much carbon was emitted in manufacturing the jacket, and how much waste it would create. The advert concludes: 'Don't buy what you don't need. Think twice before you buy anything.'

Critics argued that the advertisement was a hypocritical marketing ploy to increase sales. While its advert contributed to a bump in sales, Patagonia actually grew by 27% in the subsequent two years, attaining revenues of $575 million in 2013 (Voight, 2013). The company recognizes that while they are reducing the footprint of individual products, their footprint is increasing as a whole as the company grows.

Despite the accusations of duplicity Chouinard talks openly about the dilemmas of growing a company and its impact on the planet, and is seen as a champion of getting people to think about sustainable consumption. Patagonia launched a Responsible Economy Initiative in 2013, communicating problems of consumerism with graphics such as 'see that thing, want that thing, tire of that thing, discard that thing, forget that thing, see that (new) thing'. Patagonia has made product repair and recycling a growing part of its business model, and is trying second-hand clothing sales. It has invested in Yerdle, a web startup whose stated mission is to reduce new-product purchases by 25%, as a way for people, and even the company itself, to swap or give away used Patagonia gear. 'Our mission is to face the question of growth both by bringing it up and by looking at our own situation as a business fully ensnared in the global industrial economy.'

The Sharing Economy has generated millions of new micro-entrepreneurs, and communal economies, allowing citizens to make use of their unused assets, unlock new markets, bypass large corporations, gain access to the economy and generate revenue in entirely new ways. The development of the sharing economy has been facilitated by the use of the Internet, social media, and mobile devices which have helped create networks of shared interests and trust, and simplified the logistics of collective use. It is also helping empower people by redeveloping community relationships, building trust through peer-to-peer reviews, building what Botsman calls 'reputational capital'. And as product service and redistribution systems become established, it helps save on resources and creates less waste. As Botsman and Rogers point out, the more we share, the less we need to produce and waste, the better it is for the environment. Thus proponents of the Sharing Economy argue that it is fairer, more transparent, low carbon and creates community. PwC (2015) estimates that the potential value of the main sectors of the Sharing Economy will be about $335 billion by 2025 (see Case Study 2.8).

CASE STUDY 2.8

Airbnb

Airbnb is a private company, founded in 2008 by Brian Cheskye, Joe Gebbian and Nathan Biecharczyk, and located in San Francisco, US. Airbnb provides a website, or 'community marketplace' for people to list and book online unique accommodation around the world. It does not own any rooms itself. People rent out their lodgings including private rooms, entire homes and apartments, boats, tree houses, tepees, igloos, castles, and private islands amongst others. Users register and create a personal profile online. Every lodging is associated with a host whose profile includes reviews, recommendations and ratings by previous guests, which help build credible reputation.

Airbnb makes its money by charging a commission on both the traveller and the host. It has helped many hosts (sometimes jobless) access the economy and generate new revenue streams, and helped consumers discover new and cheaper ways of travelling. It has been criticized on security, regulatory and social discrimination grounds. Nevertheless, it has had a meteoric rise since 2008 when the founders, who could not afford the rent for their apartment, rented out their living room and accommodated guests on air mattresses. By 2015 it had over 1.2 million listings in 34,000 cities in 190 countries, and received over 35 million guests. It had a market capital valuation of over \$20 billion after a raising funding of \$1 billion in 2015, and in terms of size has disrupted top hotel brands such as Hilton and Marriott, and is poised to become the largest hospitality brand in the world (Airbnb, 2015).

The Sharing Economy is not without its critics, however, many of whom point to the regulatory and political battles that the Sharing Economy has catalysed, particularly in the disruption of the hotel industry by Airbnb (see Case Study 2.8), and taxi services by Uber. Others see the Sharing Economy as predatory and exploitative, and complain that some of the large sharing platforms are not 'sharing the wealth'. For a thoughtful discussion, see Schor (2014).

2.4.9 Energy: Powering the Future

How will the new economy be powered? It is evident that we are in the midst of an energy revolution, or 'oil-and-gas versus renewables civil war' as Leggett (2001) puts it. The Intergovernmental Panel on Climate Change (IPCC) makes the case that if we are to avoid ruinous climate change, governments need to set carbon budgets, significantly reduce the amount of fossil fuels being burned, and transit to a low carbon economy. The EU, for example, has set a target to get 20% of energy from renewables by 2020. However, the move to renewable energies has been thwarted by the advent of the shale boom and fracking for oil and gas, and lower oil prices. Leggett argues that the traditional energy industries and their political and financial power bases are failing society and creating dangerous risks that could crash economies.

The energy debate is highly politicized. On the scientific front, while the majority of climate scientists agree that climate change is the result of the burning of fossil fuels, oil companies are known to be funding 'climate denier' organizations, and lobbying against climate change legislation, which creates uncertainty amongst institutional investors. On the economic side, NGOs such as 350.org, have helped mobilize fossil-fuel divestment campaigns with the slogan 'Keep it in the Ground' and have helped persuade nearly 400 institutions (such as pension funds, universities and faith organizations) to divest from fossil fuels (Carrington & Howard, 2015). Meanwhile subsidies for oil, coal and gas, which amount to $5.3 trillion per year, are continuing to work against the transition to the use of renewable energies (IMF, 2015). In the public sphere, there are global and local protests such as the Greenpeace Campaign to stop drilling in the Arctic, and anti-fracking protests such those in Sussex and Lancashire in the UK (see Case Study 2.9), but there is also widespread resistance to renewable energy installations from the NIMBY (Not In My Back Yard) public.

In his book *The Third Industrial Revolution: How Lateral Power is Transforming Energy, the Economy and the World*, Rifkin (2011) explores how renewable energy and internet technology are merging to create a powerful energy revolution. He presents a vision of hundreds of millions of people producing their own green energy in their homes, offices, and factories, and sharing it with each other in an 'energy internet', just as we create and share information online now. This revolution will radically transform old power relationships and energy infrastructures, and create thousands of new businesses and millions of jobs. Such a vision runs parallel

CASE STUDY 2.9
REPOWERBalcombe, UK

Balcombe is a small village in Sussex, and the site of one of the UK's biggest anti-fracking protests in 2013. The UK energy company Cuadrilla was planning to use the controversial hydraulic fracturing (fracking) technique to extract oil from beneath the village. People were concerned that fracking would pollute groundwater, generate toxic waste and create earthquakes, and more than 1,000 people set up camp in the village to protest against the company. The protest won widespread support and Cuadrilla finally abandoned its plans.

The village subsequently set up a co-operative energy group called REPOWERBalcombe, which aims to generate 100% of Balcombe's electricity demand through community-owned locally-generated renewable energy. Solar panels have been installed on the roofs of a local farm and primary school, where the students can learn about renewable energy. The co-operative also plans to install a 5 MW solar farm that will provide enough electricity for all 760 homes in the village as well as another nearby settlement.

Local people have financially supported the project, and funding has also been obtained through the energy crowdfunding platform Abundance (which has nearly 2,000 investors and has invested over £11 million in energy projects in the UK since 2011). Part of the money generated from the solar energy in Balcombe will go into a community benefit fund. Anyone in the area can become a member of the co-operative by investing £250, and members have a say in how the co-operative is run, as well as receiving a financial return. The example shows the power of local people to take the energy future into their own hands, and the possibilities of alternative ownership, funding and business models to create clean energy (REPOWER Balcombe, 2015).

with another social transition underway, in which consumers are also becoming producers, or 'prosumers', a term coined by futurologist Alvin Toffler in 1980 to denote the blurring of the roles of producer and consumer, a transition which is also being facilitated by the internet. This vision of energy revolution is already being implemented in off grid schemes across parts of Africa and Asia (see Case Study 2.10).

Despite the many social and political challenges, and a recent drop in oil price, real progress is being made in the transition to renewable energies, and renewable energy supply is growing at a much faster rate than anticipated. The cost of solar power has come down, and solar is now cheap enough to compete with oil, kerosene, and diesel, particularly in developing markets. Solar electricity is anticipated to become even more competitive globally due to declining costs of solar panels. In markets dependent on coal for electricity generation, the ratio of coal wholesale electricity to solar electricity was 7:1 four years ago. This ratio is now 2:1 and is expected to approach 1:1 over the next few years (Deutsche Bank, 2015).

As part of its Mission Zero commitment, Interface has committed to source 100% of its energy needs from renewable sources by 2020, by improving energy efficiency and increasing the use of renewable energy. Many of its factories have installed renewable energy systems, and are already using 100% clean energy. IKEA is on track to become energy independent, producing as much renewable energy as it consumes in its buildings. The company has invested around $1.7 billion in wind and solar since 2009. It owns and operates over 300 off site wind turbines and has installed 700,000 solar panels on its buildings. Apple, Facebook, and Google all have long-term goals to use 100% renewable energy, and all have taken concrete steps towards that goal.

Over half of Sweden's energy now comes from renewables, and Denmark plans to abandon fossil fuels by 2050. The transition to renewables is also yielding innovative

CASE STUDY 2.10
Grameen Shakti, Bangladesh

Grameen Shakti (GS) is a renewable energy initiative established in Bangladesh in 1996 by Muhammad Yunus, initially to provide renewable energy technologies to off grid rural people. By 2012 it had installed 1 million Solar Home Systems (SHS), and is considered one of the most successful renewable companies in the world, benefiting disadvantaged groups, businesses, and the environment. GS operates a small loans scheme that enables poor households to buy a SHS. It has also created thousands of jobs and helped empower women. Local production and assembly centres are run by female engineers and technicians. GS has also helping power mosques and schools, and unleashed new income-generating possibilities. Businesses such as mobile phone shops, electronic repair shops, agricultural and livestock farms, rural hospitals and vaccination centres have grown up. On average, GS installs over 1,000 SHS per day, working with a labour force of 12,000 young people. GS also helps reduce carbon emissions by replacing millions of litres of polluting kerosene used in lamps and stoves. GS aims to install another million SHS by 2016 (Grameen Shakti, 2015).

ownership and funding models. Countries such as Germany and Denmark have made progress on renewables, partly because they have a large and mixed ownership base which creates public support for policy. Danish communities have the right to invest and profit from wind turbine programmes. Germany has over 800 renewable energy co-operatives (Kappes, 2014), and Europe has an estimated 2,400 renewable energy co-operatives (EASME, 2015). Community energy schemes are also using the internet to attract crowdfunding through sites such as the Trillion Fund, a crowdfunding platform offering peer-to-peer loans and other investments in clean energy in the UK. Developing countries are also spearheading innovation, with the use of mobile technologies. For example, enterprises such as Off Grid Electric, 'the world's first massively scalable "solar energy as a service" company' is selling pay-as-you-go solar that can be paid for daily using your mobile phone, akin to setting up a micro-utility. Numerous polls indicate that the general public is in favour of renewable energy, although the transition is fraught with political and legislative struggles.

2.4.10 Technology: Vital Connections

How is business using technology and data in ways that are good for people and planet?

Technology is a driving force of innovation and value generation in business. Since the start of the Industrial Revolution over 200 years ago, there have been at least five distinct waves of innovation, associated with new technologies such as mechanization, steam power, electricity, petrochemicals, information and communications, which have transformed society. Each has unleashed new opportunities for business, generated new markets, sources of value, and growth, and ended with a global depression. According to Bradfield-Moody and Nogrady (2010) we are now on the cusp of a sixth wave of technological innovation, driven by sustainability challenges, that will unleash new markets and drive a shift away from resource dependence to new ways of living.

Mason (2015) argues that information technology has the potential to reshape work, production and value, to destroy an economy based on markets and private ownership, and to create a more socially just and sustainable global economy (see Case Study 2.11). The growth of Web 2.0 technologies (see Definition box), social media, and information technologies is rapidly transforming business models. The internet has created an era of 'radical transparency' and made business operations much more visible, and has helped mobilize citizen action (Laszlo & Zhexembayeva, 2011). The internet and social media also have the potential to accelerate the awareness and acceptance of sustainable technologies, and raise money for projects through crowdfunding.

WEB 2.0

Web 2.0 technologies (which emphasize user-generated content) started in 2002. There are over 3 billion internet users today. Around 40% of the world population has an internet connection, while in 1995 it was less than 1%. About half the internet users are from Asia. There were 4 billion mobile phone users in 2012, and this is estimated to grow to about 5.5 billion by 2017. Facebook only started in 2004, but by the end of 2015 was being used by about 1.5 billion users worldwide (Statistics Portal, 2015).

CASE STUDY 2.11
EcoSchool, Zimbabwe

EcoSchool is one of the latest initiatives of Econet Wireless. EcoSchool provides a digital education platform that gives students and educators cheap access to world-class educational content from across the globe. Customers pay a small fee for access to a tablet, and subscription to an EcoSchool App, which gives access to books and other educational materials. It works with publishers to distribute e-textbooks, which reduces the cost of textbooks by about 50%. With growing telecommunications infrastructure, it is regarded as one of the best ways to democratize education and expand the scope of education in Zimbabwe. It can be used in rural and urban areas, by young and old, rich and poor, and helps improve the lives of disadvantaged people. EcoSchool was founded in Zimbabwe by 28-year-old Teresa Mbagaya, who had previously worked on the education team at Google. She joined Econet in 2013, and launched three education services in Zimbabwe. She is listed as one of *Forbes'* top 30 African entrepreneurs in 2015.

Econet Wireless was founded in 1993 by Strive Masiyiwa in Zimbabwe, and is a privately-held diversified telecommunications group with operations and investments in Africa, Europe, South America, North America and the East Asia Pacific Rim, offering products and services in the core areas of mobile and fixed telephony services, and broadband, internet, satellite and fibre-optic networks. Strive Masiyiwa is recognized as one of Africa's leading business voices and most generous philanthropists. He contributes to major initiatives such as fighting Ebola and reducing hunger, and helped found the Carbon War Room with Richard Branson. He and his wife are members of Giving Pledge and finance the Higher Life Foundation, which provides scholarships to over 42,000 African orphans.

Source: EcoSchool (2015); Econet Wireless (2015).

The 'Internet of Things' (IoT), a term coined by Kevin Ashton in 1999, refers to a seamless connection between everyday things online, facilitated through easy to use apps on computers, tablets and smart phones. The IoT has the potential to increase revenues, reduce costs and foster more sustainable lifestyles across the globe (see Case Study 2.12). Smart technologies are allowing individuals and institutions to manage domestic appliances (heating, fridges, washing machines) and energy consumption, hire cars, do shopping, track the health care of patients, and manage endangered species. It is also expected to generate new business models, such as usage-based insurance calculated on real-time driving data.

In 1984, only 1,000 devices were connected to the Internet. In 2010, there were 10 billion connected devices; and by 2020, it is predicted that there will be 50 billion connected devices (Evans, 2011). Forecasts regarding the future value of the IoT industry vary widely. Bradley *et al.* (2013) predict that the IoT will generate $14.4 trillion in value 'at stake' (increased revenues and decreased costs); while Gartner Inc. predicts it will generate an industry worth $309 billion, mostly in services, by 2020, and $1.9 trillion in global economic value-added through sales into diverse end markets. Many African nations are spearheading the broadband and wireless communications revolution, which is helping launch new projects and businesses. For example, the Olleh Rwandan Networks, a public-private partnership

CASE STUDY 2.12
Farmerline, Ghana

Farmerline is a company in Ghana, founded in 2012 by Aloysius Attah, that delivers useful agricultural information to smallholder farmers through SMS messages and a voice service (for those who cannot read). Smallholder farmers living in rural regions typically lack internet access, training, formal education, and financing assistance. Farmerline's vision is to empower small-scale farmers to become more prosperous by using technology and increased information access to improve their harvest and income. Mobile phones are proving to be one of the most important tools for business development in emerging markets, and there has been unprecedented, rapid growth in mobile phone adoption in Africa within the last five years.

Through Farmerline services, agricultural workers send messages such as weather forecast alerts, market prices, new farming techniques, agrochemical applications and inputs and finance to farmers and fishermen at subsidized fees. It also enables farmers to call the system for advice. More than 2,000 smallholder farmers and fishermen are currently benefiting from the web-based mobile communication services offered by the company, and there are plans to reach 2 million farmers over the next ten years and to achieve an 80% increase in income per 0.4 hectares (1 acre) across West Africa. Revenues are currently generated through selling services to farmers, grants and equity investment (Farmerline, 2015).

between the government of Rwanda and Korean Telecom, has recently launched 4G Long Term Evolution (LTE) technology using Rwanda's national fibre-optic infrastructure.

Big data, which refers to the increased ability to collect, combine, analyse and share data in real time, over vast areas (a term first used by NASA and popularized in 2003) can help us tackle sustainability problems on large scales. Environmental issues often span long periods of time, far-flung areas, and have layers of complexity. Unassisted, people do not have the skills to deal with problems of such complexity and scale, but such data can provide human-centred solutions (Tomlinson, 2010). The use of big data is creating new business models across different sectors. For example, it is improving the way we operate our buildings and helping users to develop energy-saving behaviour. In the transportation sector, big data is used to optimize use of infrastructure such as roads and railways and to design planes. One study shows that integrating big data efficiently could save the American health care sector $300 billion annually (Groves *et al.*, 2013).

There are worries that the personal data collected by retailers providing knowledge of our personal preferences, the personalization of marketing, and the 'click-and-buy' convenience of e-shopping will promote even more unsustainable consumption, increasing pollution and pressure on resources. Manyika *et al.* (2013) estimate that access to open data could help unlock $3 to $5 trillion globally across seven economic sectors. But there are also serious concerns about who owns and controls that data and how it is used. There are also the ever-increasing threats of e-fraud and cyber-attacks from professional hackers. It is important to remember that technology is a double-edged sword, and the power to use it for good or bad is in our own hands.

3D printing technologies (sometimes known as AM or additive manufacturing) are also revolutionizing production processes. 3D printing involves processes in which successive layers of material are laid down under computer control to create three-dimensional objects, of almost any shape. 3D printing has applications in every manufacturing sector including aerospace, defence, cars, computers, medical supplies, and food. It is anticipated to have far-reaching implications for the economy and culture, as highly customized, distributed printing can be done on demand, redefining resource use, supply chains, freight systems, legislation, and possibly leading to the resurgence of localized manufacturing hubs (Sharma, 2014).

2.5 Conclusion: Metamorphosis

Change is also a contested process, and is mediated through relationships of power. The metamorphosis of a caterpillar to a chrysalis, of a chrysalis to a butterfly, can be a useful metaphor in understanding the difficulties in transitioning from one paradigm to another. Metamorphosis means 'to change form' and this transformation does not happen without a struggle between old and new forms. The term 'chrysalis' comes from the same etymological root as 'crisis' or 'crossroad'.

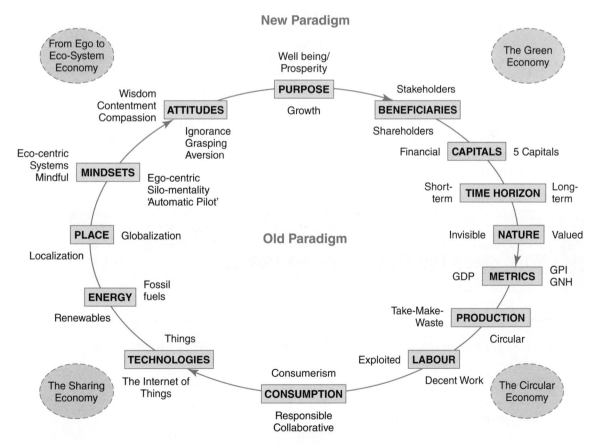

FIGURE 2.1 Old Paradigm/New Paradigm.

Take the example of the Monarch butterfly. The caterpillar of the Monarch but-terfly feeds on the milkweed plant, until it is bloated and cannot eat any more food. It then pupates, by weaving a silken thread and hanging itself upside down under a branch or leaf, and creating a tough outer skin as a protection against predators; it is then called a chrysalis. The chrysalis undergoes a radical inner transformation. Enzymes dissolve the body of the caterpillar into a kind of 'soup', and so called 'imaginal cells' – which contain the blueprint for all the features of the new organism – start to develop and inform the new growth. However, part of the immune system of the caterpillar tries to kill these off. Eventually there is a critical mass of imaginal cells which cluster and grow into a new organism. After a period of some time a butterfly emerges from the chrysalis. It is a completely different-looking creature to the caterpillar with dif-ferent behaviour, but it has been formed from exactly the same elements. What has changed is that a new informing idea has replaced the old paradigm.

Following the metaphor of metamorphosis, we might argue that business, society and self are in a process of transformation, with many internal conflicts, as an old system resists change and a new one struggles to emerge. It also suggests the need for groups to link together to support the development of a critical mass that will coalesce to form new systems.

There are also many new examples of innovative business approaches, present-ing a vision of greater potential, and providing new ways in which business can potentially become a power for good, in co-creating a better world. And all this 'reworking' requires transformations at the levels of business, economy and self (see Figure 2.1 Old Paradigm / New Paradigm). This chapter introduced ten ideas of change for good, intended to provide a starting point for discussion and to stimulate debate. Further transformative ideas are introduced throughout this volume, and in the conclusion.

In *Chapter 1* we concluded that our one planet predicament is essentially a symp-tom of 'disconnection'. Despite their supposed strengths, conventional economic and business approaches have (perhaps unwittingly) driven a profound divide between people and nature, self and others, money and real wealth, and body and soul.

One Planet Mindsets and values, on the other hand, are essentially those that are helping drive conscious 'reconnection' or 'restoration' of these divided parts.

GROUP EXERCISE 2.1

What does a One Planet Business look like?

Aims

◆ To identify the design principles and their key ele-ments needed to build a One Planet Business.

◆ To help summarize the key challenges and oppor-tunities arising from the current crises which are transforming business and society.

Set up

◆ *Class Size:* Suitable for class sessions with 15 – 50 participants.

◆ *Room Format:* Café style format with tables seating about 5 people.

◆ *Groups:* Participants to be divided into diverse teams of about 5 people, taking into account gender, culture, occupation, age, etc.

◆ *Themes:* Pre-select key principles to explore (e.g. mindsets, markets, metrics, etc.) and prepare flip chart sheets, with corresponding titles, one for each table.

◆ *Resources: see chapter 15, Table 15.2 Towards a One Planet Business: 20 Snapshots of Change for Good,* for potential themes.

◆ *Materials:* Provide pens for writing and/or drawing.

◆ *Minimum time required:* 1 hour (depending on the number of rounds of discussion).

Process

◆ *Introduction:* host introduces the discussion topic in plenary, including the aims and method of the exercise.

◆ *Question:* host invites each group to brainstorm ideas in relation to their particular theme on their table, emphasizing the shift from 'what's not working' to 'new approaches' in building a One Planet Business (the flip chart paper can be divided into two sections).

◆ *Collaborative Learning:* participants take it in turns to share ideas, listen to each other, and record key ideas on paper, either in words or drawings. Host encourages everyone in the group to participate.

◆ *Conclusion:* host invites participants to place the sheets on the wall and to make a 'gallery tour' with the class. The group representative is invited to report on key points, inviting additional insights from the wider group, including any important design principles missing. An alternative approach is to share key points from the table discussion in plenary to help make collective knowledge visible.

Methodology inspired by World Café Process.

References

Addey, J. (2005). *Harmonic anthology.* Tempe: American Federation of Astrology.

Airbnb. (2015). Retrieved from https://www.airbnb.co.uk/ (accessed 2015, October 29).

B Corps. (2015). Retrieved from https://www.bcorporation. net/(accessed 2015, October 29).

Bateson, G. (1972). *Steps to an ecology of mind.* Chicago and London: University of Chicago Press.

Benyus, J. (1997). *Biomimicry: Innovation inspired by nature.* New York: Harper Collins.

Botsman, R., & Rogers, R. (2010). *What's mine is yours: The rise of collaborative consumption.* New York: Harper Collins.

Bradfield-Moody, J., & Nogrady, B. (2010). *The sixth wave: How to survive in a resource constrained world.* North Sydney: Random House.

Bradley, J., Barbier, J., & Handler. D. (2013). Embracing the internet of everything to capture your share of $14.4 trillion. *White Paper.* Cisco. Retrieved from http://www. cisco.com/web/about/ac79/docs/innov/IoE_Economy.pdf (accessed 2015, October 10).

Carrington, D., & Howard, E. (2015). Institutions worth $2.6 trillion have now pulled investments out of fossil fuels. *The Guardian* (2015, September 22). Retrieved from http://www.theguardian.com/environment/2015/sep/22/ leonardo-dicaprio-joins-26tn-fossil-fuel-divestment-movement (accessed 2015, October 29).

Changeux, J-P. (2012). *The good, the true and the beautiful: A neuronal approach.* USA: Yale University Press.

Charles HRH The Prince of Wales. (2010). *Harmony: A new way of looking at our world.* New York: HarperCollins.

Chen, X., & Kelly, T. (2015). B-Corps – A growing form of social enterprise. *Journal of Leadership & Organizational Studies, 22*(1), 102–114.

Chouinard, Y., & Gallagher, N. (2004). Don't buy this shirt unless you need it. *Patagonia Environmental and Social Responsibility.* Retrieved from http://www. patagonia.com/eu/enGB/patagonia.go?assetid=9093 (2015, October 9).

Collot d'Escury, A. (2014). Can China kickstart its circular economy and kick its smog? *Guardian Sustainable*

Business (2014, January 15). Retrieved from http://www. theguardian.com/sustainable-business/china-recycling-waste-circular-economy (accessed 2015, October 9).

Confino, J. (2011). Talk point: When will business adopt a values-based approach? *Guardian Sustainable Business*, (2011, November 17). Retrieved from http://www. theguardian.com/sustainable-business/talk-point-values-approach-business (accessed 2015, October 8).

Crane, A., Palazzo, G., Spence, L., & Matten, D. (2014). Contesting the value of 'creating shared value'. *California Management Review, 56*(2), 130.

DaVinci 2.0. (2014). Retrieved from http://www.pointloma. edu/experience/academics/centers-institutes/fermanian-business-economic-institute/forecasting-and-expert-commentary/da-vinci-index-b (accessed 2015, October 8).

Deloitte. (2015). The Deloitte millennial survey 2015: Mind the gaps. Retrieved from http://www2.deloitte.com/global/en/pages/about-deloitte/articles/millennialsurvey. html (accessed 2014, October 29).

Deutsche Bank. (2015). Crossing the chasm: Solar grid parity in a low oil price era. Retrieved from https://www.db. com/cr/en/docs/solar_report_full_length.pdf

Dharma Life. (2015). Retrieved from http://www.dharma.net. in/(accessed 2015, October 9).

EASME (Executive Agency for Small and Medium-sized Enterprises). (2015). Spreading the model of renewable energy cooperatives (2015, March 28). Retrieved from https://ec.europa.eu/easme/en/news/spreading-model-renewable-energy-cooperatives (accessed 2015, October 29).

Econet Wireless. (2015). Retrieved from http://www. econetwireless.com/(accessed 2015, October 29).

EcoSchool. (2015). Retrieved from https://www.ecoschool. co.zw/(accessed 2015, October 29).

Elkington, J. (2012). *Zeronauts: Breaking the sustainability barrier*. London: Routledge.

Ellen MacArthur Foundation. (2012). *Towards the circular economy vol. 1: An economic and business rationale for an accelerated transition*. Isle of Wight, UK: Ellen MacArthur Foundation Publishing.

Encyclical Letter *Laudato Si' of the Holy Father Francis on Care for our Common Home*. (2015). Retrieved from http://w2.vatican.va/content/francesco/en/encyclicals/documents/papa-francesco_20150524_enciclica-laudato-si. html (accessed 2015, October 30).

Evans, D. (2011). The internet of things. How the next evolution of the internet is changing everything. *White Paper*. Cisco. Retrieved from http://www. cisco.com/web/about/ac79/docs/innov/IoT_IBSG_0411FINAL.pdf

Farmerline. (2015). Retrieved from http://farmerline.org/ (accessed 2015, October 29).

Forum for the Future. (2015). The five capitals. Retrieved from https://www.forumforthefuture.org/project/five-capitals/overview (accessed 2015, October 8).

Freeman, R., Harrison, J., & Wicks, A. (2007). *Managing for stakeholders: Survival, reputation and success*. Yale: Yale University Press.

Friedman, M. (1970). The social responsibility of business is to increase its profits. *The New York Times Magazine* (1970, September 13).

Gartner. (2013). Gartner says the internet of things installed base will grow to 26 billion units by 2020 (2013, December 12). Retrieved from http://www.Gartner.Com/Newsroom/Id/2636073 (accessed 2015, October 10).

Geng, Y., & Doberstein, B. (2008, June). Developing the circular economy in China: Challenges and opportunities for achieving 'leapfrog development'. *The International Journal of Sustainable Development and World Ecology*.

Global Times. (2013). 'China sets up association to promote circular economy. Retrieved from http://www.globaltimes. cn/content/828920.shtml#.UtWXCTGWVWg

Gore, A., & Blood, D. (2012). *Sustainable capitalism*. London: Generation Investment Management LLP.

Grameen Shakti. (2015). Retrieved from http://www.gshakti. org/(accessed 2015, October 29).

Groves, P., Kayyali, B., Knott, D., & van Kuiken, S. (2013). The big data revolution in healthcar:. Accelerating value and innovation. McKinsey&Company Report. Retrieved from http://www.mckinsey.com/insights/health_systems_and_services/the_big-data_revolution_in_us_health_care

Hart, S. (2005). *Capitalism at the crossroads. The unlimited business opportunities in solving the world's most difficult problems*. New Jersey: Wharton School Publishing.

Hawken, P., Lovins, A., & Lovins, H. (2000). *Natural capitalism: Creating the next Industrial Revolution*. Boston: Little, Brown and Company.

Hussain, S. (2014). 'Dharma Life: Making profits through rural entrepreneurs. *Forbes India* (2014, July 4). Retrieved from http://forbesindia.com/article/work-in-progress/dharma-lifes-making-profits-through-rural-entrepreneurs/38116/1 (accessed 2015, October 9).

Hutchins, G. (2014). *Illusion of separation: Exploring the cause of our current crises*. Edinburgh: Floris Books.

IKEA. (2015). People and planet. Retrieved from http:// www.ikea.com/ms/en_US/this-is-ikea/people-and-planet/ (accessed 2015, October 8).

IMF. (2015). Counting the cost of energy subsidies. Retrieved from http://www.imf.org/external/pubs/ft/survey/so/2015/new070215a.htm

IRENA (International Renewable Energy Agency). (2015). *Renewable energy and jobs: Annual review 2015*. Retrieved from http://www.irena.org/menu/index.aspx?mnu=Subcat&PriMenuID=36&CatID=141&SubcatID=585 (accessed 2015, October 29).

Jeanrenaud, S. (2002): *People-oriented approaches in global conservation: Is the leopard changing its spots?* London: International Institute for Environment and Development (IIED) and Brighton: Institute for Development Studies (IDS).

Jeanrenaud, S., Adarves-Yorno, I., & Forsans, N. (2015). Exploring a one planet mindset and its relevance in a transition to a sustainable economy. *Building Sustainable Legacies. The New Frontier of Societal Value Co-creation*, 5. Sheffield, UK: Greenleaf Publishing.

Kappes, A. (2014). Cooperatives as builders of sustainability: Tradition meets innovation: Experiences from the rise of renewable energy cooperatives in Germany. Retrieved from http://ica.coop/sites/default/files/attachments/DGRV_Kappes_Paper%20on%20RE%20Coops_10_2014.pdf

Kelly, M., & White, A. (2007). Corporate design: The missing organizational and public policy issue of our time. *Corporation 20/20*. Boston: The Tellus Institute. Retrieved from http://www.corporation2020.org/pdfs/CorporateDesign.pdf

Klein, N. (2014). This changes everything: Capitalism vs the climate. Retrieved from https://www.youtube.com/watch?v=WPQI1Lui42c

Korten, D. (2001). *When corporations rule the world* (2nd ed.). San Francisco: Berrett-Koehler Publishers, Kumarian Press.

Korten, D. (2010). *Agenda for a new economy: From phantom wealth to real wealth*. San Francisco: Berrett-Koehler Publishers Inc.

Korten, D. (2015). *Change the story, change the future: A living economy for a living earth*. A Report to the Club of Rome. Oakland, CA: Berrett-Koehler Publishers.

Kotler, P. (2015). *Confronting capitalism: Real solutions for a troubled economic system*. New York: Amacom.

Laszlo, C., & Zhexembayeva, N. (2011). *Embedded sustainability*. Stanford: Stanford University Press.

Leggett. J. (2001). *The carbon war: Global warming and the end of the oil era*. New York: Routledge.

Lin, L. (2014). China's water pollution will be more difficult to fix than its dirty air. *China Dialogue* (2014, February 17). Retrieved from https://www.chinadialogue.net/blog/6726-China-s-water-pollution-will-be-more-difficult-to-fix-than-its-dirty-air/en

LOHAS (Lifestyles of Health and Sustainability). (2015). Retrieved from http://www.lohas.com/(accessed 2015, October 9).

Louv, R. (2005). *Last child in the woods: Saving our children from nature-deficit disorder*. North Carolina: Algonquin Books of Chapel Hill.

Mackey, J., & Sisodia, R. (2014). *Conscious capitalism: Liberating the heroic spirit of business*. Boston: Harvard Business Review Press.

Manyika, J., Chui, M., Groves, P., Farrell, D., Van Kuiken, S., & Almasi Doshi, E. (2013). *Open data: Unlocking innovation and performance with liquid information*. McKinsey& Company Global Institute Report. Retrieved from http://www.mckinsey.com/insights/business_technology/open_data_unlocking_innovation_and_performance_with_liquid_information

Mason, P. (2015). *Post capitalism: A guide to our future*. London: Allen Lane.

McDonough, W., & Braungart, M. (2002). *Cradle to Cradle: Remaking the way we make things*. New York: North Point Press.

Mckeag, T. (2012). Auspicious forms. *Zygote Quarterly*, *2*(1), 14–35. Retrieved from http://issuu.com/eggermont/docs/zq_issue_02final/15?e=15278665/11095381

Meadows, D. (1999). *leverage points: Places to intervene in a system*. The Sustainability Institute. Hartland: VT.

Murray, A. (2011). *The sustainable self*. London: Earthscan.

Natura. (2014). Retrieved from https://www.bcorporation.net/community/natura (accessed 2014, October 8).

O'Brien, K., & Sygna, L. (2013). Responding to climate change: The three spheres of transformation. *Proceedings of Transformation in a Changing Climate*, June, *16–23*. Oslo, Norway: University of Oslo.

Pirson, M., Steinvorth, U., Largacha-Martinez, C., & Dierksmeier, C. (Eds.). (2014). *From capitalistic to humanistic business*. London: Palgrave Macmillan.

Porritt, J. (2005). *Capitalism as if the world matters*. Oxon: Earthscan.

Porter, M. E., & Kramer, M. R. (2011). Creating shared value. *Harvard Business Review*, January/February. Retrieved from http://www.waterhealth.com/sites/default/files/Harvard_Buiness_Review_Shared_Value.pdf

Poschen, P. (2015). *Decent work, green jobs and the sustainable economy*. Sheffield: Greenleaf Publishing.

PwC. (2015). *The sharing economy*. Consumer Intelligence Series. Retrieved from http://www.pwc.com/CISsharing (accessed 2015, October 10).

REPOWER Balcombe. (2015). Retrieved from http://www.repowerbalcombe.com/(accessed 2015, October 10).

Rifkin, J. (2011). *The third Industrial Revolution: How lateral power is transforming energy, the economy and the world*. New York: Palgrave Macmillan.

Scharmer, O., & Kaufer, K. (2013). *Leading from the emerging future: From ego-system to eco-system economies*. San Francisco: Berrett-Koehler Publishers.

Schor, J. (2014). Debating the Sharing Economy. *The Great Transition Initiative*. The Tellus Institute. Retrieved from http://www.tellus.org/pub/Schor_Debating_the_Sharing_Economy.pdf (accessed 2015, October 9).

Schröter, M., van der Zanden, E., van Oudenhoven, A., Remme, R., Serna-Chavez, H., de Groot, R., & Opdam, P. (2014). Ecosystem services as a contested concept: A synthesis of critique and counter-arguments. *Conservation Letters*, *7*(6), 514–523.

Sebastian, I. (2015, April). Doing business in a wellbeing economy. In *Reframing the game: The transition to a new sustainable economy*. A special issue of *Building Sustainable Legacies*, 5.

Seigel, D. (2014). The self is not defined by the boundaries of our skin. *Psychology Today*. Retrieved from https://www.psychologytoday.com/blog/inspire-rewire/201402/the-self-is-not-defined-the-boundaries-our-skin (accessed 2014, February 28).

Shankleman, J. (2014). Tim Cook tells climate change sceptics to ditch Apple shares. *Guardian Sustainable Business* (2014, March 3). Retrieved from http://www.theguardian.com/environment/2014/mar/03/tim-cook-climate-change-sceptics-ditch-apple-shares

Sharma, R. (2014). The future of 3D printing and manufacturing. *Forbes* (2014, January 4). Retrieved from http://www.forbes.com/sites/rakeshsharma/2014/01/15/1255/(accessed 2015, October 10).

Sisodia, R., Sheth, J., & Wolfe, D. (2014). *Firms of endearment: How world-class companies profit from passion and purpose* (2nd ed.). New Jersey: Pearson Education.

Statistics Portal. (2015). Retrieved from http://www.statista.com/statistic-portal/(accessed 2015, October 10).

Sukhdev, P. (2012). *Corporation 2020: Transforming business for tomorrow's world.* Washington: Island Press.

Tomlinson, B. (2010). *Greening through IT: Information technology for environmental sustainability.* Cambridge, MA: MIT Press.

Townsend, M. (2012). Capitalism 2.0: Are we edging towards a sustainable economy? 2degrees (4-part blog series). Retrieved from https://www.2degreesnetwork.com/groups/2degrees-community/resources/capitalism-20-we-edging-towards-sustainable-economy/(accessed 2015, October 8).

Townsend, M. (2013). Could Mindfulness hold the key to unlock a sustainable future? 2degrees (4-part blog series) (2013, April 23). Retrieved from https://www.2degreesnetwork.com/groups/2degrees-community/resources/could-mindfulness-hold-key-unlock-sustainable-future/(accessed 2015, October 7).

Townsend, M., & Zarnett, B. (2013). *A journey in search of Capitalism 2.0.* Earthshine & Toronto Sustainability Speaker Series. Retrieved from http://www.earthshinesolutions.com/docs/A-Journey-in-Search-of-CAP2_Clean-Slate_Oct_2013.pdf (accessed 2015, January 16).

UNEP (United Nations Environment Programme). (2011). Towards a green economy: Pathways to sustainable development and poverty eradication. Retrieved from http://www.unep.org/greeneconomy/GreenEconomyReport/tabid/29846/Default.aspx

UNEP. (2015). *Sustainable consumption and production and the SDGs.* UNEP Post 2015 Note #2. Retrieved from http://www.unep.org/post2015/Portals/50240/Documents/UNEP%20Publications/UNEPBriefingNote2.pdf

Voight, J. (2013). Patagonia is taking on a provocative anti-growth position: Is it all just a marketing ploy? *ADWEEK* (2013, September 29). Retrieved from http://www.adweek.com/news/advertising-branding/patagonia-taking-provocative-anti-growth-position-152782 (accessed 2015, October 29).

Volans. (2013). *Breakthrough: Business leaders, market revolutions.* London: Volans.

Watson, B. (2014). 'Natura joins B Corps: Will other big business embrace sustainability certification? *Guardian Sustainable Business* (2014, December 12). Retrieved from http://www.theguardian.com/sustainable-business/2014/dec/12/b-corps-certification-sustainability-natura

Winograd, M., & Hais, M. (2014). How millennials could upend Wall Street and corporate America. Brookings. *The Initiative on 21st Century Capitalism.* Retrieved from http://www.brookings.edu/research/papers/2014/05/millenials-upend-wall-street-corporate-america-winograd-hais (accessed 2015, October 29).

World Economic Forum (WEF). (2014). *Towards the Circular Economy: Accelerating the scale-up across global supply chains.* Prepared in collaboration with the Ellen MacArthur Foundation and McKinsey&Company. Retrieved from http://www3.weforum.org/docs/WEF_ENV_TowardsCircularEconomy_Report_2014.pdf

Xiaofei, D. (2014). Waste recycling the green way. *China Today* (2014, May 5). Retrieved from http://www.chinatoday.com.cn/english/economy/2014-05/05/content_617183.htm (accessed 2015, October 29).

Yuan, Z., Bi, J., & Moriguichi, M. (2006). The circular economy: A new development strategy in China. *Journal of Industrial Ecology, 10*(1–2).

3 Leading

Jonathan Gosling and Prasad Kaipa

'To whom are leaders responsible; and is there a kind of sensitivity, a way of being in the world, consonant with sustainability?'

Bolden *et al.*, 2011, p. 116

LEARNING OUTCOMES

The aim of this chapter is to:

1. Expose the historical roots of the way we think about leadership, and what is special about now.

2. Clarify what is involved in leading and how it relates to the kind of work to be done.

3. Compare the terminologies and meanings associated with leading in different languages and cultures.

4. Introduce and discuss the association of leadership with wisdom.

5. Consider ways of getting and using power and influence, and the risks and benefits.

6. Consider whether leadership changes in different situations.

7. Consider what might be special about leading transitions towards more sustainable business.

8. Promote self-awareness in personal responses to authority.

9. Set out the principal characteristics of One Planet Leadership.

10. Inspire confidence and creativity in taking up leadership, and supporting others who do so.

Introduction

In today's world we face major transitions in regards to how we organize, how we create wealth, and what we consider to be legitimate distributions of wealth and power.

Leading is about taking initiative and influencing others. This means exerting power, working with the structures and social norms that govern legitimate authority – and sometimes stretching these expectations.

Leading involves relationships – at the very least, between leaders and followers, so it always mobilizes emotions as well as reason (along with instinct and intuition). In fact, leading is best when it touches the intuitive sense of a possible goodness and beauty, inviting us to aspire to better ways of living and making a living.

However, much depends on which 'goods' we are seeking, who benefits, and how we go about achieving those goods. There are too many examples of leaders sacrificing their followers for the sake of an apparently noble end that turns out to be little more than self-aggrandizement, or that could have been more wisely pursued by less leadership and more co-operation. So leading is never a neutral act: it requires us to make difficult choices about aims and intentions, and also about the means to fulfil them. See Case Study 3.1.

Leading will be, more than ever, a significant factor in the technical innovations to come, and also in expressing and realizing values that we live by. Leading allows one to take an idea or a design and to manifest it through oneself or others; without leadership, innovation is stillborn. And as we will see in this chapter, finding new ways of relating to nature will open up new possibilities for creativity and community. This inevitably changes to our assumptions about power and authority. If caring becomes more important than conquering, leading will be quite different. Where will we find it, how can we practise it, and who will lead us to new ways of leading?

CASE STUDY 3.1
Volkswagen

VW, if it wants to really be the best, will have to change a lot: a single-minded focus on market share, an obsessive desire to outperform Toyota, caused willful blindness to the effects within the production process. Urged to get around tougher emissions targets, software engineers designed a program to cheat the testing regime. Targets were met – until the trick was uncovered and VW lost billions in value in 2015.

This is a case of a company that used a sustainability narrative but did not fundamentally change its business. It is a case of outrageous greenwash – and a cautionary tale about organizational leadership. VW claimed it had to be more sustainable, it was just cheating on the metrics.

VW probably had changed from a company dedicated to excellent engineering to one driven by market share statistics. The underlying point is that VW is a car company reliant on a fossil fuel, unsustainable technology. Instead of grasping the opportunity afforded by their size and engineering capability, their leadership took them back into a business model based on the most cynical modes of exploitation.

3.0 Sustainability and Leadership

Leadership is undoubtedly a powerful force in human affairs, and it always has been. All around the world, people put their hopes and trust in the hands of those they consider to be wiser, bolder, more insightful, or skilful. Sometimes this is realistic: a guide can get us out of the wilderness, a wise elder can help us see many sides of a situation and choose when and how to act, and a brilliant entrepreneur can draw us into unforeseen opportunities. But sometimes these hopes are not so realistic: no single leader is going to ease the pressures on health care systems, stop climate change, or remove carbon subsidies. Leadership works where it is melded with other processes: co-operation, collaboration, autonomous activism, bureaucratic proce- dures, audits, and even – maybe especially – practical philosophy: working out what really matters. Bringing all these together is a key aspect of leading. Too often we are told that leadership is completely different to management. While it's true that they are different concepts, leadership is valuable in enabling good management.

But is there something special about *now* that renders leadership particularly important? Yes and no. The challenges of sustainability *described in the Chapter 1* certainly require us to make radical, sometimes transformative and disruptive, changes to the way we do business. But the world has been through major changes in the past; what is different this time is that we feel the effects of complexity, know broadly what to do, and just have to get organized to do it. This makes it different to the big upheavals of the past 500 years.

A resilient response to upheaval depended heavily on resources. The pastoral and hunting societies of Australia, Africa and the Americas that had sustained themselves for thousands of years were turned upside down by colonial invasions. As a result, these communities produced some outstanding leaders, but there was nothing in their exist- ing means that could halt this turmoil. By contrast, the Indian subcontinent had been invaded and colonized repeatedly for a thousand years, and (not to deny the terrible suffering and destruction caused by successive empires) Indian culture evolved the capacity to respond creatively. This included leaders at every level, but much more than leadership: the arts, culture and profound, diverse philosophies enabled adaptation and growth. Europe, on the other hand, witnessed catastrophic plagues and almost continu- ous war through the Middle Ages, and evolved an aristocratic, male-dominated hierar- chy deeply imbued with a conviction that it was naturally endowed with the authority and ability – even the destiny – to lead. It took the devastating wars of the 20th century to shake this conviction; but there was an earlier existential threat to European civilization – one that can teach us much about leadership and sustainability.

The 14th century plague appropriately called the Black Death killed millions – in some areas only one out of four survived. Unaware of the microbial causes of the disease, people sought to explain this disaster as a punishment from God, or as a necessary cleansing of the world prior to miraculous salvation. People therefore looked to leaders offering distraction, rescue or – perversely – to plunge into the inevitable destruction. *As we will see later in this chapter*, such historical responses to crisis have impacted modern beliefs about leadership. However modest and rational a leader, they will inevitably be caught up in these kinds of unconscious, deeply-rooted cultural expectations – especially in the face of widespread existential anxiety such as that caused by climate change and potential economic collapse. In this respect our current situation is not much different to previous periods of turbulence. But there are two reasons to think that we might be facing more radically convulsive conditions, and that the demands on leadership will be different too.

Firstly, the Industrial Revolution ushered us into a mechanistic relationship with nature. For the first time, humans were able to harness water and then steam power in ways that gave us leverage over natural processes – but at the cost of becoming tied to the machines we created. This introduced a relationship to nature that valued her conquest and control through industrial processes. But now that we are confronted with limits to growth, the values of conquest and control are no longer adequate, and leaders will have to model reciprocity and harmony with natural processes and systems.

Secondly, we are now in a position to consciously create global-level governance (of trade, production, energy, etc.). The 2015 UN Sustainable Development Goals are the most prominent programmes that articulate the priorities and key agendas of such governance *(see chapter 15, Box 15.1)*.

Leaders in business, governments, international agencies and NGOs are called to contribute to these agendas beyond the particular interests of their own organizations; and beyond the foreseeable interests of their own generation. This is a perspective that has arisen gradually over the past 200 years (along with industrial globalization, as its counterpart), and is now characteristic of a 'One Planet' perspective.

Together, these two factors imply that we are in a new era known as the anthropocene, in which human activity changes many natural conditions in ways that are of geological impact, i.e., that affect the planet and its systems (Crutzen & Stoermer, 2000). Hitherto, leadership has been studied, described and judged on the basis of its role in purely human affairs. A One Planet perspective on leadership requires us to assess these human affairs in relation to our 'safe operating space' on the planet (Rokström *et al.* 2009).

Governance is a crucial aspect of 'One Planet Leadership', but there are many others, including leadership of the innovation that is already such a powerful and characteristic feature of our time. Putting all these together, it becomes clear that we need leaders who are both smart and wise. We will say more about this *later in the chapter*, but begin with some essential background to leadership.

3.1 What is Leadership?

Leadership sounds simple enough – influencing others to strive for shared goals and outcomes. But in fact definitions of leadership are notoriously slippery. In an early review of leadership research, Stogdill (1974, p. 259) concluded that there are 'almost as many definitions of leadership as there are persons who have attempted to define the concept'; even earlier, Chester Barnard (1948) famously said 'leadership has been the subject of an extraordinary amount of dogmatically stated nonsense'. Since then, the definitions have multiplied, though as we shall see, not all of them are nonsense.

In this section we will explain why it turns out to be so difficult to define and then outline the most common ways in which people have sought to analyse leadership.

To understand the problem, let's start with the simple definition at the start of this section, 'influencing others to strive for shared goals and outcomes'.

A leader might influence others to strive, but so do many other factors. If an advertisement for toothpaste influences thousands of people to clean their teeth with that brand of toothpaste, are they all followers of the advert? If a fire in a night-club influences partygoers to strive for the exit and the shared goal of escape, is that leadership? Does any kind of influence count, or are some specifically 'leadership'? What counts as shared goals? In a large auto company, are the salespeople, the paint shop workers and the executive directors really striving for shared goals? They may have a common interest that the company sells cars and keeps them employed, but actually the executives with a profit-related bonus have an interest in reducing the pay of workers and the security of salespeople. So is 'shared goal' a kind of trickery? And in any case, workers often feel managed, not led; they strive for their own personal sense of accomplishment and appropriate pay, as a response to the lack of leadership. So what's the added value of leadership, if any? These and many other questions make the issue more complicated – and that is before we question whether the 'shared objectives' matter. Is leadership that influences a purchasing decision the same as leadership that inspires a social movement, orchestrates a coup d'état or takes a country to war? Note that we are still at the level of definitions. We haven't yet started to question which *acts* count as leadership: speeches, visions, caring, and so forth; let alone how to do it.

At the core, these difficulties express some fundamental philosophical differences. For some people, leadership is a 'thing' that adheres to and characterizes a person or group. In this view, some people are leaders – they have the qualities of leaders, described as traits, styles or behaviours *(more about this below)*.

For others, leadership is just a name we give to some social arrangements. It might describe who seems to be expressing collective preferences for a group, organization or society: for example, millions of people follow celebrities when choosing what to buy or which charity to favour. And sometimes a mass of people pitch themselves into action as if led by a common revelation – often an injustice perpetrated by the authorities, such as a police shooting. Here the question is not, 'Who has the qualities of a leader?' nor 'What should leaders do?' but rather 'What are people following and who benefits from this?'

These differences are so deeply rooted that one influential writer on leadership, Keith Grint (2001), describes it as an 'essentially contested concept', and sets out four ways of thinking about it:

1   Leadership can be seen as the property of a *person*, focusing on the personal attributes of the 'leader'.

2   It can be defined by *results*, so we identify leaders as those who achieve particular outcomes.

3   It can be a *position* in a hierarchy or team, a role taken on behalf of others and fulfilling certain responsibilities.

4   Leadership may be approached as a *process*, sets of relations and interactions that give rise to effects that we recognize as 'leadership'.

To these, Peter Case *et al.* (2015) add shared *purpose*.

There is, of course, truth in all of these, and the implication is that we should try not to get stuck in any one perspective, but to remember that if we insist on a simplistic understanding of leadership, we are likely to be missing something important. This is especially true of the common tendency to romanticize the heroic contribution of some individuals, imagining their greatness explains the most extensive and complex social outcomes. Individuals *can* be great, and they *can* make extraordinary impacts on other people and processes. But they are always just part of the picture, and it helps to ask *why* they were enabled to be so great at this time and place. For example, we might admire Nelson Mandela's undoubted greatness, but we would not understand much about the end of apartheid if we think his greatness was all it took.

There are two further difficulties we should consider before settling into a good-enough definition: the moral question – can a good leader do bad (e.g., 'Was Hitler a good leader?'); and the cultural question – is leadership a culturally-specific concept that has outlived its usefulness?

3.1.1 The Moral Question

Peter Drucker (quoted in *Fortune*, 1994, February 21) said that:

> *Leadership is all hype. We've had three great leaders in this century – Hitler, Stalin and Mao.*

On a more modest scale, many of us have experienced leaders whose ruthless ambition has had a huge impact and sometimes given them personal success. Does this count as good leadership? In this book we are taking a moral position; such leaders might be effective in pursuing their objectives, but that's not enough. We are looking for leadership that improves well-being, that cares for people and planet, and that deepens human sensitivity and wisdom. This may not be possible without conflict; sometimes leaders (and most of us) are faced with choosing between evils, and the outcomes of our actions are never certain – so even the best of leaders will sometimes cause suffering and anger.

As Barbara Kellerman says, 'leaders are like the rest of us: trustworthy and deceitful, cowardly and brave, greedy and generous' (2004, p. 45). Thus leadership is often described in dualistic terms, with its light and dark sides. Lurking in the shadows are psychological perversities of narcissism and megalomania, arguably characteristic of the people who most want to be leaders, and yet tendencies that render them toxic to normal organizations. These, of course, are not limited to leaders: there are sufficient dependency-oriented personality disorders to ensure enough compliant followers to keep everyone happy! In fact some influential critics have suggested that leadership is simply 'an alienating social myth' that disempowers followers and sustains semi-totalitarian cultures (Gemmill & Oakley, 1992). But that's not the line we are taking: we accept that no one is perfect and that leadership is a morally hazardous pursuit. Mistakes, faults, failings and guilt are normal concomitants of action. Good leadership, though, is determined by the purposes, the practices and the person – how one treats the burdens and the benefits of power.

3.1.2 The Cultural Question

An equally thorny issue is whether leadership is a culturally-specific concept. The English word 'leadership' can be traced back to the Anglo-Saxon '*lead*', meaning 'to travel' and subsequently adapted, around 1200 CE, to mean 'to guide' (Grace, 2003).

The term 'leader' was used to describe statesmen from around 1300 CE, and by the early 19th century was applied to the heads of organizations in a recognized function called 'leadership'. In the English-speaking world, history has been taught as if human progress is largely composed of the actions of political, military and cultural leadership. However it is interesting to note, for example, that in French there is no comparable word, history seems to have proceeded none the less, and the lack of a terminology for leadership has not deterred Napoleon or his biographers. In modern German the term '*führer*', somewhat closer to 'guide', now has terrifying connotations; and in Russian the closest term 'лидерство' is simply a transliteration from English – the closest indigenous terms are 'руководство' which refers to management (literally 'handling situations') and 'превосходство' which implies unambiguous hierarchical supremacy and dominance, in which gentle persuasion and influence has little place. One influential author has suggested that leadership is a western obsession, 'a 20th century concept [. . .] related to the democratization of Western Civilisation' (Rost, 1991, p. 43), and by no means a universally accepted necessity.

All of these caveats have inspired scholars, including some of the most respected in management and organization studies, to come up with the most tortuous definitions. For example, Alvesson *et al.* (2016) contend:

We here therefore constrain leadership to be about:

People involved in an *asymmetrical* (unequal*) relationship* (formally or informally, permanently or temporarily, but not only momentarily) *involving followers.* Leaders (here seen as *one* type of high influential persons, regardless of whether they are formally superiors or not) are *interpersonally trying to define meaning/reality for others* (low influential persons) *that are inclined to (on a largely voluntary basis) accept such meaning-making and reality-defining influencing acts.*

Alvesson and colleagues make a good point – several points – but we will nonetheless stick with our simpler definition, acknowledging its assumptions and partiality: leadership is all about influencing others to strive for shared goals and outcomes – in particular, outcomes in harmony with One Planet business.

What this means in practice has been described by Simon Western (2013) in his influential concept of eco-leadership. To appreciate what he means, it is helpful to recognize changes in the way that leadership has been thought about over the past century, described in Figure 3.1.

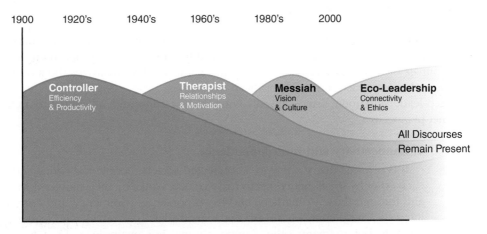

FIGURE 3.1   Discourses of Leadership. *Source:* Western, 2013, p. 150.

At the height of the Industrial Revolution, mass production, mass urbanization and mass mobilization (in war and in communist states) projected the need for leaders to control these tremendous processes. By the middle of the 20th century, wealth production shifted towards knowledge-based services and the welfare state. Now leaders were expected to care for their followers, the conditions in which they worked and the development of their potential. But in the face of globalization, migration, digitization, and the dawning clarity of environmental disaster, leaders were expected to assume the mantle of hoped-for Messianic saviours. Writers of popular leadership literature called for 'transformational leaders', claiming these extraordinary people could radically change followers' perspectives, desires and capabilities, thus bringing about wholesale change in commitment and productivity. It is not clear that members of organizations asked to be transformed in this way, but the idea was appealing to aspirant leaders, boards of directors and government policy-makers. This fuelled a surge in the leadership development industry, as consultants and business schools offered to convert aspirants into the Messiahs who would solve the complex problems confronting company directors and governments.

Needless to say, the hopes vested in this approach were seldom met, although many people would probably agree that we do need transformation and it's nice to be inspired to strive for it.

Simon Western therefore detects a fourth discourse about leadership, arising from the growing recognition of profound and ubiquitous interconnectivity. The success of one organization can no longer ignore potential harm to other parts of the system – whether this is oppression in the supply chain, waste in the production process, or a burden of pollution for future generations. Sorting out such plural, often conflicting, interests requires more than charisma and positional power: hence the growing awareness of what Western calls 'eco-leadership'.

Eco-leadership is a contemporary discourse, an emerging archetype for leadership that gives prominence to:

1   Connectivity and interdependence.
2   Systemic ethics.
3   Leadership spirit.
4   Organizational belonging.

We will consider each of these in more depth, but first we should emphasize that Western positions eco-leadership as an addition to – not a replacement for – discourses of control, therapy and Messianism. Table 3.1 summarizes the assumptions and characteristics of each of these discourses.

Eco-leadership, then, brings the following to the foreground, all central to a One Planet perspective:

1. Connectivity and interdependence

It is obvious that we live in a connected society. People are connected to each other by social networks; to massive data banks by their mobile devices, and through these to markets; and to corporate, governmental and criminal interests. These connections are not organized as hierarchies with leaders at the top, but in many other configurations. For example, a food trading

TABLE 3.1 Characteristics of Four Discourses of Leadership

Discourse	Controller	Therapist	Messiah	Eco-leadership
Vision Aims	**Iron cage** Maximizes production through transactional exchange, control and coercion	**Motivate to produce** Maximizes production though increased motivation, personal growth and team work	**Culture control** Maximizes production through identifying with the brand's strong culture, and leader's values and vision Meaning and salvation come through active followership and being part of a believing community	**Holistic and sustainable** Success is redefined in this new paradigm. Quality, sustainability and social responsibility are connected, therefore company success is measured differently from short-term profit
Source of authority	**From above** *Science* The boss/owner passes authority down the pyramid (position power) and management control gain authority from scientific rationalism	**From within** *Humanism* Drawing on personal internalized authority and the power gained through self-actualization and collaborative teamwork	**From beyond** *Charisma* The leader embodies the values, vision and culture from which they gain authority	**From the eco-system** *Interdependence* Eco-leaders draw authority from nature, networks and the belief in interdependence and connectivity
Perceptions of employees	**Robots** Employees are seen as human assets, working as unthinking robotic machines, with little personal identity or autonomy	**Clients** Are healed and made whole through reparation and creativity at work	**Disciples** Following the leader and learn to be more like them. Create an identity within a community of believers.	**Actors within a network** Employees are part of a network, with agency and with autonomy, yet also part of an interdependent, connected, greater whole
Leads what?	**Body** Controller focuses on the body to maximize efficient production, via incentives and coercion (e.g., piece work and discipline)	**Psyche** Therapist focuses on the psyche to understand motivation, designs job enrichment, creates spaces for self-actualizing behaviours	**Soul** Messiah works with the soul. Followers align themselves to the vision, a cause greater than the self (the company). The Messiah is the role model, linking success with personal salvation	**System** Eco-leaders lead through paradox, by distributing leadership throughout the system They make spaces for leadership to flourish

(Continued)

TABLE 3.1 (*Continued*)

Discourse	Controller	Therapist	Messiah	Eco-leadership
Organizational metaphor	**Machine** Takes technical and rational view of world, thinks in closed systems, tries to control internal environment to maximize efficiency	**Human organism** Creates the conditions for personal and team growth, linking this to organizational growth and success.	**Community** The Messiah leads a community (sometimes a cult). The emphasis is on strong cultures, the brand before the individual	**Eco-system** Leads through connections and linking the network. Organization is seen as a network of dispersed leadership held together by strong cultures
Control	**Bureaucratic** Control via manipulation and strict policing	**Humanistic** Control by emotional management and therapeutic governance. Paternalistic benevolence	**Culture** Culture control Workers internalize the cultural norms which become an internalized organizational ideal. Policing is via self and peers. Open-plan offices, lack of privacy and peer surveillance are techniques of control	**Self-regulating systems** Control resides in the system itself The eco-system requires resources and nurturing to self-regulate. However if resources are overused it may atrophy or it can be supported if diverse actors are connected and their interdependence understood and cherished

Source: Western, 2013, pp. 283–284.

company can link to farmers around the world, negotiating prices and logistics as a node in a web; but farmers can also be accessing other customers and agreeing contracts on future prices at the same time, evading the centralizing power of the node. Soon they might connect directly with retailers, dis-intermediating the traders but melding into logistics. Seed companies watching the trade immediately change their stock and price policy, which is spotted by ecologists concerned that introduced seeds will diminish the biodiversity inherent in local varieties, and derivative traders alter the odds on potential production next year. And so on. This degree of connectivity creates inherent interdependency and it can be so tangled that leadership *of* the connections is impossible; but leadership *in the midst* of it all is necessary. Furthermore, experience teaches us that connecting with other people opens us to connection with nature. As Western says, 'Eco-leadership is to continually work within these multiplicities; leadership is understood within a network of other actors and agents (both human and non-human)' (2013, p. 256).

To emphasize this point, eco-leadership implies a deepening connectivity to and interdependence with nature as well as with other humans. As argued above, our One Planet predicament results from the disconnect between people and nature, economy and ecology. One Planet approaches are helping to consciously develop a sense of self, participating in a living, breathing, self-organizing natural system. Note the bi-annual WWF assessment of the regenerative capacity of the earth's eco-systems is called the *Living Planet Report* (http://wwf.panda.org/about_our_earth/all_publications/living_planet_report/). This makes the point that the earth is living, imbued with life of which we humans are a part; and we are also able to act in ways that impact and even alter the behaviour of some life processes. Eco-leadership is excited by this awesome complexity of the tangled web of life, and also humbled by its electrifying beauty. Of course it would be wrong to romanticize nature, as if all 'natural' processes are characterized by harmony and kindness. Nature is seen as red in tooth and claw by some, perhaps justifying competitive, self-centred, aggressive behaviours – which have suited a particular economic logic and approach. But many contemporary biologists are striving to reclaim a view of nature in which collaboration and altruism are also noticed, as much as competition. It's all in our biology – but we haven't noticed it, and have been taught different things about the 'laws of the nature' (https://evolution-institute.org).

2. Systemic ethics

Appreciating the value of a system requires transcendence of particular sectional interests. To think systemically is to tune into the flow of connectivity. It is a way of conceiving the world as if it were a massively complicated circuit board, with switches and currents and amplifiers and resistors. It is rationalistic, and although it aims at being holistic, it is a way of thinking that is nonetheless reductionist – because it rests on the notion of the conceptualization of the system-as-a-whole.

Systemic ethics values any thing because of its connections to everything else, its influence on systemic flows. As a result, human agency – the power to affect changes – is understood in the context of much larger natural forces; this applies to collective human activity as well as individual action, so that 'goods' such as wealth are valued in a wider context. The economy is a subsystem of the ecology, so an ethical sensibility and the language appropriate to ethical decisions should be correspondingly inclusive and respectful of all that gives life.

3. Leadership spirit

Life is inherently comprehensive; it is a *sine qua non*; the ground of nature, of human being and experience – therefore of knowledge and language, and the possibility of any kind of 'system'. Appreciating the value of life requires intuition and imagination, faculties beyond instrumental rationalism.

> *Leadership spirit means to draw from the spring from which human spirit and ethics flow. . .which (I hope) is universal, yet reflects the diversity of sources that inspire it, whether humanism, different religions and spiritual beliefs, or deep ecology for example.*
>
> *(Western, 2013, p. 262)*

To get at what this means we can start with the popular but contradictory notion of 'living systems'. This is evocatively referred to by Habermas as the 'colonization of the lifeworld by the system' (1987, p. 325), referring to the way that substantive goods (that are good-in-themselves and not only for what they can achieve) such as insight, love and life are reduced or dismissed by instrumental rationality, which values any thing only as a means to other ends. The danger with systems thinking is that it sees each thing as valuable only in terms of its contribution to the system. But the system is a fiction of human thought: the real world is not bounded in this way.

Spirituality falls easily into this trap: too often we are told that spiritual practices, meditation or mindfulness are justifiable because they increase productivity or effectiveness of a system. This is like saying that truth is good because it builds trust: it might well do that much of the time (not always), but truth is good in itself. (However elusive, truth is the good that every thought desires – even the thought that truth is impossible is itself a truth-claim.)

Case and Gosling (2010), following an extensive critique of the literature and referring especially to the spiritual leadership theories of Fry and Slocum (2008), suggest three ways in which spirituality is legitimized in the workplace:

1. Spiritual leadership – a discourse that serves to appropriate and control the bodies, minds, emotions and souls of employees in the interests of corporate or other partial interests.
2. Working life – especially the challenges of leadership – provides the material and context for personal spiritual journeys; this is a form of instrumentalism, because work is seen as a means to the end of fuller life.
3. Spirituality and working life – ambition, power and glory – are incommensurable. There is therefore no inherent or necessary connection – in fact a disconnection from leadership might be more spiritually beneficial.

In practice, eco-leadership calls for an awareness of all three of these logics because what they have in common is a concern for the sacred in life. They also imply caution about the potential for religious zeal to become misleading or oppressive.

4. Organizational belonging

The organization is the subject here, and belonging is the verb; 'what the organization belongs to' is a proper concern of leadership, as well as how it enacts this belonging. Of course all organizations enact this 'belonging' through their operations, contributing goods and services. Markets are a way for commercial firms to belong to society, connecting through their customers, suppliers and employees. There are purely transactional aspects, but belonging through a market implies responsibility for the ethical conduct of that market, sustaining trust and optimizing its overall societal and environmental benefits. This is sometimes pursued through 'corporate social responsibility' (CSR), and targeted ways of extending 'shared value' amongst wider stakeholders. However, the point here is that eco-leadership involves a conscious intent for organizational belonging. (To be clear, this is not the same as the extent to which employees feel they belong to the organization, which is sometimes called 'engagement').

In summary, Simon Western approaches leadership as a feature of social discourses, enacted in ways that fit the zeitgeist. Eco-leadership, he claims, is emerging now; but there are still calls for controlling, therapeutic and Messianic leaders too.

GROUP EXERCISE 3.1

1 Which is the dominant leadership discourse in each of the organizations you are currently involved in (including non-work organizations such as sports, religious, political, social and educational groups)?

2 Would a change of leader be enough to change the discourse?

3 How do you attend to your spiritual self; and what part does work play in this?

CASE STUDY 3.2
Globally Responsible Leadership Initiative

Founded in 2004 '[t]o catalyse globally responsible leadership and practice in organisations and societies worldwide', the GRLI is now a partnership of over 50 companies and business schools. They focus specifically on strengthening the discourse of (in Western's terms) eco-leadership, and on taking action to influence leaders at forums such as the UN and through the longer-term influence of business education.

(Continued)

The GRLI's definition of responsible leadership is similar to the features we have discussed under eco-leadership (see Figure 3.2).

GRLI statements amount to a kind of manifesto which businesses and individual leaders can sign up to. Much of the content is contestable; for example, the concept of 'laws', as if drawn from theoretical physics or maths, rather mis-states the constructed and contentious claims about human capacity to 'consider every action in the context of its effect on the whole system'. This calls for a kind of omniscience, so the GRLI laws should perhaps be read as a statement of intent rather than a contract.

Globally Responsible Leadership Initiative (www.grli.org)

'Globally responsible leadership is the global exercise of ethical, values-based leadership in the pursuit of economic and societal progress and sustainable development. It is based on a fundamental recognition of the interconnectedness of the world.'

In the 2008 'GRLI's Call for Action', responsible leadership was described as ' . . . the art of motivating, communicating, empowering, and convincing people to engage with a new vision of sustainable development and the necessary change that this implies. Leadership is based on moral authority. Moral authority requires convictions, character and talent'.

The Three Laws of Globally Responsible Leadership

1. The Law of the Environment
The natural system is not a stakeholder in our businesses; it is the ultimate foundation of the rules.

2. The Law of Interconnectedness
Everything, everywhere is linked in a single system, therefore every action must be considered in the context of its effect on the whole system.

3. The Law of Engagement
Globally responsible leaders must become engaged in solving the dilemmas that confront us as a consequence of the first two laws.

FIGURE 3.2 Globally Responsible Leadership Initiative. *Source:* GRLI, www.grli.org.

Nonetheless we have arrived at a workable understanding of what One Planet Leadership is concerned with (not yet how to do it). It will attend to connectivity and interdependence, systemic ethics, leadership spirit and organizational belonging. It will operate with the assumptions underpinning globally responsible leadership, expressed by the GRLI as The Law of the Environment, The Law of Interconnectedness and The Law of Engagement.

Next we should deal with. . .

3.2 Some Nagging Questions about Leadership

Are some people better suited to this form of leadership than others? What if all this spirituality and sensitivity doesn't come naturally? Are these really the traits of new leaders – or is this wishful thinking?

Leadership has often been associated with the idea that a leader is someone with a bundle of traits – most of them 'good'. Courage, intelligence and foresight feature

FIGURE 3.3   Word Cloud of Characteristics of Leading Individuals at UK Universities. *Source:* Bolden *et al.*, 2012, p. 16.

on most lists; but the word cloud in Figure 3.3 showing the traits that UK academics identified in their leaders indicates that not all are positive. (Bolden *et al.*, 2012).

These are the traits that intelligent, experienced organization members considered most characteristic of the people actually in leadership positions, and are probably arecognizable in many sectors beyond universities. Some are obviously desirable, others less so, but overall this is probably a realistic assessment of what is needed to get power and hold onto it, at least in established bureaucratic hierarchies. Are we suggesting that eco-leadership can somehow avoid egocentric, conspiratorial back-stabbing? Isn't this how power works?

This is an important question, because we should know if we are being unrealistically optimistic. There are two parts to the answer, and to address it we will look more closely at the findings from this study of academics because it exposes dynamics that are common to many knowledge-intensive work settings, and the tensions within bureaucracies.

Firstly, institutional leadership often creates a world of its own. A detailed content analysis of the survey items listed in the word cloud shows how these are related (see Table 3.2).

Characteristics associated with 'strategic' include high-level thinking *and* the ambition to get into a position where that is called for. That seems to call for dogmatic determination, sometimes ruthlessness. In a context of bureaucratic conservatism, resistant to change and innovation, it's no wonder the energy is turned inwards. But perhaps most tellingly, academics looked on their leaders as incompetent and failed researchers. This is significant not because it is true, but because it tells us something important about how leadership is perceived in professional organizations (it is the same in health, law, accountancy, education, and many other sectors).

TABLE 3.2   Thematic analysis of additional traits

Category	Characteristic traits/qualities
Strategic	Visionary, inspirational, ambitious, goal-orientated
Committed	Self-belief, self-confident, conviction, fair, ethical
Socially adept	Good networkers, communicators, team-workers
Dogmatic	Determined, ruthless, self-serving, individualist, egotistical, lacking integrity, manipulative, controlling, unable to accept criticism
Bureaucratic	Meeting-oriented, paper-pushers, follow directives, afraid of change, reactive, dislike ambiguity, not prepared to rock the boat
Incompetent	A failed academic, inexperienced, ignorant of history, liars

Source: Bolden *et al.*, 2012, p. 16.

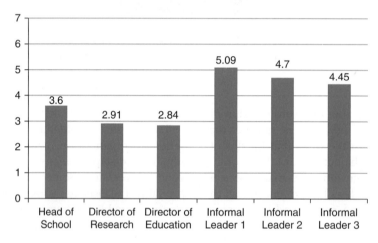

FIGURE 3.4   Perception of Formal and Informal Leaders' Leadership Behaviours. *Source:* Bolden *et al.*, 2012, p. 17.

In the survey reported here, respondents were asked to name up to three other people who influenced their work – the people they actually 'follow'. These were almost never the same as the first list, the official post-holders in the hierarchy. They were instead other professional academics, people whose work and way of working earned respect. Figure 3.4 shows that these 'informal' leaders had more influence than the hierarchical position-holders (Head of School, Directors of Research and Education), even when the people filling those positions were themselves academics. From a followers' point of view, taking a managerial role might discount one's leadership effectiveness.

But what is meant by 'providing leadership'? One might expect leaders to influence in the following five ways (see Figure 3.5).

Figure 3.6 shows in more detail who provided each of these functions.

Structures:	Provides you with structure in your work.
Inspires:	Inspires you in your work.
Represents:	Represents you and your work – in other words, embodies what you stand for.
Mentors:	Provides you with mentorship in your work.
Influences:	Influences you through their leadership.

FIGURE 3.5   Formal and Informal Leaders' Leadership Behaviours. *Source:* Bolden *et al.*, 2012, p. 17.

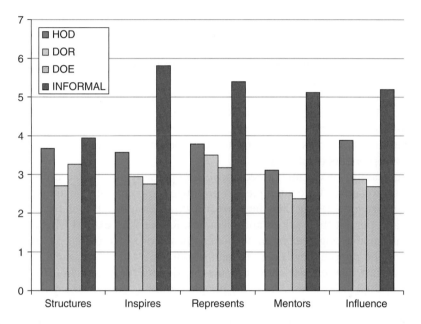

FIGURE 3.6   Comparison of Formal and Informal Leaders on Leadership Behaviours. *Source:* Bolden *et al.*, 2011, p. 19.

Here the academics are saying they follow the super-academics – much like a soccer player who in their mind would like to play as well as the best but makes independent decisions on the field to develop a distinct style and strength. Professionals look for leadership in those who are prototypical of their profession – and they look upon management of the institution, the wider organization, as incidental rather than integral to their profession. This insight is neatly summarized by Haslam, Reicher and Platow in *The new psychology of leadership* (2011) as follows:

- A leader is someone who embodies (is *prototypical* of) a social identity that is shared with other group members – and who exerts influence on this basis.
- Leadership can be seen as a process of social identity management that centres on a leader's ability to create, co-ordinate, and embody a shared, special sense of 'us'.
- Without social identity there can be no leadership: we can only be led if there is a 'we' to lead.

Therefore a leader will be accepted if they are seen as:

- **Being one of us** leaders as ingroup prototypes.
- **Doing it for us** leaders as ingroup champions.
- **Crafting a sense of us** leaders as entrepreneurs of identity.
- **Making us matter** leaders as embedders of identity.

This helps us make sense of the ambivalence that academics express about their hierarchical super-ordinates. Like many other professionals, they see them as managers, and might respect them as such; but ridicule their claims to leadership.

There are significant implications for eco-leadership and One Planet Leaders. It is not enough to have the right attitudes or personal traits: leaders will be followed only if they embody the identity-ideals of their community. In fact, leaders have to do more: they extend the possibilities of a shared identity, uncovering or creating new ways of being this or that category of person. Thus social entrepreneurs are attempting to extend the meaning of being an entrepreneur, of being a businessperson, and of being a social activist. When we demand that corporate boards and company executives take into account more than the interests of their shareholders, we are asking them to extend the meaning of 'being in business'; in other words, to act as entrepreneurs of identity.

In the example of VW mentioned above, and possibly also for UK universities, the corporate executives have attempted to prioritize the competitive market position of their organizations. Doing this, they pressurize professionals to behave in ways that reduce and pervert their values and identities. Rather than extend what it means to be an automotive engineer or an academic, these corporate managers are cynically exploiting the people they see as 'human resources'.

By contrast, leaders as 'entrepreneurs of identity' draw on 'human resource–*fulness*' of their colleagues. And some people would go further to say that:

> *What we have discovered, and rediscovered, is that leadership is not the private reserve of a few charismatic men and women. It is a process ordinary people use when they are bringing forward the best from themselves and others. What we've discovered is that people make extraordinary things happen by liberating the leader within everyone.*
>
> (Kouzes & Posner, 2002, p. xxiii)

There is one important aspect to our first 'nagging question': 'Are some people better suited to this than others?'

Eco-leadership calls for the sorts of skills and attitudes that are supposedly typical of women: would we achieve this kind of change by a more determined shift from male-dominated power structures? The answer depends on whether you think that qualities and behaviours are essential gender characteristics; or become associated with genders as a function of organizational and social dynamics. Are women naturally more co-operative than men, or have they learnt to connect, co-operate and engage deeply with others in order to survive organizational life that excludes them from positions in which direct authority would be possible?

One test of this is to consider organizations that are almost exclusively female at all levels, such as schools of nursing: are these free of the kinds of competitiveness and bullying that seem so common in typically male-dominated organizations such as investment banking? The answer is pretty clear – there is as much bullying and competition in nursing schools as anywhere else, though not expressed via displays of machismo, one hopes. So a reasonable hypothesis might be that preferences and skills for collaboration are developed most amongst those marginalized by dominant power structures, whether the demarcation is by gender, ethnicity or some other factor. Conversely, those who have enjoyed ready access to power and privilege (typically middle-class men) might have to make a particular effort to recognize such insights and attitudes. Indeed, many profound philosophies of leadership stress the importance of empathetic appreciation of powerlessness. Some would argue that this empathy is a necessary condition for properly inclusive organizations, taking into account the interests of voiceless stakeholders, including animals, plants and nature as a whole, not typically represented in decision-making senior leadership teams.

So in conclusion, it turns out it's not about the person, but about whether that person represents the group they aspire to lead.

3.2.1 Now to a Second Nagging Question

'Is eco-leadership appropriate to every situation?' Surely leading a small team of entrepreneurs in a tech start-up is not the same as leading a huge workforce in a low-tech mining operation, or a public health service spread out across a whole country. Does leading a response to crisis justify an authoritarianism that would be unacceptable in day-to-day operations? This question is usually answered by some variety of contingency model, advocating a leadership style to suit each situation, bearing in mind urgency and complexity of tasks, sophistication of employees, culture of the organization, and other environmental variables.

Contingency Theories: It Depends on the Situation   Fiedler's contingency theory (1964, 1967) assumed managers are either task- or relationship-oriented. Task-oriented managers focus on the job in hand and tend to do better in situations that have good leader-member relationships and structured tasks, and where their position of power is either accepted without question or is irrelevant because people get on with things themselves. Facing an unstructured task, they need a strong authority position in which to enact a more directive leadership style. Relationship-oriented managers do better where the task and staff relations are problematic – and unsurprisingly they exhibit a more participative style of leadership. This sounds very neat: how nice to have a perfect fit. In the real world, however, situations are a mix of conditions, organizations include a range of complex and simple tasks, and managers and leaders have to adapt to each other all the time. This turns out to be a theory that scores high on conceptual clarity but low on practicality.

Hersey and Blanchard (1969, 1993) agreed that leaders can adapt styles to suit the skill and maturity of the workforce, from directing to coaching, supporting and at the highest levels, delegating large parts of the work. Hugely popular, situational theory has been a favourite of leadership courses promising a formula for success, but a brief review of the UK universities example discussed above indicates its limitations. Academics, like other professionals, are pretty high in 'skill and maturity', but delegating control to them seems to be difficult for university managers. Perhaps academics can't be trusted to act in the best interests of the institution as a whole; and perhaps they would give priority to research over teaching. In other words, situational theory ignores the political realities of organizations, their inherent pluralism.

So we come to the key problem with contingency models – that all the parts are moving: there is no neutral point from which to diagnose a situation, or even describe an organization. We will briefly consider two models that usefully illustrate this point, and will bring us back to a more robust conception of One Planet Leadership.

Perspectives on What Organizations Are   An organization is not a simple thing: it can be conceived in ways that foreground some features and justify certain authority arrangements. Burrell and Morgan (1979) suggest three main perspectives – *unitarist, pluralist* and *radical*.

Unitarists talk of an organization as a single entity – they say things like 'we are all in the same boat' and we should 'sing from the same hymn sheet'. They see the world as a unity in which parts can slot together harmoniously – so that businesses can produce wealth and well-being without necessarily harming the environment, exploiting people or perverting government. If there is conflict it is probably caused by a few troublemakers who can be reformed or disposed of. The ideal is of a team united around a common aim and leader.

Pluralists assume that the world is made up of multiple stakeholders pursing their own interests, not always easily reconciled. They see organizations as a negotiated order in which diverse interest groups live with a good-enough arrangement most of the time – but that harmony has to be worked at; conflict and negotiation are normal, and whatever the current distribution of power, it is at least contestable.

A more *radical* understanding of systemic inequality sees most organizations – especially capitalist businesses – as complicit in the domination and exploitation of people and nature. This is not something likely to be changed by goodwill alone: organizational and management practices create too many pockets of vested interests, so change that will actually make a difference to this exploitation is likely to involve confrontation and even conflict. Radical perspectives are informed by diverse intellectual traditions. Marxism has provided much of the conceptual analysis, pointing to the fact that capitalism is built on determined exploitation of natural and human 'resources'. But the radical sentiment is found also in deep-green ecology, dissenting theologies (the Quakers have a particularly long history of skepticism towards formal authority structures), and of course millennarian movements calling for a clean sweep of capitalist or 'western' society.

All of these approaches are important for our understanding of One Planet Leadership. An ideal of a world in harmony is hard to resist, and is implicit in our title – One Planet. But any attempt to persuade us that we should all just settle down and get along together should rightly be met with a question about whose interests are served by the *status quo*. Eco-leadership is rooted in pluralist assumptions, and calls for leadership that is able to constantly negotiate its legitimacy amongst multiple interest groups. But we should also stay alert to the radical insights into systemic bias; and some important social movements inspired by this radicalism will develop forms of autonomist leadership that are an important aspect of One Planet Leadership (Simon Western, author of the eco-leadership ideas *described above*, has also written on this. See Western, 2014). We can see how any one organization can encompass all three perspectives; often senior management will hold a unitarist view, middle and junior management assert the pluralist, while workers (and perhaps suppliers and conservationists) have a more radical understanding of how power works.

The three perspectives are summarized in Table 3.3.

TABLE 3.3 Three Approaches to Conflict and Power

	Unitarist	Pluralist	Radical
Interests	Places emphasis on the achievement of common objectives. The organization is viewed as being united under the umbrella of common goals and striving towards their achievement in the manner of a well-integrated team	Places emphasis on the diversity of individual and group interests. The organization is regarded as a loose coalition which has only a passing interest in the formal goals of the organization	Places emphasis on the oppositional nature of 'class' and sectional interests. Organization is viewed as a battleground where rival forces (e.g., management and unions) strive for the achievement of largely incompatible ends
Conflict	Regards conflict as a rare and transient phenomenon that can be removed through appropriate managerial action. Where it does arise, it is usually attributed to the activities of deviants and troublemakers	Regards conflict as an inherent and ineradicable characteristic of organizational affairs and stresses its potentially positive or functional aspects	Regards organizational conflict as inevitable and part of wider conflicts in society. It is recognized that conflicts may be suppressed and thus often exist as latent rather than manifest characteristics of both organizations and society
Power	Largely ignores the role of power in organizational life. Concepts such as authority, leadership and control tend to be preferred means of describing the managerial prerogative of guiding the organization towards the achievement of common interests	Regards power as a crucial variable. Power is the medium through which conflicts of interest are alleviated and resolved. The organization is viewed as a plurality of power holders drawing their power from a variety of sources	Regards power as a key feature of an organization. Power is unequally distributed and viewed as a reflection of power relations in society at large, and closely linked to wider processes of social control, e.g., control of economic power, the legal system and education. Power is seen as a form of manipulation and suppression

Source: Linstead *et al.*, 2009, p. 397. Adapted from Burrell and Morgan, 1979, p. 388.

Addressing the question, 'Is leadership necessary in every situation?', someone taking any of the three perspectives – unitarist, pluralist and radical – would say, 'Yes – but the purposes, methods and approach will differ depending on your perspective'. Contingency and situational theories (such as those proposed by Fiedler or Hersey and Blanchard) assume there are some uncontroversial objective descriptions of the environment, the organization, and the staff. We can now see that how we describe the situation is itself a matter of perspective, and perhaps related to our own preferences and interests. We will consider one more model that will help us to distinguish One Planet Leadership amongst all these moving categories. This is taken from an influential article by Keith Grint (2005) in which he distinguishes three ways to look at and characterize 'the situation' – in particular, what kind of problem do we think we are facing?

Perspectives on the situation   According to Grint, we face problems as *tame*, *critical* or *wicked*. A *tame* problem is one with which we know what's going on, and we probably know more or less how to resolve it, even if we don't yet have all the

resources and can foresee difficulties along the way. This applies to many complicated and persistent organizational problems, such as 'how to run a hospital' or 'how
to clean up our supply chain'.

A *wicked* problem is not just complicated – it is complex: it is intractable, there is
no plausible end point, no commonly agreed way to address it and probably not
even an agreed description of the problem. Addressing climate change, 'peace in the
Middle East', population policy, can all be described as 'wicked', because all are
characterized by inescapable uncertainty.

Grint suggests that while tame problems can be approached with management,
wicked problems call for leadership – especially to ask the right questions and invite
collaborative responses, rather than responding to anxious demands for immediate
answers.

The demand for immediate answers is appropriate if the problem is seen as *critical*, if it needs urgent resolution. In that case the response is to take command,
because neither the certainties of management nor the questions of leadership are
necessary.

That seems simple enough: a critical problem needs command, a tame problem
needs management, and a wicked problem needs leadership. This is represented in
Figure 3.7.

But situations are not so easily categorized. We might hear of a 'nursing crisis' in our health care system to which CEOs are called to respond with commanding certainty. But we all know that directing resources to provide more
nursing simply shifts the pressure to other parts of the system. Describing the
problem as 'critical' might make some people feel they have galvanized action,
but overall it has probably made things worse. This dynamic is particularly
endemic in environmental discourses. We face a 'climate crisis'; and the situation is indeed dire, but not really solvable by a few ruthlessly applied reforms
(unless one is able to totally ignore the demands of energy-hungry industry,

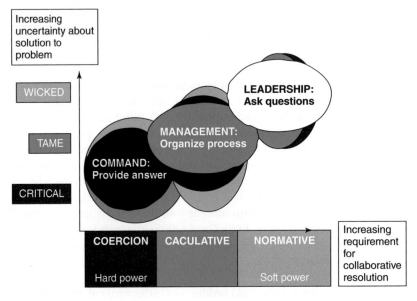

FIGURE 3.7 A Typology of Problems, Power and Authority. *Source:* Grint, 2005, p. 1477.

CASE STUDY 3.3
Malaria

The impact of this terrible disease has been successfully controlled in some places by determined managerial work in developing new treatments, improved testing, drug distribution, information-management and local health care. But in others malaria remains a persistent threat because many actively avoid their government officials, local businesses develop cheaper versions of antimalarial drugs that allow resistant strains to build up, and funding shifts to face more 'critical' diseases. Mostly it persists along with other features of poverty. Because of these dynamics Sri Lanka, which had reduced malaria to just 17 cases in 1963, had over 500,000 by 1969. A focus on 'critical' problems had undone years of careful management. Yet by 2011 the Sri Lankan health ministry could declare the effective elimination of malaria, thanks to the determined, long-term managerial response. Sri Lanka is an island

though, and even throughout years of civil war, Sri Lankans co-operated on the anti-malaria campaign because its leaders understood its wicked-ness and sustained a collaborative approach. One important factor, hard to replicate, is that Sri Lankan independence from the British Empire was motivated in part by the failure of the colonial administration to release medicines to fight a malaria epidemic in 1930 – resulting in as many as 400,000 deaths. This was the injustice that prompted many to join the independence struggle. Fighting malaria is intimately linked to the fight for independence in the Sri Lankan identity. This creates an almost subconscious unitarism even in the midst of a deadly civil war – and it is this intuition of common humanity that is conjured by leadership in the face of wicked problems. No heroic leaders, but plenty of leadership!

billions of poor people, and so on). Another example is the global fight against malaria (see Case Study 3.3).

So 'the situation' is constructed, sometimes intentionally, often in the diverse polyphony of public discourse and the media. Grint gives a telling example: in the wake of the 9/11 2001 attacks on the World Trade Center and the Pentagon, President Bush declared a 'war on terror', defining the moment as a 'crisis' calling for a 'command' response. But if any situation can be described as 'wicked', this was it! And of course this definition was no accident: many in the US administration at the time had been involved for years in negotiations in the oil-producing Middle East, supporting the Mujahideen in Afghanistan and Saddam Hussein in Iraq. They knew its long and entangled history. No, this was a moment when leadership might have been appropriate and possible, but the opportunity was lost to the desire for command – at terrible human and strategic cost.

Keith Grint uses this example to suggest that far from being obvious, the definition of a problem as tame, wicked or critical is the outcome of a power-play and:

. . . partly rests in the decision makers' access to – and preference for – particular forms of power, and herein lies the irony of 'leadership': it remains the most difficult of approaches and one that many decision-makers will try to avoid at all costs because it implies that: 1) the leader does not have the answer; 2) that the

> *leader's role is to make the followers face up to their responsibilities (often an unpopular task) . . .; 3) that the 'answer' to the problem is going to take a long time to construct and that it will only ever be 'more appropriate' rather than 'the best'; and 4) that it will require constant effort to maintain. It is far easier, then, to opt either for a Management solution – engaging a tried and trusted process – or a Command solution – enforcing the answer upon followers – some of whom may prefer to be shown 'the answer' anyway.*
>
> (Grint, 2005, p. 1475)

This now brings into focus the likely character of One Planet Leadership – difficult, uncertain and sometimes unpopular.

It means that we should be suspicious of commanding, Messianic leaders; and be tolerant of leaders who are unable to chart a clear and unambiguous path ahead. Grint goes on to describe the relative capabilities required for command, management and leadership with another persuasive example:

> *A police officer coming upon a train crash need not spend a lot of time, effort or rhetorical skill in persuading on-lookers to move away; she or he may simply Command them to move. However, for that same police officer to operate as a Manager in a police training academy requires a much more sophisticated array of skills and behaviours in order to train police cadets in the art of policing; and many of these techniques and processes are already well known, tried and tested. But to develop a new policing strategy for Iraq might mean more than Commanding civilians and more than simply training up Iraqi cadets through Management processes; instead it might require a whole new framework for constituting a post-Baathist society and that may necessitate sophisticated Leadership.*
>
> (Grint, 2005, p. 1479)

Analogies are clear in, for example, conservation campaigning organizations. Direct action to save a habitat may be more suited to command; running a national campaigning, educational and fundraising NGO requires more sophisticated managerial approaches. But developing a global policy and enforcement framework with multiple stakeholders across all sectors of society in vastly differing cultures and economies calls for leadership of quite a different order.

> *Some problems are so complex that you have to be highly intelligent and well informed just to be undecided about them.*
>
> (Attributed to Laurence J. Peter, quoted in Grint, 2005, p. 1468)

We should acknowledge that Grint's 2005 typology of problems and forms of authority is constructed to expose the weaknesses of contingency theories, showing that the process of defining a problem is 'an element in the competition between different accounts, between different interests and between different decision-makers' (Grint (2005), pp. 1491–1492). But the lessons are important, because they show why leadership is not just about providing vision and inspiration, still less about offering solutions to intractable problems. Rather, One Planet Leadership is more often about ensuring the conditions in which solutions can be negotiated. Margaret Wheatley puts it more evocatively: 'Leadership is shifting from Hero to Host' (Wheatley & Freize, 2011).

This is all consonant with the findings of other researchers across many sectors and countries (see, for example, Table 3.4).

TABLE 3.4 Summary of What Makes a Good Leader

Leadership practices inventory (Kouzes & Posner, 2002, 2003)	Characteristics of outstanding leaders (Tamkin *et al.*, 2010)	Characteristics of wise leaders (Kaipa & Radjou, 2013)
1 Model the way 2 Inspire a shared vision 3 Challenge the process 4 Enable others to act 5 Encourage the heart	1 Think systemically and act long term 2 Bring meaning to life 3 Apply the spirit not the letter of the law 4 Grow people through performance 5 Are self-aware and authentic to leadership first, their own needs second 6 Understand that talk is work 7 Give time and space to others 8 Put 'we' before 'me' 9 Take deeper breaths and hold them longer	1 Perspective/outlook: has a systemic/holistic perspective/outlook that integrates diverse, even polarizing, worldviews 2 Action orientation: acts authentically and appropriately for the larger benefit 3 Role clarity: leads from the front or from behind, allowing others to shine; practises 'detached engagement' – engaged in action without ego entanglement 4 Decision logic: applies discernment to make decisions that are ethical and yet pragmatic 5 Fortitude: knows when to let go and when to hold on to power and control 6 Motivation: operates out of enlightened self-interest

Source: Adapted from Bolden *et al.*, 2011, p. 40.

3.3 Bringing it All Home: How to Conduct Yourself in Leadership

So what are the personal implications for someone taking up the duty of One Planet Leadership? Clearly it takes more than being 'smart', though that is also important. It also takes wisdom, by which we mean practical knowledge of how to do good. In this final section we will explain this know-how and illustrate some ways of practising it. For more details of modern wisdom practices in a western tradition (derived from ancient Greek and Roman philosophy) see Case and Gosling (2007); and for equally modern practices derived from Vedantic and Buddhist traditions see Kaipa and Radjou (2013).

We have described the need to encompass very different ways of being smart – system and lifeworld, instrumental and substantive, managing and leading. Running a business, one has to attend both to operations and to innovation. It is tough to do both at once, but it is very important to move between them to avoid capture by one or the other.

If we imagine leadership as a state-dependent phenomenon, it swings from one state to another like a pendulum. Wise leadership is in the swing of the pendulum from one end to another, from one kind of smart leadership to another kind of smart leadership.

Kaipa and Radjou (2013) describe this in terms of functional and business leadership. One end of the smartness spectrum is *functional smartness*. It is not leadership of specific functions like marketing, R&D or sales, but leadership with an operational focus. When we excel at execution, produce predictable results quarter after quarter and try to address what we can control and where we can impact (like cost, quality, delivery and customer satisfaction) we are operating on the functional smart side of the spectrum. This kind of leadership creates a strong management foundation for the organization and helps it to operate like a lean and well-oiled machine, and hence it is about management excellence in a predictable, less complicated context.

While the functional smart approach focuses on operational efficiencies on one end of the smartness spectrum, *business smart* leadership is about creating the future on the other end of the spectrum. It is about bringing in innovation, increasing brand value and competitiveness, connecting with stakeholders and enhancing the business ecosystem through which the organization can grow. This kind of smartness allows people to take risks, become entrepreneurial and focus on vision and opportunity.

While the functional smart and business smart approaches define the movement of the pendulum in two different directions, wise leadership is balancing the two polarized directions (see Figure 3.8).

Notice that if the pendulum stops swinging it rests in a static position, like a serene monk sitting on the top of the mountain disengaged from leadership roles though perhaps dispensing appropriate wisdom to leaders when they seek advice. A wise leader, on the other hand, is in action and is engaged with the world and the organization though balancing the perspectives, actions, decisions and motivation between one extreme and the other. To do this requires awareness of one's own state of mind (see Case Study 3.4), one's preferences for 'smarts' – operations or business, systems or lifeworlds. The wise leader values the pleasures and excellences of each, but is not attached to either. This is one of the great benefits of the current popularity of 'mindfulness', because it is through mindfulness that one becomes able to separate the self from varying states of mind and emotion. In the pendulum model, mindfulness locates one's consciousness at the axis of the pendulum, though still engaged in the swing between one kind of smart and another. In fact one may say that smart leadership has all the answers and wise leadership is about asking the right questions – and using these to evolve considered responses (rather than reactions).

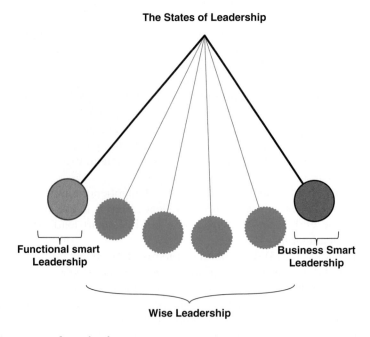

The States of Leadership

Functional smart Leadership

Business Smart Leadership

Wise Leadership

FIGURE 3.8 The States of Leadership.

CASE STUDY 3.4
Yoga

Throughout history leaders have spoken about the exercises and disciplines that enhance wisdom. Marcus Aurelius, a Roman emperor caught up in constant political and military turmoil, wrote *Meditations* as a record of how stoic mindfulness can enable wise leadership in the face of (what we would call) wicked, tame and critical problems. Marcus Aurelius and other stoics describe mental disciplines that enable them to use everyday events as material for exercising their wisdom: as if the problems they face become metaphorical weights and exercise machines for developing the moral 'body' (Case & Gosling, 2007). In Vedantic traditions this is known as *yoga*, integrating physical, mental and spiritual awareness and agility.

Within yoga, chakras are a powerful developmental framework for developing self in the context of others. Though often presented as an interior persona process, it is becoming clear that it is ecological in nature. That means, what is happening inside and what is happening outside are interlinked and happen together, whether we acknowledge them or not.

Prasad Kaipa (co-author of this chapter) is a yoga and leadership scholar. He structures personal leadership development as progress through the chakras, a journey of release from the fears that block our creative energy and potential (see Figure 3.9).

From fear for one's survival – almost a hunter vs hunted syndrome – we evolve to having desires; short term maybe, but potent drivers to experience a release of creative flow and that could get us into a different state of mind. Having once experienced this, one wants to keep having those desires fulfilled again and again, greedy perhaps, but also to develop an ability to access power and control beyond the fear.

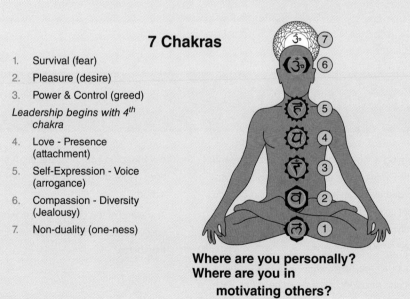

7 Chakras

1. Survival (fear)
2. Pleasure (desire)
3. Power & Control (greed)

Leadership begins with 4th chakra

4. Love - Presence (attachment)
5. Self-Expression - Voice (arrogance)
6. Compassion - Diversity (Jealousy)
7. Non-duality (one-ness)

**Where are you personally?
Where are you in
motivating others?**

FIGURE 3.9 Seven Chakras as Stages of Leadership Development and their Shadow Aspects. *Source:* Kaipa and Radjou, 2013.

(Continued)

The move from third chakra to fourth is quite different, as there is no direct correlation between subjective personal experience, and what comes to you in external circumstances. In other words, you break the cause and effect cycle and discover that you love for the sake of love and expect nothing in return *(see the discussion of instrumental and substantive goods earlier in this chapter)*. An example is the ideal of unconditional love of parent for child: 'we love them for who they are and want to take care of them, protect them and give willingly and with love'. According to Kaipa, this is the first stage of leadership, whereas the previous three stages represent management via fear, incentives and power/control.

The fifth chakra, at the throat, is the next developmental step; where people find their authentic voice, allowing them to speak independently of cultural and communal habits, conveying a sense of authenticity and presence. This is where visionary leadership becomes possible. Unfortunately it is also a place where people can get caught up with their arrogance or ego: having found their voice, they want to hear more of it, and drown out all others!

The sixth chakra cannot be reached without the help of a teacher, mentor or preceptor (in the spiritual sense). It is the source of charisma, multiplied when used for noble purposes. It comes with acceptance of the limits to one's control over outcomes, but confidence in the gifts one has and acceptance of personal role (agency), without jealousy of other leaders.

The seventh chakra represents becoming part of the one world. You lead as a servant leader with no unique identity and with the crystal-clear sense that you are just an instrument of the world and you are doing what needs to be done — nothing more and nothing less.

Progress through the chakras is not linear, because as one moves into each, new understandings and capabilities give rise to new risks. It is as if by shining a brighter light further into the world, new objects come into view and with them, new shadows. This is why we talk of yoga as continuous practice. It is not that we practise yoga in order to be wise; rather, the practice of yoga (spiritual exercise) is the practice of wisdom. The practice of leading is itself an opportunity to practise yoga and to open the higher chakras.

GROUP EXERCISE 3.2

1   Becoming a wise leader requires discipline and practice. Think of one action that is wise that you are proud of and another which is smart but you are not proud of. (You may find it easier to start by identifying decisions, actions and communication that are smart but not wise.)

2   Then pick one new 'wiser' action, possibly a particular decision or a way to be 'wiser' each day based on your own standards and expectations. Note down *why* it is a wiser decision or action.

3   At the end of this course, write down your experiences and reflect on whether you are wiser now than before.

GROUP EXERCISE 3.3

Classroom activities

1   Work in groups of three or four. Interview each other about your best and worst experiences of leading and being led. Compare and contrast these experiences.

2   In groups of three to five consider:

What is your 'north star' or noble purpose?

The values that have remained precious to you throughout life.

How have these influenced decisions you have made, and the way you have acted in critical moments?

Personal study aids

1   Collect three stories from today's headlines.

Who is taking initiative, to what ends, on whose behalf, and with what legitimacy?

2   Identify three decisions/actions that you need to take this week.

How do you bring wisdom/smartness in making those decisions and taking those actions?

Summary

Pulling all this together we can see that One Planet Leadership is an emerging discourse arising from the aware-ness of human dependency on the lifeworld and on natural systems; and the unprecedented scale of impact on natural processes. It has roots in the historical development of authority relations in hierarchical and bureaucratic forms of organization, and is influenced by autonomist and egalitarian ideals.

One Planet Leadership will likely be characterized by the qualities of eco leadership: connectivity and inter-dependence, systemic ethics, leadership spirit and organizational belonging. It will operate with the assump-tions underpinning globally responsible leadership: expressed by the GRLI as The Law of the Environment, The Law of Interconnectedness and The Law of Engagement.

One Planet Leaders will be authorized by their community because they both represent and extend the identity opportunities of community members. They will recognize the desire for unity, welcome the expression of pluralism and take cues from radical perspectives on inequalities and injustices. And One Planet Leadership will tackle the wicked problems that make the path to sustainability so difficult.

Individuals may aspire to play a role as One Planet Leaders themselves or to influence the direction and coherence of collective action through others. In either case, they will want to engage in practices of self-discipline and self-improvement; however they go about doing this is likely to be derived from long-established philosophical traditions.

QUESTIONS FOR CLASS DISCUSSION (WITH SUGGESTED ANSWERS IN THE INSTRUCTORS' GUIDE)

1. What are the qualities needed for leading national and local responses to rising sea levels? Consider both individual and collective qualities.

2. Examine the arguments (for and against) that leading is essentially a spiritual quest or calling.

3. What if leading is not about you but about developing leadership in others? How would you act differently if your job is to make others in your team/organization better than you are in every aspect?

References

Alvesson, M., Blom, M., & Sveningsson, S. (2016). *Reflexive leadership: Organizing in an imperfect world*. London: Sage.

Barnard, C. I. (1948). *Organizations and management*. Cambridge, MA: Harvard University Press.

Bolden, R., Hawkins, B., Gosling, J., & Taylor S. (2011). *Exploring leadership: Individual, organizational and societal perspectives*. Oxford: Oxford University Press.

Bolden, R., Gosling, J., O'Brien, A., Peters, K., Ryan, M., & Haslam A. (2012). *Emerging concepts of academic leadership*. London: Leadership Foundation for Higher Education. doi:10.13140/2.1.1957.6009

Burrell, G., & Morgan, G. (1979). *Sociological paradigms and organizational analysis*. London: Heinemann.

Case, P., Evans, L., Fabinyi, M., Cohen, P., Hicks, C., Prideaux, M., & Mills, D. (2015). Rethinking environmental leadership: The social construction of leaders and leadership in discourses of ecological crisis, development, and conservation. *Leadership*. doi:10.1177/1742715015577887

Case, P., & Gosling, J. (2007). Wisdom of the moment: Premodern perspectives on organizational action. *Social Epistemology, special issue on wisdom and stupidity in management, 22*(4).

Case, P., & Gosling, J. (2010). The spiritual organization: Critical reflections on the instrumentality of workplace spirituality. *Journal of Management, Spirituality and Religion, 7*(4).

Crutzen, P. J., & Stoermer, E. F. (2000) *The Anthropocene in Global Change Newsletter, 41*, 17–18. International Geosphere-Biosphere Programme. Retrieved from http://www.igbp.net/download/18.316f18321323470177580001401/NL41.pdf

Fiedler, F. E. (1964). A contingency model of leadership effectiveness. In L. Berkowitz (Ed.). *Advances in experimental social psychology*. New York: Academic Press.

Fiedler, F. E. (1967). *A theory of leadership effectiveness*. New York: McGraw-Hill.

Fry, L., & Slocum, J. (2008). Maximising the triple bottom line through spiritual leadership. *Organizational Dynamics, 37*, 86–96.

Gemmill, G., & Oakley, J. (1992). Leadership: An alienating social myth? *Human Relations, 45*(2), 113–129.

Grace, M. (2003). The origins of leadership: The etymology of leadership. Paper presented at the Annual Conference of the International Leadership Association. Guadalajara, Mexico.

Grint, K. (2001). *The arts of leadership*. Oxford: Oxford University Press.

Grint, K. (2005). Problems, problems, problems: The social construction of 'leadership'. *Human Relations, 58*(11), 1467–1494.

Habermas, J. (1987) *Theory of communicative action* (Vol. 2). Boston: Beacon Press.

Haslam, S. A., Reicher, S. D., & Platow, M. J. (2011). *The new psychology of leadership: Identity, influence and power*. Hove and New York: Psychology Press.

Hersey, P., & Blanchard, K. (1969). Life-cycle theory of leadership. *Training and Development Journal, 2*, 26–34.

Hersey, P., & Blanchard, K. (1993). *Management of organizational behaviour: Utilizing human resources* (6th ed.). Englewood Cliffs, NJ: Prentice-Hall.

Kaipa, P., & Radjou, N. (2013). *From smart to wise: Acting and leading with wisdom*. San Francisco: Jossey-Bass.

Kellerman, B. (2004). *Bad leadership: What it is, how it happens, why it matters*. Boston, MA: Harvard Business School Press.

Kouzes, J. M., & Posner, B. Z. (2002). *The leadership challenge* (3rd ed.). San Francisco: Jossey-Bass.

Kouzes, J. M., & Posner, B. Z. (2003). *Leadership practices inventory* (3rd ed.). San Francisco: Jossey-Bass.

Linstead, S., Fulop, L., & Lilly, S. (2009). *Management and organization: A critical text*. London: Palgrave.

Rockström, J. Steffen, W., Noone, K., Persson, Å., Chapin, F. S. III, Lambin, E. F., Lenton, T. M., Scheffer, M., Folke, C. Schellnhuber, H. J., Nykvist, B., De Wit, C. A., Hughes, T., van der Leeuw, S., Rodhe, H., Sörlin, S., Snyder, P. K., Costanza, R., Svedin, U., Falkenmark, M., Karlberg, L., Corell, R. W., Fabry, V. J., Hansen, J., Walker, B., Liverman, D., Richardson, K., Crutzen, P., & Foley, J. (2009). A safe operating space for humanity. *Nature, 461*, 472–475.

Rost, J. (1991). *Leadership for the twenty-first century.* Westport, CT: Praeger.

Stodgill, R. M. (1974) *Handbook of leadership: A survey of theory and research.* New York: Free Press.

Tamkin, P., Pearson, G., Hirsh, W., & Constable, S. (2010). *Exceeding expectation: The principles of outstanding leadership.* London: Work Foundation.

Western, S. (2013). *Leadership: A critical text* (2nd ed.). London: Sage.

Western, S. (2014). Autonomist leadership in leaderless movements: Anarchists leading the way. *Ephemera, 14*(4), 673–698.

Wheatley, M., & Freize, D. (2011). Leadership in the age of complexity: From hero to host. *Resurgence, 264.*

4 Valuing

Catherine Cameron

Link to : http://www.resourceobservatory.com

'You can have "growth" – for now – or you can have "sustainable" forever, but not both.

This is a message brought to you by the laws of compound interest and the laws of nature.'
Jeremy Grantham, 'Your grandchildren have no value (and other deficiencies of capitalism)'[1]

LEARNING OUTCOMES

The aim of this chapter is to:

1. Review the megatrends facing the planet.

2. Summarize why an externalities approach can be misleading.

3. Review early work on the limits to growth.

4. Examine the limits to GDP as a measure of value.

5. Consider the range of alternative measures available and the current practice.

This chapter explores the need for economic thinking and measurement that reflects the world as it is today and will likely be tomorrow. Economics as still taught in many institutions today harks back to its 19th century European roots. The world has changed a lot since then. In this chapter you will learn about the concepts of growth, new ways of valuing and measuring what matters, and consider why reframing growth is essential for the successful 21st century business.

Questions for you to consider in the course of this chapter

Why should MBA students consider the debates about growth and GDP?

What do we mean by value?

What are the limits to growth?

How will this insight benefit you in a business context?

We will explore these questions and illustrate how businesses are reframing growth.

Our natural systems face unprecedented environmental challenges, along with social and financial challenges. These system level challenges are not one-offs, or outliers. These are the new normal. An approach to valuing is therefore required that adequately and accurately reflects this. At a minimum this would reflect a better approach to risk management.

---

[1] Jeremy Grantham is the co-founder and chief investment strategist of GMO, an asset management firm. It is one of the largest firms in the world with over $122 billion in assets under management. *GMO Quarterly Newsletter* (2012, February).

Introduction

Global Megatrends

There are a number of big shifts occurring globally. Loosely defined these are referred to as global megatrends. Identifying such global megatrends has been a growth industry over the last few years with a number of sustainability practitioners, collaborations and advisory firms developing their own lists of megatrends. One such is summarized here as:[2]

1   Demographic and social change – with a growing middle class in Asia.
2   Shift in global economic power – moving steadily from West to East.
3   Rapid urbanization – we are now in a more urban than rural world.
4   Climate change and resource scarcity – threats and finite resources
5   Technological breakthroughs – digital transformation at a great pace and large scale.

The developing and emerging economies are driving these megatrends and will be most impacted by them. It is anticipated that by 2030, if not before, the E7 will take over from the G7 economies in leading the new world order. The E7 are currently defined as the four BRICs (Brazil, Russia, India and China) plus Mexico, Indonesia and Turkey. As William Gibson put it: 'The future is already here, it is just not very evenly distributed.'[3]

The Trouble with Negative Externalities

In neo-classical economics an externality is the cost or benefit that affects a party that did not choose to incur that cost or benefit. Externalities can arise as a result of market failure. That is a situation where the allocation of goods and services by a free market is not efficient. Externalities can be positive or negative. Pollution is usually cited as the example of a negative externality, since those who emitted the pollution are not those who suffer from it (pay for it). Pollution from burning fossil fuels has long been understood to lead to damage to public health, to crops and to infrastructure. What is now realized is that the burning of fossil fuels leads to the emission of CO_2 that directly leads to climate change, which adversely affects us at a planetary scale. *The Stern Review* (2006) recognized the need to take the economic concept of externality to scale:

Climate change presents a unique challenge for economics: it is the greatest and widest ranging market failure ever seen.

---

[2] http://www.pwc.com/gx/en/issues/megatrends/index.jhtml (accessed 2014, 16 December). See also BITC, http://www.bitc.org.uk/issues/marketplace-sustainability/global-mega-trends or the European Environmental Agency, http://www.eea.europa.eu/themes/scenarios/global-megatends (accessed 2014, 16 December).
[3] William Gibson, an American-Canadian writer who coined the term cyberspace. Quoted in 1993.

The review went on to say that:

The economic analysis must therefore be global, deal with long time horizons, have the economics of risk and uncertainty at centre stage, and examine the possibility of major, non-marginal change.

This is a succinct summary of the valuing challenge to be explored in this chapter. We first explore the concept of the limits to growth and the limitations of the GDP measure.

Growth and Limits

Economic growth has played a role in advancing society by capturing the increases in GDP or GNP, which can in turn enable improvements in outcomes such as better health, higher levels of education, improved infrastructure, transport and communications, and financial independence. For countries at an earlier stage of development, growth is often still regarded as a first step on the road to achieving a higher standard of living for the population. Since 1972, however, when the Club of Rome produced a report called *The Limits to Growth* (Meadows *et al.*), our understanding of the limits to growth emerged. The report used systems dynamics theory and computer modelling to analyse the long-term causes and consequences of growth in the world's population and material economy. It asked questions such as, 'Are current policies leading to a sustainable future or collapse?' and 'What can be done to create a human economy that provides sufficiently for all?'

Twelve scenarios from the *The Limits to Growth*'s World3 computer model showed different possible patterns of world development over the two centuries from 1900 to 2100. These illustrated how world population and resource use interact with a variety of limits. In reality, limits to growth (LTG) take many forms, but the LTG analysis focused principally on the planet's physical limits in the form of exhaustible natural resources and the finite capacity of the earth to absorb emissions from industry and agriculture. In every realistic scenario the model found that these limits force an end to growth sometime in the 21st century. This can take many forms, for a variety of causes. It could be collapse or it could also be a smooth adaptation of the human footprint to the carrying capacity of the planet. By specifying major changes in policies the model can generate scenarios with an orderly end to growth followed by a long period of relatively high human welfare. *The Limits to Growth* attracted significant controversy and rejection of its scenarios at the time of publication, however, the data available to the present day agrees worryingly well with the projections, as Figure 4.1 illustrates.

The basic conclusions of the LTG stem from 'an understanding of the dynamic patterns of behaviour that are obvious, persistent and common features of the global systems: erodible limits, incessant pursuit of growth and delays in society's responses to approaching limits.' *The next section* explores the origins of the incessant pursuit of growth.

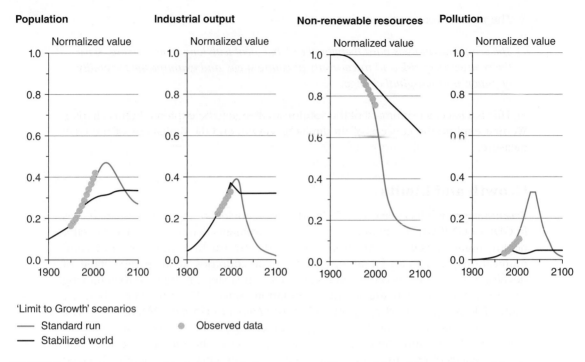

FIGURE 4.1 Comparing *Limit to Growth* Scenarios to Observed Local Data. *Source:* Meadows *et al.*, 1972.

4.0 The Limits to GDP and GNP as Measures of Value

The Impossible Hamster.[4]

New Economics Foundation

This section first reviews the definition, origins and measurement of growth, and highlights its shortcomings. It then explores the fact that what look like small numbers can have big impacts at a global level that are not sustainable. It then considers the relationship between growth and debt.

4.0.1 A Review of Growth Definitions, Valuation and Evolution

Economic growth is simply the increase in the amount of the goods and services produced by an economy over time. It is conventionally measured as the percentage rate of increase in *real gross domestic product, or real GDP*. Classical growth theory

---

[4] Go to https://www.youtube.com/watch?v=bqz3R1NpXzM to see the New Economics Foundation 'Impossible Hamster' animation. This entertaining 1.09 minute cartoon takes you through the reasons why endless growth does not work. Nature does not do this and the early economists did not plan to pursue it. The primacy of GDP is a recent phenomenon.

at the macro level assumes that output (Y) = consumption (C) + investment (I) + government (G) + (exports (X) − imports (M)). The relationship can be written as follows:[5]

$$Y = C + I + G + (X - M)$$

Growth in output results from increases in production factors (physical capital and labour) and productivity, that rises as a result of technological change, including changes in organization and practices. The environment does not play an explicit productive role in this approach. Nor is there a mainstream economic theory that treats resources as if they are finite, although more recently ecological economists have sought to correct this, e.g., Herman Daly, Paul Hawken.[6]

Economic growth can be measured by the increase in the amount of goods and services produced by an economy over time. This is the percentage increase in real gross domestic or national product (i.e., adjusted for inflation).

Gross Domestic Product (GDP) refers to the market value of all officially recognized final goods and services produced *within* a country in a given period.

Gross National Product (GNP) is the market value of all products and services produced in one year by labour and property supplied by the *residents* of a country.

Unlike GDP, which defines production based on the geographical *location* of production, GNP allocates production based on *ownership.*

There are numerous economic growth theories, including the role of increasing productivity, the enabling role of technology, the role of energy conversion, the role of cognitive wealth or the unified growth theory. Recent critiques of economic growth have looked at resource depletion arguments, negative environmental impacts of growth, impacts of greenhouse gas (GHG) emissions on the planet and the need for more equitable growth, as well as empirical observations that, after certain thresholds in developed countries, continuing growth in income and consumption do not lead to higher reported levels of well-being.

As *The Limits to Growth: The 30 Year Update* (Meadows *et al.*, 2004) put it:

> *Public discussions of economic matters are full of confusion, much of which comes from a failure to distinguish between money and the real things money stands for. Our emphasis is placed on the physical economy, the real things to which the Earth's limits apply, not the money economy, which is a social invention not constrained by the physical laws of the planet.*

Some early warnings about the shortcomings of the GNP measure The recognition of the shortcomings a focus on the growth of GNP have been well understood since the early study of political economy. A short chronological sample of critiques is provided *below.*

---

[5] Classical growth theory at the level of the firm assumes that output (Y) is produced using technology (A), physical capital (K), and labour (L). The relationship can be written as follows:

$$Y = f(A, k, L)$$

[6] It can be argued that natural capital is implicitly included within physical capital. The assumption is made that natural capital and physical capital are fully substitutable. The history of Nauru highlights the absurdity of this assumption; see http://en.wikipedia.org/wiki/Nauru.

In 1848 John Stuart Mill looked upon political economy

. . .not as a thing in itself, but as a fragment of a greater whole; a branch of social philosophy, so interlinked with all the other branches that its conclusions [. . .] are only true subject to interference & counter-action from causes not directly within its scope.

Mill expresses concern that the then cornerstones of British economic growth – the division of labour (including the increasing simplicity and repetitiveness of the work) and the growing size of factories and businesses – led to a spiritual and moral deadening.

Simon Kuznets, one of the principal architects of what became the standard way of creating national accounting systems, declared in 1933 that:

. . .the welfare of a nation can scarcely be inferred from a measurement of the national income [and went on to warn in 1962] Distinctions must be kept in mind between quantity and quality of growth, between its costs and return, and between the short and the long term. Goals for more growth should specify more growth of what and for what.

After WWII Schumacher (1973) highlighted that growth had 'subtly moved from being a means to an end, to an end in itself.' Schumacher also introduced the importance of appropriate scale into economics, as well as being one of the first to distinguish between exhaustible and renewable resources. In particular, he noted that an economy cannot continue indefinitely by converting its stocks to income. He also questioned the whole purpose of the economy highlighting that 'good work' and community were important elements of well-being and were being undermined by the pursuit of growth as an end in itself.

Almost from the moment that a system of national accounts was introduced in the UK, one of its key architects, Keynes (1963), warned not to:

overestimate the importance of the economic problem, or sacrifice to its supposed necessities other matters of greater and more permanent significance.

He also understood and recognized that economic growth was originally a means to an end:

The day is not far off when the economic problem will take the back seat where it belongs, and the arena of the heart and the head will be occupied or reoccupied, by our real problems – the problems of life and of human relations, of creation and behaviour and religion.

The shortcomings of GNP as a measure of value   GNP has become the standard measure of the size of an economy and has for several decades been the default metric for economic progress and success. Since at least the post-WWII era the presumption has been that as long as GNP is growing the other things to which we aspire (whether health, wealth, happiness, etc.) will follow through a 'trickle down' process. GNP can be a useful measure in providing information about the state of the economy, as it does now, on lack of growth, stagnation and recession. All these terms currently have negative connotations in mainstream media coverage. This short-term immediate information on whether or not an economy is in recession is very different from recognizing the impacts of growth in the long run, year on year, bigger and bigger.

Immediately after WWII there was an urgent need to rebuild nations and economies, therefore the maximization of production was strongly linked to improving the material welfare of people. However, this focus on increasing production then became the main foundation of the United Nations System of National Accounts, so complementary measures of welfare and societal progress were not pursued. The raft of recent initiatives indicates a growing recognition that the simple GNP measure is not adequate (or is being misused), hence the rise in measures to supplement this, or in some instances provide an alternative (see Box 4.1).

BOX 4.1

The Principle Flaws of GDP as a Measure of Value

1   It is neutral in its measurement of goods and services, adding up 'goods' and 'bads' together. This has also been called 'not measuring filth' by Herman Daly, e.g., nuclear waste, the Dead Zone in the Gulf of Mexico, congestion, pollution, wells drying up. So it fails to capture the negative consequences of growth, including rising GHG emissions, whilst defensive and restorative expenditures such as cleaning up the 'bads', e.g., as oil spills, show up as positively contributing to GDP. A subset of this point is that it does not take account of risk. So a short-term borrowing and spending spree would provide a boost to GDP that would be misleading in the longer term. Or more recently, as Paul Hawken put it: 'At present, we are stealing the future, selling it in the present, and calling it GDP.'

2   Not measuring positive aspects of our lives which are not monetized, such as the natural environment, caring for children, the sick or elderly, housework, or working in the community. As a result GDP can mask the breakdown of social structures and natural habitats; and worse, it can capture this breakdown as economic gain. So the depletion of finite natural capital, whilst treating it as income, is a failing of GDP.

3   It does not capture other aspects that contribute to our well-being and quality of life such as education, health, infant and child mortality, and life expectancy.

4   Empirically, GDP growth can lead to widening inequality – and adverse impacts on social indicators and well-being. The Asian Development Bank's (ADB) Asia 2012 report highlights a recent example of this, showing that inequality widened in the three countries that have been key drivers of the region's rapid economic growth, China, India and Indonesia. The ADB report notes that with a more even distribution of the benefits of growth another 240 million people would have moved out of poverty in the 45 country region (Rhee, 2012).

A famous campaign speech by Robert Kennedy in 1968 at the University of Kansas captures these points:

> Too much and too long, we seem to have surrendered community excellence and community values in the mere accumulation of material things. Our Gross National Product, now, is over eight hundred billion dollars a year, but that GNP counts air pollution and

cigarette advertising and ambulances to clear our highways of carnage. It counts special locks for our doors and the jails for those who break them. It counts the destruction of our redwoods and the loss of our natural wonder in chaotic sprawl. It counts napalm and the cost of a nuclear warhead, and armoured cars for police who fight riots in our streets. It counts the television programs that glorify violence in order to sell toys to our children.

Yet the Gross National Product does not allow for the health of our children, the quality of their education, or the joy of their play. It does not include the beauty of our poetry or the strength of our marriages, the intelligence of our public debate or the integrity of our public officials. It measures neither our wit nor our courage, neither our wisdom nor our learning, neither our compassion nor our devotion to our country; it measures everything, in short, except that which makes life worthwhile.

Source: Retrieved from http://www.jfklibrary.org/Research/Research-Aids/Ready-Reference/RFK-Speeches/Remarks-of-Robert-F-Kennedy-at-the-University-of-Kansas-March-18-1968.aspx.

5   GDP does not take fully or consistently into account improvements in quality and new goods. This is particularly the case with any big changes in technology. So in the last 20 years the move to a digital and interconnected world is captured differently by different countries depending on the hedonic index that they use. So the role of mobile phones, computers and cameras (often now all in one hand-held device compared to two decades ago) is not reflected. Nor are the transformative roles of, e.g., new medicines and medical techniques (keyhole surgery, mapping the human genome, stem cell research, treatment for heart attacks and some cancers, antiretroviral therapy (ART) for HIV, MRI scanning).

6   Using a GDP per capita average ignores the distribution of incomes within a country. Thomas Piketty's book, *Capitalism in the Twenty-first Century*, explores at some length the shortcomings of growth from the perspective of increasing inequality. See also Wilkinson and Pickett's *The Spirit Level*, which highlights the risks of increasing and widening inequality leading to a range of adverse developments, including lower health and social outcomes for all, with more crime and social breakdown.

Along with this there is the challenge of the rise in intangible services in mature economies, which are not susceptible to the same measurement as in an older primary- or secondary-based economy (e.g., agriculture, coal, oil and gas or cars, white and electronic goods and widgets). It is much harder to measure tertiary services like health care (which will be a rising proportion of services in mature economies with ageing populations) and other intangible services such as entertainment.

4.0.2   Small Numbers with Big Impacts

It is helpful to be aware that what can at first appear to be low or small rates of growth, e.g., a 2% annual increase, can have big impacts over long periods of time, as with the US GDP per capita which has grown at an exponential rate of 2% p.a. for the last 200 years. This is due to the power of exponential growth, with its classic hockey stick curve. A growth rate of 2.5% p.a. leads to a doubling of GDP within 29 years, whilst a growth rate of 8% p.a. (a rate met or exceeded by China between 1998 and 2010) leads to a doubling of GDP within 10 years. The challenge of exponential growth of GDP is that the amount that is added grows larger each year.

The outcome is 'speeding up' the use of finite resources that each country needs to keep its GDP measure of production growing. Taken globally this puts huge pressure on all resources, as the compound impacts grow ever larger in a finite world. *The 'Impossible Hamster' link provided at the beginning of this section illustrates this point.*

Ruchir Sharma (2012) highlights that the richer a country is, the harder it is to grow national wealth at a rapid pace. This is now China's position. Very few nations are able to achieve long-term rapid growth. Sharma's whole premise is about searching out where the best growth rates are to come from in the years ahead, recognizing that this is becoming harder. He identifies smaller economies starting from a lower base as those with most potential now, as:

> *China is on the verge of a natural slow down . . . in 1998 for China to grow its $1 trillion economy by 10% it had to expand its economics activities by $100 billion and consume 10% of the world's industrial commodities (oil, copper, steel). In 2011 to grow its $6 trillion economy that fast it needed to expand by $600 billion pa and consume 30% of the world's industrial commodities.*

Even at a 5% to 6% growth rate China will remain the largest single contributor to global growth in the years ahead. An annual growth rate per country can lull the observer into a false sense of what is possible or desirable. Growth at 2% p.a. from 2050 to 2100 would mean a global economy 40 times the size of the economy in 2009 (Jackson, 2009). Or as *The Limits to Growth: The 30 Year Update* succinctly put it, 'often a declining growth rate still produces a rising absolute increment, when a smaller percentage is multiplied by a much larger base.'

4.0.3   Growth and Debt

Importance of growth to a debt-based system: some history   There is a long history of borrowing (whether by governments, individuals or firms), together with a historical prejudice against it, whether expressed in the Bible or as captured by Shakespeare in *Hamlet*: 'Neither a borrower nor a lender be; For loan oft loses both itself and friend, And borrowing dulls the edge of husbandry.'

Borrowing by governments is usually for three main reasons: for investment, for war or for consumption. In the US in 1949 there was a policy disagreement amongst the Council of Economic Advisers to the President about the choice to be made between 'guns or butter'. Those favouring borrowing for consumption argued that an expanding economy (i.e., growth) permitted large defence expenditures without sacrificing an increased standard of living. So the either/or dilemma on war/consumption was neatly avoided because of growth. Those against resigned, warning about the dangers of budget deficits and increased funding of 'wasteful' defence costs.[7]

Current practice   The conventional wisdom has shifted now, so that growth is required *in order* to at least service debt. This goes hand in hand with an understanding that with increased productivity, employment will reduce over time without growth. This means that the challenge of transition to a low-growth economy has these two aspects to overcome.

---

[7] Edwin Nourse, Chairman, Council of Economic Advisers to President Harry Truman.

Since the late 1960s the US has run a deficit, however, although national debt grew, as a percentage of the growing economy it did not increase rapidly. But since the 1970s actuaries have warned that given the ageing of the baby boomers, a fiscal crunch would occur in the US sometime between 2010 and the 2020s. The Clinton administration's economic policies were designed in part to generate budget surpluses that could pay off the deficit before the baby boomers retired and began to draw on Social Security and Medicare. As a result, from 1993 to 2001, the debt to GDP ratio went from 49% to 33%. However, this policy decision was reversed by the incoming administration of George W. Bush. By 2011 debt was equal to GDP at some $14 trillion. By 2012 it reached 119% of GDP: '[w]e are at the outer edge of 200 years of experience' (Friedman & Mandelbaum, 2011) as we enter new territory on how much debt an economy can handle.

In *Breakout Nations*, Sharma compares countries' debt indicators as a means of assessing their breakout potential or the reverse, their vulnerability. He highlights that in India total public debt to GDP is 70%, one of the highest for any major developing country. In China official government debt is low at some 30% of GDP but the debt of companies and households is some 130% of GDP, among the highest levels in emerging markets. This is partly because Beijing ordered banks to issue a huge increase in credit in response to the 2008 crisis. If shadow banking is included, the ratio of debt to GDP rises to 200%: 'levels unseen before, fueling a consumption boom' (Sharma, 2012).

Overall Sharma suggests that 'the liquidity fueled turbo charged boom of the last decade . . . is now unraveling as the cost of funding growth rises', whilst observing that 'never have so many nations grown so fast for so long as they did in the last decade.' He posits that the era of debt-fuelled growth is now coming to an end and suggests that 'failure to sustain growth is the general rule, and that rule is likely to reassert itself in the coming decade'.

Instability

> 'Unbalanced, unco-ordinated and unsustainable.'
> Chinese Premier Wen Jiabao, describing Chinese growth in 2008

The risk of economic instability is reinforced by Coyle (2011), who states that 'market economies are unstable' with 'constant vulnerability to boom and bust', e.g., the mid-1970s OPEC oil price spike or 2008 near-collapse of the global financial system. She suggests that in mature (developed) economies, economic policy has 'borrowed from the future on a significant scale, both through the accumulation of debt in order to finance consumption now, or through the depletion of natural resources and social capital.' The 2008 financial crash was 'an indication of a system wide failure.'

This reasoning is even further developed by Reinhart and Rogoff in their book, *This Time is Different: Eight Centuries of Financial Folly*, in which they highlight the belief by the markets that, this time, there will not be a crash, only for there to be a crash. Learning from debt crises, whether sovereign external debt, domestic debt, banking crises, inflation and modern currency crashes or the most recent subprime crisis, their empirical analysis covers 66 countries over nearly eight centuries and finds a 'near universality of default' in sovereign external debt.

Reinhart and Rogoff examine the fact that the US exhibited all the standard indicators of a country on the verge of a financial crisis prior to the 2008 crash. They find that, on average, government debt rises by 86% in the three years following a banking crisis. 'Again and again countries, individuals, and firms take on excessive debt in good times without enough awareness of the risks that will follow when the inevitable recession hits.' They emphasize that 'the strong connection between financial markets and real economic activity, particularly when financial markets cease to function . . . has made so many of the crises . . . such spectacular historic events.' In contrast, the collapse of the dot.com bubble in global stock markets in 2001 was largely confined to technology stocks and the effect on the real economy was a relatively mild recession. 'Bubbles are far more dangerous when they are fueled by debt, as in the case of the global housing price explosion of the early 2000s.'

Super interconnectedness   What is different this time is the super interconnectedness of the global system, with fragile, highly-leveraged economies, with a concomitant vulnerability to market crises of confidence, e.g., in the Eurozone after the 2008 crisis.

Reinhart and Rogoff suggest that there is a role for multilateral finance institutions, such as the IMF, in both gathering and monitoring data. They propose a new independent international institution to develop and enforce international financial regulations (particularly so that such regulation is independent of national political pressure). However, such a call is predicated on belief in the effectiveness of such institutional approaches in the past. In the complex, non-linear systems that we have now, this may not be an appropriate response, even supposing such an institution could effectively play the role of an enforcer. We have seen how rapidly crisis and collapse can emerge, e.g., in the US, Iceland and Greece, and the risk of contagion and market sentiment.

Uncertainty   In times of uncertainty globalized, highly efficient and standardized economic systems are vulnerable to shocks, as recent events show, with a high risk of contagion due to interconnectedness of systems. There is therefore a need to build in diversity, buffers and redundancy; to promote and enhance resilience. Resilience indicators are increasingly being used to measure the 'health' of systems (ecological, social, economic) rather than a focus on growth. *We will return to this point later in this chapter.*

Different macroeconomic approaches to debt   Approaches to debt and growth vary depending on the underlying approach to value, leading to different policy choices. These can be very broadly characterized as follows:

1   Austerity (monetarism).
2   Prosperity through growth (Keynesian).
3   Prosperity through green growth (green new deal).
4   Prosperity without growth (ecological economics; steady state approaches).

4.1   The Range of Alternative Measures and Current Practice

4.1.1   Going Beyond GDP/GNP: The Range of Other Ways to Value

'Not everything that counts can be measured.

Not everything that can be measured counts.'

Albert Einstein

There have been several attempts to produce an adjusted or alternative growth measure to GDP/GNP. Some of the leading suggestions include:

1   The Report by the Commission on the Measurement of Economic Performance and Social Progress, led by Joseph Stiglitz and Amartya Sen, with Nick Stern and other luminaries, endorsed by the then President of France, Nicolas Sarkozy, in 2009 and in a subsequent book, *Mis-measuring Our Lives*, in 2010.

> *There is a huge distance between standard measures of important socioeconomic variables like growth, inflation, inequalities etc . . . and widespread perceptions. Our statistical apparatus, which may have served us well in a not-too-distant past, is in need of serious revisions.*

The Commission looked at three main areas:

1. The limits of GDP as an indicator of progress or economic performance.
2. The quality of life, a broader view of well-being.
3. Sustainable development and the environment.

It concluded by recommending that conventional economic statistics and reporting should be supplemented with a much wider range of measures including environmental measures and direct measures of well-being.

2   A joint EC, EU Parliament, WWF, Club of Rome and OECD report, *Beyond GDP: Measuring Progress, True Wealth and the Well-being of Nations*, was published in 2007. This has led to the ongoing Beyond GDP initiative which is developing indicators that are as clear and appealing as GDP, but more inclusive of environmental and social aspects of progress.[8]

3   The Human Development Index (HDI) was developed in 1990 as a supplement to the GDP measure. It was created in 1990 by economist Mahbub ul Haq and based on the work of Amartya Sen. It is the most widely used example of this type. Structurally, it consists of three elements:

1. Standard of living (GDP per capita).
2. Life expectancy at birth.
3. Knowledge: a composite measure of education that includes data on literacy and school enrolment.

In 2010 Amartya Sen observed that 'HDI is people-centered . . . GDP is commodity-centered.' The HDI is one of the UN's key headline indicators,

---

[8] www.beyond-gdp.eu/.

and is considered a useful and meaningful measure of a country's development. Norway has been top of the UN's HDI list since 2000, with the poorest African countries at the bottom.

4   The Index of Sustainable Economic Welfare was created in 1989 by Herman Daly and John Cobb.

This index adjusts for the failure to discriminate between 'goods' and 'bads' and thus presents a truer picture. The index includes estimations of the economic cost of many environmental externalities, such as pollution and environmental degradation. A key element is the redefinition of defensive household expenditure (e.g., repair bills, medical bills) and expenditure arising from crime and divorce as costs, and therefore as deductions, rather than additions, to GDP.

5   'Gross National Happiness' (GNH)[9] is a term coined in 1972 by the King of Bhutan as an alternative to GDP. The four pillars of GNH are sustainable development, cultural values, natural environment and good governance. These have then been further classified into nine domains: psychological well-being, health, education, time use, cultural diversity and resilience, good governance, community vitality, ecological diversity and resilience, and living standards. There are 33 indicators to measure the equally weighted nine domains from which the single figure index is constructed. Although there is no exact quantitative definition of GNH, elements that contribute to it are subject to quantitative measurement. Low rates of infant mortality, for instance, correlate positively with subjective expressions of well-being or happiness within a country. The indicators include the concept of 'sufficiency' or, as Coyle characterizes it, 'enough', a concept wholly missing from the GNP measure of growth, where more is always better.

A second-generation GNH concept, treating happiness as a socioeconomic development metric, was proposed in 2006 by Med Jones, the President of the International Institute of Management. The metric measures socioeconomic development by tracking seven development areas including the nation's mental and emotional health. GNH value is proposed to be an index function of the total average per capita of the following measures:

1. Economic wellness: indicated via direct survey and statistical measurement of economic metrics such as consumer debt, average income to consumer price index ratio and income distribution, savings.

2. Environmental wellness: indicated via direct survey and statistical measurement of environmental metrics such as pollution, noise and traffic.

3. Physical wellness: indicated via statistical measurement of physical health metrics such as severe illnesses and obesity.

4. Mental wellness: indicated via direct survey and statistical measurement of mental health metrics such as usage of antidepressants and rise or decline of psychotherapy patients.

5. Workplace wellness: indicated via direct survey and statistical measurement of labour metrics such as jobless claims, job change, workplace complaints and lawsuits.

---

[9] www.grossnationalhappiness.com.

6. Social wellness: indicated via direct survey and statistical measurement of social metrics such as discrimination, safety, divorce rates, complaints of domestic conflicts, and family lawsuits, public lawsuits, crime rates.

7. Political wellness: indicated via direct survey and statistical measurement of political metrics such as the quality of local democracy, individual freedom, and foreign conflicts.

These components further evolved with the development of the One Planet Living Framework by Bioregional and the WWF, as shown in Figure 4.2.

6 The Happy Planet Index (HPI) was developed by the New Economics Foundation (nef) as an efficiency measure that shows the ecological efficiency (unit of environmental output) with which human well-being (long, happy and sustainable lives) is delivered. It was first published in 2006, updated in 2009, 2012 and 2014. The HPI reflects the average years of happy life produced by a given society, nation or group of nations, per unit of planetary resources consumed. It has three separate indicators: life expectancy, experienced well-being and ecological footprint. The first two are multiplied and then divided by the third. A simple traffic light coding system then maps 151 countries. The HPI finds that high levels of resource consumption do *not* reliably produce high levels of well-being and that it is possible to produce these levels without excessive consumption. Costa Rica ranks first in the index, with Vietnam second, the UK 31st, the US 105th, and the three countries at the bottom are Qatar, Chad and Botswana. An interactive map and full index is available at www.happyplanetindex.org/data/.

'Measure what is measurable, and make measurable what is not so.'

Galileo Galilei

7 The trend now appears to be moving towards the approach advocated by Galileo, developing a more nuanced dashboard style approach, as identified by the EU 'Beyond GDP' work and Stiglitz, Sen and Fitoussi (2010). Australia

FIGURE 4.2 The One Planet Living Framework. *Source:* Bioregional website: www.bioregional.com/oneplanetliving

already does this through Measuring Australia's Progress (MAP) with four categories: individuals, the economy, the environment and living together. Canada and Germany have Indexes of Well-being. The OECD has a Better Life Index (Figure 4.3)[10]. This scores 11 areas which enables comparison across countries and regions. The areas are: housing, income, jobs, community, education, environment, civic engagement, health, life satisfaction, safety, and work-life balance. A total of 36 countries now report across these 11 areas (the 34 OECD countries plus Russia and Brazil. Over time a further four countries will join: China, India, Indonesia and South Africa. This set of indicators looks very similar to the now 40-year-old Bhutan GNH measure.

8 *The many elements of happiness and well-being approach* has been further developed and adopted by a range of businesses, most recently by the Aldersgate Group.[11] The December 2014 launch of their report, *An Economy That Works*, highlighted the many elements of happiness and well-being in Figure 4.4. This clearly suggests that GDP is only one component of well-being.

> 'A sustainable future depends on a radical redesign of the global economy that takes into account economic, environmental and social impacts. An Economy That Works *has a framework that can move us farther faster.*'
>
> Dan Hendrix, Chairman and CEO, Interface

9 In the US 20 states are working on 'beyond GDP' metrics. In 2012 Vermont became the first state to pass a law introducing a new metric for measuring economic performance and success. The Genuine Progress Indicator (GPI)

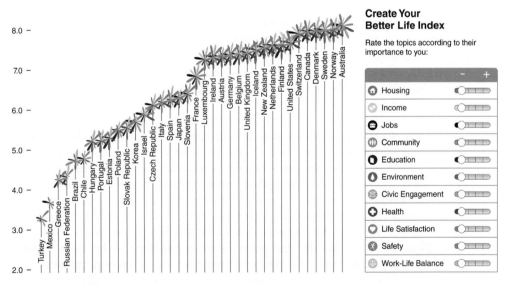

FIGURE 4.3 OECD Better Life Index, Displayed by Rank, All Topics Evenly Weighted. *Source:* OECD, http://www.oecdbetterlifeindex.org.

---

[10] http://www.oecdbetterlifeindex.org.
[11] The Aldersgate Group is an alliance of leaders from business, politics and society that drives action for a sustainable economy.

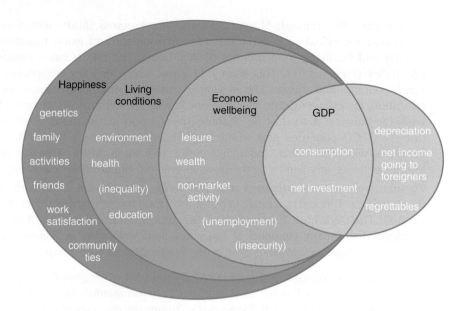

FIGURE 4.4 The Many Elements of Happiness and Well-being. *Source:* The Aldersgate Group, 2014.

takes into account economic, social and natural assets and impacts. It includes measures of welfare, equity, justice and efficiency.[12] In 2011 Vermont's GPI was 40% lower than its GDP, due to rising income inequality and a heavy dependence on fossil fuels. There are 26 ways that GPI can increase, all measured in US dollars. These include increasing energy efficiency, reducing the income gap, and preserving wetlands, forests and farmland.

10 *The valuation of nature, ecosystems, biodiversity* has been a flourishing growth area over the last few years. The importance of ecosystems and biodiversity is explained in aan animation at https://www.youtube.com/watch?v=-bE-Pydad7U (8.55 minutes). The Economics of Ecosystems and Biodiversity is a global initiative launched in 2007, led by Pavan Sukdev, which seeks to explain why it was so important to economies and businesses to recognize the many services delivered by ecosystems and biodiversity, and how important it is not to underestimate the value of these to all beneficiaries, i.e., all of us in some way.[13]An update on the progress made so far is available in The Economics of Ecosystems and Biodiversity (TEEB) Challenges and Responses report published in September 2014 (Sukhdev *et al.*). Its goal is the mainstreaming of the economics of nature. The key points are summarized in Table 4.1. Note that the first point identifies valuation as having a major role to play. Companies increasingly recognize the interconnectedness of their businesses within the environments in which they operate. See, e.g., a video showing that Marks and Spencer are making payments to highland

---

[12] http://accd.vermont.gov/sites/accd/files/Documents/business/CEDS/VT%202020%20CEDS.pdf.
[13] http://www.teebweb.org.

TABLE 4.1   TEEB Challenges and Responses Summary 2014

The TEEB initiative seeks to draw attention to the invisibility of nature in the economic choices we make across the domains of international, national, and local policy-making, public administration, and business. TEEB sees this invisibility as a key driver of the ongoing depletion of ecosystems and biodiversity.

1. TEEB sees valuation, in its diverse social contexts and its many forms, as an important human institution that has a major role to play in stemming the rising tide of degradation of ecosystems and the loss of biodiversity.

2. TEEB has been associated with several challenges and pitfalls that relate to valuation, such as issues of subjectivity, incommensurability, and ecological and economic uncertainty. These legitimate concerns are each specifically addressed by TEEB through its layered approach to valuation, in order to recognize, demonstrate and capture nature's values in appropriate social and ecological contexts.

3. TEEB has also wrongly been associated with the ideas of "putting a price on Nature" or of commodifying or privatizing the global commons. However, TEEB is anything but a cost–benefit based stewardship model for the Earth and its living fabric of ecosystems and biodiversity.

4. TEEB recognizes that values are a product of different worldviews and perceptions on the relationship of humans and nature, and treats them as legitimate and valid in their respective socio-cultural contexts.

5. TEEB argues that the most ethical response for us in the face of risk and uncertainty is not to sit idly until we have perfect information to act, but rather risk to err on the side of precaution and conservation.

6. TEEB argues that, in the absence of valuation, essential and declining ecosystem services are already being 'traded' as commodities, sometimes for an implicit price of zero.

7. A whole range of policy responses is required to solve the largely public goods problems underlying biodiversity loss and ecosystem service degradation - such as changes in land use planning, regulation, community access rights, and schemes for payments for ecosystem services.

8. In the business context, TEEB and 'Corporation 2020' both argue that corporate impacts and dependencies on biodiversity and ecosystem services should be measured and valued as an integral part of management practise and of statutory reporting and disclosure.

9. The TEEB 'community' today represents a wide and strong support base of several hundred economists, ecologists, social scientists, policymakers, administrators, and business professionals, and growing rapidly.

10. The process of identifying nature's values is not to be taken as an end in itself. It should be treated as a means to better communicate and take account of nature's importance in policy- and decision-making, with particular respect to human well-being and to the conservation of natural commons for reasons of inter- and intra-generational equity.

Source: Sukhdev et al. (2014).

communities in Kenya to protect the ecosystem services that are essential to their cut flower industry downstream, at https://www.youtube.com/watch?v=VGHqb1DD3Y0.

Note that the systems thinking approach put forward by TEEB should not be confused with the idea of 'putting a price on nature' or capturing the benefits for commercial gain. The simple goal is the mainstreaming of the economics of nature. This will make it harder to place damage to nature in the negative externalities box *discussed in sections 4.0 and 4.0.1.*

4.1.2 Growth and Limits: A Shift in the Narrative

The Steady or Stationary State   History teaches us that earlier economists from Adam Smith to John Maynard Keynes believed that growth would be a transitional stage and we would then be able to move to a steady or stationary state economy.[14] Smith (1776) reasoned that all economies would eventually reach 'a stationary state' when they had 'acquired that full complement of riches which the nature of [their] soil and climate, and [their] situation with respect to other societies allowed [them] to acquire, which therefore advance not further and which was not going backwards'.
John Stuart Mill (1848) stated that:

> *the increase in wealth is not boundless. The end of growth leads to a stationary state . . . It is scarcely necessary to remark that a stationary condition of capital and population implies no stationary state of human improvement. There would be as much scope as ever for all kinds of mental culture, and moral and social progress, as much room for improving the Art of Living and much more likelihood of its being improved, when minds cease to be engrossed by the art of getting on.*

Paul Gilding predicts a failure of growth, with desperate attempts to restart it, followed by a recognition that the end of growth is being caused by hitting the planet's physical limits. Hence the need 'to design an economy that is rich in progress and increasing prosperity, but not destructive in physical impact' (Gilding, 2011). This could include a cap on and trade system for key resources, shifting the burden of taxation from things we want more of (e.g., jobs) to things we want less of (e.g., pollution, overuse of finite resources). There are a number of other similar proposals, e.g., from the New Economics Foundation (nef), from Tim Jackson and from the Center for the Advancement of the Steady State Economy (CASSE).[15]
As Herman Daly (2008) has commented:

> *The closer the economy approaches the scale of the whole earth the more it will have to conform to the physical behaviour mode of the earth. That behaviour mode is steady state – a system that permits qualitative development but not aggregate quantative growth.*

Daly has long maintained that:

> *Uneconomic growth – the quantative expansion of the economic subsystem – increases environmental and social costs faster than production benefits, making us poorer not richer, at least in high consumption countries.*

A more conservative proposition comes from Friedman and Mandelbaum for 'sustainable economic growth' in *That Used To Be Us* (2011). They posit that the US needs to cut spending, increase revenues and invest in the future all at the same time. 'It may be possible to grow effectively without a plan but there is no way to shrink effectively without a plan.'

---

[14] Although, interestingly, if we go back further than Adam Smith, we find that the economic doctrine of mercantilism viewed government control of foreign trade of great importance for ensuring prosperity and security (16th to late 18th centuries).
[15] www.steadystate.org.

Limits to Growth

'Instead of the goal of maximum linear growth in GDP we should be thinking of maximum well being for minimal planetary input.'

Sir Ian Cheshire, CEO, Kingfisher[16]

As referred to in section 4.0 the limits to growth were explored in the report to the Club of Rome in 1972 (Meadows *et al.*), in the *The Limits to Growth: The 30 Year Update* in 2004 (Meadows *et al.*) and in *2052: A Global Forecast for the Next 40 Years* (Randers, 2012). *The Limits to Growth* reported that global ecological constraints (related to resource use and emissions) would have a significant influence on global developments in the 21st century. It developed the World3 model to simulate inter-actions, with five variables (world population, food production, industrial output, pollution and resource depletion) and three scenarios. It found that in two of the three scenarios, overshoot and collapse occurred by the mid to latter part of the century[17]. A third scenario resulted in a stabilized world.

The 30 Year Update (Meadows *et al.*, 2004) highlighted that:

. . . absolute global rates of change are greater now than ever before in the history of our species. Such change is driven mainly by exponential growth in both popula-tion and the material economy. Growth has been the dominant behaviour of the world socio economic system for more than 200 years.

The update presented 11 possible scenarios for the future, to 2100. *As stated above*, early scenarios show a tendency to overshoot and collapse, and in the last four the modelling assumes deliberate action is taken to stabilize one or more of the variables in order to avoid this.

The updated World3 model provides the following key messages in *2052* (Randers, 2012):

- The global population will stagnate earlier than expected because fertility will fall dramatically in the increasingly urbanized population. Population will peak at 8.1 billion people in 2040 and then decline.
- The global GDP will grow more slowly than expected, because of the lower population growth and declining growth rates in (gross labour) productivity. Global GDP will reach 2.2 times current levels in 2050.
- Productivity growth will be slower than in the past because economies are maturing, because of increased social strife, and because of negative interference from extreme weather.
- The growth rate in global consumption will slow because a greater share of GDP will have to be allocated to investment – in order to solve the problems created by climate change, resource scarcity, and biodiversity loss. Global consumption will peak in 2045.
- As a positive consequence of increased investments in the decades ahead (albeit often involuntary and in reaction to crisis), resource and climate problems will not become catastrophic before 2052. But there will be much

---

[16] Aldersgate Group (2014).

[17] *'Collapse: How societies choose to fail or survive'*, Jared Diamond, 2005, for a history of the collapse of societies over the centuries.

unnecessary suffering from unabated climate damage in the generations around the middle of the century.

- The lack of a dedicated and forceful human response in the first half of the 21st century will put the world on a dangerous and unstoppable track towards self-reinforcing global warming in the second half of the century.
- Slow growth in per capita consumption in much of the world (and stagnation in the rich world) will lead to increased social tension and conflict, which will further reduce orderly productivity growth.
- The short-term focus of capitalism and democracy will ensure that the wise decisions needed for long-term well-being will not be made in time.
- The global population will be increasingly urban and unwilling to protect nature for its own sake. Biodiversity will suffer.
- The impact will differ between the five regions analysed, which are:
  - US.
  - OECD, excluding US (the rest of the industrialized world).
  - China.
  - BRISE (Brazil, Russia, India, South Africa and ten other big emerging economies).
  - Rest of the world (the 2.2 billion people at the bottom of the income ladder).
- The current global economic elite, particularly the US, will live with stagnant per capita consumption for the next generation. China will be the winner. BRISE will make progress. The rest of the world will remain poor. All – and particularly the poor – will live in an increasingly disorderly and climate-damaged world.
- The world in 2052 will certainly not be flat, in the sense of being a level playing field with equal opportunity and connectedness.[18]

4.1.3 Growth and Disruption: Overshoot

The model results of World3 point to overshoot and collapse (or non-linearity) as does any mathematical model of exponential growth. The Intergovernmental Panel on Climate Change (IPCC) scenarios point to the likelihood of overshoot at a 'safe' level of GHG emissions and a breach of the 2°C temperature limit before 2100 under six of the seven main scenarios.[19] An IEA report published in November 2011 warned that we had only five years or fewer left to radically reduce our energy consumption or change our energy mix in order to avoid dangerous global warming.

Paul Gilding (2011) has recently explored what might happen in the coming decades. He suggests a possible scenario where first we address the challenge of climate change in a 'One–Degree War', an idea developed jointly with Jorgen Randers. A Coalition of the Cooling (China, US and EU 27) agree to act together.[20] Adding Russia, India, Japan and Brazil gets to 67% of global emissions. In Phase I, with a start date of 2018, the first five years are a Climate War to achieve a global reduction of 50% of GHG emissions. Phase II is Climate Neutrality over 15 years to achieve zero

---

[18] A reference to Tom Friedman's *The World is flat: A brief history of the 21st century.*

[19] IPCC *Fifth Assessment Report*, SPM, Table 1. Available at http://www.ipcc.ch/pdf/assessment-report/ar5/syr/SYR_AR5_SPMcorr1.pdf.

[20] 60 countries have now ratified the COP21 December 2015 Paris Agreement accounting for almost half of global GHG emissions. www.unfccc.int/paris_agreement/items/9444.php (accessed 2016, 22 September).

net emissions. Phase III is Climate Recovery to 2100. Gilding then moves on to what he characterizes as 'the elephant in the room – growth doesn't work . . . Despite 50-odd years of investigation, science and talk about the limits to growth, little has changed.'

4.1.4 Finite Planetary Limits

'At some point there obviously are physical limits to economic "growth." The economy, after all, is an open subsystem of a larger, but finite, 'ecosystem' which supplies its raw materials and absorbs its wastes.

The growth of the economic subsystem is limited by the size of the overall ecosystem, and by its dependence on the ecosystem.'

Bliese, 1999

The idea of finite planetary limits has been given more impetus with the work of Johann Rockström of the Stockholm Resilience Centre and Will Steffen of the Australian National University. In 2009, together with a group of 26 leading academics, they developed the framework of nine planetary boundaries (Rockström *et al.*, 2009). The concept has excited considerable attention and has now been endorsed by the UN. *See Chapter 1 for more details.*

This idea has subsequently been developed by Oxfam to suggest that planetary boundaries can be combined with social boundaries within a single framework (Raworth, 2012). The social foundation forms an inner boundary, below which are many dimensions of human deprivation, and the environmental ceiling forms an outer boundary. Between these two areas there is a doughnut-shaped area 'which represents an environmentally and socially just space for humanity to thrive'. *See Chapter 1 for more details.*

There is an implicit recognition of the limits to growth and the idea of finite planetary limits in the Unilever Sustainable Living Plan (SLP) (Case Study 4.1) which centres on the idea of doubling its size whilst halving its footprint. This is a good example of the concept of decoupling growth from production. However, it does not get away from the idea of growth. Even if all companies and economies were to adopt this plan we would still have growth. Tim Jackson (2009) explores the weakness of this approach in his book *Prosperity Without Growth*, where he shows the impossibility of achieving absolute decoupling.

Unilever describe the SLP as its 'blueprint for sustainable growth.'

Marks and Spencer provides an illuminating case study of a company that has become more ambitious in its sustainability strategy over three iterations in the last seven years (Case Study 4.2). It originally positioned Plan A as a sustainability strategy that supported doing less harm. Within two years the company found that it generated a good financial return as well as brand value. The most recent iteration has moved across from doing less harm to doing good, 'restoring the natural environment and improving people's lives'.

There is an explicit recognition of the need to eliminate adverse impacts by a pioneering company Interface, which started its journey to Mission Zero in 1994 (see Case Study 4.3). Interface took a more radical approach than Unilever, much earlier. The Interface founder and chair Ray Anderson (1994) challenged Interface to pursue a vision:

To be the first company that, by its deeds, shows the entire world what sustainability is in all its dimensions: people, process, product, place and profits – and in doing so, becomes restorative through the power of influence.

CASE STUDY 4.1

Unilever: Sustainable Living Plan

In 2010 Unilever announced their Sustainable Living Plan (SLP). This contained the then-radical proposition that they would achieve doubling through halving: doubling in size whilst halving their footprint. So in essence this was a growth plan, but recognizing the need to do this whilst reducing adverse impacts, promoting positive impacts and reducing environmental impacts. Unilever describe the SLP as their blueprint for sustainable growth.

The Plan set three big goals, as shown in the figure below:

5 Waste and packaging: halve the waste associated with the disposal of their products.

6 Sustainable sourcing: source 100% of their agricultural raw material sustainably.

7 Fairness in the workplace: advance human rights across their operations and extended supply chain.

8 Opportunities for women: empower 5 million women.

9 Inclusive business: have a positive impact on the lives of 5.5 million people.

Under these three goals Unilever made nine commitments to achieve by 2020. It also made it clear that it did not know how it was going to achieve all of them, but by setting targets it intended to drive change within the company and inspire innovation.

1 Health and hygiene: help more than a billion people improve their health and hygiene.

2 Improving nutrition: work to improve the taste and nutritional quality of all their products.

3 Greenhouse gases: halve the greenhouse gas impact of their products across the life cycle.

4 Water use: halve the water associated with the consumer use of their products.

These goals are a mixture of specific hard targets, e.g., Commitment 3 on GHG reduction, and more generalized commitments, e.g., Commitment 2 on improving nutrition. Several of them extend beyond Unilever's direct operations and down its extended supply chain, e.g., Commitments 7, 8 and 9.

Unilever embarked on a programme of training and change management throughout the organization to support the plan.

Source: Unilever Sustainable Living Plan, 2010. Retrieved from http://www.unilever.co.uk/sustainable-living-2014/unilever-sustainable-living-plan/ (accessed 2014, December 18.

QUESTIONS FOR CLASS DISCUSSION

1. What do these company case studies have in common? What differentiates them?
2. How does setting targets help?
3. Who else do companies need to implement these approaches?

CASE STUDY 4.2
Marks and Spencer: Plan A

Marks and Spencer announced a plan for change when it launched Plan A in 2007, with 100 commitments to achieve in five years. This was updated and Plan A 2020 was introduced with 100 new, revised and existing commitments, with the ultimate goal of becoming the world's most sustainable major retailer.

The evolution of Plan A is shown in the figure below: from 1980s corporate philanthropy to the ambition to be a business that is carbon positive, wastes nothing, restores the natural environment and improves people's lives by 2030. The new pillars of Plan A 2020 are Inspiration, Intouch, Integrity and Innovation.

Recent achievements include zero carbon emissions by cutting emissions and purchasing carbon offsets. In April 2013 M&S extended its scope of responsibility to include all M&S-operated joint venture stores, offices, warehouses and delivery fleets worldwide. M&S also achieved zero operational and construction waste to landfill in the UK and Republic of Ireland. Further, 100% of the palm oil in M&S products is certified by the Roundtable on Sustainable Palm Oil.

Looking ahead, under the Innovation pillar M&S now has a circular economy opportunity commitment, 66, to have completed a detailed review of circular economy opportunities across all parts of the business

M&S'S LONG-TERM PLAN TO MAKE THE BUSINESS MORE SUSTAINABLE

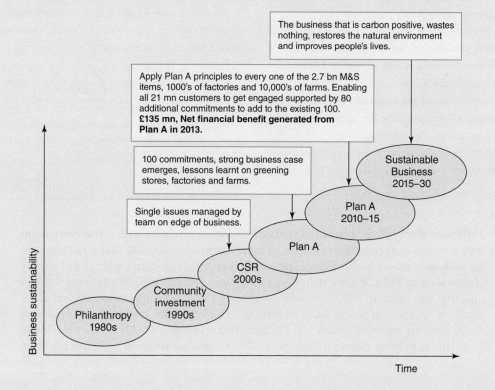

(Continued)

by 2016, together with commitment 67, the aim to publish a report outlining the policy steps that M&S believes would accelerate the journey towards creating a sustainable economy.

M&S CEO Mark Bolland has said, 'We know we cannot deliver Plan A alone and so are stepping up our efforts to lead with others by participating in broader coalitions to deliver sector wide change.'

Source: Marks and Spencer. (2013). Plan A 2020. Retrieved from http://corporate.marksandspencer.com/plan-a/about-plan-a (accessed 2014, December 18).

CASE STUDY 4.3
Interface: Mission Zero

Interface is the world's largest designer and maker of carpet tiles. It has had an ambitious plan since 1994 called Mission Zero. CEO Ray Anderson likened the journey to full sustainability to climbing 'a mountain higher than Everest'. Interface identified seven fronts on Mount Sustainability.

Front 1: eliminate waste: eliminate all forms of waste in every area of the business.

Front 2: benign emissions: eliminate toxic substances from products, vehicles and facilities.

Front 3: renewable energy: operate facilities with 100% renewable energy.

Front 4: closing the loop: redesign processes and products efficiently to close the technical loop using recycled and bio-based materials.

Front 5: efficient transportation: transport people and products efficiently to eliminate waste and emissions.

Front 6: Sensitizing stakeholders: create a culture that uses sustainability principles to improve the lives and livelihoods of all our stakeholders.

Front 7: Redesign commerce: create a new business model that demonstrates and supports the value of sustainability based commerce.

Interface has designed a metrics system to measure its progress, Ecometrics, and it also measures its impact on people through Sociometrics. On Front 1 there has been a 90% decrease in waste to landfill from carpet factories since 1996. On Front 3, 35% of its total energy use is from renewable sources, with five out of seven factories operating with 100% renewable energy.

Source: Interface. (2014). Mission Zero. Retrieved from http://www.interfaceglobal.com/Sustainability/Interface-Story.aspx (accessed 2014, December 18).

Different Entry Points in the Approach to Value and Growth   The entry point for a revision in approach to value runs from government level to major multinationals such as Unilever and Interface, national companies operating with global supply chains such as M&S. It also includes cities, towns and villages. At city level the C40 initiative was created in 2005 to address climate risks and impacts locally and globally.[21] An increase in scope and ambition is reflected in the Rockefeller Foundation creation of an initiative called 100 Resilient Cities (100RC) in 2013 (see Case Study 4.4). This is helping cities around the world become more resilient to the physical,

---

[21] http://www.c040.org/about.

CASE STUDY 4.4

100 Resilient Cities

100RC supports the adoption and incorporation of a view of resilience that includes not just shocks such as earthquakes, fires or floods but also the stresses that weaken the fabric of a city on a day-to-day or cyclical basis. Examples of these stresses include high unemployment; an overtaxed or inefficient public transportation system; endemic violence; or chronic food and water shortages. By addressing both the shocks and the stresses, a city becomes more able to respond to adverse events, and is overall better able to deliver basic functions in both good times and bad, to all populations. 100RC describes its approach as holistic and proactive. 100 RC states that:

> While sustainability is about putting the world into long-term balance amidst the depletion of natural resources, resilience looks for ways to make systems endure and even thrive in an

imbalanced world. Resilience is also broader than DRR [disaster risk reduction], as the latter concept is about reducing the damage caused by natural hazards while resilience is about developing a proactive and integrated plan addressing both shocks and stresses, from natural disasters and to adverse socio-economic trends. In essence, resilience doesn't involve merely coping and adaptive strategies, but also transformative actions to make cities better, for both the short and long-term, the good times and bad.

100RC has developed a City Resilience Framework, working with the firm ARUP, available at http://www.100resilientcities.org/resilience#/-_/.

Source: http://www.100resilientcities.org

social and economic challenges that are a growing part of the 21st century. At town level the Transition Town movement originated in 2006 and now has over 1,100 initiatives in over 43 countries.[22]

4.2 Rethinking Growth

'GDP tells you nothing about sustainability.'

Joseph Stiglitz

4.2.1 What is the Purpose of Growth?

Earlier economists[23] have recognized that the optimum or desirable rate of growth is not the maximum possible growth now, but rather growth that takes due account of the future, including the future health of the economy. The big question posed by

---

[22] https://www.transitionnetwork.org/map.
[23] Frank Ramsey, Partha Dasgupta.

Diane Coyle was, 'How to run the economy as if the future mattered?' Or, as *The Limits to Growth: The 30 Year Update* (Meadows *et al.*, 2004) asked, 'Growth of what? For whom? At what cost? Paid by whom? What is the real need here and what is the most direct and efficient way for those who have the need to satisfy it? How much is enough? What are the obligations to share?'

A consultation with over 400 business leaders asked them to explain the purpose of a good economy (Cambridge Institute for Sustainability Leadership, 2006). Their response was, 'The fundamental purpose of a good economy is to steadily improve the well-being of all people, now and in the future, with due regard to equity, within the constraints of nature, through the active engagement of all its participants.'

They identified ten attributes of a good economy; that it would be:

1 Fulfilling.
2 Inclusive.
3 Farsighted.
4 Developing.
5 Equitable.
6 Participatory.
7 Innovative.
8 Sustainable.
9 Diverse.
10 Accessible.

They also identified ten failings of current economies, as shown in Table 4.2.

4.2.2 Green Growth, Sometimes Referred to as Low Carbon, Climate Resilient Growth[24]

New characterizations of growth move beyond the simple measure of increasing GDP and towards a more balanced view, closer to what has been called sustainable development. If growth is 'quantitative increase in the physical dimensions of the economy', i.e., producing more and more, then sustainable development suggests a more balanced 'qualitative improvement' across a range of indicators. The conventional definition from the 1987 Brundtland Commission[25] is development that 'meets the needs of the present without compromising the ability of future generations to meet their own needs.' A new, simpler, shorter version is 'Enough, for all, forever.'[26]

---

[24] The OECD defines green growth as being 'about able to foster economic growth and development, while ensuring that the earth's natural assets continue to provide the resources and environmental services on which our wellbeing relies.' Retrieved from http://www.oecd.org/greengrowth and http://www.oecdobserver.org/news/fullstory.php/aid/3542/The_OECD_Green_Growth_Strategy.html#sthash.2yMm9TGA.dpuf (accessed 2015, September 21).

[25] *Our Common Future*, also known as the *Brundtland Report*, was published in 1987 by the UN World Commission on Environment and Development (WCED). Its targets were multilateralism and interdependence of nations in the search for a sustainable development path.

[26] Professor Paul Younger, Newcastle University Campaign for Sustainability, 2012.

TABLE 4.2 10 Failings of Current Economies

Failing	Description
1. Lack of education	There is a lack of education and awareness around the links between the economy and sustainability
2. Governance failings	Governments and institutions are ineffective in providing good governance and appropriate policies
3. Short-term focus	Political processes, economic pressures and financial markets prejudice against long-term thinking
4. Unfair distribution	The economy creates and maintains inequity in opportunity, power, wealth and well-being
5. Human weakness	Traits such as selfishness and greed are encouraged and exacerbated by the capitalist system
6. Inappropriate incentives	Market failure and protectionist interventions create incentives for unjust and unsustainable trade
7. Cost externalization	Prices fail to capture social and environmental costs and therefore undervalue people and nature
8. Divided purpose	There is a lack of collective consensus on the long-term purpose or goals of a good economy
9. Unsuitable values	The values underlying the current economic system may be incompatible with sustainability
10. Misleading measures	Current economic measures are poor indicators of quality of life, social well-being and environmental integrity

Source: CISL (2006).

This newer version of growth has been called 'green growth' or even more recently and specifically 'low carbon, climate resilient growth'. It has strong advocates from the Grantham Research Institute, led by Lord Stern and the Korean-based Global Green Growth Institute. As Stern (2006) has stated:

> *We can and must, now and simultaneously, handle the short-term crisis, foster sound development and economic growth in the medium term, and protect the planet from devastating climate change in the long term. To try to set the three tasks against each other as a three-horse race is as confused analytically as it is dangerous economically and environmentally. In particular, the developed world must demonstrate for all, especially the developing world, that low-carbon growth is not only possible, but that it can be a productive, efficient and attractive route to overcome world poverty. It is indeed the only sustainable route.*

The World Bank has recently joined the queue endorsing the concept of Inclusive Green Growth in a new policy paper.[27] This states that:

---

[27] http://siteresources.worldbank.org/EXTSDNET/Resources/Inclusive_Green_Growth_May_2012.pdf.

Inclusive green growth is the pathway to sustainable development. Green growth also requires improved indicators to monitor economic performance. National accounting indicators like GDP measure only short-term economic growth, whereas indicators like comprehensive wealth – including natural capital – help us determine if growth is sustainable in the long run.

GGGI is working in 16 countries and plans to expand work in 10 more.[28] Countries as diverse as the EU and India are pursuing policies with strong green growth elements. Even if they are not, they are labelled this way, such is the popularity of the term. The World Bank identifies the four channels for green growth as input, efficiency, stimulus and innovation effects. The GGGI suggests that the four keys to success are institutionalization, technology, capacity building and financing. This is an essentially technocratic approach to what is a politically and socially challenging country-level transition, with a unique set of drivers and barriers in each country.

QUESTIONS FOR CLASS DISCUSSION

1. What is good about the green growth approach? Why is it so popular?
2. What is the major shortcoming of the green growth approach?

Summary

'Growth will be at the expense of future generations, but it makes the GNP numbers look good today.'

T. S. Eliot, 1949

Valuation – both of *what* and *how* – is key to developing an appropriate response to the system-level challenges facing our planet. GDP is a limited measure that was never intended to achieve the dominant position it occupied in the late 20th century. There are now a range of other reasonable options available. These can be used as well as, or instead of, GDP, depending on the user and purpose of the valuation. These options have high-level backing from a respectable number of established governments, companies and cities. The importance of including environmental and social measures of value, alongside economic measures, is now widely supported.

There is significant attraction and traction to the green growth path, but the limits of this approach are apparent, if weight is given to the earlier arguments *in this chapter*, such as ecological and social boundaries.

---

[28] http://gggi.org/about-gggi/programs-plan-history/update. Green Growth Planning, 2012.

The time-frame is important. Using the work that defined a safe and just space for humanity *in section 4.1.4* (Raworth, 2012) and the findings from the World3 model (Randers, 2012) suggests the overwhelming importance of living within planetary boundaries. These are not linear limits, but tipping points, beyond which the system shifts into more unstable and undesirable states which are not susceptible to modelling or management. This has relevance to insurance, accounting and actuarial work around risk and uncertainty, as it introduces the precautionary principle through the recognition of safe operating limits. It is consistent with current scientific research.

The main points from this chapter are:

♦ Growth (GDP/GNP) is not a good measure of overall value.

♦ This is now widely recognized, with a number of other measures of value available.

♦ These measures incorporate social and environmental metrics on equal footing with economic metrics.

♦ Several governments have developed alternative measures.

♦ Cities and towns are also rethinking what to value and how to measure it.

♦ Companies and alliances of companies are at the forefront of practical work revaluing, and then measuring, what matters. The transition now is from reducing impact to a closed loop model.

QUESTIONS FOR CLASS DISCUSSION

1 List the principal failings of GDP/GNP as a measure of value.
2 Discuss at least three of the alternative measures of value, their advantages and shortcomings.
3 Compare the approaches of three countries to growth, e.g., Bhutan, Norway and the US.
4 Compare the approaches of at least three companies to measuring value.

References

Abdallah, S., Michaelson. J., Shah, S., Stoll, L., & Marks, N. (2012). *The happy planet index: 2012 report: A global index of sustainable well-being.* London: New Economics Foundation.

The Aldersgate Group. (2014). *An economy that works.* Retrieved from http://aneconomythatworks.org/content/uploads/2014/12/AETW-Report-LowRes.pdf.

Anderson, R. (1994). *Confessions of a radical industrialist: Profits, people, purpose: Doing business by respecting the earth.* New York: St Martin's Press.

Bliese, J. R. F. (1999). Conservatism and the ideology of growth. *Modern Age,* 41(2), 117.

Cambridge Institute for Sustainability Leadership (CISL). (2006). *The sustainable economy dialogue: Report and reflections.* Retrieved from http://www.cisl.cam.ac.uk/publications/publication-pdfs/sed-report.pdf

Coyle, D. (2011). *The economics of enough: How to run the economy as if the future matters.* Princeton, NJ: Princeton University Press.

EC, EU Parliament, WWF, Club of Rome and OECD joint report. (2007). Beyond GDP: Measuring progress, true wealth and the well-being of nations. Conference Proceedings. Retrieved from http://ec.europa.eu/environment/beyond_gdp/proceedings/bgdp_proceedings_intro_ses1.pdf

Eliot, T. S. (1949) *Christianity and culture.* New York: Harcourt Brace.

Daly, H. *A Steady-State Economy.* Sustainable Development Commission. Retrieved from http://www.sd-commission.org.uk/publications/downloads/Herman_Daly_thinkpiece.pdf (accessed 2008, April 24).

Diamond, J. (2005). *Collapse.* New York: Viking.

Friedman, T. (2005). *The world is flat: A brief history of the 21st century*. London: Allen Lane.

Friedman, T., & Mandelbaum, M. (2011). *That used to be us*. London: Little, Brown.

Gilding, P. (2011). *The great disruption: How the climate crisis will transform the global economy*. London: Bloomsbury.

IEA. (2011, November). *World energy outlook 2012*. Paris: OECD Publishing.

Jackson, T. (2009). *Prosperity without growth*. London: Earthscan.

Jones, M. (2006). *The American pursuit of unhappiness: Gross National Happiness (GNH), a new socioeconomic policy*. Executive White Paper. Las Vegas, NV: International Institute of Management.

Keynes, J. M. (1963) *Essays in persuasion*, New York: W. W. Norton & Co.

Kuznets, S. (1933). *Seasonal variations in industry and trade*. New York: NBER.

Meadows, D., Randers, J., Meadows, D., & Behrens, W. W. (1972). *The limits to growth*. Report for the Club of Rome. New York: Universe Books.

Meadows, D., Randers, J., & Meadows, D. (2004). *The limits to growth: The 30 year update*. White River Junction, VA: Chelsea Green.

Mill, J. S. (1848). *Principles of political economy* (7th edn., 1909). London: Longmans, Green and Co.

Randers, J. (2012). *2052: A global forecast for the next 40 years*. White River Junction, VT: Chelsea Green Publishing.

Reinhart, C. M., & Rogoff, K. S. (2009). *This time is different: Eight centuries of financial folly*. Princeton, NJ: Princeton University Press.

Raworth, K. (2012, February). *A safe and just space for humanity: Can we live within the doughnut?* Oxford: Oxfam Discussion Paper. Available at https://www.oxfam.org/sites/www.oxfam.org/files/dp-a-safe-and-just-space-for-humanity-130212-en.pdf

Rhee, C. (2012). *Asian development outlook 2012: Confronting rising inequality in Asia*. Asian Development Bank. Retrieved from http://hdl.handle.net/11540/108. License: CC BY 3.0 IGO

Rockström, J., Steffen, W., Noone, K., Persson, Å., Chapin III, F. S., Lambin, E., Lenton, T. M., Scheffer, M., Folke, C., Schellnhuber, H., Nykvist, B., De Wit, C. A., Hughes, T., van der Leeuw, S., Rodhe, H., Sörlin, S., Snyder, P. K., Costanza, R., Svedin, U., Falkenmark, M., Karlberg, L., Corell, R. W., Fabry, V. J., Hansen, J., Walker, B., Liverman, D., Richardson, K., Crutzen, P., & Foley, J. (2009). *A safe operating space for humanity. Nature*, 461 (2009, September 23). Available at http://www.nature.com/nature/journal/v461/n7263/full/461472a.html

Schumacher, E. F. (1973) *Small is beautiful. Economics as if people matter*. London: Blond and Briggs.

Sen, A. (2010). *The idea of justice*. London: Penguin.

Sharma, R. (2012). *Breakout nations: In pursuit of the next economic miracles*. London: Penguin.

Smith, A. (1904). *An enquiry into the nature and causes of the wealth of nations* (1776, 5th ed.). London: Methuen and Co.

Stern Review. (2006). *The economics of climate change*. Cambridge: Cambridge University Press.

Stiglitz, J., Sen, A., & Fitoussi, J-P. (2009). Report by the Commission on the Measurement of Economic Performance and Social Progress, 9. Retrieved from http://www.stiglitz-sen-fitoussi.fr/en/index.htm

Stiglitz, J., Sen, A., & Fitoussi, J-P. (2010). *Mis-measuring our lives: Why GDP doesn't add up*. New York: The New Press.

Sukhdev, P., Wittmer, H., & Miller, D. (2014). The economics of ecosystems and biodiversity (TEEB): Challenges and responses. In Helm, D., & Hepburn, C. (Eds.). *Nature in the balance: The economics of biodiversity*. Oxford: Oxford University Press.

Wilkinson, N., & Pickett, K. (2009). *The spirit level: Why more equal societies almost always do better*. London: Allen Lane.

5 Collaborating

Ward Crawford

'There exists but one system of ethics for men and for all nations – to be grateful, to be faithful to all engagements under all circumstances, to be open and generous, promoting in the long run even the interests of both.'

Thomas Jefferson

LEARNING OUTCOMES

This chapter will enable you to:

1. Develop a flexible approach to how people and organizations work together, balancing the benefits and costs of both competition and collaboration.

2. Understand the basic principles, drivers and structures associated with initiating and managing collaborative arrangements.

3. Understand the key areas of risk and opportunity associated with collaborations between stakeholders.

4. Recognize the relevance and usefulness of different stakeholder perceptions of value.

5. Understand and describe some basic approaches to overcoming conflict and disagreement.

Interacting with others is an everyday part of human society, but rarely follows the ethical framework for 'all engagements under all circumstances' suggested by Thomas Jefferson. Even he, it seems, found it hard to keep to those particular guidelines.

This chapter looks at how particular social interactions can be transformed into collaboration, and at how the development of this as a capability can contribute to our facing the sustainability challenges implicit in the words 'One Planet – in spite of our differences'.

We will consider collaboration across various dimensions of human interaction: between people sharing very similar outlooks and working towards closely aligned objectives, such as the collaborative activities within large organizations considered by Hansen (2009); between different organizations sharing an operational environment, but perhaps representing quite different sectoral ambitions and aims, such as the approaches to partnership for sustainability considered by Gray and Stites (2013); and those many occasions when a multiplicity of disparate stakeholders come together around a particular issue, each championing their own interests, perspectives and hopes, such as the analysis of multistakeholder processes considered by Hemmati (2002).

The chapter also reflects an observation that much business education fails to recognize the complexities and difficulties of working alongside others in shared environments, especially where this spans organizational or sectoral boundaries.

Introduction

To start with, however, a simple question must be posed: 'Why collaborate at all?' Collaboration is not an activity performed on its own, for its own sake: rather, it is undertaken to facilitate something else of describable purpose and desired outcome. That may be the implementation of a project or change programme, the development of policies or standards, the creation of an environment suitable for the accumulation of knowledge, or the support of innovation. Whatever the reason, collaboration is a facilitating activity that is expected to help make it easier to address an identified challenge, the effects of which are judged to impact on more than one party, and that makes it relevant for all of them to work together. And there are few challenges as big, complex or relevant as the ones humankind must face together over the coming decades.

A host of 'compacts', 'consortia', 'alliances', 'partnerships' and 'multilateral initiatives' have been initiated in response; yet the evidence of just how well we can do this is patchy at best. After the Rio +20 meeting in 2012 closed without agreement on binding commitments to reduce global carbon emissions, the environmental commentator George Monbiot (2012) – never one to resist a contentious statement – wrote that 'the greatest failure of collective leadership since the First World War . . . marks, more or less, the end of the multilateral effort to protect the biosphere'.

Yet in spite of such high-profile failures suggesting otherwise, we all know by experience that working with and through other people to get more than the simplest of things done is not only necessary, but is fortunately also possible. This is as true whether trying to meet a set of personal objectives at home or work, or developing an idea or project spanning multiple organizational boundaries and involving lots of people from different backgrounds. The bigger the task or the problem, the greater the number of people likely to be involved – and the more likely that plenty of people will want to be involved. And what is true for individuals or groups is even more the case for organizations. So just how can we make such interactions more fruitful? How can we be more successful at turning them into successful collaborations?

5.0 Images of Working Together

An immediate challenge is the variety of language used. Words such as 'collaboration', 'partnership', 'co-operation' and 'alliance' are often used interchangeably, or at least with a degree of flexibility that makes it hard to understand just what sort of interaction is being described, what forms of relationship are implied, what actions and behaviours might be involved, or what timescales are being proposed. The same words are used to describe formal, highly invested engagements expected to last many years, as well as short-term arrangements assumed as needing limited commitment. Even the word 'collaborator' by itself can carry negative connotations. This section explores this variety of meaning, and its impact on our willingness to commit ourselves alongside others in common purpose.

5.0.1 Relationships

Our first image for the exploration of the language of collaboration is that of the relationship. It is one with which we are all intimately familiar through our own personal and family experiences, and by extension it reveals much about how people approach working together.

Relationships are rarely fixed; rather, they tend towards ever closer or ever more distant levels of engagement and commitment. The motivations and factors that influence the direction of travel are therefore important: is this particular relationship disposable, for the short term only; or is it one that I want to last, and to see develop and grow? And if so, what does that say about what I will put into it, and what I expect to gain from it?

This suggests that relationships might often imply – unpleasant as it might seem – considerations of 'exchange', where value of various kinds is transacted between parties to satisfy their differing needs. Expressed in the language of commerce, this is the relationship between a customer and a supplier, one supplying goods or services in exchange for money, or bartered for other goods of equivalent value. Neither are there any restrictions on what these 'other goods' might be. The complexity created by this potential, and by different perceptions of what they might be worth, is at the root of many relationship problems; but it can also be leveraged to create opportunities for closer and more valued levels of connectivity. But even when this latter dynamic is in place it can be seen that exchange-based transactional relationships remain as simple variations on the customer/supplier interaction, albeit with both roles being held simultaneously by both parties.

This commercial imagery also reveals that the permanence of the relationship might be limited where a 'customer' begins to perceive the 'supplier's' offer as undifferentiated or easily replicated at lower invested cost, in which case access to an alternative (that is, a competitor) may lead to switching and so to the end of that particular engagement. And indeed, that may be the correct response, as there can be no assumption of permanence to any collaboration unless all parties find it of value to themselves. It is in establishing how this value is surfaced and made visible that marks the continuance of a successful **transactional** relationship.

Longer lasting and closer relationships, however, show greater degrees of affiliation between parties, with each prepared to change aspects of their own behaviour and actions – their 'offer' – to facilitate the effectiveness, efficiency, or simply the satisfaction of the other. There is a willingness to compromise some aspect of internal perspective of value in a way that suits the other party, and allows the relationship to continue and develop. Returning to the language of commerce, such **facilitative** relationships create a degree of differentiation from alternatives by improving the compatibility of the parties one with each other, making collaboration more valuable and more likely to last. Such thinking is at the core of collaborative approaches to supply chain management, such as Collaborative Planning, Forecasting and Replenishment (CPFR).

Taking this further means making reciprocated commitments of resources with the sole purpose of enhancing the relationship, with the benefit of that investment often concentrated with the other party, but in ways that integrate the way the parties are equipped to work together. This also makes the severing of the relationship more difficult and costly for all concerned. Möller and Wilson (1995) called this stage of development in a relationship **integrative**.

There is nothing to suggest that any particular relationship could or should progress linearly from being transactional in nature, through a facilitative phase, to reach an integrative zenith; a relationship might exhibit aspects of all three forms simultaneously, sitting anywhere in the relationship zone illustrated in Figure 5.1. And so too might a collaborative venture need to be constantly reshaped to reflect the changing needs and value perceptions of some participants, with the others changing or even compromising their own in response.

5.0.2 Systems

Systems theories are rooted primarily in the biological and engineering sciences: the former has introduced consideration of environmental influences and ecosystems adaptation, as developed into a 'General Systems Theory' by von Bertalanffy (1956); the latter has put more emphasis on outcomes, measurement and control. Both are concerned with how distinct and separate elements or components can work together within a bigger, shared context. Systems Theory is a complex topic in itself, so as an image to explore the language and meaning of collaboration we will look only at the ways in which systems are described (see Figure 5.2).

First of all, these 'distinct and separate elements or components' can be regarded as **subsystems**; only when they operate together can the potential of the system as a whole be observed, even if each in its own way achieves a clear outcome. But this creates something of a Russian Doll problem; at what point does one stop defining any collection of subsystems as anything other than yet another subsystem? This question leads to a conclusion that systems must have **boundaries**, within which system activities and subsystems operate. Outside this boundary lies the **environment**

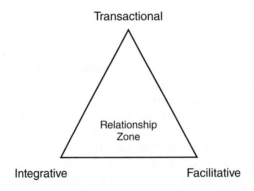

FIGURE 5.1 The Relationship Zone.

GROUP EXERCISE 5.1

Consider your own personal relationships. In what ways might the other people concerned think that you have treated them in a transactional way, or how have you felt being treated that way? In what ways are you facilitative? How do you demonstrate being integrative? How have misunderstandings in what approaches are most appropriate damaged past relationships?

within which the system operates and is contained, and from which **drivers** shape system responses. Without a boundary it is impossible to define a system, and this is a key issue when applying systems thinking to collaboration; there will always be actual or potential stakeholders wishing to extend the boundary to include themselves. The concept of the boundary is implicit in the One Planet idea.

Systems also illustrate the concepts of **emergence** and **hierarchy**: when individual components and subsystems interact, they allow a property to emerge that could not exist before in any of the component parts, at any lower hierarchical level. This can be a source of great potential and innovation: many opportunities for 'Big Data' for instance, both commercial and for wider societal benefit, have emerged through the interaction between different technological and social developments, not originally planned or predicted when those individual initiatives were introduced. For instance, the adoption by many people of a 'quantified life', capturing reams of data about their own physiological responses and changes, and communicated constantly

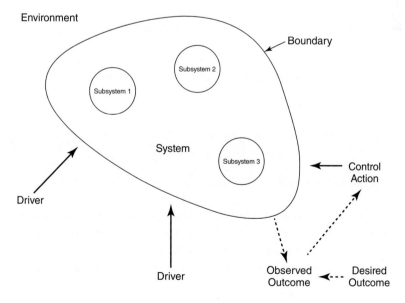

FIGURE 5.2 Simplified Systems Model.

via social media, is providing medical researchers with analytical opportunities undreamt of just a few years past: an unplanned collaboration is being made possible. But emergence is also seen in the many unintended consequences flowing from the ways individually positive innovations interact with each other: the pharmaceutical industry is as much concerned with the way a new drug will interact with other active compounds as in any side effects of that drug alone. The concept of emergence also has great relevance in collaboration: none of the parties involved needs to actually set a common aim as its own individual objective, if the act of collaborating with others allows it to emerge. In systems thinking emergence is not the same as outcome, but the two can in time be conflated if an unexpected but determinable outcome arises.

Our final systems theory principle is that a system will exhibit characteristics of **communication** and **control** in **adaptation**; that is, if there is some specific outcome expected of the system (even if that is simply expressed as 'continuance') then there must be the measurement and communication of any differences between actual and expected states, to prompt system components to adjust their actions such that any gap is closed. James Lovelock (1995) has popularized the idea of the planet Earth as a single adaptive system that he calls by the name of the Greek goddess Gaia. Gaia as a system may well adapt such that she will continue; that will not however guarantee that all subsystems contained within her boundary, including the many activities of humankind, would themselves continue unchanged. Many may have to be altered or even expunged in the pursuit of Gaia's adaptation.

5.0.3 Networks

There is much more to the study of Network Theory than can be summarized here, but its key focus on the position of an entity within a network of other actors, and the variety of roles and functions it can take in that network, has much to inform our consideration of the language of collaboration. One particular interpretation of network theory is the Value Net, a term coined by Nalebuff, Brandenburger and Maulana (1996) to challenge the simplified linearity inherent in the concept of the Value Chain in commercial relationships. They in turn simplify the complex workings of the commercial ecosystem into just four network interactions: between an entity and

GROUP EXERCISE 5.2

Consider the issue of intergovernmental efforts to tackle climate change using systems concepts and principles. Draw this out as a system using the simplified systems model illustrated in *Figure 5.2*, identifying where you have found evidence of emergence, and compare your version with one developed by others. What similarities are there, and what is different? How would you adjust your model in response?

each of its grouped customers, suppliers, competitors and what they defined as complementors. It is thinking about this last grouping that interests us most here, as it has much to reveal about the potential for collaboration in networks.

In its simplest form a complementor is another entity (or group of entities) that creates opportunities for mutual benefit for a different entity: a typical example is that a construction company building roads has no direct commercial relationship with automobile manufacturers, but each is essential to the sustainable success of the other. Another example is the mutual interdependence between the increased computing power of ever faster microprocessors and the processing demands of ever more complex software: each depends on the progress of the other.

More relevant, however, is how different players in a network might redefine their roles, and develop characteristics more akin to complementors than to more traditionally defined roles such as suppliers, customers or even competitors. A customer might also be a complementor if their consumption of an offering makes it more relevant to other users: passionate early adopters fulfil this role in fashion and technology. Similarly a supplier of a required input might be capable of broadening the market for a later-stage offering, thereby becoming a complementor (see *Case Study 5.1* on Green and Black's *later in this chapter*). Much regulatory effort to encourage competition is rooted in an economic judgement that this will grow overall economic value by enforcing complementarity in growing a market.

Competitors might also choose voluntarily to influence their common environments, paying due attention to the constraints imposed by competition law. An example is the creation of the 'Java Fund' in 1996, initiated by a number of otherwise fiercely competitive hardware and software companies to seed an ecosystem for the Java platform: all participants benefited from its increased relevance and developing critical mass. Initiatives like this are called 'open' complements, as participation in the ecosystem is freely open to all. Complements can also be closed, limiting access to participants in some way; the siting of branded coffee shops in bookstores is a common example of this. Another interpretation of this was described Pisano and Verganti (2008) as they considered open and closed forms of collaboration in resourcing innovation, reflecting different approaches to defining the roles and contributions of the various participants, and how their contributions might be managed.

A development of Network Theory in this context is the work done by Greve *et al.* (2014), where the formal and deliberate construction of portfolios of networked relationships to develop degrees of what they called 'Network Advantage' is described, including efforts to bring more distant connections together in ways that exploit the advantages of weak ties identified by Granovetter (1983). They too consider forms of complementarity, with partners combining different capabilities and knowledge – that is, different resources – to meet determined objectives. This is contrasted with compatible partnerships where resources are much more similar, and where their combination instead focuses on bringing scale advantages. This kind of language also reveals some blurring of the lines between Network Theory and Resource-Based Views (RBV), which consider organizations as working to construct a unique portfolio of resources with which they can compete – some of which they will be happy to learn through collaborations with other organizations within their networks, and also Resource Dependency Theory, where those portfolios of resources are not learned and adopted, but rather accessed or influenced vicariously through a network of partnerships.

5.0.4 Metaphors

There are many other images used in the language of collaboration: metaphors can help explore these. We construct metaphors when we use one thing to describe something else, often taking the characteristics of the familiar to help illuminate those of the unfamiliar. They can prompt us to 'understand the complex and para-doxical' (Morgan, 1986, p.13), and indeed some of the metaphors suggested by Morgan in his analysis of organizations also reflect ways in which individuals and organizations are described when working together.

For instance, when we think of **machines** we are prompted with images of (relative) predictability and control: design a mechanism properly, apply the right level of measurement, feedback and control, and the same things might be expected to happen each time it operates – a desired outcome is suggested as more or less certain and predictable. Such mechanistic (or deterministic) thinking is quite domi-nant in much business education and also in the way many organizations plan and organize their activities; in a collaborative engagement this can lead to expectations that all parties will play their roles exactly as expected and as planned, and create vulnerabilities when this does not happen.

Thinking of **organisms**, however, is much less suggestive of certainty; it brings to mind Darwinian notions of adaptation and survival, of fitting to environmental forces, and of the development of ecosystems dependent on the mutual contribu-tions of all the entities within them. Important also is the analysis of the ontology (the biological development) of each entity and of its ecosystem, and the narrative of how each and all are established, grow and develop, and decline and fall, both singly and together. In the context of collaboration, the biological term 'symbiosis' is used widely to describe the close linkage of operational entities through the use of waste outputs as necessary inputs: the International Institute for Sustainable Development (IISD) (2013) describes a case study of this in practice in an industrial zone in Kalundborg in Denmark.

Thinking about **culture** meanwhile suggests the social norms shaping how peo-ple choose to work together. Important in this is the role of shared social identities built around commonly held beliefs, values and norms in establishing effective relationships; and also in setting the criteria for the leadership of groups towards common goals, a theme developed by Reicher, Haslam and Hopkins (2005). Also prompted is consideration of those beliefs that become established as rigidly held positions, any conflict with which creates barriers between 'us' and 'them'. The issue of cultural awareness, both in terms of leveraging benefits from exploiting differ-ences as well as avoiding pitfalls, is of vital importance in collaborative activities, and there is a large body of work developing the theme as it pertains to collabora-tive working; in this chapter we will limit our consideration of it to the 'soft skills' necessary to manage agreement where many factors, including cultural ones, can raise barriers against effective outcomes, or be surfaced as differences in perspective that can be translated in alternative approaches to value creation.

Whatever the metaphor used, what quickly emerges is that collaboration is implic-itly recognized as involving complexity; any implication that a certainty of outcome can be predicted in turn demands that things must be kept simple, tightly bounded, and very easily described. The reality of working together means acknowledging the complexity that arises from the involvement of different individuals or organizations, or of different groups within apparently homogenous entities; this inevitably pre-sents scope for misunderstandings and uncertainty. And that makes it hard.

> **GROUP EXERCISE 5.3**
>
> What other metaphors can you think of that could reflect collaboration? How would you characterize these? How might this change if the people involved came from very different backgrounds? What ideas and issues does your metaphor suggest for making successful collaboration more likely? (Try some of these: a computer network; an orchestra; a rock band; a formal garden.)

5.1 Choosing Collaboration

A paradox of effective collaboration is that it requires every partner to be released to act fully and wholly on their own behalf while being trusted to contribute to the success of others. Irrespective therefore of participants' individual interests, successful collaboration requires all those involved to establish mutual respect, and actively to surface shared and common interests while negotiating any compromises or accommodations needed to deal with inevitable tensions and conflicts.

5.1.1 Lessons from a Competitive World

This is a challenging assertion where one form of human social interaction dominates like no other, especially in the world of work – competition. It is commonplace to organize the culture and objectives of an organization around a single focus, of doing better than the competition, however that is defined. It might be expressed as a claim of a 'leading' market position, or of 'superior' shareholder returns, or by asserting 'greater' social benefits than possible with an alternative: each is a statement of competitive intent. This attitude is common across all sectors of society, and is not just confined to business: charities and NGOs can be extremely competitive when it comes to securing advantaged access to funding, as are public sector departments in the run-up to budget settlements. Competition has an almost overwhelming impact on how people position themselves at work, and in how they are appraised for their performance by the groups or organizations they are part of.

This is not at all to say that competition is *per se* a 'bad' thing – it is at the heart of the modern economic system, driving the efficient allocation of resources, the removal of wasted effort through the failure of the unsuccessful, and the creation of new opportunities for innovation. Porter (1980) developed the understanding and analysis of competition as a structure for establishing strategy: but it is also apparent that his early expression of this as a model of 'five forces' assumed much mechanistic predictability, to the extent that the relevant competitive pressures could be bounded, identified and quantified. All that we have seen so far in this chapter suggests that complexity, adaptation and emergence must also play their part in competitive systems, and observation would support this (see Definition box). What is known as 'the tragedy of the commons', where multiple competitors consume the available resources contained within a fixed boundary, is an obvious example.

So neither is it the case that we can simply differentiate between competitive *markets* and collaborative *societies*: many believe that the collapse of the ecosystem on Easter Island was driven by a competitive society, much as many argue that the failure to secure agreement on a successor to the Kyoto Agreement at Copenhagen also reflects competition within a global human society; while we have previously discussed examples where markets have become collaborative.

Rather, both competition and collaboration must be seen to have a part to play in creating better future outcomes in all environments; but it is too often the case that the risks of pure competition are ignored while the opportunities of collaboration are forgotten. It is often necessary to make collaboration a formal and deliberate choice.

SHARED VALUE

Thirty years after first promoting his five competitive forces Michael Porter reflected some of this changing perspective by proposing mutual interdependence as an alternative strategic platform, one of 'Shared Value' (Porter and Kramer, 2011), where 'successful businesses need successful communities' and vice versa. Emerson (2003) had earlier proposed Blended Value as describing this potential to integrate social and financial returns in prioritizing corporate action, but Porter and Kramer were more specific in terms of how this might be implemented: they argued that 'products and markets could be re-conceived', 'productivity in the supply chain redefined', and the 'development of local clusters enabled'. What each of these actions would actually mean to any particular business would however depend very much on its environment, its strategy, and on how it engaged with its stakeholders; and this exposes a limitation of the approach. Sharing Value between businesses and the communities within which they operate suggests a very tightly drawn system boundary, isolated from a much more inclusive ecosystem reflecting ecological and political factors amongst many others. Too tightly drawn a boundary is restrictive.

And while competition might be expected to yield better value outcomes for the winners, collaboration of any kind should be expected to incur costs for all without any guarantee of return. Collaboration requires the commitment of resources, not least that of peoples' time, requiring attention and effort that could otherwise be focused entirely on achieving competitive goals. Hansen (2009) looked at this extensively in the context of internal collaboration across large organizations, stressing that collaboration presented opportunity costs: he argued that only if the projected return on a collaborative effort could be expected to exceed the total of all the costs involved, including the value of opportunities foregone, could it be commercially justified.

This observation is vitally important when seeking to collaborate with commercial partners working in competitive environments, especially across sectoral boundaries where perceptions of value may differ wildly. Many proponents of 'social value' will for instance reject the notion of 'commercial justification' if the two are in apparent opposition, a position that would be anathema to any business leader charged with allocating resources. But equally, the variety of different possible returns envisioned by diverse stakeholders can add complexity – and thus opportunity – to the calculation of value potential, and so to the attractiveness of a collaborative choice. We will return to this theme of differences in value perception later in this chapter.

5.1.2   The Emergence of Collaboration

Competition has many drivers, from the simple desire held by some to 'win', through to an imperative felt by most to survive. Whatever its root, it is an example of self-interest in practice. The assumption that such self-interest dominates for all people in all environments and in all their social interactions is reflected in traditional neoclassical economic models, and in the concept of people as a collection of self-maximizing rational actors acting with perfect knowledge – '*Homo economicus*' as it has been coined. (An amusing exploration of what this would mean in practice is described in a podcast by Dubner (2015)). Whether we agree with the premise or not, it is a useful starting point in questioning how collaborative choices and behaviours can emerge – and at times dominate – even where such a choice is suboptimal at the individual 'rational' level.

The simplest way to explore the assumed dominance of unalloyed self-interest is to use the Prisoner's Dilemma. The outline is well known: two accomplices are held separately, unable to confer or collaborate, and each is offered a deal. If one incriminates the other while the other does not, then the 'defector' is punished least severely, and the accomplice most so; if both stay silent and choose to co-operate with each other, both will be punished at a low level; while if both defect and accuse each other, both are punished at a medium level – and importantly, at a level that is worse than if both choose independently to co-operate. Logic – that is, rational decision making – demands that defection is the determined choice for all participants at all times, for it yields the optimum individual outcome irrespective of whatever decision is made by the other party. Viewed this way, the assumption of self-interest alongside rationality suggests that collaboration doesn't stand a chance where it requires any one party to risk giving up something in order to share an uncertain, though potentially better, outcome with others. Fortunately, life isn't as simple as the game theorists would suggest.

For in real life very few interactions are singular, one-off, and determined in isolation as in the Prisoner's Dilemma. Most instead are sequential, unfolding and developing over an unpredictable number of contacts, engagements, and interactions. Of course, if the structure of a series of engagements is fixed and finite, and the outcomes for the players knowable or discernible, then it would be possible for any participant to work backwards from a known end point and to develop an optimum self-maximizing strategy – which would also, for *Homo economicus* at least, lead to rational choices and competitive decision-making. However, in most engagements between people the end point is unknown and is uncertain; you may just have to deal with this person again at some point in the future. Once this is recognized the decision-making process must change, in recognition that future decisions will be based on observed and factual accounts of past behaviours. In other words, if you think you might have to work with someone again, you'll think carefully about how you treat them this time.

Axelrod (1984) modelled this idea by running a computer tournament between 15 different strategies for participating in a long, essentially undetermined, sequence of Prisoner's Dilemma problems. He discovered that a very simple rule emerged as the most successful strategy for individual players, which he called 'Tit for Tat'. An experience of defection in one round was responded to by an act of defection in the next round of play with that player, while an experience of co-operation was met with automatic co-operation. Where any initial engagement was co-operative, the rewards to both participants over time far exceeded those available to less altruistically inclined players.

Nowak and Highfield (2011) describe how Axelrod's experiment was repeated, but modified to reflect real world environments where random or chance mutation – often, errors or mistakes – can occur, or where a population of collaborators is infiltrated by a few of the purely self-interested. In Axelrod's Tit for Tat strategy, a single defection would move the players into a cycle of reciprocated defection; Nowak's innovation of 'Generous Tit for Tat' created the opportunity for random acts of forgiveness, allowing a return to a cycle of mutual co-operation. Put simply, even where self-interest exists, a strategy of altruism based on a validated basis of trust with a little bit of forbearance can allow collaboration to emerge.

But Nowak also demonstrated that any population of unconditional cooperators or altruists will in time be overwhelmed by the appearance of just a few selfish defectors; and even though collaboration might develop again in time, for a period the purely self-interested may claim the lion's share of the value available. Collaborative benefits in an ecosystem can be compromised by a few players choosing to use competitive responses to achieve immediate, albeit temporary and short-term advantage. No collaborative arrangement should be structured without maintaining vigilance regarding this possibility.

One further insight resulting from this short exploration of game theory in collaboration is the relevance of **reputation**. The examples given above are all of a type, illustrating direct reciprocity; that is, the players have direct, personal and immediate experience of the actions of the other players, and react accordingly based on their developing sense of how much these others can be trusted. But **indirect reciprocity** can also apply, where knowledge of the behaviour of other players is shared openly across an ecosystem. This is the basis for the ratings system on Amazon Marketplace, eBay and the like. Each positive (or altruistic) action can influence the way in which the whole population will deal with you in future. This prompts consideration of the importance of participating in social environments where reputation is established: fail to build a positive reputation, even if you are in fact trustworthy, and you will be disadvantaged for a while when an ecosystem shifts into a more collaborative phase. The role of reputation also has bearing on the validity given to the outcomes of a collaboration: the more respected the participants, the greater the value will be attached to the fruits of their engagement by those on the outside.

This recognition of the importance of reputation also suggests that one common interpretation of the Prisoner's Dilemma is flawed: there is no such thing as a singular interaction; every engagement should instead be viewed as being one more in a long, indeterminate sequence. There may be no formal expectation of repeating an interaction with a particular party, but future interactions with others are very likely to have taken your actions in that one into account.

And so, irrespective of any belief in the truth of the self-maximizing rational actor, or concerns about the dominance of competitive behaviours in one-off interactions, the theory demonstrates why collaboration can emerge. Apparently altruistic actions can lead to higher value outcomes for the individual party, as well as for the ecosystem as a whole (see Case Study 5.1).

CASE STUDY 5.1
Green and Black's

Green and Black's (G&B), a small company specializing in the marketing and sales of premium chocolate confectionery, started life as a single product within an established health foods business in the UK in the early 1990s, and grew slowly at first. It was acquired in 2003 by Cadbury Schweppes, at the time the largest confectionery company in the world, and itself later acquired by Kraft Foods before being spun off as part of Mondelez International. With revenues growing rapidly, by 2006 G&B was outselling its new parent in a number of key segments and markets, including in the chocolate category in the US. From being an interesting but niche competitor, G&B was by this stage established as a significant challenger brand in a number of key international markets. Its business model was also being copied by both established competitors and by numerous start-ups: an offering based on high-quality product with carefully designed flavours developed for adult consumers, supported by packaging designs that communicated a premium positioning, was growing consumption in consumer segments that had beforehand shown limited involvement in the confectionery category. This was combined with Fairtrade and organic certifications to communicate high ethical standards, a retail price point that made it an accessible indulgence, and the leveraging of copious spare capacity in the European chocolate industry to outsource its manufacturing and technical requirements to ICAM, a very highly-regarded and technically capable Italian supplier.

This success came with some unexpected problems, not least of which was that it was consuming more than 25% of the world crop of organic cacao, and forecasted exceeding 50% of an increased level of supply within a few years. However its relationships with key suppliers in the Dominican Republic, a source of the higher-quality Trinitario beans used in its production and developed through introductions from ICAM, revealed that the great majority of cacao grown there was being poorly and inexpertly processed, and sold into the low-value commodity market. In discussion with the Conacado co-operative, owned by and representing many thousands of small growers, an option emerged that could make much of this secondary market available for use within just a couple of years – equivalent to almost doubling the world supply of organic cacao, while establishing a high-quality benchmark for the whole market. It required a sub-million US dollar investment by G&B in Conacado in improved drying and handling facilities, together with the provision of technical knowledge regarding, amongst other things, organic certification and improved processing standards. The management of Conacado was enthusiastic, as commercial pressures in the cacao market were undermining the viability of smaller growers, many of which were questioning the value of their participation in the co-operative, reflected in a multi-year trend showing a reduction in membership numbers. Importantly, this increased level of supply would not be secured only for G&B use – it would be available on the open market.

With the approval of Cadbury, the investment in facilities and the transfer of knowledge soon took place, being positioned as part of its own global corporate social responsibility activities, alongside a long-standing initiative supporting community development and cocoa production in Ghana, its own primary source of cacao.

As a result of the work done with Conacado, the pressures on the price premium for high-quality organic cacao reduced, and in time supply levels increased. The action secured the capacity of the market to supply G&B and its growing set of competitors with the high-quality inputs they all needed. It also helped to establish the viability and relevance of Conacado to its members. And it helped to transform the incomes of many family growers, who saw the cash margin on their crops rise from, in some cases, a few tens of dollars per tonne to many hundreds of dollars per tonne and more.

GROUP EXERCISE 5.4

In what ways were the actions of G&B altruistic (collaborative) and in what ways were they selfish (competitive)?

Map out the various players involved, and list what you think their main interests would have been concerning the initiative. What issues do you think they would have had to face as potential barriers to their involvement and commitment?

5.2   The Theory and Practice of Collaboration

So far we have looked at examples illustrating how, whatever the language used to describe them, acts of collaboration are evident all around us. We have also looked at why this happens in spite of what might be expected in environments otherwise characterized as competitive and dominated by expressions of self-interest. Now we look at a few models, which have been developed to guide the practice of collaboration, how it might work, and who might be involved.

5.2.1   Characterizing Collaboration

There is no shortage of attempts at describing the structure or organization of collaborative initiatives: Gray and Stites (2013) identified and reviewed more than 275 academic articles related to the subject published between 2000 and 2012, to investigate approaches to partnering between organizations for sustainability purposes. Earlier, Wood and Gray (1991) had looked at a number of more general collaborations, and their list of key concepts is as good a summary as any.

They proposed that in framing collaboration:

1   It will be possible to identify a number of separate entities, or stakeholders, each with an interest in the desired outcome of the initiative; and that while the absolute number of stakeholders might not be determined, only some need be actively engaged at any time.

2   A definition, or description, can be made of a perceived problem or challenge, bounded to some meaningful extent, a change in the future state of which is to be addressed;

3   All participants intend to act in some way that impacts on issues related to the challenge, or to make decisions which demonstrate their active participation.

4   The independence of decision making power or autonomy of all stakeholders can be recognized, even where this is shared or abrogated by choice.

5   A relationship exists between all participating stakeholders for a period of time through some kind of interactive process, which is orientated toward effecting change; and

6   There is agreement amongst participating stakeholders regarding a set of shared rules, norms and structures which define how the interactive process will establish and evolve: this agreement might be either formal or informal in nature.

(Adapted from Wood and Gray, 1991.)

While these concepts might be recognizable across many forms of collaboration, the initial understanding of their meaning can vary quite widely amongst participants of even quite similar backgrounds. A useful starting point therefore, not made explicit in this listing, is to ensure a thorough process of dialogue amongst stakeholders very early on, used to explore and surface just what those differences in understanding might be. This reflects an important aspect of what is called Dialogue Theory, which proposes that the opinions and perspectives of individual participants in an interaction can be changed through the very process of interaction, with others' perspectives being acknowledged and respected without requiring compromise of one's own. Recognizing this as relevant at the very start of an interaction may make it more apparent – and easier to assure – as the relationship develops. It is also important to note that a decision to collaborate does not guarantee a successful outcome for any or all of the participants; but creating a good structure and process might just improve the chances of success.

5.2.2 Crossing Sectors

There has been much interest in the potential for cross-sector partnerships in recent years, brought about in large part by changed approaches in a number of major NGOs and intergovernmental bodies acknowledging the influence of many multinational companies and their role as stakeholders. But what is meant by 'crossing sectors'?

It is usual to differentiate between three distinct expressions of power structures in modern societies: the private sector, representing organizations owned ultimately by private individuals and resourced by capital provided by them in return for dividends and capital growth; the public sector, representing organizations and structures controlled by appointees of government, and funded by taxation and government borrowing; and the civic (or civil) sector, representing organizations and structures that bridge the private and the public sectors, drawing funding from

---

GROUP EXERCISE 5.5

Consider an example where you have observed or participated in a collaborative initiative. Use the concepts of stakeholders, problem situation, autonomy, interactive process, and shared structures to describe what happened, and what did not. What actions or decisions resulted? Was the collaboration judged a success by external observers? Can you identify any examples of how participants' perspectives altered through their involvement?

across all parts of society and which have their own independent structures of governance. Examples of the civic sector are religious, voluntary and not-for-profit organizations, although there can be a degree of overlap between the sectors, often indicated by increased levels of influence over governance in return for funding. Claims extolling the benefits of cross-sectoral collaboration are widespread, but so too are complaints about the difficulties encountered in making such arrangements work well, which have grown out of increased experience. The challenges involved have even helped create a new facilitative role, that of the 'partnership broker' (see http://www.partnershipbrokers.org/).

The attraction of cross-sector partnerships is founded on a range of expected benefits acting as drivers of value, alongside the breaking down of barriers between sectors – not least in challenging prior judgements regarding others' perceptions, positions and interests. It is also reflective of an acceptance that each party can genuinely contribute from their own experience judgements that will lead to better outcomes, and not be driven solely out of self-interest. Many of the benefits expected will be relevant to any collaborative initiative, and will include amongst others: increased levels of innovation through the mixing of experience and understanding; gaining access to capabilities, networks, and resources; increasing the speed of learning and access to knowledge; extending reach beyond existing boundaries and networks; increasing the efficiency of and return on investments; sharing risks; and enhancing or managing reputations through association with other parties. Being able to surface expected benefits is also critical in setting out plans, objectives and expectations, and of course in helping to secure the commitment of resources in advance.

An important criticism is that such approaches can be extended too far in the setting of policies and regulations, allowing private sector organizations undue influence. This criticism, however, can equally be levelled at the motivations of other sectoral participants, who may be just as eager to shape outcomes to their own benefit: good process will surface these issues within the collaboration, and ensure that external communication differentiates between participants' lobbying for individually desired outcomes, and contributing to a shared one.

An excellent source of research, case studies and guidance on the operation and intricacies of cross-sectoral partnerships (which has also helped to inform this section) can be found via the Partnering Initiative (www.thepartneringinitiative.org).

CASE STUDY 5.2
The UN Global Compact

A very visible and well-documented example of a multisector collaboration is the United Nations Global Compact initiative, which was launched in July 2000 with the objective of creating a structure to support the widespread global adoption of corporate sustainability practices. It presented a model that would guide the development, implementation and communication of corporate policies and practices designed to

(Continued)

'contribute to a more sustainable and inclusive global economy' (UN, 2011). It has been in place for long enough to highlight a number of the issues related to such cross-sectoral initiatives.

The Compact was established not as a regulatory framework, but as a voluntary initiative. Companies signing up to the Compact would commit to a number of actions, including:

- referencing a set of Ten Principles within their governance structures, at the highest level;
- communicating specific actions and their progress, on an annual basis;
- promoting the UN Global Compact across their stakeholder networks;
- participating in cross-sectoral partnership projects; and
- making an annual financial contribution to the Compact, based on company turnover.

Governance of the Global Compact is centred on a cross-sector Board that meets annually, bringing together representatives from business, civil society, labour organizations, and seven UN agencies. Senior executives of all stakeholders and members attend a tri-annual conference, or Leaders' Summit. Support is provided by a New York-based Executive Director and Office, a team co-ordinating activities across UN agencies, and donor states resourcing individual programmes and initiatives. There are also local self-governing geographic networks, also structured to involve cross-sector participants.

Criticism of the Compact has centred on accusations that many companies signed up initially simply to enhance their CSR credentials and public image, but did not reflect its principles in their subsequently observed strategies and operations. Under pressure to address this, the number of corporate signatories had fallen by more than 3,000 by mid-2012 from its 2008 peak of around 8,500 (Confino, 2012) through active intervention by the Compact's Executive Office.

The UN Compact drew on a number of existing multilateral agreements, including the Universal Declaration of Human Rights and the Rio Declaration on Environment and Development, to develop its Ten Principles, and 'asks companies to embrace, support and enact' these 'within their sphere of influence'.

The Ten Principles are:

Human Rights

- Principle 1: Businesses should support and respect the protection of internationally proclaimed human rights; and
- Principle 2: make sure that they are not complicit in human rights abuses.

Labour

- Principle 3: Businesses should uphold the freedom of association and the effective recognition of the right to collective bargaining;
- Principle 4: the elimination of all forms of forced and compulsory labour;
- Principle 5: the effective abolition of child labour; and
- Principle 6: the elimination of discrimination in respect of employment and occupation.

Environment

- Principle 7: Businesses should support a precautionary approach to environmental challenges;
- Principle 8: undertake initiatives to promote greater environmental responsibility; and
- Principle 9: encourage the development and diffusion of environmentally friendly technologies.

Anti-corruption

- Principle 10: Businesses should work against corruption in all its forms, including extortion and bribery.

Less than 10% of global multinationals are signatories to the UN Global Compact. Given the expressed objective of the Compact, what do you think might be holding them back? Would you describe the Compact as a success, or as a failure? How does its governance contribute to this?

A number of different stakeholder groups from all three sectors are represented in the governance structures of the UN Global Compact, providing a mix of perspectives on what effective adoption of many of the Ten Principles might mean. Take one of those perspectives (business, NGO, labour, UN agency, donor country) and dialogue the Principles with someone representing a constituency from a different sector (public, private or civic). Note the word 'dialogue' – the objective of this exercise is to build understanding of different perspectives, not to argue the worth of your own.

5.2.3 Multistakeholder Collaborations

Cross-sectoral collaborations (or partnerships) will typically involve a more limited number of participants than seen in the UN Global Compact (see Case Study 5.2). But sometimes an activity or initiative will impinge on the interests of a great number of other interested parties, not necessarily encompassing the different perspectives that challenge cross-sectoral engagements; this merits particular attention regarding how they might be managed in practice. It is important, however, to differentiate these from more typical communications processes, put in place to manage the fallout from a previous or planned action.

Two well-presented and argued approaches have been developed by Hemmati (2002) and Tennyson (2011), both relevant to situations where the number as well as the type of stakeholder increases the complexity and scale of what is intended. Their recommendations for process management reflect key aspects of Stakeholder Theory, in particular the view that organizations must be conscious of the impact of their decisions and actions on others, both in terms of what might be helpful as well as those that may be interpreted as potentially harmful.

The recommendations are very similar to what would be regarded as good practice for managing any complex project, identifying the need to: specify desired outcomes; evidence leadership through setting objectives and overcoming barriers; create detailed action plans; identify and secure resources; and ensure measurement and review of outcomes. What is significant, however, is that the formal management of multistakeholder arrangements will typically sit outside any existing single organizational entity, and will therefore lack many of the processes and resources that people have become accustomed to in 'getting things done'. Every activity needs to be resourced, and its effectiveness and appropriateness reviewed, whether formally or informally; and unless relevant time and effort is given to ensuring that is adequate, the desired collaborative benefits may not arise. Successful collaborations will always have some level of resource dedicated to them, whether in a secretariat or executive body of some sort: the choices will depend very much on the circumstances, the degree to which the collaboration trends towards more formal definitions of 'partnership', and on the willingness of stakeholders to contribute resources.

It is also worth noting that multistakeholder collaborations will be initiated at some distinct point of time; and while this may sometimes be through third party facilitation or via introduction, its creation will be capable of being traced back to a choice that has been made by one or more initiating parties. This suggests that good collaborative process can and perhaps should include the scoping and appraisal of potential partners with the aim of finding good fit in values and likely commitment to reaching a sustainable outcome.

The success of a multistakeholder collaboration will also depend greatly on the development of relationships across the various organizational boundaries, and particularly at senior levels. Commitments should be secured as widely as possible across all participant organizations, extending the reach of understanding and support for the initiative such that a small number of changes to key personnel does not see it undermined. See Case Study 5.3.

GROUP EXERCISE 5.7

What multistakeholder collaborations have you participated in, at work or elsewhere? What was the driver for its initiation? How were the participants determined?

Can its success or failure be explained by reference to the suggestions for good structure and process outlined above?

CASE STUDY 5.3
The Marine Stewardship Council

The Marine Stewardship Council (MSC) was co-founded in 1998 by the conservation NGO the World Wide Fund for Nature (WWF) and the global food and personal care company, Unilever, with the aim of addressing declining fisheries stocks in the world's oceans. As a private environmental standard-setting organization, the MSC draws together a very broad set of stakeholders representing fishery companies, their customers in industrial and consumer goods markets, scientific researchers, the nations and states encompassing fishery rights, and environmental groups, amongst others. The aim is to forge a link between standards of fisheries use and their markets, and to create awareness of the standard such that market pricing and demand moves in favour of those abiding by it. While consumers are an important influence in this, by far the greatest impact can be found through the adoption of sustainable supply chain practices by major retail and seafood product companies: their requirements for certification to relevant standards drive their adoption elsewhere in the supply chain.

(Continued)

The MSC standard is built around three principles: that a fishing activity must be at a level which ensures it can continue indefinitely; that fishing operations must be managed to maintain the structure, productivity, function and diversity of the ecosystem; and that the fishery must comply with relevant laws and have a management system that is responsive to changing circumstances (MSC, 2015). These three principles are then further developed into 31 performance indicators, which can be scored against a defined (and improving) level of Global Best Practice. Fisheries seeking approval against the standard will be assessed against these performance indicators, and required to meet the global best practice level within the certification period.

In the early years of its operation, the MSC gave much discretion to assessment teams in determining their scoring of the performance indicators; this led to some inconsistency, and criticism from a number of quarters, including both industrial and environmental stakeholders. Frequent changes to the standards – albeit reflecting improving best practice – also gave a sense of instability and change, not always confirmed by fisheries science, and this further undermined confidence. In 2014 the MSC initiated a multiyear review process, drawing on very wide consultation including consumers, as well as stakeholder participation, with the aim building greater confidence in the worth, validity and sustainability of the standard.

GROUP EXERCISE 5.8

How does the use of the word 'stewardship' shape your thinking about the MSC and its aims, and the way it has approached stakeholder management ?

Research a similar private standards-setting organization, such as the World Fair Trade Organization, the Better Cotton Initiative, or any other that you know of or can identify: how does its governance structure reflect collaborative objectives across multiple stakeholder groups?

5.2.4 Stakeholder Salience

Various concepts in Stakeholder Theory have run throughout this chapter, but the introduction of the idea that some stakeholders can be more salient or relevant than others is worth further consideration. That some stakeholders might be formally included in a collaboration implies that others might be formally excluded. Given all that has been discussed regarding openness, complexity and the importance of boundary setting, this can have serious implications for the implementation and management of any collaborative initiative.

A key challenge is determining who is actively entitled to be considered a stakeholder in any form of interaction, and whether this judgement, from whatever perspective it has been formed, is valid from all other perspectives. Mitchell, Agle and Wood (1997) suggested that this judgement can be aided by appraising three attributes related to salience – of Power, of Legitimacy, and of Urgency. **Power** reflects the ability of one party to apply to another any aspect of coercion, utility (rewards, or the promise of them) or norms – the pressure that certain behaviours or actions are either acceptable or not in the context of that relationship. **Legitimacy** arises when one entity can shape the actions of another through some socially developed system of appraisal or approbation; it is surfaced most when it impinges on ideas of autonomy or control. **Urgency** meanwhile reflects the degree to which an entity believes that its perceived needs merit an immediate response; although of course judgements of time importance and criticality may differ widely. Determining which of these attributes was present would allow a stakeholder to be classified: demonstrate all three, and it would certainly be regarded as a critical or salient stakeholder.

It is, however, difficult to see how, except for the simplest and most tightly drawn of issues, such a model of stakeholder identification and classification can help in practical terms, other than in surfacing the likelihood that every type of stakeholder will emerge, seeking to exercise whatever power they can muster while asserting both their legitimacy and the urgency of their claims. Hence most collaborations will need plans in place to cope with the potential appearance of self-appointed stakeholders, often from the most unexpected of places and representing the most diverse of perspectives. See Definition box.

STAKEHOLDER THEORY

Parmar et al. (2010) developed Stakeholder Theory to provide a justification for a more open, inclusive and necessarily flexible approach to judging salience. This starts with an observation that the 'public' no longer shows the level of trust in business organizations that was once a given, a change driven by revelations of a series of corporate scandals including those of Parmalat and Enron, incomprehension regarding levels of executive pay, and anger for what are regarded as avoidable environmental and social crises, all blamed on the actions of a few business entities. They argue that a new relationship with business is demanded, that requires value to be created for all stakeholders and not just shareholders, and that 'this set of stakeholder relationships . . . defines the business'. In such an environment and given these expectations, businesses can no longer expect to take sole ownership of determining stakeholder salience. Whether this public distrust also impacts on the freedom of the public and civic sectors to act in future is yet to emerge, but the indications are that it is likely: the public will expect 'big organizations', whatever sector notionally represented, to exhibit fully open and inclusive stakeholder processes.

5.3 Managing Collaborative (Dis)Agreement

There will always be what Rittel and Webber (1973) defined as 'wicked' problems, those where either simple circumstance or, in the case of collaborations, the participation of stakeholders with apparently irreconcilably contradictory positions, mean that no satisfactory way forward appears possible. Many such stakeholder positions can be rooted in precious cultural or political systems of belief; even the simple act of acknowledging a point of difference might imply a loss, or be judged as such if the parties concerned are formally representative of a larger group. When such stakeholders come face to face they can easily see each other, and be seen, as extremists; or their agreement to engage with each other might be portrayed by external commentators as evidence of weakness or betrayal. They will be encouraged to deal only in absolutes, calling upon their own systems of morals and beliefs alone, and countenancing no deviation from the paths marked out by these. They should not be influenced by any persuasion or logical argument.

One answer to dealing with such stakeholders is for the others engaged with them to apply whatever force or coercion can be mustered, by whatever means and through whatever leverage can be found; however, they might find themselves in turn facing similar expressions of power. But the evidence of history and in diplomacy and politics suggests that recourse to coercion, what is called 'power over', is unlikely to achieve anything other than to create fault-lines for future failure. Instead, there has to be a way of establishing, if only on the thinnest of ice, a form of connection upon which a more secure and solid path to future accommodation can be built. And so even if in the heat of the moment there seems little chance of success, all disagreements can be approached with an expectation that a constructive agreement of some kind is possible. Fisher and Ury (1981) suggest that in the context of negotiation this can be helped by differentiating between the '**positions**' that people hold dear, and will work hard to defend and extend, and the '**interests**' that they will wish to satisfy, and find representative of a successful outcome. In the context of disagreements in collaborations we can make this more meaningful by equating position with the nature of power as it is revealed in the relationships, and interests with how perceptions of value are surfaced and addressed; and by managing the interaction in ways that keep emotional responses to disagreement controlled. The effective application of these three approaches combine to reflect the 'soft skills' that make some people more successful in their collaborations than others.

5.3.1   Prioritizing 'Power With'

The economist Kenneth Boulding (1989) defined 'power' as the ability to change the future, and so for our purpose of developing collaboration as a necessary capability in working together to achieve better future outcomes it is an important consideration. For Boulding, changing the future meant changing the actions of other people by exerting power over them, or through them, or with them.

'**Power Over**': Boulding characterized as the use of force and coercion, reflecting the ability to dominate another person or group, bending them to one's will through force or threat supported by relative hierarchical position or strength. Typically much attention is paid to Power Over when used to establish or sustain these inequalities, or to imply a hierarchy of relationship rather than confirming equity. Less hierarchical is the use of '**Power Through**', which reflects the capacity to act and achieve goals by trading or exchanging resources or capabilities with others offering complementary competence. There may still be recognizable differences in scale or potential impact between parties, but in Power Through there is an acknowledgement of dependence and mutual need.

'**Power With**', however, assumes greater equity of role, competence and acknowledged interdependence. It reflects the capacity to work and collaborate with others, pooling and integrating mutually compatible resources to achieve a common objective. Power With implies being able to move beyond a number of individual fixed positions, and jointly to focus on a common enterprise. Recognizing that power is not just about force thus opens new opportunities to secure agreement: opportunities to create Power With need to be prioritized, and a willingness to identify and develop them exhibited. A similar perspective, drawn from politics, is Joseph Nye's (2004, p. 34) '**Soft Power**': 'When you can get others to admire your ideals and to want what you want, you do not have to spend as much on sticks and carrots to move them in your direction.'

5.3.2 Interpreting Dimensions of Value

If redefining the meaning of power means that positions can to some degree be put aside, then redefining the meaning of value means that interests can be better surfaced and more richly satisfied. And as we saw earlier, the creation of value for all participants as well as for the ecosystem as a whole is necessary if collaboration is to emerge and be sustained. The recognition that perceptions of value can vary greatly between people, and that they are also fluid and dynamic, is a foundational consideration in securing agreement.

The way in which businesses shape and communicate their offers to meet customers' needs is revealing. While their ultimate aim is to translate an offering into some form of economic return, the offering itself will be presented in a way that suggests value to the customer such that it makes them more willing to enter into an exchange. Hence the offerings of food manufacturers are presented as delicious and appealing; of soft beverage manufacturers as refreshing; of luxury goods companies as bestowing status; of holiday companies as providing relaxation; of vitamin supplement businesses as supporting a healthy lifestyle. In each instance value offered reflects a promise of needs met. The number of different types of **value** that can be imagined are probably as numerous as the variety of needs that people express; their relative importance in turn will be shaped by the **values** and systems of ethics and beliefs held by the individuals concerned. One particular type or aspect of value cannot therefore be assumed as judged equally by all people, nor even equally by one person at all times.

With such potential for variety and complexity it is useful to simplify matters by categorizing expressions of value as representing one of three distinct types. Value that can be accumulated or saved for future or subsequent consumption can be characterized as representing forms of **Wealth**: money is an obvious example, but knowledge or information are similar in nature, and so too is time; many commercial offerings are sold on the basis of convenience, of the promise of time saved now to be used more enjoyably later. Meanwhile expressions that validate respect, honour or position can be categorized as representing **Worth**. This understanding is at the heart of the luxury goods and fashion industries; they are adept at encouraging people to conflate relative positions of social standing with the ownership of physical goods. Finally, there are many expressions of value that are based on assertions of the capacity to grow and to flourish, in body, mind and spirit: these can be characterized as representing expressions of **Well-being**. Spa companies do this well, and so too do many charities and good causes when they invite us to align our acts of giving with the needs of the less well off, or with threatened nature.

So whatever differences there might be in the determined interests expressed by participants in a collaboration, it will always be possible to explore how those can be satisfied by interpreting them as different expressions of equal value that can be matched, exchanged or simply satisfied. The soft skills required, however, include not only being able to interpret these expressions of value, but also helping others to understand one's own. And of course, expressions of value need not be singular: they can involve degrees of all three types simultaneously, as illustrated in Figure 5.3.

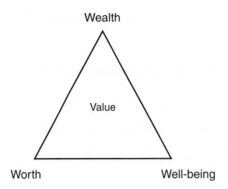

Worth   Well-being

FIGURE 5.3   Dimensions of Value.

GROUP EXERCISE 5.9

A popular structure for understanding human needs was expressed by Maslow (1943). **Physiological** needs such as food, warmth, shelter, clothing and reproduction are the most basic and essential; providing the security or stability of these represents **Safety** needs; once these are evident, and in turn, Maslow suggested the need for **Belonging**, **Self-esteem** and **Self-actualization**.

Consider examples of how value is demonstrated when any or all of these needs are met. For instance, 'access to justice' creates value by providing safety and security. Categorize your examples of value as being one or more of Wealth, Worth, or Well-being.

5.3.3 Demonstrating Respect

Even where positions have been put aside and interests satisfied, ensuring a lasting agreement to work together can remain difficult. While we have already referred to the role of trust in making collaboration work better, it is possible to trust someone and still fundamentally disagree with them about the way forward. So alongside sharing Power With and exploring dimensions of value we must consider the role of expressing respect for one another in helping to overcome barriers to agreement.

Roger Fisher was a key player in the Harvard Negotiation Project and a co-author of *Getting to Yes*, the go-to book on negotiating, published in 1981 and in print ever since. He was regarded, before his death in 2012, as one of the world's leading theorists and practitioners in the art and science of negotiation. The original title of his final book is revealing, however: it was called *Beyond Reason* before being retitled as *Building Agreement*. A lifetime of experience had taught Fisher that getting people to co-operate fully usually involved getting them to deal with their own personal emotional responses to the way other people were dealing with them. Fisher's insight was that the way in which these emotional responses were promoted or managed would either create a collaborative, co-operative environment open to integrating interests and finding accommodation – or not.

Fisher and his co-author Shapiro (2005) defined these emotional responses as relating to Appreciation, Affiliation, Autonomy, Status and Role. To a greater or lesser degree each of these can be seen to reflect the communication and perception of '**respect**'. Considering this perspective in the context of an ongoing collaborative engagement, rather than as part of smoothing the path to negotiating resolution to a single conflict, helps confirm its relevance to our purpose.

Active listening, and asking meaningful, insightful questions, demonstrates an **appreciation** of the thinking processes that someone else has followed in reaching their position. Such an expression of appreciation does not automatically imply agreement, but it does express respect, and allows conversation to develop and issues to be explored and revisited. It does not suggest that one is right and the other is wrong; and by expressing respect it invites the others involved to be similarly appreciative.

Such a non-adversarial approach might also demonstrate a desire to look for connections that are authentic and valid. This search for **affiliation** goes beyond the caricature of a salesperson trying to create a feeling of shared identity, which is too easily recognized as manipulative. Treating other people as if they were indeed 'the same' and not 'different' implies respect for them as equals, encouraging a sense of belonging and common purpose or identity.

Respect is also expressed when people are given the freedom to make or influence decisions relevant to their own judgements of their roles and positions. Impinging on this sense of **autonomy** will for most people feel highly disrespectful, implying a hierarchy of authority or power. It will also damage trust by suggesting an agenda to create just such a hierarchy.

This is similar to the way in which giving people a sense that their expertise or quality of judgement is respected confers **status**; it is an aspect of demonstrating Power With. And even where it might be judged that someone is conferring on themselves a degree of status that others might question, it is still possible to be courteous.

These emotional responses relate in combination to the **roles** people perceive themselves taking in a collaboration. If they can be encouraged to feel that their involvement in and contribution to the collaboration is appreciated and valued, then these roles will be made meaningful to them even where they are not represented by formal labels. This once more demonstrates respect for people as individuals doing what they need to do, inviting them to be more open to integrating their own interests with those of others.

Demonstrating respect for others is a simple and effective way of establishing trust; equally, any demonstration of a lack of respect will create significant barriers to success for any joint enterprise, not least one that has been approached as a 'collaboration'.

GROUP EXERCISE 5.10

Consider an instance when you were working with other people and found yourself in a position of disagreement with the way things were headed. What evidence was there of power being exerted over, through or with you? How were the different participants' needs being met, and what value and values did this represent? How did the disagreement influence the way the people involved showed respect for each other?

In retrospect, what would you have done differently?

Summary

We started this chapter with an assertion that 'there are few problems as big as the ones humankind will face over the coming decades'. To tackle these effectively will require every part of society to contribute to its fullest, leveraging the investment and innovative capacities of the private sector, the regulatory expertise and commitment to accountability of the public sector, and the passion and energy of the civic sector, all integrated and combined in a myriad of collaborations.

This chapter draws out a number of key considerations for people working together to make this happen:

◆ Collaboration is commonplace and desired when people work together, no matter how dominant or relevant we think purely self-interested competitive behaviours might be.

◆ Collaboration can emerge, yielding outcomes that are optimal to both an ecosystem and its constituents, but will always be vulnerable to exploitation.

◆ Good governance in terms of structure and processes will not guarantee good outcomes in all collaborations at all times, but poor governance will make failure a great deal more likely.

◆ Assessment of stakeholder salience will always be challenged, so preparation must be made to accommodate potential stakeholders of the most unexpected kind.

◆ No matter how well structured the process, collaborators will disagree at times. Expressions of 'power over' can only make matters worse.

◆ The recognition and surfacing of different dimensions of value can underpin the co-creation of new value for individual participants, and for the ecosystem as a whole.

◆ The development of relationships beyond simple transactional exchange can be built through engagements based on respect, inclusivity, equity and trust, encouraging the integration of interests and a commitment to a shared and common goal. Whatever the outcome, this in itself would be a successful collaboration.

QUESTIONS FOR CLASS DISCUSSION

1. **Forms of collaboration:** In the commercial world a common approach to establishing a more visible and lasting level of commitment between partners in a collaboration or 'alliance' is to create a joint venture. Research the S-LCD joint venture formed between the technology giants Samsung and Sony, and discuss this as a form of collaboration.

2. **Governance:** A number of cross-border economic collaborations exist around the world, including ASEAN, MERCOSUR, and NAFTA. Research one of these, or another equivalent arrangement of your choice, identifying and discussing its governance structures and processes. How are multiple sectoral interests represented and their influence demonstrated?

3. **Cross-sector collaborations:** Many large multinational companies formally participate in a number of 'partnerships' with NGOs in areas related to their operations. Identify an example of this, discussing how the choice and selection of partners contributes to mutually important interests and concerns.

4. **Stakeholders:** Investigate the partnership model developed by the GAVI Vaccine Alliance. How is the management of its stakeholders reflected in its structure, governance, and objectives?

5. **Agreement:** Carbon markets are proposed by many as making an important contribution in securing reductions in overall carbon emissions, but are usually negotiated in the face of much opposition. Analyse the development of regional (or common jurisdiction) carbon markets such as the EU-ETS and discuss what issues of power, value or respect might be relevant in making the agreement to multijurisdictional initiatives more likely.

References

Axelrod, R. (1984). *The evolution of cooperation.* New York: Basic Books.

Bertalanffy, L. von (1956). General system theory. *General Systems, 1*(1), 11–17.

Boulding, K. E. (1989). *Three faces of power.* London: Sage Publications.

Confino, J. (2012). Cleaning up the global compact: Dealing with corporate free riders. *The Guardian Newspaper.* Retrieved from http://www.theguardian.com/sustainable-business/cleaning-up-un-global-compact-green-wash (accessed 2014, June 14).

Dubner, S. J. (2015) Should we really behave like economists say we do? *Freakonomics Radio Podcasts.* Retrieved from http://freakonomics.com/2015/06/04/should-we-really-behave-like-economists-say-we-do-a-new-freakonomics-radio-podcast/(accessed 2015, September 9).

Emerson, J. (2003). The blended value proposition: Integrating social and financial returns. *California Management Review, 45*(4) 35–51.

Fisher, R., & Shapiro, D. (2005). *Beyond reason: Using emotions as you negotiate.* New York, NY: Viking Penguin.

Fisher, R., & Ury, W. (1981). *Getting to yes.* Boston: Houghton Mifflin.

Gray, B., & Stites, J. P. (2013). *Sustainability through partnerships: Capitalising on collaboration.* Network for Business Sustainability. Retrieved from nbs.net/knowledge (accessed 2014, March 12).

Granovetter, M. (1983). The strength of weak ties: A network theory revisited. *Sociological Theory, 1*(1), 201–233.

Greve, H., Rowley, T., & Shipilov, A. (2014). *Network advantage.* Chichester: John Wiley & Sons.

Hansen, M. T. (2009). When internal collaboration is bad for your company. *Harvard Business Review, 87*(4), 82–88.

Hemmati, M. (2002). *Multi-stakeholder processes for governance and sustainability.* London: Earthscan.

IISD. (2013). Kalundborg case study. *IISD business and sustainable development: A global guide.* Retrieved from https://www.iisd.org/business/viewcasestudy.aspx?id=77 (accessed 2015, September 9).

Lovelock, J. (1995). *The ages of Gaia: A biography of our living earth.* Oxford: Oxford University Press.

Marine Stewardship Council (MSC). (2015). MSC fisheries standard. Marine Stewardship Council. Retrieved from https://www.msc.org/about-us/standards/fisheries-standard (accessed 2015, July 15).

Maslow, A. H. (1943). A theory of human motivation. *Psychological Review, 50*(4), 370.

Mitchell, R. K., Agle, B. R., & Wood, D. J. (1997). Toward a theory of stakeholder identification and salience: Defining the principle of who and what really counts. *Academy of Management Review, 22*(4), 853–886.

Monbiot, G. (2012). After Rio, we know: Governments have given up on the planet. *The Guardian Newspaper* (2012, June 26), 29.

Morgan, M. (1986). *Images of organisation*. London: Sage Publications.

Möller, K., & Wilson, D. T. (Eds.). (1995). *Business marketing: An interaction and network perspective*. New York: Springer.

Nalebuff, B. J., Brandenburger, A., & Maulana, A. (1996). *Co-opetition*. London: HarperCollinsBusiness.

Nowak, M. A., & Highfield., R. (2011). *SuperCooperators*. New York: Free Press.

Nye, J. S. (2004). *Soft power: The means to success in world politics*. Cambridge, MA: Perseus Books.

Parmar, B. L., Freeman, R. E., Harrison, J. S., Wicks, A. C., Purnell, L., & De Colle, S. (2010). Stakeholder theory: The state of the art. *The Academy of Management Annals*, *4*(1), 403–445.

Pisano, G. P., & Verganti, R. (2008). Which kind of collaboration is right for you. *Harvard Business Review*, *86*(12), 78–86.

Porter, M. (1980). *Competitive strategy*. New York: The Free Press.

Porter, M. E., & Kramer, M. R. (2011). Creating shared value. *Harvard Business Review*, *89*(1/2), 62–77.

Reicher, S., Haslam, S. A., & Hopkins, N. (2005). Social identity and the dynamics of leadership: Leaders and followers as collaborative agents in the transformation of social reality. *The Leadership Quarterly*, *16*(4), 547–568.

Rittel, H. W., & Webber, M. M. (1973). Dilemmas in a general theory of planning. *Policy Sciences*, *4*(2), 155–169.

Tennyson, R. (2011). *The partnering tool-book*. London: The Partnering Initiative. Retrieved from http://thepartneringinitiative.org/tpi-tools/toolbook-series/the-partnering-toolbook/(accessed 24 June 2014, June 24).

Wood, D. J., & Gray, B. (1991). Toward a comprehensive theory of collaboration. *The Journal of Applied Behavioural Science*, *27*(2), 139–162.

UN. (2011). *Corporate sustainability in the world economy*. United Nations Global Compact Office. Retrieved from https://www.unglobalcompact.org/resources/240 (accessed 24 June 2014, June 24).

6 Strategizing: Does Your Business Have a Strategy for a Resource Depleted World?

Nadya Zhexembayeva and Judith Jordan

'The Stone Age didn't end because we ran out of stones.'

Sheik Ahmed Zaki Yamani, Former Oil Minister, Saudi Arabia

'Green tech may provide a way past peak oil. There is no escape from peak water.'

Gus Lubin, Journalist

'We buy things we don't need with money we don't have to impress people we don't like.'

Dave Ramsey, Finance Specialist and Author

LEARNING OUTCOMES

The aim of this chapter is to:

1. Highlight key sustainability challenges that impact business strategy today.

2. Explore different strategic responses to these sustainability challenges.

3. Demonstrate how sustainability challenges can be turned into strategic competitive advantage.

Introduction

For most of the history of modern business, we have enjoyed falling prices on nearly all raw materials – making us dangerously oblivious to the shaky foundations of our global market economy. But the tide is turning: with the prices for resources finally catching up with the ever-diminishing stocks, the new era is upon us. It is time to look into the facts – and prepare a solid strategy for dealing with them.

Welcome to a Resource-Depleted World

Like his father and grandfather before him, Al Cattone has been living off the sea all his life. For the Gloucester fisherman, who spent over 30 years braving the Atlantic's waters, fishing is 'not so much a job as it is an identity'.[1] But this legacy is coming to an abrupt end. In light of the extreme decline of cod stocks, the New England Fishery Management Council voted to slash cod catch rates by 77% in an area from Cape Cod to Nova Scotia. The destruction of fishing communities across the region is expected to follow, with a domino effect on seafood processors, wholesalers, distributors and retailers – an entire industrial ecosystem. But the unpopular move is backed by the harsh reality: the cod stocks today are very far from healthy, with some communities netting a bare 7% of moderate targets set by the National Oceanic and Atmospheric Administration.

In his struggle and sadness, Al is not alone. In the UK, the modern fishing fleet must work 17 times harder for the same catch as their sail-powered 1880s counterparts.[2] In Northern Japan, the entire fishing industry has been in 'terminal decline', with the 2011 tsunami only accelerating the collapse.[3] Recently, the *Financial Times* has become one of the most vocal voices of the fish crisis, alerting the world to the fish stock decline that is more severe than predicted: 'More than half of fisheries worldwide face shrinking stocks, with most of these in worse condition than previously thought, leading to yearly economic losses of $50 billion.'[4] And if the proven losses of the present are not enough, the projected losses of the future exceed every possible flight of the imagination. According to a Stanford University study, overfishing could take all wild seafood off our tables by 2048. 'Unless we fundamentally change the way we manage all the oceans' species together, as working ecosystems, then this century is the last century of wild seafood,' warns marine biologist Stephen Palumbi (Biello, 2006).

In its easy maths and empty plates impact, the story of fish serves as a perfect metaphor for the entire world of resources upon which our economy is built. Whether it is fish or oil, clean water or gold, vitamin C or helium, social or climate stability, the ocean of resources is running dry, creating havoc for the market worldwide.

6.0 Oil, Water, and a Touch of Hurricane Katrina: The New Business Reality

The problem of declining resources is not new. Long before current frameworks, such as The Natural Step,[5] put declining resources at the centre of attention, the issue of resource scarcity enjoyed the devotion of theorists and practitioners alike. From Plato[6] in the 4th century BC, to Thomas Malthus in 1798 to the Club of Rome

---

[1] See more on New England fish stock in the 2013, February 4 CNN article, *Historic cod fishing cuts threaten centuries-old industry in New England.*

[2] This UK study is explored in a 2010, May 4 *Guardian* article, *Study suggests decline in UK fish stocks more severe than thought.*

[3] Bloomberg's 2011, April 25 article has more, see *Tsunami quickens 'terminal decline' of northern Japan's fishing industry.*

[4] See 2012, September 28 *FT* article at http://www.ft.com/intl/cms/s/2/73d14032-088e-11e2-b37e-00144feabdc0.html#axzz2Tg8ciFAK.

[5] The Natural Steps website offers a number of free resources and toolkits at http://www.naturalstep.org/.

in 1972 (Meadows *et al.*, 1972), a parade of esteemed thinkers drew our attention to the looming collapse – to no avail. Hardly any change in the behaviour of businesses, governments, and consumers alike have been inspired by this powerful outcry – if anything, the global market grew tired of the warnings and deaf to the calls for radically new business models. Why?

While the theory of resource decline seemed strong and sound, for nearly two centuries the actual market reality had been telling exactly the opposite story. McKinsey's 2011 report on Resource Revolution puts it best:

> *During most of the 20th century, resource prices – of food, water, energy, steel, for example – declined, despite strong growth in the world's population and even stronger growth in GDP . . . During the 20th century, the price of key resources, as measured by MGI's index, fell by almost half in real terms. This was astounding given that the global population quadrupled in this era and global economic output increased by approximately 20-fold, together resulting in a jump in demand for different resources of between 600 and 2,000 percent. Resource prices declined because of faster technological progress and the discovery of new, low-cost sources of supply.*

In essence, what the declining prices on resources have been telling us for so long is that we can have our cake and eat it too – grow our population, increase our consumption, and keep cutting the prices, all at the same time.

But that was then.

The now looks drastically different – and the speed of waking up to this new reality will determine who will survive and who will vanish in the new era. Each year, we work with about 5,000 senior managers directly, and our conversations so far suggest that the majority are not yet fully awake to this new world of a rapidly collapsing resource base. So, here are a few alarm sirens for you –the general trends that are beyond striking:

- Since the turn of the 21st century, *real* commodity prices increased *147%*.
- At minimum, *$1 trillion more* annual investment in the resource system is necessary to meet future resource demands.
- *3 billion more* middle-class consumers are expected to be in the global economy by 2030, all putting new pressures on resource demand (McKinsey, 2011).

And the particularities are no less alarming. Whatever key aspect of business – or life – we are to consider, declining resources are unravelling the very foundation on which we built our economy.

Those involved in the energy debate have been struggling for decades with the question of how much oil and other fossil fuel is left – with no agreement in sight. What we do have agreement on is the demand for and the cost of energy. By 2030, world energy use is expected to go up by *36%* of the 2011 baseline (BP, 2013), and the past decade has seen a *100% increase in the average cost* to bring a new oil well online. Demand and supply pressures together create a perfect storm for any business – not because we are running out of oil or any other resource, but because the price of energy is becoming so unpredictable.

---

[6] See, for example, *The Dialogues of Plato*, translated by B. Jowett.

Figure 6.1 presents is a simple visualization of this volatility: the price of oil from January 1986 to August 2013 is plotted using nominal data from the Energy Information Administration on spot prices of a barrel of Brent petroleum, converted to August 2013 US dollars using US Consumer Price Index for All Urban Consumers (CPI-U) to show a more realistic picture. It turned out to be a rather exciting roller-coaster ride!

Imagine that we run a company producing chairs – perhaps the very chair in which you are now sitting. Many of the raw materials the chair requires are petroleum-derived – or petroleum dependent. Now, imagine that we are trying to set a sound pricing policy for our beautiful chair and, naturally, need a somewhat stable cost structure. How do you manage the up-and-down jumps in the price of oil – and all dependent products – of the like we have seen in the last five years?[7]

If the price of oil seem remote for you, however, the next group of resources cannot possibly leave you disinterested. Do you know anybody who doesn't eat?

Whenever one talks about food, it is assumed that availability is an issue. Yet, when 40% of food in the US is not eaten – amounting to $165 billion a year in waste[8] – clearly, when it comes to the developed world, availability is not an issue. Accessibility of food is becoming a strategic concern. Like a risotto or rice pudding? Of the top ten rice-producing countries of the world, the first two – China and India – produce and control more than the other eight combined.[9] If your company or your supplier depends on rice production, such dependency creates real strategic concern – and the story of the 2008 rice crisis only underlines this risk. The Global Rice Crisis took place in the early part of 2008, when the international trading price of rice jumped dramatically, increasing more than 300% from $300 to $1,200 per ton in just four months.[10] Now, try to run a business with this resource craziness.

Perhaps rice is not your food of choice – and access to Indian resources is far from one of your business challenges. Yet the global decline of food resources

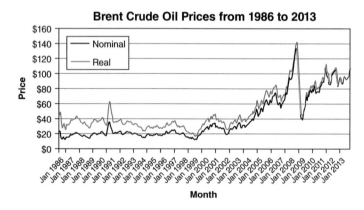

FIGURE 6.1   Volatility in Brent Crude Oil Prices from January 1986 to August 2013.

---

[7] We are very thankful to Wikipedia for sharing this data at http://en.wikipedia.org/wiki/Price_of_petroleum.

[8] See CNN article from April 2012, *40% of US food wasted, report says* at http://news.blogs.cnn.com/2012/08/22/40-of-u-s-food-wasted-report-says/.

[9] See full detail at http://www.mapsofworld.com/world-top-ten/rice-producing-countries.html.

[10] See full story of the 2008 World Rice Crisis at http://en.wikipedia.org/wiki/2008_global_rice_crisis.

touches every person and every company – if we look at the level of nutritional composition of our most precious produce. A 2004 study shows an average decline of 20% of vitamin C, 6% of protein, 16% of calcium, 9% of phosphorus, 15% of iron, and 38% of riboflavin from 1950 to 1999 across 43 garden crops (Davis *et al.*, 2004). We can already foresee a beautiful ripe tomato with absolutely no nutritional value.

From a discussion of food we run straight into another essential resource – used in every sphere of business across the global value chain: water. Water is the new oil, says the conventional wisdom of the 21st century. So, how much water did you use today? If you skipped the shower today, you might have saved 10 to15 litres. A nice bath, and you are probably hitting around 100 litres.

If you had a cup of coffee this morning, some toast and an egg, you have already consumed about 450 litres (or about 120 gallons) of water – enough for three typical baths! And if these words catch you after a nice steak, you might be surprised that a half-pounder would 'cost' you a whopping 3,850 litres (1,017 gallons). These calculations are based on the Global Water Footprint Standard,[11] developed through the joint efforts of scientists to allow companies and consumers to deal with the growing water shortages. And when it comes to disruption of corporate competitiveness and profitability, the shortages are no joke.

Already today, as clean water supply is seeing significant mismatches with demand, an estimated 1.1 billion people lack access to safe drinking water.[12] No wonder that Paul Bulcke, CEO of one of the largest food corporations of the world, Nestlé, is calling water scarcity the greatest threat to food security in the future:

> *By 2030, the demand for water is forecast to be 50% higher than today, withdrawals could exceed natural renewal by over 60%, resulting in water scarcity for a third of the world's population . . . It is anticipated that there will be up to 30% shortfalls in global cereal production by 2030 due to water scarcity . . . This is a loss equivalent to the entire grain crops of India and the United States combined . . . Resource shortages lead to price increases and volatility.*[13]

6.1 Searching for a Disappeared Resource? Check your landfill

About 1.6 tonnes of raw materials are spent to produce a single computer (UN, 2004), which on its own weighs around 13 kilos. More than 47.4 million computers were thrown out in 2012 in the US alone, and no more than 25% were recycled (*Businessweek*, 2013). If we apply that percentage to one computer, with only 25% of that weight recycled, it means that barely 0.19%, or one fifth of 1% of all originally mined materials would be recycled – 99.81% would be wasted.

It would go to waste not because the materials mined and processed have no value, but rather because we have not been designing products and processes with

---

[11] Full details and the manual on the Global Water Footprint Standard can be found at http://www .waterfootprint.org/?page=files/GlobalWaterFootprintStandard.

[12] You can find plenty of up-to-date data at the World Water Council (www.worldwatercouncil.org).

[13] You can find the full detail on Paul Bulcke's lecture at http://www.nestle.com/media/newsandfeatures/ city-food-lecture.

that value in mind. Our throwaway economy works on the assumption that it is easier to make a new product than to reuse resources already processed. But, as we enter the 21st century, 'throwaway' has gone away. The UK warned it would run out of landfill space by 2018 (*The Independent*, 2010). Dubai has approached this limit already, in 2012, when one of its two key landfills reached its capacity, and was on the brink of overflowing.[14] The Naples and Bangalore rubbish crises became so famous that they reached the pages of the most prestigious media outlets, *The New York Times* among them.

With global landfills overextended to the very top of their capacity, no wonder that waste overspills in every direction. Most of us have heard of giant waste fields floating in our oceans. No scientist is ready to take on the question of the size of any of the fields – the state of Massachusetts? The territory of the Netherlands? The Moon? CNN refers to it as an 'enormous, amorphous, nasty soup that stretches for hundreds of miles.'

For environmentalists, the answer to the question of waste might imply activism (and pessimism). But for entrepreneurs and managers, the implication is rather different. Bill McDonough and the rest of the 'cradle to cradle' crowd made it into a simple formula: 'Waste equals Food.' In other words, hundreds of miles of plastic floating in the ocean is indeed a disaster: it is also a whole lot of wasted petroleum that could, if approached with innovative intelligence, be turned into a business opportunity.

6.2 The Strategic Challenge of Sustainability: Stakeholders are calling

In its broadest sense strategy is the means by which organizations achieve their objectives and strategizing refers to the processes and practices that bring strategies into being. Businesses are composed of many different individuals and groups, each with their own agendas and objectives. As a consequence businesses often have multiple goals, some of which, at times, conflict. This pluralism – inherent to strategizing – means that the processes of analysing, deciding and doing are not linear; nor are they abstracted from the human characteristics of the people involved. Consequently the actual strategies that companies realize emerge as they go along, mixing deliberate intentions with *ad hoc* solutions that open new opportunities or create unforeseen problems. This can be represented in Henry Mintzberg's model in Figure 6.2.

When we understand that strategy arises from a pluralistic and contested process, we have to focus on *how* to think, analyse, choose and act, in order to make things happen. Hence we might look at strategizing as a large and creative set of practices, ranging from technical analyses to group co-ordination, rhetoric, selling, experimenting, innovating and so forth. As the resource crunch calls into question the security of entire value chains and the flood of waste puts a limit on growth, these trends do not go unnoticed among those with interests in business organizations –

---

[14] Full detail at http://www.thenational.ae/news/uae-news/dubai-running-out-of-landfill-space-to-dump-its-rubbish.

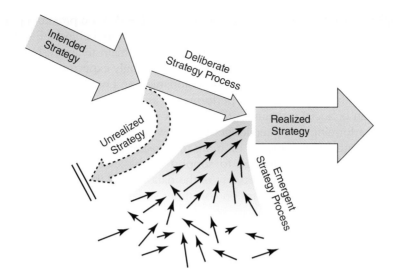

FIGURE 6.2   Mintzberg's Model.

the company's key stakeholders. So strategizing requires ever more demanding skills, more adaptability and capabilities. Gosling and Mintzberg have described five mindsets crucial to this work: reflection, essential for learning and to stay in touch with personal and collective values; analysis, to discover how all the parts of a situation can be made to fit together in constructive ways; worldliness, to appreciate the values and interests of people with very different worldviews to one's own; collaboration, in recognition of superior value always being an outcome of connecting with others; and action, the desire and the skills to craft positive change.

Investors, regulators, employees and, most importantly, customers and consumers increasingly *expect* sound social and environmental performance from the marketplace. This imposes new pressure on companies to develop strategies for sustainability but also creates new opportunities for profit and growth. Understanding the changing expectations of key stakeholders is, therefore, a good starting point for our analysis.

6.2.1   Stakeholder Group #1: Customers

The story of Daniel Lubetzky and the success of his venture, PeaceWorks, is illustrative of the change that is taking place in customers' preferences. Created in 1994 as a 'not-only-for-profit-company', PeaceWorks produces specialty food, such as vegetable spreads and energy bars, by bringing together buyers and sellers divided by conflict, such as Israelis and Arabs. With significant growth in sales, product portfolio, and distribution network, and ongoing community support, including four consecutive wins of the Fast Company Social Capitalist Award, the company's track record speaks volumes about the new expectations of customers and society at large.[15]

---

[15] You will find more information on PeaceWorks on their site, http://peaceworks.com.

Companies like PeaceWorks are niche players dependent on premium prices, but their emergence and success does not capture the full story behind the shift in market demand that is taking place. The real story is that mainstream customers across an array of markets and geographic areas are increasingly expecting social and environmental performance from the brands, companies, and products they choose but, more importantly, they want these performance improvements to be realized without any green or social premium. Consumers want products that are more affordable, better performing, healthier, longer-lasting, with added appeal – in other words, it is 'smarter' rather than 'greener' or 'more responsible' that they are after.

What evidence is there though to support claims such as the one above? To address this question a short overview of the data behind these claims is provided, together with a short commentary on consumer surveys and what they do (and do not) mean.

Consumers appear to say one thing . . . As early as 2006, a National Consumers League and Fleishman-Hillard survey (2007) of US consumers reported the social responsibility of a company as being the number one determining factor of brand loyalty (35% of respondents), well ahead of product price and availability (each receiving 20% of respondents' votes). Four years later it became clear that concerns for the environment were not limited to the consumers from developed economies – the 2010 World Economic Forum report suggested that such concern was as strong in the developing world, 'and in some areas stronger as they are often more directly affected, for example by water pollution' A recent Deloitte report (2009) suggests that while much of consumer behaviour is still dictated by price, quality, and convenience, a huge number, 95%, of American consumers report that they are willing to 'buy green'. A BBMG survey (2009) that combined a national poll of 2,000 consumers with ethnographic interviews supports the Deloitte findings: nearly seven in ten Americans (67%) agree that 'even in tough economic times, it is important to purchase products with social and environmental benefits'.

. . . but do another! All of the above surveys – suggesting the existence of the green consumer – are very encouraging, BUT . . . the relatively high level of *interest* in green products does not appear to be backed by *action*. In the Deloitte study, only 10% strongly agree that they are in fact willing to pay more for green. The vast majority of consumers are clearly unwilling to fork over more money at the checkout counter (MIT, 2009)[16].

If sustainability is on the radar screen of consumer expectations, why is it not translating into the opening of wallets in the act of purchase? From a review of consumer studies, we conclude that the gap between stated expectations and the purchase act exists for three reasons:

1   Perceptions: a majority of the consumers surveyed perceive green products as more costly, unavailable and poor in quality when compared to conventional counterparts (Dublin, 2010).

2   Trust: there is a gap between consumers' interest in green products and their confidence in green marketing claims. According to the BBMG study, nearly

---

[16] Consumer unwillingness to pay more is reaffirmed by MIT's 2009 *The Business of Sustainability* report, which finds that currently, 'insufficient customer demand or needs' is ranked as the most significant roadblock to addressing sustainability concerns (with 26% of managers ranking it as number one).

one in four US consumers (23%) say they have 'no way of knowing' if a product is green or if it actually does what it claims.

3   Survey language: plenty of evidence exists that the very surveys designed to measure consumer expectations are driving the myth of the green and social premium. Here is a typical headline: '53 percent of consumers say they would be willing to pay some type of premium for televisions with green attributes' (CEA, 2008). Who wants to pay a premium, and what is a green attribute anyway? Consumers are presented with two assumptions to digest and accept – sustainability comes at a price and they are getting green benefits or social responsibility in exchange.

By contrast, mainstream sustainability leaders are offering competitively-priced, smarter products, whether they are Clorox cleaning sprays that are biodegradable and safer for human health or GE hybrid locomotives that save 15% in fuel costs for the CFO of a railroad company. Asking the question, 'Would you buy a green product?', is very different from offering a smarter product that is priced competitively – one that is higher quality and better for human health and the environment.

It is no wonder that Wal-Mart sold 190,000 organic cotton yoga outfits in 10 weeks on its first try (Wal-Mart 2008). Once a company dares to debunk the myth of the green and social premium and offer products with sustainability performance at competitive prices and quality, customers are quick to prefer them over conventional alternatives – providing an often hard-to-imitate advantage in a highly competitive world.

It is clear that consumer expectations are shifting. Yet serving the end consumer is only one part of the deal; increasingly, companies located in the middle of a value chain find the most pressure coming from their direct customers in business-to-business relationships. IBM, Pepsi, Ikea, Ford, and Kaiser Permanente are among those setting new, tougher standards. Procter & Gamble has now come out with its own Supplier Scorecard,[17] after being subjected for several years to Wal-Mart's scorecard as a supplier itself – not particularly unexpected. But we must admit that receiving a letter from a missile manufacturing company, one of our business education clients, explaining the new sustainability demands for all suppliers to the company, was at least mildly surprising.

Customer and consumer expectations go well beyond questions about the *use* of the final product. Fuelled by information on declining resources and catalysed daily by NGOs and consumer activist groups, customers and consumers are demanding a completely new relationship to their providers of products and services. A mere satisfaction with price, quality and availability is no longer good enough – consumers are expecting to be co-creators in nearly all aspects of business, from product development and manufacturing to packaging and sales. No, they are not eager to compromise on quality and price, but they are ready to pay for smarter solutions featuring embedded ecological and social intelligence (Environmental Leader, 2010). Trendwatching.com's '10 Crucial Consumer Trends for 2010' put it best:

Ruthless capitalism went out of fashion way before the crisis hit. This year, prepare for 'business as unusual'. For the first time, there's a global understanding, if not a

---

[17] See http://www.sustainablelifemedia.com/content/story/design/p_g_launchces_supply_chain_scorecard.

feeling of urgency *that sustainability, in every possible meaning of the word, is the only way forward. How that should or shouldn't impact consumer societies is of course still part of a raging debate, but at least there is a debate. Meanwhile, in mature consumer societies, companies will have to do more than just embrace the notion of being a good corporate citizen. To truly prosper, they will have to 'move with the culture'. This may mean displaying greater transparency and honesty, or having conversations as opposed to one-way advertising, or championing collaboration instead of an us-versus-them mentality.*

The monumental shift in customer and consumer expectations can be best described as follows: we are increasingly moving from a focus on green products to offering customer-oriented solutions, and that makes all the difference.

The outside-in expectations from customers are made increasingly more urgent as another wave of expectations is putting pressure on companies from the inside-out. This new wave comes from the employees.

6.2.2 Stakeholder Group #2: Employees

In 1997, McKinsey & Co published the results of a year-long study involving 77 companies and nearly 6,000 managers. The now legendary report predicted a major talent war over 20 years following its publication – whereby all-round intelligent, technologically savvy, globally aware, operationally astute professionals would become a highly fought-over resource (Chambers *et al.*, 1998). With demand significantly outstripping supply, McKinsey offered four strategies to bring the best professionals on board:

- *Go with the Winner:* attracting those eager to join a high-performing company.
- *Big Risk, Big Reward:* appealing to those who crave challenge and risk.
- *Lifestyle:* focused on those attracted by a flexible work–life balance and a great quality of life.
- *Save the World:* crucial for those driven by an inspiring mission and sense of purpose.

Nearly three-quarters of the way through the projected time-line, it is interesting to see if 'Save the World' continues to place among the top 'attractors' for potential employees. 'Yes, it does!' says Net Impact, an association of sustainability-minded MBA providers. Already back in 2006, Net Impact polled 2,100 MBA students in 87 programmes in the US and Canada, discovering that nearly 80% of soon-to-be MBAs polled wanted to find socially responsible employment at some point in their careers, while 59% reported they would seek such opportunity immediately after graduation (Knight, 2006).

While Net Impact focused on talent in the western world, Douglas Ready, Linda Hill and Jay Conger turned their attention to emerging markets. Their 2008 report, featured in the *Harvard Business Review*, suggests four key factors that determine a company's success in attracting the most talented employees: 'brand', 'opportunity', 'culture', and 'purpose'.

Sounds familiar? Indeed, the 2008 *HBR* report offers many parallels to the 1997 McKinsey survey. These and many other studies (see, e.g., Turban and Greening, 1997; WBCSD, 2005) are all starting to sing in unison: a company's contribution to making the world a better place features prominently among the distinct factors that determine whether a recruitment effort succeeds or fails. Furthermore, a business commitment to strong social and environmental performance matters even more once the coveted employees are finally recruited. At that point a completely different dimension of employment kicks in: engagement.

Engagement represents, perhaps, the most touchy-feely and fuzzy word in the lexicon of management, so let us offer a brief definition of it. An 'engaged employee' is one who 'is fully involved in, and enthusiastic about, his or her work, and thus will act in a way that furthers their organization's interests' (Wikipedia, 2010). An estimated $300 billion is lost in the US economy due to disengaged employees (Saks, 2006). In contrast, high engagement has been shown to lead to increased self-efficacy and a nearly one-third increase in work-related performance (Luthans & Peterson, 2001). For example, engagement studies with data-entry personnel showed a tenfold increase in productivity by engaged employees (Buckingham & Coffman, 1999). Employees that are engaged were also found to have 38% higher probability of success on productivity measures and 44% higher success on customer loyalty and employee retention (Harter & Schmidt, 2002).

Now, if employee engagement is so important when it comes to company performance, how can we get more of it? Interestingly enough, embedding social and environmental considerations into the company's purpose, strategy, and operations might just be the best way to go. While the exact relationship between company commitment to social and environmental excellence and employee engagement has long been debated, it is only very recently that such a relationship was measured in a scholarly manner, proving that when employees perceive their company to be a good corporate citizen, their engagement, along with creative involvement and deep, high-quality relationships, goes up (see, e.g., Glavas and Piderit, 2009). Bob Stiller, Chairman of the Board of Green Mountain Coffee Roasters, describes this connection between business sustainability and employee engagement:

> *I've learned that people are motivated and more willing to go the extra mile to make the company successful when there's a higher good associated with it. It's no longer just a job. Work becomes meaningful and this makes us more competitive. Everyone realizes we can't do good unless we're profitable. The two go hand in hand.*
>
> Business as an Agent of World Benefit, 2005

Whether we are talking about attraction, retention, or engagement, sustainability seems to be the cornerstone of new employee expectations. Moved by the rapidly declining availability of resources, and equipped by instantly available and highly targeted sustainability intelligence, employees are putting forth new demands to business. Some companies are quick to integrate social and environmental performance into their people strategies and policies, thus creating a source of differentiation in a highly competitive talent market. Timberland, ING and Ford are just a few of thousands of companies that offer their teams up to 40 hours' paid time off to volunteer every year. Target goes a step further by sponsoring www.VolunteerMatch.org, which makes it easy for any company to engage its employees or consumers in volunteer efforts; while the youth non-profit, Junior Achievement, produces a comprehensive report making a strong business case for offering such benefits to employees (Junior Achievement, 2009). But volunteer programmes are among the least innovative ways to use a company's sustainability record as a new source of attraction, retention and engagement of precious talent. A number of other ideas can be considered for your company's 'social compensation' package: Burt's Bees calculates bonuses in part on how well the company meets energy conservation goals (Story, 2008), which employees and management set together. The offshoot is reduced energy costs, and employee engagement and buy-in because they have a hand in setting the energy reduction goal and, of course, in providing a boon to the environment. The auditing and tax firm KPMG awards 16 service-committed employees with a $1,000 donation for their favorite non-profit (Cause Capitalism, 2009). Gap Inc. was in the news for a series of grants that support employees' philanthropic work (Gap Inc., 2009). Pepsi takes it further and offers thousands of dollars to fund ideas for a better world submitted by everyone and anyone – and it is the community vote that makes the difference in project selection.[18] The talent-capture innovations keep rolling in.

6.2.3   Stakeholder Group #3: Investors

If the customers and employees are not the ones that have the greatest power in your business, perhaps the voice of investors will get your company to listen. From a small fringe in the 1970s to the present day trillions of dollars in total assets under management (Social Investment Forum, 2007), the rise of Socially Responsible Investment (SRI) is remarkable. A broad-based approach to investing that includes screening, shareholder advocacy, and community investing, SRI is perhaps best known for the rapid growth in funds that exclude so-called 'sin-stocks' such as tobacco, armaments, and gambling. In some countries, SRI now encompasses 11% of total assets under management (Social Investment Forum, 2010) – a hefty chunk of the investment market.

It is, however, the other 89% of mainstream investment that is the real news of the day. The amount of attention coming from the 'normal' investor is what companies are suddenly attuning to.

The involvement of the mainstream investment community in the field of climate change illustrates the new reality. A highly contested, tension-causing topic, climate change is hardly one to incite 'save-the-world' action and *Kumbaya* singing from the gray pinstripe universe of finance. Yet it is the investment community represented by the Ceres' Investor Network on Climate Risk (INCR) that so proudly reported a record 95 climate change-related shareholder resolutions filed by March 2010, a massive 40% increase over the year-earlier proxy period (INCR, 2010). Uniting asset managers, state and city treasurers and comptrollers, public and labour pension funds, and other institutional investors, the US-based INCR represents an investor group with nearly $10 trillion in assets. INCR's UK counterpart, the Carbon Disclosure Project, acts on behalf of 475 investors representing total assets of $55 trillion – and uses its power to force the world's largest publically traded companies to disclose their emissions. In 2009, a total of 409 out of the 500 largest companies responded to the Carbon Disclosure Project's request, up from 383 in the previous year. While France, Germany, Japan, the UK and the US represent 70% of the total emissions disclosed, the response rate from the BRIC countries has doubled since 2008 to 44%, with Brazil reaching a 100% response rate (Carbon Disclosure Project, 2009).

---

[18] See full details of the Pepsi Refresh Project at http://www.refresheverything.com/.

The efforts of investors are heavily influenced by the insurance industry, which is one of the most important drivers of the newfound affection of business for climate change action. Imagine that you are a US-based insurer, reviewing the following statistic: American insurers 'have experienced growth in weather-related catastrophe losses from levels of about $1 billion per year in the 1970s to an average of $17 billion per year over the past decade, far out-stripping growth in premiums, populations, and inflation during the same period' (London Climate Change Partnership, 2006). What action will you take?

While you are catching your breath, here is the Allstate response: run! In 2005, Allstate refused to renew policies with 95,000 homeowners and 16,000 commercial property owners in Florida. Allstate CEO Ed Liddy made the logic behind the decision painfully clear: 'We are girding for the onslaught of the next hurricane season. What's new is the intensity of this (storm) cycle could be a lot worse than things that we've seen before' (Lynch, 2006) If the insurers are running, no wonder that investors are calling, and as the spread of such guidelines as the Equator Principles illustrates, climate change is only one of many environmental and social concerns on investors' agendas. These Principles, launched in 2003 with the first ten global financial institutions – ABN AMRO Bank, N. V., Barclays plc, Citigroup, Inc., Crédit Lyonnais, Credit Suisse First Boston, HVB Group, Rabobank Group, The Royal Bank of Scotland, WestLB AG, and Westpac Banking Corporation – offer standards for determining, assessing and managing social and environmental risk in project financing. Seventy global players have signed on to the Equator Principles in the first six years of its existence (Equator Principles, 2010).

For some, rising investor expectations can be a tough pill to swallow, but others are quick to leverage outstanding social and environmental performance as a way to attract new capital. Intermediaries are also taking notice – connecting the socially and environmentally-savvy investors with top performers – and making money on it.

6.2.4 Stakeholder Group #4: Regulators

Customers, employees, investors all impact our daily business decisions, but we cannot forget about one more essential stakeholder: the regulators. In 2008, China launched a surprise crackdown on plastic bags, banning outright the production of some designs and forbidding shops from handing out free bags (Shipeng & Graham-Harrison, 2008).This was only a year after San Francisco became the first US city to ban plastic bags in supermarkets (Goodyear, 2007). Also in 2008, Calgary became the first city in Canada to make illegal trans-fats from restaurants and fast food chains (CBC News, 2007), while the Brazilian state of Mato Grosso became the first Latin American state to pass a Waste, Electrical and Electronic Equipment (WEEE) bill (SEI, 2010), focused specifically on electronic waste prevention. In 2009, the US National Association of Insurance Commissioners made climate change risk disclosure mandatory for all insurance companies with annual policies over $500 million (Ceres, 2009). In 2010, the UK launched its first mandatory carbon trading scheme, initially called the Carbon Reduction Commitment, and later renamed the CRC Energy Efficiency Scheme (Carbon Trust, 2010). Also in a single month in 2010, South Africa passed 47 amendments and extensions to its sustainability legislation and regulation (Polity.org.za, 2010), ranging from chemical management to atmospheric emissions to fertilizers and everything in between.

The data speaks for itself here, but let us try to make the point even more explicit: whether it is an act of leadership or a desperate reaction to the pressures of NGOs and activist voters, governments are taking social and environmental issues to heart, adding new laws and regulations to the pressures shaping the business environment. The question is: 'Will your company ride the wave of legislative changes to get ahead of the curve, or wait until the waters drag it under?'

By all accounts, the Whirlpool Corporation is keeping its head above water (no pun intended) while making the government a close friend and ally. A maker of household appliances, the company has been consistently preparing ever-stricter regulations – demanding higher energy and water efficiency – and receives government support for its pro-sustainability research and development efforts. In 2009, Whirlpool received a $19.3 million grant from the US stimulus project to develop 'smart appliances' with the ability to communicate with the grid, cutting the energy use during peak hours and going full steam during the low-demand periods. But it is not just future products that give the appliance maker advantage via its relationship with new pro-sustainability regulation: in the same year, Whirlpool launched a comprehensive 'Cash for Appliances' website (Whirlpool, 2010) to help American consumers get reimbursed by the US Department of Energy (Appolo Blog, 2010).

Could it be that compliance is simply no longer enough? Is it time to readjust business attitudes to speed up (rather than slow down) sustainability regulation?

Whether it is customers, employees, investors, regulators, or society at large pushing for change, the expectations of business are going up rapidly. As the decline of resources continues to take centre stage in an increasingly transparent world, sustainability is rapidly becoming a must – a new standard for business to follow, reach, and exceed.

6.3 Strategic Responses: What Strategies Have Businesses Adopted? What More Can They Do?

With new sustainability pressures challenging the ability of businesses to survive and prosper, firms need to adapt and change. This section outlines some of the strategies that companies have adopted in the face of the new resource-depleted, waste-full, stakeholder-awakened market reality *(Strategies 1 and 2)* and considers other more positive strategic responses *(Strategies 3 and 4)*.

Strategy theory (see, e.g., Barney, 1991 or Grant, 1991) suggests that to be successful a firm needs to create a distinctive value proposition that meets the needs of its chosen set of customers. The firm gains a competitive advantage by leveraging its unique resources and capabilities and configuring its activities in ways that rivals find hard to replicate. But, as the discussion of Strategy Responses 1 and 2 reveals, the strategic focus of many firms has been too narrow. Responses to social and environmental concerns are often framed in terms of overcoming obstacles to business success – costs that companies have to incur to meet legal constraints (Strategy #1) – or public relations exercises that firms need to engage in to project a positive corporate image (Strategy #2). By focusing its gaze on the needs and concerns of its immediate customers, a firm can miss opportunities and overlook the ways in which broader societal issues are affecting the ways in which it configures its value chain (the set of activities involved in creating, producing, selling, distributing and supporting its products or services). By addressing societal concerns companies are often able to add value and differentiate themselves from rivals (Strategy #3) and spur innovation (Strategy #4).

6.3.1 Strategy #1: Trade-off sustainability

The earliest (and, in our experience, the most widespread) strategic response to the challenges of decreasing resources and increasing social and environmental expectations is to consider green and social responsibility as an added cost – an inevitable trade-off with profits. A paper in the *Journal of Economic Perspectives* argues that tougher environmental regulation must, by its very nature, reduce profits (Palmer *et al.*, 1995). This widespread belief is captured here:

> *The idea that a business could ever 'do well by doing good' . . . seems to violate economic logic . . . any business that tried to provide or preserve more environmental quality than is lawfully required would incur higher costs than its competitors, and its customers would abandon it in search of lower prices.*
>
> Reinhardt, 2000

In short, if it is better for society and the environment, it must cost more for business.

One reason for the widespread trade-off assumption can be attributed to the initial dominance of awareness-raising efforts such as Rachel Carson's *Silent Spring*, Ralph Nader's *Unsafe at Any Speed* and Thomas Berry's *The Dream of the Earth* – each of them powerful works built on the pioneering legacy of Aldo Leopold, dating back to the 1940s.

> *Early models discussing the integration of the natural environment into organizational decision-making and strategy were primarily derived from the deep ecology literature. Rather than addressing the issue of competitive advantage, they presented a conflict between the economy and ecology and thus between financial and environmental performance.*
>
> Sharma *et al.*, 2005

In just one of many examples, a 1994 *Harvard Business Review* article suggests that there is a necessary trade-off between profit and environmental improvement. 'Ambitious environmental goals have real economics costs. As a society, we may rightly choose those goals despite their costs, but we must do so knowingly,' say the McKinsey authors (Walley & Whitehead, 1994).

The message that sustainability comes with a significant price tag is common but increasingly subject to challenge. Porter and Kramer (2011, p. 65) argue that 'social harms and weaknesses frequently create internal costs or firms – such as wasted energy or raw materials, costly accidents and the need for remedial training to compensate for inadequacies in education'. From their perspective, addressing societal concerns becomes a way of avoiding uncomfortable trade-offs rather than accepting them.

6.3.2   Strategy #2: Bolt-on sustainability

Many companies 'bolt-on' sustainability like an afterthought to their core strategies, despite their best intentions. They trumpet green initiatives and social philanthropy that lie at the margins of the business, with symbolic wins that inadvertently highlight the unsustainability of the rest of their activities. If Nike's *Considered* line of footwear is sustainable, what are its other products? If the 2011 Chevrolet Cruze touts its use of eco-friendly cartridge oil filters,[19] what do GM's other vehicles use? Sustainability becomes programmatic, a headquarters' endeavour pinned onto one person or one department charged with finding and communicating those things that the company is doing anyway and that can be now repackaged as sustainability leadership. This is what can be called a 'bolt-on sustainability strategy' (Laszlo & Zhexembayeva, 2011).

A good tip-off that sustainability is bolted-on is when it is declared to be a separate strategy, one that is *de facto* parallel to the company's main business. Another is internal teams working without the close collaboration of suppliers, customers, NGOs, and other stakeholders. A third is viewing corporate responsibility as a balancing act in which economic interests are traded-off against social and environmental targets. We can of course point to obvious cases such as Exxon-Mobil's[20] corporate citizenship strategy,[21] promoted through its corporate-level sustainability working group. But the reality is that the vast majority of companies pursue bolt-on green and social responsibility projects that are poorly integrated with the rest of their value added activities.

Ask yourself: 'Does your company have a separate function or department responsible for sustainability performance with its own dedicated link on the corporate website?' 'Does it have flagship green products – like the Chevy Volt, priced at nearly double its petrol equivalent – for which customers must pay extra?'

We have all heard real-life stories of bolt-on sustainability. You might even find familiar the case of the Sustainability Manager hired at a telecommunications company. After a year on the job, they produce a glossy sustainability report, largely designed by external consultants, that brilliantly covers topics ranging from ethics to information security. On environmental protection alone, the report highlights double-digit successes in energy conservation across major data centres, paper recycling and hybrid cars for sales fleets. The problem: business unit heads run the other way when they see the manager coming, the CEO never mentions sustainability in quarterly webcasts with analysts, and hardly a single employee believes sustainability is anything other than a public relations exercise. The wireless group fails to address core sustainability issues such as Electromagnetic Frequency Radiation (EMF) risk to cell phone users; the broadband and fixed line businesses are only barely compliant with WEEE and Restriction of Hazardous Substances (RoHS) regulations on heavy metals, toxic chemicals and recycling of electronic equipment. Opportunities to serve the poor in emerging markets are largely ignored, and the company is a laggard on making products available to disabled and aging customers.

---

[19] http://gmauthority.com/blog/2010/05/chevy-cruze-engines-to-get-easy-change-environmentally-friendly-oil-filter/.

[20] See, e.g., http://www.exxonmobil.com/corporate/news_speeches_20090617_sks.aspx (accessed 2010, July 11), in which sustainability is referred to as a balancing act.

[21] http://www.exxonmobil.com/Corporate/community_ccr_sustainability.aspx.

Also familiar might be the case of the specialty chemicals supplier's offsite meeting of its top executives. A consultant is asked to brief the top team on sustainability and what it means for the core business. The briefing is followed by a heated discussion about the growing attacks by international NGOs, opinion leaders, government agencies, and consumer groups who increasingly view the company's product portfolio as harmful to human health and the environment. 'Our strategy in the core business is hugely profitable,' comments the CEO. 'Even with declining market shares and growing regulatory pressures, we can continue to make money doing what we've always done.' Two years later the company has in place several sustainability initiatives from green packaging and employee well-being programmes to a foundation for educating young women in emerging countries. But its core business is increasingly demonized worldwide, sales are down and employee turnover is at an all-time high, even though for the time being profits remain strong.

Stories of bolted-on sustainability are, unfortunately, all too common. They produce self-reinforcing narratives about sustainability and corporate social responsibility being necessary costs rather than profit opportunities. With the bolt-on approach prevailing in practice, it is no surprise that much of today's sustainability efforts bring about cynicism among both corporate managers and social activists, with little value created for either party. Yet there are viable alternatives – built on radically different theory, principles, and practices – that are increasingly pursued by leading businesses of different sizes and shapes around the globe.

6.3.3 Strategy #3: Embedded sustainability

We know how to meet the demands of shareholder value – and years of thinking about managerial excellence has produced remarkable expertise in this area. We also know how to create stakeholder value: traditional approaches such as CSR and philanthropy that predictably lead to trade-offs and added costs. What we are still discovering is how to meet both shareholder and other stakeholder requirements in the core business – without mediocrity and without compromise – creating value for the company that cannot be disentangled from the value it creates for society and the environment.

Embedded sustainability is a strategic response to sustainability challenges that allows us to do just that. Defined as 'the incorporation of environmental, health and social value into the company's core business with no trade-off in price or quality (i.e., with no social or green premium)', embedded sustainability is all about integrating social and environmental thinking into the very DNA of the company.

The goal is not green or social responsibility for its own sake. It is meeting new market expectations in ways that strengthen the company's current strategy or help it to develop a better one. At its best, it is invisible, similar to quality, yet still capable of hugely motivating employees and creating loyalty in consumers and supply chain partners.

As you ponder the idea of embedded sustainability, consider the story of US-based GOJO Industries, Inc. Founded in 1946 with the first one-step heavy duty hand cleaner and the 1952 introduction of the first portion-controlled dispenser for tough soils markets, GOJO today is a mid-size private company focused on safeguarding resources and advancing public health for future generations. It helped set industry standards for sustainable skincare in introducing the world's first green certified hand soap and instant hand sanitizers. As a member of the United States

Green Building Council (USGBC), GOJO was instrumental in the inclusion of hand hygiene requirements within Leadership in Energy and Environmental Design – Existing Buildings: Operations and Maintenance (LEED – EBOM.)

Recent advancements include SMART FLEX™ technology, the company's light-weight, recyclable PET refill bottle made with 30% less material. The new bottle offers the same durability as a standard rigid HDPE bottle. Another is the Plastics to Playgrounds programme, enabling it to divert more than 50% of its solid waste from landfills through a partnership with a local toy manufacturer, reducing environmental impact while having a positive impact on the lives of children.

In 2010, GOJO declared ambitious long-range sustainability goals as part of its core strategy. The company is striving to 'bring well-being to one billion people every day by 2020' through efforts to improve hand hygiene when soap and water are not available. It is continuing to target reductions in water usage, solid waste and greenhouse gases. It also sponsors scientific research to advance quality of life and reduce risks to well-being. For example, after a university study (Gerba, 2006, 2007) revealed the vulnerability of refillable bulk soap dispensers to bacterial contamination, the company is working to educate the industry about unnecessary health risks of bulk hand soap contamination.

With its emphasis on innovation and continuous learning, GOJO is just one more example of an industry leader committed to embedding social and environmental sustainability into its business; a company that declares itself 'passionate about creating a healthy world by delivering solutions that positively impact people, places and the environment'.[22]

Another small- to mid-sized company example is Bohinj Park Hotel. Envisioned as one of the first 'green' hotels in Eastern Europe, Bohinj Park Hotel could hardly bet on price premium to make its business model viable. Instead of focusing only on marginal but highly visible environmental and social performance such as soaps, towels, and the usual hotel eco-efficiency practices, the hotel and resort has environmental performance embedded into its very walls. Combining geothermal and co-generation technologies, the hotel produces its own energy for all hotel operations, including the usually heat-demanding workings of an aqua park. Water is continuously recycled throughout the system, with heat collected from the warm shower water before it is reused for toilet flushing. Floor heating ensures comfort, while special cool-heat grids (inaudible and energy effective) significantly outperform classic air-conditioning systems. Wall and window insulation is fortified by a one-of-a-kind insulated roof, while LED lighting and wireless room controls allow for optimal room performance independent of particular guest behaviour. Socio-economic development of a remote Bohinj region is also embedded in hotel operations: it is one of the largest local food consumer, employer, and community activists, with all health and wellness amenities open free to local residents throughout the entire year. It is no surprise that the Bohinj Park Hotel generates 17.22 kg of CO_2 per guest per night, an enormous tenfold difference compared to 174.82 kg produced by 'standard' hotels in the region. As for the financial impact, the company managed to move energy expenses from the first to the last item in its cost structure, with energy representing only 14% of overall expenditure. The savings are then channelled into

---

[22] GOJO Industries, Inc. The authors would like to thank Argerie Vasilakes, Nicole Koharik and David Searle for providing information on the company.

other activities of the hotel, such as food and catering, allowing the company to produce superior performance without price premium.

Embedding sustainability into the very DNA of the company is one of the most advanced approaches to preparing a strategic response to social and environmental strategies. Yet there is one more – an entirely new strategy – that takes it to a whole new level.

6.3.4 Strategy #4: Overfished Ocean Strategy

One can think of the global economy in which we are living today as one long line. The line starts with all the companies that are mining, growing, or rearing something – those are our only options when it comes to raw materials. The line finishes with all the companies managing a not very sexy business, but increasingly a lucrative one – waste. All other businesses – large and small, products and services – are between these two dots. That is our entire global economy. One giant supply chain.

It is *linear* – as there is only one straight line from the beginning to the end. It is *throwaway* – as, generally speaking, we only use what we mine once, throwing away most of the resources just the way you throw away a plastic fork after one time use. And it is *collapsing* – as we are running of things to mine and places to trash.

But a transformation is taking place. For most businesses, this transformation is invisible. For some bearing its crushing impacts, it is disastrous. Yet some see it as the greatest opportunity of the 21st century – the chance to swim in new waters and to develop what Kim and Mauborgne (2005) refer to as 'a blue ocean strategy'.

The basis of Kim and Mauborgne's argument is that companies succeed not by battling competitors but by creating 'blue oceans' of uncontested space. They coin the term 'red oceans' and 'blue oceans' to denote different market contexts. Red oceans refer to known market spaces where industry boundaries are defined and firms battle with rivals to try and gain a competitive advantage. Oceans are depicted as red because they are characterized by 'bloody battles' and cut-throat competition. In contrast, blue oceans are market spaces that are not inhabited. They are unexplored and untroubled by competition. As Kim and Mauborne (2005) put it:

> *The only way to beat the competition is to stop trying to beat the competition. In red oceans, the industry boundaries are defined and accepted, and the competitive rules of the game are known. In blue oceans, competition is irrelevant because the rules of the game are waiting to be set.*

Firms that swim in blue oceans create and capture new demand and, rather than accepting conventional trade-offs, seek to align their activities in ways that achieve both low cost and differentiation.

Kim and Mauborgne's ideas are in striking contrast to Michael Porter's positioning view. With the powerful advice of the latter, for decades companies claimed their victory by finding the best spot – a unique position on the crowded competitive landscape,[23] represented in the well-known 'five forces' model in Figure 6.3.

---

[23] The work of Michael Porter, such as *Competitive Strategy: Techniques for Analysing Industries and Competitors* (1980), is the best illustration of the positioning approach.

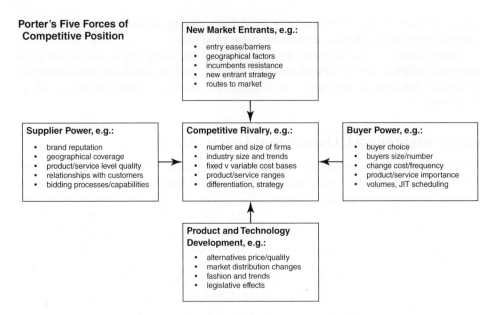

FIGURE 6.3   Porter's Five Forces of Competitive Position.

Following the fresh invitation of Kim and Mauborgne, other companies strived to avoid the crowd by discovering a new market space – swimming into the blue ocean waters far away from shark-filled, blood-red existing markets. (For more on this approach see Kim and Mauborgne, 2005). What a great idea! However, at the core, the blue ocean companies studied by the authors operate and invent within the same resource constraints as their red ocean counterparts, oblivious to the collapsing linear economy and all the pressures associated with it. As the linear throwaway economy is approaching its collapse, this *old* economic order is running its course. Whether red, blue or rainbow-coloured, the oceans are becoming excruciatingly empty, and those managers that deeply understand and master this shift are able to use the new reality to power up radical innovation and secure a remarkable competitive advantage. As they ride ahead of the wave, new products, new business models, new markets, and new profits follow. If the open-mindedness of the Blue Ocean Strategy is used and applied to sustainability challenges – you get to the *Overfished Ocean Strategy*.

The Overfished Ocean Strategy is best explained by looking at real life examples as illustrated by Case Studies 6.1, 6.2 and 6.3.

In their unexpected take on resource intelligence, TerraCycle, BMW and Swiss Re are not alone. OMV, an integrated oil and gas company, which supplies 200 million people in Central and Eastern Europe with energy, calls it *Resourcefulness*. This term, which smells of ingenuity in the age of the Great Depression, catches the new essence of survival. 'As one of the leading European oil and gas companies, OMV faces major challenges to which only innovative thinking can be the answer,' OMV explains. 'Global energy requirements are increasing significantly. At the same time, environmental protection and social justice are of growing importance. The demands placed on us grow as we expand our operations. This is why we made being careful with our resources one of our basic business principles.' OMV Resourcefulness

CASE STUDY 6.1
TerraCycle

TerraCycle is one of the businesses that has embraced the new approach. Known as the company that produced the world's first product made from 100% post-consumer rubbish, TerraCycle has 'outsmarted waste' by engaging more than 20 million people in collecting waste in over 20 countries and diverting billions of units of waste. Now a company that turns waste into over 1,500 different products, TerraCycle was once a laughing stock of the entrepreneurship competition. Founded by then barely 20-year-old Princeton dropout Tom Szaky, the company's first product was far from glamorous, but made up for it with a great name: Worm Poop. An all-natural fertilizer, Worm Poop is packaged in recycled plastic bottles, which the company collects in part through a US-wide recycling programme. *The New York Times'* Rob Walker got in on the action:

> You don't hear much about worms, or their waste, from the various big-box retailers, globe-trotting

pundits and good-looking guests of Oprah Winfrey who appear to be leading the conversation about environmental concern these days. But TerraCycle's plant food is actually a mass-oriented variation on something that hard-core eco-people talk about all the time: the worm bin. Containers filled with shredded newspaper and worms, such bins are used for composting food scraps. Worms eat this waste and digest it, and 'compost exits the worm through its tail end,' one online guide explains. These 'castings,' the result of vermicomposting (to use more formal gardening terms), happen to make good plant food.*

TerraCycle now sells at major retailers ranging from Wal-Mart to Whole Foods Market. Look who is laughing now!

*See the entire 2007 *New York Times* article at http://www.nytimes.com/2007/05/20/magazine/20wwln-consumed-t.html?_r=0.

CASE STUDY 6.2
Bayerische Motoren Werke AG

Also known as BMW, Bayerische Motoren Werke AG is another company that is successfully navigating the murky waters of resource crunch. The company moved well beyond selling products to selling services of deep meaning – and from a car company transformed itself into a mobility company. Focusing on mobility – a service rather than a product – allows the company to focus on radical innovation and open doors to completely a new business opportunity. Take the DriveNow car

sharing service of BMW i, MINI and SIXT, which allows a person in a densely-populated urban area to enjoy the benefits of a personal car without owning one. The idea, as BWM explains, is simple: 'The mobility concept is based on the motto "pick up anywhere, drop off anywhere". Billing is per minute, fuel costs and parking charges in public car parks are included. Users can locate available cars using the app, website or just on the street. A chip in the driving license acts as an electronic key.'*

(Continued)

ParkatmyHouse – a strategic investment by BMW i Ventures – is another example of BMW's remarkable resource intelligence and ingenuity. A simple online market place – powered by an app – allows people who own private parking places to connect with people who are searching for one. Imagine the savings of time, fuel, CO_2 emissions and more gained – and money made – on this simple solution. And for BMW itself, having a stronger parking infrastructure is essential for future sales: if we have good parking, we are ready to drive cars, right?

Mobility services are not the only radical innovation coming out of BMW. In an effort to protect and defend profits, the company decided to harness winds thrashing across eastern Germany to secure power as costs rise as a result of Germany's €550 billion ($740 billion) shift away from nuclear energy. BMW's transitions seem deceptively simple. Yet, when the market forces inspire you to shift your focus from designing cars to designing mobility, disruptive innovation follows – any designer and engineer will tell you that most innovation happens on the verge of the impossible. Similarly deceptive is the move towards control of the entire energy value chain – but the numbers and the endorsement of business analysts, such as Bloomberg's 2013 review, speak volumes. 'At BMW's Leipzig plant, the four 2.5-megawatt turbines from Nordex SE will eventually generate about 26 gigawatt-hours of electricity a year, or about 23 percent of the plant's total consumption,' said Jury Witschnig, head of sustainability strategy at the Munich-based manufacturer. The automaker seeks eventually to get all its power from renewables, compared with 28 percent in 2011 – both to cut its carbon output and benefit from falling prices for wind and solar energy. 'There will definitely be more such projects' from renewable sources, Witschnig said. 'Energy prices are part of the business case, and in Leipzig wind power was cheaper than other options.'**

But that is not all. BMW's rapid marriage to the energy business is a sign of remarkable foresight. As the legislation continues to pressure for less and less emissions (Euro VI requirements being one such pressure), the movement away from combustion engines appears inevitable. Electric vehicles are one alternative – and looking at the fast pace of model launch in this domain, it seems to be a viable option. Yet, when you manufacture combustion engines, the emissions are fully in your control – as your engineers are the ones designing an intelligent (or not so) motor. When we move to electricity, however, that control disappears, as emissions are now dependent on the efficiencies of power plants. And that is exactly why BMW's tango with energy production is so ingenious: it gives control back to the hands of the company – way (way!!) ahead of the competition.

*You can find a lot more about the new mobility efforts of BMW at the BMW i Mobility Services page at http://www.bmw.com/com/en/insights/corporation/bmwi/mobility_services.html#drivenow.

**You can explore the entire Bloomberg analysis of BMW's recent energy moves at http://www.bloomberg.com/news/2013-02-18/bmw-adds-wind-power-to-sidestep-merkel-s-power-bill.html.

CASE STUDY 6.3
Swiss Re

Swiss Re is another giant riding ahead of the wave – and turning disappearing resources into a thriving business model. As a 150-year-old reinsurer with over $33 billion in revenues as of 2012, Swiss Re's primary product is insurance for insurers, so the company can hardly be equated to coal-burning plant or the meth-

(Continued)

ane gas industry. A company rooted in Swiss rationality and conservatism, the reinsurer surprised the entirely industry, taking on stable climate as business risk – and opportunity – as early as 1994. By 2007, Swiss Re introduced a number of financial tools for dealing with risks of climate change. Nelson Schwartz of *Fortune* magazine explains:

> Buyers can bet on future heat waves or cold snaps with puts and calls on specific periods of time and temperature, much as conventional options have a preset strike price for a stock. So a farmer in India might be able to buy insurance from a local insurer in case the usual monsoon rains fail to arrive, or, conversely, his fields are flooded.

In the following years, the company upgraded its entire portfolio and pricing to respond to the rising cost of climate change. Speaking to Bloomberg TV in 2009, Swiss Re's senior climate advisor Andreas Spiegel took no prisoners, estimating weather-related losses at $40 billion annually:

> Weather-related insured losses are rising and the intensity of weather-related events such as hurricanes is going up as well. We are integrating these risks in our pricing, trying to quantify certain aspects of climate change and integrating them into our models. Climate and weather-related risks are a part of our core business. More and more, we see this as a business opportunity as adaptation to climate change is about managing risks in the long term. And that is our business.*

*You can learn more about Swiss Re and its climate change business, starting with the report on Andreas Spiegel's contribution to Bloomberg TV, at http://www.swissre.com/rethinking/insurers_and_climate.html.

Strategy[24] demands that every one of its 29,000 employees faces the fundamental question of the collapse of the linear throwaway economy – and takes it as a productive challenge. As such, it is a strategy that deliberately tackles both *natural* and *human* resources. On one hand, the company runs extensive eco-efficiency and eco-innovation programmes to reinvent the way it provides for the energy needs of its customers. Hydrogen (fuel cell) mobility, biofuels, water and carbon management all fall under this umbrella. On the other hand, OMV looks at diversity and skills, and community engagement, as key resources of the future – and runs comprehensive programmes to protect and grow this capital. At the company's biggest refinery the surprise is that even the apprentices – high-school leavers being trained and employed by OMV – look at the issues of resources in a broader sense. 'We sell something that is disappearing. So, the question for us is what to sell next, so that all of us don't disappear either,' said a shy 16-year-old.

Trendwatching.com, the leading consumer trend company, names the new wave of strategic resource intelligence as among the most important trends of recent years. Giving it a sassy name – *Eco-Superior* – the company flagged this trend in 2011 among its 11 most important consumer demands for the year, and again in 2013 as one that is here to stay. Here is why:

> *When it comes to 'green consumption', expect a rise in ECO-SUPERIOR products: products that are not only eco-friendly, but superior to polluting incumbents in every possible way. Think a combination of eco-friendly yet superior functionality, superior design, and/or superior savings.*

---

[24] You can find an in-depth overview of the OMV Resourcefulness approach at http://www.omv.com/.

Among the products and innovation highlighted by the trend watcher is the Throw & Grow confetti offered by the Netherlands-based gift store Niko Niko. The confetti is made of biodegradable material embedded with wildflower seeds – so when the confetti is used, it can be left on the ground or discarded in soil to disintegrate naturally and grow into flowers. Another innovation on the list is a billboard that generates drinkable water – 9,000 litres of it in three months – thanks to Peru's University of Technology and Engineering (UTEC). The Torre de Especialidades building of the Mexico City hospital also makes the cut – as it now absorbs and breaks down chemicals in the surrounding air. Using Prosolve370e tiles developed by Berlin-based design firm Elegant Embellishments, the building features tiles painted with titanium dioxide, which interacts with UV light to break down pollution into less toxic chemicals.[25]

Together with Lush, OMV, and Trendwatching.com, Design Hotels elevated the search for innovation for a resource-deprived world to the level of core strategy. A 20-year-old company that represents and markets a carefully selected collection of 250 independent hotels in over 40 countries across the globe, Design Hotels calls this new strategic effort 'Finding Infinity'. 'We live in the age of sound bites, of short-attention spans, of celebrity worship. First-term politicians seem to want only one thing: second term.' Is there a vaccine against our collective short-sidedness? For Design Hotels, there is. With a goal of replacing today's fuels with clean and endlessly renewable alternatives, the company has initiated a 'full-speed-ahead-no-time-to-lose movement . . . setting a path for a future based on infinite resources.' The company has joined intellectual forces with a number of inventors and change-makers, such as a young Australian engineer named Ross Harding, who created Finding Infinity, an organization that invents solutions for a new economy. The resulting programme, named 'Design Hotels is Finding Infinity',[26] attacks the essential problem of the disappearing linear economy. 'The world is powered by fuels that will run out in two lifetimes. This is not our problem – it's our opportunity!' – begs the powerful partnership. Pursuing this opportunity is what we call the *Overfished Ocean Strategy*.

GROUP EXERCISE

Select a company of your choice, which offers a sustainable product or service. Search the website of the company and visit the point of sale (PoS).

How would you categorize its strategy in terms of the four strategic responses outlined in the chapter?

Explore the key features of its strategy in detail, and make suggestions of ways in which the company may further improve.

---

[25] Eco-Superior appeared as one of five trends for July–August 2013, briefing downloadable at http://www.trendwatching.com/trends/pdf/2013-07%20TRENDS%20REFRESHED.pdf.

[26] Design Hotels™'s Finding Infinity initiative is presented further on the company website at http://www.designhotels.com/specials/finding_infinity.

QUESTIONS FOR CLASS DISCUSSION

1. How, and in what ways, are stakeholders pushing firms to adopt more environmentally friendly strategies?

2. What do you understand by the term 'trade-off'. What trade-offs are involved in the development of a green/environmentally sustainable strategy? Can these trade-offs be avoided or overcome?

3. Explain what is meant by a 'bolt-on' strategy. Why are bolt-on strategies unlikely to succeed in the long run?

4. What are the key differences between Porter's positioning view of strategy and the 'overfished ocean' view of strategy?

5. Compare and contrast embedded strategies with overfished ocean strategies.

Summary

Going beyond trade-off, bolt-on, and embedded approaches to sustainability, with the help of the Overfished Ocean Strategy, a new economy is being born – transforming the collapsing linear throwaway economy into a more lasting, more abundant, more sustainable version of itself. The transformation brings about a new economic reality, where we compete and win using a radically new set of rules. While the companies, people, and projects pioneering these new rules are still very rare, there are enough of them to suggest the first few essential principles that allow managers to innovate their way into a new world.

References

Appolo Blog. (2010). Whirlpool website helps consumers access energy-efficient appliance rebates (accessed 2010, May 23). Retrieved from http://apolloalliance.org/blog/?p=451

Barney, J. B. (1991). Firm resources and sustained competitive advantage. *Journal of Management, 17,* 99–120.

BBMG. (2009). Conscious consumer report: Redefining value in a new economy. [ref]

Bearse, S., Capozucca, P., Favret, L. and Lynch, B. (2009). Finding the green in today's shoppers. Sustainability trends and new shopper insights. Deloitte. Available at gmaonline.org. Accessed 8/09/16.

Berns, M., Townend, A., Khayat, Z., Balagopal, B., Reeves, M., Hopkins, M. and Kruschwitz, N. (2009). The Business of Sustainability: Findings and Insights from the First Annual Business of Sustainability Survey and Global Thought Leaders' Research Project. MIT: North Hollywood, C.A. U.S.

Biello, D. (2006). Overfishing could take seafood off the menu by 2049. *Scientific American,* November.

Bloomberg Businessweek. (2013). The complex business of recycling e-waste. Retrieved from http://www.businessweek.com/articles/2013-01-08/the-complex-business-of-recycling-e-waste

BP. (2013, January). BP Energy Outlook 2030.

Buckingham, M., & Coffman, C. (1999). *First, break all the rules: What the world's greatest managers do differently.* New York: Simon & Schuster.

Business as an Agent of World Benefit. (2005). Green Mountain Coffee goes to source (accessed 2007, July 10). Retrieved from http://worldbenefit.case.edu/innovation/bankInnovationView.cfm?idArchive=195

Carbon Disclosure Project. (2009). Carbon Disclosure Project 2009 global 500 report. Retrieved from https://www.cdproject.net/CDPResults/CDP_2009_Global_500_Report_with_Industry_Snapshots.pdf

Carbon Trust. (2010). Carbon reduction commitment (accessed 2010, May 30). Retrieved from http://www.carbontrust.co.uk/policy-legislation/business-public-sector/pages/carbon-reduction-commitment.aspx

Cause Capitalism. (2009). What's the social compensation package? 5 ways to attract talent without a checkbook (accessed 2010, May 30). Retrieved from http://causecapitalism.com/social-compensation/

CBC News. (2007). Calgary moves against trans fats (accessed 2010, May 30). Retrieved from http://www.cbc.ca/canada/story/2007/12/29/calgary-fats.html

CEA. (2008). Consumer desire for 'green' electronics on the rise, says CEA (accessed 2010, May 20). Retrieved from http://www.ce.org/Press/CurrentNews/press_release_detail.asp?id=11649

Ceres. (2009). Regulators require insurers to disclose climate change risks and strategies (accessed 2010, May 23). Retrieved from http://www.ceres.org/Page.aspx?pid=1062

Chambers, E. G., Foulton, M., Handfield-Jones, H., Hankin, S. M., & Michaels III, E. G. (1998). *The McKinsey Quarterly, 3*, 44–57.

Davis, D. R., Epp, M. D., & Riordan, H. D. (2004). Changes in USDA food composition data for 43 garden crops, 1950 to 1999. *Journal of the American College of Nutrition, 23*(6), 669–682.

Dublin, J. (2010). Will the mainstream buy green to save the Earth? (Accessed 2010, May 20.) Retrieved from http://www.sustainablelifemedia.com/content/column/brands/will_mainstream_buy_green_to_save_earth

Environmental Leader. (2010). Businesses fail to engage consumers on environmental issues (accessed 2010, May 21). Retrieved from http://www.environmentalleader.com/2010/05/20/americans-want-to-share-environmental-responsibility-with-businesses/

Fleishman-Hillard. (2007). *Rethinking Corporate Social Responsibility: A Fleishman-Hillard/National Consumers League Study.* Fleishman-Hillard Inc. St Louis, U.S.

Gap Inc. (2009). Gap Inc. employees honored with Global Founders' Award for dedication to giving back to their community (accessed 2010, May 30). Retrieved from http://www.csrwire.com/press/press_release/27522-Gap-Inc-Employees-Honored-With-Global-Founders-Award-for-Dedication-to-Giving-Back-to-Their-Community

Gerba, C. P. (2006, 2007). Bulk soap contamination. Unpublished studies. University of Arizona.

Glavas, A., & Piderit, S. K. (2009). How does doing good matter? Effects of corporate citizenship on employees. *Journal of Corporate Citizenship* (accessed 2010, May 21). Retrieved from http://www.greenleafpublishing.com/productdetail.kmod?productid=3124

GMA & Deloitte. (2009). Finding the green in today's shoppers: Sustainability trends and new shopper insights (accessed 2010, May 20). Retrieved from http://www.gmabrands.com/publications/greenshopper09.pdf

Goodyear, C. (2007). S. F. First city to ban plastic shopping bags (accessed 2010, May 30). Retrieved from http://articles.sfgate.com/2007-03-28/news/17235798_1_compostable-bags-plastic-bags-california-grocers-association

Grant, R. M. (1991). The resource-based theory of competitive advantage. *California Management Review, 3*, 114–135.

Harter, J. K., & Schmidt, F. L. (2002). *Employee engagement, satisfaction, and business unit-level outcomes: Meta-analysis.* Gallup Technical Report.

Investor Network on Climate Risk. (2010). Investors file a record 95 climate change-related resolutions: A 40% increase over 2009 proxy season (accessed 2010, May 23). Retrieved from http://www.incr.com/Page.aspx?pid=1222

Junior Achievement. (2009). The benefits of employee volunteer program (accessed 2010, May 21). Retrieved from www.handsonnetwork.org/resources/download/1536

Kim, W. C., & Mauborgne, R. (2005). *Blue ocean strategy: How to create uncontested market space and make competition irrelevant.* Boston, US: Harvard Business Press.

Knight, R. (2006). Business students portrayed as ethically minded in study. *Financial Times* (accessed 2010, May 21). Retrieved from http://www.ft.com/cms/s/ee45a804-63c5-11db-bc82-0000779e2340.html

Laslo, C. and Zhemembayeva, N. (2011). *Embedded Sustainability: The Next Big Competitive Challenge.* Stanford, U.S.: Stanford University Press.

London Climate Change Partnership: Finance Sub-Group. (2006). Adapting to climate change: Business as usual? (Accessed 2010, May 23.) Retrieved from http://www.london.gov.uk/lccp/publications/docs/business-as-usual.pdf

Luthans, F., & Peterson, S. J. (2001). Employee engagement and manager self-efficacy: Implications for managerial effectiveness and development. *Journal of Management Development, 21*, 376–387.

Lynch. D. J. (2006). Corporate America warms to fight against global warming (accessed 2010, May 23). Retrieved from http://www.usatoday.com/weather/climate/2006-05-31-business-globalwarming_x.htm

Malthus, T. (1970). *An essay on the principle of population* [1798]. New York: Penguin.

McKinsey. (2011). Resource revolution: Meeting the world's energy, materials, food, and water needs.

Meadows, D. H., Meadows, D. L., Randers, J., & Behrens III, W. (1972) *Limits to growth.* Report for the Club of Rome. New York: New American Library.

Palmer, K., Oates, W., & Portney, P. (1995). Tightening environmental standards: The benefit-cost or the no-cost paradigm? *Journal of Economic Perspectives, 4*, 121.

Polity.org.za. (2010). Warburton Attorney's monthly sustainability legislation, regulation and parliamentary update (accessed 2010, May 30). Retrieved from http://www.polity.org.za/article/monthly-sustainability-legislation-regulation-and-parliamentary-update-march-2010-2010-04-09

Porter, M. (1980). *Competitive strategy: Techniques for analysing industries and competitors.* New York: Free Press.

Porter, M. E., & Kraner, M. R. (2011). Creating shared value. *Harvard Business Review*, Jan/Feb, 62–67.

Ready, D. A., Hill, L. A., & Conger, J. A. (2008). Winning the race for talent in emerging markets. *Harvard Business Review, 86*(11), 62–70.

Reinhardt, F. (2000) *Down to earth: Applying business principles to environmental management.* Boston, US: Harvard Business Press, 5.

Saks, A. M. (2006). Antecedents and consequences of employee engagement. *Journal of Managerial Psychology, 21*(7), 600–619.

SEI. (2010). International legislation and policy (accessed 2010, May 30). Retrieved from http://www.sustainelectronics.illinois.edu/policy/international.cfm

Sharma, S., & Alberto Aragon-Correa, J. (2005). Corporate environmental strategy and competitive advantage: A review from the past to the future. In Sharma, S., & Alberto Aragon-Correa, J. (Eds.). *Corporate environmental strategy and competitive advantage.* (2005). Cheltenham, UK: Edward Elgar Publishing Limited, 1.

Shipeng, G., & Graham-Harrison, E. (2008). China launches surprise crackdown on plastic bags (accessed 2010, May 30). Retrieved from http://www.reuters.com/article/idUSPEK25589820080108

Social Investment Forum. (2007). 2007 report on socially responsible investing trends in the United States (accessed 2010, May 23). Retrieved from http://www.socialinvest.org/resources/pubs/documents/FINALExecSummary_2007_SIF_Trends_wlinks.pdf

Social Investment Forum. (2010). Socially responsible investing basics for individuals (accessed 2010, May 23). Retrieved from http://www.socialinvest.org/resources/sriguide/

Story, L. (2008). Can Burt's Bees turn Clorox green? (Accessed 2010, May 30.) Retrieved from http://www.nytimes.com/2008/01/06/business/06bees.html?pagewanted=all

The Equator Principles. (2010). About the Equator Principles (accessed 2010, May 23). Retrieved from http://www.equator-principles.com/documents/AbouttheEquatorPrinciples.pdf

The Independent. (2010). UK warned it will run out of landfill sites in eight years. Retrieved from http://www.independent.co.uk/news/uk/home-news/uk-warned-it-will-run-out-of-landfill-sites-in-eight-years-2021136.html

Trendwatching.com. (2010). 10 crucial consumer trends for 2010 (accessed 2010, May 21). Retrieved from http://trendwatching.com/trends/10trends2010/

Turban, D. B., & Greening, D. W. (1997). Corporate social performance and organizational attractiveness to prospective employees. *Academy of Management Journal, 40,* 658–672.

UN. (2004). *Computers and the environment: Understanding and managing their impacts.* Dordrecht, Netherlands: Kluwer Academic Publishers and UNU.

Walley, N., & Whitehead, B. (1994). It's not easy being green. *Harvard Business Review,* May/June, 46–51.

Wal-Mart. (2008). Walmart Stores, Inc., offering environmentally friendly textile options to customers (accessed 2010, May 21). Retrieved from http://walmartstores.com/download/2310.pdf

Whirlpool. (2010). Cash for appliances: Every kind of green (accessed 2010, May 23). Retrieved from http://www.whirlpool.com/content.jsp?sectionId=1338&dcsref=http://www.whirlpool.com/assets/images/home/wp_homepage_031609.swf

Wikipedia. (2010). Employee engagement (accessed 2010, May 21). Retrieved from http://en.wikipedia.org/wiki/Employee_engagement

World Business Council for Sustainable Development. (2005). Driving success: Human resources and sustainable development (accessed 2007, July 10). Retrieved from http://www.wbcsd.org/web/publications/hr.pdf

World Economic Forum. (2010). Redesigning business value: A roadmap for sustainable consumption (accessed 2010, May 20). Retrieved from http://www.weforum.org/pdf/sustainableconsumption/DrivingSustainableConsumptionreport.pdf

7 Organizing

Morgen Witzel

Introduction

Organization – that is, a group of people brought together for a common purpose – is an essential feature of human civilization. Over the course of our lives, each of us belongs to a number of organizations in which we have different functions and play different roles. We use organizations to help us meet our own personal goals but, importantly, belonging to an organization has a purpose of its own. Most human beings have a deeply felt need to associate with others like themselves, and we are happiest and most fulfilled when we are part of an organization whose purpose and goals align with our own.

Organizing, then, is not just a matter of creating a technically efficient system. Organizations of any kind, including businesses, are sociotechnical systems (Pasmore, 1988); i.e., as well as the technical elements of design and structure, who reports to whom and who has what responsibilities, they are also social systems comprised of people with their own individual needs and wants. Whether people belong willingly to an organization, whether they are willing to identify with and support its ends and goals, depends in very large part on whether they accept those ends and goals as valid.

Purely technical approaches to organization often focus on structure. It is assumed that if the organization is designed with the correct structure, then everything else will fall into place. This view harks back to the work of Alfred Chandler (1962), who opined that 'structure follows strategy', i.e., that an organization first identifies its strategy and sets its goals, and then designs an appropriate organization to achieve that goal. This approach has been heavily criticized, not least by Miles and Snow (1978) who argue that the interrelationship between structure and strategy is rather more complex than that, but Chandlerian views of organization remain widespread. Following on from Chandler, the view has developed that there is a 'right' form of organization that is best suited to businesses pursuing sustainability, and arguments have been advanced variously in favour of virtual organizations, matrix organizations, and more democratic and devolved organizations with higher levels of employee responsibility (Mohman and Shani, 2011).

This chapter takes the perspective that there is no one 'right' form of organizing for sustainability. While it can be – and has been – argued that sustainability requires radical new forms of organization, it is argued instead that the *form* of organization is largely irrelevant. Any form of organization can be adapted to sustainability needs. The key variables are not structure and form, but purpose, mission and values. Following Miles and Snow's concept of 'organizational fitness for purpose', the chapter will show how the key elements in making an organization fit to pursue a sustainability agenda lie on the social, not the technical, side of the sociotechnical system. This means that thinking about organization has to fit into a broader pattern of systems thinking that embraces the whole organization and its environment. In particular, organizations pursuing a sustainability agenda require three things: motivated people who buy into that agenda and are willing to pursue it, a supportive and enabling culture that allows them to pursue their goals and the goals of the organization, and requisite knowledge. These three aspects will be discussed in turn, and then concluded with a consideration of the concept of the employer brand, a powerful tool which brings all three together and can be used as a vehicle for taking an organization towards sustainability.

7.0   Organizations and Sustainability

Before going further, however, we need to make clear our terms of reference. Discussions of organization and sustainability often confuse two separate but related terms: 'sustainable organization', and 'organization with sustainability as its goal'. The two concepts do not entirely overlap. It is entirely possible to have organizations that are internally sustainable but contribute nothing in terms of environmental or social sustainability; equally, it is possible to have an organization that has strong sustainability goals but is not in itself sustainable (and therefore will not last long enough to meet those goals).

When most people think of sustainability and organizations, they think of the second concept, i.e., an organization which has sustainability as one of its key purposes and goals. That is the organization's purpose, and its strategy will – or should – be closely linked to that. The Chandlerian view would be that the organization, having set its strategy, then adapts itself to best meet that strategy. The question is, how best can it do so?

To that question, there is no single answer. Much depends on the nature of the organization. Variables will include the industry in which the organization is working; the size of the organization; skill levels among employees; the management capacity of the organization; employees' own beliefs and views about sustainability; the culture of the organization; the financial health of the organization; how the company itself defines 'sustainability'; and last but not least, the ability of the organization's leaders to unite and draw people together.

It is quite possible for two similar organizations to take different approaches to sustainability and still reach their goals, whatever those goals might be. Sustainability is a big room, and not every company can see into every corner of it. For whatever reason, idealistic or pragmatic, it is likely that companies will try to carve out some part of the sustainability domain and make it their own. As Charles Lindblom (1959) has pointed out, few organizations are comfortable with big, audacious goals. They are better suited to 'muddling through', taking a few steps at a time and adapting and adjusting as they go along, and this is true of creating and maintaining organizations as well. This does not mean that companies cannot be extremely successful and make important contributions within those limited domains, however, and one of our first and most important understandings should be that the power of a company to act in any given situation is always limited and bounded.

One of the things that binds and constrains companies' ability to act is their organization, their existing sociotechnical system. In this sense, start-up organizations have more freedom; they can create an organization from scratch, whereas previously existing organizations must undergo the expensive and risky business of restructuring or reorganizing if they wish to adopt a new strategy. Unsurprisingly, many choose to compromise and limit their strategic choices to what their organizations are capable of achieving, at least with only limited reorganization and readjustment.

This might seem lamentable from a sustainability perspective, but there is sense to this approach. An organization cannot achieve a sustainability-related goal unless the organization is itself coherent, effective and efficient; financially, technically and socially. As Witzel (2015) points out, organizational restructuring is often wasteful and inefficient and consumes resources that could be used to further other purposes – such as sustainability. Sometimes, it can be better to keep the imperfect organization we have, warts and all, in the knowledge that it will reach at least some of its goals, than to reach too far in pursuit of the perfect organizational form and then fall flat. Seventy per cent of something might turn out to be better than 100 per cent of nothing.

This point is brought into sharp relief when we consider the question of structure. The futile quest for a perfect organizational structure has been going on for over a century (Kanigel, 1997). The arguments for new organizational forms *were mentioned above*. But the organizational structure that might be perfect in one setting simply will not work in others. Virtual organization is ideally suited to consultancies and other knowledge-based businesses with low levels of tangible assets and dispersed patterns of working (Warner and Witzel, 2004). A virtual steel mill, on the other hand, simply would not work; steel mills require synergistic efforts of large numbers of people and technologies. Matrix organizations have been shown to be effective in knowledge-based and science-based organizations such as research laboratories, but they have failed in other settings.

The belief that democracy and empowerment will lead to sustainability is seductive (Uys & Campbell, 2005; Witzel, 2010), but has never been empirically proven. What we *do* know is that not all democratic action necessarily leads to sustainability. Adolf Hitler and Emperor Napoleon III both came to power through democratic means, and even though Hitler was a passionate environmentalist, neither regime can be said to have been sustainable on any level. Al-Qaida is distinguished by decentralized control and high levels of local empowerment, yet few if any would regard it as an organization dedicated to sustainability.

This brings us back to the concept of fitness for purpose. Rather than focusing only on technical structure, we need to consider whether the organization has the right culture, mindset, beliefs and knowledge to pursue its sustainability agenda. One recent study, Jia *et al.* (2016) demonstrates this very well. Jia and his colleagues studied nine companies in China, both domestic and foreign, which are pursuing sustainability initiatives. The companies, including Sony, Tetra Pak, Nestlé, Volvo and the Chinese property management company Vanke, all have quite different structures. Some are relatively decentralized, others have tight command and control. Some focus on empowerment, others take a more directive approach. One of the two things they have in common is that all have been successful, so far, in developing practices dedicated to greater sustainability. (The second thing is that they spread their message of sustainability outside the organization, up and down the supply chain and engage with other stakeholders; an important aspect of sustainability which lies outside the scope of this chapter.)

We need, therefore, to look beyond the purely technical issues of organizational structure and look deeper into the social aspects of organization. Getting these right must be the first priority; once this is done, the problems of technical organization can be solved on a pragmatic, case-by-case basis, choosing the right organizational form for the time and place, rather than searching for the non-existent perfect form.

7.1 Motivating People

People join any organization, be it a company, a sporting club, a political party or a church, for reasons which are personal to them. In every case, however, they are seeking satisfaction of a need, or a set of needs. As managers, in order to understand the people in our organizations, we need to understand why they come to work for us in the first place.

One of the most important attempts at understanding human motivation in the workplace was made by the behavioural psychologist Abraham Maslow (1954). Maslow's 'hierarchy of needs' will be familiar to many readers, and I shall sum it up here very briefly. Maslow posited that there were five basic human needs, which are presented here in ascending order of importance:

- Self-actualization.
- Self-esteem.
- Love, or 'belongingness'.
- Safety.
- Food and water.

Maslow argued that we will always try to satisfy the low-order needs first. If we lack food, then our efforts to find food will take priority over all other needs; once we have sufficient food, we then seek safety for ourselves and our families; once we are assured of safety, we then seek the society of others and friendship and love through belonging to peer groups, and so on up the scale. It is important to remember that people can slide down the scale as well as go up it, so a natural disaster, war or even a local event such as the closure of a company throwing people out of work can send people back to searching for ways of satisfying lower-order needs.

Maslow's hierarchy has been criticized for being too simplistic, and it has also been pointed out that the hierarchy has never been empirically proven. I include it none the less because it provides a very useful starting point for a discussion of motivation at work. Why do people work? Why do they join businesses as employees, and submit to the authority of their boss or superior (Witzel, 2015)?

These are questions with many answers, and we need to be aware of the plurality of answers depending on time and place. In a poverty-stricken country, people may well work for no other reason than that they need money to buy food and shelter for themselves and their families; this could well be the most important need of all.

This is, however, relatively rare. For the most part, although we continue to work to earn money to help us to survive, we also work for social reasons. There are literally hundreds of studies of work, beginning with the Hawthorne experiments in the 1920s (Mayo, 1933), showing that we join companies in hopes that they will offer us work that is fulfilling and interesting. We seek work that makes us feel good about ourselves and bolsters our self-esteem; we want to feel that our work results in something good and meaningful for the communities in which we live. Workers at the Tata Group in India, for example, are proud of the fact that their employers contribute to many social causes in India – indirectly through the work of the Tata Trusts, and directly through the CSR initiatives of the individual companies (Witzel, 2010), and feel that their work is part of a larger project of national development. And finally, we may feel that through work we can achieve self-actualization, a sense of true purpose and fulfilment. In Maslow's view, scientists and creative people are most likely to achieve this sense of self-actualization through work.

Thus to say, as many employers do, that people 'only come to work for the money' is not technically correct. They come to earn money, which they then use in order to satisfy their needs. Nor is the earning of money the only means through which needs are satisfied; many other factors are in play as well. Another early scholar of workplace motivation, Frederick Herzberg (1966), expanded on Maslow's work and developed a dual system of motivational factors. The first group of motivational factors, which he terms 'actualization factors', are very similar to Maslow's hierarchy of needs. People work, says Herzberg, because work gives them opportunities for achievement, recognition, responsibility and personal growth. The second group he terms environmental or 'hygiene' factors, things that are external to the person and in some cases beyond the person's control. They include remuneration (pay, bonuses, pensions and so on) but also such issues as working conditions, job security, the quality of management and even factors in one's personal life, which can affect motivation at work.

The importance of these 'hygiene' factors has been highlighted many times by researchers over the years. One of the first large-scale studies of motivation, the Hawthorne experiments conducted at a Western Electric telephone equipment assembly plant over the course of a decade in the 1920s and 1930s found that issues such as factors in the personal lives of workers can be very powerful motivators, or demotivators (Mayo, 1933; Roethlisberger & Dickson, 1939). The researchers noted one case of a young female worker whose productivity for some months had been very poor, but then suddenly shot up to high levels. Investigating, they found that the girl had been living at home with her parents and been very unhappy. Her decision to move out and take an apartment of her own coincided exactly with her rise in productivity.

Understanding motivation is the key to the successful management of people. That is, of course, more easily said than done. Every human being is unique, and each has a set of needs and motivations that differs from those of the people around them, even if only subtly. One of the most perplexing problems that managers face on a daily basis is how to reconcile and harmonize the activities of people with often wildly different motivations. Theorizing can in some cases do more harm than good. The psychologist Douglas McGregor, for example, postulated that there are two theories of how to manage people, Theory X and Theory Y (McGregor, 1960). Theory X assumes that most people lack ambition or interest in their work and will only work productively if coerced into doing so. Theory Y assumes that people are self-motivated and ambitious and will naturally seek responsibility and the chance to express themselves creatively. In reality both cases apply. In any large organization it is likely that there will be Theory X people and Theory Y people. Nor are the categories mutually exclusive, and in particular, Theory Y people can become demotivated and lose interest in their work and slip over to the Theory X side. Understanding 'who' is motivated by 'what' is an important but time-consuming task.

As well as understanding the factors that motivate employees and managers, we also need to understand what motivates the organizations that employ them. What are their goals? Why do they exist in the first place, what are they trying to achieve? Are the goals of the organization and its members congruent, or are they widely at variance? Emerson (1913) made the point that one of the reasons for breakdowns in relationships between workers and management is a fundamental misunderstanding by each party as to what the other wants. Workers sell their *time*, said Emerson, in exchange for wages. But what companies are buying is *output*, not time. Their need is for finished products, delivered services and so on, and the time taken to produce these is relevant only as a measure of efficient production. Thus companies think the goal is to do as much as possible in the time available, while workers have no motivation to work harder than they must. If both were in fact motivated by the same thing – such as service to customers or to community, or the desire to achieve social and/or environmental sustainability – much of this misunderstanding would disappear.

Motivation is vitally important both for organizations seeking to be sustainable in their own right and for those that have sustainability as a strategic goal. If the employees are willing to commit to the organization and, at least in part, share its goals and make them their own, the organization stands a better chance of long-term survival. Similarly, this goal congruence is necessary if employees are to work towards achieving goals related to social and environmental stability. If employees do not see these things as important – if these goals do not fit in with their own needs – then the organization will at best struggle to make progress towards those goals. Case Study 7.1 of Titan Industries demonstrates this principle.

CASE STUDY 7.1
Titan

Titan is India's largest watchmaker, and the fifth largest watchmaker by volume in the world. At the time of writing it accounts for about 60% of branded watch sales in India, and is expanding into overseas markets with a distribution deal in North America signed in 2012. Titan employs around 6,000 people, nearly all in India. It offers a number of watch brands including sport and luxury brands; the flashy Fastrack brand has become particularly popular with young Indians. Titan is also known as an innovative company. In 2002 Titan engineers created The Edge, the world's thinnest watch, with a total thickness including casing of just 3.5 mm. In the 1990s the company branched out into jewellery, and its Tanishq jewellery chain is now the largest branded jewellery retailer in India.

Titan was founded in 1987 as a joint venture between the Tata Group and the Tamil Nadu State Development Corporation (the name Titan comes from 'TI' for Tata Industries and 'TAN' for Tamil Nadu). Today Tata owns a 25% stake, the Tamil Nadu government 27%, and the rest owned by various investors.

Watchmaking requires precision engineering and high levels of skill. The original idea was to locate the new company in Bengaluru (Bangalore) where there was already an established watchmaking industry and plenty of skilled staff. The Tamil Nadu government, however, had hoped to use the new venture to kick-start development in some of the more impoverished areas of the state. Titan's Managing Director, Xerxes Desai, also believed in this vision and proposed to the board that the company set up in the small city of Hosur, in northern Tamil Nadu. The area was almost entirely dependent on agriculture and there were no skilled engineers, but it had a good education system. Desai's plan was to recruit a workforce from the most talented young people in the area and, in his words, to

'turn them into world-class horologists'. After a heated debate, Desai got his way.

Four hundred boys and girls, most just out of school, were recruited in the area around Hosur and brought into the city. Engineers from Bengaluru came down to train them in watchmaking, but every aspect of their new lives required assistance. None, for example, had ever had a bank account or knew how one worked. Most had never eaten with a knife and fork; many had never used a flush toilet. Titan provided 'housemasters' who became in effect adoptive parents and taught the young engineers the basic skills they needed for modern living. Many were also short of money, and Titan advanced them pocket money against their wages while they underwent training. The same system has continued ever since; Titan still recruits young people in the areas where it operates and trains them from scratch.

Titan pays generous salaries and benefits, but it also opens doors for its employees. They are encouraged to study for degrees while working, and the company pays their tuition fees. Talented graduates are promoted through the organizations. Others, moved by the entrepreneurial spirit, leave to start businesses of their own, and there is now a cluster of ancillary businesses around Hosur making watch-straps and other components. In every case Titan supported the new entrepreneurs financially – even if they started a business that had nothing to do with the watch industry.

Titan measures its income and profits, but it also measures the social development impact of its venture, using a measure that it calls 'lives transformed'. It is estimated that more than 200,000 people have been touched directly or indirectly by Titan and had their lives improved. Some people, as noted, have set up businesses and are now providing employment. Others used their wages to help family members move out of

(Continued)

poverty. 'I never went to university', explains one young woman at Titan, 'but thanks to my job here, all of my brothers and sisters have.' Once deeply impoverished, the Hosur region now has many amenities including better sanitation and health care.

Titan's employer brand is a very powerful one. Employees know what the company stands for and are deeply committed to it. This does not mean that relations between workers and management are always smooth. There was a lengthy strike at Hosur in 2003 when plant managers bungled an attempt to introduce performance-related pay. Managing Director Bhaskar Bhat says frankly that this was due to incompetence on the part of some managers. 'I used to say that the workers loved the company but hated the management,' he says. It is interesting that Titan workers feel so much a part of their company that they will challenge their own managers if they feel it is necessary to protect that company and culture.

What does all this mean for sustainability? Quite simply, if an organization wishes to pursue a sustainability agenda, it needs employees who regard sustainability as important. They must be willing to work for sustainability and support its principles. In this area, at least, those who argue for industrial democracy as the key to sustainability are correct; people must work willingly towards this goal. It is difficult if not impossible to impose sustainability at the point of a bayonet.

This brings us back to goal congruence. Again, the issue is easy for start-ups; when recruiting first-time employees, one simply selects those who have the same goals as well as the required skills and competencies, and integrates them into the organization's social framework. The task is harder when managers wish to reform or reorient an existing organization, which has not traditionally placed much value on sustainability, towards a sustainability agenda. Faced with lack of interest in or even outright opposition to the notion of sustainability, leaders apparently have two choices:

1   Educate, train, persuade and cajole staff to put aside their previously-held notions and adapt their thinking towards sustainability, or
2   Move recalcitrant staff out of the organization and replace them with people who share the leaders' views and are willing to work towards a sustainability agenda.

It would be pleasant to think that option 1 will always work, as it did so spectacularly in the case of Interface (Anderson & White, 2013). But resistance by staff – and other stakeholders including customers and shareholders – can slow sustainability initiatives or even derail them altogether, as in the case of Iceland Frozen Foods' attempted move into organic produce in the early 1990s. Iceland did eventually press ahead and now has a wide range of organic produce, but its first attempt met with widespread resistance.

Firing people who do not agree with our views on sustainability may seem like a brutal solution, and not entirely in keeping with our values as managers and leaders dedicated to sustainability. But the ethical dilemma is this: which does the more harm? Making redundant staff who will try to block sustainability initiatives? Or leaving them in place, and letting the initiatives fail?

7.1.1 Organizations as Human Systems

Coming to terms with variations in human motivation requires us to raise the level of examination and see organizations as 'human systems', social entities where human beings come together in order to share interests and pursue goals. This is how the first societies were created. People banded together for mutual defence, or to exploit a particular natural resource, or for spiritual purposes such as the worship of a deity or force of nature, or perhaps for a mixture of all three.

Others join organizations because they feel they want to contribute to the greater good, and/or to seek self-actualization. The members of a championship sporting team will be motivated by the desire to win. This gives them the esteem of others and self-esteem, even perhaps a degree of self-actualization; the exact benefit will depend on the individual. If one player plays the game because they enjoy the money and want to spend it on big houses and fast cars, while another could not care less about the money and plays because they feel this is what they were born to do, it does not greatly matter; so long as the team's management are aware of this and build slightly different relationships with each player. Burrell and Morgan (1989) referred to 'unitary' and 'pluralistic' organizations. In the first category, all members share a common motivation; in the second, members may have quite different motivations, and it is the task of the leader to establish and create agreement to common aims. Either type of organization can be equally successful: there is no either/or choice.

It is the quality of these relationships that often makes the difference in terms of organizational success. Relationships can generally take one of two forms: *enabling* relationships which help people to meet their own needs while at the same time working towards the goals of the organization, or *coercive* relationships which ignore the needs of the individual and insist that they be sublimated to that of the group. Frederick Emery, one of the leading early members of the London-based Tavistock Group, believed that many organizations adopt formal and rational organizational structures that are 'alienating' to their employees and ultimately result in coercive relationships. He argued that this is both demotivating for workers and ultimately damaging to the organizations themselves as the workers become less committed and less willing to work (Emery & Trist, 1965).

The French sociologist Michel Foucault went still further, arguing that one of the purposes of organizations is to enforce conformity among their members. Those who fail to conform, e.g., by not wearing a staff uniform, are punished for their transgression. Again, in Foucault's view, organizations exist to sublimate the needs of their members to the needs of the organization (Foucault, 1977).

However, this does not necessarily have to be the case. Emery and his colleague Eric Trist at the Tavistock Institute for Human Relations were influenced by the psychological principle of *gestalt*, or 'wholeness', and proposed that organizations should be developed that would match the needs of individuals to those of the organization. They proposed the concept of a 'sociotechnical organization'. This organization would still exercise a degree of control, and if we stop and think about it, we can see instances where some form of control is essential. Industrial plants require strict enforcement of health and safety rules if accidents are to be avoided and lives saved; financial institutions require compliance departments to prevent fraud; hotels and restaurants need food hygiene inspection to protect the health of guests, and so on. At the same time, however, the Tavistock Group argued that people should regulate their own activities as far as possible. This would draw them into the organization and help them to identify its goals as their own. Case Study 7.2 of Cadbury Brothers shows how this can be done.

CASE STUDY 7.2
Cadbury Brothers

The chocolate maker Cadbury Brothers (later Cadbury-Schweppes) was founded in the early 19th century. The Cadbury family were Quakers who abstained from alcohol, tobacco, coffee and tea, believing that these contained harmful stimulants. Chocolate, on the other hand, was perceived at the time to be nourishing and health giving and this was therefore seen as an ethically sound industry. Despite this, Cadbury Brothers did not really prosper at first, and when George Cadbury and his brother Richard inherited the firm in 1860 it was still a small, struggling family business.

By the mid-1870s, however, Cadbury Brothers had begun to expand and had outgrown its premises in central Birmingham. George Cadbury's solution was to follow the example of other reform-minded business leaders such as Titus Salt, moving his business out of Birmingham to a greenfield site at Bourneville and creating a 'model village' with houses, shops, places of worship and other amenities for his employees. Workers at Bourneville were provided with housing, education for themselves and their children, health care and exercise facilities.

It is as philanthropists that George Cadbury and his son and successor Edward are best known, and the Cadbury firm is often discussed as if the company's leaders were motivated only by a desire to create social reform and do good. In fact, the philanthropic face of Cadbury Brothers was only the tip of the iceberg. What the Cadburys were doing was investing in their workforce. They understood fully that healthy, happy, well-educated workers would also be more productive, and that this in turn would be good for the company. Many of the benefits provided at Bourneville had this dual purpose in mind. For example, the company built swimming baths near the factory and encouraged employees to use these. The result was better health

and fitness, but also improved employee hygiene: an important issue in food production. Cadbury Brothers also cut working hours from ten hours per shift to eight, not only because this was kinder to the workers but because George Cadbury had read research showing that employees on eight-hour shifts were more productive than those working ten hours.

Edward Cadbury, in his book *Experiments in Industrial Organization*, maintained that the company's success was based on three elements. The first was the provision of welfare and benefits, *as described above*, which enabled employees and their families to live happier and healthier lives. The second was a fair wages policy with a good basic rate supplemented by productivity bonuses. The third, and from our perspective the most interesting, was the engagement of employees with the company and their strong support for its strategy and goals.

Two particular channels were used to secure engagement. The first was an employee suggestion scheme. Many companies try these schemes and often they fail, usually because employees see that the company does not take their suggestions seriously. Cadbury Brothers demonstrated its commitment to the scheme. All employees were encouraged to make suggestions for new products, new production methods, new administrative procedures, or as Edward Cadbury said, 'any suggestion on any other subject, so long as it relates to the works at Bourneville in some way'. Around 20% of suggestions on average were accepted, and 5% to10% were put into practice. Prizes were given for inventive ideas, even if they were not accepted, thus encouraging people to keep thinking.

The second channel was the creation of works committees. There were two of these committees, one for male employees and one for female workers. The separate committee for women was judged necessary

(Continued)

so that women would have a clear voice and not be shut out by their male colleagues (recall that this was the late Victorian era, when women had few public rights and could not vote in elections). To make it clear that the women's committee was equal to that of the men, Edward Cadbury himself chaired the women's committee, the only man to do so.

The committees had a powerful voice in the running of the company. Each included a mix of people, some nominated by the directors, some by foremen and section heads, others by the shop floor. The committees functioned almost as surrogate boards of directors. They had power of scrutiny over every aspect of the business and every strategic decision; they approved plans for new machinery and buildings, oversaw health and safety matters, dealt with employee complaints and made grants to employees who were in financial distress. If they disapproved of a plan, then the plan was shelved, even if it had come from one of the Cadburys themselves.

Superficially, Cadbury Brothers is just another example of Victorian industrial paternalism. But if we look under the surface we find a powerful and flexible organization with a very strong employer brand and high levels of staff loyalty and commitment; and most of all, an organization dedicated to knowledge creation and innovation at every level. The Canadian management consultant Herbert Casson summed up the situation in four words: 'At Cadbury, everybody thinks.'

Cadbury Brothers was regarded at the time as one of the best-run companies in Britain, if not the world. By 1880 it has risen from its Midlands roots and was marketing nationally. By 1900 it was the largest British chocolate maker with an annual turnover in access of £1 million. By 1920 turnover had increased to £8 million and Cadbury was now the largest confectioner in the world, a position it would hold for another three decades. Investing in social sustainability and investing in people made Cadbury Brothers a sustainable and powerful business; and as students of its more recent history will know, it was when Cadbury broke with tradition and ceases its social commitments that its troubles began. In 2011 the company was bought by its American rival Kraft, and now only its consumer brands remain.

To our two choices given previously, then, we can add a third:

3   Create or develop an organizational culture, which has sustainability at its heart. Those individuals who share the values of sustainability will be attracted to it; those who do not will select themselves out and leave of their own accord.

7.2 Organizational Culture

Congruity of goals between employees and organization is heavily influenced by the organization's culture. There are various definitions of organizational culture, but for the purposes of this chapter we can take it as meaning the prevailing beliefs, myths, folklore, customs and practices, which are shared by the greater majority of the organization's members. Not everything in a culture has to be rational or logical, and indeed there is a good chance that much of it will be quite illogical and irrational (I once referred in class to culture as 'our bundle of shared irrationalities'). Organizational cultures take time to build up, and the strongest are usually found in organizations that have been around for some time. The prevailing culture of the Tata Group is heavily influenced by the example of the group's founder, Jamsetji Tata, and the ethos and values that he promulgated. Today, managers and employees across the group still sometimes look to his memory for example.

Cultures are also hard to manage, and often develop in unexpected ways. This is because everyone participates in the creation of a culture; it is not something that management can create out of nothing. At best, managers can attempt to influence the development of a culture through relationships with employees and personal example. Not all of these attempts succeed.

At IBM in the 1970s and 1980s, senior executives prided themselves on their corporate culture which they believed to be dynamic, open and innovative. IBM had for years been at the head of new developments in the computer industry, and executives still believed this to be the case. They proudly told outsiders that the company was a place where maverick, out-of-the-box thinking was encouraged, and talked of 'wild ducks' whose role was to test and challenge orthodox thinking on every issue. In fact, this culture did not exist. Conformity had become the watchword at IBM, where employees even had to wear the same colour of suit, and mavericks had long since been stamped out. 'What happened to all the wild ducks?' ran the bitter joke at lower levels of the organization. 'They all got shot.'

And as a result, IBM was no longer the dynamic company that its leaders imagined it to be, and was becoming increasingly easy prey for more agile competitors. By the end of the 1980s the company was facing collapse, and it took many years and much hard work and sacrifice to rebuild the company and its culture.

Culture is one of those things, like organization itself, that develops naturally whenever people begin to do things together. One of the most influential writers on organizational culture, Edgar Schein, argued that there is a cyclical connection between people and culture. 'Individuals create organizations that develop cultures', he wrote, 'and organizations acculturate individuals. The balance between individual and organizational autonomy is a perpetual struggle forever modulated by dynamic "psychological contracts" between employer and employed' (Schein, 2007, p. 9).

These 'psychological contracts' bring us back to the reasons why people join organizations in the first place, and are part of the social side of the sociotechnical system. Formal contracts lay down the duties of employees and spell out the remuneration and other benefits they will receive in return. Psychological contracts deal with all the rest; the belongingness and self-esteem that the employee expects, the commitment to goals that the employer hopes for. There is a process of emotional give-and-take that goes on between each employee and the organization.

Different organizational cultures will, however, regulate that process of emotional exchange in different ways. One useful method for understanding this process is role theory (Mead, 1934; Parsons, 1951). Role theory argues that as members of organizations we play roles, a little bit as actors do on stage. This is especially true of employees in customer-facing posts, who are often quite aware that they 'put on a face' when dealing with customers, sometimes adopting a persona different from their real one. Other employees and managers also adopt roles, though they are not always aware that they are doing so. In any group situation, we naturally try to think what the other members of the group expect of us. Once we think we know what that is, our need for belongingness encourages us to respond and we adopt a persona, which we think makes us more attractive to the other members of the group.

This can be a positive force, encouraging contact and helping people to overcome their own inhibitions and fears and work effectively with others. It can also lead to negative reactions such as unhealthy levels of peer pressure (for example, to commit illegal or dangerous acts), groupthink and a tendency to herding, following the lead of others in the group rather than thinking for oneself.

One of the most commented-upon aspects of role theory is the idea of 'role stress'. Sometimes, pressures from outside force people into roles, which make them uncomfortable. This can mean issues such as the peer pressure *described above*, but it can also be simply a matter of the wrong person in the wrong job. A shy introvert will not make a good customer sales representative; an outgoing extrovert might well be uncomfortable if tasked with doing endless hours of desk-work on a computer; each would be a 'square peg in a round hole'. Neither will have their needs satisfied and their work might well suffer as they become stressed by the incompatibility of their own persona and the roles they are expected to play. Some companies spend much time searching for the right role for their employees. N. R. Narayana Murthy, the former chief executive of Infosys, explained that his company had a policy of rotating underperforming people into new jobs. If a new employee did not perform well, Infosys assumed that this was the fault of the company for putting this employee into a job for which they were not suited. An investigation would then try to determine what role would suit this employee best.

Charles Handy has classified corporate cultures into four different sets, depending on the roles that people are expected to play (Handy, 1976). These are as follows:

- Role culture.
- Task culture.
- Power culture.
- Person culture.

In a *role* culture, the role that an employee plays is dictated largely by the post that they hold. People with higher posts tend to expect respect and deference from those beneath them, and relationships are based on formal hierarchies with orders transmitted down from above. People are expected to know their place in the hierarchy and play their role accordingly.

Task cultures, on the other hand, accord status to what the employee does, what their work entails. In these cultures, certain departments or business functions will be seen as more important than the others: traders in a financial institution, doctors in a hospital or R&D teams in a software house might serve as examples. These parts of the organization are, as the saying goes, 'more equal than others' and are looked up to by members of the other parts. Roles are adjusted accordingly depending on which part of the organization the employee belongs to.

Power cultures have a hierarchy based on what the person controls, what levers of power they are able to pull and how well they are able to reward those who are loyal to them. Power cultures often create informal hierarchies and loci of authority quite apart from the official organizational structure. Power can also be located in any part of the organization where dominant individuals have taken power into their own hands.

Finally, *person* cultures are based on who people are, on their personalities and characters rather than on external factors. These cultures probably enable people to play roles that most nearly resemble their real selves. These cultures are also very rare, as they tend to be highly decentralized with everyone going their own way and doing what they feel needs to be done with minimal supervision or direction. Handy suggests that barristers' chambers and hippie communes are the most commonly found examples of person culture.

Of course these are generalizations, and in many organizations elements of two, three or even all four cultures will be present. It is important, in our experience, not to be too judgemental about particular cultures or try to rank them in order from 'worst' to 'best'. It is tempting to see person cultures as being some sort of ideal, and indeed some organizations do have such cultures, but they are not without their weaknesses: for example, who ultimately takes responsibility when failures occur? Who exercises oversight to ensure that everyone is pulling their weight and working towards the common goal? Very high levels of trust are clearly needed for these organizations to work. Similarly, we can see role cultures as being mindless bureaucracies where everyone kowtows to authority; but *as we saw earlier*, some bureaucracies are remarkably efficient.

In the end cultures, like organizations and like people, are unique. They evolve and adapt over time, as Schein suggested, through the processes of personal interactions that go on within organizations. Creating and maintaining a culture that is focused on sustainability requires constant attention to those interactions. It follows therefore that communication and knowledge dissemination must play a key role in those interactions and relationships, and it is only through communication that top management can hope to exercise any influence over how a culture develops.

Creating a culture that will enable and support sustainability requires attention to all these elements, including role and power. Where does power reside in the organization? How can that power be harnessed to create and drive a culture? What roles do people play? How congruent are their roles with their own self-image and expectations? Can their roles be adjusted in ways that make them more aware of sustainability issues? Will empowerment set them free? Or will they continue to require guidance and direction; or, more commonly still, will they require a mixture of freedom and guidance? Once again, finding the right recipe will be unique to the organization and its circumstances. What is certain is that none of the factors discussed above can be ignored.

7.3 Requisite Knowledge

Knowledge is the lifeblood of any organization. If we examine any successful organization, we will see that it not only values knowledge but has learned how to use and disseminate knowledge very well; the *Cadbury case study* shows this particularly clearly. At the same time, it can be observed that ignorance is the enemy of sustainability. Most arguments advanced against sustainability are founded on ignorance – be it genuine lack of knowing or wilful blindness – of both the state of the world today and of the genuine principles of successful business (Witzel, 2015).

Achieving sustainability goals requires knowledge, and requires also that knowledge be circulated in ways that make it meaningful for the entire organization. Lack of circulating knowledge carries with it two dangers. The first is that people will fail to understand what is truly expected of them and – even more important – why. Without an understanding of purpose, their motivation will weaken and the company's culture could be undermined. Ultimately, their work might descend into rote, going through the motions. The second risk is the opposite; that people will remain highly motivated but will not understand the requirements of the situation. They might set out to solve the wrong problems, or take on problems that are too big and risky while ignoring simpler, easier solutions. There is, after all, nothing more harmful to a company than doing the wrong thing extremely well. When failure comes, as it ultimately will, the result could once again be disillusionment and lack of motivation.

Hence the stress on *requisite* knowledge, the knowledge the organization and its members need to carry through sustainability goals.

Nonaka and Takeuchi, in *The Knowledge-creating Company* (1995), make a clear link between culture and knowledge. They affirm that knowledge is the key to such vital business activities as innovation and maintaining customer relationships, but also argue that it plays a more general role. The circulation of knowledge within an organization also affects its culture. Organizations where knowledge circulates freely tend to be more open and less hierarchical and encourage people to voice opinions and discuss ideas. Organizations with internal silos and barriers to communication are less effective at circulating knowledge and thus more hierarchical and less flexible. The same point is made by former Intel CEO Andrew Grove in his book *Only the Paranoid Survive* (1996). Grove, speaking from personal experience, also points out that organizations with good communications systems that diffuse knowledge freely are also better equipped to adapt and survive in times of crisis.

'Knowledge', of course, is a complicated concept. It is often confused with 'information', for example, when in fact there is a distinct difference between the two. Some knowledge also takes fairly concrete forms and is easy to pass on to others, while other forms of knowledge are more vague and harder to pin down. Michael Polanyi (1966) drew a distinction between *explicit knowledge* and *tacit knowledge*. Explicit knowledge is that which we can easily write down or make clear in a form understandable to others. A marketer might know the demographics of the key market segments for their products; a jockey might know the layout of a racecourse and be able to draw a map of it; an engineer might have at their fingertips knowledge about the strength and hardness of certain materials. Tacit knowledge, on the other hand, is much harder to explain to others. The marketer might have an instinctive understanding of how customers behave but struggle to explain that to others; a jockey knows when to push a horse to the front and make a break for the finishing line but cannot explain exactly how they know this; even the engineer might struggle to explain to non-engineers how and why they make certain decisions about which materials to use when. Nonaka and Takeuchi, commenting on this, remark that tacit knowledge is often the most valuable because it is proprietary. If it can be unlocked and used within an organization, it can be an important source of competitive advantage, particularly because competitors will find it difficult to replicate that knowledge.

Max Boisot (1987, 1995) has expanded on Polanyi's concept to create two dimensions. Knowledge, says Boisot, can be *codified*, easy to set down on paper or onscreen and made explicit, or *uncodified*, difficult to make explicit or in other words, tacit knowledge. Secondly, knowledge can be *diffused*, i.e., easily shared and made public, or *undiffused*, difficult to share and understand widely. Highly technical knowledge such as, say, how to enrich uranium or how to build a Large Hadron Collider, could be considered undiffused. Using these two dimensions, Boisot creates a fourfold classification of knowledge (see Table 7.1).

TABLE 7.1   Boisot's Fourfold Classification of Knowledge

	Undiffused	Diffused
Codified	Proprietary knowledge	Public knowledge
Uncodified	Personal knowledge	Common sense

Again it is important not to see any of these forms of knowledge as superior. All organizations need access to all four – not least to common sense! Boisot's work makes us recognize that there are different forms of knowledge with different sources, and requiring different methods to create, acquire and manage knowledge.

One issue confronting organizations that intend to make sustainability a goal is that too much existing knowledge on the subject within those organizations is uncodified and undiffused. Getting the sustainability message across requires more attention to codification and diffusion, at least within the organization. What are the facts, insofar as they can be reliably ascertained? What is the cost-benefit trade-off? What specifically are the organization's goals? At the same time, though, the tacit dimension must not be neglected. As we saw earlier when discussing motivation, people do make emotional connections with organizations and are more likely to become committed to the organization's goals if their work also makes them feel good personally. Both dimensions are equally important, and neither can be neglected. A good communications strategy recognizes this and concentrates on both simultaneously in a co-ordinated way. Following on from Boisot, Nonaka and Takuechi (1995) developed the SECI model (socialization, externalization, combination and internalization) as an attempt to bring out tacit knowledge and make it more explicit. They acknowledged, however, that most organizations are very bad at doing this, and this remains true today.

7.4 The Employer Brand

'Brand' is an emotive word for some, who equate the use of brands with 'pressure marketing' and hard selling of brands, persuading people to buy things that – it is said – they do not really need. Unscrupulous companies do use brands in this way, of course, but at heart a brand is something much more complex. A brand is a bundle of perceptions. In part it represents what the organization believes about itself and would like others to believe about it; in large part, however, it is the perceptions of the organization by its stakeholders, perceptions created through their interactions with the organization and, importantly, with each other.

Among those stakeholders, of course, are employees. As Hatch and Schultz (2008) point out, as part of its overall corporate brand, every organization has an 'employer brand', the set of perceptions of the organization held by its employees. Just as with any other brand, employer brands are 'co-created' by the employer and the employees. The latter will of course discuss their perceptions of their employer during coffee or tea breaks, at lunch, after hours in their homes or the pub and, increasingly, in social media spaces. Their impressions of the employer help to create the brand.

Employer brand management consists in telling a clear and consistent story to employees so as to gain their attention and encourage them to understand the employer's position and actions and, ultimately, to commit to the employer's vision of the world and identify it with their own needs and goals. This must be done. As has often been said of brands, if you don't tell your story, someone else will tell it for you; and their version of the story may be incorrect, unpleasant and damaging. Good brands are based on truth and trust, and the story the employer tells must be founded on those two things.

In order to tell the brand story successfully, employers need to look at the factors *we have discussed above*. They need to understand their employees and what motivates them. What do they want/need to hear? The story should appeal to all employees wherever they are on the hierarchy of needs, helping them to empathize with the employer's position and compare it with their own.

The culture of the organization must be understood and the story must reflect that culture in a realistic way. Recall the example of IBM, which told a brand story which employees knew to be untrue. Sometimes this truth-telling may require some painful honesty and candour on the part of the employer. Generally, however, employees will respect this candour and it will make them more inclined to sympathy. And finally, *as we have just seen*, the channels of communication must be open and the employer must be able to communicate the story on both a practical and an emotional level, simultaneously.

The creation of a powerful employer brand, *as the Titan and Cadbury case studies show clearly*, can have very strong results in terms of performance and productivity. Both of these companies, in a short space of time, became industry leaders – and leaders in sustainability practices.

Organizations that are moving towards a sustainability agenda will have many barriers to overcome. Not the least of these may be the scepticism of employees who think the organization is merely indulging in a 'greenwash' or may even doubt the entire project and feel it is unnecessary and threatening to themselves personally. Argyris (1971) described how employees can sometimes engage in 'defensive routines', deliberate attempts to slow down or thwart a particular strategy with which they do not agree. Using the concept of the employer brand allows organizations to influence the thinking of their employees in a positive way and encourage them to see the benefits of the proposed strategy.

Ultimately, the employer brand can convert employees into what Ind (2001) calls 'brand champions', enthusiastic ambassadors for the organization who will help spread its ideas and reputation among other stakeholders and influence them in turn. Nayar (2010) goes so far as to subvert conventional wisdom and insist that employees are the most important stakeholder group of all. Get them on side, says Nayar, help them to share in the company's vision and turn them into enthusiastic brand supporters, and they will deliver top-class customer service of their own volition, with little guidance or direction needed from senior managers. The importance of this idea for a sustainability agenda should be clear. Employees who believe in the organization's vision for sustainability and support it enthusiastically will think creatively, come up with innovations, and generally drive the agenda through. Those who do not believe in this vision will at best work passively, and at worst attempt to subvert the project.

Summary

Every organization is in some way unique. This is as it should be, for each organization should be configured so as to best meet its particular goals while at the same time satisfying the needs of its members. Clearly the ideal situation is one where those goals and needs are closely congruent. In order to achieve this, organizations need to worry less about finding the ideal structure, and more about understanding their own culture, the motivations of their members on an individual and group basis, the social aspect of the sociotechnical system, and be sure that there are clear channels of communication.

(Continued)

There is, of course, nothing terribly staggering or new about all of this. It has been observed that most of our business organizations are dysfunctional; they do not meet their goals, sustainability-related or otherwise, and they act as psychic prisons that constrain people rather than enabling them to do their job. Does this mean that we need to scrap our existing models of organization entirely? As we observed earlier, there have been several attempts at doing so, but none has so far been satisfactory. Or do we simply need to get better at doing the basics of organization? My argument is in favour of the latter. If we look around at our own organizations, the ones we are members of today, how many factors are there that drag at us and demotivate us? How much of our organization's culture enables us, and how much constrains us? Are we given the knowledge we really need to do our jobs well?

Interface (Anderson & White, 2013) provides an example of an organization that does all these things very well. It is tempting then to think that, in order to succeed, all we need to do is become like Interface. But Cadbury did all these things very well too, and there was no rush to follow the Cadbury model. Why? Because business leaders were not interested? Or because they found the Cadbury model interesting but could not make it work in their own organizations? The answer in most cases, if we look at contemporary reactions to Cadbury, is the latter. Again, we must make the point: every organization is unique, and its needs are unique too. Leaders need to find the right recipe of motivation, culture and knowledge that is needed for that company, in that place, at that time.

The role of leadership has already been discussed elsewhere in this volume *(see Chapter 3)*, but readers are encouraged to refer closely to that chapter once this one has been read, and even perhaps combine some of the exercises or do them in tandem in order to make the linkage clear.

GROUP EXERCISE

Working in small groups, discuss the concept of roles in organizations. What organizations do each of you currently belong to – business, recreational, family, university, etc.? What roles do you play? Are you always comfortable with these roles? Comparing notes should enable you to understand how other people perceive their own roles.

Working in small groups, discuss the notion that companies do (or do not) need to be organized differently in the context of sustainability challenges. Provide a reason for your point of view. Give examples of what might need to change, or stay the same.

Working in small groups, discuss how you would communicate knowledge about sustainability to an organization's staff – feel free to draw on your own organization and its members as examples. What kind of knowledge do people need? What levels of resistance might be encountered? What channels would best enable meaningful communication?

Working in small groups, consider the concept of the employer brand. Think of organizations you have worked for in the past. Of what did their employer brand consist? Did these organizations directly manage their employer brand, and if so, how successful were they at doing so?

QUESTIONS FOR CLASS DISCUSSION

1. Every organization has its own needs, and every individual in those organizations has their own needs. How can these needs be balanced, especially if they compete with each other?

2. How important are Herzberg's hygiene factors in determining organizational success? How can these factors be managed?

3. How would you go about incorporating a vision for and agenda for sustainability in an existing corporate culture?

4. How might knowledge differ from information? What kinds of knowledge are needed in order to achieve sustainability?

References

Anderson, R. C., & White, R. (2013). *Confessions of a radical industrialist: profits, people, purpose: Doing business by respecting the earth.* New York: St. Martin's Press.

Argyris, C. (1971). *Management and organizational development.* New York: McGraw-Hill.

Boisot, M. (1987). *Information and organizations: The manager as anthropologist.* London: Fontana.

Boisot, M. (1995). *Information space: A framework for learning in organizations.* Institutions and Culture, London: Routledge.

Burrell, G., & Morgan, G. (1989). *Social paradigms and organizational analysis.* Aldershot: Ashgate.

Chandler, A. D. (1962). *Strategy and Structure: Chapters in the History of American Industrial Enterprise,* Cambridge, MA: MIT Press.

Emerson, H. (1913). *The twelve principles of efficiency.* New York: The Engineering Magazine Co.

Emery, F. E., & Trist, E. L. (1965) The causal texture of organizational environments. *Human Relations, 18,* 21–32.

Foucault, M. (1977). *Discipline and punish: Birth of the prison* (trans. Alan Sheridan). London: Allen Lane.

Grove, A. (1996). *Only the paranoid survive: How to exploit the crisis points that challenge every company and career.* New York: HarperCollins.

Handy, C. (1976). *Understanding organizations.* London: Penguin.

Hatch, M. J., & Schultz, M. (2008). *Taking brand initiative: How companies can align strategy, culture and identity through corporate branding.* San Francisco: Jossey-Bass.

Herzberg, F. (1966). *Work and the nature of man.* Cleveland: World Publishing Company.

Ind, N. (2001). *Living the brand: How to transform every member of your organization into a brand champion.* London: Kogan Page.

Jia, F., Gosling, J., & Witzel, M. (2016). *Sustainable champions.* Sheffield: Greenleaf.

Kanigel, R. (1997). *The one best way: Frederick Taylor and the enigma of efficiency.* New York: Viking Penguin.

Lindblom, C. E. (1959). The science of muddling through. *Public Administration Review, 19,* 79–88.

Maslow, A. (1954). *Motivation and personality.* New York: Harper & Bros.

Mayo, E. (1933). *The human problems of an industrial civilization.* New York: Macmillan.

McGregor, D. (1960). *The human side of enterprise.* New York: McGraw-Hill.

Mead, G. (1934). *Mind, self and society.* Chicago: University of Chicago Press.

Miles, R. E., & Snow, C. C. (1978). *Organizational strategy, structure and process.* New York: McGraw-Hill.

Mohman, S. A., & Shani, A. B. (Eds.). (2011). *Organizing for sustainable effectiveness.* London: Emerald.

Nayar, V. (2010). *Employees first, customers second: Turning conventional management upside down.* Boston: Harvard Business Press.

Nonaka, I., & Takeuchi, H. (1995). *The knowledge-creating company: How Japanese companies create the dynamics of innovation.* Oxford: Oxford University Press.

Parsons, T. (1951). *The social system.* Cambridge, MA: Harvard University Press.

Pasmore, W. (1988). *Designing effective organizations: The sociotechnical perspective.* New York: Wiley.

Polanyi, M. (1966). *The tacit dimension.* New York: Doubleday.

Roethlisberger, F., & Dickson, W. J. (1939). *Management and the worker.* Cambridge, MA: Harvard University Press.

Schein, E. H. (1997). From brainwashing to organizational therapy. *European Business Forum, 31,* 6–9.

Uys, P., & Campbell, M. (2005). *Structure and sustainability: An analysis of the organization of educational technology leadership and support at Australian universities.* Retrieved from http://www.ascilite.org.au/conferences/brisbane05/blogs/proceedings/80_Uys.pdf

Warner, M., & Witzel, M. (2004). *Managing in virtual organizations.* London: International Thomson Business Press.

Witzel, M. (2010). *Tata: The evolution of a corporate brand.* New Delhi: Penguin India.

Witzel, M. (2012). *A history of management thought.* London: Routledge.

Witzel, M. (2015). *Managing for success: Spotting danger signals – and fixing problems before they happen.* London: Bloomsbury.

8 Investing: Responsible Investment and its Role in a Sustainable Economy

Rory Sullivan

LEARNING OUTCOMES

This chapter will enable you to:

1. Understand how investors influence the companies in which they are invested.

2. Understand the different responsible investment strategies, and their relationship to mainstream investment practice.

3. Understand the potential contribution that responsible investment might make to the goals of a more sustainable economy.

4. Critically analyse the literature on responsible investment and its relationship to the goals of sustainable development.

Introduction

There is growing interest in the potential contribution that large institutional investors might make to the goals of a socially and environmentally sustainable economic system (see Definition box).

Over 1,300 institutional investors (pension funds, investment managers, insurance companies) have signed up to the Principles for Responsible Investment,[1] committing themselves to taking account of environmental, social and governance issues in their investment processes and in their dialogue with the companies in which they are invested.

The question this raises is whether, and under what conditions, these commitments contribute to the wider goals of a socially and environmentally sustainable economic system.

Over the past 30 years, in particular since the fall of the Berlin Wall and the end of the Cold War, debates around sustainable development have broadened from an emphasis on the roles and responsibilities of government to a broader discussion on the

---

[1] https://www.unpri.org/directory/ (accessed 2016, September 7).

roles and responsibilities of companies. In these debates, concern has been expressed about the adverse social and environmental impacts (e.g., global warming, biodiversity loss, resource depletion) of globalization and about the perceived power and influence of corporations *vis-à-vis* national governments. There has been heated discussion about the responsibilities and accountabilities of corporations in a globalized economy, heightened by examples and allegations of corporate wrongdoing and inappropriate influence on government, both in the developed and the developing countries.

More recently, there has been a focus on the role played by the investors in these companies. There are various reasons: investor pressure to deliver short-term profits may lead companies to put these ahead of corporate responsibility; recognition that environmental and social issues may affect investment returns as a result of litigation (e.g., tobacco, asbestosis, product liability), regulation, taxation and company failure as a consequence of probity failings (e.g., Enron); demand from regulators, clients, beneficiaries and stakeholders such as trade unions and non-governmental organizations for more sustainable approaches to investment (see, e.g., *Business for Social Responsibility*, 2008; Gitman *et al.*, 2009; Kiernan, 2009; Sullivan, 2011; for historic perspectives on the evolution of investor interest in responsible investment, see Sparkes, 2002 and Sullivan & Mackenzie, 2006).

INSTITUTIONAL INVESTORS

This chapter focuses on what is referred to as the institutional investment market,[2] which is a general term for investments managed or controlled by insurance companies, pension funds and investment managers in pension funds, mutual funds and other investment vehicles. Institutional investors invest on behalf of large numbers of individuals who have their pensions and savings invested in these funds.

Many pension funds operate under trust law. This imposes a 'fiduciary' obligation on the trustees and fund managers involved to serve the interests of those whose money is invested in these funds.

QUESTION FOR CLASS DISCUSSION

Do you agree with the argument (see, e.g., UNEPFI, 2005; Hawley *et al.*, 2014; Sullivan *et al.*, 2015) that fiduciary duty creates a positive duty on investors to pay attention to environmental, social and governance issues in their investment practices and in their dialogue with companies?

The investment industry has responded to these pressures. Perhaps the clearest evidence of this is that over 300 asset owners (pension funds) and 1,000 investment managers[3] have signed the Principles for Responsible Investment (see Box 8.1), committing themselves to taking account of environmental, social and governance issues in their investment processes and to encouraging the companies in which they invest to adopt higher standards of corporate governance and corporate responsibility.

---

[2] The institutional investment market is just one part of the wider financial system. For a wider discussion of the global financial system, of the key actors in the system and of their role in financing sustainable development, see the website and publications of the UNEP Inquiry into the Design of a Sustainable Financial System at www.unep.org/inquiry/ (accessed 2016, September 7).

[3] https://www.unpri.org/directory/ (accessed 2016, September 7).

BOX 8.1

The Principles for Responsible Investment[4]

As institutional investors, we have a duty to act in the best long-term interests of our beneficiaries. In this fiduciary role, we believe that environmental, social, and corporate governance (ESG) issues can affect the performance of investment portfolios (to varying degrees across companies, sectors, regions, asset classes and through time). We also recognize that applying these Principles may better align investors with broader objectives of society. Therefore, where consistent with our fiduciary responsibilities, we commit to the following:

Principle 1: We will incorporate ESG issues into investment analysis and decision-making processes.

Principle 2: We will be active owners and incorporate ESG issues into our ownership policies and practices.

Principle 3: We will seek appropriate disclosure on ESG issues by the entities in which we invest.

Principle 4: We will promote acceptance and implementation of the Principles within the investment industry.

Principle 5: We will work together to enhance our effectiveness in implementing the Principles.

Principle 6: We will each report on our activities and progress towards implementing the Principles.

8.0 Mechanics of Influence: How do Investors Influence Companies?

In broad terms, investors exert influence through the share or asset price, and through the dialogue (engagement and voting) that they have with companies.

Share prices (or other financial measures, e.g., the cost of capital) provide companies with a broad measure of how they are perceived by financial markets. Investors tend to focus on how the company and its share price will perform over the next year or two years at most. This does not mean that these investors are unaware of or do not analyse issues that are likely to impact on companies beyond this one- or two-year time horizon. What it does mean is that investors tend to focus on short-term factors in their investment decisions and to be less interested in investments that provide longer-term returns, or that mitigate risks that may occur at some point in the future (Sullivan, 2011).

There is evidence that companies respond to the signals sent to them by the financial markets; e.g., concern about the market reaction to a failure to meet earnings expectations might cause companies to engage in earnings management to meet these market expectations (see Dallas, 2012, p. 269) and the references cited therein). This statement should be qualified by acknowledging that there are a variety of reasons why companies may behave in this way, such as the desire to build

---

[4] https://www.unpri.org/about/the-six-principles (accessed 2016, September 7).

the firm's credibility with capital markets, to maintain or increase their stock prices, to convey future growth prospects, and to achieve particular credit ratings (Bhojraj & Libby, 2005; Graham *et. al.*, 2005, 2006). That is, while short-termism is a factor, there are a variety of other factors at play in the relationship between companies and their investors.

The manner in which investors use their formal rights (e.g., to vote proxies, call meetings) and their informal influence (often referred to as engagement) also signals to companies the issues that are seen as important by investors (Sullivan and Mackenzie, 2006, pp. 151–157, 332–346; Sullivan, 2014). The general arguments for companies to take a proactive approach to communicating with investors on long-term and sustainability-related issues are that regular engagement increases mutual trust between companies and their investors (Godfrey *et al.*, 2009), that constructive challenge by institutional shareholders of strategy and capital expenditure is a necessary and invaluable part of the value creation process (ICSA, 2013, p. 5) and that engagement enables shareholders to better understand the business (Cronin & Mellor, 2011, p. 4). In practice, however, many companies criticize investors for focusing primarily on near-term financial performance, quarterly earnings and remuneration, interpreting this as a sign that investors have less interest in longer-term business drivers or in sustainability-related issues. These perceptions are compounded by the fact that investors are often not forthcoming about their views on the long-term prospects for the company, or how they use the information provided by companies in their investment decision-making (Sullivan, 2011).

8.1 What is Responsible Investment?

Responsible investment is an approach to investment that explicitly acknowledges the relevance to the investor of environmental, social and governance factors, and the long-term health and stability of the market as a whole.[5] Underpinning this is the recognition that the generation of long-term sustainable returns is dependent on stable, well-functioning and well-governed social, environmental and economic systems. From an investment perspective, it suggests that investors should research, analyse and evaluate environmental, social and governance issues as a fundamental part of assessing the value and performance of an investment over the medium and longer term, and that this analysis should inform asset allocation, stock selection, portfolio construction, shareholder engagement and voting.

At a very high level, responsible investment can be differentiated from conventional approaches to investment in that the goal is the creation of sustainable, long-term investment returns and not just short-term returns, and that explicit attention is paid to the impacts of investment activities on the stability and health of social, economic and environmental systems.

---

[5] http://2xjmlj8428u1a2k5o34l1m71.wpengine.netdna-cdn.com/wp-content/uploads/1.Whatis responsibleinvestment.pdf (accessed 2015, April 29).

8.1.1 A Typology of Strategies

While the *prima facie* argument that environmental and social issues can be financially significant is now widely accepted, there is no consensus about how these issues actually affect investment returns or on how best to integrate them into investment processes. Table 8.1 presents a typology of the major responsible investment strategies presently in use. These range from 'traditional' negative screening approaches (i.e., where companies are excluded because of their ethical characteristics) through to the more mainstream approaches of engagement and enhanced analysis that have emerged over the past ten years (for data on the market share of these different strategies, see Global Sustainable Investment Alliance (2014)).

Even though *Table 8.1* sets out the recognized major approaches to responsible investment, these approaches are not homogeneous. The reality is that terms such as 'ethical investment' and 'responsible investment' conceal a variety of investment

TABLE 8.1   Major Responsible Investment Strategies

Strategy	Description
Negative screening	Negative screening involves avoiding (i.e., not investing in) companies on the basis of specified criteria. The criteria can be defined in a range of ways, including by product (e.g., alcohol, tobacco), by activity (e.g., gambling), by sector (e.g., oil, mining, banking), by reference to international norms (e.g., non-compliance with international standards or principles such as those from the United Nations or the International Labour Organization) or by management practice (e.g., the absence of human rights policies).
Positive screening	Positive screening involves preferentially investing in companies on the basis of specified criteria. In a similar manner to negative screening, the criteria can be defined in a number of ways, including by product (e.g., renewable energy technologies), by activity (e.g., education services), by sector (e.g., health care), by reference to international norms (e.g., complying with international standards or principles such as those from the United Nations or the International Labour Organization) or by management practice (e.g., high-quality policies and reporting on human rights).
Best in class	Best in class involves preferentially investing in companies with better governance and management processes (e.g., more comprehensive policies, better reporting) and/or with better environmental or social performance (e.g., lower greenhouse gas emissions per unit of production). Best in class may be defined by reference to a specific sector (e.g., mining) or across a defined investment universe (e.g., the FTSE100 Index of the 100 largest publicly listed companies in the UK).
Thematic investment	Thematic investment involves the selection of companies on the basis of investment opportunities driven by themes such as climate change or demographic change.
Engagement/ activism	Engagement (or activism) involves investors using their formal rights (e.g., the ability to vote shareholdings, the ability to call an emergency general meeting) and informal influence to encourage companies to improve their management systems, their performance or their reporting.
Integrated analysis (or enhanced analysis)	Integrated analysis involves the proactive consideration of environmental and social factors in investment research and decision-making. Integrated analysis can be quantitative (e.g., generating data on costs and revenues for use in discounted cash flow models, modifying business growth assumptions), qualitative (e.g., providing an alternative perspective on a company's quality of management or risk management processes, providing a ranking of companies on one of more dimensions of their corporate responsibility performance) or a combination of both.

Source: Sullivan, 2011.

strategies and philosophies (see, generally, Business for Social Responsibility, 2008; Sandberg *et al.*, 2009). Some of the dimensions on which responsible investment strategies vary include (Sullivan, 2011, pp. 11–13):

- *The relative importance of environmental and social issues to the investment process.* Specifically, (a) do these issues outweigh financial considerations, (b) are they explicitly considered as an integral part of discussions around a company's quality of management, or (c) are they researched but with no requirement for the results of this research to be explicitly considered in investment decision-making?

- *The specific issues that are of concern.* The breadth of topics that could be covered in a responsible investment strategy is well illustrated by the following quote from analysts at Société Générale:

  > *In a typical day, we can look at issues as diverse as calculating our own quantitative sustainability ratings; identifying long-term ESG [environmental, social, governance] considerations for the luxury goods sector; identifying the carbon footprint of a car manufacturer; arguing over a utility company's carbon dioxide-derived windfall profits; screening companies with potential involvement in producing cluster bombs; debating the nutrition benefits of a certain range of margarines; and assessing the consequences of the last European Court of Justice ruling on the minimum wage in Germany*
  >
  > (Lucas-Leclin & Nahal, 2008, p. 43).

- *The specific data points that are used in investment evaluations.* For example, the assessment of a company's governance systems could be made on the basis of (among others) (a) the existence (or not) of a board committee for corporate responsibility, (b) the range of topics covered in a corporate responsibility report, (c) the quality of environmental policies (e.g., climate change), (d) the robustness of the company's risk identification and risk assessment processes, (e) evidence of the company identifying and exploiting new business opportunities, and (f) the company's performance against its own policies and targets.

- *Whether the responsible investment strategy applies to an individual fund, to a specific asset class or across all asset classes.* It is not uncommon for investment managers to have multiple investment strategies depending on the specific funds that they manage. To further complicate the matter, it is common to find multiple strategies applied to a single product (e.g., a negatively screened fund may also have an engagement strategy, and environmental and social factors may be explicitly considered in investment decisions).

- *How the responsible investment strategy is implemented.* To take just one responsible investment strategy – negative screening – there is a wide variation in the screens that are applied in ethical or negatively screened funds and an even greater variation in how these screens are interpreted. In an extremely critical assessment of socially responsible investment mutual funds, Hawken (2004) highlighted the lack of clarity on screening criteria, the fact that virtually any stock can be considered 'acceptable' depending on the interpretation of the screening criteria, the fact that most of the screening criteria had very little to do with sustainable development, and the generally limited focus on the companies' products and activities.

- *What the investment manager sees as material (or relevant) to the investment decision.*
- *The level of the organization's commitment to the responsible investment strategy,* in terms of the resources allocated to responsible investment, the level of CEO or senior management involvement, the calibre of individuals charged with managing responsible investment activities within the organization and the level of transparency around the actions taken and the outcomes achieved.

8.1.2 Materiality and Time-frames, and their Implications for Responsible Investment

Even though there is a wide variation in the responsible investment strategies that can be adopted, the idea of materiality underpins virtually every responsible investment strategy. Materiality (or, more specifically, financial materiality) is widely used to describe the financial significance of a particular issue. Information is defined as 'material' if its omission, mis-statement or non-disclosure has the potential to adversely affect decisions about the allocation of scarce resources made by the users of the financial report or the discharge of accountability by the management or governing body of the entity.

While there is no consensus on the precise threshold or quantitative level at which an issue becomes material', a general accounting rule of thumb is that companies should disclose events that lead to impacts of greater than 10% on a key financial performance indicator (such as profit, turnover or revenues), whereas impacts of less than 5% are generally not considered material (Sullivan, 2011, p. 123). Investors generally use a similar rule of thumb. That is, they are interested in issues that have impacts of at least 5% or 10% on key financial performance indicators or on share prices, and will tend to have less interest in impacts below this level. Because of the manner in which mainstream investors define financial materiality, the vast majority of environmental and social issues are not considered financially material (see, e.g., the views presented in Campbell and Slack, 2008, pp. 23–24).

There are a number of important nuances in investors' definition of materiality. First, the assessment of the risk faced by a company requires that attention is paid to the company's exposure, its markets and its quality of management. For instance, when considering the financial implications of greenhouse gas emissions, investors do not just consider the total volume of greenhouse gases emitted. They also consider the likelihood that the company will be required to reduce some or all of its greenhouse gas emissions, the degree of emissions reductions likely to be required and the time-frames over which these will be required, the capital and operating costs associated with the company reducing its emissions, whether the company is required to absorb some or all of the costs of the emissions reductions it is required to make, and the company's quality of management (both of climate change specifically and of environmental and social issues in general) (Sullivan & Kozak, 2009; Sullivan, Crossley & Kozak, 2008). See Definition box.

STRANDED ASSETS

The Carbon Tracker Initiative defines stranded assets as:

> ... fossil fuel energy and generation resources which, at some time prior to the end of their economic life (as assumed at the investment decision point), are no longer able to earn an economic return (i.e. meet the company's internal rate of return), as a result of changes in the market and regulatory environment associated with the transition to a low-carbon economy.[6]

The Carbon Tracker Initiative introduced the concept of stranded assets to encourage investors to think about the implications of not adjusting their investment portfolios in line with the emissions trajectories required to limit global warming. It has suggested that assets might be stranded because of regulation (e.g., due to a change in policy or legislation), economics (e.g., due to a change in relative costs) or physical impacts (e.g., floods, droughts).

The Carbon Tracker Initiative states that it aims to prevent stranded assets by identifying where capital expenditure may be allocated to investments which may not yield the expected returns in a low-demand, low-price scenario.

QUESTIONS FOR CLASS DISCUSSION

1. What sorts of assets are at particular risk of stranding as a result of the introduction of a carbon price (or a carbon tax)?
2. How would investors assess the risks to their portfolios as a result of the introduction of a carbon price (or a carbon tax)?
3. What actions might investors take to mitigate the risks associated with asset stranding?
4. What challenges might they encounter when trying to manage or mitigate these risks?

Second, materiality is as much a relative as an absolute question. That is, the importance of the costs (or benefits) associated with a specific environmental or social impact is defined by the size, scale and activities of the business. For example, the significance of a company having to pay £10 million to reduce its greenhouse gas emissions is critically dependent on the company's turnover and profits. If the company's profit is £20 million, greenhouse gas emission reduction costs are clearly material, whereas if the company's profit is £1 billion, investors are likely to spend less time dwelling on its greenhouse gas emissions.

Third, time-frames are critical. For most investors, the time-frame of interest is relatively short, with most attention being paid to how the company and its share price will perform over the next year or two years at most (see Box 8.2). Issues that may impact on the business beyond that time (e.g., regulation that takes effect a number of years in the future) are unlikely to receive much attention. Expressed another way, investors are likely to be very interested in an environmental or social issue that has an impact of 10% on a key financial indicator over the next one to two years but may have less interest if the issue may have a 50% impact on the same financial indicator over the next five to ten years (Sullivan, 2011).

---

[6] http://www.carbontracker.org/resources/ (accessed 2015, April 29).

BOX 8.2

Why is Short-termism an Issue?

The case for companies to take account of sustainability-related issues in their strategic planning and capital investment decisions is compelling. To provide just one example, 93% of the CEOs that participated in a 2013 UN Global Compact-Accenture CEO study on sustainability stated that they considered sustainability as important to the future success of their business, with 76% stating that they believed that embedding sustainability into core business would drive revenue growth and new opportunities (Accenture & UN Global Compact, 2013, p. 35).

Yet, these CEOs also expressed frustration that their efforts are constrained by current market structures, incentives and expectations. One of the key constraints is pressure from investors for companies to focus on short-term financial performance, often at the expense of the longer-term needs of their businesses (see, e.g., Graham *et al.*, 2005). Short-termism refers to the excessive focus of some corporate leaders, investors, and analysts on short-term, quarterly earnings and a corresponding lack of attention to strategy, fundamentals, and long-term value creation. Short-termism in companies can manifest itself in a variety of ways, including:

◆ Lower expenditures on research and development.

◆ The foregoing of investment opportunities in physical assets or in intangibles such as product development, employee skills and customer reputation, with a positive long-term net present value, in order to satisfy the market's short-term performance expectations.

◆ Accounting adjustments that maximize short-term earnings and stock prices, rather than the long-term value of the corporation.

◆ A bias towards high dividend payouts and share buybacks, at the expense of investment.

◆ Remuneration structures that reward short- rather than long-term performance and that skew management's incentives towards actions that provide short-term boosts to the share price.

◆ A lack of attention to longer-term risks in the company's products, services or business strategy.

◆ An excessive focus on restructuring, financial re-engineering or mergers and acquisitions rather than on organic growth or on developing the operational capabilities of the business (Aspen Institute, 2009; Brochet *et al.*, 2012; CFA, 2006; Dallas, 2012, pp. 266–272, 277–280; Graham *et al.*, 2005; Kay, 2012, pp. 12–14; Rappaport, 2005).

The most common explanation for short-termism in listed companies is pressure from the financial markets. In this account, financial market participants face considerable short-term performance pressures from their clients and from the media, with the benchmarking and evaluation of investment managers based on their one-month and three-month investment performance a seemingly inescapable part of the investment landscape.

Even those investment organizations that should, at least in theory, be classed as long-term investors, too often appear to be primarily interested in short-term performance. For example, asset owners – whose investment time horizons should extend many decades into the future – often focus on quarterly or even monthly investment portfolio performance. This results in investment managers seeing this as the *de facto* time horizon over which their performance is being assessed. This emphasis on short-term financial performance tends to be reinforced by the manner in which investment management mandates (i.e., the contracts between asset owners and asset managers) are structured and monitored. These mandates often require investment managers to report quarterly, or more frequently, on investment performance, again reinforcing the perception that short-term investment performance is of primary importance. While mandate design and investment manager monitoring are important issues, the emphasis on short-term investment performance also reflects some of the regulatory and other requirements that asset owners have to meet. For example, in the wake of the global financial crisis, regulatory bodies have placed much more emphasis on short-term performance management and reporting, especially in situations where pension funds have shortfalls against their liabilities.

Source: Adapted from Sullivan (2014).

Fourth, the 'net present value' of a future environmental or social impact is lower than the financial effects if the environmental or social impact occurred today because:

(a) investors discount the future (i.e., they use a non-zero positive discount rate to account for future impacts on the business);

(b) investors frequently exclude high-consequence but low-probability events completely from their calculations (on the grounds that the likelihood of these occurring over the time-frame of interest to the investor is relatively low); and

(c) investors are, very often correctly, sceptical that governments will act to correct market failures and, even if governments do act, generally assume that firms that are disadvantaged will be compensated in some way (see, e.g., Waygood *et al.* 2006).

These dynamics are well illustrated in the case of climate change adaptation, which (from an investment perspective) can be characterized as occurring at some point in the future (albeit acknowledging that certain effects of changing weather patterns are already being seen), with a significant probabilistic element. While the scientific predictions are increasingly robust, there are significant uncertainties around the actual impacts that will be seen, the specific locations where these will occur and how public policy-makers will respond (not least, in relation to the trade-offs that will need to be made between mitigation, or emissions reductions, and adaptation). The result has been that investors have, to date, not paid much attention to adaptation in their investment research (Pfeifer & Sullivan, 2008; Sullivan, Russell & Robins, 2008; Sullivan *et al.*, 2009).

From a stakeholder perspective, the most important point to take from this discussion is that the investor definition of materiality differs significantly from the definitions adopted by stakeholders (see, e.g., Faux, 2002). Mainstream investors' focus on financial materiality means that wider ethical values (other than to the extent that these manifest themselves as impacts on the business through, e.g., regulation, damage to brand or reputation, increased costs) tend to be excluded from the assessments made. Even investors with a particular interest in social or environmental matters tend to confine their interest to a relatively narrow set of topics (e.g., the specific screens in a negatively screened fund) rather than the spectrum of social and environmental issues that may be of concern.

8.2 So What Can Responsible Investment Deliver?

8.2.1 Disclosure?

Investors have played an important role in encouraging companies to report on their social and environmental performance even where the company does not have any (in the eyes of mainstream investors) financially material environmental or social impacts. Investors have supported the work of the Global Reporting Initiative (GRI)[7] and have encouraged companies to report against the GRI's reporting frameworks. Investors have also established and supported a series of issue-specific reporting frameworks, including CDP[8] (previously the Carbon Disclosure Project), the Access to Medicines Index[9] and the Forest Footprint Disclosure Project.[10] While there are clearly a variety of factors at play, it is probably fair to say that, across the board, investors have made an important contribution to increasing the number of companies that report on their corporate responsibility performance.

It is also fair to say that the quality of this information continues to fall short of that required by investors and other stakeholders (Sullivan & Gouldson, 2012; Sullivan, 2011, 2014). This can, at least in part, be attributed to the fact that despite calling for more disclosure, many investors do not actually use the corporate responsibility information published by companies. This is not necessarily a contradictory statement. The reason many investors have supported various disclosure initiatives is that they recognize the public goods and other benefits (e.g., improved stakeholder dialogue, the creation of incentives for companies to improve their performance, allowing investors to demonstrate their responsible investment credentials) that accrue from this support. Many companies have, therefore, concluded that these issues are not a priority for investors and so have tended to be reactive rather than proactive in communicating their corporate responsibility performance.

8.2.2 Performance?

The huge increase in the number of investors that have made commitments to responsible investment (i.e., to taking account of environmental and social issues in their investment processes and to encouraging high standards of corporate responsibility performance in the companies in which they are invested) represents one of the most important developments in the corporate responsibility area in recent years. Investors' views on corporate responsibility matters and the way in which investors use corporate responsibility information in their research and decision-making are critical influences on how companies manage and report their corporate responsibility performance. There is a substantial body of evidence that investor engagement has contributed to companies improving their social and environmental management systems and processes, focusing on environmental and social issues as potential drivers of business value, and improving their reporting and performance

---

[7] http://www.globalreporting.org
[8] http://www.cdproject.net
[9] http://www.atmindex.org
[10] http://www.forestdisclosure.com

(in particular when there is a clear business case for action) in these areas (see, e.g., Sullivan & Mackenzie, 2006).

The growing interest in the integration of environmental, social and governance issues into investment decision-making should provide further support to investor engagement and increase the pressure from investors for companies to improve their corporate responsibility performance. As responsible investment matures, it is likely that we will see more complex approaches that make greater use of performance data emerge over time. It is, however, important to recognize that investment integration is not a trivial task, and remains very much a work in progress even among the leaders in the responsible investment field. Many aspects of corporate responsibility performance are difficult to define in quantitative terms or performance measures because these issues have yet to be agreed (see, e.g., the discussion of social issues in Box 8.3).

QUESTIONS FOR CLASS DISCUSSION

You represent a human rights NGO that is concerned about a proposed major oil development and 250 km-long oil pipeline in West Africa. The construction of the project and the pipeline will require 7,000 people to permanently leave their homes. You have evidence that families along the pipeline route have been threatened with violence if they do not leave their homes and land. You have been offered a meeting with a large UK institutional investor which holds 2.4% of the issued share capital of the company. The investor is a signatory to the Principles for Responsible Investment.

1. What would your objectives for this meeting be?

2. What would you expect the investor to do (or offer to do) about the project?

3. What could you do to encourage the investor to take further action?

BOX 8.3
Addressing Social Issues in Investment Practice

The arguments around the business importance of social issues (i.e., human rights, labour, employees, community) are generally accepted after, e.g., the damage to high-profile brands such as Nike and Gap following allegations about their use of sweatshops. In practice, however, social issues continue to receive far less attention than environmental issues in investment practice. Most investors tend to pay relatively little attention to these issues until a problem emerges, and tend to be reactive rather than proactive in including these issues in their investment research and decision-making. There are a variety of reasons for this: many social issues are presented in qualitative terms, making it difficult to integrate them into conventional investment research and decision-making processes; there is a general lack of mainstream investor interest in social issues of any sort; and there are significant weaknesses in corporate reporting that make assessing performance, comparing companies or linking performance on social issues to investment performance very difficult (see further Roca & Manta 2010, pp. 25–26).

Despite the theoretical potential for responsible investment to create a more holistic dialogue between companies and their investors, it is important not to overstate the role that enhanced analysis and engagement can make to improving corporate responsibility performance. Simply because investors have made commitments to responsible investment does not mean that they will systematically reward companies that effectively manage their social or environmental issues, or be willing to pay a premium for companies that are recognized leaders for their corporate responsibility performance.

Investors' focus on those issues that are financially material over relatively short time-frames, signals to companies that short-term performance is more important than long-term performance, and that most environmental and social issues are simply not of interest to investors. This, in turn, creates the risk that company management will prioritize maximizing short-term profit rather than taking a more long-term, wider and deeper approach to value creation (Sullivan, 2014). Even if investors' time-frames were extended and the materiality tests liberalized, there is a fundamental limit to the changes that can be effected in the absence of effective public policy or other incentives for companies to be more responsible or take action to reduce their negative impacts (or maximize their positive impacts). In the vast majority of cases, social and environmental issues are important to investors for instrumental rather than inherent reasons. That is, investors want to know whether and how these issues will affect a company's strategy, cash flows, profits or balance sheet, and they use financial materiality to determine which of these are of sufficient magnitude to warrant further analysis. Even in funds where social and environmental concerns trump financial performance (e.g., negatively screened funds), once a company has met the criteria specified, the analysis is then almost entirely couched in financial terms and the final decision on whether to invest or not is inevitably one that is based on financial criteria.[11] This has important consequences. It means that investors are – from an investment perspective – unlikely to be particularly interested in most aspects of the company's corporate responsibility performance. It also suggests that there may not be a premium (in terms of share price) for companies that do a particularly good job of managing their corporate responsibility issues.

While this analysis, and its associated conclusion, suggests that investors effectively encourage companies to ignore corporate responsibility issues, a more positive picture emerges when we look at investment practice. Mainstream investors expect companies to effectively manage their environmental and social impacts; the fact that this message is not routinely communicated in company–investor meetings does not mean that investors are not supportive of companies effectively managing their environmental and social risks. Investors recognize that regulatory pressures and stakeholder demands and expectations are increasing and that companies need to position themselves to respond effectively to these.

8.2.3 Externalities?

While the focus of this chapter is on the manner in which individual investors make investment decisions, it is important to recognize that, as yet, relatively little attention has been paid to the wider social and environmental externalities associated with

---

[11] As a clarification, the term 'financial criteria' frequently encompasses qualitative metrics including views on a company's quality of management.

modern investment practice. In fact, prevailing approaches to responsible investment largely focus on individual companies and are mainly directed towards monitoring and managing the ethical and investment risks to these companies. The
broader ethical issues associated with systemic risk, at least to date, have not received
anything like the same attention. Even in the wake of the global financial crisis –
where it became very clear that the governance, incentives and risk management of
banks was not a matter for institutions in isolation but could create serious damage
for the rest of the system and the wider economy – the ethical responsibilities of
investors, regulators and the international community to vulnerable populations in
the case of systemic shocks are rarely debated. Yet, as illustrated in the emerging
markets example in Box 8.4, it is clear that investors do bear some responsibility for
managing these wider systemic risks. As an integral part of discussions about the
social and environmental responsibilities of investors, there is a clear need for targeted discussion of these issues both within the fund management industry and
within wider discussions on financial stability.

BOX 8.4
Responsible Investment, Capital Flows and Emerging Markets

Over the past 20 years, emerging markets have become
an essential part of global investment funds. In the face
of stagnant economies, enormous debt burdens and
ageing populations across the developed world, the
emerging markets have been billed as the likely drivers
of global economic growth in the years ahead.

Rapid inflows of foreign capital can, however, create major problems for emerging markets, including
rapid credit expansion, rising asset prices and overheating, and strengthening currencies. Emerging markets also raise many questions for investors concerned
about social and environmental impacts. Investors
often cannot rely on legal and institutional structures
to provide operating certainty or to protect their economic interests. Emerging markets are instead often
characterized by endemic problems of lack of governance, corruption, absence of the rule of law, inequality,
abject poverty, violation of human rights, weak institutions, lack of transparency and lack of environmental
protection.

Many investors in these markets assume that economic growth, supported by domestic and foreign
investment, will provide the catalyst which will lead
many countries to address these structural problems.
The logic is that foreign investment catalyses economic
growth, and that poverty reduction, improvements to
institutional and regulatory frameworks, and increased
government revenues for social programmes will
follow as a result of this growth.

It cannot simply be assumed, however, that a few
years of high rates of economic growth and strong
financial markets will automatically translate into
domestic momentum to address the problems that
have constrained growth for so long in the past. A
study by Hausmann et al. (2005) identified 83 instances
of growth accelerations in developing countries
between the mid-1950s and 2005. Only a small handful
of these, though, turned into sustained, higher levels
of economic growth over the long term that led to a
marked convergence in living standards with the

advanced economies. In most cases, the growth acceleration collapsed and petered out in the face of a chronic inability to institute the needed institutional transformation and tackle problems like endemic corruption, lack of infrastructure and lack of human development. In fact, far from providing a catalyst for positive change, fund inflows can actually exacerbate these problems by widening the gulf between those who stand to benefit from growing economic prosperity and those who are largely excluded or exploited by the process, which can inflame social tensions, imperil the sustainability of the economic boom, and actually strengthen distorted power structures.

Mainstream financial analysis generally fails to capture the complex institutional and power dynamics involved in the process of institutional transformation which is essential to turn financial inflows to emerging markets into sustainable economic growth. Structural transformation does not follow inevitably as a result of economic growth. In fact, it depends upon the choices of the power elite in given societies, who can easily choose to sequester the gains from financial inflows and economic growth for themselves. This can directly imperil the sustainability of the growth take-off, and the potential benefits of poverty reduction and the rule of law, and can even exacerbate the problems of gross inequality, deprivation and human rights violations. It can also make an economy more susceptible to an external shock like a financial crisis as funds are misallocated across the economy. Even where a ruling party has a strong will to implement reform, this can be an uphill challenge in the face of strongly ingrained patterns of privilege, poverty and corruption, and reforms can easily be derailed, or they can make the security and living conditions of the poor more precarious than they were before.

A further concern is the extent to which the narrative of emerging market growth has significantly magnified the exposure of emerging markets to systemic risks in the international financial system. Given the size of the inflows and the globally interconnected nature of financial markets, emerging markets are now critically exposed to destabilization by a sudden withdrawal of funds by foreign investors. As we saw with the global contagion during the Asian financial crisis and again in the post-Lehman global crisis, market chaos – combined with financial regulation which can trigger one-way markets in an attempt to liquidate assets and maintain capital/liquidity ratios – is rapidly, almost instantaneously, transmitted around the world. The massive growth in the exposure of investment funds to emerging markets means that the risk of systemic disruption has also greatly increased for these countries, and this can have devastating long-term impacts on economies and people. This is compounded by the fact that most emerging market countries only have rudimentary social protection systems in place and large swathes of the population are extremely vulnerable to the effects of an economic downturn. In China alone it has been estimated that over 20 million workers were laid off almost overnight as a response to the post-Lehman downturn (Anderlini & Dyer, 2009).

It is difficult to develop tools to address this problem because it is in essence a collective action issue that revolves around systemic stability, frequently compounded by regulatory provisions regarding solvency and liquidity which can force selling. It is also difficult to know when markets have reached a tipping point. On the one hand it would be impossible for any one individual fund manager to have much of an overall effect on systemic risk by pulling funds out early when markets appear to be overheating (if this point can be effectively determined), but on the other, a fund manager has ethical obligations to investors not to lose their life savings by refusing to sell in a market rout. Ethical issues cut both ways, but there is an urgent need for further exploration within the fund management community and the regulatory community of how they can meet their ethical obligations to the world's vulnerable populations in regard to systemic risk.

Source: Adapted from Dowell-Jones (2012).

QUESTIONS FOR CLASS DISCUSSION

1. What policy measures or frameworks might help to reduce the vulnerability of emerging market populations to financial and economic shocks?
2. What is the potential contribution of responsible investment (or of investors with commitments to responsible investment) to the development and implementation of these measures?

8.3 Conclusion

Despite the enthusiasm for responsible investment, the signals that *are* being sent by investors through their investment decisions and their routine dialogue with companies are swamping the more positive messages that they *wish* to send about the value they assign to good corporate responsibility performance. This suggests that investors need to much more proactively ask companies about how they are managing risks and opportunities related to corporate responsibility, communicate their expectations of how environmental and social issues should be managed, and explain exactly how these issues are taken into account in their investment analysis. Unless investors provide these signals, companies will not understand the reasons informing investment decisions, or whether or not these decisions were informed by the company's environmental or social performance.

It is important to be realistic about the extent to which this new-found enthusiasm for responsible investment can or will drive change within companies. The vast majority of investors – including those that could be classed as 'responsible investors' and those offering ethical or environmental investment products – are evaluated over relatively short time-frames. Even those that fully accept their responsibilities as long-term investors will face significant pressure to concentrate on shorter-term performance. Moreover, there are many situations where encouraging companies to be 'responsible' (e.g., to significantly reduce their greenhouse gas emissions, to ensure a living wage is paid throughout their supply chains) runs counter to companies' short-term or even longer-term interests (Sullivan & Mackenzie, 2009). In these situations, no matter how progressive the signals from their investors, companies will find it extremely difficult to fully respond to this type of engagement.

Summary

The growth in the number of investors that have made commitments to responsible investment is one of the most significant changes that have been seen in the investment industry. There is evidence that responsible investment has contributed to marked improvements in corporate governance; in the quality of corporate reporting on environmental, social and governance issues; and in the manner in which companies manage social and environmental impacts.

The pressures on investors, however, to deliver short-term financial returns, the focus on risk and opportunity at the portfolio level, and the weaknesses in wider policy frameworks for sustainable development suggest that prevailing approaches to responsible investment are just one part of a wider discussion around the social responsibilities of the investment sector.

References

Accenture and UN Global Compact (2013), *UN Global Compact-Accenture CEO Study on Sustainability 2013.* New York: Accenture and UN Global Compact.

Anderlini, J., & Dyer, J. (2009). Downturn causes 20m job losses in China *Financial Times* (2009, February 2).

Aspen Institute. (2009). *Overcoming short-termism: A call for a more responsible approach to investment and business management.* Washington, DC: Aspen Institute.

Bhojraj, S., & Libby, R. (2005). Capital market pressure, disclosure frequency-induced earnings/cash flow conflicts, and managerial myopia. *The Accounting Review, 80*(1), 1–20.

Brochet, F., Loumioti, M., & Serafeim, G. (2012, August). Short-termism, investor clientele, and firm risk. *Harvard Business School Accounting & Management Unit Working Paper,* No. 12-072.

Business for Social Responsibility. (2008). *Environmental, social and governance: Moving to mainstream investing?* San Francisco: Business for Social Responsibility.

Campbell, D., & Slack, R. (2008). *Narrative reporting: Analysts' perceptions of its value and relevance.* London: Association of Chartered Certified Accountants.

CFA Centre for Financial Market Integrity and Business Roundtable Institute for Corporate Ethics. (2006). *Breaking the short-term cycle: Discussion and recommendations on how corporate leaders, asset managers, investors and analysts can refocus on long-term value.* New York: CFA Centre for Financial Market Integrity.

Cronin, C., & Mellor J. (2011). *An investigation into stewardship. engagement between investors and public companies: Impediments and their resolution.* London: Foundation for Governance Research and Education (FGRE), CFA Institute, European Capital Markets Institute (ECMI) and Centre for European Policy Studies (CEPS).

Dallas, L. (2012). Short-termism, the financial crisis, and corporate governance. *The Journal of Corporation Law, 37*(2), 264–363.

Dowell-Jones, M. (2012). Investing in emerging markets: The ethical context. *Journal of Corporate Citizenship, 48*(winter), 75–90.

Faux, J. (2002). A stakeholder perspective of material disclosure thresholds for environmental events. *Asian Review of Accounting, 10*(2), 3–16.

Gitman, L., Chorn, B., & Fargo, B. (2009). *ESG in the mainstream: The role for companies and investors in environmental, social and governance integration.* San Francisco: Business for Social Responsibility.

Global Sustainable Investment Alliance (GSIA). (2014). *Global sustainable investment review 2014.* Retrieved from http://www.gsi-alliance.org/wp-content/uploads/2015/02/GSIA_Review_download.pdf (accessed 2015, April 29).

Godfrey, P., Merrill, C., & Hansen, J. (2009). The relationship between corporate social responsibility and shareholder value: An empirical test of the risk management hypothesis. *Strategic Management Journal, 30*(4), 425–445.

Graham, J., Harvey, C., Rajgopal, S. (2005). 'The Economic Implications of Corporate Financial Reporting', *Journal of Accounting and Economics, 40*(1), 3–73.

Graham, J., Harvey, C., & Rajgopal, S. (2006). Value destruction and financial reporting decisions. *Financial Analysts Journal, 62*, 27–39.

Hausmann, R., Pritchett, L., & Rodrik, D. (2005). Growth accelerations. *Journal of Economic Growth, 10*, 303–329.

Hawken, P. (2004). *Socially responsible investing.* Sausalito, CA: The Natural Capital Institute.

Hawley, J., Hoepner, A., Johnson, K., Sandberg, J., & Waitzer, E. (Eds.). (2014). *Cambridge handbook of institutional investment and fiduciary duty.* Cambridge: Cambridge University Press.

Institute of Chartered Secretaries and Administrators (ICSA) (2013), *Enhancing Stewardship Dialogue.* London: ICSA.

Kay, J. (2012). *The Kay review of UK equity markets and long-term decision making: Final report – July 2012.* London: Department for Business, Innovation and Skills.

Kiernan, M. (2009). *Investing in a sustainable world.* New York: Amacom.

Lucas-Leclin, V., & Nahal, S. (2008). Sustainability analysis. In Krosinsky, C. and Robins, N. (Eds.). (2008). *Sustainable investing: The art of long-term performance.* London: Earthscan, 41–56.

Pfeifer, S., & Sullivan, R. (2008). Public policy, institutional investors and climate change: A UK case-study. *Climatic Change, 89*, 245–262.

Rappaport, A. (2005). The economics of short-term performance obsession. *Financial Analysts Journal, 61*(3), 65–79.

Roca, R., & Manta, F. (2010). *Values added: The challenges of integrating human rights into the financial sector.* Copenhagen: The Danish Institute for Human Rights.

Sandberg, J., Juravle, C., Hedesstrom, T., & Hamilton, I. (2009). The heterogeneity of socially responsible investment. *Journal of Business Ethics, 87*(4), 519–533.

Sparkes, R. (2002). *Socially responsible investment: A global revolution.* Chichester: John Wiley & Sons.

Sullivan, R. (2011). *Valuing corporate responsibility: How do investors really use corporate responsibility information?* Sheffield: Greenleaf Publishing.

Sullivan, R. (2014). *Coping, shifting, changing: Strategies for managing the impacts of investor short-termism on corporate sustainability.* New York: Global Compact LEAD and London: Principles for Responsible Investment.

Sullivan, R., Crossley, R., & Kozak, J. (2008). Corporate greenhouse gas emissions management: The state of play. In Sullivan, R. (Ed.). (2008). *Corporate responses to climate change.* Sheffield: Greenleaf Publishing, 9–25.

Sullivan, R., & Gouldson, A. (2012). Does voluntary carbon reporting meet investors' needs? *Journal of Cleaner Production, 36*, 60–67.

Sullivan, R., & Kozak, J. (2009). Investor case-studies. Climate change: Just one more investment issue? In Oulton, W. (Ed.). (2009). *Investment opportunities for a low carbon world*. London: GMB Publishing, 270–280.

Sullivan, R., & Mackenzie, C. (Eds.). (2006). *Responsible investment*. Sheffield: Greenleaf Publishing.

Sullivan, R., & Mackenzie, C. (2009). Finance and investment. In Staib, R. (Ed.). (2009). *Business management and environmental stewardship*. Basingstoke: Palgrave Macmillan, 215–225.

Sullivan, R., Martindale, W., Feller, E., & Bordon, A. (2015). *21st century fiduciary duty*. London: Principles for Responsible Investment.

Sullivan, R., Russell, D., & Robins, N. (2008). *Managing the unavoidable: Understanding the investment implications of adapting to climate change*. London: Insight Investment, Henderson Global Investors, USS and Railpen.

Sullivan, R., Russell, D., Beloe, S., Curtiss, F., & Firth, J. (2009). *Managing the unavoidable: Investment implications of a changing climate*. London:Acclimatise, Henderson Global Investors, Insight Investment, Railpen and USS.

United Nations Environment Programme Finance Initiative (UNEP FI). (2005). *A legal framework for the integration of environmental, social and governance issues into institutional investment*. Nairobi: UNEP FI.

Waygood, S., Erler, S., Wehrmeyer, W., & Jeswani, H. (2006). Integrated investment analysis: Investment implications of the REACH regulation. In Sullivan, R. and Mackenzie, C. (Eds.). (2006). *Responsible investment*. Sheffield: Greenleaf Publishing, 62–80.

9 Innovating

John Bessant[1] and Palie Smart

LEARNING OUTCOMES

The aim of this chapter is to:

1. Establish the key concepts and theories relating to sustainability-orientated innovation.

2. Recognize the range of contexts for sustainability-orientated innovation opportunities facing business.

3. Decipher and articulate the value of organizational responses to managing sustainability-orientated innovation.

Introduction

The Innovation Imperative

The challenge of innovation is hard to ignore for anyone concerned with management and leadership in business. Quite simply if an organization does not change what to offer the world (its products or services) and the ways it creates and delivers those offerings (its processes) then it risks being left behind in an increasingly competitive race – and at the limit may not survive. And this is a message as much for public and third sector organizations as for those in the commercial world – the challenges of a hostile and uncertain environment mean that innovation has become an imperative for long-term business survival and societal progression.

One of the key dimensions of that uncertain environment lies in the area of sustainability – living and working in a world of 7 billion people with rising expectations, providing energy, food and resource security, dealing with climate change, tackling pollution and a host of other issues will require massive change in products, services, processes, marketing approaches and the underlying business models which frame them. The way we do business and indeed the way we innovate will need to change to keep pace with this shift.

[1] We acknowledge the support of the Theo and Friedl Schoeeler Foundation, Germany and the EPSRC Centre for Innovative Manufacturing in Industrial Sustainability for the work underpinning this chapter.

There is plenty of discussion about the need for sustainability-orientated innovation – simply staying as we are is unlikely to be an option (Adams, *et al.*, 2015; Adams *et al.* 2013). The evidence underpinning concern about sustainability is extensive (MEA, 2005; UNEP, 2007; Rockstrom *et al.*, 2009) For example, the WWF suggests that lifestyles in the developed world at present require the resources of around two planets and if emerging economies follow the same trajectory this will rise to two and a half by 2050 (WWF, 2010). Others draw attention to the implications of reaching 'peak' availability of key strategic energy and physical resources (Brown, 2011; Scheinberg, 2007). Some even gloomier commentators point out that most of the wars which we have fought as human beings have been over resources – and that we have a conflict-filled future to look forward to as a result of the growing imbalances and shortages!

Sustainability-orientated innovation reaches beyond the boundaries of any one organization to create new and sustainable value that is shared amongst a greater number of stakeholders. A gradual shift away from solely focusing on shareholder value towards stakeholder value can be observed in much of the emerging literature on this topic.

Of course there are also optimists who see real opportunities in the picture. For example, a Price Waterhouse Coopers report suggests significant market potential in the provision of 'green' goods and services; their estimate was as high as 3% of global GDP. The global market for 'green products and services' was recently estimated as a $3.2 trillion business opportunity, while UK consumer spending on 'sustainable' products and services was last reported at more than £36 billion – bigger even than alcohol and tobacco sales combined. Significantly, investment in sustainability projects held up throughout the recent recession, suggesting a combination of enforced compliance with increasingly tough legislation and a perception of the major opportunities implicit in this agenda. (In a BCG/MIT survey (2010) 60% of companies increased their investment with the 'embracers' in the survey sample indicating plans to take this further, raising investments by a further 24%) (Boston Consulting Group, 2011). UNEP's (2011) report illustrates how 'greening the economy' is already becoming a powerful new engine of growth in the 21st century. The World Business Council for Sustainable Development's (WBCSD) Vision 2050 sets out new opportunities for businesses in responding to sustainability challenges, promoting whole system perspectives (WBCSD, 2010).

And we should not forget that there is a sense in which we have seen this all before – back in the 1970s there was a wave of concern about reaching 'the limits to growth' and many influential commentators predicted massive changes in a negative direction. In the event we are still around and have managed to survive their worst forecasts – but not by standing still. The period since the publication of the influential Club of Rome report in 1972 (Meadows *et al.*) has been one of continuing and radical *innovation* – of changes to products, services and processes which give us hope that we can meet the sustainability challenge. (For examples, see Meadows *et al.*, 1972; Hart, 1995, 1997; Bradbury & Clair, 1999; Jansson *et al.*, 2000; Paramanathan *et al.*, 2004; Porter & Kramer, 2006; Nidumolu *et al.*, 2009; Hansen *et al.*, 2009; Cole *et al.*, 1973.) Nonetheless we should also recognize the need to exercise the precautionary principle as we move forward – a point highlighted by Richard Owen and colleagues with the term 'responsible innovation' (Owen *et al.*, 2013).

This increasing evidence suggests that the adoption of sustainability targets as part of mainstream innovation strategy is accelerating and that an increasing number of organizations are moving into this space. Arguably the debate has shifted from early 'cosmetic' activity (in which organizations sought to improve their profile or strengthen their corporate social responsibility image through high-profile activities designed to show their 'green' credentials, through a second phase in which increasingly strong legislation provides a degree of forced compliance. The frontier is now one along which leading organizations are seeking to exploit opportunities within this emerging space, as they recognize the need for innovation to deal with resource instability and scarcity, energy security and systemic efficiencies across their supply chains.

But what does this mean for how we organize and manage innovation? Are our current models for handling the process sufficient – or will the nature and pace of change be so disruptive that it requires radically new approaches? What kinds of innovation ecosystem might emerge and how will incumbent players position themselves within it? What opportunities exist for entrepreneurs and how can they best frame their activities to ride the waves of radical change? What new skills will we need within – and between – our organizations? What tools, techniques and approaches will help equip established players and aspiring new entrants to manage effectively? In the face of radical change, what do we need to do more of, less of and differently in the ways we manage innovation? This chapter will explore some of these issues and outline a framework for thinking about – and working with – sustainability-orientated innovation (SOI).

9.0 Innovation Strategy

Perhaps the most important question in innovation lies in deciding *what* to change – and it is a problem for all but the simplest organization because it involves making choices about where and how to use increasingly scarce and valuable resources. Which directions offer the best return – e.g., choosing between improving productivity through the use of a new technology or working method or opening up new market growth through launching a new product or service? The question is made doubly difficult because of the uncertainty involved – by its very nature innovation is about the unknown. Will the new technology work? Will the market actually adopt the new product or service? What unexpected events – competitor behaviour, government policy, changes in the economic system – might surprise us as we take our idea and project forward? The only way we can reduce this uncertainty is by actually carrying out the project – so at the outset we need to make assessments of risk. What is the best balance between incremental innovation projects and more radical bets? How much do we spend on low risk 'doing what we do but better' projects as opposed to those expeditions into uncharted territory which offer something completely different but have a high risk of failure? And if we do too much of the former what is the risk of being surprised by a competitor doing something completely different which upsets the applecart of our particular business and leaves us vulnerable?

Innovation strategy is about making these choices and trying to build a balanced portfolio of future projects. Rather than simply throwing the chips down randomly on the roulette wheel and gambling we need to undertake a systematic exploration of the possible directions in which we could make changes. It is easy to fall into the trap of thinking that innovation is confined to a few directions of change – the reality is, of course, that there is a wide area of innovation space available but we do not always explore it fully. For entrepreneurs this is good news because it means there will always be opportunities to find space to do something new and different; for established players it represents a challenge to make sure we are not going to be unpleasantly surprised by new ideas coming from places we had not expected. We can map this space along four directions (see Figure 9.1), a bit like an 'innovation compass', which define the ways in which we might innovate:

- 'product innovation' – changes in the things (products/services) an organization offers;
- 'process innovation' – changes in the ways in which they are created and delivered;
- 'position innovation' – changes in the context in which the products/services are introduced;
- 'paradigm innovation' – changes in the underlying mental models which frame what the organization does.

(These concepts are as applicable in the public and not-for-profit sectors as in the commercial world of innovation. The Humanitarian Innovation Fund, e.g., uses them as a backdrop to evaluating and supporting innovation projects in humanitarian aid.)

Table 9.1 gives some examples of these potential directions. In reality, of course, various combinations of incremental and radical innovation across these fields are possible. They key issue for any organization is to ensure that it explores its options

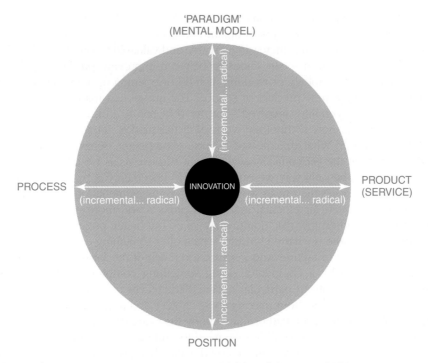

FIGURE 9.1 Exploring innovation space. *Source:* Tidd and Bessant, 2009.

TABLE 9.1 Potential directions for innovation strategy

Innovation type	Incremental – do what we do but better	Radical – do something different
'Product' – what we offer the world	Windows 7 and 8 replacing Vista and XP – essentially improving on existing software idea New versions of established car models, e.g., the VW Golf essentially improving on established car design Improved performance incandescent light bulbs CDs replacing vinyl records – essentially improving on the storage technology	New to the world software, e.g., the first speech recognition program Toyota Prius – bringing a new concept – hybrid engines. Tesla – high-performance electric car. LED-based lighting, using completely different and more energy efficient principles Spotify and other music streaming services – changing the pattern from owning your own collection to renting a vast library of music
Process – how we create and deliver that offering	Improved fixed line telephone services Extended range of stockbroking services Improved auction house operations Improved factory operations efficiency through upgraded equipment Improved range of banking services delivered at branch banks Improved retailing logistics	Skype and other VOIP systems Online share trading eBay Toyota Production System and other 'lean' approaches Online banking and now mobile banking in Kenya, Philippines – using phones as an alternative to banking systems Online shopping
Position – where we target that offering and the story we tell about it	Haagen Dazs changing the target market for ice cream from children to adults Airlines segmenting service offering for different passenger groups – Virgin Upper Class, BA Premium Economy, etc. Dell and others segmenting and customizing computer configuration for individual users Online support for traditional higher education courses Banking services targeted at key segments – students, retired people, etc.	Addressing underserved markets, e.g., the Tata Nano aimed at emerging but relatively poor Indian market with car priced around $2,000. Low cost airlines opening up air travel to those previously unable to afford it – creating new market and also disrupting existing one Variations on the 'One laptop per child' project, e.g., Indian government $20 computer for schools University of Phoenix and others, building large education businesses via online approaches to reach different markets 'Bottom of the pyramid' approaches using a similar principle but tapping into huge and very different high-volume/low-margin markets – Aravind eye care, Cemex construction products

(Continued)

TABLE 9.1 *(Continued)*

Innovation type	Incremental – do what we do but better	Radical – do something different
Paradigm – how we frame what we do	Bausch and Lomb – moved from 'eye wear' to 'eye care' as their business model, effectively letting go of the old business of spectacles, sunglasses (Raybans) and contact lenses, all of which were becoming commodity businesses. Instead they moved into newer, high-tech fields like laser surgery equipment, specialist optical devices and research in artificial eyesight Dyson redefining the home appliance market in terms of high-performance engineered products Rolls Royce – from high-quality aero engines to becoming a service company offering 'power by the hour' IBM – from being a machine maker to a service and solution company – selling off its computer making and building up its consultancy and service side	Grameen Bank and other microfinance models – rethinking the assumptions about credit and the poor iTunes platform – a complete system of personalized entertainment Cirque du Soleil – redefining the circus experience Amazon, Google, Skype – redefining industries like retailing, advertising and telecoms through online models Linux, Mozilla, Apache – moving from passive users to active communities of users co-creating new products and services

Source: Tidd and Bessant, 2009.

thoroughly – it may choose not to pursue every idea but it is important to avoid being surprised.

With such a framework we can now begin to see where and how sustainability-orientated innovation might take place. At the incremental end of the innovation spectrum we could make some incremental changes to our processes, improving their efficiency or reducing their carbon footprint. Or we could modify our products to offer a 'greener' dimension like reduced energy consumption or improved recyclability. Such 'do better' incremental innovations are becoming increasingly widespread – not surprisingly driven in large measure by an increasing weight of regulation which is forcing improvements (Adams *et al.*, 2013).

We could also place some bigger bets, setting ourselves stretch targets (like 100% recyclability of all products or only using sustainable sources of raw material) and then working out solutions to these major challenges. These projects are by nature higher risk but offer significant benefits if we can get them right. The famous example of Interface Flor, the world's most successful floor coverings company, provides a good illustration of such radical stretch thinking. Ray Anderson's vision and commitment over a sustained period as Chief Executive helped shape a radical innovation agenda which took the company along some very rocky and unmapped roads – but which led to significant strategic advantage being created through sustainability-orientated radical innovation in products, services, processes and business models.

At the limit we could move from focusing on our own strategy and what we – as a single organization – can change and look to system level changes which involve us as part of a wider network of suppliers, customers and other players. Such 'ecosystem innovation' is an emerging field of interest – it is very difficult to achieve because of the problems in co-ordinating and focusing the efforts of many different stakeholders, not all of whom share the same sense of direction or motivation. But co-evolving a new system model changes the parameters for innovation, offering step change increases along several performance dimensions.

We have seen this in the past – for example Henry Ford's contribution was not the invention of the motor car (he was a comparative latecomer to the industry) but in rethinking the whole system, from mining iron ore at one end to repair and service of cars once they had been sold at the other end. The system had broad reach – it not only focused on a radically new production system (process innovation) but also on a dramatically different standardized product concept. It opened up huge market opportunity by targeting mass market rather than luxury consumers (position innovation) and it integrated innovation across a broad front – financial service innovation to help people buy and insure their cars, human resource innovation to mobilize a workforce for his factories drawn from a population with low or no skills in the area and with huge diversity of cultural backgrounds (many of his early employees could not speak English). This system-level innovation took over a decade to perfect – but when in place it became the dominant model not just for the car industry but for an increasing set of other manufacturing and eventually service industries – the mass production paradigm. Table 9.2 summarizes this set of possibilities.

It is clear that there are different levels of innovative activity ranging from simple 'cosmetic' statements, through incremental change ('doing what we do but better'), to radical, new to the world approaches (Adams *et al.*, 2013). In the sustainability space a number of frameworks have been proposed to take account of this, e.g., Prahalad suggests five steps moving from 'viewing compliance as an opportunity', through 'making value chains sustainable' and 'designing sustainable products and services', to 'designing new business models'. His fifth stage focuses on 'creating next practice platforms' – implying a system level change (Nidumolu *et al.*, 2009). The consultancy A. D. Little has a similar model, whilst the Boston Consulting Group classifies SLO companies in terms of the extent to which they embrace such principles (Boston Consulting Group, 2011). They represent versions of what are termed 'maturity models' (Paulk, *et al.*, 1993) (Aguilera, 2007) and we can synthesize them in Table 9.3.

TABLE 9.2 Ecosystem Innovation

Innovation target	Examples
Product/service offering	'Green' products, design for greener manufacture and/recycling, service models replacing consumption/ownership models
Process innovation	Improved and novel manufacturing processes, lean systems inside the organization and across supply chain, green logistics
Position innovation	Rebranding the organization as 'green', meeting needs of underserved communities, e.g., bottom of pyramid
'Paradigm' innovation – changing business models (i.e., buisness model innovation)	System level change, multi-organization innovation, servitization (moving from manufacturing to service emphasis)

TABLE 9.3 Outline Maturity Model for Sustainability-orientated Innovation

Level	Characteristics	Examples
0 **Passive/cosmetic**	No activity, or 'cosmetic' public relations based statements of intent	
1 **Operational optimization**	'Do what we do but better' innovation, taking waste out, reducing footprint of existing processes, efficiency enhancing	Compliance with externally imposed regulation Commitment to frameworks like Forest Stewardship Council Greening of existing processes, products and inter-organizational value chains
2 **Organizational transformation**	Creation of new products, processes, services which open up innovation space	New technologies – solar, etc. New process routes and architectures, e.g., low-energy bioprocessing instead of thermal cracking
3 **System building innovation**	Creation of new business models at system level involving reframing of the way value is created and often extending across multiple organizations	Interface Flor reinventing itself as an integrated 'green' company and positively impacting society

A number of writers have looked at the idea of different types of sustainability-orientated innovations (SOI) and at the levels of novelty, and Figure 9.2 offers an emerging model on which we can place the reported experience of a wide variety of organizations trying to work in the SOI space (Adams *et al.*, 2013).

FIGURE 9.2 Model for Developing Sustainability-orientated Innovation. *Source:* Adams *et al.*, 2015.

Not surprisingly most of the reported examples of SOI have concentrated so far around the 'do better' agenda. Many of the 'eco-efficiency' type of projects (WBCSD, 2000) which involve finding new and more efficient ways of 'doing more with less' would fall into this category. For example, reducing carbon footprint through supply chain improvements or switching to less energy- or resource-intensive products and services which deliver equivalent value can generate significant savings. 3M, for example, saved nearly $1.4 billion over a four-year period and prevented billions of dollars of pollutants entering the environment through their Pollution-Prevention-Pays (3P) programmes (3M, 2011). GE Industrial saved $12.8 million per year by using high-efficiency lights in their plants. One of Alcoa's facilities in France achieved an 85% reduction in water consumption leading to a $40,000 per year reduction in operating costs (Senge *et al.*, 2008).

QUESTIONS FOR CLASS DISCUSSION

Why have most organizational responses to sustainability challenges focused on the efficiency agenda?

But there are an increasing number of activities which climb up the ladder, moving into radical innovation within the organization. Interface Flor have been active in this space for over 20 years and provide an excellent illustration of what can be achieved – and also the economic case for doing so. Interface has cut greenhouse gas emissions by 82%, fossil fuel consumption by 60%, waste by 66%, water use by 75%; and increased sales by 66%, doubled earnings and raised profit margins. To quote Ray Anderson, founder and chairman:

> As we climb Mount Sustainability with the four sustainability principles on top, we are doing better than ever on bottom-line business. This is not at the cost of social or ecological systems, but at the cost of our competitors who still haven't got it.

As a global manufacturer of modular carpet tiles, Interface looked to nature for design inspiration for a carpet tile, an action which has significantly reduced waste going to landfill and increased company revenue. Biomimicry, innovation inspired by nature, has become a source of design inspiration for a whole new industrial paradigm that seeks to work with the laws of nature, rather than against them (Benyus, 1997). Biomimicry literally means 'to imitate life' and the approach encourages innovators to ask the question, 'How would nature do business?' By learning from natural forms, processes and systems, innovators can extract design principles to help solve human sustainability issues (Chang, 2010) (see Box 9.1).

Large companies like Lafarge, Nokia-Siemens Networks and Sony provide an increasingly wide library of examples (Gosling *et al.*, 2012). For example, Philips have been working for some time on a mixture of 'do better', 'do different' and 'breakthrough' projects in their SOI activity (Seebode *et al.*, 2012). Since 2004 they have been working on 'green' products which offer significant environmental improvements in one or more Green Key Focal Areas: energy efficiency, packaging, hazardous substances, weight, recycling and disposal, and lifetime reliability.

For example, the Consumer Lifestyle division has recently launched the first Cradle-to-Cradle inspired products, such as the Performer EnergyCare vacuum

BOX 9.1
Biomimicry at Product, Process and System Levels*

Product

Interface Flor's design was inspired by the pattern of the forest floor, which appears homogenous but actually consists of many unique parts, arranged in a pattern of 'organized chaos'. Using this design principle enables Interface's 'Entropy' carpet tile to be manufactured with a variety of patterns, and using different dye batches. Waste is eliminated during the manufacturing process, as well as during carpet installation itself. This tile has been the most popular product in the company's history, and has saved the company, as well as consumers, millions of dollars in avoided waste elimination costs (Anderson & White, 2009).

Process

Biomimicry has also inspired new approaches to decision-making within organizations. Nature provides many fascinating examples of group behaviour; and social insects such as ants and bees, which are highly organized, can exhibit useful, functional and intelligent outcomes which seem well beyond the capabilities of any individual in the group. This is a phenomenon known as 'swarm intelligence' (Bonabeau & Meyer, 2001). What is interesting about social insects is that they are self-organized and decentralized. There is no master agent directing activities, and they function without supervision. Individuals interact according to simple rules, and the co-ordination of the swarm arises from the thousands of exchanges of information between individuals in the colony. This allows the group to be flexible and adapt quickly to internal and external conditions. Solutions to complex problems are robust and emergent, rather than pre-planned. Swarm intelligence generates algorithms that have been applied to solve complex problems, e.g., in airline logistics, telecom networks, and internet applications. So called 'honey

bee democracy' has also inspired goal-orientated decision-making in more collaborative management cultures (Seeley, 2010).

System

Ideas from the natural world have also inspired new ways of thinking about wider production and consumption systems, such as the shift away from the linear, take-make-waste models of the industrial paradigm, to circular systems such as Cradle-to-Cradle manufacturing (McDonough & Braungart, 2002), closed loop production (Abdallah et al., 2011), and circular economy principles (Ellen MacArthur Foundation, 2013). The Cradle-to-Cradle (C2C) model, for example, aims to mimic the planet's natural cyclical nutrient flows, its use of solar energy, and its creation of diversity and abundance. In nature, e.g., there is no such thing as waste: 'waste = food', and materials are continuously recycled to nourish new organisms. Several companies have been inspired by C2C innovation, including Interface, Desso, Herman Miller, and Rhoner textiles.

Some of the principles underpinning Cradle-to-Cradle innovation include:

- Designing with ecological and human health in mind. This involves analysing all the ingredients in the manufacturing process, and eradicating and phasing out all carcinogenic and other harmful chemicals.

- Developing a new framing of material flows in industry, and managing biological (organic) and technical (inorganic) nutrient flows in two separate cycles.

- Designing products with disassembly and the future use of products in mind; and refining the notion of recycling into 'downcycling' and 'upcycling' value chains.

◆ Moving from a product to a service economy, in which products are reconceived as services that consumers can rent for a defined period, and which helps conserve resources.

◆ Promoting the concept of eco-effectiveness, which strives 'to do good' for people and planet, rather than eco-efficiency which aims 'to do less harm'.

◆ Preparing to learn: being adaptable and flexible to permit new ways to grow.

◆ Promoting fair labour practices and intergenerational responsibility.

*Thanks to Sally Jeanrenaud for some examples of product, process and system applications of biomimicry.

cleaner, made from 50% post-industrial plastics and 25% from bio-based plastics. It is extremely energy-efficient, but it earns its designation as a green product primarily because it scores so highly in the focal area of recycling.

Another example is the award-winning Econova LED TV. This high-performance LED TV consumes 60% less power than its predecessor. Even the remote control is efficient – powered by solar energy. In addition, the TV is completely free of PVC and brominated flame retardants, and 60% of the aluminum used in the set is recycled.

In 2010 green products accounted for 37.5% of Philips' sales, resulting from an investment of around €1bn. By 2015 the plan is for this to be 50%.

There are also some examples where attempts are being made at system-level changes. For example, Nike is actively engaged in system-innovation because it recognizes that business is entering an era of unprecedented risk and volatility, brought about by challenges such as resource scarcity, climate change, greater transparency and consumer demands. It realizes that current business models based on abundant raw materials, cheap labour and endless consumption cannot be sustained over the long term. Its supply chain includes contracts with about 900 factories, and its operations use more than 16,000 different materials. Environmental risks and social pressures therefore have the potential to undermine profits in major ways. See Box 9.2.

Other examples of system-level changes include considerable efforts to mobilize across supply chains, e.g., in Marks and Spencer's Plan A programme. The floor coverings maker, Desso, have made extensive efforts in this direction, working hard to change the overall culture and operational logic across a wide network of often sceptical supply partners (Howard & Jeanrenaud, 2012). Interface Flor is running a variety of experiments, e.g., their 'Net Works' programme is attempting to mobilize a novel supply route for Nylon 6, an important raw material in their business of carpet tile manufacture. Whilst this normally comes from a petrochemical feedstock, Interface is attempting to mobilize fishermen in the Philippines to recycle their damaged and discarded nets as a source of recyclable material – in the process not only contributing to a resource-saving innovation but also to poverty reduction and economic development at the 'bottom of the pyramid'.

We know how powerful system change can be – but also how difficult it is to bring about. It involves multiple stakeholders whose views have to be somehow incorporated in a single methodology. It needs a sense of shared vision which is rich and exciting enough to bring people in to share it. It needs ways of co-ordinating and interconnecting solutions which have 'emergent properties' – the whole is greater

BOX 9.2

A Systems Innovation Strategy: Nike and the LAUNCH Initiative

Nike has developed a system innovation strategy because it recognizes that the only effective long-term solution is to play a role in changing the systems in which it operates. It has a team that focuses on shaping the system around the company to ensure its success in that system. It builds networks with others within and across its sector to create a shared vision on a number of system innovation initiatives and to generate new markets. And its system level initiatives are designed to take new practices to scale.

It is involved in several systems-building initiatives including a project to help transform its materials system. Some 60% of the environmental footprint of a pair of Nike shoes is embedded in the materials used to make them, so materials is a big issue for the company. It developed the Nike Materials Sustainability Index, that helps designers select better materials, and has made this an open source so that everyone can take up the approach.

However, Nike also recognizes that creating sustainable materials is too great a challenge for one company to tackle on its own. To get the level of innovation in raw materials, rethinking manufacturing to create a closed loop, new chemical approaches, and access and engagement with the consumer requires 'getting the whole system in the room' to develop more pioneering practices and to change the rules of the game.

Nike has thus entered a strategic partnership with NASA, USAID and the US State Department called LAUNCH that is promoting game-changing solutions to issues such as water, energy and health. Each year it announces an innovation challenge and then supports the best ideas and businesses submitted.

LAUNCH is currently involved in transforming the materials system. The global apparel industry is worth $1 trillion a year, and employs 40 million people. By 2015 it is predicted to produce 400 billion m^2 of fabric a year. The current project, which started in 2013, brings together 150 experts in the materials supply chain to explore the challenges of the system, find leverage points and start to find ways forward.

The 'bringing the system into the room approach' employs techniques such as gaming and system mapping to enable principal actors to work together to diagnose the key changes required to shift the system, such as consumer engagement, land use and raw material innovation, green chemistry and closed loop manufacturing. It helps generates promising new solutions and alliances, that are fed into the LAUNCH acceleration process so that they can be developed and brought to scale. Such networks can more effectively take solutions to scale because key people such as designers or manufacturers are already part of the system.

Source: Adapted from Draper, 2013.

than the sum of the parts. We can see the beginnings of this shift in many of the exciting projects underway around sustainability, e.g., companies like IBM working on water management for whole regions as part of a 'Smart Planet' experiment in the Dublin Bay area of Ireland. Or Grameen Shakti, a rural renewable energy initiative in Bangladesh, which fosters collaboration between the micro-finance sector, suppliers of solar energy equipment and consumers, enabling millions of poor households to leapfrog to new energy systems. It is generating new employment opportunities, increasing rural incomes, empowering women, and reducing the use of environmentally polluting kerosene. Grameen Shakti is the world largest and fastest growing rural renewable energy company in the world (Grameen Foundation, 2011).

Unilever's Sustainable Living Plan is committed to a ten-year journey towards sustainable growth. Its impact is felt right across the value chain – it ise taking responsibility not just for its own direct operations but for its suppliers, distributors and, crucially, for how its consumers use their brands.

To do this effectively, Unilever builds partnerships with multiple stakeholders including suppliers, NGOs, consumers, aims to create a better future in which billions of people can increase their quality of life without increasing their environmental footprint. The new plan is fuelling innovation, generating markets and saving money (Unilever, 2011).

Innovations can arise from developing unusual partnerships across sectors. For example, the GreenZone, in Umea, Sweden, designed by architect Anders Nyquist, is an early example of holistic planning. It involves a block of interconnected businesses, including a car dealership, a petrol station and carwash, and a fast food restaurant. The buildings are connected, allowing a recycling and sharing of heat.

9.1 How Can We Innovate? Innovation as a Management Process

Deciding on the 'what?', the question of where to innovate, is only half of the story. The other major challenge involves finding ways of organizing and managing the process itself. Unlike the cartoon image, innovation requires a little more than just a light-bulb moment as an idea flashes above someone's head. In reality it involves a learning journey, growing and shaping the original trigger idea into something which can spread across a population and create value. As Figure 9.3 shows, travelling along this road means finding answers to some key questions.

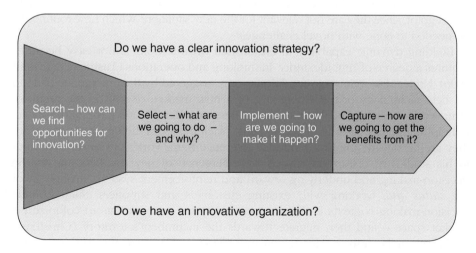

FIGURE 9.3 Simple model of the innovation process. *Source:* Tidd and Bessant, 2009.

QUESTIONS FOR CLASS DISCUSSION

1. Can you identify the sustainability priorities of a chief innovation officer on the process above?
2. Imagine a conversation between the chief innovation officer and the chief sustainability officer on some of these issues.

No organization starts with a perfect model of the innovation process. Instead it is something it builds up through a learning process, trying out new behaviours and hanging on to those which work. Eventually these patterns of repeated and learned behaviours – 'routines' – become embedded in 'the way we do things around here' and take shape in the form of policies, procedures and rules (Nelson & Winter 1982; Zollo & Winter, 2002). They will vary between organizations – everyone finds their own particular way of answering the basic questions and some recipes work better than others. This is beneficial since it allows us to learn not only through experience but by watching how others manage the innovation task and grafting on useful new approaches and ideas.

The strength of routines is that they provide a structured set of responses which help the organization manage the change process needed to cope with an uncertain environment. But therein also lies their weakness – they represent well-established approaches which work in a particular 'selection environment' where the kind of signals for change are well understood. Established organizations know which technologies to explore, which competitors to monitor, which markets to listen to for the 'voice of the customer' and which suppliers to develop close relationships with. The risk is that they lose the ability to deal with sudden discontinuous shifts in their environment – they find it difficult to 'think outside the box' and their core routines become barriers to finding different ways of working more suited to the new conditions (Teece *et al.*, 1997).

This is the challenge of 'dynamic capability' – successful innovation management requires a regular reappraisal and reconfiguration of routines to take account of shifting external events (Makadok, 2001). Of the routines in place, which ones should we develop further because they are still appropriate? And which ones should we let go of, since they are not relevant for the new situation? Which new routines will be needed to cope with novel challenges?

Building dynamic capability in established organizations is not easy because it requires a degree of 'ambidexterity' in thinking and operations (Tushman & O'Reilly, 1996). Under 'discontinuous' conditions – e.g., triggered by the emergence of a radical new technology or the emergence of a new market, or shift in the regulatory framework – established heuristics and internal rules for resource allocation are unhelpful and may actively militate against placing bets on the new options because they are far outside the firm's 'normal' reference framework. As Christensen argues in his studies of disruption caused by emergence of new markets, the existing decision-making and underlying reward and reinforcement systems strongly favour the *status quo*, working with existing customers and suppliers. Such bounded decision-making contexts create an opportunity for new entrants to colonize new market space – and then migrate towards the incumbent's territory (Christensen, 1997). In similar fashion Henderson and Clark (1990) argue that shifting to new 'architectures' – new configurations involving new knowledge sets and their arrangements – poses problems for established incumbents.

Sustainability-orientated innovation, especially at the more novel end of the spectrum *we discussed earlier*, is likely to raise this problem of dynamic capability because it forces firms to learn new approaches and let go of old ones around the core search, select and implement questions. By its nature SOI involves working with different knowledge components – new technologies, new markets, new social traditions, new environmental or regulatory conditions, etc. – and firms need to develop enhanced absorptive capacity for handling this (Zahra & George, 2002). In particular they need the capability (and enabling tools and methods) to acquire, assimilate and exploit new knowledge and to work at a systems level.

We can see this pattern of reconfiguration of routines taking place inside many organizations which are trying to respond to the SOI challenge in strategic fashion. Philips, for instance, have a long-standing commitment to sustainability principles; e.g., in the early 20th century their employees benefited from schools, housing and pension schemes. They have also been a key actor in several international sustainability initiatives. In the early 1970s, Philips participated in the Club of Rome's 'Limits to Growth' dialogue and in 1974 the first corporate environmental function was established. Initially this function created transparency on how Philips complied with environmental laws, and health and safety regulations. Later, in 2003, a structured sustainable supply chain programme was also introduced.

But the growing importance of SOI paved the way in 1998 to the launch of explicit corporate strategies – the EcoVision programmes – which set corporate sustainability-related targets. The first formal green innovation targets were introduced in 2007 in EcoVision4 and in 2010, Philips published Vision 2015, declaring their aspiration 'to be a global leader in health and well-being . . . to simply make a difference to people's lives with meaningful, sustainable innovations.[2]

Philips EcoVision5[3] programme for 2010–2015 establishes concrete targets for sustainable innovation:

- To bring care to 500 million people.
- To improve the energy efficiency of our overall portfolio by 50%.
- To double the amount of recycled materials in our products as well as to double the collection and recycling of Philips products.

Philips have reconfigured their innovation routines to deliver this programme with a growing shift towards more open and user-centric approaches. Figure 9.4 gives an overview. For example, 'search' strategies based on 'conventional' R&D or market research may need to shift to take account of new signals giving early warning of newly-emerging innovation trajectories (Bessant & Von Stamm, 2007). In the case of Philips there has been a marked shift from being an R&D-led business to one with a much stronger market orientation and this is now moving into the social and

---

[2] More background information to be found at http://www.philips.com/about/company/missionandvision valuesandstrategy/vision2015.page.

[3] More information to be found at: http://www.philips.com/about/sustainability/index.page.

PHILIPS

Innovation in Philips, evolution (of recent decades)

	Technology led	&	End-user driven (since 1990's)	&	Sustainability driven (emerging)
Core contribution	ENABLE		EXPERIENCE		Health & Well-being
High level benefit	Independence from environment		Self-expression (independence from community)		Interdependence with nature and society/community ???
R&D capabilities	Physics, chemistry, math engineering, material science		& Psychology, pedagogle, medicine, UI, software dev., biology, bio-chemistry, industrial design		& (Social) system design, ecology, geology, sociology, anthropology ??? ... T.b.d.
Fields of Research	Technology		& Technology in application Market research Socio-cultural trend research		& technology/solution impact on individual, society, environment ???
Type of solutions	Standardized & mass hardware → devices & components		& customization via censors, software, UI, → smart & convenient solutions, branding		& (context) knowledge → resilient systems & systems of systems ???
Way of working	Closed research		Open innovation		Co-creation respecting sustainability principles ???
Innovation process	R&D → "Free" research, technology shapes product development		& milestone driven projects, eco-desing 1.0, and user insights & value proposition house		& cradle 2 cradle; life's principles, book-casting, eco-design 2.0.etc. ???
Leading business model (in Philips)	Sell hardware products		& enable experience by celling solutions and services		???

FIGURE 9.4 Evolution of Innovation within Philips. *Source:* Philips, http://www.philips.com/about/sustainability/index.page.

human development domain (Tidd & Bessant, 2009). An indicator here is the growth of new functions within established organizations associated with searching and building links into the emerging sustainability communities.

Similarly, resource allocation systems will need to shift to embed SOI values and criteria into established frameworks such as stage gate systems (Bessant et al., 2009). Developing explicit criteria, and measuring performance against these, will become an important driver of behaviour change within innovation systems. The example of green products within Philips is an indicator of this process at work, and similar cases can be found in fields like greenhouse gas emissions. However, it could be argued that these represent improvement innovations – essentially doing what is already done in more sustainable fashion. As such they can fit within an existing approach; the challenge may come to innovation management systems when more radical business cases need to be considered which represent significant leaps into the unknown.

Implementing SOI at the level of 'doing what we do but better' will require adaptation in terms of pathways, skills, project management arrangements, etc. – and the emerging evidence is that this adaptation is being accommodated within 'embracer' organizations. However more radical SOI projects may need to follow novel pathways, especially when they involve external partners and new configurations of knowledge – 'architectural innovations'. The challenge here is one of learning to work with new and unusual partners and raises issues around 'finding, forming and performing' within new innovation networks (Birkinshaw et al., 2007). Table 9.4 summarizes these challenges.

TABLE 9.4 Key Innovation Management Challenges Associated with Radical Sustainability-orientated Innovations

Innovation activity	Challenges in radical SLO
Search	Peripheral vision – searching in unfamiliar fields (sectors, technologies, markets, etc.) Reframing Finding, forming, performing in new networks
Selection	Resource allocation under high uncertainty Cognitive dissonance Not invented here
Implementation	Internal mobilization – new skills, structures, etc. Crossing the chasm and the diffusion problem New appropriate language
Innovation strategy	Need for a clear framework within which to locate search, select, implement – a 'roadmap for the future' New corporate paradigm – criteria based on sustainability – people, profit, planet, etc.

9.4 Emergent routines for SOI

We can map this innovation management challenge as in Figure 9.5. The vertical axis refers to the familiar 'incremental/radical' dimension in innovation whilst the second relates to 'environmental complexity' – the number of elements *and* their potential interactions. Rising complexity means that it becomes increasingly difficult to predict a particular state because of the increasing number of potential configurations of these elements.

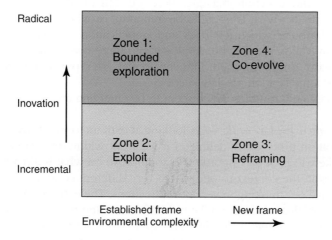

FIGURE 9.5 Simplified Map of Innovation Space.

In this way we capture the 'component/architecture' challenge *outlined above*. Firms can innovate at component level – the left-hand side – in both incremental and radical fashion but such changes take place within an assumed core configuration of technological and market elements – the dominant architecture. Moving to the right introduces the problem of new and emergent architectures arising out of alternative ways of framing amongst complex elements. Arguably SOI represents a significant challenge to innovation management because it requires bringing in multiple new elements and stakeholders.

Zones 1 and 2 represent 'business as usual' innovation space within which established routines for search, select and implement work well. But on the right-hand side there are configurations which require the development of new routines and the modification – or even abandonment – of existing ones. This favours new entrant entrepreneurs over established players that have both a 'learning' and an 'unlearning' challenge around such configurations of innovation management routines.

Reconfiguration can take place at an incremental level (zone 3) – essentially finding new ways of 'doing what we already do'. The case of 'lean' thinking provides an example; the extreme conditions of post-war Japan brought new elements into the frame as far as manufacturing was concerned. Faced with shortages of skilled labour, reliable energy sources or key raw materials, firms like Toyota were unable to follow the established mass production trajectories which dominated innovation thinking. Instead they developed an alternative approach to process innovation based around minimizing waste. This led to a radically different performance in terms of key productivity indicators but it also involved a suite of new innovation management routines (e.g., the development of effective employee involvement, concurrent engineering, kaizen tools and methods, etc.).

Zone 4 represents the 'edge of chaos' complex environment where innovation emerges as a product of a process of co-evolution. Rather than the end point of a predefined trajectory it is the result of complex interactions between independent elements. Processes of amplification and feedback reinforce what begin as small shifts in direction – attractor basins – and gradually define a trajectory. (This is the pattern in the 'ferment' state/fluid state before a dominant design emerges (Utterback, 1994)). Search and selection strategies here are difficult since it is, by definition, impossible to predict what is going to be important or where the initial emergence will start, and around which feedback and amplification will happen. Under such conditions innovation strategy breaks down into three core principles: be in there, be in there early, and be in there influentially (i.e., in a position to be part of the feedback and amplification mechanisms).

Amongst key new routines which seem to be emerging are:

(a) *Learning to explore at the edge*, looking at extreme contexts for triggers to the innovation process. By definition if we work within an established field we are likely to pick up opportunities to improve on what is already there – but if we shift the context to one where very different conditions are found this can drive our thinking in very new directions. The extreme challenge, e.g., of providing clean water for millions in Africa or rural Asia, may also provide the stimulus for some quite different approaches to water management and treatment in the developed world. An increasing number of smart players in the corporate sector are using situations like this as 'laboratories' to explore radically different innovation options which may provide the seeds for a transformation back in their core markets. In health care, e.g, delivering to a population where the skill base is low or non-existent, where infrastructures are rudimentary, where average incomes are less than $2 per day, has led to the emergence of fundamentally different models which might also have relevance for first world countries (Bessant, *et al.*, 2012).

(b) *System level working*, exploring opportunities with multiple stakeholders to co-evolve viable systems for SOI. This opens up the innovation process in a way that is distinct from open innovation (Chesbrough, 2006) activities at the level of product development. There is potential to operate collaboratively on a grand scale. It is here that we witness the powerful engagement of business-led coalitions (Grayson & Nelson, 2013) that are spearheading a range of sustainability issues, some of which have very important implications for system level working for, e.g., redefining growth and national competiveness for a more sustainable world.

(c) *Cradle-to-cradle – circular thinking*. McDonough and Braungart (2002) reject the traditional concept of eco-efficiency or 'doing more with less', widely promoted in the 1990s by organizations such as the WBCSD (1992, 2000) and argue that solving environmental problems through the '4 Rs' of waste management (Reduce, Reuse, Recycle and Regulate), while worthy environmental goals, only work to make the old destructive system a bit less so. Approaches which attempt to be 'less bad' are no longer good enough. Instead they promote the concept of 'eco-effectiveness' which aims to generate positive social, natural and economic values simultaneously.

Summary

This chapter highlights the opportunities to 'do better' and 'do different' in the contexts of SOI. To reach the higher echelons of this model, perhaps one of the biggest underlying challenges is for organizations to rethink their governance and bring to bear a fresh outlook that privileges innovation with sustainability in mind and respect, encompassing:

1   The mutual dependency of business in society for sustainable value creation.

2   Long-termism as a feature of more radical sustainability-orientated innovations and ultimately framing western democratic notions of 'conscious', 'responsible' and 'sustainable' capitalism.

3   Discontinuous and system level changes that have potential to go beyond eco-effectiveness agendas and provide multiple pathways to improving organizational change management and learning capabilities.

4   Collective attempts through business-led coalitions to redefine growth and national competiveness – where inclusive and sustainable growth is a prime focus.

5   Political debate regarding the appropriate level of voluntary vs. involuntary corporate action for sustainability-orientated innovation. To what degree can/should regulation and strategic choice influence the management of innovation?

(Continued)

6 Grappling with understanding their organization's context complexity and specificity affects innovation outcomes.

7 Enhanced awareness of hyper-connectivity, collaborating with usual partners in increasingly unusual ways through broad-range social media.

8 Anticipation of unintended consequences of future innovations and development of anticipatory, adaptive and reflexive responses to ensure their success.

9 Deep engagement with different stakeholder groups to establish the legitimacy (and manage divergence) of perspectives exposed by potential ethical rifts.

10 An explicit consideration of social justice and ethics in innovation management practice.

In doing so, sustainability-orientated innovations will be borne out of governance regimes that advocate stewardship, encouraging greater levels of responsibility, accountability and transparency in how we manage innovation in the future.

References

3M. (2011). 3M's Sustainability Strategy and Waste Minimization. http://mntap.umn.edu/events/wastemin2011/3M_Sustainability.pdf

Abdallah, T., Diabat, A. and Simchi-Levi, D. (2012). Sustainable supply chain design: A closed-loop formulation and sensitivity analysis. *Production Planning and Control*, 23(2–3), 120–133.

Adams, R., Jeanrenaud, S., Bessant, J., Overy, P., & Denyer, D. (2013). *Sustainability-orientated innovation: A systematic review of the literature*. Ottawa, Canada: Network for Business Sustainability.

Adams, R., Jeanrenaud, S., Bessant, J., Denyer, D., & Overy, P. (2015). Sustainability-orientated innovation: A systematic review. *International Journal of Management Reviews*. doi:10.1111/ijmr.12068

Aguilera, R. V. (2007). Putting the S back in corporate social responsibility: A multilevel theory of social change in organizations. *Academy of Management Review*, 32(3).

Anderson, W., & White, V. (2009) Exploring consumer preferences for home energy display functionality. Report to the Energy Saving Trust. *Design*, 123, 49.

Benyus, J. (1997). *Biomimicry: Innovation inspired by nature*. New York, NY: Harper-Collins.

Bessant, J., & Von Stamm, B. (2007). *Twelve search strategies that could save your organisation*. London: AIM Executive Briefing.

Bessant, J., B. Von Stamm, K. M. Moeslein and A.-K. Neyer (2011). "Backing outsiders: selection strategies for discontinuous innovation." R&D Management 40(4): 345–356.

Bessant, J., Rush, H., & Trifilova, A. (2012). 'Jumping the tracks': Crisis-driven social innovation and the development of novel trajectories. *Die Unternehmung [Swiss Journal of Business Research and Practice]*, 66(3), 221–242.

Birkinshaw, J., Bessant, J., & Delbridge, R. (2007). Finding, forming, and performing: Creating networks for discontinuous innovation. *California Management Review*, 49(3), 67–84.

Bonabeau, E., & Meyer, C. (2001) Swarm intelligence. A whole new way to think about business. *Harvard Business Review*, 79(5), 106–114, 165.

Boston Consulting Group. (2011). *Sustainability: The embracers seize the advantage*. Boston: Boston Consulting Group.

Bradbury, H., & Clair, J. A. (1999) Promoting sustainable organizations with Sweden's Natural Step. *Academy of Management Executives*, 13(4), 63–74.

Brown, L. R. (2011). *World on the edge: How to prevent environmental and economic collapse*. New York, NY: W. W. Norton.

Chang, Z. K. (2010) *Biomimicry: Tool for innovation at all levels of organization*. Herndon, VA: Strategic Sustainability Consulting.

Chesbrough, H. W. (2006). *Open innovation: The new imperative for creating and profiting from technology*. Cambridge, Mass.: Harvard Business Press.

Christensen, C. (1997). *The innovator's dilemma*. Cambridge, MA: Harvard Business School Press.

Cole, H., Freeman, C., Jahoda, M., & Pavitt, K. L. R. (1973). *Thinking About the future: Critique of 'Limits to Growth'*. Lincoln, UK: Anybook Ltd.

Draper, S. (2013). *Creating the big shift: systems innovation for sustainability*. London: Forum for the Future. Retrieved from http://www.forumforthefuture.org/sites/default/files/images/Forum/Documents/SI%20document%20v4.2%20web%20spreads_1.pdf

Gosling, J., Jia, F., Trifilova, A., & Bessant, J. (2012). Building capabilities in sustainability-led innovation: Some examples from China. ISPIM 13th Annual Conference. Barcelona: ISPIM.

Grameen Foundation. (2011). *Two steps backward for innovation to end poverty*. Retrieved from http://www.grameenfoundation.org/blog/two-steps-backward-innovation-end-poverty#.WAIfcPl9600

Grayson, D., & Nelson, J. (2013). *Corporate responsibility coalitions: The past, present, and future of alliances for sustainable capitalism*. Stanford: Stanford University Press.

Hansen, E. G., Grosse-Dunker, F. and Reichwald, R. (2009). Sustainability innovation cube: Framework to evaluate sustainability-orientated innovations. *International Journal of Innovation Management*, 13(04), 683–713.

Hart, S. L. (1995). *A natural-resource-based view of the firm*. Academy of Management Review, 20(4), 986–1014.

Hart, S. (1997). Beyond greening: Strategies for a sustainable world. *Harvard Business Review*, 75(1), 66–67.

Henderson, R., & Clark, K. (1990). Architectural innovation: The reconfiguration of existing product technologies and the failure of established firms. *Administrative Science Quarterly*, 35(1), 9–30.

Howard, M., & Jeanrenaud, J. (2012). *Desso case study*. Cranfield European Case Clearing House.

Jansson, N. K., Levin, S., Lubchenco, J., Mäler, K. G., Simpson, D., Starrett, D., Tilman, D., & Walker, B. (2000, July). The value of nature and the nature of value. *Science*, 289(5478), 395–396.

Macarthur, E., 2013. Towards the Circular *Economy: Opportunities for the consumer goods sector*. Ellen MacArthur Foundation.

Makadok, R. (2001). Towards a synthesis of the resource-based and dynamic capability views of rent creation. *Strategic Management Journal*, 22(5), 387–395.

McDonough, W., & Braungart, M. (2002). *Cradle to cradle: Remaking the way we make things*. Old Saybrook, CT: Tantor Media.

MEA. (2005). *Ecosystems and human well-being*. Washington, DC: Island Press.

Meadows, D., Meadows, D. L., Randers, J., & Behrens III, W. (1972). *The Limits to Growth*. New York, NY: Universe Books.

Nelson, R., & Winter, S. (1982). *An evolutionary theory of economic change*. Cambridge, Mass.: Harvard University Press.

Network, G. F., 2010. *Living Planet Report 2010*. WWF International, Switzerland.

Nidumolu, R., Prahalad, C., & Rangaswami, M. (2009). Why sustainability is not the key driver of innovation. *Harvard Business Review*, (September), 57–61.

Owen, R., Bessant, J., & and Heintz, M. (Eds.). (2013). *Responsible innovation*. Chichester: John Wiley and Sons.

Paramanathan, S., Farrukh, C., Phaal, R. and Probert, D. (2004). Implementing industrial sustainability: The research issues in technology management. *R&D Management*, 34(5), 527–538.

Paulk, M., Curtis, B., Chrissis, M. B. & Weber, C. V. (1993). *Capability maturity model, version 1.1*. IEEE software, 10(4), pp.18–27.

Porter, M., & Kramer, M. (2006). Strategy and society: The link between competitive advantage and corporate social responsibility. *Harvard Business Review*, 8, 78–92.

Rockström, J. Steffen, W., Noone, K., Persson, Å., Chapin III, F. S., Lambin, E., Lenton, T. M., Scheffer, M., Folke, C., Schellnhuber, H., Nykvist, B., De Wit, C. A., Hughes, T., van der Leeuw, S., Rodhe, H., Sörlin, S., Snyder, P. K., Costanza, R., Svedin, U., Falkenmark, M., Karlberg, L., Corell, R. W., Fabry, V. J., Hansen, J., Walker, B., Liverman, D., Richardson, K., Crutzen, P., & Foley, J. (2009). Planetary boundaries: Exploring the safe operating space for humanity. *Ecology and Society*, 14(2), 32–64.

Schimdheiny, S. with WBCSD (1992). *Changing Course: A global business perspective on development and the environment*. Cambridge, Massachusetts: MIT Press.

Seebode, D., Jeanrenaud, S., & Bessant, J. (2012). Managing innovation for sustainability. *R&D Management*, 42(3), 195–206.

Seeley, T. D. (2010). *Honeybee democracy*. Princeton, NJ: Princeton University Press.

Senge, P., Smith, B., Kruschwitz, N., Laur, J. and Schley, S. (2008). *The necessary revolution: How individuals and organizations are working together to create a sustainable world*. New York, NY: Doubleday.

Teece, D., Pisano, G., & Shuen, A. (1997). Dynamic capabilities and strategic management. *Strategic Management Journal*, 18(7), 509–533.

Tidd, J., & Bessant, J. (2009). *Managing innovation: Integrating technological, market and organizational change*. Chichester: John Wiley and Sons.

Tushman, M., & O'Reilly, C. (1996). Ambidextrous organizations: Managing evolutionary and revolutionary change. *California Management Review*, 38(4), 8–30.

UNEP. (2007). *Global Environmental Outlook*. Nairobi, Kenya: United Nations Environment Programme.

UNEP. (2011). *Towards a green economy: Pathways to sustainable development and poverty eradication*. Nairobi, Kenya: United Nations Environment Programme.

Unilever. (2011). *Unilever Sustainable Living Plan*. retrieved from https://www.unilever.com/sustainable-living/

Utterback, J. M. (1994). *Mastering the dynamics of innovation*. Boston, MA: Harvard Business School Press.

WBCSD. (2010). *Vision 2050: The new agenda for business*. Geneva: World Business Council for Sustainable Development.

WBCSD. (2000). *Eco-efficiency: Creating more value with less impact*. World Business Council for Sustainable Development, 1–32.

Zahra, S., & George, G. (2002). Absorptive capacity: A review, reconceptualization, and extension. *Academy of Management Review*, 17(2), 185–203.

10 Operating: The Sustainable Supply Chain

Mickey Howard, Fu Jia and Zhaohui Wu

LEARNING OUTCOMES

This chapter will enable you to:

1. Discuss the significance of supply strategy and sustainable practice in relation to examples from industry.

2. Explain how companies design their closed loop supply chain.

3. Evaluate the stakeholder engagement approach of MNCs for achieving sustainability in their supply chain.

4. Understand and be aware of sustainability standards, certification and measures.

Introduction

This chapter will look at some of the key operations and implementation issues involved with managing a sustainable enterprise. This includes understanding sustainability and the interplay between profit on the one hand, and environmental and societal interests on the other. We introduce four main themes which represent the primary operating challenges for sustainable supply chains:

1   Transition to the triple bottom line.
2   Closed-loop supply chain design.
3   Certification and measurement.
4   Stakeholder management.

In order to provide real life context, we include four examples of global sustainable businesses, their postures regarding sustainability, the strategies they employ, and how they overcome the operational challenges posed by adopting more sustainable business practice.

Operating the sustainable supply chain requires defining the key principles that guide the decisions a business makes. Such principles define the company's position on profitability, the natural environment (local and planet-wide) and society. It should include all the stakeholders involved with the company. And it should contain guidelines for decision-making that optimize outcomes for all these players. Ultimately, the transformation of a business to a more sustainable model often requires fundamental changes in product and process design. In many ways, it may be easier to create a sustainable business from the foundations upwards.

10.0 Transition to the Triple Bottom Line

Sustainable businesses abide by the triple bottom line. Unlike standard accounting practices, which focus solely on monetary gain, the triple bottom line encompasses two additional dimensions: environmental and societal robustness. Together with the financial balance, they form the triple bottom line. These three measures are sometimes referred to as the 3Ps: planet, people and profit.

Sustainable businesses hold themselves responsible to all their stakeholders. Single bottom line companies generally pledge themselves to their shareholders, and frequently their customers and employees. Government regulators, trade groups and NGOs can also influence corporate behaviour. Triple bottom line companies include their employees and the communities in which they operate as important stakeholders, as well. If the business is a small store, its stakeholders are necessarily limited numerically and geographically. A medium-sized business, however, may have stakeholders around the world. High performance across all three dimensions of the triple bottom line is possible, suggesting that organizations can truly be sustainable. Yet companies with the highest operational performance tend to be the least sustainable. A short-term perspective suggests that being sustainable is not as profitable as ignoring the social and environmental elements of the triple bottom line. Public pressure and resource shortages, however, are changing the question from *if* it pays to be responsible, to *how* to be responsible.

10.0.1 Environmental Sustainability

Does it pay to be green? Improved environmental performance is linked to improved economic and operational performance. There are limits to this relationship and some organizations have failed, in spite of being green. Nonetheless, energy efficiency, waste reduction, and design for the environment generally reduce operating costs. The use of 'lean thinking' has been a popular tool for reducing waste for many decades in sectors such as the automotive and aerospace industries. Derived from Japanese management practices where any non-value adding and unnecessary use of resources (e.g., inventory, manpower, energy) is classed as waste or '*muda*', the terms 'lean' and 'just-in-time' are used almost interchangeably in manufacturing and supply chain circles. Today, lean process improvement techniques are increasingly being used to explore ways of reducing waste in an environmental management context, such as the CO_2 emissions from logistics and transportation networks.

A sustainable business strives to minimize environmental impact by managing energy consumption and use of non-renewable resources, while reducing waste.

Companies that observe the triple bottom line assess all environmental, social, and financial costs. This includes material procurement, manufacturing and shipping, and reuse, recycling or disposal.

In an evolving regulatory world, adopting sound environmental policies before new requirements come into effect can position a company for additional improvements, and can attract customers who operate in a stricter regulatory environment, or want to manufacture products that will be compliant when new regulations come into effect.

Additionally, incorporating an environmental perspective into existing management practices can lead to higher performance. The best practice often comprises a combination of new and existing methods. Economic and non-economic elements of sustainability need to be aligned and sustainability has to be part of the daily conversation, not an isolated add-on. Sustainability is the responsibility of every employee at every level of the organization.

10.0.2 Social Sustainability

Social performance has not been addressed as extensively as environmental performance. Some studies and anecdotal evidence suggest a positive relationship between social performance and economic performance. Theoretically at least, social responsibility is linked to positive organizational outcomes.

Social and environmental sustainability work together. Every improvement to a company's environmental bottom line benefits its workers and its community. Decreasing emissions, toxic waste and pollution will benefit society as a whole. Social sustainability is often measured in reduced clean-up expenses, lower health care costs, or gains in efficiency and productivity due to greener operations. Other benefits that may accrue to a sustainable business include lower employee turnover, higher dedication and the ability to recruit a more talented and dedicated workforce. Sustainable business practices can also be used as an internal and external marketing tool. Regardless, environmental and social sustainability are often seen as enemies of financial gains, and direct societal costs and benefits can be difficult to quantify.

Notwithstanding its fiduciary commitment to shareholders, a company may consciously sacrifice some short-term profit in order to be sustainable in the long term, in order to focus on its community, the environment, its workers, it suppliers and its customers as much as does on its shareholders.

10.0.3 Financial Sustainability

Of course, to be sustainable, a business must make a profit. That is, it must remain in business. But sustainable enterprises take more than money into account. They look at the overall impacts and benefits the company has on the environment and the society in which it operates. The long-term view suggests that in order to remain in business, a company needs healthy workers and customers, and they need a world in which they can live. In calculating overall profits, a sustainable company will account for both the beneficial and harmful impacts it has had on people and the planet. A business showing a small profit may consider itself successful if the community thrives as a result of its activities.

10.0.4 Approaches to the Triple Bottom Line

Existing companies attempting to make themselves more sustainable can adopt any of three basic approaches towards the triple bottom line: environment first, 'equal footing' or opportunity first. In the environment first posture, a company will capitalize on environmental issues; success is seen as contingent on the accomplishment of environmental goals. In the equal footing posture, business is conducted sustainably for the benefit of all stakeholders. In such organizations, environmental and social issues are integrated and viewed as equally important. These companies may forgo profits and growth in favour of providing good pay and benefits, and stability to their communities.

The opportunity first posture differs from the previous two in that efforts to 'green' the company may be recent, *ad hoc*, and driven by monetary happenstance rather than operating principles. Opportunity first companies may use environmental or social sustainability to differentiate themselves and achieve economic goals or to appeal to customers seeking sustainable goods or services. The organic food industry has seen this in recent years, with large corporations creating or buying organic labels to capitalize on food-buying trends. Regardless, as these companies realize greater profits from their sustainable operations, those operations will grow.

10.1 Industrial Ecology and Closing the Loop

In the natural world, everything is recycled. Waste products from one organism provide nutrition for another. A common example is cow dung: cows eat and digest grass and drop dung. Bacteria live and thrive on nutrients in the dung, and as those nutrients are broken into simpler forms, fungi appear. Animals eat the fungi, while additional nutrients and elements are released into the soil to support plant growth. Herbivores feed on the plants, carnivores feed on the herbivores, and when a plant or animal dies, bacteria decompose its biomass, and similar circular processes continue on several scales.

Just as ecology examines the flow of materials and energy through a pasture (or other natural system), industrial ecology quantifies those same flows through an industrial system. Its primary concern is with shifting industrial processes from a linear model (an 'open' loop) in which resources and capital eventually become waste, to a closed-loop system where wastes from one process become inputs for another. It looks beyond conventional inputs and outputs to focus on life cycle design, co-location of industrial facilities (also known as industrial symbiosis), producer responsibility (product stewardship), and eco-effectiveness. Table 10.1 compares characteristics of natural and industrial systems.

10.1.1 Circular Economy

The circular economy is a development strategy to balance economic growth against the limits to raw materials and energy. Closely related to industrial ecology, it deals with the flow of energy and materials through multiple processes. Thus, the circular economy addresses consumption as well as production. The first basic goal is to develop efficient processes. The next objective is to develop a network that benefits production systems as well as the environment. Techniques include shared infrastructure, exchange of by-products, and waste recycling, among others.

TABLE 10.1   Comparison of Natural and Industrial Systems

Natural ecosystem	Organizational level	Industrial ecosystem
Environment	Systems/organizational levels	Market
Food chain/web		Supply chain/network
Ecological niche		Market niche
Ecosystem (forest, meadow, seashore, etc.)		Industrial park
Organism	Population and products	Company
Food (meat, fruit, seed, etc.)		Product or service
Natural selection	Processes	Competition
Succession		Economic cycles
Adaptation		Innovation
Mutation		Design for environment

The final developmental stage of a circular economy (the 'climax community', to use a phrase from the study of ecology)[1], is the evolution of the industrial park into an eco-municipality. Whereas the eco-industrial park focuses only on sustainable production, the eco-city includes the notion of sustainable consumption. Figure 10.1 shows several nested systems within a circular economy.

10.1.2   Closed-loop Supply Chains

In a circular economy, one company's waste can be another company's production input. A closed-loop supply chain may implement that strategy, but the chain aims to recover used or worn products for reuse by the same company by adopting a 'cradle-to-cradle' approach to manufacturing. Traditional supply chains operate in one direction: materials, components, and subassemblies move from upstream suppliers to downstream manufacturers and vendors (e.g., distributors, retailers).

A closed-loop supply chain features a reverse supply chain. Reverse supply chains have shipping and tracking systems in place, just as traditional supply chains. However, they begin with used products and return them to the manufacturer for disassembly and reuse or recycling. For example, a field technician will determine if a piece of equipment such as a printer or heating, ventilating and air conditioning (HVAC) unit can be repaired or needs replacing. If the machine is irremediable, they will ship it back to the manufacturing/recycling facility. There it is disassembled and its usable components are returned to the appropriate tiers of the manufacturing line for reuse, thereby closing the loop. Standard components (e.g., computer RAM) and any salvaged materials (e.g., gold contacts, or copper wiring) can be sold or reused.

When components cannot be disassembled before recycling, the process often involves 'grind and sort' which recovers less value. If the raw materials can be used again, the loop remains closed. In other scenarios, certain materials (rubber or plastics, for

---

[1] The term 'climax community' is rarely used in ecological studies, in that it implies a static system. Natural systems that seem to have reached a steady state are actually in flux, a state of dynamic stability.

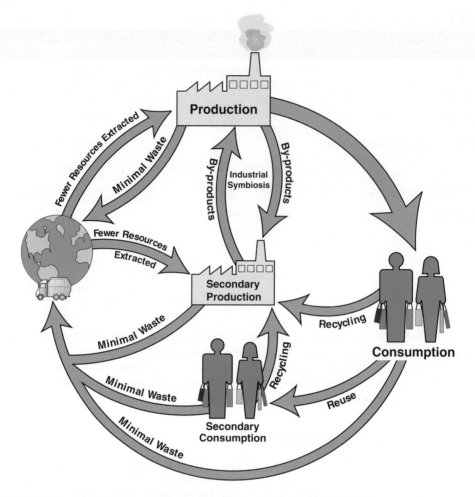

FIGURE 10.1 Closed Loops and Circular Economies in Industrial Ecology.
Source: Department of Natural Resources and Parks. King County, WA: US.

instance) are incinerated as fuel to generate power. Only in the worst possible case are materials sent to a landfill site and this practice is increasingly being legislated against by regional authorities.

10.1.3 Practices for closing the loop

A number of common tools and practices exist for creating closed-loop supply chain operations. Life cycle assessment or 'LCA' (also known as life cycle analysis) examines a product's environmental impacts over the entire lifespan, from raw material through manufacture, distribution, use, and final disposition. An LCA is defined in ISO standards 14040 and 14044, which can be used to compare the environmental impacts of similar products.

Industrial co-location (found in eco-industrial parks) allows businesses to co-operate in efforts to reduce waste and pollution, share resources, and sustain development. A hypothetical example would be one plant that required pure water for its processes and another that could use 'gray' water equally well. If the first plant can identify the contaminants in its effluent, the one resource could be used twice, with both companies sharing the expense of the clean water.

Eco-design (or design for the environment) is intended to minimize pollution and waste. It has three main elements. *Design for environmental manufacturing* ensures that the extraction and processing of raw material are safe. *Design for environmental packaging* aims to reduce or eliminate packaging and shipping materials. *Design for disposal or reuse* minimizes the product's impact at the end of its life cycle. *Product stewardship*, which includes disposal or recycling expenses in the initial cost of the product, extends this idea.

Many companies did not pursue end-of-life (EOL) management until recently because of the expense involved. But changes in customer concern and regulation have brought EOL issues to the fore. EOL design and manufacture closes the supply loop by eliminating waste while improving the efficiency and efficacy of reuse, refurbishment and recycling.

Companies merely seeking to comply with regulations may outsource the recycling process. While this may be cost-effective, it provides little recovery of materials. It does not impact the supply chain, since the company can choose to use recycled materials in manufacturing or not. If a company recycles onsite, it can simply recycle and reuse any reclaimed materials or it can recycle with disassembly and refurbishment/remanufacture. The additional handling and processing costs may be mitigated or even surpassed by the value of the recovered components or materials. More and more companies are designing for disassembly to minimize the costs and maximize the returns of this process. Design strategies include modular product designs (easy to dismantle and redirect components), material choice (use of easy-to-recycle materials that require little or no additional chemical or physical processing), snap or push-to-fit parts instead of glued or screwed assemblies (fewer parts and materials), non-toxic components (to minimize any impact the recycling process may have,) and use of common materials (to eliminate separating, sorting and processing different materials).

10.2 Sustainability Standards, Certification and Measures

Certification is a method that has traditionally been used to assess the risk of nonconformance in areas such as quality and delivery. It verifies compliance with regulations banning hazardous materials, dangerous environmental practices, unethical labour policies, and so on. Certification is one of the few areas where social issues such as the use of sweatshop labour are addressed. It is usually done by an accredited third party.

ISO 9000 and ISO 14000 are management standards, developed by the International Organization for Standardization (ISO), that specify a system to assure quality for manufacturing processes. ISO 9000 sets standards for quality management, while ISO 14000 addresses environmental management. ISO 9001 and 14001 cover the requirements that companies must fulfil to receive ISO 9000 and 14000 certification. Taken together, they allow companies and organizations to ensure that products and services meet customer needs and that their processes meet regulatory requirements.

The ISO 14000 'family of standards' in particular addresses environmental management, using a framework similar to the ISO 9000 standard. As companies focus increasingly on sustainable operations, ISO 14000 provides them with tools to manage environmental impact and improve environmental performance. It specifies methods to identify every operation that impacts the environment, as well as procedures for handling and disposal of hazardous materials and waste, and compliance with environmental laws. Different standards within the family focus on environmental management systems, life cycle analysis, communications and auditing. The standard can be used by any organization, including businesses and government agencies, to assure an organization's stakeholders that environmental impact is being monitored, documented and improved. Benefits to adopting the standard can include reduced waste management costs, energy and materials savings, and good public relations. ISO 14000 is seen most often in large multinational corporations that encourage their suppliers to apply for ISO certification as well. Table 10.2 lists some of the ISO 14000 standards and the areas they cover.

Both ISO 9000 and 14000 focus on internal processes without necessarily addressing performance as viewed from outside the organization. But while quality management is an internal concern (with ramifications for customers and employees), environmental management is directly concerned with the external environment. Moreover, when an entity interacts with its environment, it becomes part of a larger system: ISO standards do not fully deal with environmental concerns.

The EU recently adopted a more stringent environmental standard, EMAS, or the Eco-Management and Audit Scheme, a globally-accepted standard. ISO 14000 is a fundamental part of EMAS, but EMAS adds additional elements – stricter measurement and evaluation of environmental performance, in particular. The evaluation is based on extensive assessment of environmental impact, a year-by-year comparison of performance, and independent verification. A company's performance is judged against objectives and targets, and continuous improvement is a requirement. EMAS also requires employee participation in environmental initiatives, recognizing that although management determines environmental policy, employees implement environmental practices.

TABLE 10.2 ISO 14000 Standards and Areas Covered

Standard	Areas of coverage
ISO 14001	Environmental management systems: requirements with guidance for use
ISO 14004	Environmental management systems: principles, systems and support techniques
ISO 14006	Environmental management systems: guidelines for incorporating eco-design
ISO 14015	Environmental assessment of sites and organizations
ISO 14020 to 14025	Environmental labels and declarations
ISO 14030	Post-production environmental assessment
ISO 14031	Guidelines for environmental performance evaluation
ISO 14040 to 14049	Life cycle assessment, pre-production planning and environment goal setting
ISO 14050	Terms and definitions
ISO 14062	Improvements to environmental impact goals
ISO 14063	Environmental communication: guidelines and examples
ISO 14064	Measuring, quantifying and reducing greenhouse gas emissions
ISO 19011	Audit protocol for both 14000 and 9000 series standards

SA 8000 (Social Accountability 8000) is a certifiable norm that focuses on labour rights in global supply chains. The standard is defined by Social Accountability International (SAI), with the help of NGOs, labour unions and corporations. SAI is a non-governmental, international, multistakeholder organization dedicated to improving workplaces and communities by developing and implementing socially responsible standards. It convenes key stakeholders to develop consensus-based voluntary standards, conducts cost-benefit research, accredits auditors, provides training and technical assistance, and assists corporations in improving social compliance in their supply chains. In 1997, SAI launched SA 8000 – a voluntary standard for workplaces, based on ILO and UN conventions – which is currently used by businesses and governments around the world and is recognized as one of the strongest workplace standards (see http://www.sa-intl.org).

The standard covers issues including child labour, liveable wages, work hours and complaint resolution. It is based, in part, on the *United Nations Convention on the Rights of the Child* and the *Universal Declaration of Human Rights*. As of September, 2013, over 2 million workers were covered in more than 3,000 SA 8000-certified facilities worldwide. Table 10.3 details some of its provisions.

There are other globally-recognized certifications, many of which are specific to particular industries. The Forest Stewardship Council (FSC) is an international association that allows forest owners, timber industries and social and environmental NGOs to find solutions to forest management issues. It was formed to promote responsible forest management. The FSC sets standards for sustainable forestry and logging, offers certification and provides for labelling of sustainably-harvested forest products. Similarly, the Marine Stewardship Council (MSC) is an international not-for-profit agency comprising commercial fishermen and environmental NGOs.

TABLE 10.3   SA 8000 provisions

Area of coverage	Specifications
Forced labour	Zero tolerance. No deposits or fees required to work. No denial of salary, benefits, property or documents to coerce continued work. Right to leave premises after shift. Free to quit. No use of human trafficking.
Child labour	No child labour and/or conditional employment of such workers. Written policies and procedures for remediation of children found working at facility. Financial and other support for such children.
Work hours	Compliance with laws and standards. Work week (excepting paid overtime) not to exceed 48 hours. Six consecutive work days followed by one day off. No compulsory overtime, unless negotiated in collective bargaining.
Wages	Right to living wage. Legal minimum wage, sufficient to meet basic needs and discretionary income. No disciplinary deductions (with some exceptions). Wages and benefits clearly communicated. Convenient form of pay. Premium for overtime. No outsourcing of child labour; no false apprenticeships; no short-term contracts to avoid obligations.
Health and safety	Safe and healthy workplace. Accident prevention. Senior management to ensure OSH. OSH instruction for workers. Accident documentation and reporting. Protective equipment and medical attention. Risk removal and reduction. Hygiene: toilet, potable water, clean food storage. Liveable dormitories. Right to evacuate from danger.

(Continued)

TABLE 10.3 (*Continued*)

Area of coverage	Specifications
Discipline	Dignity and respect for workers. No corporal punishment. No mental or physical abuse. No harsh or inhumane treatment.
Discrimination	No discrimination based on race, origin, religion, disability, gender or sexual orientation, union membership, political opinions or age. No discrimination in hiring, pay, training, promotion, termination, or retirement. No interference with tenets, beliefs or practices. No threatening, abusive, exploitative or coercive behaviour at workplace or company facilities. No pregnancy or virginity tests.
Collective bargaining	Right to form and join unions. Right to collective bargaining. Freedom from retaliation. No discrimination against employees in worker organizations. Workplace access to union or trade organization representation.

They certify sustainably-managed fisheries and offer a label to identify seafood products that originate in such waters. Box 10.1 lists the FSC principles.

It is perhaps instructive to note that since minerals and petroleum are strictly non-renewable, there are no certifications of sustainability for those industries. The American Petroleum Institute (API) does, however, offer ISO 14001 certification to provide assurance that efforts to minimize environmental impact are ongoing, as well as OSHA 18001 certification (Occupational Safety and Health Administration: a US government agency) to cover worker safety issues in that industry.

C2C® (Cradle-to-Cradle®)[2] certification is administered by the Cradle to Cradle Products Innovation Institute. The certification 'provides a path to manufacturing

---

BOX 10.1

Forest Stewardship Council Principles and Criteria

Principle 1: Compliance with all applicable laws and treaties.

Principle 2: Clearly defined, long-term land tenure and use rights.

Principle 3: Recognition of and respect for indigenous people's rights.

Principle 4: Long-term social and economic well-being of forest workers and local communities. Respect of workers' rights in compliance with International Labour Organization (ILO) conventions.

Principle 5: Equitable sharing of benefits derived from the forest.

Principle 6: Reduction of environmental impact of logging and maintenance of forest ecology.

Principle 7: Appropriate and continuously updated management plan.

Principle 8: Appropriate monitoring and assessment to assess the forest condition, management activities, and social and environmental impacts.

Principle 9: Maintenance of High Conservation Value Forests.

Principle 10: Plantations must reduce the pressures on forests and promote restoration and conservation.

---

[2] Cradle-to-Cradle® is the registered trademark of McDonough Braungart Design Chemistry (MBDC).

healthy and sustainable products for our world.' It has five criteria: material health (harm-free materials), material neutralization, renewable energy and carbon management, water stewardship, and social fairness. Case Study 10.1 *looks more closely at the C2C® standard*.

10.2.1 TQEM, Eco-efficiency and Eco-effectiveness

Continuous improvement regimens (TQM, JIT, lean practices and others) have long been considered best practices. A critical goal of a lean system is waste reduction, which in turn reduces pollution and resource consumption. So it makes sense that they are linked to improved environmental performance.

Total Quality Environmental Management (TQEM) leads to simultaneous improvements in operational and environmental performance. However, TQEM and similar

---

CASE STUDY 10.1
Desso: Closing the Loop through Supply Chain Redesign

This case examines the carpet manufacturer Desso, based in the Netherlands, after its decision to adopt the Cradle-to-Cradle® philosophy and redesign its products and processes using environmentally-friendly principles. Although the company had embraced sustainability initiatives such as green energy before it was acquired in 2007, no one in the organization had considered adopting a concept as bold as Cradle-to-Cradle® as a primary operating principle.

Cradle-to-Cradle® (C2C®) is a play on the phrase 'cradle to grave'. C2C® promotes the use of non-toxic materials and sustainable manufacturing systems in which products are designed for disassembly and safe recycling. The concept was popularized by McDonough and Braungart in their book *Cradle to Cradle: Remaking the Way We Make Things*. Originally published in 2002, the book is now considered a classic. Phrases such as 'cradle to grave' refer to the linear manufacturing model dating from the Industrial Revolution. While the extract-use-discard system provided the foundation of the modern economy, it also resulted in waste, pollution, resource depletion and loss of biodiversity.

C2C® considers the end of a product's useful life, at which point it is disassembled and its materials used as inputs for other manufacturing processes. C2C® takes its

inspiration from nature. The model mimics the planet's natural nutrient flows, its use of solar energy, and its creation of diversity and abundance. In nature, there is no such thing as waste: materials are continuously recycled to nourish new organisms. However, asking customers and suppliers to change a lifetime of ingrained habits demands enterprise-wide metamorphosis. Such a paradigm shift can severely disrupt a business. Regardless, Desso took on the challenge in the midst of the worst worldwide recession in over 50 years. As C2C® implementation gathered momentum the management team began to appreciate the complexity of transforming the organization and its supply chain. The shift involved material sourcing, information sharing with suppliers and customers, and a commitment to surpass regulatory requirements, all while designing products from an environmental perspective.

The objective was to have every product support the C2C® vision by 2020. Initially the new management team had to decide which product from the existing portfolio to start with. They chose carpet tiles, a popular product with commercial customers particularly in busy office environments. The idea behind carpet tiles is fundamentally sound: tiles in high-traffic areas where carpet wears out quickly can be replaced without having to pull up the

(Continued)

entire carpet; waste reduction is intrinsic to the design. But traditional carpet tiles were composed of around 120 ingredients, some toxic, even though they complied with regulations (such as REACH (Registration, Evaluation, Authorization and Restriction of Chemicals) and CE (Conformité Européenne) labelling). They also contained elements not allowed by Cradle-to-Cradle® criteria.

A major component of a typical carpet tile is the bitumen used as backing. This is the thick residue left after oil and gasoline have been refined from crude oil. Although it is a 'natural' material, it may contain a number of uncontrollable chemical compounds, making recycling difficult and leading to the dumping of used carpet tiles in landfill sites.

Desso's carpet tile production line was one of the first to benefit from the company's new operating principle, though it required considerable collaboration with architects, regulatory agencies, and suppliers to decide how to replace the bitumen used in the backing material. Together with EPEA[3] and Dow Chemical they developed a new backing called EcoBase™ with a polyolefin-based layer that can be completely and safely recycled. The backing is specifically designed for disassembly and recycling in Desso's own production plant. Carpet tiles with EcoBase® have achieved Cradle-to-Cradle® Silver Certification, with up to 97% of the materials positively defined.[4]

A particular challenge for the company is the Take Back initiative, which the company has offered since 2008. Under this system the company offers to retrieve used carpet tiles, including those manufactured by competitors, from buildings undergoing refurbishment (a practice termed 'urban mining') and to recycle them at the Desso plant in Waalwijk. Desso's Take Back and recycling process is called ReFinity® which separates the post-consumer carpet into its main components, either for recycling into new carpet yarn, or for downcycling into road building materials or use as secondary fuel in the cement industry.

Encouraging independent carpet fitters to collaborate is one issue, but identifying the material used in the tiles which may have been manufactured a decade ago is another. Old tiles may also have a high bitumen content which is non-recyclable. While Desso is currently exploring the use of incinerated material for use in cement, its objective is to separate the yarn and other fibre for reuse. Desso has evolved a process of separation which involves shredding and fluffing. A supplier has developed a dye-removal process that produces a white yarn. Other methods had been tried, including direct extrusion of the fibre, but it left the colour which made it unsuitable for light-coloured carpet. The innovative recycling method means that yarn can be reused indefinitely, with only a little loss of material with each cycle. Innovation on the scale envisaged by Desso through the implementation of C2C® requires significant investment in time, resources and technologies. To develop the yarn recycling process, e.g., has taken the company several years. 'It takes guts. . .it's about challenging the framework and thinking outside the box,' explains the company's sustainability director.

Adopting the Cradle-to-Cradle® approach is hard because it means rethinking the traditional supply chain, and the once-peripheral issues of product end-of-life and disposal become central to the solution. C2C® requires more than minor adjustment. Rather than outsourcing responsibility to suppliers, the prime manufacturer must persuade partners to accept new legislation and co-operate through information sharing, process improvement, product design and materials research. C2C® disrupts traditional notions of 'upstream-downstream' and supply chain hierarchies in conventional business circles.

---

[3] Environmental Protection Encouragement Agency (EPEA) GmbH, founded by Michael Braungart who works with clients worldwide to apply the Cradle-to-Cradle® methodology to the design of new processes, products and services.
[4] 'Positively defined' means all ingredients have been assessed as either Green (optimal) or Yellow (tolerable) according to the Cradle-to-Cradle® assessment criteria, as described in the Cradle-to-Cradle® Certification Program Version 2.1.1, prepared by MBDC, September 2008, and updated January 2010.

(Continued)

Identifying appropriate supply chain partners was vital to Desso's adoption of a circular economy approach. For example, Aquafil, based in Trento, Italy, has been offering premium materials to commercial carpet makers for years, based on recycling polymers from such waste as old fishing nets. Aquafil knows there is a growing market for supplying high-quality industrial fibres with a guaranteed percentage of recycled material. And while the process of breaking down, cleansing and reconditioning the polymer is complex, it uses far fewer resources than conventional processes. There are also at least two secondary benefits to Aquafil's pioneering work: fishermen can realize a profit from worn-out nets, and Aquafil estimates that tens of thousands of sea turtles and other creatures are saved from an untimely death, tangled in otherwise discarded nets.

The concept of Design for the Environment (DFE) and the circular economy are significant today because they introduce new rules to the game of pricing and incentive structures. They require co-operation from all stakeholders, including regulators and NGOs. C2C® rethinks the way materials are upcycled or downcycled, and presents the idea of emulating nature's cycles to create a new model of design, production and consumption. C2C® reframes our understanding of supply chain strategy, because instead of a linear approach leading to landfill, it brings the concept of a cyclical, closed-loop supply system to life.

efforts focus on incremental change and avoid large-scale innovation. TQEM may improve the eco-efficiency of an existing operation, but can hinder eco-effectiveness in situations that call for radical change.

As we saw in the case of ISO 14000 vs. EMAS perspectives, companies must direct their attention beyond their manufacturing processes and analyse the products they make to embrace eco-efficacy. For example, one automobile company may reduce energy consumption on their production line, but if they build gas-guzzlers, the net impact on the environment is still negative. On the other hand, another car-maker might undertake an enormous one-time expenditure of energy to overhaul their processes. But if the cars they produce are more fuel efficient, the net savings in energy consumption and pollution can be huge:

$$(\text{Improved rate per kilometre}) \times (\text{Hundreds of thousands of cars})$$
$$= (\text{Vast reduction in resource consumption}).$$

As another automotive example, the batteries used in electric and hybrid cars have an acknowledged negative environmental impact. But the increased fuel efficiency mitigates that impact, so electrics and hybrids are a more eco-effective approach to transportation. This is the core difference between eco-efficiency and eco-effectiveness (or eco-efficacy). Developing an eco-effective approach towards business requires analysing the total impact a product has on the environment, from resource extraction to manufacturing, and throughout the product's life cycle. An operation must achieve eco-efficiency before it can consider eco-efficacy.

Development of eco-effective products demands a holistic viewpoint – something most non-sustainable companies lack. That viewpoint includes identifying products and services that damage the environment, developing a market for sustainable goods and services, and creation of a green supply network. When this approach is recognized as a best practice, sustainable innovation will be seen as a winning strategy, not a burden.

10.3 Stakeholder Management

A stakeholder in a business is defined as 'any group or individual who can affect or is affected by the achievement of the organization's objectives'. Traditionally, firms dealt solely with the needs and wishes of investors, employees, suppliers, and customers. A sustainable business today will likely be called upon to respond to those traditional stakeholders, along with government agencies, NGOs, trade unions, the competition, financial institutions, the community, the media and the public at large. Some sources refer to the natural environment as a stakeholder as well (though it is usually represented by proxy in negotiations). These parties will probably have different, often competing, requests and demands. Both internal and external stakeholders may take part in any given decision-making process, so it is necessary to manage a variety of interests and expectations. Effective stakeholder management requires engagement and communication, and there are established methods to gather information, acknowledge participation and arrive at a decision.

If this is not handled well, a company or project manager risks delays or cancellation. In identifying stakeholders, it is important to consider the impact of the project from their point of view, given their concepts of justice, fairness and social rights. The best way to manage stakeholders is to identify them, and what they see as potential problems associated with a project. By meeting with them in the planning phase, it may be possible to settle any differences. Negotiation, mitigation and compromise will likely come into play. Stakeholder management also involves assessing the relative strength of each individual stakeholder or group and planning around their requirements, ideally gaining their buy-in and support for the project.

Stakeholders may support or oppose a given activity. It is possible to forge positive relationships with stakeholders, including those antagonistic to company or project goals. The first step is to identify them. Catalogue the people and groups who are affected by the company or project, who can influence it, or have a vested interest in its success or failure. There are several ways to characterize and rank their relative importance.

One method, adapted from Mitchell, Agle and Wood (1997), ranks stakeholders based on their saliency. It bases saliency on three qualitative attributes: power, legitimacy and urgency. Power measures a stakeholder's ability to carry out their will in spite of opposition. Legitimacy is linked to what or how much a stakeholder has at risk. A legitimate voluntary stakeholder might be an investor, a manager whose career depends on a project, or a long-standing employee who relies on the company for their livelihood. A legitimate involuntary stakeholder could be a neighboring homeowner with concerns about a proposed facility expansion and how it will affect their property value. Urgency can cover time-sensitivity or how important the outcome of the activity is to a stakeholder. The more attributes a stakeholder has, the more salient that stakeholder is.

Figure 10.2 maps out types of stakeholders and their attributes. A dormant stakeholder may wield power, but lacking investment (of financial or human capital) and urgency, chooses not to take an interest. Similarly, discretionary stakeholders are invested but have no power or urgency, and thus may choose to participate in decision-making or not. The demanding stakeholder views the outcome as critical, but lacks the power and legitimacy to alter the situation significantly. Stakeholders with two attributes, being more salient, will be more directly involved and more

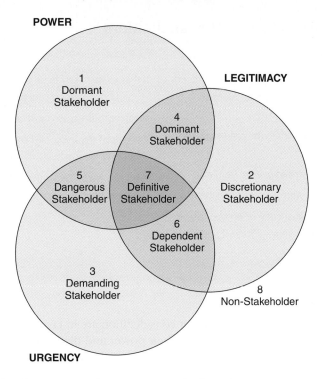

FIGURE 10.2 Stakeholder Typography. *Source:* Mitchell et al., 1997.

influential. And a definitive stakeholder, possessing all three attributes, will be among the most influential of participants when decisions are made.

A simpler classification method positions stakeholders on an x, y-plane, based on degree of power and interest (interest essentially combines urgency and legitimacy). Figure 10.3 shows the matrix resulting from this model. The stakeholder matrix

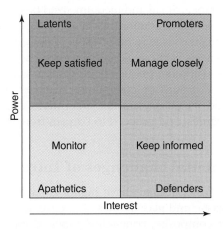

FIGURE 10.3 Stakeholder Matrix.

What is their opinion of the project? Is it based on good information? Can you share more information or correct wrong impressions?

Who influences their opinions? Who influences their opinion of the project?

What information do they need or want from you?

What is the best way of communicating with them?

How are they invested (financially or emotionally) in the project? Is their involvement/interest positive or negative?

If they are not likely to be positive, what will win them around to support your project?

What motivates them most of all?

If you don't think you will be able to win them around, how will you manage their opposition?

Who else might be influenced by their opinions? Do these people become stakeholders in their own right?

assumes that all the stakeholders under consideration are in favour of an activity, and breaks them into four groups based on their power and degree of involvement.

In this model, it is wise to engage and communicate with 'promoters' (high-interest, high-power stakeholders) closely. It makes sense to inform them of current issues, progress (or setbacks), and project status. High-power, low-interest participants ('latent stakeholders') should be kept up-to-date, but with less-detailed reports on board meetings or steering committee decisions. High-interest, low-power promoters should be kept informed, and low-power, low-interest 'apathetics' should be monitored and informed, but not necessarily engaged in decision-making. Box 10.2 lists a few questions to consider when classifying stakeholders.

The hierarchical structure of large corporations can impede stakeholder management. Communication may require executive approval, and decisions are made slowly, often from a distance. Small and medium-sized businesses hold an advantage in that they have fewer levels of administration and can reach decisions quickly. On the other hand, large businesses may have teams of lawyers and negotiators to deal with governmental agencies at the regional or national scale. Small businesses lack the firepower, but they will more frequently be dealing with entities on the scale of local governments, civic groups or community alliances. And while big business relies on its brand and its image, smaller enterprises can establish mutual trust among and between parties, and proceed to bargain from there.

10.3.1 Environmental challenges of Tetra Pak packaging

Tetra Pak brick and pillow packages have higher capacity and are easier to pack, ship and store than plastic and glass bottles (see Case Study 10.2). Tetra packaging is made of a six-layer composite, containing paper, aluminium and polyethylene. Figure 10.5 details the layers. The packages exclude air and light, but pose other

Tetra Pak: Creating the Triple Bottom Line

Tetra Pak (TP) is the largest food processing and packaging company in the world. The company provides packaging, filling machines and processing equipment for dairy products, beverages and other prepared foods. It works with its customers and suppliers to provide safe, innovative and environmentally sound products that each day meet the needs of hundreds of millions of people.

Its commitment regarding sustainability includes minimizing environmental impact, helping its customers build their businesses, helping to maintain reliable food supplies, and supporting the communities in which it operates.

When TP entered China in 1972, per capita consumption of milk was negligible. Dairies were scattered across the countryside, serving only local or regional markets. The dairy industry had little or no support, and few or no standards. Since then, TP has been a major player in the emerging dairy industry. The company has grown with increased demand and it has leveraged its technologies to shape China's dairy industry. However, as it has integrated sustainability into management, it has faced challenges as local competitors' operations have caught up with the innovations it introduced.

Over the past decade, China's dairy industry has grown around 20% per year, becoming the world's fourth largest dairy producer. TP works with the four largest dairies in China, supplying packaging, processing equipment and services to them all. Ultra-high temperature milk (UHT, the most popular kind in China) is generally packaged in aseptic 'bricks'. TP dominates the market for this type of packaging, with a 70% – 90% share. The bricks can last up to a year with no refrigeration. Distribution and storage costs are reduced, as is environmental impact, and shelf life is increased. Figure 10.4 shows a variety of TP packaging. TP cartons have been criticized for being hard to recycle. Recycling requires specialized plants; otherwise the cartons end up in landfills. The company has implemented measures to reduce this impact, including a carbon management plan.

The brick-shaped Tetra Brik   The pillow-shaped Tetra Fino

FIGURE 10.4 Tetra Pak Containers.

problems such as the layers being difficult to separate and recycle. One layer is aluminium, which does not decompose in landfills and can damage crops and poison grazing animals if it seeps into soil or water. The packages cannot be incinerated and end up discarded. In some areas, piles of Tetra packages are visible in the landscape. In addition, Tetra packaging is expensive, accounting for as much as 40% of product cost.

10.3.2 KAM: Working with Customers

Key Account Management (KAM) is instrumental in TP's collaboration. The company sends a KAM team, including experts on strategic development, technology, quality development, and sales and administration to new customers' plants. Customer employees also join the team. In return, TP requires a guaranteed purchasing volume from these customers. With its expertise throughout the dairy industry ('from cow to consumer'), TP considers itself a service provider, delivering integrated business solutions to its customers. TP provides technical service and marketing support to its customers, as well as consulting services to their customers. It has committed to support 'the entire dairy sector in any country'. Its value chain activities touch multiple tiers of suppliers and customers (see Figure 10.6).

TP began to work with the company Yili in 1996. Yili bought its first filling machine from TP and started producing UHT milk and other dairy products. UHT milk allowed the company to expand to far-flung markets. To date, Yili has bought more than 200 filling machines from TP and the annual purchases exceed 10 billion packages. After 15 years, the co-operation between Yili and TP has expanded from equipment and packaging to marketing, training, technical innovation and product development.

TP also offers financial services. For companies put off by the large investment, TP provides its Tetra Fino filling lines for a down payment of 20%. If the customer purchases a set amount of packaging, TP excuses the remaining debt. The customer can invest this capital, and TP increases its market share. TP provides a programme

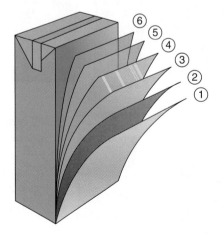

1. Polyethylene - preventing water

2. Paper board - stabilizing and supporting

3. Polyethylene - bonding

4. Foil: blocking oxygen, light and odour

5. Polyethylene - bonding

5. Polyethylene - sealing

FIGURE 10.5   Tetra Pak Six-layer Package Material.

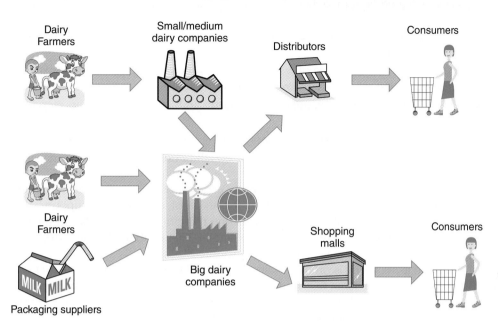

FIGURE 10.6 Dairy Supply Chain Structure in China.

named Tetra PlantMaster that allows plant managers to use standard software to collect and use real time production information. TP also works with other stakeholders, including NGOs (e.g., the World Wildlife Federation (WWF) and the China Green Foundation (CGF)), universities, government institutions, forestry companies, recyclers, and even rubbish collectors.

10.3.3 FSC Certification

To maximize the recycled paper content of its packages, TP instituted a forestry guideline – even though it does not do business directly with forestry companies. The company's goal is to use wood fibre from forests with FSC certification. Since 2006, TP has been worked with the WWF and the CGF to support certification. In certifying the YongAn forest in southern China, TP funded the certification process and expenses of the other stakeholders involved (ministries, academics and the expert team from China). In July 2010, TP earned the FSC certification seal.

10.3.4 Creating a Recycling System

Although the carbon footprint for a Tetra carton is less than the same-volume plastic or glass package, the quantity of TP packaging still poses a serious environmental issue. TP cartons have been criticized for being more difficult to recycle than other materials. The problem is that existing recycling plants lack the necessary processes and equipment, so TP is working with cities to build a recycling infrastructure. It is also advancing other approaches:

1 Package design with recyclability measured at every stage of product development.
2 Co-operation with beverage companies, municipalities, industry groups and communities to ensure recovery of Tetra packages.
3 Recycling its own manufacturing waste and supporting other recycling initiatives.
4 Developing new recycling technologies.
5 Incorporating recycling performance into the evaluations of local managers.

In 2007, the company was involved in the creation of China's Circular Economy Law, providing funds and co-ordination for stakeholders. TP also supports the Circular Economy Committee, helping to define recycling standards. The company increased its own recycling from almost nothing in 2004 to about 15% in 2010, redirecting almost 71,300 tonnes of 'misplaced resources'.

Although its recycling is on the rise in China, it still lags behind the global average (30%) and the rate in some EU countries (70%). TP is aware that a circular economy can only be achieved if there is a robust recycling chain, and that success depends on stakeholder commitment and co-operation. It has identified three key areas that need additional support: technology, infrastructure and awareness. It must also establish a uniform collection and classification system in China, where waste coding systems are still vague.

TP has taken three steps to establish its recycling supply chain in China. First is to increase the collection of used packaging. TP trains waste collectors and helped establish the collection network. In Shanghai, TP works closely with Shanghai Green World. More than 1,000 Shanghai residents now sort rubbish into recyclables and non-recyclables. According to Wen Yucheng, owner and General Manager of Shanghai Green World, 'Tetra Pak does not only focus on used packaging, it aims to establish a system for recycling'. Second, TP provides recycling companies with recycling and manufacturing technologies (see Table 10.4). When properly separated, the value of recycled materials increases by nearly a third: a boon for the recyclers.

Lastly, TP works with paper processors, providing one company with technology, production lines and equipment leases, and helping another with raw materials

TABLE 10.4 Recycling Technology for Tetra Cartons

Technology	Application of renewed materials
Hydro-pulping	Renewed paper, materials for plastic and aluminium items
Wood, plastic, composites	Indoor furniture, gardening, industrial pallets
HB clad plate	Rubbish bin
Pyrolysis	Plastic granular and aluminium power

procurement. One difficulty is that in China, only large paper mills receive government support. TP's used packaging is low in volume and difficult to process, so it is difficult for small recyclers to expand. Without government support, they have to deal with waste water on their own. Nonetheless, more than ten companies in China are producing renewed materials using waste Tetra cartons, and a recycling value chain is taking shape (see Table 10.5). TP's experience in China proves it can be done, even in a market lacking clear waste management legislation.

10.3.5 Social Sustainability

TP has worked with the National School Milk Office (NSMO) in China since its creation in 2000. The NSMO includes representatives from the ministries of Finance, Agriculture, Education, Industry and Information Technology, Commerce, Health, and the National Development and Reform Commission (NDRC). In that time, TP has supported the NSMO's three activities: milk quality management, management of appointed milk processors and promotion, all with the goal of providing healthy milk in schools.

For the past five years, TP has invested heavily to improve raw milk quality. Regarding the company's motivation, Zhang Shuyi, head of the Steering and Building Committee, said, 'As a successful company, it has the same goal as the society'. In the case of the School Milk Programme, the common goal is children's health. Mr Zhang further pointed out:

> In China, students receive nine years of compulsory education. After nine years of milk consumption at school, a child would have the habit of drinking milk. . .This child will probably instill the concept of drinking milk to his own children . . .Generation by generation . . . there would be a great demand for the whole dairy industry.

Hence benefits accrue to all: the child, society and Tetra Pak. See Case Study 10.3.

TABLE 10.5   Tetra Pak Value Chain Activities

Supply chain operations	Activities
Raw material production/farm level	◆ Support for the training of farmers ◆ Equipment financing ◆ Food product development
Processing plant level	◆ Investment feasibility analyses ◆ Commercial financing of processing and packaging plants ◆ Management support and training ◆ Food product development ◆ Market development
Distribution level	◆ Support for market development
Consumers/school meal	◆ Wide support for the establishment of school feeding programmes ◆ Consumer information

CASE STUDY 10.3
Loftex: Certification and Measurement in Energy Efficient Operations

'Wal-Mart is our biggest customer. About 20% of our revenue is from Wal-Mart. We have other clients, domestic and overseas, but if we can meet the energy efficiency needs of Wal-Mart, we can meet the needs of other customers.' So says Mr. Jia Peili, a manager at Loftex, a large bath towel manufacturer in Binzhou City in Shandong Province, China.

At its 2008 supplier summit, Wal-Mart notified its suppliers that it would require a 20% reduction in energy consumption in all their operations. This coincided with a major energy-saving goal in the Chinese central government's eleventh Five Year Plan, between 2006 and 2010. In as much as Loftex is state-owned, the mandate was clear: cut energy use significantly and immediately. Within a year, the company had achieved that goal, winning Wal-Mart's Innovative Vendor of the Year award.

Over the past three decades, China's economic boom has created a strong export-oriented manufacturing sector, sometimes called the 'world factory'. At the same time, business and physical climates have changed across the world. Globalization has imposed increased competitive pressure, while environmental concerns have made carbon footprint, waste and pollution as important as bottom-line profitability. Buyers, governments and policy-makers have begun to pay attention to the environmental impact of manufacturing taking place in China. Businesses in China, particularly those that function as suppliers to the global market, are paying attention too.

Buyers seeking to reduce their carbon footprint are pushing their Chinese suppliers to cut energy use, because most of the energy produced and consumed in China comes from coal. For many western buyers, managing the Energy Efficiency (EE) of suppliers in China is a crucial element of their environmental sustainability initiatives.

While the Chinese central government considers EE an important economic development initiative, it also views it as a social issue. The worsening pollution and fatal accidents in coal mines have created a public health crisis and social unrest.

Energy management is often considered as part of quality management, because the energy management system, ISO 50001 (released in 2011), is an extension of ISO 9000 and ISO 14000. Nonetheless, there are factors beyond the influence of quality based decision-making. EE initiatives are unique. Since energy is not generally budgeted to specific activities, the incentive to save energy is low as compared to efforts to conserve materials. Energy-associated cost savings often do not provide direct financial incentives and paybacks. In addition, the environmental impact of energy consumption and waste is not obvious, as carbon emission is externalized to the society at large.

The transition from a planned economy to free-market state capitalism exposed Chinese companies to new pressures, including a growing awareness of sustainability and government demands to deal with environmental degradation. Export-oriented manufacturers often face competing demands from stakeholders: western buyers; government agencies at various levels; and NGOs that monitor trade, and social and environmental issues.

Finally, Chinese manufacturers are forced to deal with rationed electricity and 'brown-outs' which compel them to conserve electricity, especially in the summer, when electricity is diverted for residential use. The business landscape has changed in China, and energy efficiency has become a key consideration in operations. Loftex is a leading company, so the local government has high expectations regarding energy savings. One manager said the local government views their performance on energy savings as part of the district's political performance, and is pushing the company to do more.

When Wal-Mart notified its suppliers of its new requirements, Loftex responded quickly. Managers called for suggestions, which resulted in more than 190 ideas. They classified these as high-, middle- and low-cost. If an idea proved feasible, the low- and middle-cost changes moved forward promptly. High-cost undertakings were analysed most closely before implementation. While the expected payback period was two to three years, all green-lighted projects broke even within a year. By the end of 2009, Loftex had put 171 ideas into effect. The company also called in third-party analysts to conduct 'clean energy' audits, and arranged training workshops based on the results.

Several factors played into Loftex's rapid adoption of energy-saving ideas: company culture encourages everyone to feel responsible for performance, company image, China's energy policies, and soaring energy prices. Nonetheless, it was their largest customer's dictate that spurred them into action.

Many of the early changes were obvious, others less so. Overhead lighting fixtures had four tubes. However, workers had enough light with only three tubes, so one tube was removed from each fixture. Some equipment had lighted control panels or interior lights for maintenance purposes. These lights were generally left on, even when the machine was running and there was no need to access the controls or interior. This was just a bad habit, so employees began to turn off unnecessary lights. One employee called these ideas 'so simple, they would not be thought of in the past'. These simple ideas came from every part of the factory.

All the low- and no-cost changes are classified as 'management-based'. Implementation required little more than a go-ahead from a mid-level supervisor. Energy efficiency through management also includes employee training, focused on establishing work routines, work teams and reward systems to nurture environmental awareness. The objective is to reduce energy consumption and waste in existing production processes. The training is simple, emphasizing common sense practices such as stopping leaks and reducing non-productive use of electricity, water and steam. Employee education promotes frugality and waste reduction, which align with traditional Chinese virtues and are easily understood by migrant workers. EE through management is about people. Employees who feel connected to their managers and the company are more likely to participate in programmes that require their co-operation.

One other management-based change not only saved energy, but extended the life of machinery: retrofitting machines with power inverters to adjust motor speed. Motors often ran continuously at the maximum-delivery speed, which was rarely needed in practice. Installing an inverter in the controls allowed them to save up to 60% to 70% in energy-intensive applications.

High-cost energy efficiency efforts fall into two categories: technology and equipment upgrades, and process-oriented change. EE through equipment upgrades includes investing in newer and more energy efficient production equipment, for instance replacing boilers that burn heavy oil with more efficient electrical boilers.

Process-oriented EE initiative focuses on drastic changes and innovation to reduce energy needs. Process-oriented measures suggest several strategies, such as overhauling steam and heat supply systems to reduce energy consumption, reconfiguring process layout or integration of production processes to use less energy. Process-oriented EE activities require deep understanding of production processes and technical expertise.

Several stages of towel manufacturing take place at the Loftex plant. Piece dyeing passes the fabric through a high-temperature dye solution and then through rollers to distribute the dye and remove excess liquid. The fabric undergoes two separate wet treatments, followed by an antimicrobial finish. Finally, the fabric undergoes extensive tumble drying. The heat involved in both wet and dry treatments requires great energy expenditure. The carbon impact is also high.

(Continued)

Using the old process, the heat (i.e., energy) from dyeing was wasted. One of the engineering managers suggested heat exchangers that heat cold water while hot water is discharged. This relatively simple process reconfiguration means nearly all the energy is recovered. On the surface, process-oriented EE appears similar to equipment upgrades. However, it differs from equipment-focused EE initiatives on two counts. First, equipment-focused EE focuses on the energy savings potentials of stand-alone equipment, whereas process-oriented EE initiatives consider how the equipment fits into the overall needs and condition of the company. Managers incorporate production information (production schedule, volume) into process designs to reduce energy usage. Second, in process-oriented EE, a cascade of changes and improvements is possible when processes are combined. In another process-based initiative, engineers combined scouring, bleaching and dyeing in one container. These steps had previously taken place in three separate containers. The change cut hot water use by 40%.

The aggressive investment necessary to implement such sweeping changes derives from the administrative mandate: the command-and-control approach inherited from the planned economy era enables speedy decisions regarding capital investment. Managers talked about their EE actions as ways to achieve goals set out by the central government.

10.3.6 C.A.F.E. practices

To manage its complex supply chain, Starbucks implemented a formalized set of supplier development and certification processes called Coffee And Farmer Equity (or 'C.A.F.E.') practices (see Case Study 10.4). The non-profit organization Conservation International (CI) supports and evaluates the program in multiple ways, including through impact assessment. SCS Global Services, a third-party auditing firm, trains and oversees independent verification organizations responsible for assessing suppliers according to the C.A.F.E. Practices requirements (or 'Scorecard').

CASE STUDY 10.4

Starbucks: Stakeholder Management, Supplier Sourcing and Selection

Starbucks is the largest coffee-house company in the world, with over 20,000 locations in 64 countries. The company has always focused on high-quality products and treating its employees well. It pays above-market wages and provides health insurance to its American workers, something their competitors do not do. The company's rapid growth has made maintaining its supply of high-quality inputs (generally agricultural products) a top priority. Because it sources from developing counties, Starbucks faces close scrutiny for its suppliers' labour and environmental practices. Its supply chain is made up of many small suppliers in 26 countries. There is no clearly-defined tiered structure. Some suppliers are vertically integrated; they grow crops and handle processing, sorting, grading, packaging and shipping. But most only handle some of these processes, and Starbucks must oversee them all.

An evaluation checklist of C.A.F.E. practices rates farmers, processors, farmers/ processors and suppliers according to these criteria, awards points for compliance, and sets minimum and preferred point totals. Table 10.6 lists C.A.F.E. practices criteria.

Starbucks does not simply push higher operating expenses on its suppliers. Farmers with high overall scores are eligible for a one time strategic premium. Social responsibility standards include several 'zero tolerance' categories, which closely follow SA 8000 provisions *(refer to Table 10.3).*

TABLE 10.6 C.A.F.E. Practices Evaluation Checklist

Economic accountability	
Incentives for sustainability	Economic transparency
	Equity of financial reward
Financial viability	Financial viability
Social responsibility	
Hiring practices and employment policies	Minimum/living wage
	Overtime
	Freedom of association/collective bargaining
	Vacation/sick leave regulation
	Child labour/discrimination/forced labour (zero tolerance)
Worker conditions	Access to housing, water and sanitary facilities
	Access to education
	Access to medical care
	Access to training, health and safety
Environmental sustainability – coffee growing	
Protecting water resources	Watercourse protection
	Water quality protection
Soil resources	Controlling surface erosion
	Improving soil quality
Conserving biodiversity	Maintaining coffee shade canopy and natural vegetation
	Protecting wildlife
	Conservation areas and ecological reserves
Management and monitoring	Pest and disease management and reducing chemical use
	Farm management and practices

(Continued)

TABLE 10.6 *(Continued)*

Economic accountability	
Environmental sustainability – coffee processing	
– wet milling	
Water conservation	Minimizing water consumption
	Reducing wastewater impacts
Waste management	Operations/beneficial reuse
Energy use	Energy conservation/impacts
– dry milling	
Waste management	Operations/beneficial reuse
Energy use	Energy conservation/impacts

Source: C.A.F.E. Practices Generic Evaluation Guidelines (2004, November 9).

In 2012, 90% of Starbucks coffee (over 222 million kilos) had been verified by C.A.F.E. practices. By 2015, Starbucks goal is that 100% of the coffee will be verified or certified, either through C.A.F.E. practices, Fairtrade or another audit system. These practices have costs, but also significant short- and long-term benefits for farmers, suppliers, and the company. Starbucks has mitigated the environmental and social impact of farming and improved the livelihood of its growers.

10.3.7 In-store operations

In spite of its successful supply chain practices, Starbucks faces challenges in retail operations. Retail locations are leased, making it difficult to improve energy efficiency. Even seemingly simple changes run into roadblocks. Cups are regulated as food containers, where strict rules apply to material reuse. So it took great efforts to introduce a cup with even a small amount of reclaimed content. Starbucks began using the new paper cups, with 10% recycled content, in 2004. They were the first food containers ever to incorporate recycled material, winning an award from the US National Recycling Coalition. In 2004, Starbucks also shrank the paper napkins and rubbish bags used in stores, decreasing solid waste production. In 2014, Starbucks ranked number 11 on the EPA's overall national list of green power purchasers and fifth on retail operations.

Before 2009, the company had used a system with continuously-flowing water to rinse utensils. Though it wasted as much as 27 million litres a day, the system was required by some health codes. In 2009, it introduced a new system that eliminated the continuous flow, but met health requirements. Starbucks estimates it saves up to 680 litres of water each day, in every store.

In 2004, workers at a Manhattan Starbucks organized a union. They complained that $7.75 an hour was not a living wage in New York City and that the lack of guaranteed weekly hours made their lives precarious. Twelve workers submitted union cards to the National Labor Relations Board (NLRB), requesting an election to certify the union. Starbucks appealed, the NLRB agreed to review the appeal, and the union withdrew the petition. According to the company, the withdrawal was due to a lack of interest. The efforts to organize the Starbucks Workers Union continue to this day at Starbucks locations around the world.

Starbucks has enjoyed dramatic growth and high margins for over a decade. In addition, it has implemented sound environmental practices to manage its supply chain. But regulatory constraints make similar advances on the retail side difficult. So the inbound chain has become more sustainable while the overall environmental impact of the outbound chain is increasing.

Summary

Each of the four cases in this chapter touches on several topics within the larger subject of sustainable business practices.

Desso, a long-established company, recreated itself by embracing a new business paradigm, based on examples set by natural cycles and processes.

It worked with architects, regulators and customers to prove the viability of the concepts of closed-loop supply chains and Cradle-to-Cradle® business practices. It was among the first companies to achieve C2C® certification.

Tetra Pak was an established company before it entered China. Its main product was a packaging system for a product almost no one there used. It arrived with two big missions:

◆ To create a customer base for its product.
◆ To build a green supply/recycling chain for its product.

To establish its market Tetra Pak worked with stakeholders at every level of society and government, including local farmers, businesses, educational institutions, trade associations and regional dairies. Responding to these stakeholders and following its own path, the company essentially created an industry from the ground up, and followed by ensuring that it could maintain its business sustainably by introducing a recycling industry and infrastructure.

Loftex received mandates from its two most influential stakeholders to reduce energy consumption: its largest customer and the central government of China. The company embraced the challenge and undertook both incremental and large-scale systemic changes in its operations, surpassing its goals in subsequent years. By upholding the principles of ISO 50001, it is likely to extend its success.

Starbucks began as an environmentally and socially conscious company. Then it rapidly grew to global proportions. Facing the question of how to stay green while maintaining growth and quality, the company turned to its suppliers: rather than increasing pressure, it pushed profits upstream to suppliers by paying more for beans from the most sustainable farms. In so doing, it enlisted those suppliers as strongly-committed stakeholders as well as farmers. Starbucks continues to maintain its high quality and enjoy the cachet of providing a premium product sustainably.

QUESTIONS FOR CLASS DISCUSSION

1. How do the companies approach each dimension of the triple bottom line?
2. Who are the various stakeholders in each company? How do the companies interact with their stakeholders?
3. What are the similarities and differences between roles that different stakeholders play from country to country and industry to industry?

References

McDonough, W., & Braungart, M. (2010). *Cradle to cradle: Remaking the way we make things*. New York: MacMillan.

Mitchell, R. K., Agle, B. R., & Wood, D. J. (1997). Toward a theory of stakeholder identification and salience: Defining the principle of who and what really counts. *Academy of Management Review*, 22(4), 853–886.

11 Marketing: Sustainability Marketing: Building Relationships for One Planet Living

Ken Peattie and Frank-Martin Belz

'If you can shift your thinking away from merely selling and into building trust instead, even if it costs you a few bucks in profit, you'll begin to see opportunities you never imagined once you understand what it means to 'wow' that customer by giving them more than they expected.'

Chris Zane (*Reinventing the Wheel: The Science of Creating Lifetime Customers*, 2011)

Marketing is the Devil.

Billy Bob Thornton

LEARNING OUTCOMES

The aim of this chapter is to:

1. Outline the evolution of the relationship between marketing and sustainability.

2. Frame the concept of sustainability marketing as both a natural extension of underlying trends in marketing thought and a challenge to the conventional dominant marketing management paradigm.

3. Explore a new sustainability orientated framing of the Marketing Mix concept to illustrate how sustainability marketing requires alternative approaches to key marketing ideas and creates a number of practical challenges.

4. Demonstrate how socially and environmentally responsible companies are creating innovative approaches to marketing that can transform markets, influence consumer behaviour and generate competitive advantage through greater sustainability.

Introduction

The discipline of marketing has been cast as both villain and potential saviour in the story of society's struggle to achieve a more sustainable approach to its systems of production and consumption. Although marketing traditionally seeks to persuade people to consume, it can be applied to develop more sustainable options for consumers and to encourage them to choose and adopt them. A trip to any supermarket will reveal an array of success stories for sustainability marketing, including organic and local food, low-energy light bulbs and appliances, concentrated and environmentally benign detergents, packaging recycling initiatives, and probably a few electric and hybrid vehicles in the car park. However, the question remains as to whether conventional marketing approaches have the ability to deliver substantive progress towards a One Planet society, or whether we need to rethink marketing itself.

Sustainability and Marketing – Strange Bedfellows?

Marketing is one of the most powerful forces on the planet. Applying the philosophy and tools of marketing has allowed companies to generate competitive advantage and grow their markets across international boundaries, and to build ever-closer relationships with their customers in order to maintain their loyalty (and, some would argue, their propensity to consume). Although rooted in commerce, marketing has been adopted in a wide range of contexts within society so that our public services, our politicians, our cultural heritage and our societal values are increasingly marketed to us. The critics of marketing see it as primarily focused on driving global consumption and resource use to go ever further beyond the sustainable limits of our planet and its ecosystems. Marketing's supporters point out that there is nothing about marketing as either a business philosophy or a business process that is inherently geared towards the unsustainable exploitation of resources. Whatever one feels about marketing, it is undeniably crucial in promoting a One Planet business philosophy. Marketing's role as the interface with the customer means that it has a central role in ensuring that innovative new products are developed to meet customer wants and needs, and that their benefits are effectively communicated to customers. Marketing also plays a crucial role in developing strategies for pricing, packaging and distribution. Whilst the former is important for customer acceptance, the latter two represent important contributions to the ecological footprint of businesses through the generation of waste and carbon emissions.

The move towards a One Planet economy will require novel approaches to meeting customer needs in many markets, new systems of production and consumption to emerge and prosper, and consumers to be willing to live and consume differently, and in some cases, consume less. A transition to a sustainable economy will not happen unless more sustainable lifestyles, products and services, and even the concept and benefits of sustainability itself, are marketed effectively to us. Some of those who champion sustainability, and who are concerned with the extent that marketing (and particularly commercial advertising as one of its tools) seems geared to stoking ever-increasing levels of consumption, tend to think of 'sustainability marketing' as an oxymoron. The reality is that well-intentioned attempts to launch new and more sustainable businesses, products, services and government policies have frequently floundered because they have been poorly matched to the needs and concerns of consumers and citizens. Successfully blending marketing principles and practices with sustainability concerns and the need to move towards a One Planet economy and society is a significant challenge, not least because it goes against the grain of much of the marketing discipline's conventional world view and values. However, unless we are willing and able to create, teach and practise a more sustainability orientated approach to marketing, making progress towards more sustainable systems of consumption and production will be very difficult.

From 20th to 21st Century Marketing

Marketing was one of the great success stories of the 20th century. The literal use of the word 'marketing', for the taking of products to a physical market to sell them, has been commonplace for hundreds of years. It was only in the early 20th century that it emerged as a formalized set of business practices and an academic discipline. Initially marketing had a focus on the development and selling of products, particularly in relation to distribution and retailing. Gradually, as the science of market research evolved, the data it provided, particularly when interpreted using the developing discipline of psychology, was exploited to gain insights into the motivations and behaviour of customers. By the 1950s the 'marketing philosophy' had emerged, which sought to orientate the entire business around the guiding principle of researching, understanding and meeting the wants and needs of customers. Doing this better than the competition became recognized as the route to profitability and long-term success.

During the 1950s the notion of a 'marketing mix' of key variables that the marketer has at their disposal in order to try and meet their customers' needs and expectations became the subject of much discussion. This was crystallized in 1960 with McCarthy's famous categorization of the key marketing mix variables into the 'Four Ps' of Product, Price, Place (referring to distribution) and Promotion. Once marketing research allowed a company to understand the customer and the marketing environment, a strategy could be developed for the effective targeting of a customized mix of these marketing variables at specific segments of the market.

Although by the late 1970s all the core components of what was often termed 'modern marketing management' thinking were in place (Bartels, 1988), the evolution of marketing thought and practice continued throughout the final decades of the 20th century and beyond. Partly this reflected continuing changes in the marketing environment, particularly the increasing globalization of companies, products and consumer tastes, and the rise of online technologies as a means of doing business and as a medium for marketing. The continuing evolution also reflected a fragmentation of marketing as it split into a variety of subdisciplines. Services marketing, tourism marketing, bank marketing, non-profit marketing, political marketing and arts marketing are just some of the subtypes of marketing that spun out from the core discipline. Another important marketing subdiscipline that emerged from the 1970s onwards was social marketing, the application of marketing principles and practices to promote behaviour change for societal good (Kotler & Zaltman, 1971). Although initially dominated by health care applications, social marketing has expanded more recently to include the promotion of a wide range of pro-social and pro-environmental behaviours, which represent important aspects of a sustainable lifestyle (Peattie & Peattie, 2011).

A more fundamental split was between consumer marketing, aimed at individuals and households, and industrial and organizational marketing in which other businesses or organizations represented the customer. As organizations such as companies or branches of government themselves became more committed to sustainability strategies, so their purchasing practices and behaviours as corporate or organizational customers began to incorporate sustainability concerns in their purchasing criteria and relationships with suppliers. A core part of retailer Marks and Spencer's Plan A sustainability strategy is a Fair Partner programme of initiatives aimed at improving working standards, education, opportunities, health and financial well-being of the people and communities within their supply chains. The sustainability marketing agenda has largely been led by consumer-focused manufacturers and retailers, and therefore this chapter concentrates on consumer marketing. However, there are also considerable efforts being made to develop and research sustainability orientated marketing philosophies and practices in business-to-business and organizational markets (for more details see Sharma *et al.*, 2010).

11.0 Sustainability and Marketing: An Evolving Relationship

In the latter part of the 21st century, two particularly strong challenges to the dominant marketing paradigm emerged. The first challenge was symptomatic of the disconnection between existing marketing practices, and the ecological and social realities of the wider marketing environment. This disconnect led to the emergence of macro-marketing as a subdiscipline that sought to address and integrate concerns about the social and environmental impacts of marketing activity and the relationships between markets, regulation and social welfare. In contrast to conventional micro-marketing that focused on the marketing efforts of individual companies, macro-marketing sought to systematically consider the social implications of whole industries or shared marketing practices with an emphasis on the (often unintended) impacts on environmental quality and societal welfare (Hunt, 1981). This 'big picture' view of marketing has, however, remained a field of academic interest for a specialist few, whilst mainstream marketing scholarship has become increasingly focused on the discipline's technical minutiae (Wilkie & Moore, 2003).

The perceived disconnection between marketing as it was taught and practised, and the social and ecological realities of the markets which firms operated within, also led to attempts to promote new types of marketing that were environmentally, ethically or socially orientated. The notion of societal marketing first emerged in the 1970s as an attempt to encompass broader social and ethical concerns in the development of marketing strategies alongside the demands of addressing the customer's needs and competitive pressures (Crane & Desmond, 2002). Societal marketing broadly reflected the logic of corporate social responsibility extended into marketing as a function.

In the mid-1970s the first wave of environmentally orientated marketing ideas also emerged as 'ecological marketing' (Hennion & Kinnear, 1976). This focused on those industries perceived as making the largest contribution to the overuse of resources and the generation of pollution and waste, including the oil, car and chemicals industries. It also introduced new ideas such as that of the 'responsible consumer' who differed from the traditional notion of consumers as people out to maximize the benefits and value that they could enjoy, and instead were interested in moderation and restraint (Fisk, 1974). This early ecological marketing concern was strongly driven by the oil crises and resource shortage concerns of the early 1970s. As concerns about oil receded, so did marketing's interest in the environment.

In the mid-1980s a fresh wave of environmental revelations and concerns surfaced and were reflected in the influential *Brundtland Report* (WCED, 1987) and the first Earth Summit in Rio. This rekindled marketers' interest in the environment leading to a wave of environmental concern within marketing that was characterized by a number of labels (often used interchangeably) including 'eco', 'environmental', 'green' and 'ethical'. This second era differed from the ecological marketing of the previous decade in several ways. It encompassed a much broader range of environmental issues, and saw a greater intertwining with health and social issues as appreciation grew of how global poverty in particular was a key driver of environmental degradation in many ecologically important regions. Perhaps the easiest way to understand this era is as a mixture of environmentally inspired 'eco-marketing' and socially inspired 'ethical marketing' coming together under a 'green marketing' agenda (much as the green political agenda embraces the social and environmental).

Green marketing applied to a far wider range of industries than the earlier era, going beyond the obviously polluting and resource-intensive sectors. The emergence of markets for eco-tourism holidays and ethical banking saw service industries entering the green marketing arena. Green marketing also differed from ecological marketing in the extent to which consumer concern about environmental and social issues, which was clearly visible from marketing research data, could provide opportunities for firms to differentiate their offerings on the basis of superior socio-environmental performance in the search for competitive advantage. Instead of pressure for better environmental performance being seen as a threat that might compromise competitiveness, it was recognized that it could spark innovations, resource efficiencies and consumer interest with the potential to boost competitiveness (Porter & van der Linde, 1995). Perhaps the most visible manifestation came in the retail section where the mainstream supermarkets began to compete on the basis of their environmental credentials and specialist retailers such as Body Shop became increasingly global and visible brands.

The Green Marketing era was characterized by the rapid proliferation of green consumer guides across markets and countries, and by the attention focused on a relatively small selection of iconic green companies and brands, and the entrepreneurs behind them (with Body Shop, Ben & Jerry's and Patagonia being three of the better known). It was also notable for the widespread use of environmental claims and imagery in advertising by all manner of businesses, sometimes with little connection to the environmental merits of the products being advertised. All this activity reflected attempts to integrate socio-environmental concerns into existing marketing thinking and practices, more than any attempt to change the marketing paradigm to make it substantively more sustainable. The notion that environmental concerns were not simply a threat to businesses, but had the potential to act as a source of differentiation and competitive advantage was an important step forward. It resulted in many successful niche strategists competing on a platform of social and environmental excellence, and it increased the sensitivity of larger companies to the need to be perceived as good corporate citizens and to avoid negative headlines linked to social or environmental impacts.

The second fundamental challenge to the marketing mainstream came from within the discipline, with commentators becoming critical of marketing thinking and practices and their failure to evolve to reflect the changing realities of the commercial environment. In particular it was argued that marketing was too rooted in the past and to a business logic geared to the marketing of tangible products and the individual commercial transactions that their purchase represented. Much of this criticism was encapsulated in Christian Grönroos's (2007) book, *In Search of a New Logic of Marketing*. It began with a chapter entitled *Marketing – A Discipline in Crisis*, which argued that marketing was in danger of ossifying and becoming less influential and relevant within companies because of a failure to evolve. As Grönroos phrases it: 'Mainstream marketing continues to be orientated towards doing something **to** customers, instead of seeing customers as people **with whom** something is done.' He proposes instead a vision of marketing as a process of managing relationships with customers rather than of facilitating transactions with them. This shifts the emphasis away from the selling of products to customers, and instead concentrates on the process of interacting with and delivering value, in order to build long-term relationships with customers.

11.1 Sustainability Marketing: Marketing for the 21st Century

To progress towards a genuinely more sustainable form of marketing, we would suggest that it is a logical progression from the pressures that conventional mainstream 'modern' marketing faces, both externally, as reflected in the growth in eco-marketing and ethical marketing, and from within the discipline, with the growing emphasis on relationship marketing. To contribute to sustainability and a shift to a One Planet economy, the next step in marketing's development is to merge those two sets of challenging ideas to create a new concept of 'sustainability marketing' as set out in Figure 11.1.

Sustainability marketing involves building and maintaining sustainable relationships with customers, society and the natural environment (Belz, 2006). It shares the long-term value orientation of relationship marketing, as opposed to conventional marketing's short-term transaction and profit focus. The transition to sustainability marketing in part involves the integration of socio-environmental issues and criteria with

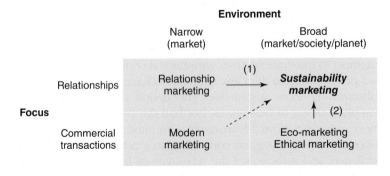

FIGURE 11.1 Towards a New Concept of Sustainability Marketing. *Source:* Belz and Peattie, 2012, p. 17.

conventional marketing thinking and processes. Therefore it requires their integration with the articulation of marketing values, the conduct of marketing research, the segmenting of markets and the targeting of customers, the setting of marketing goals and the development of marketing strategies.

The process of making conventional marketing practices and processes more sustainable is particularly visible in efforts to make key marketing processes and resources more energy and resource efficient. Such changes can provide 'win-win' benefits of the type outlined by Porter and van der Linde (1995), without any radical changes to marketing technologies, processes or customer relationships. One area for such changes is through packaging reduction and recycling. Packaging is both a major contributor to municipal waste (20%–36% across EU countries), and an important aspect of marketing through its roles in protecting products, acting as a medium for labelling information and helping to make products eye-catching, attractive and convenient for consumers. Reducing packaging allows marketers to save money and resources, and demonstrate environmental concern, without impacting on the nature of the core product or consumer experience. HP in France replaced its disposable packaging for notebook computers with a readymade carrying case (made from recycled material). This cut packaging material by 97% whilst providing the consumer with the additional benefit of a useful case. Similarly in product distribution, companies are striving to improve their efficiency in order to reduce both costs and carbon emissions. French retailer Nature & Découvertes improved their shipping and transport efficiencies by better routing, eliminating empty return journeys for trucks and optimizing vehicle loading. This reduced the distance travelled by their products by 22% over four years whilst the volume of goods moved increased by almost 30%.

Taking marketing beyond improving the eco-efficiency of existing practices to create a genuine transformation towards sustainability will require some different and innovative thinking on the part of marketing managers and scholars in four key areas:

1   Treating socio-ecological problems as a starting point of the marketing process, not as a set of externalities or constraints.
2   Understanding consumers and their behaviour more holistically.
3   Reconfiguring the marketing mix.
4   Appreciating and utilizing the transformational potential of marketing activities and relationships.

11.1.1 Socio-Ecological Problems as a Starting Point for Marketing

The conventional starting point for marketing thinking and practices has traditionally been the consumer and the notion of consumer sovereignty often encapsulated in the slogan 'The customer is King'. The marketing orientated business seeks to understand the wants and needs of the consumer through market research, and use this understanding to create desirable and affordable offerings for their target market. Although it may be well understood that the creation, marketing, use and disposal of such offerings will have significant negative socio-environmental consequences, many of these have historically been treated as 'externalities' and therefore not reflected in the prices paid by the consumer. Therefore the price of a new car will not include provision for all of the costs associated with the environmental legacy of mining ores for the metals in the car, the contribution to carbon emissions and climate change, the toll of deaths and injury from traffic accidents on the road, or even any potential health implications for the driver through in-car exposure to pollutants or the promotion of a more sedentary lifestyle. The assumption is that such external costs will be met by the taxes paid to governments by consumers, citizens and companies, although in practice many such external costs go unmet and in doing so drive the sustainability crisis. Traditionally however, unless a socio-environmental impact linked to production and consumption directly concerns consumers and influences their behaviour, or creates a strategic disadvantage or advantage in relation to competitors, it has been of little interest to marketers. Socio-environmental issues, where they have been considered at all, have typically been treated as a set of constraints, which limits what a company can and cannot do in its search for customer satisfaction. There are some problems with this perspective:

1   It gives priority to the rights and interests of the current customer over those of other (and future) people and species unquestioningly, simply on the basis that the customer wants something which is legally available and can afford to pay for it. Marketing as a profession emphasizes its positive societal contribution in delivering customer satisfaction. However, the dissatisfaction generated amongst all those who, for example, are exposed to the advertising of a desirable product, but cannot afford to purchase it, is never weighed against the satisfaction of paying customers.

2   By conceptualizing people narrowly as 'consumers', it ignores their interests in other roles. A car-buyer and driver may also be a parent, pedestrian and cyclist with a wider stake in how cars are used within their community. The notion of people as consumers also allows the satisfaction of peoples' wants and needs to be prioritized over their welfare. This is graphically illustrated by the marketing of cigarettes, a product that will ultimately kill its consumer (if nothing else does first).

3   It conceptualizes 'the customer' as a single entity with a set of common interests and a unified will that can be obeyed, not as a heterogeneous group whose members have multiple and potentially conflicting wants.

4   By envisaging social and ecological problems simply as constraints, or as limits to what can be achieved economically, it prioritizes short-term economic gain over long-term viability. Eco-footprinting data shows that collectively humankind's production and consumption behaviours are already exceeding the planet's bio-capacity and degrading the ecosystem services on which our welfare depends *(see Chapter 2)*. By the time the ecological limit on a particular economic activity is understood and proven through research data, that limit has typically already been exceeded and therefore further lowered.

5   The lack of attention to the long-term consequences of consumption may ultimately collectively disadvantage all consumers. The long-term impact of current consumption and production activities may include a destabilization of global climate systems that effectively disadvantages all citizens including consumers.

Making marketing more sustainable will be difficult if we continue to treat the customer and their wants and needs as the sole focus of marketing, and socio-environmental problems as part of the range of constraints on what the marketer can accomplish. This abstracts the consumer and their interests from the social and environmental context in which they live, and absolves the customer and the company from responsibility for the consequences of their consumption and production behaviours in a way that ignores both morality and long-term viability. The alternative is to make the starting point for marketing processes a balanced consideration of the customer and their wants and needs, and the socio-ecological problems related to the relevant production and consumption system. This can be achieved by undertaking socio-ecological life cycle assessments (LCA) of all the stages of a product's life from material sourcing and production (including down the supply chain), to purchase, use and disposal. Figure 11.2 represents a simplified environmental impact matrix for coffee as a product by employing life cycle assessment.

Gathering such information gives any company a sound basis on which to make decisions about managing the sustainability of its offerings, and on which to communicate with consumers. Timberland, for example, have led their industry by producing 'nutrition style' labelling for its footwear detailing a range of environmental impacts linked to the production of each item.

Emphasizing the socio-environmental impacts also allows for the introduction of the principle of 'consumer social responsibility' as a corollary to corporate social responsibility. Although this goes against the conventional concept of consumer sovereignty, there is growing evidence that consumers do recognize that they have

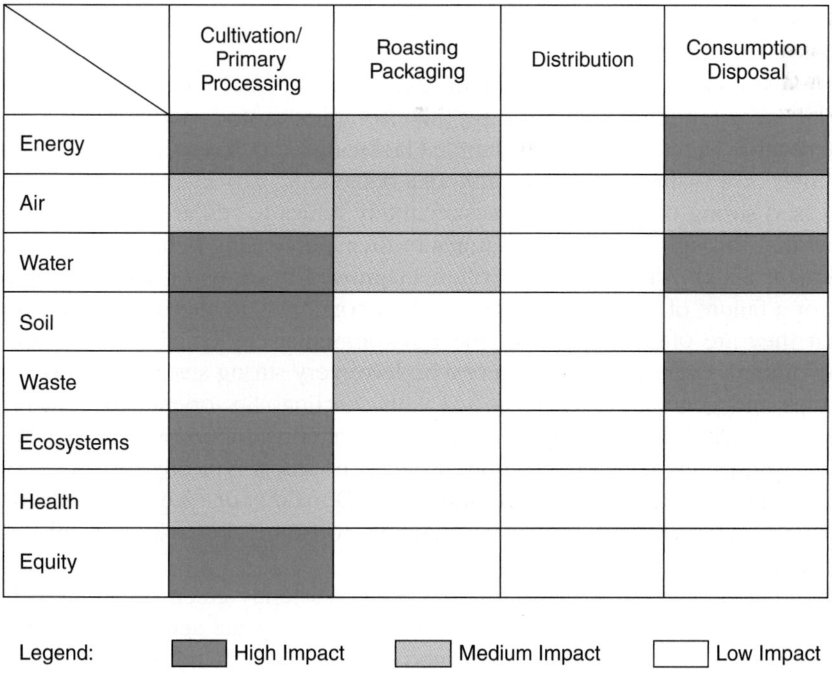

	Cultivation/ Primary Processing	Roasting Packaging	Distribution	Consumption Disposal
Energy	High	Medium		High
Air	Medium	Medium		Medium
Water	High	Medium		High
Soil	High			Medium
Waste	Medium	Medium		High
Ecosystems	High			
Health	Medium			
Equity	High			

Legend: ■ High Impact   ▨ Medium Impact   □ Low Impact

FIGURE 11.2 Lifecycle Impact Matrix for Coffee. *Source:* Belz, 1995, p. 37.

power within markets and therefore have some responsibility for the generation of problems such as climate change and for contributing toward solutions (Wells *et al.*, 2010). They are also supportive of producer and retailer strategies of choice editing, the removal of the most damaging products from the assortment offered to consumers, even though this also goes against the conventional wisdom of maximizing consumer choice. The intersection of socio-ecological problems and consumer wants creates the context for sustainability marketing and can also create significant new market opportunities for innovative companies.

11.1.2 A Holistic Approach to Understanding Consumers

The conventional marketing response to growing socio-environmental concern has been to seek out and identify specific 'green consumer' or 'ethical consumer' segments within particular markets. The logic being that if those consumers with the strongest social and environmental concerns can be identified, a specific marketing mix can be developed to appeal to them, preferably at a premium price. The late 1980s and 1990s witnessed a substantial research effort that sought to identify and segment the green consumer on a whole range of different bases (Straughan & Roberts, 1999). Many of the early efforts concerned demographic factors of age, sex, educational attainment, social class and income. Later efforts focused more on psychosocial factors such as perceived consumer effectiveness (the extent to which people felt they could make a difference), environmental knowledge, attitudes towards sustainability issues and people's sense of social identity and self perception. The most consistent result from all this research effort was inconsistency. Factors shown to be significant in influencing consumer behaviour in one study were found to be insignificant in another. The sheer variety of the range of potential influences on sustainable consumer behaviour meant that models of behaviour that sought to be realistic were rendered untestable by their complexity, and models simple enough to be testable were unrealistically simple (Jackson, 2004). There also emerged strong evidence of a 'values-action' or 'attitudes-behaviour' gap in that consumers who expressed strong concerns about sustainability issues to researchers often failed to follow that through in terms of changes to their purchasing behaviour (Kollmuss & Agyeman, 2002). Although this is often diagnosed in terms of social acceptability bias, or a failure of consumers to act on their concerns, an alternative interpretation is that they are often sceptical of the environmental credentials of what they are being offered. Even those consumers who have very strong sustainability orientated attitudes and generally back these up with sustainability orientated consumption behaviours, will still tend to have certain areas of consumption where they will not make sustainability based consumption decisions (most typically for use of private cars, foreign travel and meat consumption). McDonald *et al.* (2012) christened these consumers who were models of sustainable consumer behaviour in all respects except their consistency as 'exceptors'.

The logic behind the troubled hunt for the consistently green consumer is flawed in several ways. It overlooks a point made nearly 40 years ago by Kardash (1976) that we are all environmentally concerned consumers in that, if we are offered two products that are identical, except that one has a better environmental performance than the other, everyone (barring a contrary few) would choose the environmentally superior product. Therefore the key to understanding consumer behaviour in relation to sustainability concerns lies in understanding those factors that make more sustainable offerings different to their conventional rivals. Where more sustainable goods and services are more expensive (which may be unavoidable when they are internalizing the socio-environmental costs treated by competitors as externalities), or less convenient to use, consumers' willingness to buy them may be compromised.

Other research suggests that circumstantial factors relating to time, infrastructure and access can influence key consumption and lifestyle decisions linked to shopping, travel behaviours and the management of our homes. Behaviours linked to travel, household management and food preparation and storage are more driven by habit than by conscious decision-making. Overall the extent to which environmental knowledge and values actually drive consumer behaviour is relatively limited. This is one reason why strategies that have sought to encourage sustainable consumer behaviour through messages that promote environmental knowledge and values have generally had limited success. Those strategies that have tended to succeed are those in which the company tells a credible and compelling story that connects the sustainability attributes of a product to values that matter to customers, with the minimum compromise asked of them in terms of cost and convenience (Ottman et al., 2006).

Another shortcoming in the conventional research into sustainable consumer behaviour is the dominance of purchasing (or often purchase intention) as a specific consumer activity, even though consumption encompasses a range of behaviours that both precede and follow purchase. The importance of the moment of purchase when payment is made and ownership changes hands is obvious for economists and marketers, but from a social and ecological perspective the significance of a purchase often becomes clear only during the use and post-use phases of the consumption process. For example, for a typical European domestic dishwasher, 95% of its environmental impacts relate to the use phase (Otto, Ruminy & Mrotzek, 2006). In the context of sustainability, all the stages of consumer behaviour are important and the environmental responsibility of a consumer's car purchase will depend on how that car is driven, maintained and ultimately disposed of.

The traditional approach to understanding sustainable consumption is partly hampered by its focus on purchasing, but also by its emphasis on the motivations behind the behaviour of consumers rather than its consequences. A simple consumer behaviour that would promote a more sustainable economy would be a reduction in the consumption of meat, due to the intensity of resource inputs and greenhouse gas emissions linked to meat as a source of protein. A consumer adopting a vegetarian diet for ecological reasons would be considered a green consumer but someone doing it to save money, for religious reasons or because they don't particularly like the taste of meat, would not. Similarly a relatively affluent consumer who could afford to run a hybrid vehicle and travel to distant countries on eco-tourism trips would register as a green consumer due to their choices, whereas someone who could afford neither, would not.

For the marketing discipline to substantively move consumer behaviour towards sustainability, the hunt for the green consumer needs to be called off. Marketing a sustainability orientated product or service to a certain segment of a market, usually at a premium price, may make good short-term business sense, but it will contribute little to long-term sustainability. This will require mass markets in key sectors, such as housing, transport, food, energy and household equipment, to embrace more sustainable goods and services within the mainstream. It will also require a broadening of consumer research beyond the individual purchases of consumers to understand the sustainability of their lifestyles, their habits and how they live. Many of us consume, not just as individuals, but as part of a family or household, and the structure and nature of that household may have a greater influence on the sustainability of our lifestyles than the relationship between our socio-environmental concerns and our choices at the supermarket checkout. This is particularly the case with the growing trend towards single person households across much of Europe, which leads to much higher per capita energy and other resource consumption than shared households.

A final misconception about consumers is that it is only those in relatively affluent countries that are interested in more sustainable products, services and lifestyles. The 2014 National Geographic/Globescan 'Greendex' survey of consumer lifestyles across 18 major economies (http://environment.nationalgeographic.com/environment/greendex/) showed that the countries where environmental concern had increased most sharply between 2008 and 2014 were Brazil, Mexico, India and Argentina. These four countries, along with China, were also those with the highest proportion of consumers who, when given information about the environmental impacts of their lifestyles, then planned to make significant lifestyle improvements as a result. This contrasted with Japan, Sweden, Britain, Canada and Germany (countries traditionally associated with green consumerism), whose consumers were the least likely to respond by planning significant improvements. One explanation for this is that consumers in poorer countries are more likely to witness firsthand the social and environmental impacts of global consumption and production systems. Chinese and Indian consumers were those most likely to believe that environmental pollution was directly impacting their health. Another explanation is that for the consuming classes within these countries the 'consumer lifestyle' is newer and therefore less taken for granted or viewed as a right. Either way, consumer concern about sustainability issues is very much a global phenomenon.

Sustainability marketing requires a more holistic approach to understanding consumers, their consumption, their lifestyle, the motivations behind it and the socio-environmental consequences that go with maintaining it. Conventional mainstream marketing tends to reduce consumers to a handful of characteristics and wants, and abstract them from the rest of their lives, the rest of society and from the ecological systems that they ultimately depend on. As Eden *et al.* (2007) suggest, marketing research for sustainability needs to rediscover and get to know consumers as real and complex people, rather than treating them as superficial research constructs to make assumptions about.

11.1.3 Reconfiguring the Marketing Mix for Sustainability

Once a company has researched its market and developed an understanding of its rivals and the wants and lifestyles of consumers, it can develop a strategy to target the market and develop an advantage over competitors. That strategy is implemented through the development of a marketing mix of those variables that marketers can control and manipulate in order to win the custom and loyalty of their target market. McCarthy's (1960) four 'P' factors of Product, Price, Place and Promotion continue as the dominant mix model more than 50 years after its introduction. Despite many changes to the world and to marketing, and despite a range of criticisms levelled against the 4P mix, its simplicity and memorability have allowed it to survive.

Two of the criticisms levelled at the conventional mix are particularly important from a sustainability perspective. The first is that it is producer orientated, and therefore goes against the consumer orientation that should underpin the marketing discipline (Shaw & Jones, 2005). The notion of 'product' focuses us on what the company produces, not the benefits that the consumer enjoys. The 'price' (in most markets) is set by the producer according to the product's cost or what the producer believes the market will bear. The 'place' variable largely concerns distribution and retail and the logistics of getting the product to the consumer and the point of sale. 'Promotion' of the company and its product offering is self-explanatory, although in contemporary marketing even when the unidirectional label of promotion is used, it more often refers to 'communication' as a process. The other criticism is that McCarthy's 4P model was never intended to consider a wider range of stakeholders than customers, even when they are important to the marketing process (Silverman, 1995). As our appreciation of marketing strategy and the dynamics of consumer behaviour has extended, so has our understanding of the important role that a range of other stakeholders play in the development and execution of marketing strategies.

Given the twin challenges facing marketers of developing a greater focus on customer relationships and their management, and a need to harmonize marketing thinking and practices with the principles of sustainable development, we propose a new '4Cs' sustainability marketing mix (Belz & Peattie, 2012), below. This retains the simplicity and memorability of the original, but adopts a more genuine customer orientation.

11.2 From Products to Customer Solutions

The material goods and intangible services we purchase as consumers reflect what we perceive as solutions to a particular problem linked to a want or need. Status symbol purchases aside, we buy products for what they can do for us, not for what they are (the classic example being that although we might buy a drill, we are actually buying the ability to make holes). The advantage of envisaging what consumers purchase as a 'solution' rather than the more conventional view of a product as 'a bundle of benefits' is that it emphasizes the limitations of purchasing a product which solves one problem, whilst causing another (either for the consumer or for others). From a sustainability perspective, products and services need to address both customer problems and socio-ecological problems. So although in sustainability marketing we might be providing customers with products and services, remembering that they are solutions to particular problems too is also helpful in keeping us customer orientated. Positioning rechargeable batteries as economical and long-lasting as a solution to customer needs is more likely to be persuasive to customers than technical details about their environmental superiority (Ottman *et al.*, 2006).

Thinking in terms of customer solutions can allow a marketer to step outside the existing production/consumption system to offer something significantly different and more sustainable. A simple example relates to cars, since the benefit they provide is in terms of personal mobility; and it is access to, not ownership of, a car that provides this benefit. Therefore an obvious step towards a more sustainable solution for customers is to provide services based on access to shared cars instead of car purchase and ownership (see Case Study 11.1).

When considering the products and services that we provide to customers as solutions, defining what makes one 'sustainable' remains problematic. The answer ultimately depends upon the sustainability of the energy and material resources embedded within an offering, the social and environmental behaviours of all the companies within the supply chain behind it, how it is purchased and used, and what happens at the end of its life (if it is a tangible product). The absolute sustainability of a product will also depend upon the sustainability of the society within which it is produced and consumed, since ultimately a single component of a system is only as sustainable as the system that it is a part of. The most workable definition

---

CASE STUDY 11.1
Mobility CarSharing

Mobility is one of the pioneers of car sharing worldwide. It is a co-operative founded in 1997 and based in Lucerne (Switzerland), employing 180 people. The company offers a unique mobility solution to private and business customers: car sharing and combined mobility. Customers have access to a fleet of 2,600 cars at 1,300 locations all over Switzerland. At locations in urban areas there is a wide range of car types and models available in ten different categories: Electro, Budget, Micro, Economy, Combi, Comfort, Convertible, Fashion, Minivan and Transport. Customers choose the most suitable car according to their needs: smaller cars for singles, mid-sized cars for families, premium cars for businesspeople, fun and fashion cars for the weekend, and trucks for moving or transporting bulky goods. The cars can be booked by customers at any time from anywhere via phone or internet. Registered customers hold an electronic 'Mobility card' providing easy access to the cars and their onboard computers, which are connected to the Mobility centre via a Global Positioning System (GPS) that transfers the data.

Mobility CarSharing is a well-known brand with a high recognition rate among the Swiss population. It stands for first-class quality service in car sharing and guarantees accessibility, transportation, safety, tidiness and ecological concern. In co-operation with the Swiss rail and regional public transport companies, Mobility CarSharing offers mobility cards providing access to both car sharing and public transport. These are popular in urban areas and with commuters and are a unique solution to the mobility needs of some customer groups. In communication the simplicity of car sharing is emphasized to reach out to new customers: 'Mobility CarSharing: Quite simple. 1. Make a reservation, 2. Get access, 3. Drive, 4. Pay.'

Due to its unique offer and co-marketing with strategic partners like the Swiss railway, the growth of Mobility CarSharing has been impressive: between 1997 and 2012 the number of car sharers rose from 17,000 to 105,000. Even more important is the effect on other countries and companies by helping to inspire similar business models to emerge in most European countries and many North-American cities. Large multinational companies like Smart (as part of the Daimler group) have taken up the trend to offer Car2Go as a car sharing service as well.

Source: Belz and Peattie, 2012, pp. 174–175.

of sustainable products and services are those that offer satisfying solutions to customer needs and that offer significant improvements in social and environmental performance along the whole product life cycle in comparison to conventional or competing offers (Peattie, 1995). This definition emphasizes the following six characteristics (Belz & Peattie, 2012).

1 *Customer satisfaction*: if sustainable products and sustainable services do not satisfy customer needs, they will ultimately not survive in the market.

2 *Dual focus*: unlike purely environmental products, sustainable products have a dual focus that also includes socio-ecological aspects.

3 *Life cycle orientation*: sustainable products have to consider the whole life cycle from cradle to grave, i.e., extraction of raw materials, transportation, manufacturing, distribution, use, and post-use.

4 *Significant improvements*: sustainable products and sustainable services have to make a significant contribution to tackling (a) socio-ecological problems on a global level (macro level), or (b) specific socio-ecological problems linked to offerings identified and analysed using instruments of life cycle assessment, or (c) both.

5 *Continuous improvement*: sustainable products and services are not absolute measures, but are dependent of the state of knowledge, latest technologies and societal aspirations, which change over time. A product or service that meets customer needs and that has an extraordinary social and environmental performance today may be considered standard tomorrow. Thus, sustainable products and services have to be continuously improved regarding customer, social and environmental performances.

6 *Competing offers*: a product or service that satisfies customer needs and that provides environmental and social improvements may still lag behind competing offers. Thus, the offerings of competitors are yardsticks for improvements with regard to customer, social and environmental performances.

11.3 From Price to Consumer Cost

Everything that we buy has a monetary price, and from a rational economic perspective consumer behaviour reflects the perceived relationship between the benefits offered and the price paid. The concept of cost is applied to the producer, with their profit determined by the difference between the price paid and the costs incurred in getting their offering to the consumer. However, in many instances the consumer will weigh up other pros and cons related to a purchase beyond the monetary price, and these can encompass other elements of the consumption process beyond purchase. The notion of transaction costs is frequently used in economics to try to understand cost in a holistic way that recognizes non-monetary costs as well. A particular purchase might involve time and effort involved in researching options and getting to the point of sale, it might involve psychological costs for significant purchases in terms of worry, and if the item is a tangible and durable product like a car there may be costs linked to use, storage, maintenance, insurance and, at the end of its life, disposal.

In many markets more sustainable consumption can be encouraged through an emphasis on 'Total customer cost' as an alternative to price, which includes all the financial and non-financial transaction costs throughout the entire consumption process. Emphasizing the lifetime costs of particular solutions, rather than purchase price for products, provides opportunities to more effectively market innovative products and charging systems within some of the most important markets for sustainability such as personal transport and home ownership. One of the most visible markets where there has been a shift of emphasis from price to cost is in the marketing of low-energy light bulbs (see Case Study 11.2).

CASE STUDY 11.2

Philips 'Marathon': Saving Customer Cost through Long Life and Efficiency

Philips invented compact fluorescent bulb (CFL) technology in 1980 and has led the way in product refinement and market development ever since. Despite the advantages of the new lighting technology, such as extended lifetime, energy efficiency, and absence of heat emissions, consumers still preferred the traditional incandescent lamps for their brightness, instantaneousness and low price. Early generations of compact fluorescent light bulbs were big and bulky, forcing consumers to replace lampshades or get modification kits to make the bulbs fit some of their fixtures. Additionally, consumer dissatisfaction was caused by humming, delayed start, lack of 'dimmability', poor outdoor performance, poor light levels and colour rendition. In the 1990s, the penetration rates of CFL bulbs in the residential light market were generally disappointing, both in the US and Europe. In 1994 Philips made its first attempt to market a stand-alone CFL bulb. The product was branded EarthLight and was sold at a unit price of $15 (€10.80) versus $ 0.75 (€0.55) for incandescent bulbs. It rapidly gathered numerous public awards, but neither the awards nor the environmental benefits of the product persuaded mainstream consumers to buy the EarthLight. This situation made Philips reconsider its marketing approach in 1998. The first step was to find out through market research what was really important to consumers of light bulbs. As Steve Goldmacher,

Director of Corporate Communications for Philips Lighting in the US, explained, 'It turned out the environment wasn't their primary need. Environmental responsibility was the number four or five purchase criterion. Number one is that they wanted the bulb to last longer. Being green is wonderful, but no one wants to pay the extra nickle.' Another major problem uncovered was a high level of consumer confusion concerning CFL bulbs, especially regarding their expected lifetime.

The market research prompted Philips to react to the misunderstood consumer benefit and the consumer confusion by offering a whole series of new long-life light bulbs. Thus, it reintroduced the Earth-Light under the Marathon brand in 2000, underscoring its new 'super long life' and promising savings of over $20 (€14.40) in energy costs over its lifetime. The lifetime of the product was guaranteed, meaning that if a light bulb failed to last as long as Philips promised, the customer would be able to mail it back to the company for a refund. The market research had revealed that consumers wanted their light bulbs to have a traditional shape, so the new design of Marathon bulbs offered the look and versatility of incandescent light bulbs. To add credibility, the products were labelled with the US Environmental Protection Agency's Energy Star label. Within the new series, Marathon would be the top-line product family with a guaranteed life of five to seven years. Additionally, in 2000 Philips introduced Halogena as a middle-level product range with a guaranteed life of two years, and in 2002 DuraMax, as the entry-level product range with a guaranteed life of one year. This full-line concept would allow consumers to choose the ideal light bulb for different locations and needs. These measures, backed up by increasing sensitivity to rising utility costs and electricity shortages, led to an increase in sales of 12% in 2001 in an otherwise flat market. Due to the initial success, the full line concept has been adopted by Philips on a worldwide basis.

Source: Belz and Peattie, 2012, pp. 232–233.

11.4 From Place to Convenience

The conventional 'Place' mix variable tends to overemphasize the physical distribution of products, with conventional marketing texts focusing on the organization of distribution channels and the management of the relationships between producers and the intermediaries within them. Although this is an important operational element of marketing management, it makes little difference to the consumer providing the channel works as intended. The emphasis on the point of exchange (or the service encounter), like the emphasis on the price paid there, tends to again focus attention on purchase as an activity more than consumption as a total process encompassing the use and disposal stages. Also the conventional concept of a physical place in many markets is becoming increasingly irrelevant as elements of the consumption and production process, from purchase to customer support to product specification, move into an online environment.

From a consumer perspective, the key value that distribution efforts provide is convenience. Retailers and service providers bring together a range of goods and services in a single place with parking facilities or transport links in a way that is convenient. Whether seeking to get goods and services to consumers in stores, online, or delivered directly to their homes, the efforts of marketers are geared towards making their offerings convenient in terms of being widely available, easily accessible and convenient to access and use. Convenience is highly valued by consumers, particularly those who are cash rich/time poor, and it can be a key driver of behaviour and satisfaction. Convenience represents a challenge for sustainability marketers, since historically there has often been a trade-off between convenience and environmental performance (e.g., in the use of rechargeable batteries). While some commentators argue that successful marketing of sustainability solutions will depend on matching conventional products for convenience (Ottman *et al.*, 2006), others argue that our devotion to, and notion of, convenience may have to change (Shove, 2003).

The evolution of the retailing of sustainability orientated products saw them first emerge in specialist shops or via mail order that made them relatively inaccessible and therefore purchased only by highly motivated consumers. With the green marketing boom in the late 1980s and early 1990s mainstream retailers rapidly embraced products like organic food, recycled paper products, natural cleaning products and FairTrade coffee, making them much more conveniently accessible to consumers. Since then retailers' sustainability strategies have become increasingly sophisticated, with the introduction of energy-efficient stores, lower emission lorry fleets, packaging reductions, healthy and organic product ranges and a wealth of customer information. One of the best examples is the leading Swiss retailer Coop (see Case Study 11.3), which started its sustainability initiative and programme in the early 1990s.

One area where it will be important to facilitate consumer involvement through convenience is in product take-back strategies that aim to bring used product back into the value system for reuse, recycling or remanufacture. In some markets such as cars, electronics, packaging and batteries, Extended Producer Responsibility legislation may require companies to recover old product and packaging from consumers. In other markets there may be a compelling economic and environmental case for reclaiming old product (such as for recycled printer cartridges). Either way it requires both the establishing of reverse logistics systems to recover the material, and the building of consumer relationships and the provision of incentives to engage consumers with such systems.

CASE STUDY 11.3
Coop: Making Sustainability Convenient for Customers

Coop is the largest retailer in Switzerland and recognized as one of the sustainability leaders in retailing worldwide. Coop offers a wide variety of food and non-food products with a strong focus on sustainability. Coop Naturaplan is the best-known organic food brand in Switzerland. The sustainability retail brand was introduced in 1993, when Coop offered a basic assortment of certified organic food products. During the launch phase Naturaplan products were only offered in larger stores due to limited supplies. The market pull by the Swiss retailer led to an expansion of Swiss organic farming production capacity in the mid-1990s. Hence, Coop was able to offer its basic organic food assortment in all stores on a national level, making it widely available for Swiss consumers. In the second half of the 1990s Coop started launching numerous organic food innovations such as fresh ready-made organic salads and 'Bio-Rösti' potatoes, which offer high convenience in addition to ecological quality and health benefits. In 2013 Naturaplan celebrated its 20th birthday. The Naturaplan range by this time included over 1,600 items and was responsible for revenue of more than CHF800 million

(€650 million). Under the Naturafarm brand, Coop also stocks high-quality meat and egg products from animal-friendly, humane husbandry in Switzerland. The sales of this sustainability programme achieved around CHF450 million in 2012. The Coop Oecoplan includes products from the non-food and near-food segments with ecological value added (e.g., Fairtrade soccer balls, FSC-certified wooden products). The Coop Naturaline includes sustainable textile and cosmetic products at inexpensive prices. Put together, Coop offers a wide range of sustainable products in the areas of food and non-food, which are easy to obtain for Swiss consumers all over the country, including urban and rural areas. To acquire and enhance credibility, Coop co-operates with third parties and employs sustainability labels which are widely recognized. The 20 years of Coop's sustainability marketing strategy has made a wide range of more sustainable products easily accessible to consumers, simple to identify and find, and easy for them to understand and trust.

Source: Coop, 2014, www.coop.ch.

11.5 From Promotion to Communication

Contemporary marketers of all types are increasingly focused more on building good relationships with consumers rather than simply promoting products to them. This process may be even more important for sustainability marketers. Without effective communication it will be almost impossible to make consumers aware of sustainability solutions that have been developed, and how they will integrate with consumers' lifestyles and meet their needs. Sustainability solutions may require people to consume in different ways, to consider different types of product and service, and to take a longer-term and more multidimensional perspective in assessing their value. Effective communication to forge long-term relationships with consumers (that continue through use and post-use of the product) will also be crucial to ensure that a whole life cycle approach is taken to managing sustainable solutions.

The core components of marketing communication are the message and the medium. The traditional media available to marketers include advertising (including broadcast media, billboards and print), personal selling, exhibitions and trade shows, on-pack communication, sales promotion activity (including sampling, special offers, promotional pricing, contests, coupons and premiums), direct mail and public relations activity. More contemporary approaches also include online and mobile phone-based campaigns and experiential marketing centred on live events. The media message can seek to address one or more of a range of communication objectives that will be set according to the nature of the sustainability solution, the market it is intended for and the competitive situation it faces. Typical marketing communications objectives include:

1   Raising awareness of new products or services: public relations activity surrounding product launches or in-store sampling of new food products can be important in the effort to launch new products.

2   Informing consumers about the advantages of a particular solution they are offered, including its sustainability performance.

3   Persuading consumers to test, find out about or purchase a particular offering.

4   Rewarding customers through the offer of direct benefits in order to reinforce their loyalty or influence their behaviour.

5   Building relationships with consumers, particularly through online and interactive communication.

An important element of sustainability marketing communication is labelling, which is important in providing consumers with information about the socio-environmental performance of particular types of products and helping them to easily identify and choose sustainability solutions. In particular, third-party certified standards labels can be very important for building consumer confidence in the solution they are offered (Ottman *et al.*, 2006). Such labels can reflect the nature of the product itself (e.g., the US Energy Star label), or the production method (e.g., organic produce or carpets with the GoodWeave symbol, indicating the avoidance of child labour), the economic system underpinning production (such as FairTrade certified products) or the distribution method used (such as the airfreight labels for fresh produce introduced by retailers including Tesco and Marks and Spencer).

Despite some concerns about consumer confusion due to the proliferation of labelling schemes, the evidence suggests that consumers perceive them as adding value and will respond positively to them (D'Souza *et al.*, 2006).

One area in which conventional marketing and sustainability may intersect without truly integrating is through cause-related marketing (CRM). In CRM campaigns a company usually allies with a charitable cause in a joint promotion, which generates revenue for the charity through increased sales of specially-badged products. Although this can generate win-win benefits for both parties, such promotions also pose risks through bringing together very different types of organization with different priorities and cultures. Such campaigns allow companies to support sustainability-orientated causes through their marketing, but they depend on finding a cause that will strike consumers as a natural 'fit' and not as a cynical attempt to exploit a worthy cause. It may also raise questions amongst stakeholders about the company's sincerity if it supports an external cause without seeking to make its own business more sustainable.

Marketing communications can be a very challenging issue for sustainability marketers to get right for several reasons. Some communications media have inherent problems in relation to sustainability. The fact that direct mail is so often referred to as 'junk mail' indicates that its contribution to waste makes it a difficult medium through which to communicate a credible sustainability message. Sales promotion offers similarly are seen as trying to increase consumption levels in ways that can compromise sustainability efforts. This is particularly the case for the popular 'buy-one-get-one-free' type of offer, which when used for fresh food products can tend to lead to increased levels of food waste. This is one reason that the retailer Tesco switched some of its promotional offers to a 'buy-one-now-get-one-free-later' basis. It can also be difficult to communicate effectively about sustainability issues that are complex, multidimensional and subject to scientific uncertainty if your medium is a produce jar label that must also accommodate information on ingredients and potential allergy advice in multiple languages.

Advertising is the communication medium most readily associated with marketing, although the same challenges remain in trying to encapsulate a sustainability issue and the role an offering plays as a partial solution to it, using a one-page ad or a 30-second TV or radio slot that consumers will actually attend to. Advertising is also an element of marketing that has come in for particular criticism for its role in stoking material consumption to unsustainable levels, and in presenting unrealistic stereotypical images that can create alienation rather than consumer satisfaction (Pollay, 1986). Advertising's defenders see it as a 'mirror' that simply reflects existing societal values, whilst its critics point to mounting evidence that it can influence those values in a pernicious way (Alexander *et al.*, 2011).

Given the challenges of getting sustainable marketing communications right, it is perhaps unsurprising therefore that concerns about 'greenwashing' have escalated as the number of 'green' products and claims have increased. In their 2010 report on *The Sins of Greenwashing*, US environmental marketing firm TerraChoice studied 12,061 environmental claims in the marketing of more than 5,000 common US or Canadian consumer products. The number of product offerings on retailers' shelves being marketed as 'green' had grown by 73% compared to the previous year, and of the claims studied, only 4.5% avoided any or all forms of false or misleading claims. This was at least an improvement on the 2% found during the same exercise conducted in 2009, but it meant that over 95% of claims had elements that were vague, irrelevant, misleading, unsubstantiated or simply untrue.

It is through online media that the promise of one-way promotion evolving into two-way communication between the producer and the consumer may have the greatest scope to become a reality. The online environment provides opportunities to provide interested consumers with the full story behind the products and companies that they patronize and to interact with them. It provides unique opportunities to boost the credibility of sustainability marketing communication in the face of concerns about greenwashing (see Case Study 11.4).

Rather like Followfish, the sustainable clothing company Patagonia produces its own online 'Footprint Chronicles' which combines text, images and interviews in entertaining ways that allow consumers to understand the impact of specific products from design to delivery. This type of information makes the cradle-to-grave product life cycle transparent, and reduces the information asymmetries between producers and consumers, which can undermine consumer trust.

CASE STUDY 11.4
Followfish: Following the True Taste

Followfish is a niche player in the frozen fish market. It was founded in 2007 by a team of highly experienced and passionate fish vendors. The company offers a wide range of sustainable fish products. The organic fish products come from organic aquaculture, while the wild fish is captured according to the guidelines of the Marine Stewardship Council (MSC). All fish products are certified and labelled accordingly. In communication the company provides a special interactive feature on its packaging and website. By using a tracking code consumers can view in Google maps where the fish comes from, when it was caught, and how it was transported. This creates transparency and trust. In line with the brand name, consumers can literally or, better, digitally 'follow the fish'. The tagline 'Following the True Taste' has a double meaning: on the hand it refers to the freshness and great taste of the product, on the other it refers to the digital tracking. Aside from the tracking code and packaging Followfish mostly uses the internet and social media in communication, following a kind of

guerrilla marketing approach, which is unconventional and interactive. One of the recent campaigns was 'TunaTunes', in which a guitar maker created a ukelele out of a recycled tuna package which was then used by various musicians to create videos and performances dedicated to sustainability. Singer/songwriter Duncan Townsend composed a song called *A New Beginning* on the 'Tuna-lele' which was debuted at BioFach, the world's largest trade fair for organic food products.

Founded in 2007, Followfish was awarded the Best Food Product Innovation in 2008 in Germany. Subsequently, Followfish was listed in the assortments of the leading food retail chains in Germany. Ever since, the sustainable fish assortment and its sales have been increasing. This latest innovation is a new vegetarian organic food assortment, called FollowFood, which is based on the same principles as FollowFish, including tracking, transparency, trust and taste.

Source: Followfish, 2014, www.followfish.de.

The range of social media now available to companies is allowing them to overcome the cost and reach constraints of conventional media to find novel ways of interesting and engaging consumers in sustainability issues, and to try and build relationships with them. In the US, Wal-Mart has created a dedicated Pinterest page for its green products and services to highlight progress in making its supply chain and some products more sustainable. Levi's has used its investment in skate-parks in deprived communities in South Africa and India as a focus for an eye-catching YouTube sports video series that also highlights its contribution to social causes. Online and social media has the potential to do more than provide a channel that allows consumers access to information about the products they buy. Done effectively it can provide a two-way channel that can build relationships and turn customers and other stakeholders into brand advocates and valuable sources of information. This is particularly the case for younger 'millennial' consumers. Heineken's 'Legendary 7' online campaign to highlight its commitment to expanding sustainable ingredient sources, and the efforts of the farmers in its supply chain, encouraged interactivity through an app that scanned bottle labels and beer mats to unlock entertaining video content. Consumers were then encouraged to post their own 'selfies' in support of the 'legendary' farmers to share online. GE's 'Ecomagination' strategy includes an open innovation channel that seeks to discover new sustainability orientated technology ideas by crowdsourcing them from a global network of inventors, thinkers and product users. This allows it to access new innovative solutions and acts as part of its commitment to customer focus.

11.6 Sustainability Marketing as a Transformational Force

The conventional view of marketing is as something relatively passive, particularly through the emphasis on consumer sovereignty with the marketer cast in the role of a servant responding to consumers' needs and wants. This characterization suits many businesses since it rather absolves them of any responsibility for the socio-environmental consequences of production and consumption or for doing anything proactive to address them. It also furnishes companies reluctant to engage with the sustainability agenda with a ready-made excuse along the lines of 'Our customers aren't asking for it' (Whelan, 2013). It is disingenuous to pretend that companies lack power or are condemned only to follow. Whether it is through corporate lobbying, political donations, shareholder briefings or public relations campaigns, companies seek to wield power and influence. In the sustainability arena there is a growing trend towards companies that lead in sustainability performance, not simply seeking to capitalize on their advantage over competitors, but instead lobbying for their entire industry to improve its performance through tougher legislation or co-operative efforts.

A sustainability perspective on marketing takes a more realistic view of the power of companies and marketing, and of the relationship between the marketer and consumer. In some markets that relationship is being transformed through the introduction of supply loops to replace the conventional linear concept of supply chains. Supply loops are emerging in markets (such as for vehicles and electronics) where product take-back strategies (whether established in response to regulations or commercial opportunities) are transforming consumers from the end destination of the value chain into resuppliers of value to companies within supply loops.

Ultimately the distinction between producer and consumer may begin to blur as we increasingly understand markets as production and consumption systems and as approaches such as co-design emerge in which customers and companies work together to develop solutions to customer needs. There are many technical and professional markets in which such collaborations between producers and consumers, and a willingness for producers to take some responsibility for the welfare of consumers, are commonplace. In future such approaches will become evident across a wider range of markets as part of a move towards sustainability, and as part of marketing's evolution away from arm's length transactions and towards building lasting producer–consumer relationships.

Another blurring of conventional marketing boundaries is occurring as sustainability orientated firms increasingly seek to influence the behaviour of consumers in ways that go beyond simply marketing a product to them. An important part of the Health and Wellbeing strand of Marks and Spencer's Plan A is providing nutritional information for consumers with the explicit aim of encouraging behaviour change, and also establishing campaigns to encourage both staff and customers to become more physically active. Unilever's Sustainable Living Plan goes even further by seeking to change elements of consumer behaviour linked to the use of their products in ways that will improve health and hygiene and reduce the environmental burden. For example, one element of the Plan is to reduce the consumer's use of water (by half by 2020) when using products such as washing detergents and personal care products. In previous decades there was a very clear distinction between the sustainability marketing efforts of companies seeking to provide more sustainable products to customers, and the efforts of governments using social marketing to promote positive social and environmental behaviours amongst citizens. That distinction is rapidly disappearing, with major companies adopting behaviour change programmes as part of their sustainability strategies and governments increasingly working with relevant commercial partners in delivering their social marketing programmes.

11.7 Conclusion

It is worth noting that the need for marketing, and the need to address sustainability challenges, are both a consequence of industrialization and the separation of production and consumption activities. In pre-industrial societies markets were largely local so that producers knew their consumers, and the impact of production on the environment was evident to both. Industrialization allowed for the growth of international and mass markets, separating consumers from producers and creating a gulf in understanding that marketing later sought to bridge. The technologies of industrialization also allowed for the unsustainable exploitation of resources and ecosystem services, with the separation of consumption and production largely rendering the consequences of unsustainable production invisible to consumers. Sustainability marketing seeks to bridge the gap in understanding of consumers about production processes and their consequences. This is most obvious in markets for FairTrade products where marketers are actively seeking to make consumers aware of the plight of producer communities and the need for prices to be sufficient for farmers to live on, and for their communities to develop (Golding & Peattie, 2005).

Openness is a key part of sustainability marketing and the quest to build sustainable value relationships with consumers, and it is also very much about innovation. Partly this innovation is about technology, with new materials, new processes and new products being developed that are more resource and energy efficient and able to facilitate more sustainable consumer behaviours. Partly the innovation will need to be social, in terms of how we live and consume, and also in how we envisage, teach and practise marketing itself. It will also require technical and social innovations to be combined in the search for new business models that can address consumer needs in new ways that are profitable to make them sustainable in an economic sense. If we were to try to provide a short answer to the question, 'What would a sustainability orientated vision of marketing look like?' we would suggest the following pseudo-mnemonic, that sustainability marketing is marketing that endures forEVER (Belz & Peattie, 2012), in that it delivers solutions to our needs which are:

- *Ecologically orientated*: taking account of the ecological limits of the planet and seeking to satisfy our needs without compromising the health of ecosystems and their ability to continue delivering ecosystem services.
- *Viable*: from a technical feasibility and economic competitiveness perspective.
- *Ethical*: in promoting greater social justice and equity, or at the very least in terms of avoiding making any existing patterns of injustice worse.
- *Relationship based*: which moves away from viewing marketing in terms of economic exchanges, towards viewing it in terms of the management of relationships between businesses and their customers and other key stakeholders.

Ultimately a transition to a One Planet economy and society will not occur simply because marketers persuade consumers to choose the most sustainable brands on offer. Substantive progress will also require changes to lifestyles, household behaviours and a willingness to explore new and different ways to meet our needs, and in some cases to demand and consume less, as well as differently. That sustainability marketing agenda will need both commercial and social marketers to communicate to consumers the value of sustainability as a societal goal, and the viability, worth and attractiveness of the changes that will be required.

GROUP EXERCISE

Select a company of your choice, which offers a sustainable product or service. Search the website of the company and visit the point of sale (PoS). Describe the 4Cs of the sustainability marketing mix in detail, and make suggestions to improve it further.

Summary

Sustainability marketing represents a further development of marketing that addresses long-standing critiques of the discipline for failing to properly address the socio-environmental impacts of production and consumption, and integrates them with newer critiques based around the overemphasis within conventional marketing on tangible products and a short-term focus on transactions. It represents a fusion of green, ethical and relationship marketing.

Developing sustainability marketing strategies requires a balance between understanding and responding to consumer needs through marketing research, and addressing the socio-environmental issues linked to the production and consumption process provided by cradle-to-grave life cycle analysis of sustainability impacts.

Sustainability marketing strategies are implemented through the development of a marketing mix. To assist in making this process more orientated towards both consumers and sustainability, the conventional 4Ps marketing mix model can usefully be replaced by the four sustainability C factors of Customer Solution, Cost, Convenience and Communications.

Although the factors that influence the consumer's response to sustainability marketing propositions are varied and complex, building consumer confidence and trust through open communications and an avoidance of greenwashing is vitally important.

The creation of a One Planet society will require more than a marketing approach that encourages consumers to select the most sustainable products and brands. It will need consumer acceptance of behavioural change, alterations to lifestyles and expectations, and often radically different ways of meeting needs and generating value. For this to happen, sustainability as a societal goal and the changes that we will need to make within society for it to be achieved, will all have to be successfully marketed to us.

QUESTIONS FOR CLASS DISCUSSION

1. **General:** what are the key differences between conventional marketing and sustainability marketing?

2. **Customer solutions:** how would you define a sustainable service? What are key characteristics? What are the ecological advantages of car sharing as a sustainable service? Will car sharing substitute or supplement car ownership? Why? Why not? Discuss critically.

3. **Consumer cost:** what is the difference between price and consumer cost? Why does it make sense for sustainability marketers to emphasize the total consumer cost? Give concrete examples.

4. **Convenience:** explain the different aspects of convenience by the examples of a) fair trade food and b) electric cars.

5. **Communications:** why is the new approach of online and social media better suited for sustainability marketing than the old shotgun approach employing mass media like television? Discuss possibilities and limitations of the new sustainability communication approach.

References

Alexander, J., Crompton, T., & Shrubsole, G. (2011). Think of me as evil? Opening the ethical debates in advertising. *PIRC/WWF-UK Report*. London: PIRC/WWF.

Bartels, R. (1988). *The history of marketing thought* (3rd ed.). Homewood, Illinois: Richard D. Irwin, Inc.

Belz, F.-M. (1995). *Oekologie und wettbewerbsfaehigkeit in der lebensmittelbranche*. Bern: Paul Haupt.

Belz, F.-M. (2006). Marketing in the 21st century. *Business strategy and the environment*, 15(3), 139–144.

Belz, F.-M., & Peattie, K. (2012). *Sustainability marketing: A global perspective* (2nd ed.). Chichester: John Wiley & Sons.

Crane, A., & Desmond, J. (2002). Societal marketing and morality. *European Journal of Marketing*, 36(5/6), 548–69.

D'Souza, C., Taghian, M., & Lamb, P. (2006). An empirical study on influence of environmental labels on consumers. *Corporate Communications*, 11(2), 162–173.

Eden S., Bear, C., & Walker, G. (2007). Mucky carrots and other proxies: Problematising the knowledge-fix for sustainable and ethical consumption. *Geoforum*, 39(2), 1044–1057.

Fisk, G. (1974). *Marketing and the ecological crisis*. New York: Harper & Row.

Golding, K., & Peattie, K. (2005). In search of a golden blend: Perspectives on the marketing of fair trade coffee. *Sustainable Development*, 13(3), 154–165.

Grönroos, C. (2007). *In search of a new logic for marketing*. Chichester: John Wiley & Sons.

Hennion, K. E. II, & Kinnear, T. C. (1976). *Ecological marketing*. Chicago, IL: American Marketing Association.

Hunt, S. (1981). Macromarketing as a multidimensional concept. *Journal of Macromarketing*, 1(1), 7–8.

Jackson, T. (2004). *Motivating sustainable consumption: A review of evidence on consumer behaviour and behavioural change*. Guildford: Centre for Environmental Strategy, University of Surrey.

Kardash, W. J. (1976). Corporate responsibility and the quality of life: Developing the ecologically concerned consumer. In Henion, K. E. II, & Kinnear, T. C. (Eds.). *Ecological Marketing*. Chicago, IL: American Marketing Association.

Kollmuss, A., & Agyeman, J. (2002). Mind the gap: Why do people act environmentally and what are the barriers to pro-environmental behaviour? *Environmental Education Research*, 8(3), 240–260.

Kotler, P., & Zaltman, G. (1971). Social marketing: An approach to planned social change. *Journal of Marketing*, 35(3), 3–12.

McCarthy, E. J. (1960). *Basic marketing: A managerial approach*. Illinois: Richard D. Irwin.

McDonald, S., Oates, C. J., Alevizou, P. J., Young, C. W., & Hwang, K. (2012). Individual strategies for sustainable consumption. *Journal of Marketing Management*, 28(3/4), 445–468.

Ottman, J. A., Stafford, E. R., & Hartman, C. L. (2006). Avoiding green marketing myopia: Ways to improve consumer appeal for environmentally preferable products, *Environment*, 48, 22–36.

Otto, R., Ruminy, A., & Mrotzek, H. (2006). Assessment of the environmental impact of household appliances. *Appliance*, 63(4), 32–35.

Peattie, K. (1995). *Environmental marketing management: Meeting the green challenge*. London: Pitman Publishing.

Peattie, S., & Peattie, K. (2011). Social marketing for a sustainable environment. In Hastings, G., Bryant, C., & Angus, K. (Eds.). *The SAGE handbook of social marketing*. London: Sage, 343–358.

Pollay, R. W. (1986). The distorted mirror: Reflections on the unintended consequences of advertising. *Journal of Marketing*, 50(2), 18–36.

Porter, M.E., & van der Linde, C. (1995). Green and competitive: Ending the stalemate. *Harvard Business Review*, 73(5), 120–134.

Sharma, A., Iyer, G. R., Mehrota, A., & Krishnan, R. (2010). Sustainability and business-to-business marketing: A framework and implications. *Industrial Marketing Management*, 39(2), 330–341.

Shaw, E., & Jones, D. G. B. (2005). A history of schools of marketing thought. *Marketing Theory*, 5(3), 239–281.

Shove, E. (2003). Converging conventions of comfort, cleanliness and convenience. *Journal of Consumer Policy*, 26(4), 395–418.

Silverman, S. N. (1995). An historical review and modern assessment of the marketing mix concept. In Rassuli, K., Hollander, S. C., & Nevett, T. R. (Eds.). *Proceedings of the 7th Conference on Historical Research in Marketing*. Fort Wayne, Indiana, 25–35.

Straughan, R. D., & Roberts, J. A. (1999). Environmental segmentation alternatives: A look at green consumer behaviour in the new millennium. *Journal of Consumer Marketing*, 16(6), 558–575.

TerraChoice. (2010). *The Sins of Greenwashing: Home and family edition*. Ottowa, Ontario: TerraChoice Environmental Marketing.

WCED. (1987). *Our common future (The Brundtland Report)*. World Commission on Environment and Development. Oxford: Oxford University Press.

Wells, V., Ponting, C., & Peattie, K. (2010). Behaviour and climate change: Consumer perceptions of responsibility. *Journal of Marketing Management*, 27(7/8), 803–833.

Whelan, T. (2013). The five excuses marketeers use for failing to promote sustainability. *Guardian Online* (2013, August 12).

Wilkie, W. L., & Moore, S. E. (2003). Scholarly research in marketing: Exploring the '4 eras' of thought development. *Journal of Public Policy and Marketing*, 22(2), 116–146.

12 Accounting

Stephen Jollands

'Is education possibly a process of trading awareness for things of lesser worth?'

Leopold (1968, p. 18)

LEARNING OUTCOMES

This chapter explores the meta-question:

How can we understand whether the outcome(s) of the decisions we make move us towards a state of sustainability or to a more unsustainable state?

This meta-question leads to a whole raft of relevant questions, including the following, that are explored in this chapter:

1. What tools and techniques (i.e., financial and management accounting) are organizations currently using to provide information to decision-makers in this respect?

2. What other tools and techniques (i.e., financial and management accounting) do organizations have at their disposal to provide information to decision-makers in this respect?

3. What issues, concerns, problems, and shortcomings with these tools and techniques should the users (i.e., decision-makers) of the information be aware of in terms of using the information provided?

Introduction

There is already a lot written about traditional accounting. It is not the purpose of this chapter to recreate or summarize this vast literature. Rather it is the intention to question and debate the usefulness of traditional accounting and its extensions in a world of ecologically constrained resources and all the issues that this implies. This chapter should be read in conjunction with any of the large number of textbooks written about accounting that cover the topics discussed here. For the purposes of illustration, throughout this chapter appropriate text from Atrill and McLaney (2011), to be read in conjunction with the different sections, will be highlighted. The choice of Atrill and McLaney has been made due to it being a highly representative and appropriate text that aptly covers the broad landscape of traditional accounting. Further, as the terrain of accounting is so vast it is not possible, within these pages, to address all of the many and varied topics. Rather this chapter is designed to overview representative issues within traditional, contemporary and sustainability accounting. The absence of any given topic or issue is, therefore, by no means a statement about its relative importance but rather one of not being able to cover everything here.

12.0 Accounting and Sustainability

To address the meta-question and all of the many sub-questions we first examine what it is we mean by accounting and sustainability. We start with the question of what accounting is. Establishing possibilities of what accounting may be allows us to then examine how we can understand the issue of sustainability through the lens this provides.

12.0.1 What is Accounting?

Atrill and McLaney (2011, p. 2) note that '[a]ccounting is concerned with collecting, analysing, and communicating financial information.' From this perspective information is required to assist with decision-making but focuses on a very specific type, that which relates to the financial. It is true that accounting has become synonymous with the preparation and dissemination of financial information. However, in examining the concept of accounting we can note that this does not equate to all that it is, can be or should be. For example, an *Oxford English Dictionary* definition (Simpson & Weiner 1989, p. 88) notes that, along with the financially focused definitions, accounting is '[a]nswering for, giving a satisfactory explanation of.' Miller and Napier (1993, p. 631) state that:

> There is no 'essence' to accounting and no invariant object to which the name 'accounting' can be attached. Accounting changes in both content and form over time; it is neither solid nor immutable. New techniques are invented, or transferred from one domain to another, and new meanings and significances are attributed to existing techniques.

From this we can see that rather than narrowly examining what accounting is thought to deal with, the financial affairs of a specific organization, we should examine what it assists us to do. Specifically it assists us in the preparation of an account; which provides the explanation of events, actions, and the use of resources. Unsurprisingly, these accounts often involve financial figures, as this provides an accessible means to quantify the discharging of responsibility through a medium, money, which is understandable to many. However, *as we will see below*, when it comes to sustainability it is questionable whether the widely accepted medium of money holds sufficient meaning to translate and provide a significant account of the discharging of responsibility.

These accounts can have at least two differing purposes, *both of which are mentioned above.* The first is to provide an account that overviews events and actions. This type of account aims to provide evidence of the discharging of responsibility in relation to the use of resources. The second is to provide an account on which to base decisions. That is, the construction of information to assist a decision-maker with the process of making a specific decision.

Case Study 12.1, Josiah Wedgewood, provides an illustration of how accounting, through the construction of an account, achieves both of these purposes and in doing so gains its power. From this case we can see that accounting helps to (re)present things that are physically and spatially removed in a way that renders them mobile and understandable for the reader. Further, it is the very nature of these objects being physically and spatially removed that gives accounting its power. In other words the impossibility of presenting the objects themselves enables accounting to gain power through providing representation of them. In short, accounting gains its power through providing visibility. However, we need to be aware that where visibility is created, inevitably other things will remain invisible (Rahaman *et al.* 2004). Further, this becomes compounded when accounting moves from being seen as a means to assist with the accomplishment of a certain

---

CASE STUDY 12.1
Josiah Wedgewood

McKendrick (1970) and Hopwood (1987) provide an overview of Josiah Wedgwood, who was a famous potter. Wedgewood had very little formal education but was a pioneer in many areas including production methods, product design, the application of scientific research, and the commercial exploitation of his products. He had little use of accounting until 1772 when there was a major economic recession.

During this recession Wedgwood experienced accumulating stock, falling sales, slack demand, and cutbacks in production. In response Wedgwood developed his own detailed and sophisticated costing system, which allowed him to represent the processes involved in making and selling his pottery in an abbreviated form, and displaced the physical process into a costing book. This broke down the complexity of his vast operations into a means that allowed him to more effectively perform remote control and in doing so

allowed him to develop a number of policies to improve the running of his business.

This system included making visible the potential to gain from the economies of scale through having longer production runs and attaining a lower cost per unit, setting lower and more stable prices based on product costs that allowed the accessing of a broader market, incentivizing salespeople by putting them on commission, and reducing labour costs through paying a piecemeal rate.

Perhaps the most striking aspects was that the system allowed him to compare actual costs with accounting costs and actual profits with accounting profits. This highlighted discrepancies and the discovery of fraud. As McKendrick (1970, p. 61) notes it led to revelations 'that the housekeeper was frolicking with the cashier', that the head clerk was ill with the 'foul disease', and had 'long been in a course of extravagance & dissipation far beyond anything he has from us (in a lawful way)'.

goal to being seen as an end in itself (McMann & Nanni Jr., 1995). The tensions between visibility and invisibility as well as means versus ends are themes that run throughout this chapter.

12.0.2 Understanding Sustainability Through an Accounting Lens

With reference to *the above discussion* of what accounting can be, the next question we turn to is how can it assist us to understand the issue of sustainability? A starting point is to note that '[t]he concept of sustainability is contested and ambiguous' (Ball & Milne, 2005, p. 315). Further, with various definitions of this concept presented by many different academics and practitioners, who often utilize it loosely and ubiquitously, it becomes problematic in that the word has the potential to become meaningless. One way around this issue is to place all these various definitions into the broad dichotomy of 'strong' and 'weak' understandings.

Within this dichotomy weak definitions 'downplay questions of equity and social justice, absolute levels of material resources and energy use and the scale of developments relative to the resource base, while playing up the gains to be made by more efficient use of materials and energy relative to the outputs being produced' (Ball & Milne, 2005, p. 317). A great example of this is the concept of 'eco-efficiency'. Eco-efficiency has become a popular concept in practice and is often used by corporates to help prove they are serious about sustainability issues (Milne *et al.*, 2006). However, it has been known since the Industrial Revolution that gains in relative resource use are quickly lost through these very gains encouraging increases in absolute resource use (Alcott, 2005; Holm & Englund, 2009; Missemer, 2012).[1]

Contrasted with weak notions are strong understandings of sustainability. This requires acknowledging that 'sustainability is about maintaining natural capital or critical natural capital and learning to live off natural income' (Ball & Milne 2005, p. 315). This requires us to understand that we only have one ecosphere to rely upon, which contains limited resources, to provide us with everything we need and want. Hence these strong understandings are incompatible with the current focus on growth that is put forward by neo-classical economies and traditional accounting tools that are based on that perspective.

We can therefore translate this dichotomy into an understanding of what sustainability is with the assistance of Figure 12.1. In this we see the interrelationship between the economy, society, and ecology. An observation is that, *as presented in Chapter 1*, it is a nested set of systems. This raises the question of what the respective roles of ecology, society and the economy are. This question is, however, beyond the remit of this chapter, but nonetheless an interesting and important one to ask.

The main point of highlighting this interrelationship is that it helps us to understand what sustainability entails and how accounting can assist us with this issue. That is, we can start to understand that sustainability is a system-based concept (Gray, 1992; Milne, 1996; Milne, 2007), pertaining to a self-organizing 'living' system, where '[t]he economy is viewed as an open subsystem of the larger, but finite, closed and

---

[1] This was originally known as the 'Jevons' Paradox' but the term 'rebound effect' is now commonly used within the discipline of ecological economics.

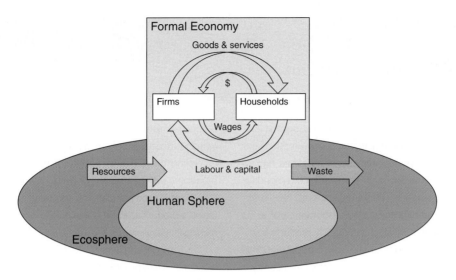

FIGURE 12.1 Understanding sustainability. *Source:* Based on Figure 2.4, Wackernagel and Rees, 1996, p. 44.

nongrowing ecosystem' (Daly, 1992, p. 186). From the ecosphere we constantly need to draw natural resources and utilize ecosystem services, such as waste assimilation, in order to sustain the human sphere (Costanza *et al.*, 1997, p. 253). Thus sustainability is a state in which no more resources are drawn from the ecosphere than can naturally be replenished and the use of those resources is equitable across the human sphere (Ball & Milne, 2005; Milne & Gray, 2007). Accounting, in the broadest sense *discussed above*, can assist through providing explanations of the events and actions that are undertaken to ensure the sustainable use of the natural resources and ecosystem services that we all rely on for our survival. Arrow *et al.* (1995, p. 521) notes that '[e]conomic activities are sustainable only if the life-support ecosystems on which they depend are resilient.' This implies that the state of sustainability requires the acknowledgement of a world of limits (Meadows *et al.*, 1972; Costanza, 1989) where the scale of economic activity cannot exceed levels consistent with the carrying capacity of the ecosphere (Daly, 1992). Accounting can provide information about the resilience of the ecosphere on which we can make better informed decisions about how to preserve and sustainably use natural resources and ecosystem services. The various accounts we currently have, while not definitively proving whether or by how much we are exceeding the carrying capacity of the ecosphere (Dryzek, 1997), show that we are not in a state of sustainability and that we are moving towards a more unsustainable state (Wackernagel & Rees, 1996; Bebbington *et al.*, 2001; Gray & Milne, 2002; Ball & Milne, 2005; WWF, 2014). Even without definitive proof, the prudent course of action is to assume that ecological limits exist and that we need to act in accordance with this assumption (Costanza, 1989; Small & Jollands, 2006).

In short, there are two aspects to the challenge of sustainability. These are an ever increasing population which requires increasing levels of natural resources and ecosystem services to sustain itself, and an ever decreasing, finite natural capital base from which these natural resources and ecosystem services are drawn. This is the basis of the ecological footprint calculation, which is overviewed in Case Study 12.2.

CASE STUDY 12.2
The Ecological Footprint

The ecological footprint is 'an accounting tool that enables us to estimate the resource consumption and waste assimilation requirements of a defined human population or economy in terms of a corresponding productive land area' (Wackernagel & Rees, 1996, p. 9).

At its most basic the ecological footprint enables us to understand how much biologically productive surface area is required to sustain a given population. This can be calculated on a worldwide basis, for a country, a region, an organization, or indeed any given population. The power of this tool is that the result, which can be understood as the demand for biologically productive surface area, can then be compared with how much of the biologically productive surface area is available, the supply side.

Through comparing demand and supply we can therefore estimate the differences between the two. If supply exceeds demand then theoretically the given population can sustain itself on what that biologically productive surface area can generate. However, if demand exceeds supply then the given population is exceeding the carrying capacity of that biologically productive surface area. The only way that this is possible is if the given population is also using up the biologically productive surface area itself and in doing so making it unavailable for the future.

Wackernagel and Rees (1996) calculated that on a worldwide average basis, demand was exceeding supply by 20%. Of concern is that since that time it has been estimated that this has increased to 50% (WWF, 2014), which indicates that we are moving away from a state of sustainability rather than towards it.

While the ecological footprint is excellent for providing visibility over resource throughput it does not extend to providing information on other areas of sustainability, such as ecosystem health, inter- and intra-generational equity, and other aspects of social sustainability.

As seen in Case Study 12.2, data from the ecological footprint calculations highlight that we are increasingly overshooting the carrying capacity of our ecosphere. This suggests that change is inevitable and we have only two related choices. The first is to choose to continue as we are and in doing so allow the change to occur unabated. The second is to choose to try to manage the changes that are occurring, which will most likely require a major shift in how our economies are organized and operated (Korten, 2010; Rockstrom & Klum, 2012; WWF, 2014).

The latter suggests the need to implement processes of 'Sustainable Development', recognized, *as overviewed in Chapter 1*, as being central to the recommendations of the *Brundtland Report* (World Commission on Environment and Development, 1987, p. 8). We should therefore distinguish sustainability, which is a dichotomous state as we either are sustainable or we are not, and sustainable development, which is the process of achieving this state. Further, we should question what it is that we are trying to sustain. The need to ask this question is due to many people assuming that sustainability is in some way automatically linked to the green movement or environmentalism. However, this is not necessarily the case. Rather sustainability focuses on sustaining us and links to how we perceive the ecosphere.

This can be exemplified through making a comparison between capitalism and Marxism. Specifically, under the current, neo-classical economics-based version of capitalism, it is perceived that there is no 'value' to anything until human labour, the only true scarce resource, is added. Despite attempts to provide a modern version of Marxism more in line with environmentalism (see, e.g., Tinker & Gray, 2003), it also has this very same underpinning. Hence the two differ not in their fundamental ideals but rather in how the 'value' that is added through human endeavour should then be distributed. In capitalism, as the providers of the capital risk most, it is believed that they deserve the largest share of the 'value' added. However, in Marxism, it is believed that those that create the added 'value', the workers, deserve the largest share of it.

So it is that in the majority of economic thought the ecosphere is merely a resource that is there for the human sphere to draw upon as it so desires. This in turn has implications for the way in which accounting is performed; *see, e.g., the discussion of natural capital accounting below*. This perspective is hardly surprising given that it is humans that need to be sustained through the continued use of the ecosphere to meet this purpose. However, in this perspective the ecosphere is merely the resource and has no value in and of itself. This means that all that is required is to maintain the ecosphere at a state that it provides enough natural resources and ecosystem services to maintain the human population. This perspective has many implications from the underpinning principle that does not grant the ecosystem any kind of intrinsic value. For example, this places the millions of other species that share the ecosystem as subservient to human interest. Not all perspectives view the ecosystem in this way. Specifically, deep ecology (Leopold, 1968; Naess, 1973; Naess, 1990) and the branches of ecological economics that draw from it, mobilizes the perspective of humans as just one small part of the ecosphere and develops the concept of value being distributed throughout it. This perspective provides great difficulties for the other branches of economics in that it requires that sustainability becomes more than just the maintenance of humans.

In closing this section we turn to Case Study 12.3, Easter Island, as an illustration of the potential for accounting to assist with averting the disaster of our ever increasing unsustainable societies. That is, we can see from this case that the people of Easter Island did not seem to have at their disposal the information required to make informed decisions about the sustainable use of the resources available to them. Further, they did not seem to have a system for the discharging of the responsibility for the ongoing sustainable use of the resources available. In short, the Easter Island case illustrates that having incomplete information, that does not link the decisions we make to the impact the resulting actions have on the ecology, may inhibit us from becoming sustainable. We now turn to overviewing the two major streams within accounting, financial accounting and management accounting, in terms of how effective they are at providing the required information in relation to sustainability. In order to do this we first examine the traditional accountings within these areas before expanding to examine some more contemporary developments.

> ## CASE STUDY 12.3
> # Easter Island
>
> Diamond (2005) provides an overview of the events that led to the collapse of society on Easter Island, which can be seen as a compelling analogy to what is currently occurring on a global scale. His description starts with the arrival of seafarers who utilized advanced technology, for their time, to this remote South Pacific island. They quickly established a society that was divided geographically into chiefdoms with different resources being located within each. Trade flourished as each area sought to acquire the resources they required to meet their needs and to fulfil their wants.
>
> In time the population grew and the respective chiefs marked their relative prosperity with giant statues, known as Moai. These monuments grew in size over time as the respective chiefs of each area strove to outdo those around them. With the population at its highest the levels of essential resources for sustaining the island's inhabitants collapsed through overconsumption. The chain of events that followed would eventually lead to the devastation of the island to such a degree that when Europeans arrived they were astounded as to how, on such a barren wasteland of an island, the great statues could have been constructed, transported, and erected.
>
> These events started with deforestation and thereby the depletion of the necessary materials for buildings, fires, statue construction and transportation. This was eventually so complete that most of the important species were extinct and the subtropical forest disappeared. Because of deforestation food shortages ensued, followed by starvation, population crash, cannibalism, and the collapse of the society into war.
>
> While this account has been subject to critique, e.g., by Hunt and Lipo (2011), and counterclaims of that critique, e.g., by Flenley and Bahn (2011), Diamond's description still provides a harrowing example of the potential consequences for us on a global scale of ignoring the concept of strong sustainability.

12.1 Financial Accounting

Traditionally financial accounting concerns itself with the preparation of numerical statements for general release to the public. Typically there are four main statements that are prepared. The first of these is the Statement of Financial Position, which is often known as the Balance Sheet, and is overviewed in Chapter 2 of Atrill and McLaney (2011). This statement aims to provide a snapshot at a moment in time of what assets the organization has and how they have been financed. The second is the Statement of Financial Performance, which is often known as the Profit and Loss Account or Income Statement, and is overviewed in Chapter 3 of Atrill and McLaney (2011). This statement aims to provide an overview of the financial performance of the organization over the previous accounting period, which is usually 12 months. The third is the Statement of Changes in Equity, with an overview provided in Atrill and McLaney (2011, pp. 140–141). This provides further details, beyond that provided in the Statement of Financial Position, of how the owners' stake in the organization has changed over the last accounting period. The final is the Statement of Cash Flow, with an overview provided in Chapter 5 of Atrill and McLaney (2011). Given the importance to an organization of having enough cash to meet its obligations as they come due, this statement overviews where cash has come from and where it has been applied over the last accounting period.

In preparing these statements, accountants are governed by sets of rules, dependent on the jurisdiction within which they are operating (see Atrill & McLaney, 2011, pp. 142–144, for futher details). Examples include the International Financial Reporting Standards, US Generally Accepted Accounting Practices (GAAP), and rules imposed on publically traded companies by the stock exchange on which they are listed. However, these rules can require a company to account for the financial events in differing ways. One of the most famous examples of this is that of Daimler-Benz, which in 1993 disclosed profits of DM0.6 billion using German GAAP but a loss of DM1.8 billion using the same data but prepared following US GAAP (Zeff, 2012, p. 817).

While these sets of rules often provide prescriptive guidance on how to record and report specific financial transactions, it is not possible to provide rules for every eventuality. Hence they usually outline a set of underlying assumptions, conventions and concepts that are provided to guide the accountant when there is no prescriptive rule to follow. In the next part of this section we examine the most common of these assumptions and concepts in order to discuss their meaning in the broader context of sustainability.

12.1.1   Underlying Assumptions, Conventions and Concepts

Relevance   (Atrill & McLaney 2011, p. 5.) Information is said to be relevant if it is capable of influencing decision-making. The information provided must have confirmatory value in terms of previous events or predictive value in terms of future events for it to be able to influence decisions. Issues around sustainability are arguably highly relevant but currently the information being provided by most organizations fails to have either confirmatory or predictive value (Gray & Milne, 2002; Gray & Milne, 2004; Birkin *et al.*, 2005; Milne *et al.*, 2006; Milne, 2013). The question therefore arises as to why an organization would provide information that should be but is not relevant to sustainability issues. *Potential explanations for this are reviewed below.*

Reliability   (Atrill & McLaney, 2011, p. 6.) For information to be useful it needs to be able to be relied upon. For this to occur it should be free from material error, a faithful representation, neutral, prudent, and complete. *As mentioned above*, sustainability is a complex issue that involves much that is unknown. Dryzek (1997) provides the analogy of a car racing towards an invisible wall, with the car representing economic activity and the wall ecological crisis. In this analogy traditional economists, who favour hitting the accelerator as there seem to be no problems ahead, are pitted against environmentalists, who favour a precautionary approach but cannot prove the existence of the invisible wall or even provide definitive evidence of where it may be. It may be argued that there is incontrovertible proof for some sustainability issues, such as anthropocentric climate change (IPCC, 2014), and hence the analogy is somewhat obsolete. However, this analogy illustrates the need for the development of tools and metrics that can provide reliable information that can be used to improve decision-making in relation to the broader issues of sustainability, such as aspects of ecosystem health, inter- and intra-generational equity, and how these relate to specific organizations. *Some of the experiments in this respect will be overviewed below.*

Comparability (Atrill & McLaney, 2011, p. 6.) Comparability requires that the measurement and display of items should be consistent over time. Further, as accounting requires decisions to be made as to how to account for specific items, the organization should disclose the accounting policies it has adopted. This will assist the user of the information to make comparisons across time and between entities. As sustainability is a contested and ambiguous concept (Milne, 1996; Ball & Milne, 2005; Gray, 2010) that can be understood in many different ways, it is probable that information will be interpreted and presented in differing ways over time and between organizations. This issue of comparability of sustainability-related information may be compounded by a lack of ecological literacy (Ball & Milne, 2005) within organizations and the lack of tools that aim to provide information in line with strong understandings of the issues.

Understandability (Atrill & McLaney, 2011, p. 6.) If information is not understood by the user then it is useless. This requires that accountants should strive to present complex information as simply as possible. Returning to the prevalence of a lack of ecological literacy (Ball & Milne, 2005), it is doubtful that accountants have the required knowledge to present the complexities of sustainability issues, let alone users being able to understand them. There are two further parts to this issue to consider. The first is that organizations typically do not employ ecologists with whom to consult and, secondly, the education system typically does not equip people with the necessary ecological literacy.

Entity (Atrill & McLaney, 2011, p. 51.) For accounting purposes the transactions relating to the organization and the owner of that organization are kept separate even if legally they are considered the same entity. In respect to sustainability, questions have been raised (see, e.g., Birkin, 1996; Ball & Milne, 2005) as to what should be considered as the entity that is accounted for. The issue stems from the idea that what gets accounted for gets sustained. So if, e.g., the entity to be accounted for was a river then all organizations operating along the river would need to account for how they have contributed to the maintenance of that entity.

Going Concern (Atrill & McLaney, 2011, pp. 53–54.) Accounting is always performed under the assumption that the entity will continue its existence into the foreseeable future. This has implications on how accounting is done. For example, when we consider asset valuations, the value that could be gained from selling the assets is not relevant. This is because if we assume the business is going to last into the foreseeable future then the assets will continue to be required and selling them is not a realistic prospect. In terms of sustainability we need to start questioning how sound this assumption is. *As mentioned above*, all the leading indicators demonstrate that we are continuing to increase the stress we place on the ecology. This is primarily driven through organizations increasing profits through increasing the resources they draw from the ecology. If this trend continues then worst case scenario predictions are that very soon we could see a catastrophic crisis in the ecosystem that, given the systems view *outlined in Figure 12.1*, will flow on to critically affect society and the economy as we know them today.

Accrual Basis (Atrill & McLaney, 2011, p. 87.) The accrual basis is a means of undertaking the recording of transactions, whereby their effects are recognized when they occur rather than when the cash flow, or cash equivalent, occurs. The going concern assumption results in the accountant having to divide the life of an organization into accounting periods, usually of a year, in order to provide the statements that outline the ongoing position and performance of the entity. As business is largely conducted on credit it is common that large numbers of transactions occur in one accounting period but the resulting cash flows occur in another. Accrual accounting is utilized in an attempt to provide a greater reflection of the economic reality of the transaction being recorded. Through the use of accrual accounting and the dividing up of the organization's life into accounting periods, our attention naturally focuses on the short term. This often creates short-termism that results in actions that are counter to those required to sustain ourselves. Hence sustainability requires an accounting that imparts a long-term focus and results in actions that reduce the level of our unsustainability.

Materiality (Atrill & McLaney, 2011, p. 7.) When accountants are preparing the financial statements they must decide whether the omission or misstatement of an item could influence decisions based on the information provided. If the answer is yes, then the item is material and should be disclosed. It could be argued that sustainability is the defining issue of our time. Information would be highly material if it accounts for how the actions of an organization result in moving us towards or away from a sustainable state. *As will be discussed below*, organizations have begun disclosing more information under the heading of sustainability. However, it is debatable whether they are disclosing the most material information.

Money Measurement (Atrill & McLaney, 2011, pp. 55–58.) Within the realm of financial accounting the only items to be recognized or included are those that can be expressed in monetary terms. Within the remit of traditional accounting valuable resources or assets of an organization, e.g., brands or human resources, may not be shown in the financial statements due to there being no reliable way of measuring them in monetary terms. When we extend the scope to include sustainability issues this becomes even more problematic as it is not clear how to or even whether we should try to monetize the ecology. For example, there is currently a hotly contested debate (see, e.g., Costanza *et al.*, 1997; Costanza, 1998; de Groot *et al.*, 2002; Ayres, 2004) around whether or not we should even try to monetize ecosystem services and natural capital or whether this will lead to the further embedding of the mindset that caused these issues in the first place (Cairns, 2001).

These assumptions, conventions and concepts have been developed in relation to the preparation of the financial statements. It may seem unfair to examine how they stack up under the broader context of sustainability. However, organizations have started to extend what they are publically reporting beyond the financial to include information on social, environmental, and sustainability related issues. It is highly likely that some of these assumptions, conventions and concepts will be utilized in the preparation of this additional information. As Gray (2010, p. 47) notes: '[o]ne convergent theme in that critique [of accounting for sustainability] has been a challenge that much of the realist and procedural baggage associated with conventional accounting is no longer apposite when seeking to account for sustainability.' *In the next part of this section* a brief overview is provided of how, what and why organizations report additional information.

12.1.2 Inclusion of Social, Environmental and Sustainability Information

Organizations increasingly provide information in relation to social, environmental, and sustainability issues. They provide this in a number of formats including within their annual report, on their websites, and through producing stand-alone sustainability reports. Like financial accounting, there are a number of differing sets of rules to guide the organization in preparing these reports. However, unlike financial accounting, in all but a few jurisdictions, e.g., France and South Africa, organizations are not mandated to provide this information or to follow any of these sets of rules.

While there are many different sets of rules perhaps the two most commonly known are the Global Reporting Initiative (GRI) and Integrated Reporting (<IR>). The GRI[2] was founded in the US in 1997 by the Coalition of Environmentally Responsible Economies (CERES) and the Tellus Institute, with claims of it being linked to the social movements of the 1970s (Brown *et al.*, 2009). It has the backing of organizations such as UNEP, with different iterations of the guidelines being developed in consultation with many differing stakeholders, including trade union groups and academics. The framework is now at its fourth iteration (known as G4) and is perhaps one of the most widely used in this area, with over 11,000 organizations stating they utilize it.

The GRI framework aims to provide a basis for organizations to report on their sustainability activities. It expressly states that it assists an organization to report on its environmental, social and economic performance and impact through a process of selecting applicable metrics from a list for each of these categories. However, even with it being based on the best of intentions, it is not without critique. For example, *if we refer back to the discussion above as to what sustainability is* we can see that to be sustainable requires the global economy to only extract a quantity of resources that can naturally be renewed. The metrics require the organization to report on its direct impacts while not having to report on the scale and scope of its operations in relation to, e.g., planetary boundaries, which are already exceeded or stressed at the global level (Rockström *et al.*, 2009; Whiteman *et al.*, 2013).

The selective nature of this framework along with it not requiring the reporting of certain important aspects of sustainability, including scale and scope of activity, has meant that claims have been made that it has been co-opted for other purposes than originally intended. An overview of these purposes is provided *in the next part of this section* as they apply to many of these frameworks, not just the GRI. However, at this point it is worth noting that companies that have potentially been involved in major scandals have been able to provide GRI compliant reports with little or no mention of these issues. A good example of this is the commodities giant Glencore Xstrata. In its 2013 report it notes that it 'meets application level A+ of the GRI guidelines, with the self-declared GRI A+ level independently assured by Deloitte LLP' (Glencore Xstrata, 2013, p. 81). However, Glencore Xstrata has been heavily criticized for possibly being involved in extremely unethical actions (see, e.g., Global Witness Limited, 2012; Sweeney, 2012), particularly in relation to its operations in the Democratic Republic of Congo and Colombia, none of which are addressed in its sustainability report.

---

[2] More details of this framework can be found at https://www.globalreporting.org/Pages/default.aspx.

As the name suggests, <IR>[3] aims to produce periodical reports that synthesize all aspects of an organization and the context within which it operates. It aims to provide a framework in which to streamline all the differing reporting needs – including financial, social, and environmental – of an organization into one concise report. <IR> developed out of the Prince of Wales convening a meeting in 2009 of differing representatives of groups with an interest in this area, including his own The Prince's Accounting for Sustainability Project and the GRI. Just like the GRI, it is also not without its critics (see, e.g., Baue & Murninghan, 2011). These criticisms include the same as levelled at the GRI and also more specifically at the lack of inclusion of wider stakeholder voices within the dialogue.

It can be argued that the weaknesses of the GRI, <IR>, and other similar frameworks is that, while they may be based on the good intention to get business to move away from solely an economic focus, they allow for a business as usual perspective to continue (Milne *et al.*, 2006; Milne, 2013) through not forcing organizations to address strong sustainability. That is, none of these frameworks represent sustainability in that they do not require organizations to report on how their operations link to the ecology in terms of scale and scope of economic activity. Even with reporting on direct social and environmental impacts, without a discussion of how the scale and scope of an organization's activity relates to stocks of natural interest and natural capital, at best, these frameworks can be seen to be adhering to a weak understanding of sustainability.

Some evidence suggests that economic (financial) performance can be enhanced through having a focus, which these frameworks can assist with, on sustainability issues. Examples include Bartolomeo *et al.* (2000) who note that an environmental focus can identify hidden costs, and Al-Tuwaijri *et al.* (2004) who note that 'good' environmental performance is associated with 'good' economic performance. However, within this evidence the economic always takes precedence. Further, it can be questioned as to whether the cause and effect looked at within this research are highly correlated. For example, in relation to the findings of Bartolomeo *et al.* (2000) we can question whether the sustainability focused actions are only due to the identification of these hidden costs. In other words, without the identification of the hidden costs would any sustainability focused actions occur? Also it could be questioned, in relation to Al-Tuwaijri *et al.* (2004), whether it is only as a result of the 'good' economic performance that we see the 'good' environmental performance. Hence we can question whether the cause and effect, as put forward by these authors, is as unidirectional as they argue.

In closing this part of the section there are a few other critiques of these frameworks that can be mentioned. The first is to question whose agenda is being put forward through the use of these frameworks. *As mentioned above* many organizations utilize these disclosures as an opportunity to further their own interests through highlighting their positive actions while obfuscating any negative actions. Further, an industry of consultants has sprung up around these movements. Of course having consultants assist organizations in their engagement with actions to address sustainability concerns and then report on it may be required and therefore a good thing. However, we need to question the ecological literacy of these consultants. For example, are consultants who come from the big consultancy and accounting firms, with

---

[3] More details of this framework can be found at http://www.theiirc.org/.

traditional business education backgrounds, really the best and most knowledgeable people to be engaging in such consulting activities? Following on from this it has to be asked why, in these frameworks, the western capitalist perspective takes precedence? It can be argued that the current sustainability issue is being caused by over-consumption in richer countries but the immediate and worst affects are being felt in poorer countries. If we view these frameworks as voluntary regulations then we can extend the issues of trying to apply western regulations on non-western countries, as highlighted by the likes of Belal and Owen (2007).

We have to question whether these frameworks really deal with what is important. Part of this is aligned to questioning what definition of sustainability they ascribe to and utilize in their development. In using these frameworks, are organizations forced to disclose information about their operations in the areas that are really controversial and that need to be opened up to public debate? While there is much ongoing debate and research into these questions, the one that has dominated the academic literature is: why do organizations provide information beyond that which is required by regulations? *In the next part of this section* we turn to briefly overviewing the most common theories put forward as to why we see organizations doing this.

12.1.3 Theories as to Why Organizations Disclose More Than is Regulated

Accountability (See, e.g., Gray *et al.*, 1996; Gray *et al.*, 1997.) From this perspective an organization has a duty to provide an account for the actions for which it is responsible. There are two interrelated parts to this. The first is an expectation that organizations will undertake certain actions and refrain from other actions. The second is that they will provide a full and honest account of the actions undertaken. Thus from this perspective reporting is responsibility driven rather than demand driven, including providing material information even if society does not demand it. While there are many critiques of this perspective (see, e.g., Parker, 2005, p. 847), one of the most significant is that it relates to how organizations should act rather than how they actually do act.

Legitimacy (See, e.g., Dowling & Pfeffer, 1975; Deegan, 2002; Deegan, 2007.) Parker (2005, p. 846) notes that: '[t]his theory according to Lindblom [(1993)] argues that an organisation is legitimised when its value system matches that of the social system of which it forms a part and that where there is a mismatch, the organisation's legitimacy is threatened.' From this perspective an organization has no inherent right to the resources it acquires and relies on society to support its access to those resources. Hence the organization has a social contract, which goes beyond its legal requirements, with relevant groups within society that have the ability to force the withdrawal of access to the resources that the organization depends upon. It is thought that the social contract has both implicit and explicit expectations of how the organization should act. But as values within society change over time an organization must make sure that it changes how it acts accordingly. An organization may utilize voluntary reporting of sustainability information in order to demonstrate its alignment with societal expectations.

Stakeholder (See, e.g., Roberts, 1992; Gray *et al.*, 1995.) This perspective overlaps with legitimacy theory. The difference arises from the recognition that there may be a number of differing specific stakeholder groups that an organization needs to be aware of. This results in a number of different social contracts being formed. Further different stakeholder groups will have differing power in relation to being able to coerce the organization. Thus while legitimacy theory looks at how an organization interacts with society as a whole, stakeholder theory looks at how it interacts with specific stakeholder groups. Within stakeholder theory there are two dissimilar perspectives. The first, the ethical perspective, notes that all groups have the right to be treated equally. Thus the actions of an organization towards a group should be in relation to the impact it has on that group and not in relation to the groups' relative (economic) power. The second perspective, the managerial perspective, notes that in practice how an organization acts towards a group is in relation to how this action can further the interests of the organization. An organization will not respond to each group equally and the information contained within reports will be in relation to the expectations of the groups that are perceived to have the most potential to affect the organization's interests.

New Institutional Sociology   (See, e.g., DiMaggio & Powell, 1983; Rahaman *et al.*, 2004.) This perspective can be viewed as complimentary to legitimacy theory and stakeholder theory. It looks to understand how the practices aimed at achieving legitimacy, such as reporting practices, become institutionalized, or taken for granted, within organizations. It explores how the structures of organizations and actions of those within them are moulded by cultural, political and social forces. In this perspective accounting is one form of institutional practice and is a 'ceremonial means for symbolically demonstrating an organization's commitment to a rational course of action' (Covaleski *et al.*, 1996, p. 11). Specifically it recognizes that like all practices, accounting and reporting will be influenced by both the internal and external organizational environments and subject to differing isomorphism. The first is coercive isomorphism, where pressure to conform to certain ways of doing things are exerted by individuals or organizations. The next is mimetic isomorphism, where the pressure to reduce uncertainty leads to an organization's practices being modelled or copied from another organization's procedures. The final is normative isomorphism, where pressure is exerted to conform to practices that are in line with professional or occupational norms and rules. This perspective recognizes that usually there will be a decoupling between what the desirable practice is and the actual practices utilized by an organization and, as such, reporting will be used to construct an image that is more in line with the desirable.

Altruism   While altruism has not been utilized as an explicit perspective we can see it implicitly running through some of the literature that tries to explain why organisations account as they do. It has been defined as the 'selfless concern for the wellbeing of others' (Pearsall, 2001, p. 40) and importantly, it is where one goes beyond their duty. At an organizational level representative examples include Mirvis (2000), who examines Shell and Holliday (2001), who examines Du Pont. While each of these articles argues that the respective organizations are attempting to move towards doing the right thing it is perhaps clear that in relation to sustainability this still does not equate to altruism given that both are still exploiting non-renewable resources. More promising is individuals within organizations. For example, Ball (2007) looks at environmental accounting and reporting as a tool used from social movements in organisations' perspectives and develops the notion of 'workplace activists.' Questions that this gives rise to include: within the confines of our current capitalist organizations and societies how realistic is this, and how do we create space within which these workplace activists can operate and actually prompt real change?

Regulatory   (See, e.g., Lemon & Cahan, 1997; Milne, 2002.) In this perspective the threat of regulation prompts organizations to put in place measures to counter it. The most prolific theory in this area is the political cost hypothesis whereby groups lobbying the government result in political pressure on a specific industry or organization. An organization responds by using 'devices, such as social responsibility campaigns in the media, government lobbying and selection of accounting procedures to minimize reported earnings' (Watts & Zimmerman, 1978, p. 115). While the main part of this literature has focused on how organizations minimize their reported earnings to avoid potential political costs there has also been research on the use of social responsibility campaigns. For example, Lemon and Cahan (1997) link environmental disclosure decisions to political visibility and suggest that organizations may use sustainability related disclosures as a means of reducing the chances of new regulations. However, Milne (2002) counters this and notes that Watts and Zimmerman's (1978) reference to social lobbying was a passing remark. As such their notion of directly lobbying the government, particularly in the US, may be more in line with practice.

12.1.4 The Visibility and Invisibility Created by Sustainability Reporting

In closing this section we return to the theme of visibility and invisibility in relation to reporting. This can be illustrated with reference to an investigation of the Volta River Authority (VRA) (as outlined by Rahaman and Lawrence, 2001a; Rahaman and Lawrence 2001b; Rahaman *et al.*, 2004). The VRA was set up in the 1960s with the express aim of providing economic and social benefits for Ghanaian society through supplying electricity. The World Bank, that lent the money for the project, in order to guarantee the repayment of the loan, insisted on the VRA supplying a US aluminium company with 60 per cent of production at a set price. However, with the hyperinflation of the 1970s, costs for the VRA rose dramatically and it utilized a sophisticated costing system to 'prove' the need to increase the prices it charged for the remaining 40 per cent of production. The World Bank also insisted that the VRA provide social and environmental reports, which it did to a high level of proficiency. These highlighted many positive aspects, such as the building of schools and hospitals, but also kept silent on the most important issue. That is, the VRA did not report on how the ever increasing prices that it was forced to charge meant that it failed to deliver its fundamental mission of providing economic and social development, as the majority of local Ghanaians could not afford to purchase the electricity that was being generated.

Accounting can gain power from its ability to provide visibility, such as demonstrating how the VRA had built schools and hospitals; but it equally gains power by keeping things invisible that organizations do not wish to address. This therefore brings us back to the discussion about the reporting frameworks promoted as being about sustainability. We must ask what these frameworks, such as the GRI, <IR>, and The Prince's Accounting for Sustainability Project, make visible, and what in turn they keep invisible and, in doing so, silence. They make visible the direct social and environmental impacts of an organization, or at least that which the organization chooses to disclose. However, these frameworks are problematic as they tend to be based on a weak conception of sustainability. That is, they keep invisible the scope and scale of the organization and how this relates to maintaining natural capital and living off natural interest. In essence what these frameworks do is allow organizations to report in the name of sustainability while allowing them to remain silent about the issue of sustainability. We now turn to examine the other main area of focus, management accounting.

12.2 Management Accounting

Traditionally management accounting concerns itself with the preparation of information to be used by managers in the process of making decisions. The typical topics covered by management accounting include cost-volume-profit analysis, which is overviewed in Chapter 7 of Atrill and McLaney (2011). This technique examines how an organization's costs change in relation to changes in volume, in order to calculate things such as the level at which the organization will break-even, how many sales are needed for a desired profit, and to be able to perform 'what if' scenario testing. Another example of a topic covered in management accounting is budgeting, overviewed in Chapter 9 of Atrill and McLaney (2011). Budgeting is the process of preparing a financial plan that is designed to assist with implementing the intended strategies and tactics in order to achieve the goals of upper management. Once prepared this plan may be used to evaluate performance as the organization progresses through the time period it covers. A final example of a typical topic covered by management accounting is costing, overviewed in Chapter 8 of Atrill and McLaney (2011). Costing is the utilization of a specific method that aims to assign costs to an object in order to assist with specific decisions, such as what price to sell a product, whether a product should be discontinued or, if looking to expand, then which products to target.

It is the topic of costing that has seen the greatest emphasis in regards to sustainability. There have been a number of experiments undertaken to ascertain whether it would be possible to expand these techniques in order to enable managers to include a wider range of considerations into their decision-making. One such experiment is known as Full Cost Accounting (FCA) (see, e.g., Bebbington *et al.*, 2001; Antheaume, 2007). FCA seeks to integrate and quantify all potential costs and benefits, including those that relate to social and environmental factors that organizations would normally consider as externalities, into the economic calculations they perform. The aim of this is to ensure that a full set of broad considerations are taken into account during the decision-making process. Tools have been developed in order to assist users with the implementation of FCA, including the sustainability assessment model (SAM) (see, e.g., Baxter *et al.*, 2004; Bebbington *et al.*, 2007; Frame & Cavanagh 2009; Xing *et al.*, 2009).

Another example in this area is the Sustainable Cost Calculation (SCC), which was first proposed by Gray (1992). The SCC puts forward a way to measure how much it would cost an organization to ensure that its operations left the earth at least no worse off at the end of the accounting period. As Bebbington (1997, p. 376) notes, it is 'a powerful accounting device for disrupting business unsustainability by using the language of business and accounting to illustrate just how far away we are from a sustainable state.' One of the most notable examples of attempts to implement this in practice is provided by Bebbington and Gray (2001). They provide an overview of an unsuccessful attempt to construct an SCC within an organization, at Manaaki Whenua, Landcare Research New Zealand Ltd (hereafter Landcare). This organization has the 'aim of developing knowledge of how land eco-systems may be sustainably managed' (Bebbington & Gray 2001, p. 564). While the experiment was judged to be unsuccessful, due to its creation of foreseeable and unforeseeable tensions, '[t]he experiment, however, was successful in suggesting how the initial visualization of sustainable cost was severely and crucially mis-specified' (Bebbington & Gray 2001, p. 558). That is, the experiment highlighted many issues in attempting to produce a calculation of this sort, including: the lack of reliable data; the inability to calculate anything except how unsustainable an organization is given that what a state of sustainability looks like is indeterminable; and issues around setting the scope of what is included and excluded from the calculation.

It is interesting to contrast the experiment performed at Landcare with Puma's Environmental Profit and Loss (EP&L) account,[4] overviewed in Case Study 12.4. When contrasting the former with the latter it raises quite a few questions. To start with the former experiment was conducted within an organization that specifically researches sustainability issues and therefore contains experts that would naturally add to the conceptualization of such a calculation, albeit creating some tensions in doing so. Even with the support of this expertise it is clear that the calculation was far from complete or reflective of the true state of unsustainability of the organization. In other words it was signalled as to the types of invisibility that were created in the process of trying to make the unsustainability of the organization visible.

In contrast to this, Puma released very little information in relation to its EP&L, with many important aspects still not known that make it impossible to fully understand what this account means. So, e.g., it is not clear what the method of calculation utilized was, how the data was gathered and what decisions were made as to what to include and exclude, what expertise was drawn upon in making the calculation, and how the results will be used by Puma. Through its silence on these important aspects, a lot of invisibility is created.

Further, the visibility that is created still raises more questions than it answers. Given, e.g, that the amount calculated is substantially less than its net earnings for the same period, is the inference from this that Puma is in a state of sustainability? It is not clear what actions will result from this calculation. Will, for instance, Puma utilize €145 million of its net earnings to undo the environmental impacts that it has caused, if this is even possible in practice? And has this changed Puma's underlying focus with corresponding changes in ecological throughput? Regardless, will it prompt action truly in line with strong sustainability or just be used as part of the journey metaphor (Milne *et al.*, 2006) of creating the illusion of moving to a state of sustainability? In essence we need to question whether Puma's EP&L is being used as a means to understand what its impacts are in relation to our state of unsustainability

---

[4] Puma's parent company, Kering, has subsequently also produced an EP&L. However, for the purposes of this discussion it is more instructive to focus on Puma due to the surrounding publicity, hype and claims that were made at the time of release of their EP&L. For more information of Kering's EP&L see http://www.kering.com/en/sustainability/epl.

CASE STUDY 12.4
Puma's Environmental Profit and Loss Account

In May of 2011, accompanied by a large amount of publicity, Puma, claiming to be the first to do such a thing, released their initial results from calculating their Environmental Profit and Loss Account (EP&L), with the final version released in November 2011. In order to conduct the process of calculation they hired the services of consultants Trucost and the accountants PwC. They define the EP&L as 'a means of placing a monetary value on the environmental impacts along the entire supply chain of a given business' (Puma, 2011, p. 2). Further, they state that the entire supply chain has the meaning of '[f]rom production of raw materials to transport to stores, the total impact of bringing products to market' (Puma, 2011, p. 2). They calculated, within what they deemed to be key areas, that in 2010 the environmental impacts generated through the operations and supply chain of PUMA were €47 million for greenhouse gas emissions, €47 million for water use, €37 million for land use, €11 million for other air pollution and €3 million for waste. This meant that their calculation of the total of the environmental impacts generated through the operations and supply chain of PUMA in 2010 were valued at €145 million in 2010, in a year that saw them also calculate Net Earnings of €202.2 million.

or whether it is an ends in itself, designed to assist with the implementation of goals as outlined *in section 12.1* looking at why organizations release more information than they are regulated to. At the very least we need to question why there are not greater levels of transparency over the release of this account.

Puma's EP&L can be seen as an example of what is being labelled as natural capital accounting. The move to introduce natural capital accounting has an underpinning of wanting organizations to take ecological concerns into account, including ecosystem services (see, e.g., Juniper, 2013). What the above example tries to illustrate is that natural capital accounting is being pursued without a balanced review of its possible downside. *As the discussion at the beginning of the chapter infers*, all types of accounting are a form of technology and as such there is a need to be aware of the potential issues that may arise from them (see, e.g., Small & Jollands, 2006). For example, from an ethical perspective we can question the appropriateness of a market system where almost everything is for sale (Sandel, 2013). That is, natural capital accounting, through adding numerical values to aspects of the ecosystem, reinforces the underlying utilitarian ethos of the market system where there is a 'right' price for everything. In doing so it crowds out other perspectives, most notably that of the categorical imperative where certain acts are seen as not justifiable under any circumstances. So this then raises the question of whether the good intentions of those that support the use of natural capital accounting will be undermined by the very market system that they seek to control.

This can be seen through returning to the case of Puma, and the questions posed above, and linking it back to the discussion at the beginning of the chapter in regards to sustainability. Currently there is no evidence to suggest that Puma has changed from being a market driven, consumer goods company. As such their focus on increasing the growth of their sales will still demand increasing levels of ecological throughput, despite any efficiency they gain in production or sourcing of materials *(see below)*. In such a situation natural capital accounting will suggest trade-offs to be made at the 'right' price rather than decisions being made about actions that should not be taken or resources that should not be used regardless of the situation. This will mean that at best Puma is aligned with weak conceptions of sustainability where the implementation of strong sustainability is required to sustain our futures.

Beyond the area of costing and natural capital accounting there have been several other noted examples of management accounts that have been adjusted or created to try to provide information about sustainability to managers. An example of where an adjustment has been made is the Balanced Scorecard (BSC) (see, e.g., Kaplan and Norton, 1992; Kaplan and Norton, 1996 for further details on the BSC). The BSC aims to be a strategic planning and management system that aligns the activities of the business with the intended strategy. It groups together – in the four perspectives of learning and growth, business processes, customers, and financial - both financial and non-financial metrics in order to provide a broader and more balanced view of how the organization is performing. The rationale behind the perspectives is that they promote thinking about the cause and effect links between these four areas. That is, improvements in the performance of employees, as reflected in the learning and growth perspective, will flow through to having better business processes, which will in turn create happier customers and corresponding improvements in the financials. However, the BSC is not without its critics (see, e.g., Nørreklit, 2000; Nørreklit, 2003), including questioning of whether the cause and effect between the perspectives are as linear as the BSC suggests. Notwithstanding these critiques attempts have been made to extend the balanced scorecard to include a fifth perspective that is focused on either ethical concerns or environmental concerns (see e.g., Epstein & Wisner, 2001; Figge *et al.*, 2002). However, it is debatable where this fifth perspective would fit within the BSC given the aforementioned issues with the linear cause and affect assumptions. For example, if the organization still has as its goal the increasing of profit through increasing sales, which in turn requires more ecological throughput, then at best this fifth perspective will reflect weak notions of sustainability and therefore it is arguable whether this moves beyond a 'business as usual' mindset.

Management accounting tools that have also been created in relation to sustainability issues include the ecological footprint *that is outlined in Case Study 12.2.* Another example is the carbon footprint, which is an offshoot of the ecological footprint. The carbon footprint aims to provide an account of the throughput of carbon and carbon-equivalent greenhouse gases, which have been linked to the causing of anthropocentric climate change (IPCC, 2014). There is potential for carbon footprints to assist in many ways in regards to alleviating the causes of anthropocentric climate change. For instance, those accountants and managers that use this tool will be required to acquire knowledge around the greenhouse gases and how they are made to be equivalent (MacKenzie, 2009). Therefore this tool, and those that examine aspects of issues relating to sustainability, have the potential to improve the ecological literacy (Ball & Milne, 2005) of those that engage with them and in doing so act upon the decisions these people make. However, with reference to the discussion of Puma's EP&L *above*, regardless of the visibility that these tools create there are many potential actions that may result, of which only some will be in line with strong sustainability. Specifically, in relation to the carbon footprint, many organizations have utilized carbon offsetting schemes. However, as the parody website www.cheatneutral.com points out, these schemes do not address the fundamental underlying problems of reducing the practices that create the greenhouse gas emissions in the first place.

Another example of the creation of sustainability focused management accounting is the tools and techniques that can collectively be grouped under the label of Environmental Management Accounting (EMA). A good example to illustrate the types of techniques that are covered under this term is Material Flow Cost Accounting (MFCA). MFCA calculates the cost of waste produced in making a product and thereby tries to motivate the efficient use of resources. That is, by putting a cost to the waste and having this included in the cost of the product it tries to ensure as much of the inputs make it into the final product rather than ending up as waste. However, like all EMA that has been labelled as 'ecological modernism' by some (see, e.g., Everett and Neu, 2000), MFCA is not without its critique, *as the example below illustrates.*

In the example in Table 12.1, if the starting point is state 1, then MFCA will prompt us, through putting a cost to the 50% of inputs that end up as waste, to think about how we can move to state 2. Once state 2 is reached then our relative performance has improved, as we are now only wasting 37.5% of the inputs. We may also think that we are now more environmentally friendly as we are only utilizing 80 kg of inputs to make our 50 units of the final product. However, the problem here is that what is being made visible, the relative performance, is keeping invisible something that is far more important in terms of sustainability, the absolute performance. This is best illustrated with reference to Table 12.2:

The scenario that is presented in Table 12.2 is the ongoing operations of an organization, with just the initial eight weeks shown. This organization is utilizing MFCA in order to improve the relative use of the inputs. It achieves this by reducing the relative amount of waste from 50% to 37.5% between weeks 1 and 2 and then through reducing the relative amount of waste from 37.5% to 30% between weeks 4 and 5. However, Table 12.2 also illustrates that, like all organizations, it aims to improve its profits through improving its sales. These improvements in relative efficiency will flow through to the product costing the organization less to produce and in turn enabling it to reduce the selling price it charges to customers. This decrease

TABLE 12.1   Improvements in Efficiency Moving from State 1 to State 2

State 1		
Input	Production	Sold
100 kg	50 kg goes to product 50 kg goes to waste	50 units sold 50% of material wasted
State 2		
Input	Production	Sold
80 kg	50 kg goes to product 30 kg goes to waste	50 units sold 37.5% of material wasted

TABLE 12.2 Relative Versus Absolute Over Time

Week	Sold	Input	Product	Waste	Relative
1	50 units	100 kg	50 kg	50 kg	50%
2	50 units	80 kg	50 kg	30 kg	37.5%
3	60 units	96 kg	60 kg	36 kg	37.5%
4	70 units	112 kg	70 kg	42 kg	37.5%
5	70 units	100 kg	70 kg	30 kg	30%
6	77 units	110 kg	77 kg	33 kg	30%
7	84 units	120 kg	84 kg	36 kg	30%
8	91 units	130 kg	91 kg	39 kg	30%
Absolute		848 kg			

in price increases demand for the product and the number of units sold, as shown in the table. As sales increase the absolute amount of inputs utilized will also increase. In effect the savings in wasted resources are used for advertising purposes and lead to increased sales. These extra sales result in increased absolute levels of resource throughput. In this example the first relative efficiency gains are overcome in absolute terms when sales increase to 63 units. Further, this example illustrates that over the course of the eight weeks the absolute resources used are 848 kg. We therefore need to ask questions as to what type of input the 848 kg represents. There is a large difference between these resources being renewable and across all organizations no more of them being utilized as can be constantly renewed, versus these inputs being non-renewable natural capital. Further, this example illustrates the issue, *which we referred to above*, of Jevons' Paradox, commonly referred to as the rebound effect. That is, we know that gains in efficiency, as measured by relative metrics, usually encourage absolute increases in environmental effects. This is why it is often noted that eco-efficiency subscribes to a weak conception of sustainability. In finishing this example we note again that these EMA tools are not in themselves bad. They should, rather, be looked at as a means of telling us something about relative performance, and this relative performance and the output of these tools should not become ends in themselves. So, e.g., if these tools are also used in conjunction with other tools that make visible other aspects of absolute resource throughput, the nature of the resources being utilized, and the absolute effect this has on the ecology, then there is potential to not fall victim to Jevons' Paradox.

One final example of an emerging technique is that of Net Positive.[5] The motivation for this is that natural capital is being extracted at a rate faster than it can naturally be replenished. Therefore, Net Positive aims for organizations to have a positive rather than a negative impact on natural capital. This of course will require measurement

---

[5] Refer to http://www.forumforthefuture.org/project/net-positive-group/overview for further details.

and so comes under the broad definition of accounting, which we opened this chapter. Organizations such as Lafarge, Kingfisher Group and BT have made commitments to and begun to experiment with this technique. However, as with all the techniques *overviewed above*, it has weaknesses as well as its strengths. Specifically, due to it being relatively new, it is still unclear as to what being Net Positive really means and whether in practice it is even possible. Also, like all of the techniques considered, the main challenge lies in making sure it is used as a means to address sustainability issues and that it is not co-opted into being a means of allowing business to continue as usual through obfuscating a reality of inaction (Milne *et al.*, 2006).

The use of a whole raft of supporting tools and techniques, including those usually labelled as accounting, by an organization to make visible a variety of aspects in relation to its performance and to guide managers into making decisions that are in line with its strategy and beliefs comes under the collective title of Management Control Systems (MCS). Bisbe and Otley (2004, p. 709) define MCS as 'the set of procedures that managers and other organisational participants use in order to help ensure the achievement of their goals and the goals of their organisations and it encompasses formal control systems as well as informal personal and social controls.' These systems are utilized to implement the intended strategy of managers and to identify emergent strategy as it arises. However, in relation to sustainability and the issues raised *above* we can refer to Ball and Milne (2005), who provide a comprehensive critique of how the MCS we see currently being employed in practice by organizations exacerbate these issues rather than help in addressing them. The chapter concludes with this in mind.

12.3 Conclusion: Addressing the meta- and sub-questions

We started this chapter by outlining a meta-question and a series of sub-questions. In concluding we return to each of these questions in turn. Starting with the meta-question, it asked how we can understand whether the outcome(s) of the decisions we make move us towards a state of sustainability or to a more unsustainable state. We have overviewed how accounting is so much more than it is typically perceived to be. However, the one thing that all accounts have in common is that they are a source of information that can be drawn upon in the decision-making process. *As has been outlined above*, these accounts are not always as objective as they appear to be. Further, as we have seen, every type of account has the potential to provide visibility over a certain aspect of what it focuses on. However, no account can provide visibility over all aspects and therefore in using an account we must be aware not only of the visibility that it creates but in turn what remains invisible. After all, the quality of the decisions we make will always be affected by the basis on which we make that decision. In terms of sustainability we must therefore ask, in relation to the accounts we employ, how they relate to the strong conception and whether key aspects still remain invisible through their use. We now turn to the sub-questions in order to explore this further.

The first of the sub-questions was what tools and techniques (i.e., financial and management accounting) are organizations currently using to provide information to decision-makers in this respect? In relation to this question we have explored whether traditional accounting has moved beyond its narrow focus on merely the financial aspects of an organization. In terms of financial accounting there is no doubt that it has become more sophisticated over the years as the types of transactions needing to be recorded have also become more complicated. But we have seen that despite the increased sophistication it is still reliant on the subjective judgements of the preparer. Further, the sophistication is reliant on the cumbersome supporting infrastructure of accounting standards. Despite all this sophistication and standards it is still open to misuse, as in the cases of ENRON and Worldcom. Given this fragility of financial accounting, which has developed over hundreds of years, it is not surprising that social, environmental, and sustainability reporting[6] has not fared much better, particularly given its relative infancy. Further, we have seen that management accounting has the potential to provide visibility over these issues for decision-makers but, again, it is reliant on how these tools and techniques are designed and used, and whether the resulting actions are in line with strong conceptions of sustainability.

This therefore brings us to the second sub-question, which is, what other tools and techniques (i.e., financial and management accounting) do organizations have at their disposal to provide information to decision-makers in this respect? We have overviewed several examples of accounts that can make visible aspects of sustainability. These included the ecological footprint and its offshoot the carbon footprint, the sustainable cost calculation, and full cost accounting. We saw in relation to these how Puma had implemented its EP&L. This reminded us that the way in which these are utilized, specifically as a means or as an end, is as important as how they are calculated. Given that any of these will only ever offer some aspect of what is being made visible, it is important to use a variety of tools that support each other and highlight differing information. In regards to sustainability there are many more techniques that we could have covered here, including the notion of 'burden to base' put forward by Birkin (1996), or those highlighted by Ball and Milne (2005) aimed at dematerialization, including material inputs per unit of service, the ecological rucksack, surface area per unit of service, and ecotoxic exposure equivalent per unit of service.

The need for a number of accounts that make visible differing aspects brings us to our third and final sub-question, which is: what issues, concerns, problems, and shortcomings with these tools and techniques should the users (i.e., decision-makers) be aware of in terms of using the information provided? While we have covered most of these points in the previous couple of paragraphs, it may help to again return to the example of the ecological footprint. The ecological footprint is a great measure for making visible the throughput of ecological resources and in doing so providing a notion of the scale and scope of the organization's operations. However, if this account is taken in isolation then one of the major things that will remain invisible

---

[6] With reference to the above discussion, specifically the discussion of what sustainability is, we should note that sustainability reporting is somewhat different to social and environmental reporting. The former requires the acknowledgement of much more than the latter including planetary boundaries, scale and scope of operations, and inter- and intra-generational equity. The latter, however, only reports on the direct social and environmental impacts of the organization. However, in practice, these terms are often used interchangeably and thereby erroneously by organizations.

is the health of underlying ecosystem that these resources are being drawn from. This could arguably lead to a situation whereby an organization, while reducing its footprint, is still creating great harm as it is drawing all of its resources from one specific part of the ecosystem and in doing so decimating that specific area, which may in turn impact on the greater ecology. This example, therefore, demonstrates the need for a management control system of various accounts that make visible differing aspects of strong sustainability. Even with this in place users and decision-makers still need to constantly question what aspects remain invisible. This needs to be done in a way that addresses concerns around intra- and inter-generational equity. Above all it is clear that traditional accounting as we know it needs to radically change in order to play its part in averting Easter Island-like consequences on a global scale.

Summary

This chapter covered the following points:

1   Accounting is much more than the narrowly focused preparation of financial information but rather is the preparation of an account, in its broadest sense, which provides the explanation of events, actions, and the use of resources.

2   Accounts will make visible certain aspects of what they are trying to focus on and in doing so will draw attention away from other aspects that will remain invisible.

3   In practice many new accounts, tools and techniques are being developed in the name of sustainability; many of these have a limited relation to a strong conception of sustainability and are being utilized for a variety of purposes other than addressing concerns over sustainability issues.

4   It is the resulting actions that these accounts prompt that are important, not the accounts themselves, and therefore they should be viewed as part of the means to achieving improvements towards attaining a state of sustainability rather than ends in themselves.

5   Decision-makers within organizations need a management control system full of accounts that support each other through providing visibility over differing aspects of sustainability issues.

QUESTIONS FOR CLASS DISCUSSION

1. Define what accounting is and how this contrasts with commonly held views of the subject.
2. How can accounting help us to understand sustainability issues?
3. What are some of the issues in trying to provide an account of sustainability?

References

Al-Tuwaijri, S. A., Christensen, T. E., & Hughes II, K. E. (2004). The relations among environmental disclosure, environmental performance, and economic performance: A simultaneous equations approach. *Accounting, Organizations and Society, 29*(5, 6), 447–471.

Alcott, B. (2005). Jevons' paradox. *Ecological Economics, 54*(1), 9–21.

Antheaume, N. (2007). Full cost accounting: Adam Smith meets Rachel Carson? In Unerman, J., Bebbington, J., & O'Dwyer, B. *Sustainability accounting and accountability*. London: Routledge, 211–225.

Arrow, K., B. Bolin, Costanza, R., Dasgupta, P., Folke, C., Holling, C. S., Jansson, B.-O., Simon, L., Mäler, K.-G., Perrings, C., & Pimentel, D. (1995). Economic growth, carrying capacity, and the environment. *Science. 268*(5210), 520–521.

Atrill, P., & McLaney, E. (2011). *Accounting and finance for non-specialists*. Harlow: Pearson.

Ayres, R. U. (2004). On the life cycle metaphor: Where ecology and economics diverge. *Ecological Economics, 48*(4), 425–438.

Ball, A. (2007). Environmental accounting as workplace activism. *Critical Perspectives on Accounting, 18*(7), 759–778.

Ball, A., & Milne, M. J. (2005). Sustainability and management control. In Berry, A. J., Broadbent, J., & and Otley, D. *Management control: Theories, issues, and performance*. Basingstoke and New York: Palgrave Macmillan, 314–337.

Bartolomeo, M., Bennett, M., Bouma, J. J., Heydkamp, P., James, P., & Wolters, T. (2000). Environmental management accounting in Europe: Current practice and future potential. *European Accounting Review, 9*(1), 31–52.

Baue, B., & Murninghan, M. (2011). *Integrated reporting in a disintegrating world. The Guardian*. Retrieved from theguardian.com.

Baxter, T., Bebbington, J., & Cutteridge, D. (2004). Sustainability assessment model: modelling economic, resource, environmental and social flows of a project. *Triple Bottom Line: Does It All Add Up?* A. Henriques and J. Richardson. London, Earthscan, 113–120.

Bebbington, J. (1997). Engagement, education and sustainability: A review essay on environmental accounting. *Accounting, Auditing & Accountability Journal, 10*(3), 365–381.

Bebbington, J., Brown, J., & Frame, B. (2007). Accounting technologies and sustainability assessment models. *Ecological Economics, 61*(2–3), 224–236.

Bebbington, J., & Gray, R. (2001). An account of sustainability: Failure, success and a reconceptualization. *Critical Perspectives on Accounting, 12*(5), 557–588.

Bebbington, J., Gray, R. H., Hibbitt, C., & Kirk, E. (2001). *Full cost accounting: An agenda for action*. London, Association of Chartered Certified Accountants.

Belal, A. R., & Owen, D. (2007). The views of corporate managers on the current state of, and future prospects for, social reporting in Bangladesh. *Accounting, Auditing & Accountability Journal, 20*(3), 472–494.

Birkin, F. (1996). The ecological accountant: From the cogito to thinking like a mountain. *Critical Perspectives on Accounting, 7*(3), 231–257.

Birkin, F., Edwards, P., & Woodward, D. (2005). Accounting's contribution to a conscious cultural evolution: An end to sustainable development. *Critical Perspectives on Accounting, 16*(3), 185–208.

Bisbe, J., & Otley, D. (2004). The effects of the interactive use of management control systems on product innovation. *Accounting, Organizations and Society, 29*(8), 709–737.

Brown, H. S., de Jong, M., & Lessidrenska, T. (2009). The rise of the Global Reporting Initiative: A case of institutional entrepreneurship. *Environmental Politics,* 18(2), 182–200.

Cairns, J. (2001). Sustainability, exceptionalism, and exemptionalism. *Ecosystem Health, 7*(3), 147–154.

Costanza, R. (1989). What is ecological economics? *Ecological Economics, 1*(1), 1–7.

Costanza, R. (1998). The value of ecosystem services. *Ecological Economics, 25*(1), 1–2.

Costanza, R., D'Arge, R., De Groot, R., Farber, S., Grasso, M., Hannon, B., Limburg, K., Naeem, S., O'Neill, R. V., Paruelo, J., Raskin, R. G., Sutton, P., & Van Den Belt, M. (1997). The value of the world's ecosystem services and natural capital. *Nature, 387*(6630), 253–260.

Covaleski, M. A., Dirsmith, M. W., & Samuel, S. (1996). Managerial Accounting Research: The Contributions of Organizational and Sociological Theories. *Journal of Management Accounting Research, 8*, 1–35.

Daly, H. E. (1992). Allocation, distribution, and scale: Towards an economics that is efficient, just, and sustainable. *Ecological Economics, 6*(3), 185–193.

de Groot, R. S., Wilson, M. A., & Boumans, R. M. J. (2002). A typology for the classification, description and valuation of ecosystem functions, goods and services. *Ecological Economics, 41*(3), 393–408.

Deegan, C. (2002). The legitimising effect of social and environmental disclosures: A theoretical foundation. *Accounting, Auditing & Accountability Journal, 15*(3), 282–311.

Deegan, C. (2007). Organizational legitimacy as a motive for sustainability reporting. In Unerman, J., Bebbington, J., & O'Dwyer, B. *Sustainability accounting and accountability*. London: Routledge, 127–149.

Diamond, J. M. (2005). *Collapse: How societies choose to fail or survive*. New York: Viking.

DiMaggio, P. J., & Powell, W. W. (1983). The iron cage revisited: Institutional isomorphism and collective rationality in organizational fields. *American Sociological Review, 48*(2), 147–160.

Dowling, J., & Pfeffer, J. (1975). Organizational legitimacy: Social values and organizational behavior. *The Pacific Sociological Review*, *18*(1), 122–136.

Dryzek, J. S. (1997). *The politics of the earth: Environmental discourses*. Oxford and New York: Oxford University Press.

Epstein, M. J., & Wisner, P. S. (2001). Using a balanced scorecard to implement sustainability. *Environmental Quality Management*, *11*(2), 1–10.

Everett, J., & Neu, D. (2000). Ecological modernization and the limits of environmental accounting? *Accounting Forum*, *24*(1), 5–29.

Figge, F., Hahn, T., Schaltegger, S., & Wagner, M. (2002). The Sustainability Balanced Scorecard - linking sustainability management to business strategy. *Business Strategy and the Environment*, *11*(5), 269.

Flenley, J., & Bahn, P. (2011). Review of Hunt, T. and Lipo, C. *The statues that walked: Unraveling the mystery of Easter Island*. *Rapa Nui Journal*, *25*(2), 60–62.

Frame, B., & Cavanagh, J. (2009). Experiences of sustainability assessment: An awkward adolescence. *Accounting Forum*, *33*(3), 195–208.

Glencore Xstrata. (2013). *Glencore Xstrata Sustainability Report 2013*. Baar, Switzerland, 107.

Global Witness Limited. (2012). *Annual Review 2012*. London, 32.

Gray, R. (1992). Accounting and environmentalism: An exploration of the challenge of gently accounting for accountability, transparency and sustainability. *Accounting, Organizations and Society*, *17*(5), 399–425.

Gray, R. (2010). Is accounting for sustainability actually accounting for sustainability [. . .] and how would we know? An exploration of narratives of organisations and the planet. *Accounting, Organizations and Society*, *35*(1), 47–62.

Gray, R., Dey, C., Owen, D., Evans, R., & Zadek, S. (1997). Struggling with the praxis of social accounting: Stakeholders, accountability, audits and procedures. *Accounting, Auditing & Accountability Journal*, *10*(3), 325–364.

Gray, R., Kouhy, R., & Lavers, S. (1995). Corporate social and environmental reporting: A review of the literature and a longitudinal study of UK disclosure. *Accounting, Auditing & Accountability Journal*, *8*(2), 47–77.

Gray, R., & Milne, M. J. (2002). Sustainability reporting: Who's kidding whom? *Chartered Accountants Journal*, *81*(6), 66–70.

Gray, R., & Milne, M. J. (2004). Towards reporting on the triple bottom line: Mirages, methods, and myths. In Henriques, A., & Richardson, J. *Triple bottom line: Does it all add up?* London: Earthscan, 70–80.

Gray, R., Owen, D., & Adams, C. (1996). *Accounting & accountability: changes and challenges in corporate social and environmental reporting*. London : New York Prentice Hall.

Holliday, C. (2001). Sustainable growth, the DuPont way. *Harvard Business Review*, *79*(8), 129–134.

Holm, S.-O., & Englund, G. (2009). Increased ecoefficiency and gross rebound effect: Evidence from USA and six European countries 1960–2002. *Ecological Economics*, *68*(3), 879–887.

Hopwood, A. G. (1987). The archeology of accounting systems. *Accounting, Organizations and Society*, *12*(3), 207–234.

Hunt, T., & Lipo, C. (2011). *The statues that walked: Unraveling the mystery of Easter Island*. New York: Free Press.

IPCC (2014). *Climate change 2014: Impacts, adaptation, and vulnerability. Part A: Global and sectoral aspects. Contribution of Working Group II to the Fifth Assessment Report Of The Intergovernmental Panel On Climate Change*. Cambridge and New York: Cambridge University Press.

Juniper, T. (2013). *What has nature ever done for us? How money really does grow on trees*. London: Profile Books.

Kaplan, R. S., & Norton, D. P. (1992). The balanced scorecard: Measures that drive performance. *Harvard Business Review*, *70*(1), 71–79.

Kaplan, R. S., & Norton, D. P. (1996). *The balanced scorecard: Translating strategy into action*. Boston, MA: Harvard Business School Press.

Korten, D. (2010). *Agenda for a new economy: From phantom wealth to real wealth*. San Francisco: Berrett-Koehler Publishers, Inc.

Lemon, A. J., & Cahan, S. F. (1997). Environmental legislation and environmental disclosures: Some evidence from New Zealand. *Asian Review of Accounting*, *5*(1), 78–105.

Leopold, A. (1968). *A Sand County almanac and sketches here and there*. New York: Oxford University Press.

Lindblom, C. K. (1993). *The implications of organizational legitimacy for corporate social performance and disclosure*. Paper at Critical Perspectives on Accounting Conference. New York.

MacKenzie, D. (2009). Making things the same: Gases, emission rights and the politics of carbon markets. *Accounting, Organizations and Society*, *34*(3–4), 440–455.

McKendrick, N. (1970). Josiah Wedgwood and cost accounting in the industrial revolution. *The Economic History Review*, *23*(1), 45–67.

McMann, P. J., & Nanni Jr., A. J. (1995). Means versus ends: A review of the literature on Japanese management accounting. *Management Accounting Research*, *6*(4), 313–346.

Meadows, D. H., Meadows, D. L., Randers, J., & Behrens III, W. W. (1972). *The limits to growth: a report for the club of Rome's project on the predicament of mankind*. New York, Universe Books.

Miller, P., & Napier, C. (1993). Genealogies of calculation. *Accounting, Organizations and Society*, *18*(7–8), 631–647.

Milne, M. (2013). Phantasmagoria, sustain-a-babbling in social and environmental reporting. In Jack, L., Davison, J., & Craig, R. *The Routledge companion to accounting communication*. London: Routledge, 135–153.

Milne, M. J. (1996). On sustainability: The environment and management accounting. *Management Accounting Research*, *7*(1), 135–161.

Milne, M. J. (2002). Positive accounting theory, political costs and social disclosure analyses: A critical look. *Critical Perspectives on Accounting*, *13*(3), 369–395.

Milne, M. J. (2007). Downsizing reg (me and you)! Addressing the 'real' sustainability agenda at work and home. In Mathews, M. R., Gray, R., & Guthrie, J. *Social accounting, mega accounting and beyond: A festschrift in honour of M. R. Mathews*. St. Andrews: Centre for Social and Environmental Accounting Research, 50–66.

Milne, M. J., & Gray, R. (2007). Future prospects for corporate sustainability reporting. In Unerman, J., Bebbington, J., & O'Dwyer, B. *Sustainability accounting and accountability*. London: Routledge, 184–207.

Milne, M. J., Kearins, K., & Walton, S. (2006). Creating Adventures in Wonderland: The Journey Metaphor and Environmental Sustainability. *Organization, 13*(6), 801–839.

Mirvis, P. H. (2000). Transformation at Shell: Commerce and citizenship. *Business and Society Review, 105*(1), 63–84.

Missemer, A. (2012). William Stanley Jevons' *The Coal Question* (1865), beyond the rebound effect. *Ecological Economics, 82*, 97–103.

Naess, A. (1973). The shallow and the deep, long-range ecology movement: A summary. *Inquiry, 16*(1–4), 95–100.

Naess, A. (1990). *Ecology, community and lifestyle: Outline of an ecosophy*. Cambridge: Cambridge University Press.

Nørreklit, H. (2000). The balance on the balanced scorecard: A critical analysis of some of its assumptions. *Management Accounting Research, 11*(1), 65–88.

Nørreklit, H. (2003). The balanced scorecard: What is the score? A rhetorical analysis of the balanced scorecard. *Accounting, Organizations and Society, 28*(6), 591–619.

Parker, L. D. (2005). Social and environmental accountability research: A view from the commentary box. *Accounting, Auditing & Accountability Journal, 18*(6), 842–860.

Pearsall, J. (2001). *The concise Oxford dictionary*. Oxford: Oxford University Press.

PUMA. (2011). *PUMA's environmental profit and loss account for the year ended 31 December 2010*. Retrieved from http://about.puma.com/damfiles/default/sustainability/environment/e-p-l/EPL080212final-3cdfc1bdca0821c6ec1cf4b89935bb5f.pdf.

Rahaman, A. S., & Lawrence, S. (2001a). A negotiated order perspective on public sector accounting and financial control. *Accounting, Auditing & Accountability Journal, 14*(2), 147.

Rahaman, A. S., & Lawrence, S. (2001b). Public sector accounting and financial management in a developing country organisational context: A three-dimensional view. *Accounting Forum, 25*(2), 189.

Rahaman, A. S., Lawrence, S., & Roper, J. (2004). Social and environmental reporting at the VRA: institutionalised legitimacy or legitimation crisis? *Critical Perspectives on Accounting, 15*(1), 35–56.

Roberts, R. W. (1992). Determinants of corporate social responsibility disclosure: An application of stakeholder theory. *Accounting, Organizations and Society, 17*(6), 595.

Rockström, J., & Klum, M. (2012). *The human quest: Prospering within planetary boundaries*. Stockholm: Bokforlaget Max Strom.

Rockström, J., Steffen, W., Noone, K., Persson, A., Chapin, F. S., Lambin, E. F., Lenton, T. M., Scheffer, M., Folke, C., Schellnhuber, H. J., Nykvist, B., de Wit, C. A., Hughes, T., van der Leeuw, S., Rodhe, H., Sorlin, S., Snyder, P. K., Costanza, R., Svedin, U., Falkenmark, M., Karlberg, L., Corell, R. W., Fabry, V. J., Hansen, J., Walker, B., Liverman, D., Richardson, K., Crutzen, P., & Foley, J. A. (2009). A safe operating space for humanity. *Nature, 461*(7263), 472–475.

Sandel, M. J. (2013). *What money can't buy: The moral limits of markets*. London: Penguin.

Simpson, J. A., & Weiner, E. S. C. (Eds.). (1989). *The Oxford english dictionary*. Oxford: Clarendon Press.

Small, B., & Jollands, N. (2006). Technology and ecological economics: Promethean technology, Pandorian potential. *Ecological Economics, 56*(3), 343–358.

Sweeney, J. (2012). Billionaires behaving badly? *Panorama*, BBC (30 minutes).

Tinker, T., & Gray, R. (2003). Beyond a critique of pure reason: From policy to politics to praxis in environmental and social research. *Accounting, Auditing & Accountability Journal, 16*(5), 727–761.

Wackernagel, M., & Rees, W. E. (1996). *Our ecological footprint: Reducing human impact on the earth*. Gabriola Island, B.C.: New Society Publishers.

Watts, R. L., & Zimmerman, J. L. (1978). Towards a positive theory of the determination of accounting standards. *The Accounting Review, 53*(1), 112.

Whiteman, G., Walker, B., & Perego, P. (2013). Planetary Boundaries: Ecological Foundations for Corporate Sustainability. *Journal of Management Studies, 50*(2), 307–336.

World Commission on Environment and Development. (1987). *Our common future*. Oxford: Oxford University Press.

World Wide Fund for Nature. (2014). *Living planet report 2014: Species and spaces, people and places*. Gland: Switzerland.

Xing, Y., Horner, R. M. W., El-Haram, M. A., & Bebbington, J. (2009). A framework model for assessing sustainability impacts of urban development. *Accounting Forum, 33*(3), 209–224.

Zeff, S. A. (2012). The evolution of the IASC into the IASB, and the challenges it faces. *Accounting Review, 87*(3), 807–837.

13 Entrepreneurship

Tony Cooke

This chapter is dedicated to the late Ray Anderson, pioneering One Planet Entrepreneur and inspiration to a generation of sustainable business leaders.

'Innovation is the specific instrument of entrepreneurship . . . the act that endows resources with a new capacity to create wealth.'

Peter F. Drucker

'In times of major political, social, and environmental change, the number of problems requiring judgment increases and the demand for entrepreneurs rises as a result.'

Mark Casson (1982)

LEARNING OUTCOMES

By the end of this chapter you will have developed an understanding of:

1. The nature of entrepreneurship.

2. The variety of organizational contexts where entrepreneurship can have an impact.

3. One Planet Entrepreneurship: the application of entrepreneurship in relation to the environment, society and the economy.

4. Your own entrepreneurial attributes and where best to have impact as a One Planet Entrepreneur.

Introduction

The theory and practice of entrepreneurship has much to offer a One Planet approach to building sustainable businesses, not to mention public services, charities and communities. At its heart is the key concept of 'creative destruction', i.e., the ability and restless desire to shift resources out of areas of lower productivity into areas of higher productivity and, in doing so, move society beyond current paradigms towards new ways of living. Applicable at any scale from the individual to society and across a wide variety of contexts, entrepreneurship represents a collection of behaviours and skills that, provided they are morally and ethically grounded, could make a profound contribution to the achievement of sustainability goals. For aspiring change-makers wishing to maximize their own impact across business, society and the environment, understanding how best to channel their own entrepreneurial intentions in the career choices they make into the future will be critical. This chapter provides a primer on entrepreneurship that aims to frame it in the widest possible terms whilst integrating it with a number of adjacent business topics including economics, business ethics, strategy and innovation.

13.0 The 'Cult' of Entrepreneurship?

Entrepreneurship, it seems, is on everyone's lips. A Google search of 'entrepreneurship' yields 68.9 million results.[1] Political leaders revering entrepreneurship as the lifeblood of the economy. Corporate executives espousing the need for more entrepreneurship to remain competitive. Social activists believing entrepreneurship can deliver breakthrough improvements to tackling inequality, social injustice, crime and many other social issues. See Box 13.1.

BOX 13.1

On entrepreneurship . . .

Entrepreneurs embody the promise of America: the belief that if you have a good idea and are willing to work hard and see it through, you can succeed in this country. And in fulfilling this promise, entrepreneurs also play a critical role in expanding our economy and creating jobs.

Barack Obama, US President

Nobody talks of entrepreneurship as survival, but that's exactly what it is and what nurtures creative thinking.

Anita Roddick, Founder, The Body Shop

I believe that drudgery and clock-watching are a terrible betrayal of that universal, inborn entrepreneurial spirit.

Sir Richard Branson, Chairman, Virgin Group

I'm encouraging young people to become social business entrepreneurs and contribute to the world, rather than just making money. Making money is no fun. Contributing to and changing the world is a lot more fun.

Muhammad Yunus, Founder, Grameen Bank, Bangladesh

My dream is to find individuals who take financial resources and convert them into changing the world in the most positive ways.

Jacqueline Novogratz, Founder & CEO, Acumen Fund

What does an entrepreneur do? The first thing is they've given themselves permission to see a problem. Most people don't want to see problems . . . once you see a problem and you keep looking at it you'll find an answer.

Bill Drayton, Founder, Ashoka Changemakers

---

[1] Google search conducted in May 2015.

In an starkly unequal world struggling for economic growth whilst simultaneously wrestling with the immense challenge of keeping within planetary boundaries,[2] entrepreneurship is widely perceived as being able to make a critical contribution to solving the world's toughest problems.

Popular culture on TV, radio, the internet and social media in much of the developed world has seemingly become obsessed with propagating a cult around successful independent entrepreneurs, enveloping them (and entrepreneurship by extension) with an aura of heroism. Often inspiring and self-obsessed in equal measure, these caricatured media personalities are presented to the audience as a breed apart, convincing us that entrepreneurship is not something for mere mortals. Indeed, it is often inferred that one must first be successful to earn the title 'entrepreneur'. At the very least, the title tends to be reserved for those who have been through the process of setting up and running their own business, suggesting that being an entrepreneur is a binary status – you either are an entrepreneur or you are not. In reality, of course, any person undertaking such a venture would have been entrepreneurial long beforehand and quite possibly had a number of failures to their name that the tabloid media have conveniently airbrushed out of their biography.

The cult of the entrepreneur therefore provides us with an overly narrow and sanitized version of entrepreneurship and what it is to be entrepreneurial. It perpetuates the belief that entrepreneurship is relevant only in the context of independent businesses founded and led by entrepreneurs, thus limiting the application of it as a powerful idea across a much wider variety of contexts, and doing nothing to help us to arrive at a useful definition and understanding of what entrepreneurship is.

In practice, entrepreneurship is an infinitely more prosaic yet inspiring, pervasive yet perilous, phenomenon than the media, politicians and commentators would have us believe. Far from being heroic, it is as much found in everyday 'small acts of entrepreneurship' by almost everyone as it is in the game-changing, headline-grabbing actions of household name entrepreneurs.

Entrepreneurship has both the ability to create and destroy. It can generate new industries and markets whilst simultaneously destroying old ones, often simply as collateral damage. It can act as a relentless, impartial force for redeploying resources, contributing to sustainability whilst creating losers. It can radically improve our quality of life whilst threatening to undermine cultural traditions, social identity, continuity, routines and even how we organize ourselves as a society. It can contribute profoundly to society's innovation, creativity, progress and prosperity whilst, if devoid of moral purpose, strong ethics and values, also being moribund, corrupt and responsible for the worst aspects of human greed and criminality. And of course, it can result in failure – from very limited to catastrophic – with the potential to take a heavy toll on the psychological and financial health of those engaged in it, or the victims of it.

For this reason, this chapter will chart a path for the reader towards a more holistic understanding of entrepreneurship and its application in achieving business sustainability.

---

[2] Stockholm Resilience Centre, Planetary Boundaries 2.0. Retrieved from http://www.stockholmresilience .org/21/research/research-news/1-15-2015-planetary-boundaries-2.0—new-and-improved.html.

13.1 A Brief History of Entrepreneurship Theory

A good place to begin with developing an understanding of entrepreneurship is to look at the evolution of its theory. There is a wealth of useful material in the specialized entrepreneurship literature *and some of the key references are provided at the end of this chapter*, but an overview is provided here.

Entrepreneurship is a discrete yet multidisciplinary and cross-cutting field of study in its own right which owes its existence to a convergence of interest between psychology, management studies, sociology and economics (see Box 13.2). Broadly speaking, the motivation for studying entrepreneurship as a phenomenon differs between them: psychology being interested in the antecedents of an individual's entrepreneurial ability, i.e., individual characteristics, attributes and life experiences; management studies being interested in the practice of entrepreneurship within the context of the firm and its interrelationship with strategy, innovation, people, performance and competitiveness; sociology being interested in the relationships between entrepreneurship, culture and society: and economics being interested in the effects of entrepreneurship upon the economic system. Each of these fields, and more, have made valuable contributions to the understanding and meaning of entrepreneurship, as well as underlining the importance of entrepreneurship as a cross-cutting multidisciplinary subject, but we have the field of economics to thank for laying the foundation stones of entrepreneurship theory.

13.1.1 Economic Foundations

Whilst observed as a phenomenon as far back as classical Greece, it was not until 1755 that Irish-French economist Richard Cantillon (1680–1734) first coined the term 'entrepreneur' in his posthumously published *Essai sur la Nature du Commerce en General.*

BOX 13.2

On entrepreneurship . . .

'Entrepreneur' comes from the French word 'entre-prendre', meaning 'to undertake'.

Entrepreneurs are innovators who create change within markets through the carrying out of new combinations.

Joseph A. Schumpeter (1934)

Entrepreneurship is the process of creating value by bringing together a unique combination of resources to exploit an opportunity.

Howard Stevenson & Carlos Jarillo (1990)

Innovation matters, but it doesn't happen automatically. It is driven by entrepreneurship – a potent mixture of vision, passion, energy, enthusiasm, insight, judgment and plain hard work which enables good ideas to become a reality.

John Bessant & Joe Tidd (2007)

The focus of his definition was on risk – he saw the entrepreneur as someone who assumes the risk of a business in exchange for profit.

Throughout the 19th century, the entrepreneur became framed much more widely as an opportunity-seeking economic actor playing a reorganizing role in the efficient allocation of economic resources. In 1803, French economist Jean-Baptiste Say, an early pioneer of free-market thinking, expounded the role of the entrepreneur, putting him at the heart of his supply-sided economic theory which cast him as an opportunity-recognizing producer. Later, in 1848, John Stuart Mill briefly popularized the concept in *Principles of Political Economy*, but by the end of the 19th century it had fallen from use. Precisely why this was is not understood, but Mark Casson more recently argued in *The Entrepreneur: An Economic Theory* (1982) that the emergence of 'perfect information' as a simplifying assumption in economic theory during the 19th century had the effect of purging entrepreneurship from consideration, for the simple reason that perfect information left no room for uncertainty and thereby eradicated the need for judgement and risk-taking – the domain of the entrepreneur.

This is an important observation as, by the first half of the 20th century, economists began to drop the assumption of perfect information, ushering in renewed interest in entrepreneurship. American economist Frank Fetter (1863–1949), of the Austrian School, preferred to call the entrepreneur an 'enterpriser' and saw the bearing of uncertainty as the key entrepreneurial function. Fetter did not limit the entrepreneurial role to the creation of new ventures or even the introduction of new products, processes and so on. Rather, he saw entrepreneurship as lying at the very heart of day-to-day matters of production and exchange.

Another American economist, Frank H. Knight (1885–1972) of the Chicago School, who refined the earlier work of Cantillon and Say by distinguishing between risk and uncertainty, pointed out that risk relates to 'recurring events whose relative frequency is known from past experience, whereas uncertainty relates to unique events whose probability can only be subjectively estimated' (Knight, 1924). In other words, whilst an entrepreneur can exercise judgement to calculate and mitigate risks, they must bear uncertainties themselves. Profit then becomes the reward for doing so.

Joseph A. Schumpeter (1883–1950), an Austrian-born Professor of Economics at Harvard University, and thought of by many as the father of contemporary entrepreneurship theory, focused much more on the entrepreneur's critical role in innovation. In his 1934 treatise *A Theory of Economic Development*, he framed the entrepreneur rather heroically as an agent of 'novel new combinations' of economic resources, leading to the introduction of new products, processes, markets, types of organization and models of value exchange. Schumpeter saw entrepreneurs as being critical to the creation of new industries and sectors, as well as the 'creative destruction' of old industries rendered obsolete by the new. As such, Schumpeter framed entrepreneurship as a key factor in disturbing any equilibrium and driving structural change, economic growth and business cycles. History has indeed seen entrepreneurship drive the emergence of new industries such as railways and aviation, the adoption of new technologies such as the mobile phone and the creation of new models of value exchange such as collaborative consumption. Indeed, such recognition of the fundamental importance of entrepreneurship and innovation to economic development has resulted in much macroeconomic policy-making being informed by Schumpeter's theory, notably the EU's €3.6 billion innovation programme[3] as well as its main development programme for 2000–2010, the Lisbon Strategy.[4] That the latter failed to deliver against most of its objectives is perhaps symptomatic of Schumpeter's heroic, but arguably flawed, 'high-level' view of entrepreneurship which, by emphasizing game-changing but episodic innovation, leaves little room for the more prosaic and everyday, but no less important, forms of entrepreneurship that permeate society.

CREATIVE DESTRUCTION

Proposed by Austrian-American economist Joseph A. Schumpeter (1942), who defined 'creative destruction' as:

> A process of industrial mutation that constantly revolutionises the economic structure from within, incessantly destroying the old one, incessantly creating a new one.

Schumpeter considered it as 'the essence of capitalism' but that it would lead to its eventual failure as an economic system. The effects of creative destruction are referred to as 'Schumpeter's gale'.

It has become broadly synonymous with disruptive innovation as a business concept. Numerous contemporary examples exist: smartphones all but killing off the market for many other devices such as PDAs, MP3 players, watches, calculators, compasses and voice recorders; digital streaming of films (e.g., Netflix, LoveFilm, Amazon Prime) killing off DVD sales and rental (e.g., Blockbuster).

In contrast, Friedrich Hayek (1899–1992) and Israel Kirzner (1930–present), contemporaries of Schumpeter and both also Austrian School economists, saw these 'lower-level entrepreneurs' as critical in the price-setting activity in a market economy. By offering prices motivated by opportunities for making a profit, entrepreneurs arbitrage any differentials to settle market prices. Kirzner's theory (1973; 2012), developed the idea of 'entrepreneurial alertness' to opportunities, that entrepreneurs play a critical role in restoring equilibrium to the economy whenever it is out of balance. This is a particularly useful idea when thinking about entrepreneurship in relation to sustainability, and one to which we will return *later in this chapter*. However, Kirzner's analysis also cast entrepreneurs as speculators or dealers isolated from the firm, whereas in most established businesses, pricing decisions are delegated by their owners to their managers, raising the important question of whether managers can be entrepreneurial too.

In *The Entrepreneur: An Economic Theory* (1982), British economist Mark Casson argued that employment is no barrier to being an entrepreneur (see Box 13.3). Indeed, he believed it was critical to see the entrepreneurial individual in relation to their institution and its culture, rather than apart from them. For Casson, entrepreneurs are just as likely to be found within established firms as they are to be independent, and quality of judgement is a greater determinant of the entrepreneur than their employment status.

This important distinction reflects the emerging thinking on corporate entrepreneurship in the 1970s (Peterson & Berger, 1971) and 1980s (Miller, 1983; Burgelman, 1983a & b;

---

[3] European Union Competitiveness and Innovation Framework Programme. Retrieved from http://ec.europa.eu/cip/.
[4] European Union Lisbon Strategy 2000–2010 Evaluation Document. Retrieved from http://ec.europa.eu/europe2020/pdf/lisbon_strategy_evaluation_en.pdf.

BOX 13.3
On entrepreneurship . . .

The title of entrepreneur should be confined to an owner or manager who exhibits the key trait of entrepreneurship, i.e. judgment in decision making. Judgment is a capacity for making a successful decision when no obviously correct model or decision rule is available or when relevant data is unreliable or incomplete. Cantillon's entrepreneur needs judgment to speculate on future price movements, while Knight's entrepreneur requires judgment because he deals in situations that are unprecedented and unique. Schumpeter's entrepreneur needs judgment to deal with the novel situations connected with innovation.

Entrepreneurs are specialists who use judgment to deal with novel and complex problems. Sometimes they own the resources to which the problems are related, and sometimes they are stewards employed by the owners. In times of major political, social, and environmental change, the number of problems requiring judgment increases and the demand for entrepreneurs rises as a result.

Source: Mark Casson (1982).

Covin & Slevin, 1989), which focused on entrepreneurship in the context of established businesses. Corporate entrepreneurship, as a multidisciplinary subfield of entrepreneurship, represents an important body of work that has, over time, demonstrated the value that entrepreneurship can bring to established organizations in sustaining success.

13.1.2 The Entrepreneurial Mindset

Numerous studies have been conducted (Khandwalla, 1977; Miller, 1983; Covin & Slevin, 1989; Lumpkin & Dess, 1996; Kuratko *et al.* 1990; Robinson *et al.*, 1991; Lindsay, 2005) to develop and test measurement instruments for 'entrepreneurial orientation' (EO), made up of a series of attributes detectable both at an organizational level and an individual level.

Measurements of EO can provide a useful indication of the strength of preference of the individual or the organization towards each of the attributes. Whilst early measures such as the Miller/Covin-Slevin scale created a single composite score from three of the attributes (risk, innovativeness, proactiveness), later instruments added a further two (competitive aggressiveness and autonomy), though these have since been shown to be less salient than the first three. Later research has drawn into the question the logic of creating a composite score, as it requires a high score across all attributes to generate a high overall score, whereas it has been shown that all of the attributes act independently and are worthy of separate investigation. Furthermore, circumstances and context – both internal and external – have been shown to have a significant impact on the variability of all attributes over time, indicating that measurement cannot be treated as a one-off event.

ENTREPRENEURIAL ORIENTATION (EO)

Entrepreneurial Orientation is a construct developed over three decades of numerous empirical studies to identify and measure the key attributes of entrepreneurship from an individual to an organizational level. Its early development focused on its use as a unidimensional construct, but latterly it has become more commonly used as a multidimensional construct conceived as a 'decision-making proclivity favouring entrepreneurial activities' (Lumpkin & Dess, 1996). The most important attributes have been found to be:

Risk-taking appetite

A willingness to commit resources to projects, ideas or processes whose outcomes are uncertain and for which the cost of failure would be high.

Innovativeness

Experimentation, exploration and creative acts in pursuit of the successful exploitation of ideas.

Proactiveness

Engaging in forward-looking actions targeted at the exploitation of an opportunity in anticipation of future circumstances.

Competitive aggressiveness

Hostility towards competitors in the marketplace. Also used to assess individual competitiveness in the workplace.

Autonomy

The level of freedom sought in decision-making and acting.

Related to these attributes are the key aspects of entrepreneurial behaviour, which include *alertness, opportunity recognition* and *entrepreneurial intentions* (see Box 13.4). Alertness is, as it suggests, simply a heightened awareness of what is going on around oneself – the more alert, the more likely an individual or organization is to come across an opportunity. However, a proliferation of opportunities is, according to Virgin boss Sir Richard Branson, only part of the picture as 'opportunities are like buses, there's always another one coming'. The real skill is in being good at opportunity recognition, i.e., being able to distinguish between the poor and the promising opportunities. Having identified a promising opportunity, entrepreneurial intentions are then, according to psychology's theory of planned behaviour, the best indication of the likelihood of actions.

13.1.3 Nature or Nurture?

If these attributes, alertness, opportunity recognition and entrepreneurial intentions, have been linked to entrepreneurship, then one might wonder how they are acquired.

The debate has raged for decades over whether entrepreneurs are born or made, that is to say, that entrepreneurial attributes and behaviours are either innate or can, in fact, be nurtured through experiences and education (see Box 13.5). Certainly it is well established that exogenous influences and psychological conditioning can have a powerful amplifying or moderating effect on entrepreneurial attributes and

BOX 13.4

On entrepreneurship . . .

Rita Gunther McGrath and Ian MacMillan, in their best-seller *The Entrepreneurial Mindset*, highlighted five key characteristics of habitual entrepreneurs:

1   **They passionately seek new opportunities –** they stay alert, always looking for the chance to profit from change and disruption in the way that business is done. Their greatest impact is when they create entirely new business models.

2   **They pursue opportunities with enormous discipline –** they are not only alert enough to spot opportunities, but they make sure they act on them. Most maintain some form of inventory, or register, of unexplored opportunities.

3   **They pursue only the very best opportunities –** they avoid exhausting themselves and their organizations by chasing after every option.

4   **They focus on execution –** specifically, adaptive execution.

5   **They engage the energies of everyone in their domain –** they involve many people inside and outside their organization in their pursuit of an opportunity.

Source: McGrath, R. G., & MacMillan, I. (2000). *The Entrepreneurial Mindset.* Massachusetts: Harvard Business School Press.

BOX 13.5

On entrepreneurship . . .

Entrepreneurship education tends to focus on developing core entrepreneurial competencies of attitude, skills and knowledge.

Attitude

Sense of initiative
Risk propensity
Self-efficacy
Need for achievement
Structural behaviour

Skills

Creativity
Analysis

Motivation
Networking
Adaptability

Knowledge

Understanding role of entrepreneurs
Knowledge of entrepreneurship

Source: Adapted from EIM Business & Policy Research (Gibcus, *et al.,* 2012).

behaviours. Equally, a positive correlation has been shown between the overall level and quality of someone's general school and further/higher education and their entrepreneurial intentions.

Unfortunately, the picture is less conclusive for specialized entrepreneurship education, though universities and colleges around the world would no doubt prefer you not to know this. If your intentions are to undertake specialized entrepreneurial education, e.g., a module on an MBA programme or an intensive summer school programme, then it is important that you do so with realistic expectations of how it might help.

According to European Commission research (Gibcus *et al.*, 2012), entrepreneurship education can result in an improvement across attitude, skills and knowledge, all of which will increase the likelihood of success for those already intent on starting their own venture. Global Entrepreneurship Monitor (Martinez *et al.*, 2010) research has also shown that entrepreneurship education increases self-efficacy and heightens entrepreneurial intentions, and improves the likelihood of students tapping into a wider network of advisors to support them going forwards, though it has little to no effect on individuals' opportunity recognition and fear of failure.

Souitaris *et al.* (2007), however, have shown the reverse, that entrepreneurial intentions remain unaffected by an improvement in attitude, skills and knowledge alone. Inspiration, it appears, is the only factor in entrepreneurship education that makes the biggest difference to the likelihood of students pursuing an entrepreneurial career. As such, the ability of academics and external contributors to inspire students appears to be just as important as the course content. This finding demonstrates not only that emotions have an important influence upon the effect of an exogenous influence (i.e., education) on attitudes and intentions towards entrepreneurship, but also that it has wider theoretical implications for the role and importance of emotions in entrepreneurship. As Souitaris *et al.* (2007) put it, 'whether the individual "falls in love" with the entrepreneurial career and/or with an entrepreneurial opportunity is driven by emotion and personal preference (love is blind) rather than rational evaluation'. This may go some way to explain why overall statistics reveal that the overwhelming majority of students of entrepreneurship education tend to enter employment rather than self-employment. Whether or not inspiration is in short supply, perhaps the insight for educators here is that entrepreneurship education needs to focus on developing students' competencies for becoming more entrepreneurial employees and citizens rather than purely on becoming independent entrepreneurs.

Indeed, the emerging consensus on entrepreneurship education, in Europe at least, is that it should be obligatory across schools as well as higher and further education on the basis that entrepreneurial competencies are of wide application and benefit to people in all walks of life and all sections of society. Perhaps then the increasing prevalence of entrepreneurship education outside of business and management studies and alongside subjects as broad as engineering, science, medicine and law would gradually lead to a fundamental reframing of entrepreneurship at a societal and cultural level.

Whatever the potential scope, role and impact of formal entrepreneurship education, there will always be variation in entrepreneurial competencies and intentions at an individual level. It seems now that at least some of this variation can be put down to genetic predisposition. Groundbreaking research (Nicolaou *et al.*, 2008; Zhang *et al.*, 2009; Nicolaou & Shane, 2010) has now demonstrated that the tendency to be entrepreneurial can also be influenced by genetic factors. By examining the propensity of a large sample of pairs of twins (both monozygotic (different sex) and dizygotic (same sex)) towards entrepreneurial behaviour, Nicolaou & Shane (2010) found that between 37 and 42 per cent of variance in the tendency to be entrepreneurial can be accounted for by genetic factors. This heritability was found to be substantive for both males and females and influences both the expression of entrepreneurial intentions as well as the tendency to be self-employed.

So we are not all born equal, at least in terms of our entrepreneurial tendencies, but at least we also now know that entrepreneurial attributes, intentions and behaviours can be taught, acquired or inspired. This is a crucial point, as it reminds us that the possibility of being entrepreneurial, at least to some degree, is within reach of anyone and everyone. As such, we need to begin thinking about the broader potential for entrepreneurship – as a process and as a set of competencies – outside the narrow confines of independent ventures and more widely across a variety of organizational and societal contexts.

Perhaps the more morally grounded our collective entrepreneurial capabilities are, then the more likely that our entrepreneurial intentions and activities focus on the things that matter most; to the environment, to society and to the economy?

Perhaps entrepreneurship has a leading role to play in reimagining how we live by spotting previously unseen opportunities for improvement? The more prevalent our collective entrepreneurial capabilities are, the more likely we are to find a way forward to sustainability, and faster?

Perhaps the 'cult' of the entrepreneur identified at the beginning of this chapter needs to make way for a more diffuse but infinitely more useful 'culture of entrepreneurship' that transforms humanity's ability to address complex unresolved problems such as climate change, social injustice and economic inequality? In the face of dwindling natural resources and burgeoning population growth, can entrepreneurship radically improve the productivity of human resources and, in turn, our resource productivity to deliver sustainable development? Or put another way, can we imagine achieving it without entrepreneurship?

13.2 Towards One Planet Entrepreneurship

In asking these questions, we are beginning to consider the role of entrepreneurship in relation to a One Planet Approach to sustainable business. The case for sustainable business has been clearly articulated earlier in this book, based upon the work of many leading thinkers across academia, politics, NGOs and the business world. The question for this chapter is, 'can entrepreneurship help us get there?'

To answer this question, we need an organizing framework that places the theme of entrepreneurship over a useful lens for conceptualizing sustainability. The current model of choice amongst sustainable business scholars is the 3-nested dependencies model, based on the work of Bob Doppelt, Peter Senge and Bob Willard.

3-NESTED-DEPENDENCIES MODEL

This model neatly summarizes the relationship between environment, society and economy as being consecutively dependent upon each other. This is in stark contrast to what Peter Senge (2010) calls the ' calls the 'Industrial Age' point of view where the economy is the largest and most important circle, with the society and environment as much smaller circles within it. With the 3-nested- dependencies model, the economy, as the late CEO of Interface Ray Anderson puts it 'is a wholly owned subsidiary of nature'.

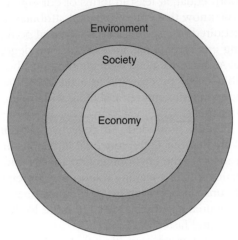

Source: **Based on work by Doppelt, 2008, Senge, *et al.*, 2010 and WIllard, 2002.**

13.2.1 One Planet . . . Who Needs Entrepreneurship?

Ironically Doppelt, Senge *et al.* and Willard do not explicitly refer to entrepreneurship at all in their highly-regarded research. Nor, for that matter, do many other pioneering scholars whose books line the shelves of students of sustainable business (see Box 13.6).

This is not to detract in any way from this collection of polemical masterpieces, many of which have been an inspiration to us, but rather to wonder why so many of these leading thinkers on sustainable business over the past three decades have omitted to make any explicit reference to entrepreneurship in their work. In fairness few, if any, would claim to be experts in the field of entrepreneurship and might therefore be forgiven for not being alert to its role in driving change and disrupting markets. We suspect that there are two reasons for this. The first is language, that is to say that the essence of entrepreneurship is implicit in their books but is represented by other, arguably more motivating, but no less loaded terms such as 'change-makers', 'innovators' and 'visionaries' – even 'zeronauts'.[5] The second is to do with the framing of entrepreneurship which, at the time that most of these books were written, was primarily conceptualized in relation to the creation of independent businesses rather than driving innovation across a wider range of organizational contexts.

---

[5]'Zeronauts' was coined by leading environmentalist John Elkington in *The Zeronauts* (2012).

BOX 13.6

(Not) on entrepreneurship . . .

The table below summarises leading sustainable business literature that makes no reference to 'entrepreneurship' (or related terms such as entrepreneur, entrepreneurial):

Author	Title
Bob Doppelt	*Leading Change Toward Sustainability*
Bob Doppelt	*The Power of Sustainable Thinking*
Peter Senge	*The Necessary Revolution*
Peter Senge	*The Fifth Discipline: The Art and Practice of the Learning Organisation*
Bob Willard	*The Sustainability Advantage: Seven Business Case Benefits of a Triple Bottom Line*
Paul Hawken, Amory Lovins & L. Hunter Lovins	*Natural Capitalism: The Next Industrial Revolution*
Paul Hawken	*The Ecology of Commerce*
Paul Hawken	*Blessed Unrest*
Aries de Geus	*The Living Company*
Stuart Hart	*Capitalism at the Crossroads*
Pavan Sukhdev	*Corporation 2020*
Stefan Heck, Matt Rogers	*Resource Revolution: How to Capture the Biggest Business Opportunity in a Century*
Michael Braungart, William McDonough	*Cradle-to-Cradle: Re-making the Way We Make Things*
Franz-Martin Belz, Ken Peattie	*Sustainability Marketing*
Vijay Govindarajan, Chris Trimble	*The Other Side of Innovation: Solving the Execution Challenge*
Richard Rumelt	*Good Strategy, Bad Strategy*
Peter Marsh	*The New Industrial Revolution: Consumers, Globalisation and the End of Mass Production*
Geoffrey A. Moore	*Escape Velocity: Free Your Company's Future from the Pull of the Past*
Jim Collins	*Good to Great*
Jim Collins, Jerry Porras	*Built to Last: Successful Habits of Visionary Companies*

When one considers the challenges that lie ahead in charting a path towards truly sustainable business – resource productivity, reimagining business models and economic paradigms, creating new markets (and destroying obsolete ones) – then it is hard to imagine how they can be faced without the risk appetite, the innovativeness, the proactiveness, the competitive aggressiveness and the need for autonomy of the entrepreneurial mindset. The fact that entrepreneurship is overlooked in so much of the sustainable business literature makes it all the more important to do justice to it within this chapter. It is also worth stressing to students of sustainable business that, given the broad conceptualization provided here of what entrepreneurship is, they should be prepared to keep entrepreneurship with them as a filter through which to engage with the classic texts listed.

Thankfully, there remain a number of leading authors on sustainable business – including John Elkington, C. K. Prahalad, Philip Kotler, Rita Gunther McGrath, Christopher Meyer and the late Ray Anderson – for whom entrepreneurship takes centre stage. Perhaps it is no coincidence that these authors also happen to be strategy professors, management consultants, entrepreneurs and marketers, for whom entrepreneurship is never far from front of mind.

Whatever the reason, it seems that entrepreneurship has some catching up to do in gaining a legitimate place in the lexicon of sustainable business literature. Whilst a niche body of 'sustainable entrepreneurship' literature has emerged in recent decades under a number of alternate labels including 'green entrepreneurship' and 'environmental entrepreneurship' and portmanteaus of 'eco-entrepreneurship', 'eco-preneurship' and 'sustainopreneurship', it has thus far achieved only limited traction with practitioners, policy-makers, the media and mainstream business scholars. This is possibly due, in part, to its narrow framing of environmental sustainability and, in part, to 'social entrepreneurship' becoming established as shorthand for all purpose-led entrepreneurship. In order to rebalance the framing of sustainable entrepreneurship and locate it firmly in the mainstream entrepreneurship literature, we propose a conceptual framework for 'One Planet Entrepreneurship' that applies entrepreneurial competencies and attributes across a variety of organizational contexts, in pursuit of delivering environmental, social and economic sustainability goals (see Figure 13.1).

No one would deny that the world needs innovation – and lots of it – to solve the sustainability challenges facing us. But we must never forget that it is entrepreneurial people who will be the ones that make it happen. As Bessant and Tidd (2007) put it:

> . . . innovation matters, but it doesn't happen automatically. It is driven by entrepreneurship – a potent mixture of vision, passion, energy, enthusiasm, insight, judgment and plain hard work which enables good ideas to become a reality. The power behind changing products, processes or services comes from individuals – whether acting alone or embedded within organisations – who make innovation happen.

13.2.2 The One Planet Entrepreneur

The One Planet Entrepreneur is proposed as an archetype of the entrepreneurial individual who applies their entrepreneurial competencies, attitudes and knowledge to solving sustainability challenges either unilaterally or, more likely, in collaboration with others. They might run their own business or social venture, but it is just as likely they will work within an established organization in the private, public or not-for-profit sector, or else be an active member of a community or network. Whatever their organizational context, they will be well networked and work comfortably across geographical, cultural and organizational boundaries.

These entrepreneurs will be relentlessly dissatisfied with the *status quo* and take a high degree of responsibility for solving the problems that they see around them. Whilst ambitious for themselves, they will be even more ambitious for solving 'big,

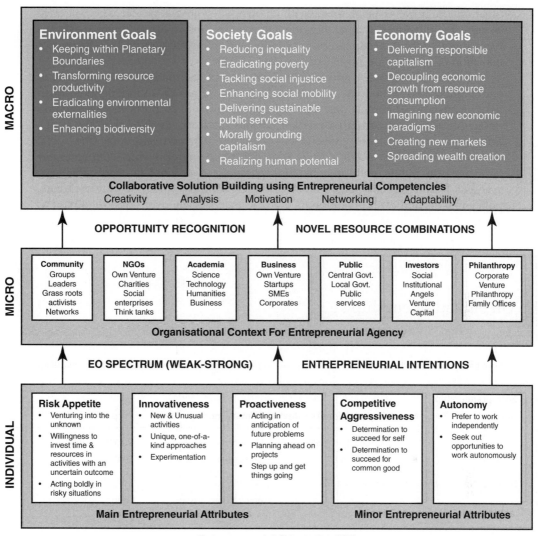

FIGURE 13.1 Conceptual Framework for One Planet Entrepreneurship.

hairy, audacious'[6] problems and, whilst they may be driven by wealth creation, social impact, escaping poverty, leaving a legacy or a combination of all of these, their motive simply provides the rocket fuel and the passion for them to act. Their staying power and commitment to problem-solving will have earned them a reputation for being trustworthy, ethical and consistent in their dealings with others.

This, coupled with their deep appreciation of the interdependency of stakeholders, positions them eminently well as honest brokers for solving the systemic problems of our environment, society and economy that are simply too big for any one

---

[6] Adapted from Jim Collins' *Good to Great* in which he talks of BHAGs (Big Hairy Audacious Goals).

organization, however large, to solve on its own. They are the people who will drive 'systems building' for sustainability-orientated innovation to apply 'a whole-systems focus to influence the redesign of institutions and infrastructures and the reconceptualiation of business purpose' (Adams *et al.*, 2012).

In the last two decades, and largely in an attempt to broaden the application of entrepreneurship orthodoxy beyond the limited confines of an independent business organizational context and a purely opportunity-driven profit motive, the taxonomy of entrepreneurship (see Box 13.7) has gradually evolved with the genus *Entrepreneur* giving rise to several new 'species': *Entrepreneur socii* (the social entrepreneur); *Entrepreneur corpus* (the corporate entrepreneur); *Entrepreneur publicus* (the public entrepreneur); *Entrepreneur magister* (the entrepreneurial academic); and *Entrepreneur communis* (the collective entrepreneur). Scholars, policy-makers and even practitioners to some extent have, over time, attempted to

BOX 13.7
On entrepreneurship . . .

The table below illustrates the taxonomy of entrepreneurship summarizing the key variables affecting classification.

Entrepreneurship 'species'	Organisational context	Primary motive	Purpose
Conventional entrepreneurship	For-profit business Startup/SME	Opportunity-driven profit seeking	Wealth creation Legacy
Social entrepreneurship	Social enterprise	Address social or environmental issue	Social/environmental/ economic impact Legacy
Corporate entrepreneurship	For-profit business Corporation	Sustain success (company) Career advancement (individual)	Sustain success of company
Public entrepreneurship	Central & local Government Public services	Public service ethos	Public good Social/environmental/ economic impact
Academic entrepreneurship	Universities R&D institutes	Opportunity-driven knowledge seeking	Knowledge creation Social/environmental/ economic impact Legacy
Collective entrepreneurship	Any organization Intra-organization	Opportunity-driven profit seeking	Exploit opportunities inaccessible to individual entrepreneurs

reinforce the differences between these 'species' and glossed over the commonalities, giving rise to diverging identities for each. The reality, of course, is that these 'species' share the same entrepreneurial DNA but apply it in very different organizational contexts, to serve different motives and purposes. It is also fair to say that these different labels are of little consequence to anyone other than the scholars and policy-makers who seek to sense-make through the lenses that they provide. They do, however, provide a shorthand for differentiating between different groups of entrepreneurs based upon three variables: organizational context, primary motive and purpose.

We have already learned that motive is largely immaterial save for its role in providing the stimulus for entrepreneurial intentions. As such, provided motive has a moral and ethical basis (i.e., it is not immoral or unethically based, e.g., criminal), then it can be discounted.

One Planet Entrepreneurship, however, results from a convergence of purpose between these different 'species' of entrepreneur. Whilst historically there has been commonality of purpose between social entrepreneurs, public entrepreneurs, entrepreneurial academics and collective entrepreneurs, sharing an outward-looking purpose of delivering social, environmental and economic impact, the conventional and corporate entrepreneurs have remained anomalies pursuing pure profits. However, once it becomes apparent that the most profitable opportunities available are in solving sustainability problems, then conventional and corporate entrepreneurs find their goals are aligned to all other 'species' of entrepreneurs.

Once this happens, and we contend that it is already happening, there is commonality of purpose between social entrepreneurs, public entrepreneurs and entrepreneurial academics (see Definition box).

THE ONE PLANET ENTREPRENEUR

An innovator pursuing opportunities to create positive social, environmental and economic value, regardless of organizational context or motive and despite uncertain outcomes.

The last element in this proposed definition is critical. In the increasingly 'VUCA' (Volatile, Uncertain, Complex and Ambiguous) world that we all inhabit, the One Planet Entrepreneur is in their element – as we have learned, judgement in the face of uncertainty is the domain of the entrepreneur.

HOW DO YOU MEASURE UP?

Take the *self-assessment test at the end of the chapter* to discover your entrepreneurial orientation as a One Planet Entrepreneur.

13.2.3 One Planet Entrepreneurship and the Environment

Concern for the impact of humans upon the environment can be traced back to pre-Roman times, for instance with soil conservation being practised across India, China and Peru for over 2,000 years. Equally, we have long recognized the importance of a healthy environment to human wellbeing. Indeed, the spread of epidemic diseases such as the black death and cholera across Europe in the 14th to 16th centuries is known to have been triggered by pollution from human activities.

However, the contemporary environmental movement rose out of concerns in the late 19th century about protection of the countryside and wilderness from creeping industrialisation across Europe and the United States. The prevailing political thinking at the time was liberalism, which held that all social and environmental problems could be solved through the free market. In stark contrast, the majority of early environmentalists argued that governments rather than markets should be responsible for protecting the environment and its resources. Gifford Pinchot (1865–1946), the first head of the US Forest Service, was a leading protagonist of the environmental movement and a firm believer in conservation as 'the wise and efficient use of resources'. Ironically, his grandson Gifford Pinchot III was the first person to coin the phrase 'intrapreneurship'[7] - entrepreneurial behaviour within established firms - whilst losing none of his forbear's fervour for sustainability.

Following decades of anti-business sentiment pervading the environmentalist movement, there has been a sea change in attitude towards seeing business as a critical player in the pursuit of environmental sustainability. Former environmental doom-mongers and once vitriolic critics of multinational corporations' environmental record are now to be found in the boardrooms of the very companies they lambasted, advising them on how to chart a path to corporate sustainability. In his 2004 speech[8] to the Commonwealth Club, environmentalist, author and entrepreneur Adam Werbach triggered this shift in thinking with a critique of environmentalism being inward-looking and failing to connect with people. Change, as Werbach contested, will not come from convincing fellow environmentalists of the need for it, or from expecting consumers to make heavy sacrifices for it. In his 2008 follow-up speech, 'The Birth of Blue', he called for a change in approach, of replacing negative talk of 'limits' with positive talk of 'possibilities' and the role of consumer activism as a powerful driving force demanding more environmentally friendly products, services and practices by the world's businesses. Werbach, himself an entrepreneur,[9] saw that the only way to deliver change on the scale necessary was to reframe sustainability as something so irresistible to consumers that they would demand it over the unsustainable alternative. His simple and compelling vision recast business in relation to the environment – business can be the solution.

The liberalist market-oriented zeitgeist appears to have now taken hold amongst the international business community, environmental NGOs and prominent environmental activists helped, no doubt, by their shared frustration with governments' continued procrastination on environmental regulation.

Regrettably, we remain some way off from Werbach's vision being realized, not least because it relies upon consumers becoming sustainability-literate enough to differentiate between more and less sustainable choices, but also because it depends upon businesses' ability to deliver more sustainable products and services without trade-offs on quality, price or performance.

---

[7] In his best-selling book *Intrapreneuring: Why You Don't Have to Leave the Corporation to Become an Entrepreneur* (1985), Pinchot introduces the idea that entrepreneurship has its rightful place within established organizations.

[8] Adam Werbach, 'The Death of Environmentalism and the Birth of the Commons Movement'.

[9] Adam Werbach founded Act Now Productions in 1998, growing it to 45 employees, before it was acquired by global advertising agency Saatchi & Saatchi, to be rebranded as their sustainability services arm, Saatchi & Saatchi S. In 2012, he co-founded Yerdle (www.yerdle.com) as a marketplace for sharing things.

What part can One Planet Entrepreneurship play in halting environmental degradation, transforming resource productivity, restoring ecosystems or improving biodiversity?

Kirzner's emphasis on alertness and opportunity recognition reminds us that it will be entrepreneurial people and, by extension, organizations that will see opportunities where others only see problems. Whilst the growing number of well-researched publications like McKinsey's 'Resource Revolution' (Dobbs *et al.*, 2011) and the subsequent book by the same name (Heck & Rogers, 2014) make a significant contribution to raising entrepreneurial alertness to the opportunities available, they can only go so far (see Case Study 13.1). Entrepreneurial competencies such as

CASE STUDY 13.1
Winnow Solutions for Food Waste

While at McKinsey & Company, Marc Zornes co-authored 'Resource Revolution', a significant research paper on resource productivity. From the report, three things became undeniably clear:

◆ Too much food is wasted in the world. It is tough to pin down the exact numbers but it is somewhere close to one third of all food grown ends up not being eaten.

◆ Solving it is one of the biggest resource productivity opportunities we face today – one third of food wasted is worth $750 billion annually.

◆ Not nearly enough attention is focused on solving this issue.

Zornes was sufficiently motivated to take action and co-founded Winnow alongside college friend Kevin Duffy in 2013, with the mission of helping the hospitality industry tackle avoidable food waste by connecting the kitchen through usable technology, in order to empower chefs to run a more efficient operation.

The technology at the heart of Winnow is a kitchen-grade smart tablet preinstalled with proprietary software linked to a set of integrated scales that measure food waste. The weight and cost of what is put in the bin is recorded automatically and Winnow's cloud platform captures data, tracking waste value and sources over time. The theory of change behind the model is simple – discovering the value of food thrown away drives behaviour. Daily reports sent to the operator's inbox pinpoint opportunities to cut waste, benchmark multiple sites and track performance.

Trials of their prototype system with Compass Group resulted in food waste being reduced by over 50%, leading to over 10 tonnes less food wasted per site per year – equivalent to over 10,000 plated meals. This level of performance has now been demonstrated across more than 200 sites in the UK, resulting in a reduction in food waste of 1 million meals and 3,680 tonnes of CO_2 saved, whilst saving customers over £2 million in reduced food purchasing costs.

These promising results have helped Winnow to raise £2.4 million in series A funding from leading institutional, corporate and angel investors including Mustard Seed (a social investment fund), D: Ax (Axel Johnson's digital venture capital fund), Alan Parker (former CEO of Whitbread) and Jeremy Oppenheim (head of McKinsey's Sustainability and Resource Productivity Practice). Now with a proven business model and heavyweight investors behind them, the future looks promising for Winnow as they aim to expand internationally.

Winnow is an example of a growing number of young 'environmental capitalist' businesses that have developed a business model that makes money whilst solving an environmental issue.

Source: www.winnowsolutions.com.

creativity, analysis and networking will be key to driving thought leadership, creating collaborations and developing the novel combinations of resources that will underpin the radically new business models required to realize this vision. In the context of an established business, developing entrepreneurship as a strategic capability is paramount, not only to becoming more responsive to customers' changing demands and innovating new products and services that deliver step changes in eco-efficiency and eco-effectiveness, but also to leading a discovery-driven process (McGrath, 2010) for finding new scalable business models that enable the business to be more profitable by doing environmental good rather than harm. Manufacturing companies, e.g., will need to find radical new ways of dematerializing and decarbonizing their products, as well as leveraging new technologies such as 3D printing if even the basic needs of another 3 billion middle-class consumers are to be met. Companies that figure out how to decouple revenue growth from net resource consumption will face fewer barriers to growth than those that do not. Successfully implementing powerful concepts such as cradle-to-cradle manufacturing, not to mention navigating a way through to new business models, will require lots of experimentation; prototyping, testing and evaluating before being ready to produce to scale. Implicit in this is the entrepreneur's ability to learn from failure, not to mention creativity and resourcefulness in their problem-solving – all important attributes of the One Planet Entrepreneur.

Important though these unilateral efforts within companies are, to realize the full potential of One Planet Entrepreneurship for the environment we need to focus on systems-building. Many of the environmental challenges we face are systems-level and, by definition, simply too big for individual organizations to solve. Unprecedented levels of collaboration will be required between competitors, industry sectors and broader stakeholders including NGOs, investors, policy-makers and communities to find practical solutions that provide individual actors with a sense of ownership and responsibility, as well as a focus to the tangible contribution they can make.

Above all, this will demand a new style of entrepreneurial leadership, not least because we are entering uncharted territory and having the courage to make decisions in the face of uncertain outcomes will be absolutely critical to success. Few in the business community are likely to disagree with this, but we must now think much more broadly than ever before about where that leadership comes from. In *Knowledge and Power* (2013), George Gilder proposes a new information theory of capitalism based on the idea that power is centralized whereas knowledge is diffuse. As such, the knowledge and insights required to solve problems are spread across society whereas the power to act largely resides with the institutions of business and government. As Gilder puts it:

. . . crony capitalism necessarily fails because it thwarts the emergence of knowledge. Knowledge comes from experiments that can either succeed or fail. A sure way to stultify an economy is to separate the knowledge dispersed around the world from the power to actually carry through these experiments of enterprise.

In other words, for entrepreneurial endeavour (regardless of organizational context) to succeed in the name of the environment (or for that matter, any other common goal), we need to become much smarter at aligning knowledge with power. We must develop new collaborative platforms for sharing perspectives, knowledge, data, insight, ideas, possible solutions, investment and implementation on an unprecedented scale. The scale of the environmental challenge demands it.

13.2.4 One Planet Entrepreneurship and Society

Around the world local and national cultures differ greatly, as does the way in which entrepreneurship is perceived and treated by society, as well as societies' abilities to create and sustain entrepreneurial activity.

Geert Hofstede's extensive research on national cultures[10] has provided us with valuable insight into the collective cultural values that different nationalities share and that have an important bearing on entrepreneurship. In particular, measures of uncertainty avoidance and power distance reveal a great deal about the propensity of a nation to embrace or reject entrepreneurship as socially acceptable behaviour. In contrast, measures of individualism and masculinity have been found to tell us surprisingly little about entrepreneurship? (Kreiser *et al.*, 2010).

Beyond this, the question of how and to what extent national culture influences the expression of entrepreneurship culture has been hotly debated since the 1930s, without conclusive evidence one way or the other. Numerous studies seeking to investigate the complex interactions amongst cultural, economic and institutional factors have singularly failed to identify variability in an entrepreneurial culture from one societal context to the next.

What we do know, however, is that entrepreneurial activity differs greatly across different societies. The Global Entrepreneurship Monitor (GEM) measures Total Entrepreneurial Activity (TEA) as well as Entrepreneurial Employee Activity (EEA), though the latter is generally at a much lower level than the former. GEM has found (Singer *et al.*, 2014) that social values can make a significant difference to attitudes towards entrepreneurial activity, particularly in terms of the perception of entrepreneurship as a good career choice, the status bestowed upon successful entrepreneurs, and the media attention devoted to entrepreneurship. Overall, GEM has demonstrated that African countries display the highest social values towards entrepreneurship and European countries (especially the EU member states) display the lowest.

The stage of economic development of the country appears to matter too, with 'factor-driven' (e.g., India, Uganda, Philippines) and 'efficiency-driven' economies (e.g., Malaysia, South Africa, China, Brazil, Colombia, Thailand) holding entrepreneurship in much higher esteem than 'innovation-driven' economies (e.g., Japan, EU, US, Taiwan, Australia, Qatar) (see Case Study 13.2). There is certainly some irony in this as the innovation-driven economies need entrepreneurship at least as much as anyone else – after all, who is it who drives innovation?

These social values manifest themselves as higher levels of TEA and entrepreneurial intentions in factor-driven and efficiency-driven economies than in innovation-driven economies, which see significantly higher levels of entrepreneurial employee activity. However, the proportion of TEA driven by necessity rather than opportunity or improvement is also higher in factor-driven and efficiency-driven economies.

---

[10] See http://geert-hofstede.com.

CASE STUDY 13.2

Juliana Rotich

Born and raised in Kenya, Juliana fought her way to win a place at the University of Missouri to read computer science. Following graduation, she worked in telecommunications and data warehousing until in 2008, when she saw an opportunity to use her skills to collect and map reports of post-election violence in Kenya.

The website she created – Ushahidi (which means 'testimony' in Swahili) – was rapidly embraced by journalists looking for real-time information crowdsourced from citizens via their mobile phones. However, Juliana was quick to recognize the opportunity for her technology's ability to support a wide range of circumstances where there was a need to organize temporal and geospatial information, not just for news reporting but also for mobilizing targeted interventions. By 2015, Ushahidi had been deployed internationally across a multitude of applications, e.g., mapping violence in the Congo;

pharmacy stockouts across Africa; eyewitness reports in the Gaza war; rescue efforts in the Haiti, Chile, New Zealand and Nepal earthquakes; pollution incidents relating to the Deepwater Horizon oil spill; roadblocks caused by winter storms in Washington DC; forest fires in Italy and Russia; and corruption in Macedonia.

From modest beginnings and, as Juliana puts it herself, a deep sense of mission to 'make, fix and help others', her leadership has been recognized internationally, including being named Schwab Social Entrepreneur of the Year in 2011, being a regular speaker on the TED circuit and becoming Chair of the World Economic Forum's Global Agenda Council on Data Driven Development.

Juliana's story is inspiring and a remarkable example of how individuals possessing an entrepreneurial mindset can have real impact in the world in a few short years.

This cultural context is immensely important as it provides a sense of a society's receptiveness to entrepreneurship – attitudes, attributes, behaviours and activities – which then underpins the level of legitimacy afforded to entrepreneurship by a country's society.

Cultural Traditions   What cultural context does not tell us a great deal about are cultural traditions and sensitivities that stand to be trodden on or eroded by entrepreneurial activities. One might imagine that cultural traditions and entrepreneurship are not happy bedfellows, not least if you cast the entrepreneur as the agent of change. Keelan and Woods (2006) would disagree, however, based upon their extensive studies of Maori entrepreneurship. Maori, as an ancient New Zealand indigenous tribe, have a strong cultural foundation in folklore. Far from discouraging entrepreneurial behaviour, this folklore is routinely used as a narrative to promote entrepreneurship. Te Ao Hurihuri ('the turning world') is a Maori philosophy that embraces constant change by seeing that the world is not static. Maori see development as an ongoing process, without end, and with people totally integrated with nature.

And Maori are not alone as an indigenous people promoting entrepreneurship. Many tribes, including Polynesians, Aborigines and the Apaches of Arizona, have a long record of entrepreneurial activity and promoting trade. Distinct from ethnic entrepreneurship, which looks more closely at the entrepreneurial activities of immigrants in their host countries, indigenous entrepreneurship tends to be more community-based and motivated by a desire for high levels of self-determination or autonomy, provided that the entrepreneurial activity remains in harmony with religious and moral beliefs.

Entrepreneurship: Religion, Morality and Ethics   Of course, religion and morality are not the preserve of indigenous tribes. They have been shown to provide the crucial foundations for entrepreneurship and economic development across society (see Case Study 13.3). Max Weber first introduced the idea that the emergence of modern capitalism in Northern Europe was in large part due to the Protestant work ethic. His theory of the 'spirit of capitalism' proposed in *The Protestant Ethic and the Spirit of Capitalism* (1905) that the ideas and *esprit* of the Protestant work ethic 'favour the rational pursuit of economic gain'. By extension, he argued that entrepreneurial activity is rooted in the value orientation of individuals, especially those of ethical values. Whilst his research was focused on Protestantism, he also argued that his theory holds true for other religions and produced separate studies on ancient Judaism, Hinduism, Buddhism and Confucianism. According to

---

CASE STUDY 13.3
Barclays Bank and the Quaker Movement

On 20 May 2015, Barclays Bank plc agreed to pay £1.53 billion in fines to the Financial Conduct Authority and four US regulators for its part in manipulating the foreign exchange markets. This came on top of a £38 million fine in 2014 for putting £16.5 billion of client assets at risk, a £330 million fine in 2013 from US energy regulators for rigging the electricity market, a £290 million fine in 2012 for rigging LIBOR (London Inter-Bank Offer Rate) and £3.95 billion in compensation paid out to customers for misselling PPI (Payment Protection Insurance) over a period of several years up to 2013. In total, Barclays has paid out over £6.1 billion in fines and compensation for its failure to suppress greed amongst its own staff.

Barclays can be traced back to two Quakers, John Freame and Thomas Gould, who established themselves as goldsmith bankers in Lombard Street in the City of London in 1690. Their business flourished, helped in no small part by their Quaker reputation for frugality, prudence and trustworthiness. Family, religious and business ties were inextricably linked and, as business

thrived, their descendants took a prominent and courageous stand against a variety of social issues including slavery and prison reform over a 250-year period.

The Quakers (more accurately known as The Society of Friends) were founded in the 1650s on the belief that there is something of God in everyone. They believed in living a simple life, often reflected in their speech and dress, and their refusal to take oaths precluded them from entering many professions. As a consequence, many Quakers established their own businesses, becoming many of the leading entrepreneurs of their time, relying upon on their own industry and moral code to become trusted and respected figures within their communities. Other prominent Quaker entrepreneurs include John Cadbury and Joseph Rowntree, and Quakers have been associated with the founding of many NGOs including Greenpeace, Amnesty International and Oxfam.

Source: www.telegraph.co.uk and Barclays Bank plc webpage 'Our Quaker Roots'.

Weber, the 'this-worldly ascetism of Puritanism' introduced during the Reformation creates the 'highest form of moral obligation of the individual to fulfil his duty in worldly affairs' – what Weber referred to as 'the calling'. This calling was observed to be particularly acute amongst the Calvinist movement, a Puritan sect of Protestantism, which preached a doctrine of predestination, i.e., certain humans are saved from damnation in a manner predetermined by God. Weber commented that 'this doctrine must above all have had one consequence for the life of a generation which surrendered to its magnificent consistency . . . a feeling of unprecedented inner loneliness'. From this cruel torment, Weber argues, the capitalist spirit was born and success in one's 'calling' came to be regarded as a 'sign' of being one of the predetermined 'chosen' ones. As such, the pursuit and accumulation of wealth was morally acceptable provided it was accompanied by a sober, industrious character. Calvinism, as Weber put it, provided the moral energy and drive for the capitalist entrepreneur.

Anderson and Smith (2007) developed this idea further by arguing that a moral imperative exists in entrepreneurship, whereby 'authenticated' entrepreneurship – in other words, that which is consistent with a socially approved moral dimension – is legitimized through comparisons made with the socially constructed view. Whilst the classical view of the political economy characterized by Adam Smith and others might have been judged to be morally constituted, the modern free market logic stands accused of breaking the link between economic rationality and moral purpose. Furthermore, as post-modernist thinking has since rejected any attempts to form normative judgements about what is deemed right and wrong, society has increasing left the responsibility for making that decision to the individual rather than institutionalizing it. Given that as a society we increasingly look to entrepreneurship for providing economic growth, Anderson and Smith (2007) argue that the morality of entrepreneurship is underpinned and informed by broader societal questions of morality. Their research on entrepreneurial criminals illustrates this point perfectly, as does examples of capitalism going badly astray, as in the recent banking crisis.

BOX 13.8
On entrepreneurship and ethics . . .

Although potential social harms may result from entrepreneurial activity, it is still clear that entrepreneurs perform necessary – often indispensable – business tasks in society. Because of the importance of their economic functions, it is appropriate to ask whether entrepreneurs have particular moral obligations to society. The present research is unclear about the precise ethical meaning of entrepreneurial responsibility and obligation. Yet this research consistently raises a number of questions: should society treat entrepreneurs differently because of the important tasks they carry out in the economy? Should ethical standards of entrepreneurial behaviour be different from those guiding other business persons in established organisations? What, if anything, is distinctive about the ethical problems encountered by contemporary entrepreneurs?

Source: Francis T. Hannafey (2003).

Francis Hannafey was one of the first to study the moral and ethical dilemmas of entrepreneurship (Hannafey, 2003) (see Box 13.8). He was interested in the difficult moral problems relating to basic fairness: personnel, customer and supplier relationships and communications, amongst other challenges. He recognized the stressful, time-constrained environments in which entrepreneurial people operate, making it difficult to find time for ethical reflection. He also recognized the societal role of entrepreneurs in disrupting 'obsolescent societal patterns'. However, he also observed that the entrepreneurial licence to disrupt was largely a function of the degree to which society had bestowed legitimacy upon entrepreneurship. Etzioni (1987) studied this particular issue in detail, providing an ethical framework for societies to use in addressing practical moral implications of entrepreneurship, but the area remains a difficult one with little definitive guidance.

Social Entrepreneurship   Partly out of dissatisfaction with the motives and goals, not to mention the recent record, of conventional entrepreneurship in addressing societal needs, social entrepreneurship has emerged as a contemporary phenomenon across the global, enjoying extremely high levels of popularity amongst the next generation of entrepreneurs. Commonly defined as 'entrepreneurial activity with an embedded social purpose' (Austin *et al.*, 2006), some of its highest profile examples have come out of developing countries in an attempt to address basic human needs such as sanitation and health care. However, social entrepreneurship is just as popular in developed countries, at levels now beginning to rival conventional entrepreneurship.

Santos takes this further by examining the interplay with positive and negative externalities whereby social entrepreneurship is best placed to act in domains with strong positive externalities where 'the potential for value creation is not matched by the potential for value appropriation because the benefits to society go far beyond the benefits accrued to transacting parties' (see Box 13.9).

BOX 13.9
A theory of social entrepreneurship . . .

Filipe Santos, in a 2009 INSEAD working paper (Santos, 2009) proposed a positive theory of social entrepreneurship in an effort to coalesce a growing body of literature that had splintered away from conventional entrepreneurship over the past two decades.

Santos' theory provides a simple theoretical framework focused not on distinctions based around organizational context or goals, but on the choice made by the entrepreneur between value creation and value appropriation:

Value creation: 'When the utility of society's members increases after accounting for the resources used in that activity.'

Value appropriation: 'Happens when the economic actor is able to capture a portion of the value created by the activity.'

Santos contention is that social entrepreneurship focuses predominantly on value creation for society whereas conventional entrepreneurship focuses predominantly on value appropriation.

Implicit in this theory is an assumption of a trade-off between value creation and value appropriation put simply, a trade-off between profit and impact s which presents the entrepreneur with a simple binary choice. In practice it is much less clear than this. Examples abound of entrepreneurs whose motives are mixed and for whom there is no trade-off between impact and profit – they want both (see Box 13.10).

Public Entrepreneurship   In any society, the state – both local and central (or federal) – accounts for hundreds of billions of dollars of expenditure and is usually the largest single employer in its respective country. It is usually the largest funder of basic science and R&D, a critical early investor in promising new industries and technologies, the main market maker and regulator, and easily the largest customer of goods and services in the economy. It has to fund, commission or deliver an array of public services from cradle to grave for its citizens. It has to protect the most vulnerable in society. It has to create appropriate policy and regulatory frameworks to support the development of entrepreneurship in the economy, the economy in society, and society in the environment. And as it works to meet these challenges, all the while demand is inexorably going up whilst resources are becoming ever more squeezed.

So, enabling economic growth and creating the market conditions for private investment is a critical role of an entrepreneurial state; but what of the hundreds of millions of public sector workers around the world carrying out their daily tasks? Against a prevailing culture of risk-averse administration, one might imagine what possible role entrepreneurial public sector workers could play (see Box 13.11). However, the immense financial constraints that governments are operating under is putting most at the point where they have a 'burning platform' sufficiently ablaze for public sector leaders to loosen their vice-like administrative grip enough to provide a 'safe space' for entrepreneurial staff to innovate.

If the state was ever in need of entrepreneurship it is now. It is imperative that it innovates in order to deliver more value for less resource, to engage citizens in new ways, to exercise sound judgement in the face of uncertainty and to take risks that no private sector business would be comfortable with – as a lender of last resort and as a sovereign power.

BOX 13.10
Social entrepreneurship in action

Blake Mycoskie, founder of TOMS, is a social entrepreneur who has built a value proposition around 'One for One' – a simple concept resulting in a pair of shoes being given to a child in need for every pair that a consumer buys.

Far from diminishing the value appropriation for TOMS by pursuing impact, Mycoskie has built a differentiated brand whose financial returns are generated because of the impact that it delivers.

In December 2014, Bain Capital acquired 50% of TOMS in a deal valuing the eight-year-old business at $625 million and demonstrating that a social business can attract traditional investors persuaded purely by the financial returns.

BOX 13.11
Public entrepreneurship in action

In *The Entrepreneurial State*, Mariana Mazzucato (2013) lays out through case studies, including Apple's iPhone, the role of the state in funding the breakthrough technologies at the heart of products, including lithium-ion batteries, signal compression, LCD displays, micro hard drives, microprocessors, cellular technology, the internet, GPS, multi-touch screens and even Siri, Apple's voice recognition system.

By taking on the risk of early development of these technologies, the US government stimulated private sector investment in their application.

13.2.5 One Planet Entrepreneurship and the Economy

We learned earlier in the chapter about the vital role that entrepreneurship plays in the economic system: Schumpeterian 'creative destruction' and the constant recombining of resources from areas of lower productivity into areas of higher productivity; Knightian bearing of uncertainty and importance of judgement; and Kirznerian alertness and opportunity-seeking behaviour. Entrepreneurship is therefore understood to play a critical role both in destabilizing the *status quo* as well as restabilizing a dynamic equilibrium.

We have learned that entrepreneurship can be applied across a wide variety of organizational and societal contexts and it is a capability that humanity needs in more plentiful supply, provided it is morally grounded in society's values and focused on solving problems that address the planet's needs as much as society's. We have also learned that whilst aspects of entrepreneurial attitudes and behaviour are hereditary, they can also be learned and developed. As such, entrepreneurship is within almost everyone's reach and, provided the societal conceptualization (and by extension legitimization) of entrepreneurship can be broadened to a more holistic level, could see greater expression across society.

And yet we start from a very low base. According to the Global Entrepreneurship Monitor (GEM) (Singer *et al.,* (2014)), the level of independent entrepreneurial activity varies considerably across the globe, with Africa accounting for by far the highest incidence across the board and only non-EU European countries scoring lower than the EU and North America. Conversely, for entrepreneurial employee activity, it is the EU and North America that see the highest levels, though these are markedly lower than for independent entrepreneurship. Even Denmark and Qatar, with the highest levels of employee entrepreneurship in the world, manage no higher than 11.5 per cent of the adult workforce engaged in entrepreneurial activity. Most countries sit below 6 per cent, with even a significant number below 1.0 per cent, including all of the BRICS[11] except Russia (which is not measured in the GEM analysis).

[11] BRICS – coined by Jim O'Neill, Chairman of Goldman Sachs Asset Management. Stands for 'Brazil, Russia, India, China and South Africa' and denotes fastest growing economies outside the G8.

This would suggest that given more investment in formal and informal entrepreneurship education alongside an improved climate for employee entrepreneurship (more commonly known as 'corporate entrepreneurship' or 'intrapreneurship'), there is tremendous potential for entrepreneurship to impact positively upon economies around the world, and in the more advanced innovation-driven economies in particular. It is also worth noting that the GEM measurements of employee entrepreneurship are based on their percentage of the adult population, rather than on a more weighted measure such as GVA or GDP per capita. They therefore take no account of the economic productivity of each entrepreneurial employee. Given that they are to be found in larger businesses with resources at their disposal and more extensive customer bases and supply chains, they are capable of having a disproportionately positive effect on the economy per capita. Therefore it could be argued that efforts at a national and international level to foster entrepreneurship should place at least as much emphasis on corporate entrepreneurship as anywhere else.

Corporate entrepreneurs have a particularly important role to play in discovery and investment in what Clayton Christensen calls 'empowering innovation' (Christensen, 2014) – game-changing technologies that disrupt marketplaces, industry sectors and even the way we live (see Box 13.12). Established businesses tend to focus most of their capital on driving what Christensen calls 'efficiency' and 'sustaining' innovations which actually create few jobs and have a low need for capital, but provide a swift payback on investment. He argues that more of the capital freed up by 'sustaining innovations' needs to be reinvested into empowering innovations that create jobs and that require capital. This used to happen routinely, argues Christensen, but in the last 15 years or so, the link has been broken and capital freed up by sustaining innovations has been continually recycled within established businesses to drive more and more sustaining innovations. In stark contrast, empowering innovations have been starved of capital – not because there is a scarcity of it (quite the reverse, as the world's corporations are awash with $1.6 trillion of cash on their balance sheets), but because their payback is not swift enough. Christensen maintains that the principal reason why companies do this is because they still measure success

BOX 13.12
League of intrapreneurs

Established in 2013 through a partnership between Ashoka Changemakers and Accenture Development Partnerships, the League of Intrapreneurs is a global movement of corporate changemakers that seeks to connect, inspire, celebrate and support entrepreneurial employees. Its growing membership includes people like Christine Gould of Syngenta, who has created a global competition, Thought For Food, to engage university students in developing bold solutions to food insecurity. Already engaging over 3,000 students across 300 universities in 52 countries, Christine is passionate about harnessing social media tools and open innovation to solve big problems.

Source: www.leagueofintrapreneurs.com, www.tffchallenge.com

using financial metrics developed for an era when capital was scarce and other resources were abundant.

In the context of One Planet Entrepreneurship, perhaps we can develop this further? Capital is now abundant and cheap whereas other resources, particularly natural resources, are now scarce and finite. What if we were to add scarce natural resources alongside abundant capital into Christensen's model? Could this lead to capital becoming the financial nutrient circulating around a virtuous resource productivity-oriented innovation cycle? See Figure 13.2.

If the capital cycle can be restored in this way, then it has the potential to fuel dramatic improvements in resource productivity. In fact, this is already showing signs of happening as progressive businesses, recognizing that innovation (particularly empowering innovation) comes from building networks and collaborative partnerships, are doing exactly that with other organizations that can bring complementary capabilities, creativity and technical expertise. We have seen in the past few years a dramatic rise in R&D spend of many companies alongside the novel use of corporate

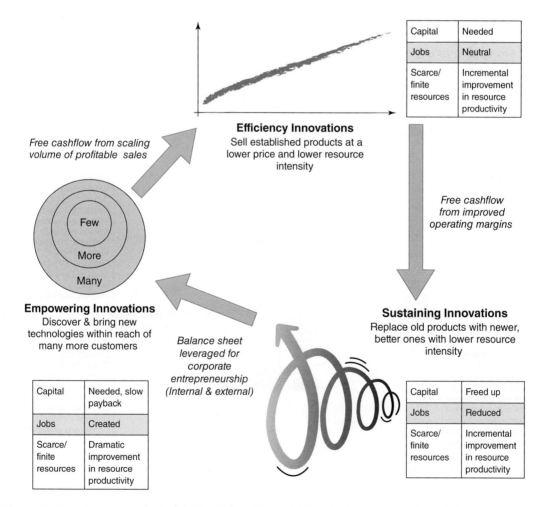

FIGURE 13.2 Conceptual Model: Capital as Financial Nutrient. *Source:* Adapted from Christensen, 2014.

entrepreneurship techniques particularly in the telecoms, technology, media & publishing, FMCG, automotive and chemical sectors.[12] Techniques and models include: open innovation platforms such as Innocentive and OpenIDEO; corporate venturing units such as those at Google, BP and Unilever; corporate-sponsored startup business incubators and accelerators such as Telefonica's *Wayra, Qualcomm Labs*, Google's *Campus* and Barclays' *Escalator* and; corporate partnerships with existing private equity houses to search on their behalf, such as P&G's partnership with Silicon Valley-based crowdfunding platform CircleUp.

All of these initiatives are designed to improve and accelerate the flow of capital to promising innovations being driven by independent entrepreneurs outside an established business. However, similar techniques can also be successfully applied internally to support entrepreneurial employees. As the pace of change quickens, competition intensifies and uncertainty becomes more prevalent, so entrepreneurship becomes an increasingly important strategic capability for organizations to develop. As McGrath (2013) points out, the pursuit of sustainable competitive advantage - for so long the focus of business strategy theory and practice - is becoming an obsolete idea being subsumed by the pursuit of a pipeline of transient sources of competitive advantage. However, achieving this demands a business at ease with change and uncertainty, alert to opportunities and ruthless in exiting older activities before they become unprofitable. This in turn demands not only strong entrepreneurial leadership and management, but also an organizational structure capable of supporting the spectrum of entrepreneurial capability across its workforce. This is no easy task and most organizations who attempt it fail, primarily because they fail to properly contextualize their efforts. As Birkinshaw's *Paradox of Corporate Entrepreneurship* model illustrates (see Figure 13.3),

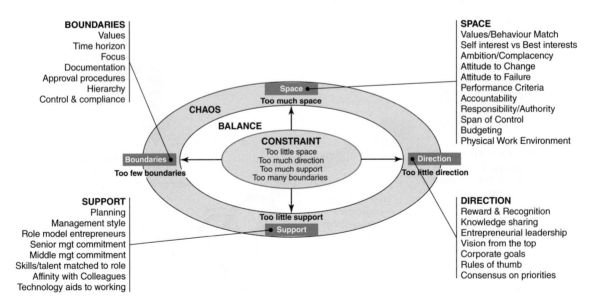

FIGURE 13.3 Organisational Factors affecting Corporate Entrepreneurship. *Source:* Cooke, 2014.

[12] BCG Perspectives. Retrieved from https://www.bcgperspectives.com/content/articles/mergers_acquisitions_growth_incubators_accelerators_venturing_more_leading_companies_search_next_big_thing/?chapter=3.

the challenge is in finding an appropriate balance between 'constraint' (necessary for optimizing for operational efficiency of the core business) and 'chaos' (necessary for opportunity-recognition, prototyping, testing and scaling new sources of competitive advantage) across four key dimensions; space, direction, support and boundaries.

In fact, there are over 30 organizational factors thought to have the potential to act as either barriers or enablers to entrepreneurship within an established organization, all of which may be perceived differently by employees at different points along an entrepreneurial spectrum. It therefore follows that some organizational factors may be more salient than others in affecting entrepreneurship within an organization and as such it should, theoretically at least, be possible to optimize an organization for entrepreneurship.

However, we simply don't know enough about how these factors interplay with each other to be certain of their effect on corporate entrepreneurial capability, but the short lifespans of businesses (Singer et al., 2014; de Geus, 1997) would suggest that most organisations fail to achieve an effective balance between constraint and chaos across these organisational factors. Further research is needed in this area if businesses are to improve upon their strategic capability of 'tuning' themselves more effectively for entrepreneurship and improving their own survival - and financial sustainability - in the process. Developing entrepreneurship as a strategic capability is therefore a fundamental of survival. After all, only by enduring can an organisation then hope to make a meaningful contribution to a sustainable economy in the long term.

Summary

This chapter has addressed the following main points:

◆ Entrepreneurship plays a vital role in the functioning and prosperity of any economy. It is responsible for 'creative destruction' that recombines resources in novel ways to create new value. It is about alertness and opportunity-seeking behaviour. It is about the bearing of uncertainty and the exercising of judgement.

◆ Entrepreneurship has application and value to a variety of organizational and societal contexts; in business (from startups to multinational corporations), in the public sector, in the not-for-profit sector, in the investment community and in communities. It is widely perceived as a positive force for change, provided that it is grounded in the morals and ethics of its society. Entrepreneurs are the people who solve problems by making innovation happen and their attributes and behaviours can be usefully applied to solving social and environmental problems.

◆ One Planet Entrepreneurship offers a useful way of thinking about entrepreneurship in pursuit of sustainability regardless of organizational context or underlying motive. This is provided as a draft conceptual framework as a basis for further discussion by students of entrepreneurship and sustainable business.

◆ A more holistic and inclusive framing of entrepreneurship has been provided in order to encourage the reader to consider their own entrepreneurial attributes and intentions, as well as informing their own career planning as an entrepreneur.

GROUP EXERCISE

In small teams of three to five people, take ten minutes to brainstorm as many different organizational and societal contexts in which you think entrepreneurship can contribute to sustainability. Write your ideas on a flipchart and appoint a spokesperson.

After ten minutes, take about five minutes per group to present your ideas to the other groups in the room.

Then, as a plenary session, spend a further 20 minutes discussing the following:

- Which organizational and societal contexts offer the most opportunity for entrepreneurs?
- What ethical considerations should be paramount in behaving entrepreneurially in those contexts?
- How would you sell the value of entrepreneurship to sceptical stakeholders in those contexts?

QUESTIONS FOR CLASS DISCUSSION

1. Is entrepreneurship better served as a solitary pursuit or in entrepreneurial teams?
2. If alertness and judgement are such important entrepreneurial traits, how do you think entrepreneurs go about identifying opportunities, and then filtering and selecting the best opportunities?
3. Take the *self-assessment test below* for Entrepreneurial Orientation (EO). Analyse your scores and then reflect on what (if anything) this means to you and your career planning.

GROUP EXERCISE

1. Think of a recent example of 'creative destruction' in action where a mature industry was disrupted by a new technology or business model. Explore whether you think this has been a good or bad thing for sustainability.
2. Examine the One Planet Entrepreneurship conceptual framework and make a list of its strengths and weaknesses. Now think about how you would improve upon it.

References

Adams, R., Jeanrenaud, S., Bessant, J., Overy, P., & Denyer, D. (2012). *Innovating for sustainability: A systematic review of the body of knowledge.* London, Ontario: Network for Business Sustainability.

Anderson, A., & Smith, R. (2007). *The moral space in entrepreneurship: An exploration of ethical imperatives and the moral legitimacy of being enterprising.* The Open Access Institutional Repository at the Robert Gordon University.

Austin, J., Stevenson, H., & Wei-Skillern, J. (2006). Social and Commercial Entrepreneurship: Same, Different or Both? *Entrepreneurship Theory and Practice*, Vol 30, issue 1, 1–22, January 2006.

Bessant, J., & Tidd, J. (2007). *Innovation and entrepreneurship.* Chichester: John Wiley & Sons.

Birkinshaw, J. (2003). The Paradox of Corporate Entrepreneurship. *Strategy + Business.* 30(spring): 46–58.

Burgelman, R. A. (1983a). A model of the interaction of strategic behavior, corporate context, and the concept of strategy. *Academy of Management Review*, 8(1), 61–71.

Burgelman, R. A. (1983b). A process model of internal corporate venturing in the diversified major firm. *Administrative Science Quarterly*, 28, 223–244.

Cantillon, R. (1755). *Essai sur la nature du commerce en general.* Higgs, H. (Ed.). London: Macmillan, 1931.

Casson, M. C. (1982). *The entrepreneur: An economic theory.* Oxford: Martin Robertson, xiv + 418 pp. (2nd. ed., Edward Elgar, 2003).

Christensen, C. M. (2014, June). The capitalist's dilemma. *Harvard Business Review.* Retrieved from https://hbr.org/2014/06/the-capitalists-dilemma. Talk also available at https://www.thersa.org/events/2013/09/the-capitalists-dilemma/

Collins, J. (2001). *Good to Great: Why Some Companies Make the Leap and Others Don't*. London: Random House.

Cooke, A. J. (2014). Fostering intrapreneurship in healthcare. *International Symposium of Healthcare Improvement and Innovation*. Prato, Italy (September 18–20).

Covin, J. G., & Slevin, D. P. (1989). Strategic management of small firms in hostile and benign environments. *Strategic Management Journal, 10*(January), 75–87.

Dobbs, R., Oppenheim, J., Thompson, F., Brinkman, M., & Zornes, M. (2011). *Resource revolution: Meeting the world's energy, materials, food and water needs*. London: McKinsey Global Institute.

Doppelt, B. (2008). *The power of sustainable thinking*. London: Earthscan.

Elkington, J. (2012). *The Zeronauts: Breaking the Sustainability Barrier*. Abingdon: Routledge.

Etzioni, A. (1987). Entrepreneurship, adaptation and legitimation: A macro-behavioural perspective. *Journal of Economic Behaviour and Organisation, 8*, 175–189.

de Geus, A. (1997). *The living company*. Massachusetts: Harvard Business School Press.

Gibcus, P., de Kok, J., Snijders, J., Smit, L., & van der Linden, B. (2012). *Effects and Impact of Entrepreneurship Programmes in Higher Education*. Brussels, European Commission, DG Enterprise.

Gilder, G. (2013). *Knowledge and power: The information theory of capitalism and how it is revolutionising the world*. Washington: Regency Publishing Inc.

Hannafey, F. (2003). Entrepreneurship and ethics: A literature review. *Journal of Business Ethics, 46*, 99–110.

Heck, S., & Rogers, M. (2014). *Resource Revolution: How to Capture the Biggest Business Opportunity in a Century*. New York: Melcher Media.

Keelan, T., & Woods, C. (2006). Mauipreneur: Understanding Maori Entrepreneurship. *The International Indigenous Journal of Entrepreneurship, Advancement, Strategy and Education, 2*(2), 1–20

Khandwalla, P. (1977). *The design of organisations*. New York: Harcourt Brace Jovanovich.

Kirzner, I. (1973). *Competition and entrepreneurship*. Chicago, IL: University of Chicago Press.

Kirzner, I. (2012)[1997]. *How markets work: Disequilibrium, entrepreneurship and discovery (2nd Ed)*. Institute of Economic Affairs.

Knight, F. H. (1924). The limitations of scientific method in economics. In *Selected essays by Frank H. Wright, vol. 1: 'What is truth' in economics?* Emmett, R. B. (Ed.). Chicago, IL: University of Chicago Press, 1–39.

Kreiser, P. M., Marino, L. D., Dickson, P. and Weaver, K. M. (2010), *Cultural Influences on Entrepreneurial Orientation: The Impact of National Culture on Risk Taking and Proactiveness in SMEs*. Entrepreneurship Theory and Practice, 34: 959–983. doi:10.1111/j.1540-6520.2010.00396.x

Kuratko, D., Montagno, R., & Hornsby, J. (1990). Developing an intrapreneurial corporate instrument for an effective entrepreneurial environment. *Strategic Management Journal, 11*, 49–58.

Lindsay, N. J. (2005). Toward a cultural model of indigenous entrepreneurial attitude. *Academy of Marketing Science Review, 5*.

Lumpkin, G. T., & Dess, G. G. (1996). Clarifying the entrepreneurial orientation construct and linking it to performance. *Academy of Management Review, 21*(1), 135–172.

Martinez, A., Levie, J., Kelley, D., Saemundsson, R., & Schott, T. (2010). *A global perspective on entrepreneurship education and training*. Massachusetts: Global Entrepreneurship Monitor.

Mazzucato, M. (2013). *The entrepreneurial state: Debunking private vs public sector myths*. London: Anthem Press.

McGrath, R. G., & MacMillan, I. (2000). *The entrepreneurial mindset*. Massachusetts: Harvard Business School Press.

McGrath, R. G. (2010). Business models: A discovery-driven approach. *Long Range Planning, 43*, 247–261.

McGrath, R. G. (2013). *The end of competitive advantage: How to keep your strategy moving as fast as your business*. Massachusetts: Harvard Business Review Press.

Miller, D. (1983). The correlates of entrepreneurship in three types of firms. *Management Science, 29*(7), 770–791.

Nicolaou, N., Shane, S., Cherkas, L., Hunkin, J., & Spector, T. (2008). Is the tendency to engage in entrepreneurship genetic? *Management Science, 54*, 167–179.

Nicolaou, N., & Shane, S. (2010). Entrepreneurship and occupational choice: Genetic and environmental influences. *Journal of Economic Behaviour & Organisation, 76*, 3–14.

Peterson, R., & Berger, D. (1971). Entrepreneurship in organisations: Evidence from the music industry. *Administrative Science Quarterly, 16*(1), 97–106.

Pinchot, G. (1985). *Intrapreneuring: Why You Don't Have to Leave the Corporation to Become an Entrepreneur*. New York: Harper & Row.

Robinson, P. B., Stimpson, D. V., Huefner, J. C., & Hunt, H. K. (1991). An attitude approach to the prediction of entrepreneurship. *Entrepreneurship Theory and Practice, 15*(4).

Santos, F. (2009). *A positive theory of social entrepreneurship*. INSEAD Faculty & Research Working Papers, 2009/23/EFE/ISIC.

Schumpeter, J. A., 1934 (2008). *The Theory of Economic Development: An Inquiry into Profits, Capital, Credit, Interest and the Business Cycle*. Translated from the German by Redvers Opie, New Brunswick (U.S.A) and London (U.K.): Transaction Publishers.

Schumpeter, J. A. (2014)[1942]. *Capitalism, socialism and democracy* (2nd ed.). Floyd, Virginia: Impact Books.

Senge, P., Smith. B., Kruschwitz, N., Laur, J., & Schley, S. (2010). *The necessary revolution: How individuals and organisations are working together to create a sustainable world*. London: Nicholas Brealey Publishing.

Singer, S., Amoros, J., & Arreola, D. (2014). *Global entrepreneurship monitor: 2014 global report*. London: Global Entrepreneurship Research Association.

Souitaris, V., Zerbinati, S., & Al-Laham, A. (2007). Do entrepreneurship programmes raise entrepreneurial intentions of science and engineering students? *Journal of Business Venturing, 22*, 566–691.

Stevenson, H. H., & Jarillo, J. C. (1990). A paradigm of entrepreneurship: Entrepreneurial management. *Strategic Management Journal, 11*, 17–27.

Weber, M. (1905). *The protestant ethic and the spirit of capitalism*. Germany.

Werbach, A. (2004). *The Death of Environmentalism and the Birth of the Commons Movement*. Speech at the Commonwealth Club, San Francisco, Dec 8 2004. [online at: http://grist.org/article/werbach-reprint/]

Willard, B. (2002). *The sustainability advantage: Seven business case benefits of a triple bottom line*. Gabriela Island, BC: New Society Publishers.

Zhang, Z., Zyphur, M., Narayanan, J., Arvey, R., Chaturvedi, S., Avolio, B., Lichtenstein, P., & Larsson, G. (2009). The Genetic Basis of Entrepreneurship: Effects of Gender and Personality. *Organisational Behaviour and Human Decision Processes, 110*(2009), 93–107.

14 Transitioning: What Does Sustainability for Business Really Mean? And When is a Business Truly Sustainable?

Thomas Dyllick and Katrin Muff

'Imagine a world where business is celebrated for its contribution to society.'
Nick Main, Deloitte

LEARNING OUTCOMES

By the end of this chapter you will:

1. Understand that despite the fact that more and more companies are integrating sustainability into their management, the state of the planet is not improving.

2. Understand how this 'big disconnect' is related to the way business sustainability has been framed and developed in theory and in practice.

3. Be familiar with different ways of defining sustainability in business and appreciate the evolution of thinking.

4. Know a simple framework for the analysis of existing and emerging models for business sustainability.

5. Understand a new typology for business sustainability, ranging from Business-as-Usual to Business Sustainability 1.0 (Refined Shareholder Value Management), Business Sustainability 2.0 (Managing for the Triple Bottom Line) to Business Sustainability 3.0 (Truly Sustainable Business).

6. Know what it means for a business to be not just sustainable but 'truly sustainable' and be familiar with some of the related challenges in putting this into practice.

Introduction

While sustainability management is becoming more widespread among major companies, the impact of their activities is not reflected in studies monitoring the state of the planet. What results from this is a 'big disconnect' between sustainable business on an organizational level and sustainable development on a global level. In this chapter[1] we address two main questions: 'How can business make an effective contribution to addressing the sustainability challenges we are facing?' And: 'When is business truly sustainable?' In a time when more and more corporations claim to manage sustainably, we need to distinguish between those companies that contribute effectively to sustainability and those that do not. We do this by clarifying the meaning of business sustainability (BST) and link it to the global sustainability challenges. We review established approaches to business sustainability in the literature and develop a typology of business sustainability with a focus on effective contributions for sustainable development (SD). This should help to assess companies on their journey towards integrating BST into their strategies and business models. And it provides a framework for scholars and professionals to engage in the transformation of business, moving from 'Business-as-Usual' to 'True Business Sustainability'. We will not address the required changes in the underlying economic model or in the model of consumer behaviour, although effective changes in these areas are clearly interrelated.

We start out by looking in more detail at this 'big disconnect' between sustainable business on an organizational level and sustainable development on a global level. We then look at studies monitoring the overall state of the planet before we move to the business level. Here we consider how models of business sustainability have been typically framed in theory and practice. In the main part of the chapter we develop a new typology for BST ranging from Business Sustainability 1.0 (Refined Shareholder Value Management), to Business Sustainability 2.0 (Managing for the Triple Bottom Line), and to Business Sustainability 3.0 (True Sustainability). Next we briefly addresses some of the challenges in managing and organizing for BST. In the final section we present our conclusions and a discussion.

14.0 Sustainable Business and Sustainable Development: The Big Disconnect

The role of business in making our world a more sustainable place is at the center of the study of sustainability management. If we follow the studies monitoring the acceptance and integration of sustainability by big companies, there is a strong consensus emerging that sustainability is having, and will continue to have, a significant material impact on company strategies and operations. More and more business executives agree that sustainability-related strategies are necessary to be competitive today and even more so in the future. More and more executives report that their organizations' commitment to sustainability has increased in the past and will develop further in the future. They report that benefits of addressing sustainability accrue not only to the environment and to society, but also to the companies themselves, through tangible benefits in the form of reduced costs and risks of doing business, as well as through intangible benefits in the form of increased brand reputation, increased attractiveness to talent and increased competiveness (Bové & Bonini, 2014; Kron *et al.*, 2013; UN Global Compact & Accenture, 2013 & 2010; Haanaes *et al.*, 2012; Haanaes *et al.*, 2011). But somehow this good news is not reflected in studies monitoring the state of our planet. Here we learn that poverty has not been eradicated, inequity is growing, hunger and malnutrition still kills a child every 6 seconds,

---

[1] This chapter builds on an earlier paper published as Dyllick and Muff (2016).

1.8 billion people do not have access to clean drinking water and sanitation, and 2.3 billion people do not have access to electricity. Further, a 4° warming scenario is now being accepted by international organizations like the World Bank and the IEA, while the international climate negotiations have failed to produce any consensus on effective global strategies to keep global warming at least below 2° (Bakker, 2012; UNEP, 2012; WWF, 2014; Gilding, 2011).

What results from this discrepancy between micro level progress and macro level deterioration is a big disconnect between company activities and the global state of the environment and society. Although there are different reasons to explain this disconnect – after all corporations are not the only relevant actors in the global sustainability arena – the current situation should be considered as a wake-up call for businesspeople and management scholars alike that their good intentions and actions have not been leading to significant sustainability improvements on a global level. In response to this disconnect, we look critically at how the concept of BST has been used in the academic literature and in the world of practice. In clarifying the meaning of BST, we do not assume this alone will solve the problem, but we believe that a better understanding of the impact of business on global sustainability will at least set the discussion on the right track.

Bansal and Gao (2006) analysed the 'organization and environment' research published in leading general management journals and found that a majority of the articles explained environmental outcomes, yet only a small fraction of these offered radically new insights about balancing economic and environmental needs. Sharma concluded that research on business sustainability has become increasingly incremental and is mostly failing to ask bold and important questions that address fundamental sustainability issues the world is facing. And although 'rigor increases every year, the questions asked become increasingly uninspiring, uninteresting, and insignificant' (Sharma, cited by Starik, 2006, p. 433).

Kallio and Nordberg (2006, p. 447) conclude rather sceptically in their analysis of the literature with regard to the environmental side of business sustainability:

> *What we do know is that eco-efficiency of companies usually increases because of environmental management. But we also know that the ecological footprint of humanity has shown no signs of getting smaller, and neither has that of the industrialized world – in fact rather to the contrary (e.g. WWF). We simply do not know to what extent corporate greening actually contributes to ecological sustainability or whether it does at all.*

They link their analysis to the skewed perspective and values of business sustainability scholars. It seems that when these authors analyse win–win strategies and solutions in their research, the debate is really about whether and how business is profiting from it, ignoring society and the environment. It is not really societal or environmental issues that are under scrutiny, but organizational issues and consequences.

Banerjee (2011) arrives at the same conclusion with regard to corporate social responsibility and links it to the primary focus in the literature, which has been on the financial impact and on the company, not on the outcomes for society. Margolis and Walsh (2003, p. 289) conclude more broadly from their appraisal of 30 years of studies on corporate social performance:

> *Although the financial effects of corporate social performance have been extensively studied, little is known about any consequences of corporate social initiatives.*

Most notable, as calls for corporate involvement increase, there is a vital need to understand how corporate efforts to redress social misery actually affect their intended beneficiaries.

In looking at some of the underlying reasons, Banerjee (2011, p. 720) suggests there are deeply rooted ideological barriers that come into play when business sustainability is approached from the dominant economic-centered paradigm. These barriers include the perspective of looking first and foremost for benefits that serve the organization (by increasing brand value, reducing risk and cost factors or embracing new revenue growth potential) rather than embracing a more balanced approach to value creation. As such, the dominant view is that business can profit from sustainability while solving the social and environmental problems of the world through new growth opportunities (Hart, 2007), through opportunities for innovation (Nidumolu *et al.*, 2009) or for profit (Prahalad & Hammond, 2002; Prahalad, 2004). The underlying assumption embedded in this win–win perspective is that business will not pursue environmental and social initiatives if these do not provide economic advantages to the business. A purely economic perspective and an ideological bias in favour of business success are therefore constraining relevant contributions of business sustainability to bring about real and noticeable improvements to the state of the planet.

Considering this brief overview of the state of the sustainability literature, we cannot help but notice the paradoxical absence of nature and society from sustainability research and the deplorable lack of bold steps to addressing environmental and social outcomes. It appears that these are connected to some fundamental shortcomings and blind spots of how the management discipline has developed:

1   *Educational shortcomings:* the knowledge and understanding of the great majority of management scholars in the environmental and sustainability fields is simply too weak to bring a similar understanding and depth to the debate as compared to the organization side (Whiteman *et al.*, 2013).

2   *A missing interdisciplinary perspective:* issues of ecological and social sustainability are typically much more complex than organizational issues and may include ecological, economic, political, social and cultural relationships which demand cross-enterprise, cross-level, cross-theoretical and interdisciplinary approaches which are rarely taught and difficult to apply.

3   *A very limited perspective on skills:* sustainability issues include cognitive, emotional and ethical elements that typically are very challenging for the researcher.

4   *Missing incentives for researchers:* theoretical research is mainly concerned with methodological rigour and contributions to established theory; the societal relevance of the questions is often of little concern for the researcher. And as normative research (what should or needs to be done) enjoys significantly less credibility than explanatory research (giving explanations, while refraining from taking a normative stance), bold and exploratory research that addresses the big issues society is facing is very rare and holds few benefits for academic researchers.

5   *Ideological prejudices:* the dominance of win–win strategies in the sustainability literature reflects the economic interests of business, but fails to take into account the public interest which was seen to be paramount for the Academy of Management at the time of its foundation more than 55 years ago (Walsh *et al.*, 2003).

14.1 Understanding Our Global Sustainability Challenges

Humanity is living far beyond the planet's means, consuming the earth's renewable resources as if we had more than one planet to draw upon. According to the estimation of humanity's global footprint, we are using the resources of 1.5 planets (WWF, 2014). At the same time, there are significant disparities between regions and their footprints. If we all consumed at the level of the European consumers, we would need the resources of three planets; at the level of the US consumers, we would need more than four planets. This is an absurd thought that becomes scary when we consider the projections for the global middle class tripling to reach 4.9 billion by 2030, with an additional 2.7 billion middle-class consumers in Asia alone (WEF & Accenture, 2012). These consumers will increase our global footprint to reach a biocapacity need of two planets by 2030. Having only one planet available, obviously this is not at all a sustainable path (Gilding, 2011). In order to assess the overall state of the planet a number of major scientific analyses have been presented, all with equally disturbing results.

The Millennium Ecosystem Assessment (MEA, 2005) is the largest assessment of the health of ecosystems ever undertaken. It was commissioned by the UN and prepared by 1,360 experts from 95 countries. It represents a consensus of the world's scientists on the rate and scale of ecosystem changes and consequences for 24 ecosystem services. Ecosystem services are services provided by nature in the form of provisioning services (wood, crops, water or genetic resources), regulating services (water purification, climate or erosion regulation) and cultural services (educational or recreational values of nature). The findings demonstrate that humans have radically altered these ecosystems in the last 50 years. While such ecosystem changes have brought economic gains, these were achieved at growing ecological costs that threaten the achievement of the UN Millennium Development goals. The overall result is sobering: 15 out of 24 (60%) ecosystem services analysed have been degraded during the past 50 years, five show mixed results, while only four have improved. Most of the services provided free by nature have become not only costly, but increasingly scarce (e.g., capture fisheries, wild foods, genetic resources, erosion regulation).

A group of renowned earth-system and environmental scientists, led by Johan Rockström of the Stockholm Resilience Centre, analysed the environmental threats of the planet and developed a 'planetary boundaries approach', defining thresholds for nine critical earth-system processes. The boundaries were defined based on best available scientific knowledge. Together they create what Rockström and collegues (2009) call a 'safe operating space for humanity'. Crossing the boundaries could lead to irreversible and, in some cases, abrupt environmental change. Such change could move the earth out of the stable state which has allowed humankind to develop safely and beneficially during the past 10,000 years. The nine processes that define the planetary boundaries include climate change, rate of biodiversity loss, nitrogen and phosphorous cycles, ozone depletion, ocean acidification, global freshwater use, change in land use, atmospheric aerosol loading, and chemical pollution. When comparing the current status of these processes with the proposed safe boundaries, Rockström *et al.* conclude that most of the first three – climate change, rate of biodiversity loss, nitrogen cycle – have already crossed their critical thresholds, while four more are rapidly approaching their thresholds – the phosphorus cycle, ocean acidification, global freshwater use, and change in land use.

Any vision of sustainable development recognizes, of course, the importance of societal well-being as an integral part of our planetary well-being. Eradicating poverty and achieving social justice is inextricably linked to ensuring ecological stability and renewal. While planetary boundaries provide an environmental ceiling defined by critical natural thresholds, there are also social boundaries defined by critical human deprivations. They represent a kind of lower limit and provide a minimal social foundation for sustainable development. Raworth (2012) presents a 'doughnut model' or 'life-safer model' to define a safe and just space for humanity, with an outer environmental boundary and an inner social boundary. Between a minimal social foundation that protects against critical human deprivations and an environmental ceiling that avoids critical planetary thresholds lies a 'safe and just space for humanity' in which to thrive.

The minimal social foundations presented are based on international human rights as laid down in the UN's Universal Declaration of Human Rights (1948), the Millennium Development Goals (2000) and the UN General Secretary's High-level Panel on Global Sustainability (2012). They include 11 social priorities enabling people to be well, productive and empowered:

- Being well: food security, adequate income, improved water and sanitation, health care.
- Being productive: through education, decent work, energy services, resilience to shocks.
- Being empowered: through gender equality, social equity, having a political voice.

Clearly, achieving sustainable development, or even just making significant steps in the right direction, presents a long-term challenge. It will need major transformations in many different areas and on different levels. Society, the economy and business are challenged to help ensure this urgent transition. The World Business Council for Sustainable Development (WBCSD) recognizes in its Vision 2050 – 'nine billion people living well and within the limits of the planet' – that the demands of a growing and more demanding population have to be met within the capacity of the existing planet. In order to achieve this goal, both a significant reduction of the ecological footprint and an improved biocapacity will be needed (WBCSD, 2010). In other words, it will not suffice to radically lower the level of resource consumption, we will also have to come up with ingenious solutions to (re)generate biocapacity, e.g., solutions that do not just reduce emissions but take emissions out of the atmosphere. The WBCSD outlines a number of significant changes required to ensure a world on track towards sustainability by 2050. Some of them demand better solutions and technological innovation that can be viewed as important business opportunities; others relate to behavioural change and social innovation (WBCSD, 2010):

- Developing radically more eco-efficient lifestyles and solutions to enable education and economic empowerment for billions of people, women in particular.
- Incorporating the cost of externalities, including carbon, water and ecosystem services.
- Doubling the agricultural output without increasing the amount of land or water used.
- Halting deforestation and increasing yields from planted forests.

- Halving carbon emissions worldwide and providing access to low-carbon mobility.
- Delivering a four- to tenfold improvement in the use of resources and materials.

Vision 2050 sets the standard of the challenge for business and society. To move from today's business-as-usual to a sustainable world in 2050 it will be necessary to rebuild the economy with new rules, to decouple economic growth from resource consumption and ecosystem degradation, to move markets toward true-value pricing and long-term value creation, and for business to make sustainability an easier choice for consumers and companies themselves (WBCSD, 2010).

The challenges of sustainable development for the future of the economy are as daunting as for the future of business. Beyond the belief that we have to somehow move from a 'brown' to a 'green economy' which, according to UNEP (2011), can be thought of as one which is low carbon, resource efficient and socially inclusive, there are no signs yet as to what such an economy and the necessary transition could possibly look like.

> *The sheer scale of this task is rarely acknowledged. In a world of 9 billion people all aspiring to Western lifestyles, the carbon intensity of every dollar of output must be at least 130 times lower in 2050 than it is today. And by the end of the century, economic activity will need to take carbon out of the atmosphere rather than adding to it.*
>
> (Jackson, 2011, p. 187.)

What society and the planet need in the next two decades is nothing short of an economic miracle. Business, with its capacity for innovation, is uniquely well-placed to generate such a miracle.

14.2 Different Approaches to Framing Business Sustainability

The basic business process can be understood as a transformation of various inputs into different kinds of outputs. We will use this simple 'input – process – output' model in order to look more deeply at existing approaches for integrating sustainability into business (see Table 14.1). On the input side we identify different *concerns* (or issues) business chooses to consider and address. On the process side we focus on different *organizational perspectives*. And on the output side we find different *values* business creates or preserves. A focus on inputs defines BST with regard to the relevant concerns considered by business (what?). A focus on perspectives defines BST with regard to the perspectives taken by business (how?). And a focus on values defines BST with regard to the values created by business (what for?).

TABLE 14.1 A Framework for Analysing Different Approaches to Business Sustainability

Input	Process	Output
Concerns	Organizational perspectives	Values created
What?	*How?*	*What for?*

14.2.1 Focusing on Concerns

Some of the early concepts of BST were focusing on concerns like 'integrating short-term and long-term aspects' and 'consuming the income, not the capital'. Another concern relates to 'being accountable for the impacts of business decisions and activities'. Let us look at these approaches in more detail.

While the relevant planning horizons for companies have become shorter and shorter, mainly driven by pressures from the financial markets, developments in the sustainability field typically require a much longer time horizon. Demographic processes, urbanization, resource depletion and renewal rates, time lags in climate change and ozone depletion, are only some examples of this. If sustainability concerns are to be taken into consideration by companies, *long-term aspects need to be given at least equal weight as short-term aspects.* This logic is well exemplified in the decision by Paul Polman (2012) after he had come in as new CEO of Unilever. As one of his first decisions, he got rid of quarterly reporting and told hedge funds and short-term investors, 'You don't belong in this company', as they were not aligned with Unilever's longer-term strategy to double revenue by 2020 while halving the company's sustainability impact.

The second approach requires business to *live off the income and preserve the capital base* (Dyllick & Hockerts, 2002). Companies have considered this as good financial management, yet the same holds true for natural and social capital which also deserves to be preserved, although it is not equally accepted or institutionalized. In times when environmental and social capitals have become scarce or strained, sustainable business has to take all three areas into consideration. Balancing economic, environmental and social capital is thus a foundation of a good sustainable business practice.

Being accountable for the impacts of business decisions and activities, a third concern, is well-defined in the ISO 26000 standard (2011) on social responsibility (which can be interpreted here as an alternative term for sustainability):

> *The essential characteristic of social responsibility is the willingness of an organization to incorporate social and environmental considerations in its decision-making and be accountable for the impacts of its decisions and activities on society and the environment. This implies both transparent and ethical behavior that contributes to sustainable development, is in compliance with applicable law and is consistent with international norms of behavior. It also implies that social responsibility is integrated throughout the organization, is practiced in its relationships and takes into account the interests of stakeholders.*

Without a doubt, accountability is an important aspect of BST, just like the other two concerns: integrating short-term and long-term aspects, and consuming the income, not the capital. They all address important parts of BST that promise to contribute to sustainable development, but there are other approaches, with a focus on organizational perspectives and values created, that we also need to look at.

14.2.2 Focusing on Organizational Perspectives

Other approaches for integrating sustainability into business involve focusing not on the concerns to be considered, but on the organizational perspectives used by business. These include 'managing risks and opportunities' and 'embedding sustainability throughout the organization'.

Some authors base their BST strategies on the dual needs of *managing risks and opportunities* which can be located on an operational or a strategic level (Steger, 2004 and 2006; Schaltegger, 2006). Others focus on managing the downside by reducing costs (e.g., resource efficiencies, regulatory burden) or risks (e.g., business risks, supply chain risks) and building the upside by increasing revenues, market share or reputation (Esty & Winston, 2009; Nidumolu *et al.*, 2009).

Embedding sustainability throughout the organization has been another prominent perspective considered to be of key importance for integrating sustainability into business. Such authors argue that simple bolt-on sustainability will not suffice to effectively manage the sustainability risks and opportunities. Business will need to embed sustainability throughout the organization in its strategies and operations, in its governance and management processes, organizational structures and culture, its auditing and reporting systems (Eccles *et al.*, 2012; Laszlo & Zhexembayeva, 2011; Belz & Peattie, 2012; Smith & Lensen, 2009; Esty & Winston, 2009; Epstein, 2008).

The ISO 26000 guidelines (2011) further clarify that the regular activities constitute the most important behaviours to be addressed, not special activities or projects. They should be an integral part of the core organizational strategy, with assigned responsibilities and accountability at all appropriate levels of the organization, and they should be reflected not only in decision-making but also in implementation activities. Finally, corporate responsibility should be based on an understanding of the broader expectations of society and an identification of and engagement with relevant stakeholders. These are considered to be fundamental conditions for business to move beyond isolated or partial strategies and to be able to make significant contributions to sustainable development on a broader level.

14.2.3 Focusing on Values Created

A third type of approach focuses neither on concerns nor on organizational perspectives, but on the particular values created or preserved by a business. These values look at the output of the business process for defining BST, not on the input or the process. The different outputs discussed in the literature are 'integrating economic, ecological and social value creation', 'creating shared value' and the 're-emergence of social purpose.

In many approaches BST has been associated with the need to contribute to *economic, ecological and social value creation*, or at least prevent their destruction. Elkington (1997) introduced the concept of the 'triple bottom line' as a new business objective, which measures more adequately the multidimensional business contributions to sustainability. Although very appealing at first sight, it has remained to a large degree unclear how the trade-offs between economic, ecological and social values are to be measured and compared.

Emerson (1983) introduced the concept of '*blended value*' that combines a company's creation of revenue with the generation of social value. Porter and Kramer

(2011) suggest that we need to redefine capitalism around '*creating shared value*', not just profit, thereby elevating the discussion to a fundamental level of the purpose of business and the economic system as a whole. Shared value creation is defined as creating economic value in a way that also creates value for society by addressing its needs and challenges. Ideally, the starting point for business planning thereby is society and its problems, rather than business itself, to unlock business opportunities.

Shared value creation may be a useful first step to resolve the stalemate created by the opposing views of shareholder value management (Friedman, 1970; Rappaport, 1986) and stakeholder value management (Freeman, 1984). By reconnecting business to society, it would help to overcome the Friedmanian fallacy of business seeing itself as being disconnected from society (Muff *et al.*, 2013). However, shared value creation is unlikely to be a sufficient approach for solving societal problems, as it is limited to those issues and concerns that promise economic value for business (Crane *et al.*, 2014; *Financial Times*, 2014). Dyllick and Hockerts (2002) asked for business to look 'beyond the business case' and go beyond eco-efficiency or socio-efficiency to become eco-effective or socio-effective, while developing effective solutions in addressing the real sustainability issues their societies are facing. Recent developments related to social business, social entrepreneurship, impact investment, benefit (B-) Corporations (Rae, 2012), *Corporation 2020* (Sukhdev, 2012), public value creation (Meynhardt, 2009) or the Economy for the Common Good movement in Europe (Felber, 2010) point to alternative organizational models that share '*goal alignment with society*' and a '*re-emergence of social purpose*' as distinguishing features.

Over the past decade *social business* (or social enterprises) and *social entrepreneurship* have assumed a prominent role in society and in academia. Social businesses use business methods and practices to generate direct social and/or environmental benefits. Fulfilment of their social mission is of primary importance, while achieving financial benefits is only of secondary importance. Sabeti (2009) speaks of an emerging 'fourth sector' of organizations oriented towards social benefits, like government agencies and NGOs, but earning their income themselves, unlike government agencies and many NGOs. The income of social businesses is mostly earned, but they may also receive contributions from private or public donors. There is a great variety of organizations and sources of income. A comprehensive support infrastructure for social businesses has been developing, including educational programmes, social business clubs and centers at business schools, incubators (e.g., the Hub), coaches, supporting foundations (Ashoka, Schwab, Skoll), government programmes (EU Social Business Initiative 2011), a special legal status for privately owned organizations that prioritize their social mission (i.e., B-Corporation or community-interest companies) and a specialized financial services industry specializing in social and impact investment. Social businesses promise a higher effectiveness in addressing sustainability challenges than commercial businesses by making social issues their primary objective.

Changing the business purpose to the common good may be too radical for existing commercial businesses, but the emergence of B-Corporations and a broad support for social businesses and social entrepreneurship demonstrate that there is a need for new organizational forms with a clear social purpose. Their further development offers new perspectives for 'true business sustainability' through new or hybrid business organizations with a purpose that reaches beyond shared value creation.

In concluding our overview of existing approaches to BST, we realize there have been many different attempts to frame business sustainability in the broader context of SD. They have mostly fallen short of reaching this ambitious goal. They include approaches based on partial or incremental improvements of an existing strategy instead of a method that looks at all kinds of concerns, organizational perspectives and values created. They include attempts that are oriented primarily towards increasing shareholder value by reducing the business footprint rather than creating sustainable value in its broader meaning. Often, such approaches are based on an inside-out perspective, demonstrating how business is contributing through its activities to improving some sustainability issue. What is rarely done, however, is to look at the relationship of business and society the other way around, by asking how business can contribute effectively to solving sustainability challenges. Such an outside-in perspective may be the crucial step needed for business to move to fully fledged or true sustainability.

14.3 Introducing a Typology for Business Sustainability

Sustainability demands an integration of social and environmental issues with economic issues. What exactly this means and what the consequences are for business is far from clear. While many companies have started to consider longer-term, social and environmental aspects in their business, they rarely ask themselves what their contribution to resolving sustainability issues on a regional or global scale could be and should be. Such a positive contribution to society and the planet, however, lies at the heart of a truly sustainable business.

We now develop a typology of business sustainability based on the above systematic analysis of different approaches in the literature. In deriving the different types we will use the three previously introduced elements of the business process model that the relevant concerns considered (inputs), the values created (outputs) and the organizational perspectives applied (processes) – thereby switching the second and third elements. Based on these three elements we develop a typology of business sustainability, using the current economic paradigm as a starting point. Starting out with 'Business-as-Usual', we add three increasingly relevant types of business sustainability, which we call *Business Sustainability 1.0, 2.0* and *3.0*. As we move up from Business Sustainability 1.0 to 2.0 and 3.0, the contribution to resolving sustainability issues increases, with Business Sustainability 3.0 representing what we consider as 'True BST'.

14.3.1 Business-as-usual: The Current Economic Paradigm

The current economic paradigm or 'Business-as-Usual' (see Figure 14.1) is based on a purely economic view of the firm and business processes. The underlying assumption is that typical economic concerns (e.g., access to cheap resources, efficient processes, striving for a strong market position) are pursued to produce economic value in the form of profit, market value or, more generally, shareholder value. Such an approach usually results in significant externalized costs which are not understood, measured or declared. The perspective is inside-out, with the business and its objectives as the starting point and main reference for all planning and action. The main beneficiaries of the economic values created are shareholders, complemented by management and customers. Economics Nobel Prize winner Milton Friedman (1970) has created the appropriate description for the current economic paradigm by stating bluntly that 'the business of business is business'.

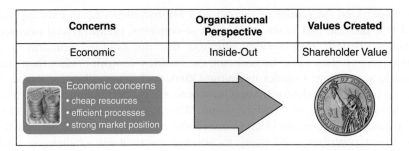

Concerns	Organizational Perspective	Values Created
Economic	Inside-Out	Shareholder Value

FIGURE 14.1 Business-as-usual: The Current Economic Paradigm.

14.3.2 Business Sustainability 1.0: Refined Shareholder Value Management

A first step in introducing sustainability to the current economic paradigm results from recognizing that there are new business challenges from outside the traditional market exchanges. Extra-market challenges result from environmental or social concerns which are typically voiced by external stakeholders like NGOs, media, legislation or government. They raise environmental and social concerns which create economic risks and opportunities for business. These new challenges are picked up and integrated in existing processes and practices without changing the basic business premise and outlook. Even if sustainability concerns are considered in decision-making and actions, business objectives remain clearly focused on creating shareholder value. The view of BST 1.0 is very well captured by SAM and PWC (2006) in their definition of corporate sustainability:

> *Corporate sustainability is an approach to business that creates shareholder value by embracing opportunities and managing risks deriving from economic, environmental and social developments.*

This widely shared view on business sustainability is often considered as representing sustainability management, although it is only a kind of refined version of shareholder value management (Hahn & Figge, 2011). In our view, it is only a first yet insufficient step towards true business sustainability.

What does BST 1.0 look like in practice? We will use two different industries to illustrate the different forms of BST in practice, banking and food, and we will look at three different aspects separately: governance, processes, and products/services. (See Box 14.1 and Box 14.2.)

The underlying objective of these activities remains economic. While introducing sustainability to business will generate positive side-effects for different sustainability issues, its main purpose is to reduce costs and business risks, to increase reputation and attractiveness for new or existing talents, and to respond to new customer demands and segments, thereby increasing profits, market positions, competitiveness and shareholder value. Business success is still evaluated from a purely economic view and remains focused on serving the business itself and its economic purposes. The values served may be somewhat refined, but still oriented towards shareholder value (see Figure 14.2).

BOX 14.1

Business Sustainability 1.0: The Case of Banking

Taking banking and looking at governance issues first, BST 1.0 means introducing new rules for compliance in areas like corruption or money laundering, in dealing with politically exposed persons or regimes, ethical codes, compensation schemes for management in the long term or pursuing stakeholder dialogues. New or integrated banking processes may be introduced for energy and climate management, sustainable purchasing, green IT, building and infrastructure, diversity, old age employment or home office solutions. In the area of banking products and services, sustainability concerns may be integrated in project finance, asset and credit management, in increasing fee transparency or introducing new products in areas like microfinance or student loans.

BOX 14.2

Business Sustainability 1.0: The Case of Food

Or, taking the food industry as another example, BST 1.0 means introducing sustainability into its governance structures by responding systematically to stakeholder concerns, by developing policies and codes covering major issues in sustainable sourcing, product development and safety, marketing and communication, but also by creating organizational, management and board structures for effective management, control and auditing. Processes and transparent procedures for energy and water efficiency, for greenhouse gas reduction, sourcing, manufacturing and transport need to be implemented. In particular, not only has sustainable and fair sourcing recently been a major concern, if one thinks of palm oil, soy, cocoa, coffee, tea, meat or fish, but also procedures for verification and certification. BST 1.0 means products reduce the environmental footprint, improve their social value and their nutritional quality (e.g., reduce sugar, salt, saturated fats, calories), reduce waste and packaging, and provide transparent and verified information to consumers.

Concerns	Organizational Perspective	Values Created
Three-dimensional Concerns	Inside-Out	Refined Shareholder Value
Social concerns / Environmental concerns / Economic concerns	→	

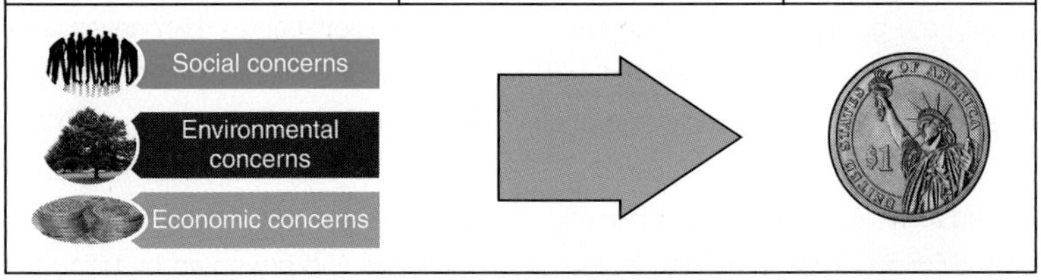

FIGURE 14.2 Business Sustainability 1.0: Refined Shareholder Value Management.

14.3.3 Business Sustainability 2.0: Managing for the Triple Bottom Line

A further step in introducing sustainability to business acknowledges that sustainability is more than just recognizing the relevance of and need to respond to social and environmental concerns, in addition to economic concerns. BST 2.0 means broadening the stakeholder perspective and pursuing a triple bottom line approach. Value creation goes beyond shareholder value and includes social and environmental values. Companies create value not just as a side-effect of their business activities, but as the result of deliberately defined goals and programmes targeted at specific sustainability issues or stakeholders. These values are not only addressed through particular programmes, but also measured and reported. This view of BST 2.0 is well expressed in the definition of business sustainability used by the Network for Business Sustainability (2012):

> *Business sustainability is often defined as managing the triple bottom line – a process by which firms manage their financial, social and environmental risks, obligations and opportunities. These three impacts are sometimes referred to as people, planet and profits.*

BST 2.0 is clearly more ambitious than BST 1.0 and represents a big step forward in making sustainability a respected and integrated business issue. It allows business to align the concerns it addresses with the values it seeks to create, by relating economic, environmental and social concerns to the triple bottom line values of sustainability. While this shift from refined shareholder value to the creation of social, economic and environmental values is a quantum leap, it is not yet what we understand as 'true sustainability' (see Box 14.3 and Box 14.4).

BOX 14.3

Business Sustainability 2.0: The Case of Banking

Applied to banking, BST 2.0 means contributing sustainability values through programmes and actions taken in the areas of governance, processes, and products/services. Instead of positive side-effects resulting from actions addressing specific concerns in these fields, results are the outcomes of purposeful action. Fighting corruption, money laundering and tax evasion are included; but also, stakeholder dialogues are deliberately pursued with the goal of making measurable contributions in these areas. Objectives are defined and their achievements are managed, measured and reported.

Programmes and activities with regard to banking processes are pursued with the goal of making measurable contributions, e.g., to reduce the CO_2 footprint or to improve diversity across all levels of employees, as well as voluntarily limiting top management compensation and the variable part of the compensation of hedge fund managers. The activities are typically embedded in the organizational and management structures. Banking products and services are created and offered around specific objectives in areas such as financing sustainable construction and living, healthy living, regional and urban development, or financing business projects for markets and entrepreneurs where new forms of collaborations and financing (e.g., microfinance) are needed. Further, responsible investment products are not only developed, but also actively marketed and promoted by trained customer service representatives to achieve defined market objectives.

BOX 14.4
Business Sustainability 2.0: The Case of Food

Taking the food industry, BST 2.0 means introducing sustainability in its governance structures. This requires that sustainability objectives are integrated in the planning and reporting cycles to define specific objectives for projects and brands, and ensuring that goals are achieved through adequate forms of incentives and accountability. Also, reporting achievements in a transparent and externally verified way is an important element. Processes and transparent procedures for reducing greenhouse gases, energy and water use, and waste from manufacturing, transport and offices need to be not only implemented but also measured and reported. Objectives and achievements with regard to sustainable sourcing need to be measured and communicated. In other words, BST 2.0 means not merely that the environmental and social footprint is minimized but that a positive footprint is achieved and measured over the whole product life cycle and per consumer use, to improve social value, nutritional quality of food, to limit waste and packaging, in a clearly defined and controlled way. Objectives and achievements need to be reported.

The underlying objective for BST 2.0 firms is to invent, produce and report measurable results in well-defined sustainable development areas, while doing this in an economically sound and profitable way. The value proposition of business is broadened to include all three dimensions of the triple bottom line (people, planet, profit) (see *page 396*, Figure 14.3). The perspective applied is still inside-out, however.

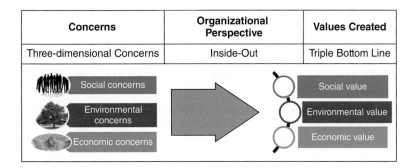

Concerns	Organizational Perspective	Values Created
Three-dimensional Concerns	Inside-Out	Triple Bottom Line

FIGURE 14.3   Business Sustainability 2.0: Managing for the Triple Bottom Line.

14.3.4 Business Sustainability 3.0: Truly Sustainable Business

A truly sustainable business reflects on questions that go beyond those so far considered. It reflects on questions such as, 'How can business contribute with its products and services to resolving pressing sustainability issues in their societies?' Or,

'How can business use its resources, competencies and experiences in such a way as to make them useful for contributing to solve some of the big economic, social or environmental challenges societies are confronted with, e.g. climate change, migration, corruption, water shortage, poverty, pandemics, youth unemployment, sovereign debt overload, or financial instability?'

Our view of Business Sustainability 3.0 may be defined as follows:

Truly sustainable business shifts its perspective from seeking to minimize its negative impacts to understanding how it can create a significant positive impact in critical and relevant areas for society and the planet. A Business Sustainability 3.0 firm looks first at the external environment within which it operates and it then asks itself what it can do to help resolve critical challenges that demand the resources and competencies it has at its disposal.

As a result, a BST 3.0 firm translates sustainability challenges into business opportunities making 'business sense' of societal and environmental issues. This follows the line of thinking suggested by Peter Drucker, who commented on the business challenge of sustainability: 'Every single social and global issue of our day is a business opportunity in disguise' (cited in Cooperrider, 2008).

Having figured out how to improve their operational effectiveness by introducing energy savings and social benefits to their supply chains or improving their products and services, truly sustainable organizations ask themselves more challenging questions such as:

1   Which of the burning environmental, societal or economic issues could be resolved by dedicating our wealth of resources, competencies, talents and experiences to them?
2   What are the benefits and contributions of our products and services to society and the environment?
3   How can we transform our operations to provide solutions (products or services) in a direct and measurable way to the paramount issues in nature and society?
4   How can we open up and develop our governance structures to respond more effectively to society's concerns?
5   What can we do individually? Where do we need to engage in sector-wide or cross-sectoral strategies?
6   And where do we need to engage in activities to change the rules of the game to bring together the divergent demands of the current economic system and of sustainable development?

A business typically starts out by reviewing pressing sustainability challenges society is facing and subsequently engages in developing new strategies and business models that resolve these challenges (although this sequence may also sometimes be reversed). The potential for contributing positively will vary largely between companies, their resources, strategies and purposes. And it will vary between different industry sectors and societal contexts. Making a positive contribution to solving sustainability issues and thus serving the common good becomes the main purpose of a truly sustainable business. In this perspective, the values created change from the triple bottom line to creating value for the common good, defined as that which benefits society and the planet as a whole, in contrast to the private good of individuals and sections of society. When this is done by commercial businesses, ways have to be found to do this in an economical way. When it is done by social or hybrid businesses, financial constraints are less stringent and the economic equation may look different.

Truly sustainable firms engage on different levels of action to increase their sustainability impact and to ease conflicts between financial demands and societal needs. As long as they act on an individual company level they can innovate their processes and products or improve their systems of governance and their transparency. The impact and reach of their activities, however, will remain limited. Engaging on a *sectoral or cross-sectorial level*, businesses can change the common approaches and practices shared by all members in an industry or along supply chains. They can do this by creating transparency, sharing best practices or defining common rules and setting standards. These collaborative partnerships will increase the impact and outreach of their sustainability strategies.

In order to create new space for economic and sustainable solutions and to scale-up the impacts, truly sustainable businesses will also have to engage in *changing the rules of the game*. After all, big sustainability issues like climate change, availability of water and loss of biodiversity cannot be solved by business alone. Also, businesses are often punished by financial and consumer markets when they engage in serious sustainability strategies, as many companies in the solar power industry are currently experiencing; or soft drink companies evaluating alternatives to address the profound and very real issue of obesity. Such companies will not be able to address the real sustainability issues they are confronted with as long as the rules of the game are not changed. Engagement for changing the collective rules of the game may take many forms and range from changing accounting rules and standards for disclosing and internalizing sustainability risks and impacts; informing and educating customers about unsustainable choices and practices; to lobbying for taxes on resource consumption, emissions or stricter standards for public health. See Box 14.5 and Box 14.6.

BST 3.0 firms see themselves as responsive citizens of society. Truly sustainable business shifts its perspective from seeking to minimize its negative impacts to understanding how it can create a significant positive impact in critical and relevant areas for society and the planet. BST 3.0 represents a very different strategic approach to business. It turns around the traditional 'inside-out' approach used by business and applies an 'outside-in' approach instead, much like social businesses do (see Figure 14.4).

The key characteristics of our BST typology are summarized in Figure 14.5.

As companies move to higher and more effective levels of BST, three important changes take place:

1   The relevant concerns considered by business shift from economic concerns to three-dimensional concerns (social, environmental and economic) related to the sustainability challenges we are collectively facing.

BOX 14.5

Business Sustainability 3.0: The Case of Banking

Banks need to address the enormous challenge of financing sustainable infrastructures for a world populated of 9 billion people in ever larger mega-cities. They will have to shift funding from unsustainable investments to strategic projects of regional relevance (securing of water, food, etc.). According to the outside-in logic, banks start out by evaluating relevant sustainability challenges in their societal contexts. They evaluate and decide what issues they can and want to contribute to. The choice will be among such issues as wealth and income inequalities, youth unemployment, climate change, energy efficiency and renewable energies, sustainable construction and living, new models of sustainable tourism, old age provisions, assisted living, financing public health or education, integration of foreigners and migrant workers. Products and services include packages of information and consultation, new forms of collaboration, public–private partnerships, new forms of financing and collaterals like microfinance or crowdfunding (e.g., www.kickstarter .com). Also, banks will have to address the grave issues of systemic risks created by their collective behaviour for societal groups (e.g., homeowners, students) and whole countries (e.g., Greece, Spain, Ireland, Iceland, Switzerland, US). The effectiveness of their strategies is measured by the contributions made and the values thereby created, for the different stakeholders and for the business itself.

BOX 14.6

Business Sustainability 3.0: The Case of Food

Food companies will need to evaluate sustainability challenges and define the relevant issues for them, depending on their exposure to issues and competencies to solve them. The choice will be among issues like alleviating poverty, access to clean and affordable water, providing healthy and affordable nutrition or supporting smallholder farmers and distributors in developing countries.

In developed countries the issues are more oriented towards fighting overconsumption and obesity, providing healthy products for different ages, contributing to public health and healthy life-styles, sustainable agriculture, production and consumption, or fighting food waste. Products and services include healthy and balanced products, new forms of health related information and education for consumers (provided collaboratively with scientific and public organizations), but also restraint from misleading and aggressive marketing.

In developing countries the issues will be different, related to fighting hunger, securing human rights, supporting smallholder farmers and distributors, securing the availability of water, energy and public health. In order to deliver organic or fair trade products to the markets (e.g., textiles, coffee, tea, cacao, bananas, chicken) whole supply chains will have to be reconstructed and controlled, reaching from third world farmers to traders, processors and end-user markets. Rule-changing strategies can be seen in the creation of new institutions securing sustainable supplies like the Marine Stewardship Council for fish and fisheries, and the roundtables on sustainable soy or palm oil. They set new standards for sustainable practices and create transparency through certification. This changes the rules of the game for all or most competitors.

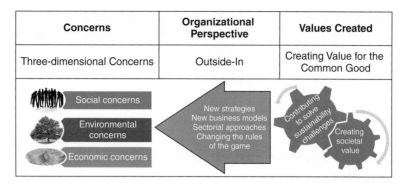

Concerns	Organizational Perspective	Values Created
Three-dimensional Concerns	Outside-In	Creating Value for the Common Good

FIGURE 14.4 Business Sustainability 3.0: Truly Sustainable Business.

BUSINESS SUSTAINABILITY TYPOLOGY (BST)	Concerns (What?)	Values Created (What for?)	Organizational Perspective (How?)
Business-as-Usual	Economic concerns	Shareholder value	Inside-out
Business Sustainability 1.0	Three-dimensional concerns	Refined shareholder value	Inside-out
Business Sustainability 2.0	Three-dimensional concerns	Triple bottom line	Inside-out
Business Sustainability 3.0	Three-dimensional concerns	Creating value for the common good	Outside-in
The key shifts involved:	1st shift: broadening the business concerns	2nd shift: expanding the values created	3rd shift: changing the perspective

FIGURE 14.5 The Business Sustainability Typology with Key Characteristics and Shifts.

2 The values created by business shifts from shareholder value to a broadened value proposition that includes all three dimensions of the triple bottom line (people, planet, profit).

3 The shift in fundamental organizational perspectives, from an inside-out perspective with a focus on the business itself to an outside-in perspective with a focus on society and the sustainability challenges it is facing. This moves the value creation perspective from the triple bottom line to creating value for the common good.

Each of these changes has different consequences. A shift in concerns broadens the business agenda to include non-business considerations in planning and actions. A shift in values created broadens the output and purpose of business activity to include non-business goals. But only a shift in organizational perspective, from inside-out to outside-in, will allow a company to develop the strategies and the business models needed to make relevant contributions to overcome societal and planetary challenges, thereby contributing to the common good. This last shift is what we consider to be the sign of true business sustainability.

14.4 Managing Business Sustainability: Organizational Characteristics

In starting out from this typology, further questions will be raised on how to organize for and manage BST 3.0. Many of the organizational changes to develop higher forms of BST run deep and span many different areas. We can only mention very briefly below how we see that these changes will play out as organizations move from BST 1.0 to BST 2.0 and on to BST 3.0 (see Table 14.4).

1 **Engagement.** From reacting to social pressures to actively engaging with stakeholders to ultimately embracing a voluntary and proactive engagement with a variety of players in search of new solutions to burning societal challenges.

2 **Primary focus.** From shareholders to stakeholders and to a focus on society and the planet.

3 **Market definition and positioning.** From reacting to outside pressures in existing markets to exploring new market opportunities and emerging segments inside or outside existing markets to ultimately transforming existing markets or defining new markets, allowing for significant repositioning. (Dyllick, 2003; Nidumolu *et al.*, 2009; Adams *et al.*, 2012 and 2015).

4 **Products and services.** From selective improvements of existing products and services in response to pressures and changing demands to systematic improvements including all relevant dimensions and the whole life cycle ('better product') to, ultimately, a 'good product' with a net positive effect on sustainability challenges (ILFI, 2015; McDonough & Braungart, 2013; Heck *et al.*, 2014; Crul *et al.*, 2009).

5 **Governance and leadership.** From primarily defensive policies, codes and guidelines to protect against diverse risks to an integration of triple bottom line objectives into policies, structures, management compensation and board management to ultimately integrating relevant societal stakeholders into decision-making processes at all levels of the organization (Eccles *et al.*, 2014).

6 **Type of CEO.** From an 'opportunity seeker' with an instrumental view on sustainability and the business case to an 'integrator', feeling responsible to all legitimate stakeholders affected by the organization to, ultimately, an 'idealist' viewing business as being in the service of society and motivated primarily to create societal value (Pless *et al.*, 2012).

TABLE 14.4 Organizational Characteristics of BST 1.0, 2.0 and 3.0

Criteria	BST 1.0	BST 2.0	BST 3.0
Engagement	Reacting to social pressures	Actively engaging with stakeholders	A voluntary and proactive engagement with a variety of players
Primary focus	Shareholders	Stakeholders	Society and the planet
Market definition and positioning	Reacting to outside pressures in existing markets	Exploring new market opportunities and emerging segments inside or outside existing markets	Transforming existing markets or defining new markets allowing for significant repositioning
Products and services	Selective improvements of existing products and services ('better product')	Systematic improvements including all relevant dimensions and the whole life cycle ('better product')	A 'good product' with a net positive effect on sustainability challenges
Governance and leadership	Primarily defensive policies, codes and guidelines to protect against risks	Integration of triple bottom line objectives in policies, structures, management compensation and board management	Integration of relevant societal stakeholders into decision-making processes at all levels of the organization
Type of CEO	Opportunity seeker	Integrator	Idealist
Organization	Centrally managed by specialized functions	Integrated in the various regular functions and divisions	Reorganizing around the societal challenges and including outside players in open and dynamic structures
Sustainability reporting	Selective reporting as a response to outside demands	Full reporting on all material aspects of the triple bottom line	Reflecting and reporting on the societal value created by the organization

7 **Organization.** From initially being centrally managed by specialized functions to increasingly becoming integrated in the various regular functions and divisions to, ultimately, reorganizing around the societal challenges they address, thereby including outside players into open and dynamic structures.

8 **Sustainability reporting.** From selective reporting as a response to outside demands to full reporting on all material aspects of the triple bottom line, as demanded by the GRI, to ultimately reflecting and reporting on the societal value created by the organization (Eccles *et al.*, 2014).

14.5   Conclusion

This chapter demonstrates that 'business sustainability' can actually be categorized into three different types. We thereby provide an answer to the question of what it means for an organization to be 'truly sustainable', namely to contribute to solving the sustainability challenges we are collectively facing and thus to create value for the common good. A core element of this answer lies in shifting the perspective from seeking to minimize negative impacts of business actions to creating a positive impact in critical and relevant areas for society and the planet. This implies a change from an 'inside-out' to an 'outside-in' approach. While we are suggesting and portraying a progression in this typology towards truly sustainable business, we do not seek to minimize or neglect achievements and contributions made by organizations that are currently operating in the BST 1.0 or 2.0 modes. It may well be a major challenge for large, existing businesses and industries to embrace the fundamental shift required to move on to BST 3.0.

Business sustainability 3.0 raises crucial questions in two different areas: 'How do we ensure that the business contributions to solving sustainability challenges and thereby creating value for the common good will indeed be done effectively and efficiently?' And: 'Is it realistic to expect commercially oriented businesses to refocus on sustainability challenges and value creation for the common good or will this be primarily the domain of social businesses?'

Dogmatic positions expressed by liberal economists like Friedman or von Hayek, which are reflected in the normative position of the shareholder value approach, question the legitimacy as well as the competency of business to address and solve social issues. The reality looks very different: businesses today are expected by stakeholders and society to address social issues and they do in fact include them in their decisions. They do this to varying degrees and with highly variable impacts which are rarely evaluated according to clear metrics and remain mostly vague and hard to assess. Furthermore, it is important to note that businesses have the right to exercise appropriate judgement in considering social issues, as exemplified by the 'business judgement rule'. This rule asserts the right of corporate directors to address societal concerns as they relate to their business, as long as their decisions are made in good faith, with the necessary care, and with the reasonable belief that they are acting in the best interests of the corporation. One could claim that corporations do indeed have all the necessary insight and knowledge about sustainability issues, maybe even more so than many other societal actors. More importantly, corporations have the resources to effectively address such issues.

The question, however, remains: 'How do we ensure that business contributions addressing sustainability challenges will indeed be effective and efficient?' Good business judgement is likely to limit business engagements in areas of little expertise. Yet to ensure effectiveness and efficiency we will need to create and develop the conditions in two interdependent areas: transparency and metrics. Transparency is required with regard to decisions and actions taken by companies in order to evaluate, compare, and improve business contributions to sustainability – but also transparency related to the effects and impacts of the actions taken. Beyond communication and reporting on such contributions, external assurance will be of the essence to satisfy the need for transparency. Effective reporting will have to focus more on depth and materiality, possibly at the expense of the breadth of issues. Furthermore, an effective assessment of the business contributions to sustainability issues requires adequate metrics and measures to assess and compare their impact. We will need to come up with issue-specific metrics that reliably indicate improvements. In this area, the Sustainability Accounting Standards Board (SASB), which is developing industry-specific metrics on the materiality of sustainability issues, offers a promising starting point (www.sasb.org; Eccles & Serafeim, 2013).

Becoming a truly sustainable business clearly *is* a challenge for companies, particularly for commercial businesses. Is it indeed realistic to expect commercially oriented corporations to focus their strategies on solving sustainability challenges and creating value for the common good? There are different issues to be considered in answering this question. First, solving sustainability problems the world is facing can be considered a strategic challenge like many other business challenges. For example, there is no reason to believe that developing renewable energy technologies is more challenging and less rewarding than exploring oilfields in the deep sea or in Arctic regions. Another example is nuclear energy, where handling it safely and economically over the whole life cycle has been shown to be a lot more challenging and costly than expected. And industry still needs to acknowledge and address the substantial new risks involved in large-scale experiments related to the exploitation of gas and tar sands. Business has always explored new opportunities in new fields and has come up with innovative and economic solutions. We need to ask the question, however, of why companies seem to have far fewer problems accepting high risks in certain highly unsustainable business areas than in some other more sustainable fields.

Second, Peter Drucker has rightly pointed out that social and global issues are 'business opportunities in disguise'. Embracing these new opportunities may well require changes in the current rules of the game. Neither is this new, however, nor so different from what we have known for a long time, although industry pressures to keep up unsustainable rules still seem to dominate. For example, global subsidies for fossil fuels are still outnumbering by a factor of six those for renewable energies (International Energy Agency, 2011, p. 507), and all attempts to change this situation have been failing. This tilted situation strongly favours entrenched and unsustainable technologies while effectively preventing new and more sustainable energy solutions from taking their place at a much faster rate.

There is without any doubt significant room for commercially oriented businesses to become truly sustainable, although such an approach requires a fundamentally different strategic approach. It invites companies to start thinking and acting from the outside-in and to remain focused on contributing to solving sustainability challenges, even if there are more economically attractive, but unsustainable, alternatives available. As long as such outside-in strategies provide not only a positive contribution to sustainability challenges, but also offer a satisfactory economic value for the shareholders, these approaches are feasible for commercial businesses. Such strategies then fall into the domain of shared value creation.

There are, though, limits to commercial businesses following the true sustainability route, in particular when they have to live up to strong shareholder pressures from financial markets. Financial markets are very short-term oriented while true sustainability strategies – like many other strategies as well – need a longer-term perspective. In addition, true BST cannot be achieved by solving sustainability issues incidentally or opportunistically, as such initiatives are typically cancelled as soon as the prospects for economic gain diminish. Instead, true sustainability requires a solid foundation in pursuing social benefit as a worthy cause as such, as it is the case with social businesses. Maybe it also helps to remind ourselves of the fact that many big and successful corporations started out as social businesses with, e.g., Henri Nestlé providing baby food to help mothers who were unable to breastfeed and William Lever, a founding father of Unilever, helping to make cleanliness, hygiene and health commonplace in Victorian England.

We agree with Peter Bakker (2012), president of the World Business Council for Sustainable Development, that business has both the opportunity and the responsibility to play an essential role in responding to and solving the societal and planetary sustainability challenges. This will only be the case, however, when business starts to live up to its possibilities by using its immense resources in a truly sustainable way. This may lead to a world where one day business will indeed be celebrated for its contribution to society and no longer criticized for achieving economic success at society's cost.

Summary

This chapter has addressed the following points:

1. Linking business contributions to the global sustainability challenges enables us to assess their value for society and the planet. This allows us to distinguish between improvements of the triple bottom line and contributions to sustainability challenges.

2. We highlighted reasons why business sustainability has been framed and developed in a very narrow way by addressing educational shortcomings, a missing interdisciplinary perspective, a very limited perspective on skills, missing incentives for researchers, and ideological prejudices.

3. We provided a framework for the comparative analysis of existing and emerging models of business sustainability, differentiating between a) the concerns considered by business, b) the organizational perspectives taken, and c) the different values created by sustainable business.

4. We developed a typology for business sustainability, ranging from Business-as-usual to Business Sustainability 1.0 (Refined Shareholder Value Management), Business Sustainability 2.0 (Managing for the Triple Bottom Line) to Business Sustainability 3.0 (Truly Sustainable Business), allowing us to categorize different approaches based on their contribution to solve sustainability challenges.

5. We have learned that truly sustainable business shifts its perspective from seeking to minimize its negative impacts to understanding how it can create a significant positive impact in critical and relevant areas for society and the planet.

References

Adams, R., Jeanrenaud, S., Bessant, J., Overy, P., & Denyer, D. (2012). *Innovating for sustainability: A systematic review of the body of knowledge*. Network for Business Sustainability. Retrieved from http://nbs.net/wp-content/uploads/NBS-Systematic-Review-Innovation.pdf

Adams, R., Jeanrenaud, S., Bessant, J., Denyer, D., & Overy, P. (2015), Sustainability-oriented innovation: A systematic review. *International Journal of Management Reviews*. doi:10.1111/ijmr.12068

Bakker. P. (2012, December 12). *Speech by the President of the World Business Council for Sustainable Development at the annual A4S (Accounting for Sustainability) event*. London. Retrieved from http://www.accountingforsustainability.org/events/forum-event

Banerjee, S. B. (2011). Embedding Sustainability across the organization: A critical perspective. *Academy of Management Learning & Education, 10*(4), 719–731.

Bansal, P., & Gao, J. (2006). Building the future by looking to the past: Examining research published on organization and environment. *Organization & Environment, 19*(4), 458–478.

Belz, F. M., & Peattie, K. (2012). *Sustainability marketing* (2nd ed.). Chichester: Wiley.

Bové, A.-T., & Bonini, S. (2014). Sustainability's strategic worth. *McKinsey global survey results*. Retrieved from http://www.mckinsey.com/insights/sustainability/sustainabilitys_strategic_worth_mckinsey_global_survey_results

Cooperrider, D. (2008, July/August). Social innovation. *BizEd*, 32–38.

Crane, A., Palazzo, G., Spence, L., & Matten, D. (2014). Contesting the value of 'creating shared value'. *California Management Review, 56*(2), 130–153.

Crul, M., Diehl, J. C., & Ryan, C. (2009). *Design for sustainability – :A step-by-step Approach*. Paris: UNEP.

Dyllick, T. (2003). Nachhaltigkeitsorientierte wettbewerbsstrategien. In Linne, G., & Schwarz, M. (Eds.). *Handbuch Nachhaltige Entwicklung*. Opladen: Leske & Budrich, 267–271.

Dyllick, T., & Muff, K. (2016). Clarifying the meaning of sustainable business. *Organization & Environment*, Vol. 29, No. 2, 156–174.

Dyllick, T., & Hockerts, K. (2002). Beyond the business case for corporate sustainability. *Business Strategy and the Environment, 11*, 130–141.

Eccles, R. G., Ioannoui I., & Serafeim G. (2014). The impact of corporate sustainability on organizational processes and performance. *Management Science, 60*(11), 2835–2857.

Eccles, R. G., & Serafeim, G. (2013, May). The performance frontier: Innovating for a sustainable strategy. *Harvard Business Review*, 50–60.

Eccles, R. G., Miller Perkins, K., & Serafeim, G. (2012). How to become a sustainable company. *MIT Sloan Management Review, 53*(4), 43–50.

Elkington, J. (1997). *Cannibals with forks: The triple bottom-line of 21st century business*. Oxford: Capstone.

Emerson, J. (1983). The blended value proposition: Integrating social and financial returns. *California Management Review, 45*(4), 35–51.

Epstein, M. (2008). *Making sustainability work*. Sheffield: Greenleaf.

Esty, D., & Winston, A. (2009). *Green to Gold*. Hoboken, NJ: Wiley.

European Commission. (2011, October 15). *Social Business Initiative*. COM (2011) 682 final. Brussels.

Felber, C. (2010). *Die Gemeinwohl-Ökonomie*. Wien: Deuticke.

Financial Times. (2014). A debate on the value of creating shared value, with contributions from Andrew Crane, April 20; Mark Kramer, April 22; Thomas Donaldson, April 23; Thomas Dyllick, April 24 *et al. FT,* Soapbox. Retrieved from http://www.ft.com/intl/cms/s/2/88013970-b34d-11e3-b09d-00144feabdc0.html#axzz3Wi3IiO6m

Freeman, R. E. (1984). *Strategic management: A stakeholder approach*. Boston: Pitman.

Friedman, M. (1970). The responsibility of business is to increase its profits. In *The New York Times Magazine* (1970, September 13). Retrieved from http://www.colorado.edu/studentgroups/libertarians/issues/friedman-soc-resp-business.html

Gilding, P. (2011). *The great disruption*. London: Bloomsbury.

Haanaes, K., Reeves, M., von Strengvelken, I., Audretsch., M., Kron, D., & Kruschwitz, N. (2012, Winter). Sustainability nears a tipping point. *MIT Sloan Management Review Research Report in collaboration with BCG*.

Haanaes, K., Arthur, D., Balagopal, B., Teck Kong, M., Reeves, M., Velken, I., Hopkins, M., & Kruschwitz, N. (2011, Winter). Sustainability: The 'embracers' seize advantage. *MIT Sloan Management Review Research Report in collaboration with BCG*.

Hahn, T., & Figge, F. (2011). Beyond the bounded instrumentality in current corporate sustainability research: Toward an inclusive notion of profitability. *Journal of Business Ethics, 104*, 325–345.

Hart, S. L. (2007). *Capitalism at the crossroads* (2nd ed.). Upper Saddle River, NJ: Wharton School Publishing.

Heck, S., Rogers, M., & Carroll, P. (2014). *Resource revolution*. New York: Melcher Media.

ILFI. (2015): *Living Product challenge 1.0 guide: Handprinting. A visionary path to a regenerative future*. International Living Future Institute: Seattle. Retrieved from https://living-future.org/sites/default/files/LPCGuide-Handprinting_final_web.pdf

International Energy Agency. (2011). *World Energy Outlook 2011*. Paris: IEA.

Jackson, T. (2011). *Prosperity without growth. Economics for a finite planet*. London: Taylor & Francis.

Kallio, T., & Nordberg, P. (2006). The evolution of organizations and natural environment discourse: Some critical remarks. *Organization & Environment, 19*(4), 439–457.

Kron, D., Kruschwitz, N., Haanaes, K., Reeves, M., & Goh, E. (2013, Winter). The innovation bottom line. *MIT Sloan Management Review Research Report in collaboration with BCG.*

Laszlo, C., & Zhexembayeva, N. (2011). *Embedded sustainability: The next big competitive advantage.* Stanford: Stanford Business Books and Sheffield: Greenleaf.

Margolis, J., & Walsh, J. (2003). Misery loves companies: Rethinking social initiatives by business. *Administrative Science Quarterly, 48*(2), 268–305.

McDonough, W., & Braungart, M. (2013). *The upcycle.* New York: Melcher Media.

Meynhardt, T. (2009). Public value inside: What is public value creation? *International Journal of Public Administration, 32*(3-49), 192–219.

Millenium Development Goals. (2000). Retrieved from www .un.org/milleniumgoals

Millenium Ecosystem Assessment (MEA). (2005). *Ecosystems and human well-being: Opportunities and challenges for industry.* Washington DC: World Resources Institute.

Muff, K., Dyllick, T., Drewell, M., North, J., Shrivastava P., & Haertle, J. (2013). *Management education for the world: A vision for business schools serving people and planet.* Cheltenham, UK: Edward Elgar.

Network for Business Sustainability. (2012). *Definition of business sustainability.* Retrieved from http://nBST.net/ about/what-we-do/

Nidumolu, R., Prahalad, C., & Rangaswami, M. (2009). Why sustainability is now the key driver of innovation. *Harvard Business Review, 87*(9), 57–64.

Pless N., Maak, T., & Waldman, D. (2012). Different approaches toward doing the right thing: Mapping the responsibility orientations of leaders. *Academy of Management Perspectives, 26*(4), 51–65.

Polman, P. (2012, June). Captain Planet: Interview with Unilever CEO Paul Polman. *Harvard Business Review,* 112–118.

Porter, M., & Kramer, M. (2011, Januaru/February). Creating shared value: How to reinvent capitalism – and unleash a wave of innovation and growth. *Harvard Business Review,* 62–77.

Prahalad, C. K. (2004). *The fortune at the bottom of the pyramid: Eradicating poverty through profits.* Upper Saddle River, NJ: Wharton School Publishing.

Prahalad, C. K., & Hammond, A. (2002). Serving the world's poor, profitably. *Harvard Business Review, 80*(9), 48–55.

Rae, A. (2012). Assessing the accountability of the benefit corporation: Will this new gray sector organization enhance corporate social responsibility? *Journal of Business Ethics, 110*(1), 133–150.

Rappaport, A. (1998). *Creating shareholder value.* New York: Free Press (first ed. 1986).

Raworth, K. (2012). A safe and just space for humanity. Can we live within a doughnut? Oxfam Discussion Papers

(accessed 2012, February). Retrieved from https://www .oxfam.org/en/research/safe-and-just-space-humanity?utm_ source=oxf.am&utm_medium=oe8&utm_content=redirect

Rockström, J., Steffen, W., Noone, K., Persson, Å., Chapin III, F. S., Lambin, E., Lenton, T. M., Scheffer, M., Folke, C., Schellnhuber, H., Nykvist, B., De Wit, C. A., Hughes, T., van der Leeuw, S., Rodhe, H., Sörlin, S., Snyder, P. K., Costanza, R., Svedin, U., Falkenmark, M., Karlberg, L., Corell, R. W., Fabry, V. J., Hansen, J., Walker, B., Liverman, D., Richardson, K., Crutzen, P., & Foley, J. (2009, September 24). A safe operating space for humanity. *Nature, 461,* 472–475.

Sabeti, H., with the Fourth Sector Network Concept Working Group. (2009). *The emerging fourth sector: Executive summary.* Washington: Aspen Institute.

SAM & PWC (2006). The Sustainability Yearbook 2006. Zurich.

Schaltegger, S. (2006). How can environmental management contribute to shareholder value? The environmental shareholder value approach. In Schaltegger, S., & Wagner, M. (Eds.). *Managing the business case for sustainability.* Sheffield: Greenleaf, 47–61.

Smith, N. C., & Lensen, G. (Eds.). (2009). *Mainstreaming corporate responsibility.* Chichester: Wiley.

Starik, M. (2006). In search of relevance and impact. *Organization & Environment, 19*(4), 431–438.

Steger, U. (2006). Building a business case for corporate sustainability. In Schaltegger, S., & Wagner, M. (Eds.). *Managing the business case for sustainability.* Sheffield: Greenleaf, 412–443.

Steger, U. (Ed.). (2004). *The business of sustainability: Building industry cases for corporate sustainability.* Houndmills, UK: Palgrave Macmillan.

Sukhdev, P. (2012). *Corporation 2020: Transforming business for tomorrow's world.* Washington: Island Press.

UN. (1948). *The universal declaration of human rights.* Geneva: United Nations. Retrieved from http://www.un. org/en/universal-declaration-human-rights/index.html

UN. (2000). *Millennium development goals.* New York: United Nations. Retrieved from http://www.un.org/ millenniumgoals/

UN Secretary-General's High Level Panel on Global Sustainability. (2012). *Resilient people, resilient planet: A future worth choosing.* New York: United Nations.

UNEP (2011). *Towards a green economy. Pathways to sustainable development and poverty eradication. A synthesis for policy makers.* Retrieved from www.unep .org/greeneconomy

UNEP. (2012). *GEO 5. Global Environmental Outlook: Summary for policy makers.* Nairobi. Retrieved from www.unep.org/geo/Geo5

UN Global Compact & Accenture. (2013). *Architects of a better world. The UN Global Compact – Accenture CEO Study on Sustainability.* Retrieved from http://www .accenture.com/SiteCollectionDocuments/PDF/Accenture- UN-Global-Compact-Acn-CEO-Study-Sustainability-2013 .PDF

UN Global Compact & Accenture. (2010). A new era for sustainability. *The UN Global Compact – Accenture CEO Study on Sustainability*. Retrieved from http://www.accenture.com/sitecollectiondocuments/pdf/accenture_a_new_era_of_sustainability_ceo_study.pdf

Walsh, J., Weber, K., & Margolis, J. (2003). Social issues and management: Our lost cause found. *Journal of Management, 29*(6), 859–881.

Whiteman, G., Walker, B., & Perego, P. M. (2013). Planetary boundaries: Ecological foundations for corporate sustainability. *Journal of Management Studies. 50*(2), 307–336.

World Business Council for Sustainable Development. (2010). *Vision 2050: The new agenda for business.* Geneva: WBCSD.

World Economic Forum (WEF) & Accenture (2012). *More with less: Scaling sustainable consumption and resource efficiency.* Geneva.

World Wildlife Fund for Nature. (2014). *Living planet report: Species and spaces, people and places.* Retrieved from http://assets.panda.org

15 Conclusion: A One Planet Approach

Sally Jeanrenaud, Jean-Paul Jeanrenaud
and Jonathan Gosling

The conclusion offers four main take-home messages, summarizing key arguments from across this volume.

1   **The Challenges: The One Planet Predicament** involves global, interlinked environmental, social, and economic challenges that pose systemic risks to business and society, but may also be the catalysts for many new business opportunities.

2   **Sustainable Business: A One Planet Approach** is pro-people, pro-planet, and pro-prosperity, and is aligned with the United Nations 2030 Sustainable Development Agenda.

3   **Change for Good** includes 'systems' as well as 'personal' transformation, renewing business, economy, and self, and can be summarized through 20 snapshots of change.

4   **Transforming Business Management Education** goes beyond adding bolt-on modules to existing business degrees, to rethinking entire curricula and ways of learning.

15.0 The Challenges: The One Planet Predicament

For the first time in human history the interlinked ecological, social, economic and political crises, and our awareness of them, is global. No matter where we look we see the effects of climate-change and extreme weather events; biodiversity loss and dwindling resources; population pressure and growing conflict; wealth concentrated in fewer and fewer hands; more and more people forced to flee persecution and oppression; wars and natural disasters.

Stuart Wallis (2011) succinctly sums up the challenges to the economy as the '4Us': Unsustainable, Unfair, Unstable and Unhappy, to which we might add a further U – Undemocratic. Otto Scharmer and Katrin Kaufer (2013) talk of three great divides: the ecological divide between people and nature; the social divide between self and other; and the spiritual divide between self and self. The challenges are summarized in Table 15.1.

TABLE 15.1 Summary of the Challenges

PEOPLE: 1% of the population and unfair. Currently 1% of the global population owns almost half the world's wealth. Wealth benefits the few and is not trickling down, and economic growth is fuelling social inequality. Growing inequalities have created a 'social disconnect' between the haves and have-nots, which is considered unethical, socially divisive, and politically corrosive; ecologically as well as economically damaging in the long term. Social dynamics challenge the orthodox economic idea that wealth trickles down and that rising GDP increases happiness and well-being. New models such as the Sharing Economy help stimulate new markets and reconnect people to others, and the economy.

PLANET: 1.5 planets and unsustainable. We are currently using 1.5 planets' worth of resources to fuel economic growth, and our current consumption patterns. Our fossil-fuel based, linear, take-make-waste economy is creating climate disruption, water shortages, loss of biodiversity, declining resources, and huge amounts of waste. The 'ecological disconnect' between people and nature is destroying our life support systems, causing human suffering, and undermining the basis of business and the economy itself. The risks to global ecological systems extend beyond national borders, and challenge the traditional economic argument that we can grow now, and clean up later. New models such as the Circular Economy can provide promising alternatives to the prevailing linear one, and help reconnect ecology and economy.

PROFIT: $5.3 trillion in subsidies and unstable. Some US$5.3 trillion dollars per annum subsidize the old fossil-fuel-based brown economy, and create barriers to building a new green one based on renewables. We have created a financial sector that favours speculation and 'phantom wealth' over investment in real wealth. This 'economic disconnect' is driving boom and bust cycles, creating debt, holding governments hostage to financiers, and undermining efforts to invest in a sustainable economy. New economic theories challenge the prevailing view that our current model can create real wealth over the long term or that growth creates jobs. New models such as the Green Economy, which values and invests in natural capital over the long term, can help reconnect ecology and economy.

POWER: $2.6 Billion in lobbying and undemocratic. Corporations in the US spend $2.6 billion per annum on lobbying the government, and this pattern of lobbying is widespread around the world. The links between big business, governments, international trade and financial institutions, influence decisions relating to taxes, subsidies, trade deals and legislation. These support private gain at the expense of the planet and people, and threaten democratic processes. Political dynamics challenge the orthodox idea that competitive capitalism is a vehicle of democracy. We need new models to help shift this growing imbalance of power, while retaining the positive elements of globalization, and helping to relocalize economies. This will lead to a much needed reconnection between people and place.

PERSON: 1 million suicides and unhappy. Rates of stress and depression are increasing, and are recognized as the number one health concern across the world. Some 1 million people die by suicide each year, and it is the leading cause of death among young people. Once a certain level of income is obtained, and basic needs have been met, there is no correlation between increased GDP and increased well-being. Materialistic values and consumerism generate chronic dissatisfaction, do not help us fulfil our human potential, and create a 'spiritual disconnect' from who we really are. The traditional economic notion of human beings as *homo economicus*, as rational, self-interested, profit-maximizing agents, has been challenged. Growing interest in non-consumptive lifestyles of health, happiness, sustainability, and world wisdom traditions, can help reconnect self with the deeper dimensions of being.

The scale and urgency of the challenges and risks we are facing is staggering in both magnitude and complexity, and many argue that we are on the brink of entire systems breakdown. In terms of society, the first signs of an impending global revolution are increasingly visible: the Arab Spring, the rise of so-called 'Islamic State' (IS), the Occupy Movement, the polarization of politics, the shifting dynamics between East and West, the growing risk of a third World War.

These trends have profound implications for the future of business and society, and are provoking a conscious and widespread desire for more wholesome ways of living and making a living across the globe. How can we make the changes? And will they be fast enough? What is clear is that if we are to prosper going forward, then there is a need for a radical change of mindsets and values to ones that embrace new ways of thinking about business, the economy, and self. There are signs that these are beginning to emerge.

15.1 Sustainable Business: A One Planet Approach

The title of this textbook begs the question: what is a One Planet approach? The various chapters highlight the importance of some key principles of a One Planet business approach which we identify as pro-people, pro-planet and pro-prosperity. This book is thus very much aligned with the new United Nation's 2030 Sustainable Development Agenda (see Box 15.1), agreed by 193 nations in 2015, and expressed as People, Planet, Prosperity, Peace, and Partnership. We suggest how a One Planet business

BOX 15.1

The United Nations 2030 Sustainable Development Goals

The UN Sustainable Development Agenda is expressed in greater granularity in 17 specific sustainable development goals.

Goal 1. End poverty in all its forms everywhere.

Goal 2. End hunger, achieve food security and improved nutrition and promote sustainable agriculture.

Goal 3. Ensure healthy lives and promote well-being for all at all ages.

Goal 4. Ensure inclusive and equitable quality education and promote lifelong learning opportunities for all.

Goal 5. Achieve gender equality and empower all women and girls.

Goal 6. Ensure availability and sustainable management of water and sanitation for all.

Goal 7. Ensure access to affordable, reliable, sustainable and modern energy for all.

Goal 8. Promote sustained, inclusive and sustainable economic growth, full and productive employment and decent work for all.

Goal 9. Build resilient infrastructure, promote inclusive and sustainable industrialization and foster innovation.

Goal 10. Reduce inequality within and among countries.

Goal 11. Make cities and human settlements inclusive, safe, resilient and sustainable.

Goal 12. Ensure sustainable consumption and production patterns.

Goal 13. Take urgent action to combat climate change and its impacts.

Goal 14. Conserve and sustainably use the oceans, seas and marine resources for sustainable development.

Goal 15. Protect, restore and promote sustainable use of terrestrial ecosystems, sustainably manage forests, combat desertification, and halt and reverse land degradation and halt biodiversity loss.

Goal 16. Promote peaceful and inclusive societies for sustainable development, provide access to justice for all and build effective, accountable and inclusive institutions at all levels.

Goal 17. Strengthen the means of implementation and revitalize the global partnership for sustainable development.

approach speaks to this agenda, and supports the need for a shift from a focus on profit, narrowly defined in financial terms, to the broader concept of prosperity. We hope that this volume will make a useful contribution to delivering this agenda.

15.1.1 People

'We are determined to end poverty and hunger, in all their forms and dimensions, and to ensure that all human beings can fulfil their potential in dignity and equality and in a healthy environment.'

UN 2030 Sustainable Development Agenda

This book demonstrates that a new generation of business is rethinking its relationships with society. This is embodied in new ways of thinking about business responsibility and purpose; and new ways of leading; strategizing; organizing; operating; marketing; and creating shared value. There is a shift away from an exclusive focus on shareholders to stakeholders, and from competition to collaboration. These approaches call for new values, skills and capabilities. Entrepreneurship, social enterprises, and models of the sharing economy and collaborative consumption are addressing problems of poverty and inequality. These are helping build relationships between citizens, allowing more people access to the economy than before, and growing new businesses attuned to local needs. In short, *Sustainable Business: A One Planet Approach* is thus **pro-people**.

15.1.2 Planet

'We are determined to protect the planet from degradation, including through sustainable consumption and production, sustainably managing its natural resources and taking urgent action on climate change, so that it can support the needs of the present and future generations.'

UN 2030 Sustainable Development Agenda

The way business is thinking about its relationship to nature has also emerged as another key theme in this volume. There is greater awareness of ecological risks to business and society. There is growing scientific understanding of planetary boundaries; of ecological footprint; of limits to growth; of the value of nature's goods and services to the economy; and the impact of negative externalities. There is also a growing understanding of how we can learn from nature for design inspiration; the role of science-based targets; and of materiality and ecologically based metrics. New business approaches are shifting from linear, cradle-to-grave approaches, which waste energy and resources, to circular, cradle-to-cradle regenerative models that provide services as well as products. *Sustainable Business: A One Planet Approach* is thus **pro-planet**.

15.1.3 Prosperity

'We are determined to ensure that all human beings can enjoy prosperous and fulfilling lives and that economic, social and technological progress occurs in harmony with nature.'

UN 2030 Sustainable Development Agenda

This book recognizes the changing role of business in society, new understandings of 'capital', ideas of well-being, and the role of investing for long-term prosperity. Its chapters have strongly emphasized the idea that business is part of society rather than apart from it. Increasingly business is defining a higher purpose; realizing that purpose and profit are not incompatible; becoming solutions providers; and making a positive net contribution to people and planet (putting back more than they take out). Some are now striving to 'be the best *for* the world', rather than just 'be the best *in* the world'. They are aiming to be restorative, and to generate value and long-term prosperity, rather than just short-term profits. *Sustainable Business: A One Planet Approach* is **pro-prosperity**.

15.1.4 Peace

'We are determined to foster peaceful, just and inclusive societies which are free from fear and violence. There can be no sustainable development without peace and no peace without sustainable development.'

UN 2030 Sustainable Development Agenda

We recognize that global environmental and social challenges, such as climate change, water insecurity, and growing inequalities can trigger social conflicts and magnify existing ones. Frequently, businesses operate in areas where conflict is endemic, and they risk getting caught up in political struggles. They either have to abandon their operations or adapt to the circumstances, putting their staff and investments at risk. One Planet business seeks long-term engagement with, and restitution of, ecosystems as well as legitimate social and political systems. This is markedly different to businesses that see war as an opportunity for sales, cheap labour, and land-grabs. We argue that businesses do have a role to play in peace-building; facilitating constructive relationships between groups; helping dispel prejudicial stereotypes; and creating the conditions that are likely to attain and maintain peace. *Sustainable Business: A One Planet Approach* is **pro-peace**.

15.1.5 Partnership

'We are determined to mobilize the means required to implement this Agenda through a revitalised Global Partnership for Sustainable Development, based on a spirit of strengthened global solidarity, focussed in particular on the needs of the poorest and most vulnerable and with the participation of all countries, all stakeholders and all people.'

UN 2030 Sustainable Development Agenda

This volume recognizes that neither formal systems of state politics; nor the self-interested politics and power dynamics of corporations; nor the plurality of civil society groups each individually pursuing their own ends, are sufficient on their own to effect a transition to a sustainable economy. People need to work together to rebalance society, and effect change. A new generation of business leaders, also part of civil society, recognizes that it needs to consciously build and foster partnerships between all stakeholders. Change for good will be achieved through building and maintaining long-term alliances between business leaders, investors, consumers and policy-makers, who are working to effect systems transformation, that will deliver well-being for community, environment and economy. *Sustainable Business: A One Planet Approach* is **pro-partnerships**.

15.2 Change for Good

Identifying an agenda and set of five generic principles *(in section 15.1)*, can help clarify complexity. However, principles also need to be made more specific to assist leaders on the ground. Table 15.2 presents 20 snapshots of change for good, summarizing many of the themes introduced in the chapters. These summarize what is being disrupted and what is already emerging as new ways of thinking about business, economy and the self. These represent a paradigm shift in the way value is conceived, generated and shared within business and society. We conclude that change for good represents a shift in thinking and practice across all business domains, and involves a 'systems' as well as 'personal' transformation.

Transforming the economy for good implies reframing the role of business in society. This reframing recognizes that businesses can become solution providers in relation to material flows; energy; food; mobility; health; finance; etc. Such transformations imply large-scale systems innovation, rather than incremental innovation, which goes beyond the boundaries of the firm. Ultimately an individual business cannot be sustainable in an unsustainable system. Systems innovation involves 'doing good by doing new things with others', recognizing that issues are too big for any one actor to solve alone. Collaboration between governments, business, investors and citizens is needed to co-create change. This involves technological innovation as well as the development of appropriate enabling conditions – policies, economic incentives, and supportive tax regimes to support a transition to a more sustainable economy.

Transforming the self for good recognizes the importance of changing from the 'inside out' as integral to wider systems transformation. This change is what Scharmer and Kaufer (2013) call the personal inversion journey, or bending the beam of attention back onto ones' own habits of heart, mind and will, and opening up to the new possibilities of what wants to be born within. It involves giving serious consideration to ones' aspirations, intentions, and attention, and taking time to commune with the deeper dimensions of our being, of others and of the universe. It involves letting go of the old, the unlearning of old habits or ways of being and doing, and being prepared to move into new, unfamiliar territory. In this way we access new possibilities, unfold our highest potential, and discover what makes us truly happy. This recognizes that if we want to change the world we have to be able to change ourselves. Reflective, contemplative and mindful practices play an important role in this domain of change, helping us reconnect to our deeper selves, to each other and to nature.

In short, such transformations give rise to potentially new states of being or, put another way – a new 'beingset' – rather than a new 'mindset'. By a new beingset we mean a new state of being which is characterized by presence, wisdom, kindness, humour, simplicity and compassion. It represents a shift from the fear- or greed-based rushing, grasping, wanting and 'doing', to the deeper dignity and sagacity of 'being'. After all, we are human 'beings' not human 'doings', and yet it is so easy to become trapped on the relentless treadmill of activity, each action spinning its own web of cause and effect, action and reaction. This is not to say that 'doing' is bad; it is just that it has got out of balance with being. Our prevailing culture, particularly in the West, also glorifies doing and achieving, and many have forgotten, or never learned, how to access deeper sources of peace and wisdom within themselves. The world's wisdom traditions point to an interesting concept: the 'paradox of action', which suggests that the more interior, unitive and spiritual the idea, the more powerful and far reaching will be its results. We need to allow for more downtime, more rest, more silence in order to access a deeper wellspring of inspiration and creativity. Doing-less and being-more might just be a more effective way of 'changing everything'.

TABLE 15.2 Towards a One Planet Business: 20 Snapshots of Change for Good

1. Mindsets: A shift in consciousness, from 'silos to systems' (i.e., from seeing things in parts, to seeing things as wholes); and from 'ego' to 'ecosystem' worldviews. A willingness to be curious and open to new models, and to question the assumptions of outdated economic orthodoxies.

2. Values: a shift in emphasis from extrinsic to intrinsic values (i.e., from achievement, wealth and status, to relationships, creativity, responsibility and well-being). From a top-down, competitive and individualistic culture, to a more egalitarian one of caring, sharing, collaborating and serving the community – including 'me', 'we' and 'MWe' which transcends both me and we.

3. Purpose: a shift from an exclusive focus on making profits for shareholders, to profits with a social purpose; and the recognition that doing good and making money are not incompatible. The rise of values-led businesses and new business models which harness new markets to deliver solutions and net positive impacts.

4. Growth: a shift from an exclusive focus on growing GDP, a measure of economic production which cannot distinguish between the quantity and quality of growth, to developing a holistic understanding of prosperity; and economies and businesses that grow human well-being and happiness, and support green and smart growth.

5. Governance: a shift from 20th century models of shareholder capitalism, which serve a small minority with short-term interests, to new models of stakeholder capitalism, which serve a wide range of social relationships to generate value over the long term (e.g., with employees, customers, suppliers, investors, regulators, local communities).

6. Nature: A shift from 'conquering nature' to 'celebrating diversity' and 'learning from nature' for design inspiration. Working with the grain of life, rather than against it. Recognizing nature as a living, self-organizing system, of abundance and fecundity – as well as limits and boundaries – and which contributes to human health and well-being.

7. Capital: a shift from an exclusive focus on financial and manufactured capital, to one that includes human, social and natural capital (i.e., which recognizes the value of skills, knowledge, relationships and natural resources, etc.) and invests in all these assets for long-term sustainability and value creation.

8. Labour: a shift from the logic that sees labour merely as a factor of production in which work is exchanged for money, to one which fosters entrepreneurship and encourages creative and purposeful work whilst serving community needs. The creation of new 'green jobs' through the transition to a low-carbon economy.

9. Production: a shift from sourcing the cheapest supplies possible, to sustainable supply chain management. An evolution from the wasteful linear take-make-waste production system, to one that embraces cradle-to-cradle manufacturing and the *Circular Economy*, which recovers and remanufactures materials and products.

(Continued)

TABLE 15.2 (*Continued*)

10. Consumption: a shift from a culture of individual hyper-consumerism to one of mindful consumption which fulfils all basic and higher human needs, and supports a better quality of life through sustainable resource use, and equitable models of collaborative consumption through the *Sharing Economy*.

11. Technology: a shift from the mass production, stockpiling and global transportation of goods, to decentralized production on demand at a local level. A shift from 'things to the internet of things'; the harnessing of big data, and use of social media to encourage sustainable outcomes.

12. Advertising: a shift from 'turning wants into needs', creating consumer demand and fuelling consumerism; to supporting choice-editing (offering only sustainable products), and accountable and responsible advertising which discloses product origin, content, life span, and disposal, thus encouraging sustainable consumption.

13. Energy: a shift from a reliance on fossil fuels, and power supplies managed by big utilities, to renewable energy resources, energy self-sufficiency, and smaller scale 'prosumer' models of production and consumption (in which consumers also become producers), facilitated through the internet.

14. Ownership: a shift from shareholder models of ownership, with their associated patterns of decision-making and wealth distribution, to different ownership models, with alternative power and authority structures, pay scales and metrics of performance, such as locally-owned or employee-owned enterprises.

15. Innovation: a shift from centrally-controlled, incremental, inward-looking innovation processes, to building innovation ecosystems that cross organizational boundaries and involve all stakeholders, to tackle systemic problems, and co-create innovative solutions that transform systems and add value to people and planet.

16. Leadership: a shift from leading business-as-usual to leading transformational change beyond the current system with vision and courage. A shift from individual 'heroic' leadership styles, to leading by convening or hosting, involving building commitment through engagement, and encouraging dispersed forms of leadership.

17. Relationships: a shift from individualism and an exclusive focus on competition, to working in long-term alliances, and collaborating with investors, consumers and policy-makers to create new systems that deliver well-being value for community, society, environment and economy.

18. Place: a shift from an exclusive focus on globalization of trade, and the global corporate chain store economy, to building local living economies, involving the relocalization of the production of food, goods and services that meet basic needs, celebrate diversity, support democratic societies, and function in harmony with nature.

19. Metrics: a shift from a focus on the financial bottom line and quarterly reporting, to measuring what matters and new metrics of success, such as triple bottom line and integrated reporting, which includes social and environmental dimensions, and recognizes the significance of long-term value creation.

20. Self: a shift from an exclusive focus on sustainability problems 'out there' (political, economic and techno fixes), to involving the personal and inner dimensions of social change 'in here', or change from the 'inside out'. The role of reflective, mindful, contemplative practices to consciously shift the inner place from which we operate.

15.3 Transforming Business Management Education

We face a tremendous but exciting challenge: learning to live sustainably on our one planet. Business education is instrumental to this change. Our conclusions relating to the contribution of business to the new sustainable development agenda, and the required transformation of economy, business and self, underscore the need for business education to play a leading role in building a sustainable future.

Curricula based on traditional business disciplines, taught as though they were morally, technically and politically neutral, are inadequate, and not fit for purpose in the 21st century. Educating business leaders and managers requires an understanding of, and consequent action based on, a profound, complex appreciation of purpose and meaning. This will happen if processes for designing and delivering management education become more open to the richer variety of knowledge, and ways of knowing, through educational experiences that foster and celebrate goodness, truth and beauty. Thus, the transformation of business management education goes beyond adding bolt-on modules to existing business degrees, to rethinking entire curricula, as well as pedagogies.

On the basis of this challenge, we see an opportunity for the transformation of business management education. We believe that business education programmes aiming to drive companies towards sustainability should:

1   **Base their research and teaching – across all business disciplines – on the premise that we live and do business on one planet** – a finite ecological system of which the economy is a subsystem.

2   **Put values, ethics, and responsibility at their core,** educating business leaders to have a strong sense of personal and organizational purpose in the service of society, locally and globally, including stewardship of the natural environment.

3   **Embrace a systems approach in their research and teaching,** reflecting the real context of business in a globalized economy, which would:

   ● Teach the skills to manage and lead in the context of complexity and ambiguity.

   ● Ensure a good understanding of the systems in which business operates and therefore of the sustainability challenge.,

   ● Support ecology: cover basic environmental science (ecosystems, climate change, natural resources), emphasizing the interactions and inter-dependencies of natural and human systems.

   ● Encompass geopolitics and economics: the rise of BRICS, the shift in economic power from West to East, market and state capitalism and other alternative systems, international trade regulations (including WTO and carbon trading, etc.)

4   **Equip business leaders with the skills and knowledge to:**
   Create new business models:

   ● Solutions-oriented business models, based on societal needs and new economic models – Low-Carbon Economy, Circular Economy, Sharing Economy, Green Economy, etc.

   ● Learning organizations, change management, innovation, and entrepreneurship.

   ● Collaboration, partnerships, intelligence through multi-stakeholder engagement.

   ● Internet, mobile technologies, 3D printing.

   Co-develop new performance measurement systems: metrics and narratives for social, ecological and financial accounting.

   Co-develop new standards for responsible management of natural, human, social, manufactured, and financial capitals.

Contribute to the world by tackling the most pressing issues, both locally and globally, through conceptual and empirical research as well as student projects, and the convening of multi-stakeholder dialogues. Global issues include human rights, anti-corruption, poverty, access to food and fresh water, climate and energy, biodiversity and ecosystems.

5　**Offer an environment and experience conducive to learning, through:**

Diversity of cultures and gender balance in students, faculty and other contributors, through recruitment and exchanges with other institutions, as well as partnerships with external stakeholders.

Experiential learning, real-life case studies and assignments, by engaging with businesses and other stakeholders.

Co-creation with students, through interactive sessions, tapping into the wealth of students' own experiences (facilitated discussions and lectures), and the co-development of the curriculum.

6　**Develop both future and existing leaders, through:**

Self-awareness, personal development, critical reflection on their practice, and experiential learning.

Life-long and shared learning, through alumni community co-ordination and executive education based on customized coaching and facilitation techniques.

Delivery by institutions that lead by example and live by the principles that they teach, particularly in terms of ethics, governance, stakeholder engagement, and operational footprint.

In relation to the One Planet MBA we would sum this up as follows:

ONE PLANET MBA

pro-people, pro-planet, pro-prosperity

O
ONE
We recognize that we only have **One** planet, but we are living as if we had 1.5 planets.

N
NEW
We explore **New** economies, new business models for sustainability, and deliver new forms of business management education.

E
ETHICS
We promote **Ethics** in business: ideas of 'higher purpose', 'values', and 'responsible business' practices.

P
PEOPLE
We examine **People** issues in business: population, consumption, poverty, inequality, human rights, power, stakeholders, and best codes of practice in business.

L
LEADERSHIP

We explore key **Leadership** issues in business, and how to become a responsible and wise leader in challenging times.

A
ALLIANCES

We promote **Alliances** and collaborative action between stakeholders to transform sectors and systems to deliver well-being value for people, planet and economy.

N
NATURE

We explore the science of **Nature** as it relates to business and economy, to understand the scale and urgency of systemic risk, as well as innovations and solutions inspired by nature.

ECONOMY

We examine key dimensions of a new **Economy**: growth, externalities, new forms of capital, sustainable finance, and the enabling conditions needed to build a sustainable economy.

T
TECHNOLOGY

We explore the role of new **Technologies** in a sustainable economy: the transition from 'take-make-waste' to designing for the Circular Economy, and the role of big data.

M
METRICS

We explore new **Metrics** in business: the triple bottom line, beyond GDP, ecological footprint, and integrated reporting, for net positive impact.

B
BUSINESS

We promote **Business** as a catalyst for a sustainable society, in driving new values and markets, supporting a more inclusive, prosperous and resilient world.

A
ACTION

We stand for practical **Action**: the *how* questions as well as the *why* and the *what*; and explore transformations at the level of business, economy and self.

References

Scharmer, O., & Kaufer, K. (2013). *Leading from the emerging future: From ego-system to eco-system economies.* San Francisco: Berrett-Koehler Publishers.

United Nations. (2015). *Transforming our world: The 2030 agenda for sustainable development.* A/RES/70/1. Retrieved from https://sustainabledevelopment.un.org/post2015/transformingourworld

Wallis, S. (2011). *The four horsemen of economics.* YaleGlobal Online. Retrieved from http://yaleglobal.yale.edu/content/four-horsemen-economics (accessed 2015, January 4).

Note: *Italic* page numbers indicate figures and tables.

3 Es: Equity, Ecology and Economy 6
3-nested-dependencies model 358
3 Ps: People, Planet and Profit 6
3D printing technologies 81
4 Ps: Product, Price, Place and Promotion 295, 304–5
4Us: Unsustainable, Unfair, Unstable and Unhappy 409
100RC (100 Resilient Cities) 143

accountability 388
    and disclosure 332
    economic 289
    SA 8000 (Social Accountability 8000) 273
accounting 319–20
    financial 326–35
    management 335–41
    meta- and sub-questions 341–3
    and sustainability 320–6
accrual basis, accounting 328–9
activism, investment strategy 229
adaptive systems 154
advertising 312
    and consumerism 23
    shifting focus of 415
affiliation and respect 173
agriculture, mobile services, Ghana 80
Airbnb 75
Aldersgate Group, 'An Economy that Works' report 133
altruism 160, 333–4
Anderson, Ray, Interface CEO 27, 60, 139, 142, 248,
        251, 358, 360
anthropocene era 8, 90
anthropocentric climate change 327, 338
appreciation and respect 173
automation 32–3
autonomy 173
    entrepreneurial mindset 354, 359, *361*
Avaaz, online campaigns 41
Axelrod, R., 'Tit for Tat' strategy 159–60

B (Benefit) Corporation 64
Balanced Scorecard (BSC) 338
banking
    compensation and fines 369
    crises 128, 129
    innovation strategies 247
    sustainability strategies 393, 394, 398

barbarization scenarios 2
Barclay's Bank 369
'beingset' (state of being) 416
belonging(ness)
    need for 205, 209, 216
    organizational 99
'best in class' strategy 229
Better Life Index, OECD *133*
big data 80, 153–4
'big disconnect' between sustainable business and
        sustainable development 382–4
biodiversity *9*, 10, 134, 135
biomimicry 68–9
    at product, process and system levels 252–3
blue ocean companies 196
BMW (Bayerische Motoren Werke) AG 197–8
Bohinj Park Hotel, embedded sustainability 194–5
bolt-on sustainability 192–3
Boulding, Kenneth 170
boundaries
    corporate entrepreneurship 376
    planetary 12, 139, 385–6
    system 153
brand, employer 220–1
Branson, Richard 55, 60, 79
Brent crude oil prices, volatility in *180*
Brundtland Report (1987, WCED) 4–5, 144, 297, 324
BST *see* business sustainability
'bullet train', Shinkansen, Japan 68
business-as-usual
    current economic paradigm 391–2
    current policies supporting 31, 34
business management education, transforming 416–19
business risks
    economic 34
    environmental 13–15
    reputational 25–6
business role
    future scenarios 3–4
    reframing 414–16
business smart leadership 112
business sustainability (BST) 381–2
    banking case 393, 394, 398
    different approaches to framing 387–91
        focusing on concerns 388
        organizational perspectives 389
        value creation 389–91
    food industry example 393, 395, 398

business sustainability (BST) (*Continued*)
  global challenges, understanding 385–7
  organizational characteristics 400–1
  and sustainable development 382–3
  typology for 391–400
    BST 1.0 (refined shareholder value management) 392–3
    BST 2.0 (managing for triple bottom line) 394–5
    BST 3.0 (truly sustainable business) 395–400
    current economic paradigm 391–2
  voluntary programmes, Lafarge 16–17

C.A.F.E. practices 288–90
C2C® (Cradle-to-Cradle®) 71, 261, 274–5
  biomimicry, Interface 252
  certification 276
  and closed-loop supply chains 269
  Desso, supply chain redesign 275–7
Cadbury Brothers 214–15
capital 64–7
  changing focus of 415
  'empowering innovation' 374–6
capital flows and emerging markets 238
capitalism
  and democracy 35
  new forms of 56
  new information theory of 366
  overhaul of, need for 42–3
  redefining around 'shared value' concept 389–90
  shareholder model 63
  'spirit of', Weber 369, 370
  and systemic inequality 106
  versus Marxism 325
car sharing 306
carbon dioxide emissions *see* greenhouse gas (GHG)
    emissions
Carbon Disclosure Project, UK 188
carbon footprint 338–9
carbon offsetting 338–9
Carbon Tracker Initiative 232
carbon trading scheme, UK 189
Casson, Mark 347, 351, 352
certification 271–7, 283, 286–90
Certified B Corps 64
chakras, yoga 113–14
challenges
  group exercise 45–6
  One Planet predicament 409–11
  understanding 385–7
change 53–4
  business 54–5
  case for 42–3
  economy 56–7
  metamorphosis 81–2
  self 57–9
  transformations 59–81
change for good 414–16
chemicals, regulation on toxic 15
child labour 21, 25, 273
China
  Circular Economy 72–3, 284–5
  debt 128

diary industry 281, 283
economic growth 37
  Loftex 286–8
  slow down in growth 127
chrysalis 81–2
Circular Economy (CE) 17, 56, 71, 268–9
  China's 72–3, 284
  Desso 277
  Marks and Spencer 141
  TetraPak 284
cities, resilience initiative 142–3
civic (civil) sector 163–4
climate change 8, 9–10
  adaptation 234
  debate 75–6
  Equator Principles 189
  financial impact 15
  and the insurance industry 189, 199
  investor action on 188–9
  IPCC 40, 75, 138
  Lafarge 16–17
  and pressure on resources 13
  regulations to curb 189–90
  Stern, Nicolas 30, 120–1, 145
  supply chain disruption 14
  trade deals ignoring 40
closed-loop supply chains 269–70
Coffee And Farmer Equity ('C.A.F.E.' practices 288–90
collaboration 149–50
  characterizing 162–3
  and competition 157–8
  cross-sector partnerships 163–6
  emergence of 159–62
  language of 150–7
  managing dis(agreements) 169–74
  multistakeholder 166–8
  prioritizing 170–1
  respect, demonstrating 172–4
  stakeholder salience 168–9
  value dimensions, interpreting 171–2
collaborative (sharing) economy 56, 73–5
collective entrepreneurship 357, 362
communications
  marketing 311–14
  systems theory 154
comparability of accounting information 327
competition 155, 157–8
competitive aggressiveness, entrepreneurial mindset 353,
    354, 359, *361*
competitiveness and leadership 104–5
compliance risks 14, 15
concentration of corporate wealth 36, 37
conflict minerals 25
consumer cost 307–9
consumer expectations 183–6
consumer trends 185–6, 199–200
consumerism 22–3
consumers/consumption
  growing consumption 20
  holistic approach to understanding 302–4
  shifting focus of 415

consumption 73–5
contingency theories, leadership 105–6
controlling leaders *93, 95–6*
convenience, consumer 309–10
conventional world scenarios 2
Coop case study 310
core entrepreneurial competencies 355
corporate culture 215–18
corporate empowerment 37–8
corporate entrepreneurship 352–3, 362, 363, 374
    paradox of 376–7
corporate lobbying 36, 38–9, 410
corporate model, transformation of 54–5
corporate power, challenges of 35–42
corporate social responsibility (CSR) 43, 99, 193, 245, 383–4
corporate sustainability *see* business sustainability
Corporation 1920, characteristics of 40
Cradle-to-Cradle (C2C) *see* C2C (Cradle-to-Cradle)
creating shared value (CSV) 66–7, 389–90
creative destruction 347, 351, 352, 373
'crisis of capitalism' 42–3
critical problems 108
cross-sector partnerships 163–6
crowdfunding 78
'cult' of entrepreneurship 348–9
cultural traditions 368–9
culture metaphor 156
culture, organizational 215–18
customer collaboration 282–3
customer cost 307–9
customer solutions 305–7

dairy industry 281–3
Daly, Herman 131, 136
DaVinci 2.0 index 69
debt and growth 127–9
'democracy deficit' 39
demographics 18, 20
deregulation 38, 40, 61
Design for the Environment (DFE) 266, 271, 277
Design Hotels 200
Desso, supply chain redesign 275–7
Dharma Life, India 70
Dialogue Theory 163
(dis)agreement on collaborative management 169–74
disclosure of environmental impacts 15, 16, 235, 334
    Carbon Disclosure Project 188
    and materiality 329
    reasons for/theories of 332–4
'disconnect'
    between sustainable business and sustainable
        development 382–4
    economic 34, 410
    of humans from nature 67
Drucker, Peter 92, 347, 396, 403
dynamic capability, building 256–7

Easter Island, ecosystem collapse 158, 325–6
eco-design 271
eco-effectiveness (eco-efficacy) 277, 366
eco-efficiency 322, 340

eco-leadership *93, 94, 95–6,* 97, 98, 99
ecological design frameworks 69
ecological footprint 11–12, 324, 342–3
ecological marketing 296–7
ecological overshoot 13
Econet Wireless, Zimbabwe 79
economic acceleration 7–9
economic globalization 38
economic growth
    alternatives to GDP/GNP 130–5
    changing focus of 414
    and debt 127–9
    definitions 122–3
    exponential growth of GDP 126–7
    flaws of GDP as a measure of value 125–6
    future scenarios 138–9
    green growth 144–6
    limits to 121–2, 137–8
    measures of 123
    purpose of 143–4
    pursuit of 28
    rethinking 143–6
    shortcomings of GNP 123–5
    'stationary/steady state' 136
    theories of 123
economic instability 128–9
economy
    entrepreneurship and 373–7
    new narratives for sustainable 56–7
EcoSchool, Zimbabwe 79
ecosystem innovation 248–9
ecosystem services 11, 135, 323, 385
EcoVision programmes, Philips 257
eco-leadership 93, 94, 97, 99
    characteristics of *95–6*
Eco-Management and Audit Scheme (EMAS) 272, 277
ECO-SUPERIOR products 199–200
eco-system economies, movement towards 56–7
education of business managers 416–19
electronic waste prevention, WEEE 189
Elkington, John 6, 389
Ellen MacArthur Foundation, Circular Economy 56, 71
embedded sustainability 193–5, 389
emergence, systems theory 153, 154
emerging markets and capital flows 238–9
Emery, Frederick, Tavistock Group 213
employees 186–8
    belonging/engagement 99, 187–8
    effect of employer brand on 220–1
    revolving door concept 39
employer brand 220–1
empowering innovation 374, 375
end-of-life (EOL) design and manufacture 271
energy demand and supply 179–80
Energy Efficiency (EE) initiative, Loftex 286–7
energy-efficient operations, Loftex 286–8
energy, transition to renewable 75–8, 415
engagement
    of employees 187–8
    investment strategy 229
    Law of 100

enhanced analysis strategy, investing 229
entity, accounting 328
Entrepreneurial Orientation (EO) 354, *361*
entrepreneurship 347–8
   'cult' of 348–9
   definitions 350
   economic foundations 350–3
   education 355–6
   and ethics 370
   history 350–7
      economic foundations 350–3
   mindset/orientation 353–4, 355, 361
   nature versus nature 354–7
   overlooked in sustainability literature 358–60
   public 362, 372, 373
   social 360, 362, 371–2, 390
   taxonomy 362
   towards One Planet 357–77
environment and entrepreneurship 363–7
environmental challenges 7–8, *9–10*
Environmental Management Accounting (EMA) 339
Environmental Profit and Loss (EP&L) account 336–7
environmental sustainability 266–7
Equator Principles 189
ethics
   and entrepreneurship 370–1
   and investment 238
   and marketing 296, 297, 298
   systemic 97–8
exploitation 19, 21
   of labour 25
externalities 30, 120–1, 237–8
extreme challenges, exploring for innovation 260–1
extreme weather events, effect on logistics and
      operations 14

facilitative relationships 151–2
failings of current economies *145*
Farmerline, Ghana 80
fertilizers
   increase in consumption *8*
   Worm Poop, TerraCycle 197
financial accounting 326–35
   assumptions, conventions and concepts 327–9
   disclosure theories 332–4
   short-termism 31, 233–4
   sustainability information reporting 330–2
   visibility and invisibility of sustainability reporting 334–5
financial capital 65
financial crises 128–9
financial risks 14, 15
financial sustainability 267
Finding Infinity initiative, Design Hotels 200
finite planetary limits 139–42
firms, past versus future 55
fish crisis 178
fish products, organic niche market 313
Fisher, Roger, negotiation 172–3
fishing nets, recycling 27
fitness for purpose 206, 208
'five forces' model, Porter 157, *196*

Followfish 313
food industry
   palm oil supply chain, Nestlé 15
   sustainability examples 393, 395, 398
   sustainable products, Coop 310
   see also Tetra Pak (TP)
food resources, global decline of 180–1
food waste 10, 180
   reduction of, Winnow 365
Forest Stewardship Council (FSC) 16, 273
   certification 283
   principles 274
formal and informal leaders *102–3*
fossil fuel subsidies 32, 76
Foxconn factories, working conditions 25
fracking, protests against 76
Friedman, Milton 35, 61, 63, 391–2
Full Cost Accounting (FCA) 335, 342
functional smartness 11–12
future scenarios 2
   global warming 383
   growth and disruption 138–9
   Limits to Growth model 121–2, 137–8
   role of business 3–4
   sustainable development 5–7

Gaia 154
game theory 159–60
garden crops, decline in nutritional value 181
Genuine Progress Indicator (GPI) 133–4
Gilder, George 366–7
Gilding, Paul 136, 138–9
Global Compact, UN 164–6
Global Entrepreneurship Monitor (GEM) 367, 373–4
Global Green Growth Institute (GGGI) 34, 145, 146
global megatrends 120
Global Reporting Initiative (GRI) 17, 235, 330, 331
global warming *see* climate change
globalization, economic 38
Globally Responsible Leadership Initiative (GRLI) 99–100
goal congruence 210, 212
going concern, accounting 328
GOJO Industries, Inc. 193–4
good economy, ten attributes of 144
governance 63–4, 400–1, 414
Grameen Shakti (GS) 77, 254–5
great transition scenarios 2
Green and Black's (G&B) 161
green consumers 302, 303
   inconsistent behaviour of 184
Green Economy, UNEP 34, 56, 69
green growth 144–6
'green jobs' 69
green marketing 297
   claims of 184–5
green products
   customers' interest in 184–5
   global market worth 244
   Philips 253, 258
greenhouse gas (GHG) emissions 9
   Apple's pledge to cut 63

and carbon footprint 338–9
    disclosure of 188
    financial implications of reducing 231, 232
    initiatives to reduce 15–17
    ISO 14064 standard 272
    reduction by Interace 251
    true cost of 30
Greenpeace 15
Grint, Keith 91, 107–10
GRLI (Globally Responsible Leadership Initiative) 99–100
Gross Domestic Product (GDP) 33–4
    alternatives ways of measuring value 130–5
    challenge of exponential 126–7
    definitions of growth 122–3
    growth and debt 127–9
    limits to as measure of value 125–6
    MNCs bigger than nations 36–7
    World3 model of the future 137
Gross National Happiness (GNH) 131–2
Gross National Product (GNP) 123
    alternative measures 130–5
    campaign speech by Robert Kennedy 125–6
    shortcomings of 123–5
'grow now, clean up later' concept 13
growth see economic growth

happiness
    elements of 133, 134
    and material consumption 73
    measure of success 26
    metrics 131, 132
    paradox 23
Happy Planet Index (HPI) 132
Hawken, Paul 3, 33–4, 125, 230–1, 359
heart, personal transformation 58
hierarchy
    of needs, Maslow 23, 172, 208–9
    and power 170, 217
    and systems 153
Hofstede, Geert, national cultures 367
holistic approach, understanding consumers 302–4
human capital 65
Human Development Index (HDI) 130–1
human rights 21, 165, 273, 386
human systems, organizations as 213–15
'hygiene' factors, Herzberg 209–10

IBM, organizational culture 216, 221
Ikea, sustainability strategy 62
Inclusive Green Growth 145–6
income inequality 22, 134
incremental innovation 246–8, 259–60
Index of Sustainable Economic Welfare 131
India
    Dharma Life 70
    Titan Industries 211–12
indirect reciprocity 160
industrial co-location 270–1
industrial ecology, closing the loop 268–71
Industrial Revolution 78, 90, 94
inequality 19, 410

economic growth causing increase in 125, 126
    growing trend of 22
    systemic 106
influence of investors over companies 227–8
informal and formal leaders 102–3
innovation 243–5
    as a management process 255–9
    emergent routines 259–61
    strategy 245–55
innovation space 246, 259
innovativeness, entrepreneurs 354, 361
instability, economic 128–9
institutional investors 226
insurance industry 189
    reinsurance 198–9
integrated analysis strategy, investing 229
Integrated Reporting (<IR>) 330, 331
integrative relationships 152
interconnectedness
    connectivity of society 94, 97
    of global system 129
    law of 100
Interface 139
    Flor 251, 252, 253
    Mission Zero 77, 142
    Net-Works initiative 27
Intergovernmental Panel on Climate Change (IPCC) 40, 75, 138
'Internet of Things' (IoT) 79
intrapreneurship 364, 374
Investor Network on Climate Risk (INCR), US 188
investors
    influence exerted on companies 227–8
    institutional 226
    stakeholder group 188–9
    see also responsible investment
invisibility created by sustainable reporting 334–5
<IR> (Integrated Reporting) 330, 331
ISO 14000 standards 271–2

jobless growth 32–3
jobs in the new economy 69–71

Kellerman, Barbara 92
Kennedy, Robert, critique of GDP 33, 125–6
Key Account Management (KAM) 282–3
Keynes, John Maynard 124, 136
Kirzner, Israel 352, 365
Klein, Naomi
    on climate change 34, 40, 53–4
    'disaster capitalism' 35
Knight, Frank H., risk vs uncertainty 351
knowledge
    Gilder's information theory of capitalism 366–7
    and innovation 257
    requisite 218–90
Kuznets, Simon 124

labour 69–71, 165
    exploitation, Apple 25
    shifting focus of 415

Lafarge, CO2 reduction targets 16–17
landfill sites, source of disappearing resources 181–2
LAUNCH Initiative, Nike 254
leadership 87–8
    controlling leaders *93, 95–6*
    defining 90–2
        cultural question 92–3
        moral question 92
    discourses *93, 95–6*
    eco-leadership 93–4, *95–6*
        connectivity and interdependence 94, 97
        organizational belongingness 99
        spirituality 98
        systemic ethics 97–8
    formal and informal 102–3
    Messianic leaders 93, 94, *95–6*, 110
    nagging questions about 100–11
    practising wisdom 111–14
    sustainability and 89–90
    therapist leaders *93, 95–6*
    traits/characteristics *101, 102, 111*
League of Intrapreneurs 374
lean thinking 260, 266, 275
legitimacy
    and accounting disclosure theories 332–3
    stakeholder saliency 169, 278–9
life cycle assessment (LCA) 270, 301
Lifecycle Impact Matrix for Coffee *301*
lifestyle behaviours/decisions 303
light bulbs, Philips 308–9
limits and growth, narrative shift 136–8
limits to growth (LTG) 121–2
Limits to Growth: The 30 Year Update (Meadows) 123, 127,
        137, 144
Limits to Growth, The (Meadows) 121–2
living livelihoods, labour 69–71
lobbying, corporate 36, 38–9, 410
Local Living Economies 42
Loftex, energy-saving ideas 286–8
LOHAS (Lifestyles of Health and Sustainability) 73

machine metaphor 156
macro-marketing 296
malaria 109
management accounting 335–41
Management Control Systems (MCS) 341
manufactured capital 65
many elements of happiness and well-being approach 133
Marine Stewardship Council (MSC) 167–8
marketing 293–5
    from 20th to 21st century 295–6
    for the 21st century 298–305
    as a transformational force 314–15
    evolution 296–8
    holistic approach to consumers 302–4
    reconfiguring the market mix 304–5
        place to convenience 309–10
        price to consumer cost 307–9
        products to customer solutions 305–7
        promotion to communication 311–14
    socio-ecological problems 299–302

Marks and Spencer 134–5
    Plan A 139, 141–2, 296, 315
Maslow, hierarchy of needs 23, 172, 208–9
Material Flow Cost Accounting (MFCA) 339
materiality
    and accounting 329
    investment strategy 231, 232
    investor definition of 234
matrix organizations 207
maturity models, innovation *250*
megatrends 120
Messianic leaders 93, 94, *95–6*, 110
metamorphosis 81–2
metaphors
    collaboration 156–7
    metamorphosis 81–2
metrics 33–4, 131–5, 415, 419
Mill, John Stuart 124, 136
Millennium Development goals (MDGs), UN 385, 386
Millennium Ecosystem Assessment (MEA) 385
mind, personal transformation 58
mindsets 414
    entrepreneurs 353–4, 355
    transformation of 59–61
minerals, mining of in conflict areas 25
Mintzberg, Henry
    on lobbying 38
    political imbalances 41
    strategizing model 182–3
Mission Zero, Interface 77, 142
MNCs (multinational companies)
    cross-sector collaborations 163–6
    power of 35–42
    tax avoidance 33
Mobility CarSharing 306
mobility services, BMW 197–8
Monarch butterfly, metamorphosis 82
money measurement 329
morality 92, 369–71
motivation 208–12
Mount Sustainability, 7 fronts, Interface 142
multinational companies (MNCs)
    cross-sector collaborations 163–6
    power of 35–42
    tax avoidance 33
multistakeholder collaborations 166–8

Natura, Brazil, social capital 66
natural capital 29, 30, 65, 67
    accounting 337–8
    Net Positive accounting 340–1
natural ecosystems versus industrial systems *269*
nature
    4 new ways of relating to 67
    changing for good 414
    design inspired by 68–9
    'disconnect' from 67
    valuation of 134–5
needs, Maslow's hierarchy of 23, 172, 208–9
negative externalities 29, 30, 55, 120–1
    GDP not taking into account 125

negative screening strategy, investment 229
negotiation 172–3
Nestlé, palm oil supply chain 15
Net Positive technique, accounting 340–1
'net present value', responsible investors 234
network theory 154–5
Net-Works initiative, Philipines 27
New Institutional Sociology 333
Nike, LAUNCH initiative 254
Nowak, M., 'Generous Tit-for-Tat' 160

oil price volatility 180
old paradigm/new paradigm transition 81–2
OMV Group 196, 199
One Planet Approach
    challenges 409–11
    change for good 414–16
    rethinking management education 416–19
    to sustainable business 411–14
One Planet Business 82–3
One Planet Entrepreneur 360–3
One Planet Entrepreneurship 357–8
    conceptual framework for *361*
    and the economy 373–7
    and the environment 363–7
    and society 367–73
One Planet Living Framework *132*
One Planet MBA 418–19
One Planet Mindset 58, 60, 61, 82
One Planet Predicament 409–11
online campaigns 15, 41, 314
openness, sustainability marketing 316
operational optimization *250*
operational risks 14
operations *see* supply chains
organisms, collaboration context 156
organizational belonging 99
organizational culture 215–18
organizational structure 207
organizations 205–6
    employer brand 220–1
    as human systems 213–15
    knowledge, requisite 218–20
    motivating people 208–12
    and sustainability 206–8
Our Common Future (WCED) 4
overconsumption 20, 332
Overfished Ocean Strategy 195–200
Oxfam Doughnut Model 24–5

Paradox of Corporate Entrepreneurship *376*
partnerships
    cross-sector 163–6
    One Planet approach 413–14
Patagonia, product repair and recycling 74
peace, One Planet approach 413
PeaceWorks 183–4
people (social challenges) 18–19
    companies' responses to 26–8
    key concepts and issues 20–5
    One Planet approach 412

reputational risks to big business 25–6
person cultures 217–18
personal data concerns 80
personal sphere, transformation of 57–9
perverse subsidies 29, 32
phantom versus real wealth 29, 31
Philips
    long-life light bulbs 308–9
    sustainability-oriented innovation 251, 253, 257–8
Piketty, T., capital and inequalities 22, 35
place (market mix) to convenience 309–10
planet (environmental challenges) 7–10
    companies' responses 15–17
    key concepts and issues 11–13
    One Planet approach 412
    risks to business 13–15
planetary boundaries 12, 139, 385–6
planetary limits, finite 139–40
plastic bags, banning of 189
Plastics to Playgrounds programme 194
pluralist approach, leadership 106, *107*
political cost hypothesis 334
pollution 30, 120, *122*
population growth *8*, *18*, 20, *122*, 137
Porter, Michael, competition strategy 157, 195–6
positive screening 229
positive screening strategy, investment 229
poverty 19, 20–1, 22
power
    cultures 217
    and prioritizing 170–1
    and stakeholder salience 168–9, 278–9
    three approaches to 106–7
power of corporates, challenges of 35–6
    campaigns to tackle 41–2
    key concepts and issues 36–41
price (market mix) to consumer cost 307–9
prioritizing, and collaboration 170–1
Prisoner's Dilemma 159–60
private sector 163
proactiveness, entrepreneurs 354, 359, *361*
problems we face 107–8
process-oriented EE (energy efficiency) 287, 288
production, C2C models 71–3
products (market mix) to customer solutions 305–7
profit (economic challenges) 28–9
    companies' responses to 34
    key concepts and issues 30–4
    risks to business 34
promotion (market mix) to marketing communications 311–14
prosperity, One Planet approach 412–13
Protestant work ethic 369
psychological contracts, employer-employee 316
public entrepreneurship 372
public sector 163
PUMA, EP&L account 336–8
purpose
    of business, changing 61–2
    entrepreneurship 362, 363
    social, re-emergence of 390
    and will 58

Quakers
   Barclay's Bank 369
   Cadbury Brothers 214
quarterly reporting 31, 55, 63
   rejection of 34, 388

radical approach, leadership 106, *107*
radical innovation 245, 246–8
   BMW 197–8
   challenges associated with 258–9
   key new routines emerging for 259–61
recycling
   Circular Economy 71–3, 268–9
   closed-loop supply chain 269–71
   Cradle-to-Cradle (C2C) products 71, 251–3, 275–7
   GOJO Industries 194
   Interface, fishing nets 27
   lack of 181–2
   product take-back strategies 310
   setting targets for 248, 257
   Starbucks 290
   TerraCycle 197
   TetraPak 283–5
refined shareholder value management 392–3
regulation 189–90
   added cost of 191
   assets stranded due to 232
   compliance risks 14, 15
   environmental disclosure decisions 334
   forcing EOL design 271
Reinhart, C.M. 128–9
reinsurers 198–9
relationships, collaborative 151–2, 415
relevance of accounting information 327
reliability of accounting information 327
religion 98, 369
renewable energy
   Grameen Shakti 77, 254–5
   Interface, Mission Zero 142
   subsidies low versus fossil fuels 32, 403
   transition to use of 75–8
reporting 55
   and disclosure 235
   short-termism 31
   see also financial accounting
REPOWERBalcombe, UK 76
reputation and collaboration 160
'reputational capital', sharing economy 74
reputational risk 14–15
   to big business 25–6
   exploitation 21
   online campaigns 41
resilience
   of cities 142–3
   climate resilient growth 145
   indicators 129
resource decline/depletion 10, 178–81, 326, 388, 410
respect and collaboration 172–4
responsibility *see* social responsibility
responsible investment 225–7
   capital flows and emerging markets 238

delivering performance 235–7
disclosure of environmental impacts 235
and externalities 237–40
goal of 228
influence, mechanics of 227–8
materiality and time-frames 231–4
principles of 227
strategies of 229–31
reverse supply chain 269
'revolving door' concept 39
'right livelihoods' 70–1
risk
   economic 34
   reputational 14–15, 25–6
   systemic 13
risk assessment/management 389
   business risks 13–15
   innovation strategy 245
   insurance industry 189, 198–9
   and materiality 231–2
risk-taking appetite, entrepreneurs 354, *361*
Rogoff, K.S. 128–9
role stress 217
role theory 216, 217
roles
   and collaboration 173
   networks 155
   in organizations 216, 217
Rotich, Juliana, entrepreneurial website 368
rules of the game, changing 254, 277, 397, 398, 403

SA 8000 provisions 273–4
'safe and just space for humanity', Raworth 24–5, 386
saliency of stakeholders 168–9, 278–9
Schumpeter, Joseph A., on entrepreneurship 351, 352
screening, investment strategy 229, 230–1
self-transformation 57–9, 416
Senge, Peter 358, 359
shared value creation 66–7, 158, 389–90
shareholder value management 392–3, *393, 399*
shareholders 63–4
Sharing Economy 56, 73–5, 410, 415
Sharma, Ruchir 127, 128
Shinkansen, Japanese railways 68
short-termism 31, *145*, 233–4, 329
situational theory, leadership 105–6
situations, perspectives on 107–10
slave labour 21, 25–6
smart leadership 111–12
smart products/appliances 185, 190
smart technologies 79
Social Accountability International (SAI) 273
social businesses 390, 404
social capital 65, 66
social challenges 18–25
social enterprises 70, 390
social entrepreneurship 271–360, 390
social issues in investment practice 236
social media 41, 74, 78, 314
social responsibility 61, 191, 192, 267, 289, 388
   campaigns 334

consumer 301–2
corporate 43, 99, 193, 245, 296, 383–4
ISO 26000 standard (2011) on 388
social sustainability 267, 285–8
Socially Responsible Investment (SRI) 188
Society of Friends (Quakers) 369
Solar Home Systems (SHS), GS 77
spirituality, leadership 98
Sri Lanka, fight against malaria 109
stakeholders
and collaboration 162–3, 166–8
disagreement between 169–70
and financial accounting disclosures 332–3
governance 63–4
management 278–80, 288
power-interest grid 279–80
saliency 168–9, 178–9
sustainability strategies 182–3
consumers/customers 183–6
employees 186–8
investors 188–9
regulators 189–90
types and attributes of 278–9
standards 271–7
Starbucks
C.A.F.E. practices 288–90
in-store operations 290–1
states of leadership *112*
status and respect 173
steady/stationary state economy 136
Stern Review (2006) 30, 120–1, 145
stockholders *see* shareholders
Stockholm Resilience Centre 12, 139, 385
stories about the future 2–7
stranded assets 232
strategic risks 13
strategies
adopted by businesses 190–200
responsible investment 229–31
strategizing 182–3
stress, work-related 23–4, 217
subsidies 29, 32, 76, 403, 410
subsystems 152, 153
suicide 19, 25, 410
SumOfUs, online campaigns 41
supply chain slaves, Thailand 25–6
supply chains 265–6
China's dairy industry *283*
climate change disrupting 14
closing the loop 268–71
Desso case study 275–7
Loftex case study 286–8
standards, certification and measures 271–7
Starbucks 288–91
Tetra Pak 280–5
triple bottom line 266–8
sustainability challenges 43, 45–6
solving 401–4
understanding 385–7
sustainability-oriented innovation (SOI) 244–5
and dynamic capability 257

efficiency agenda 251
emergent routines for 259–61
management challenges 258–9
models 249–50
Philips 257–8
strategy for 245–9
system-level changes 253–4
Sustainable Cost Calculation (SCC) 335–6
sustainable development 4–7
disconnected from sustainable business 382–4
Sustainable Development Goals (SDGs), UN 411
Sustainable Living Plan (SLP), Unilever 139–40, 255, 315
Swiss Re, reinsurance 198–9
systemic ethics 97–8
systemic risk 13, 238, 239
systems approach, business education 417
systems-level challenges 366
systems-level innovation 250
biomimicry, Interface Flor 252–3
Nike and the LAUNCH initiative 254
systems theory 152–4

take-make-waste economy 11
tame problems 107–8
task cultures 217
Tata Group, India 61, 209, 211, 215
Tavistock Group 213–14
tax avoidance 29, 33
technology 78–81
shifting focus of 415
TEEB (The Economics of Ecosystems and Biodiversity) 134–5
TerraChoice 312–13
TerraCycle 197
Tetra Pak (TP)
environmental challenges 280–2
FSC certification 283
Key Account Management (KAM) 282–3
recycling of 283–5
therapist leaders *93, 95–6*
throwaway economy 181–2, 195
collapse of 196, 199
time-frames, investment 231, 232, 237
short-termism 233–4
'Tit for Tat' strategy, game theory 159–60
Titan Industries 211–12
TOMS, social business 372
'total customer cost' versus price 307–9
Total Entrepreneurial Activity (TEA) 367
Total Quality Environmental Management (TQEM) 275–7
trade deals 39, 40
trade-off sustainability 191
transaction costs 307–8
transactional relationships 151, 152
Transatlantic Trade and Investment Partnership (TTIP) 39
transformations 59–81
business management education 416–19
capital 64–7
consumption 73–5
energy 75–8
governance 63–4

transformations (*Continued*)
labour 69–71
mindsets 59–61
nature 67–9
production 71–3
purpose 61–2
technology 78–81
Trendwatching.com 185–6, 199–200
triple bottom line 6, 17, 55
managing for 394–5, 394–5
operational challenges in transition to 266–8
Tetra Pak creating 281
Tru Cost, corporate profits 30

UN Global Compact (2015) 4, 164–6
UN Millennium Development goals (MDGs) 385, 386
UN Sustainable Development Goals (SDGs) 411
uncertainty 129
versus risk 351
understandability of accounting 328
uneconomic growth, Daly 136
UNEP 14, 31, 73, 244, 387
unfairness 21, 410
see also inequality
unhappiness 410
Unilever Sustainable Living Plan (SLP) 140
unitarist approach, leadership 106, *107*
urbanization, rapid rate of 21–2
urgency, stakeholder salience 169, 278–9

value creation
outdated model 66
shareholder value 391–2, 394
by sustainable business 389–91, 394, 399
triple bottom line 389, 395
versus value appropriation, social entrepreneurship 371–2
value dimensions, interpreting 171–2
values/valuing 119
alternative measures 130–5
externalities approach, problem with 120–1
GDP and GNP, limits of as measures of value 122–9
global megatrends 120
limits to growth 121–2, 137–8
rethinking growth 143–6
Vermont state, GPI measure 133–4
virtual organizations 207
visibility
and financial accounting 334–5
and management accounting 336
Vision 2050, WBCSD 3–4, 244, 386–7
Volkswagen (VW) 88
Volta River Authority (VRA) 334
voluntary standards 273
volunteer programmes 187–8
VUCA (Volatility, Uncertainty, Complexity and Ambiguity) world 3, 363

Wal-Mart 14, 185, 286, 287, 314
Wallis, Stuart 209–10
waste 10, 181–2
circular economy/recycling 17, 71–2, 261, 268–9, 283–5

closed-loop supply chains 269–71
Cradle-to-Cradle (C2C) philosophy 275–7
industrial ecology 268
ISO 14000 standards 271–2
products from, TerraCycle 197
reduction of 140, 141, 142, 194, 251, 252, 266
sharing economy 74
take-make-waste economy 11
watchmaking, Titan 211–12
water pollution 30
water scarcity 10, 26, 181
disruption to supply chains 14
water treatment 72
water use *8, 12*
industrial co-location 270–1
reducing 140, 251, 288, 290
watershed, restoring, NYC 65
wealth 64–5
concentration of 37
phantom 29, 31
shareholder 63
unequal distribution of 22, 410
value dimension 171, 172
Web 2.0 technologies 78
Weber, Max 369–70
Wedgwood, Josiah 321
well-being 19
and consumption 73
happiness paradox 23
many elements approach 133, *134*
measures of 131–2
societal 386
value dimension 171, 172
wellness 131–2
Werbach, Adam 364
Western, Simon, eco-leadership 94, 97, 99
Whirlpool Corporation, 'smart appliances' 190
wicked problems 107–9
will, personal transformation 58
Willard, Bob 13–14, 358, 359
Winnow, food waste solutions 365
wisdom traditions 59, 416
wise leadership 111–12
yoga 113–14
work, and sense of purpose 69–71
work-related stress 23–4
role stress 217
working together 150–7
World Bank 37–8
green growth 145–6
international poverty line (IPL) 20
and the VRA, Ghana 334
World Business Council for Sustainable Development (WBCSD) 3–4, 244, 386–7, 404
World Commission on Environment and Development (WCED) 4, 297
World Trade Organization (WTO) 38, 39
World3 model of the future 121–2, 137–8
WWF (World Wildlife Federation) 16, 244, 283

yoga and leadership 113–14